AN EQUITABLE FRAMEWORK FOR HUMANITARIAN INTERVENTION

This book aims to resolve the dilemma regarding whether armed intervention as a response to gross human rights violations is ever legally justified without Security Council authorisation. Thus far, international lawyers have been caught between giving a negative answer on the basis of the UN Charter's rules ('positivists'), and a 'turn to ethics', declaring intervention legitimate on moral grounds, while eschewing legal analysis ('moralists'). In this volume, a third solution is proposed. The idea is presented that many equitable principles may qualify as 'general principles of law recognised by civilised nations' – one of the three principal sources of international law (though a category that is often overlooked) – a conclusion based upon detailed research of both national legal systems and international law. These principles, having normative force in international law, are then used to craft an equitable framework for humanitarian intervention. It is argued that the dynamics of their operation allow them to interact with the Charter and customary law in order to fill gaps in the existing legal structure and soften the rigours of strict law in certain circumstances. It is posited that many of the moralists' arguments are justified, albeit based upon firm legal principles rather than ethical theory. The equitable framework proposed is designed to provide an answer to the question of how humanitarian intervention may be integrated into the legal realm. Certainly, this will not mean an end to controversies regarding concrete cases of humanitarian intervention. However, it will enable the framing of such controversies in legal terms, rather than as a choice between the law and morality.

Volume 45 in the series Studies in International Law

Studies in International Law

Recent titles in this series

Contracting with Sovereignty: State Contracts and International Arbitration
Ivar Alvik

Multi-Sourced Equivalent Norms in International Law
Edited by Yuval Shany and Tomer Broude

The Distinction and Relationship between *Jus ad Bellum* **and** *Jus in Bello*
Keiichiro Okimoto

International Humanitarian Law and Terrorism
Andrea Bianchi and Yasmin Naqvi

The Militarisation of Peacekeeping in the Twenty-First Century
James Sloan

Accounting for Hunger: The Right to Food in the Era of Globalisation
Edited by Olivier De Schutter and Kaitlin Y Cordes

Promises of States under International Law
Christian Eckart

Multilevel Regulation of Military and Security Contractors: The Interplay between International, European and Domestic Norms
Edited by Christine Bakker and Mirko Sossai

Europe and Extraterritorial Asylum
Maarten den Heijer

The Practice of International and National Courts and the (De) Fragmentation of International Law
Edited by Ole Kristian Fauchald and André Nollkaemper

The Politics of International Criminal Justice: A Spotlight on Germany
Ronen Steinke

Fighting Corruption in Public Procurement: A Comparative Analysis of Disqualification or Debarment Measures
Sope Williams-Elegbe

The Interception of Vessels on the High Seas: Contemporary Challenges to the Legal Order of the Oceans
Efthymios Papastavridis

Integration at the Border: The Dutch Act on Integration Abroad and International Immigration Law
Karin de Vries

For the complete list of titles in this series, see 'Studies in International Law' link at www.hartpub.co.uk/books/series.asp

An Equitable Framework for Humanitarian Intervention

Ciarán Burke

·HART·
PUBLISHING
OXFORD AND PORTLAND, OREGON
2013

Published in the United Kingdom by Hart Publishing Ltd
16C Worcester Place, Oxford, OX1 2JW
Telephone: +44 (0)1865 517530
Fax: +44 (0)1865 510710
E-mail: mail@hartpub.co.uk
Website: http://www.hartpub.co.uk

Published in North America (US and Canada) by
Hart Publishing
c/o International Specialized Book Services
920 NE 58th Avenue, Suite 300
Portland, OR 97213-3786
USA
Tel: +1 503 287 3093 or toll-free: (1) 800 944 6190
Fax: +1 503 280 8832
E-mail: orders@isbs.com
Website: http://www.isbs.com

British Library Cataloguing in Publication Data

Data Available

ISBN: 978-1-84946-404-8

Typeset by Hope Services, Abingdon
Printed and bound in Great Britain by
TJ International Ltd, Padstow

Acknowledgements

This book represents the culmination of four years of – frequently interrupted, but always enjoyable – work in the hills above Florence. Based upon a doctoral dissertation defended in the winter of 2011, the published edition has benefited from a further year's perspective, as well as allowing for a brief examination of the recent crises in Libya and Syria. While it has frequently been observed that writing a work of this kind is a solitary occupation, it could not have been completed to the present standard without the support of a number of people, to whom I offer my humble thanks.

To have been assigned to Professor Martin Scheinin as my doctoral supervisor at the European University Institute was a most fortuitous piece of luck. His confidence in my ability to follow my (often unorthodox) ideas through to their conclusion made the realisation of this book possible. Always there to offer sensible and grounded advice when I needed it, his professionalism, honesty and breadth of knowledge were invaluable throughout. Martin, thank you.

Significant thanks are also due to Professor Wouter Werner. Many of the ideas in this book grew from discussions and work completed under his tutelage while at the Vrije Universiteit, Amsterdam. The perspectives that I garnered through the Law and Politics of International Security course of which he was, and is, the director were invaluable in broadening my academic interests and perspectives.

Others have also contributed to the final shape of this edition in various ways. The critiques of Professor Francesco Francioni allowed me to bolster my argument in ways I would have not have otherwise envisaged. The same must most certainly be said of Professor Martti Koskenniemi, who took the time to compose a detailed critical assessment of an earlier draft of this text, which proved invaluable in countering many arguments against the framework as presented. Thanks are also offered to Dr Christopher Rossi of the University of Iowa, both for his inspirational work on equity in international law, and for his advice in shaping the final version of this text. I would also like to thank Dr Oonagh Breen of University College Dublin for her help.

Thanks at a more personal level are offered to those who have touched and enriched my life in the past years. My Florentine adventure has put me in contact with many colourful characters, who, through welcoming me into their lives, have enriched my own in a variety of ways. Thanks are offered to my fellow members of 'The Burning Tower', Ben Farrand,

Dennis-Jonathan Mann, Dominik Menno and Wim Muller. Making music together was truly special. Thanks are also due to everyone at IUE Calcio, as well as to Anna Bara, Conor Talbot, Râna Babaç, Costica Dumbrava, Tomasz Gabor, Bernadette van Boxel, Francisco Javier Sánchez Broto and countless others who will (hopefully!) forgive me for not naming them individually, but who have made my life a more interesting place these last years. *Grazie di cuore.*

My gratitude is finally, and most of all, offered to my parents, Noëlle and Dónal. Everything I am is thanks to them and it is to them that I dedicate this book.

Contents

Table of Cases

Table of Legislation

Introduction

THIS BOOK BRINGS together two rather unlikely legal bedfellows. On the one hand is equity, a series of general principles and doctrines devised to infuse the domestic legal systems with more flexibility in the face of legal rigidity. On the other, we have humanitarian intervention, the idea that States may intervene militarily to protect against, and put an end to, gross human rights abuses. Their interaction and interplay, while not being the most obvious one, nonetheless does much to shed light upon some otherwise rather problematic legal issues.

In 1999, the North Atlantic Treaty Organisation (NATO) responded to what it viewed as the excesses of the Serbian Government against its ethnic Albanian population in the southern province of Kosovo. A bombing campaign was launched, intended, ostensibly, to cripple Serbian military capacity, and to halt the human rights abuses being perpetrated against the Kosovars. This was done despite the lack of legal backing from the United Nations Security Council. While a specific resolution was never sought for NATO's operation, it was broadly acknowledged that the procurement of such a resolution was practically impossible. Russia's close ties with Serbia ensured that in the Security Council it was always likely to veto any such initiative. The decision to intervene, then, was, on the face of it at least, illegal.

However, the seeming illegality of NATO's intervention did not attract the condemnation from international law scholars that one might expect. Instead, by and large, the reaction was positive. This is remarkable, since international legal scholars rarely enjoy witnessing the dismissal of the rules of their own discipline by States. The reasons behind this reaction, however, are quite simple. NATO's intervention was, at the time at least, viewed primarily as an act of altruism.[1]

Kosovo was not an oil rich region, and did not dispose of key natural resources. Nor was it particularly strategically important. Furthermore, the Kosovars were a Muslim people, oppressed by a Christian Serbian Government. Therefore, accusations of profiteering, opportunism, or

[1] A certain number of authors also paralleled the Kosovo operation with that of the United States in Somalia in 1992. See S Thomashausen, *Humanitarian Intervention in an Evolving World Order: The Cases of Iraq, Somalia, Kosovo and East Timor* (Pretoria, Africa Institute of South Africa, 2002) for a more detailed discussion on this line of argument.

Western pro-Christian bias were unlikely to colour judgments. While other military interventions which had succeeded in ending gross human rights abuses had also involved other more self-interested motivations, Kosovo genuinely seemed to be a selfless act of doing the right thing in the circumstances. The fact that it was apparently, *de lege lata*, illegal meant that commentators faced a stark choice: defend the law and find themselves on the side of the human rights abusers; or embrace NATO's intervention, but weaken international law – and thereby international order – by defending breaches thereof.

The first chapter of this work recounts the debate on humanitarian intervention which was unleashed by the Kosovo crisis. In 1999 and in the first years of the twenty-first century, a myriad of scholars devised a series of opinions on the subject of the legitimacy and legality of intervention to prevent gross human rights abuses without Security Council approbation. In the first chapter, it is noted that, aside from that minority of scholars who condemned the Kosovo action as illegal, the breadth of the international legal community adopted an apologetic stance toward 'humanitarian intervention'. The justifications proffered were many and varied, and I have endeavoured to give the full flavour of the views of leading authors in this regard. However, broadly, it may be said that those theories devised to justify humanitarian intervention did not make full use of the law itself in their argumentation. Instead, they preferred to confine themselves to ethical judgments, moral stress tests and discussions on the possible future crystallisation of customary legal norms, rather than dealing with the situation at hand head-on and examining humanitarian intervention as a concept in the light of the law, since to do so would likely have resulted in a verdict of illegality and, ergo, impermissibility.

My own reaction to this trend was one of surprise. Much of the rhetoric employed by leading lawyers was far from legal. The separation of international legality from vague notions of 'legitimacy', which for many commentators suddenly seemed more important, represented a worrying and, to my mind, at least, a misguided, trend. The 'flight to ethics', as it were, seemed broadly understandable given that it was difficult for lawyers to reconcile the law with the demands of their respective consciences. However, in addition to potentially weakening international legal certainty, the flight was premature. While the regime on the use of force by States had been examined with reference to custom and treaty law in the humanitarian intervention debate, none of the leading scholars had made reference to the normatively equal third source of international law – general principles of law.[2] The basic premise of this work is that, in making

[2] I repeatedly designate general principles of law as the 'third source' of international law throughout this work. This is not intended to denigrate such principles in any way as a legal source. It is clear from the Statute of the International Court of Justice, as well as the works of leading scholars, that general principles enjoy normative parity (with certain reserva-

this oversight, the international legal community missed a trick, as it were. The humanitarian intervention debate is not the first instance where legal rigidity prevented the law from being reconcilable with a just outcome. General principles of law, and more particularly, equity, have been used to solve such problems in domestic fora in the past.

This being the case, the question which arose was whether general principles, and particularly those principles of an equitable nature, might be employed to shed light upon the humanitarian intervention debate and perhaps introduce a 'fresh' legal source, obviating the necessity for the recourse to legal and ethical theory. In the second chapter, I examine the core elements of the 'general principles of law recognised by civilised nations' category, as the third source of international law per Article 38 of the Statute of the International Court of Justice. In doing so, I conclude with the assessment that its potential for normative influence in a variety of situations is quite significant. However, in so doing, it becomes clear over the course of this chapter that equitable principles have their roots in domestic legal systems, and that in order to assess the potential modalities of operation of equity in international law, it is first necessary to look at the roots of the doctrine and how it is applied in national legal systems.

The third chapter of this work embarks upon a detailed comparative examination of the main legal families, ranging from the English common law, to the various manifestations of the civil law system. Also taken in are Muslim law, Chinese and Japanese law, the legal system of South Africa and that of the United States. Many of the principal European 'exporter' systems – those whose legal systems have been transposed elsewhere – are also treated. In this manner, it is possible to trace a common core of equitable general principles which crop up again and again in domestic legal systems, and which, therefore, represent excellent candidates for 'general principles of law recognised by civilised nations'.

Recent scholarship on general principles of international law has been close to non-existent, and many of the leading texts on the subject are several decades old. Further, a concrete test for what constitutes a general principle recognised by civilised nations has never been formulated in a manner which has garnered universal acceptance. As a result, persuasive though the evidence presented in the comparative study undertaken in chapter three may be, it is necessary to refer to international practice to determine whether a principle is in fact a general principle of international law

tions) with international conventions and customary international law – the 'first two' sources of international law. The term 'third source' is used, rather, for two purposes. First, it reflects its position in the 'list' of sources of law prescribed by Art 38(1) of the Statute of the International Court. Secondly, and rather more pertinently, general principles of law are seriously under-discussed as a normative category in international legal scholarship. Indeed, this work argues that a lack of attention to this category has been problematic in the context of the humanitarian intervention debate. A lack of attention to either of the other two principal normative categories was never likely to occur in the context of such a discussion.

possessing normative force. Mere recognition by a plurality of legal systems would not seem, on its own, to be enough. However, in terms of 'practice', understood in the usual sense when describing the actions of states, it is clear that states rarely make reference to general principles to justify their acts, and this area is unlikely to be a fruitful source of confirmation for general principles which are found in national legal systems. Therefore, cases before the International Court of Justice represent the best source of material for these purposes; the jurisprudence of the Court representing the best form of 'practice' available, especially in view of the fact that Article 38(1)(d) makes specific provision for 'judicial decisions . . . [constituting] subsidiary means for the determination of rules of law'.[3] The fourth chapter of this volume undertakes an examination of those cases before the World Court[4] which have made reference to general principles of law, particularly those of an equitable nature. The chapter concludes with the assessment that there is ample evidence in the practice of the Court – itself a subsidiary source of international law for the purpose of interpreting the content of principal sources – for one to conclude that a significant number of equitable principles have been transposed from domestic law to international law in one form or another.

The fifth and final chapter of this work concludes by proposing a framework for humanitarian intervention based upon equitable general principles. It is argued that domestic practice demonstrates that general principles operate in a manner that may on occasion derogate the strict operation of all normative categories, including constitutional norms

[3] A sharp distinction should probably be drawn here between general principles of law on the one hand, and customary international law, on the other. Of course, in order to determine the existence of customary international law, it is necessary to demonstrate consistent and widespread State practice, allied with *opinio iuris*. While the test for determining the existence of general principles of law is far less clear-cut (this is discussed in greater detail later in this work), it is clear that such principles are derived from the municipal legal systems of States. An element of international 'practice' does not qualify, *stricto sensu*, as part of any test to determine their existence. However, given that the test for determining general principles is unclear or disputed, it is clear that widespread recognition by a plurality of legal systems is not, in and of itself, enough for a general principle to be transposed into the international legal system. For example, the notion of an easement, widely recognised by a great number of legal systems, was not upheld in the 1960 *Right of Passage Over Indian Territory* case, *Right of Passage Over Indian Territory (Merits)* Judgment [1960] ICJ Rep 66. Hence, in the absence of a concrete and reliable test, and in order to bestow clarity upon the category, the judgments and opinions of the ICJ are used as a form of practice, as a means of showing which general principles of law widely recognised in national legal systems may qualify as norms of international law.

[4] The term 'World Court' is frequently employed in this text as a description both of the International Court of Justice (ICJ) – the principal judicial organ of the United Nations – and of its predecessor, the Permanent Court of International Justice (PCIJ). This is, of course, not to say that these courts are one and the same thing. However, the Statutes of the two Courts are virtually identical, their roles are similar, and as a result, for certain purposes, past practice of the two Courts is sometimes described in tandem during this work. In such sections, the term 'World Court' is employed. Wherever distinctions between the two organs and their jurisprudence are necessary, by contrast, they are referred to by their official titles.

when they clash with fundamental values. This being the case, there would seem to be potential for the derogation of *ius cogens* norms by other subsequent *ius cogens* norms combined with general principles of law. Using the principles shown to be part of the equitable international law *corpus* in previous chapters, a model is proposed, combining an *ius ad bellum* permissibility test with several conditions for the conduct of warfare by the intervening State. It is argued that there is good reason to suggest that general principles of law may indeed have a role in the humanitarian intervention conundrum, and that they may have the potential to shape a third exception to the prohibition upon the use of force by States.

The book concludes with two brief 'test scenarios', centred on two military interventions, one counterfactual, one hypothetical, but both based partly upon recent factual circumstances. An assessment of the potential invocation of the equitable theory of humanitarian intervention is presented, and some tentative remarks as to the use of general principles in international legal reasoning in concrete situations are offered.

1

The Humanitarian Intervention Discourse: A Debate on the Edges of the Law

Ainsi, la plupart des mauvaises actions des hommes sont venues au-devant d'eux, déguisées sous la forme spécieuse de la nécessité; puis, la mauvaise action commise dans un moment d'exaltation, de crainte, de délire, on voit qu'on aurait pu passer auprès d'elle en l'évitant. Le moyen qu'il eut été bon d'employer, qu'on n'a pas vu, aveugle qu'on était, se présente à vos yeux facile et simple; vous vous dîtes: comment n'ai-je pas fait ceci au lieu de faire cela?*

I. GENERAL INTRODUCTION

THE 1999 NATO (North Atlantic Treaty Organisation) intervention in Kosovo was contemporaneously accompanied by a period of stark silence from international lawyers concerning the *strict* legality of the operation.[1] Many of those who proffered comment upon the matter couched their analyses in terms of 'classical international law'[2] or 'traditional international law'.[3] The rationale that brought about this reticence to affirm the legality of NATO's actions may be easily explained: any such affirmation could be immediately demonstrated to be untrue.

The United Nations Charter, the primary legal instrument concerning the use of force by States, effectively outlaws war. Article 2(4) of the Charter represents a general prohibition upon the use of force by States at international level. There exist two exceptions to this rule, however, namely collective action authorised by the UN Security Council under Chapter VII of the UN Charter, and an inherent right enjoyed by each State, to (individually or collectively) defend itself, described in Article 51

* Alexandre Dumas (père), *Le Comte de Monte-Cristo,* 1844.

[1] M Byers and S Chesterman, 'Changing the Rules about Rules? Unilateral Humanitarian Intervention and the Future of International Law' in JL Holzgrefe and RO Keohane (eds), *Humanitarian Intervention: Ethical, Legal and Political Dilemmas* (Cambridge, Cambridge University Press, 2003) 177.

[2] See, eg C Greenwood, 'Yes, but is the war legal?', *Observer*, London, 28 March 1999.

[3] See also J Habermas, 'Bestiality and Humanity: A War on the Border between Legality and Morality' (1999) 6 *Constellations* 263, 264, who uses the term 'classical international law'.

of the Charter. However, humanitarian intervention may not be held to fall within either of these exceptions.

For the purposes of this discussion, I shall define humanitarian intervention as: (1) the threat or use of force; (2) across State borders; (3) by a State or group of States; (4) aimed at preventing or ending gross human rights violations; (5) where such violations are being committed by the violating State against individuals other than the citizens of the intervening State(s);[4] (6) without the permission of the State within the territory of which force is applied.

The above corresponds with the definition of JL Holzgrefe and Robert O Keohane,[5] but to it, I add one further tenet: (7) the intervention is not authorised by the UN Security Council. This final criterion shall limit our discussion to interventions which are not sanctioned by the Security Council, thereby avoiding confusion between authorised and unauthorised 'humanitarian' interventions.

It is clear that this type of operation, since it is not of a self-defensive nature, and since it has not received the prerequisite Security Council go-ahead, is outside of either of the two designated exceptions to Article 2(4). The above, in tandem with the fact that customary international law has not accepted a right of humanitarian intervention as lawful, renders such activities illegal, both under customary international law and Charter law.

However, in the aftermath of the NATO Kosovo operation, condemnation of the intervention as downright illegal was relatively scarce. Instead, a broad range of theories attempting to justify the legality, or at the very least, the justice of the intervention, surfaced. The reasons for this may be traced in the historical and political *Zeitgeist* and shall be discussed herein.

This work will examine a great deal of the scholarship which has been undertaken attempting to justify humanitarian intervention, particularly since 1999. It will focus on leading authors and the justificatory models and tests which they have proffered. The goal of this work is to argue that all of the scholarly models which have been identified are inadequate to do the job for which they were devised. None of the arguments resolve the conflict which arises between law and justice, and many of them do damage to international law and order. In addition, several theories which in 1999 were utilised to justify NATO's involvement in Kosovo have since been

[4] This requirement is inserted to avoid discussions about 'rescue missions', such as the Israeli 'operation Entebbe' in 1976, carried out by States to extricate and protect their citizens in situations where they are at threat from the government of the State in which they are resident. Such operations are in need of separate discussion which goes beyond the scope of this volume, but are discussed in detail in, *inter alia*, S Chesterman, *Just War or Just Peace: Humanitarian Intervention and International Law* (New York, Oxford University Press, 2001); and KE Eichensehr, 'Defending Nationals Abroad: Assessing the Lawfulness of Forcible Hostage Rescues' (2008) 88 *Virginia Journal of Internationl Law* 451.

[5] JL Holzgrefe, 'The Humanitarian Intervention Debate' in JL Holzgrefe and RO Keohane (eds), *Humanitarian Intervention: Ethical, Legal and Political Dilemmas* (Cambridge, Cambridge University Press, 2003) 18.

employed to justify other interventions where the humanitarian motives of the interveners were less apparent, notably the 2003 invasion of Iraq. The tone of this work will necessarily therefore be rather negative, seeking as it does to criticise the broad majority of scholarship in this field. This may be easier to understand if I offer some brief explanation as to the content of the later chapters of this volume. Based upon the stated deficiencies of the various proposed legitimising formulae, I shall undertake a study of whether the third source of international law – that is, general principles (almost completely ignored by scholarship in this field until now) – may hold the possibility of a third exception to the prohibition upon the use of force. It is my position, based upon my research thus far, that such an exception may indeed exist. However, the need for exploration of such a theory is only justified if the models proposed by other authors in this field are faulty. It is my contention that they are, and hence my wish to undertake the critical examination contained in this volume.

II. HISTORICAL INTRODUCTION

Following upon persistent threats and warnings of its imminent resort to the use of force, NATO, on 24 March 1999, commenced air strikes against the Federal Republic of Yugoslavia (FRY). A veritable plethora of reasons were proffered justifying this operation. The NATO operation, given its timing in the wake of the horrors of Srebrenica and Rwanda, was broadly welcomed. Someone at last seemed to be standing up for human rights. However, the legality of the operation was, on the face of it, at least, extremely suspect. This fact presented a quandary. Human rights protection is essentially enshrined within the normative framework of international law. Indeed this protection constitutes one of the three fundamental tenets of international law which underpin international relations.[6] Many legal and political commentators found themselves vexed by how to treat an ostensibly illegal military operation at least purportedly undertaken in the name of human rights protection. How could one break international law in the name of international law?

The responses composed to the NATO operation were diverse, between commentators as between intervening States and third party States. Some condemned the operation as downright illegal, while others attempted to excuse this illegality on the basis of an 'international exception'. Still others drove the debate away from the strict legality of the operation and attempted to assess its 'legitimacy', while there were also those who claimed a new norm of customary international law was developing. A great many assess-

[6] The other two being peace and self-determination. A Cassese, 'Ex iniuria ius oritur: Are We Moving owards International Legitimation of Forcible Humanitarian Countermeasures in the World Community' (1999) *European Journal of International Law* 23.

ments – some contradictory – were advanced regarding what Kosovo could mean for international law. However, if one thing has clearly emerged from the debate, it is that there is no overall consensus. This is disquieting, in that it leaves the future uncertain.

In this chapter, I shall attempt to shed some light on a selection of the principal component arguments within the humanitarian intervention debate, post-Kosovo. In doing so, I shall attempt to remain within the legal sphere as far as possible. However, it is evident that a full treatment of the debate may not be undertaken without at least a passing reference to historical debate, political comment, and the facts of the Kosovo crisis itself. Furthermore, I shall endeavour to cast a critical eye over many of the arguments adduced, in order to show the relative weaknesses of many of the proffered justifications for the Kosovo operation, and indeed for humanitarian intervention in general. Obviously, due to the breadth of scholarship which events post-Kosovo have generated, it is impossible to be exhaustive here, but I shall treat the opinions of leading commentators and indicate when opinions may be treated as exemplary of broader trends within the discourse.

An exhaustive treatment of the literature in this field would be all but impossible in a work of this length. However, I shall nonetheless endeavour to examine the principal schools of argument in this field through a thorough treatment of their usage by leading authors. The authors chosen for in-depth analysis represent some of the leading exponents of the various theories, though necessarily choices had to be made to include some rather than others for the sake of brevity. In addition, and in order to furnish a more complete picture of the doctrinal debate, I shall furnish brief commentaries via annotations and footnotes on where these authors find concurring and dissenting opinion both within and without their schools of thought.

I shall begin with the convincing argument proposed by, inter alia, Ian Brownlie, that the Kosovo intervention was illegal. Brownlie maintained this position for many years, and his research here is second to none. Thereafter, I shall treat the analysis of Bruno Simma, who epitomised the school of thought that the Kosovo action, although illegal, was only separated by what Simma dubs 'a thin red line' from international legality. I shall then refer to the position argued by Antonio Cassese and others, that while humanitarian intervention is illegal, a customary norm justifying such activities may soon evolve, and will compare this with the 'Solidarist' position defended by Nicholas Wheeler. I shall then describe a 'turn to ethics' amongst international lawyers, who have attempted to employ ethical and political rationales to bolster legal arguments, and shall demonstrate the theoretical repercussions which this process has had upon the humanitarian intervention debate. I shall also examine efforts to legitimise the intervention in a way keeping closer to the strict letter of the law, particularly the analysis of Thomas M Franck, and shall enquire whether the logic of the debate, and particularly the parallels which may be drawn between it and the long-defunct Just War doctrine are dangerous, insofar as they may be employed by the unscrupulous for their own designs. Finally, I shall attempt an in-depth appraisal of the most visible concerted and international effort to provide a new discourse combined with a legal framework for humanitarian intervention post-Kosovo, namely the Responsibility to Protect initiative.

III. 'KOSOVO' AS AN ILLEGAL OPERATION

In a memorandum treating the international law aspects of the Kosovo crisis, Ian Brownlie and CJ Apperley present a cogent case that the operation was illegal.[7] I shall deal with this treatment in some depth, as it may later be used in order to refute many of the apologist/justificatory theories submitted by other scholars. This article shall represent my major source for the 'illegality' position within the debate. It is chosen for such purposes due to its timing – shortly after the Kosovo intervention – and due to its strength of argument, as well as the fact that it typifies those who argue for the illegality of humanitarian intervention. I shall, however, refer to further concurring opinion from Brownlie himself and indeed from other sources in order to demonstrate the strength of this position. The position also represents the 'standard' positivist reading of international law that has been prevalent throughout international legal scholarship, seeing the general prohibition of the use of force and its two exceptions as a watertight, closed, regime.

Brownlie and Apperley point to the excuses proffered by the UK Government for military action, couched in: (1) UN Security Council Resolutions 1199 and 1203; (2) the assertion of a legal right 'to prevent a humanitarian catastrophe'; and (3) the fact that military action might only be undertaken in the event of Belgrade's non-acquiescence to the Contact Group's demands (the Rambouillet 'Agreement').

Further, in the British House of Commons, a customary right to humanitarian intervention was espoused, although as the authors point out, none exists. A tendency on the part of the British Government to avoid reference to any exact legal sources (such as treaties, the UN Charter, etc) was further remarkable.

Ab initio, Brownlie and Apperley appear palpably hostile to the idea of Kosovo finding legal justification. They note that the 'novel phrase' 'humanitarian catastrophe' is more often employed than the traditional nomenclature of humanitarian intervention,[8] and refer to evidence that the actual

[7] I Brownlie and CJ Apperley, 'Kosovo Crisis Inquiry: Memorandum on the International Law Aspects' (2000) 49 *ICLQ* 878.

[8] ibid, 884.

views, as opposed to those publicly expressed, by NATO legal advisors, were unfavourable to action.[9] However, this evidence, although it may point to disingenuous comportment on the part of the aforementioned actors, is simply not pertinent to a legal argument, and I struggle to grasp why Brownlie and Apperley mention it. After all, following from the *Eastern Greenland* case of 1933, government officials are estopped from denying the value of unilateral declarations when they have given others cause to believe they are to be relied upon.[10] Therefore, the fact that such declarations are not necessarily truthfully representative of the sentiments of the officials which impart them is legally irrelevant.[11]

The UN Charter, Article 2(4) prescribes that:

> All Members shall refrain in their international relations from the threat or use of force against the territorial integrity or political independence of any state, or in any other manner inconsistent with the Purposes of the United Nations.

Brownlie and Apperley point out that the *travaux préparatoires* indicate that this phrase ought to be afforded a strict interpretation, and that the second part of the phrase – 'against the territorial integrity and political independence of any state' – may not be construed to refer to a particular threshold which must be reached by threats and uses of force in order to render them illegal.[12] As Anne-Sophie Massa has pointed out, far from restricting the scope of the prohibition, these words 'were inserted as a guarantee for small states to reinforce the impermissible character of recourses to force against a state', a pleonasm of sorts.[13] Although not referred to by Brownlie, this assertion is further evidenced by the rejection

[9] ibid, 883.

[10] This dispute centred on the so-called 'Ihlen Declaration' of 22 July 1919, by the Norwegian Foreign Minister, Nils Claus Ihlen, regarding Denmark's sovereignty over Greenland. Ihlen stated that 'the plans of the Royal [Danish] Government respecting Danish sovereignty over the whole of Greenland . . . would be met with no difficulties on the part of Norway'. The PCIJ (Permanent Court of International Justice) held that the statement constituted a definitive and unconditional promise, which could be relied upon by Denmark.

[11] *Legal Status of Eastern Greenland (Denmark v Norway)* PCIJ Rep Series A/B No 53; see also *Case Concerning the Temple of Preah Vihear (Cambodia v Thailand)* (Merits) [1962] ICJ Rep 1. This position was borne out by the more recent cases *Nuclear Tests (New Zealand v France)* [1974] ICJ Rep 253 and *Nuclear Tests (Australia v France)* [1974] ICJ Rep 457. Here, the ICJ, referring to the famous Ihlen Declaration of the *Eastern Greenland* judgment, stated that a unilateral declaration, 'even though not made within the context of international negotiations, is binding. In these circumstances, nothing in the nature of a quid pro quo nor any subsequent acceptance of the declaration, nor even any reply or reaction from other States, is required for the declaration to take effect, since such a requirement would be inconsistent with the strictly unilateral nature of the juridical act by which the pronouncement by the State was made'. ([1974] ICJ Rep 267 [43] and 472 [46], respectively).

[12] A contrary interpretation is argued, inter alia, by A D'Amato, *International Law: Process and Prospects* (New York, Transnational Publishers, 1987) 57–73; F Tesón, *Humanitarian Intervention: An Inquiry into Peace, Law and Morality*, 2nd edn (Irvington, NY, Transnational Publishers 1997) 150-51; and F Abiew, *The Evolution of the Doctrine and Practice of Humanitarian Intervention* (The Hague, Kluwer Law International, 1999) 94–95.

[13] AS Massa, 'Does Humanitarian Intervention Serve Human Rights? The Case of Kosovo' (2009) 1 *Amsterdam Law Forum* 52.

of a more supple interpretation of this phrase by the International Court of Justice (ICJ) in the *Corfu Channel* case (1949).[14] Hersch Lauterpacht adopts a similar attitude.[15] This position has been confirmed 25 years after the Charter's inception in the 'Friendly Relations' Declaration,[16] which reaffirmed the principle 'concerning the duty not to intervene in matters within the domestic jurisdiction of any state, in accordance with the Charter'. Therefore, the 'qualifying clause' was intended as an extra bulwark against force, rather than 'the key to the padlock'. Indeed, as shown from the ICJ's *Nicaragua* judgment, a restrictive interpretation will be applied to any of the narrow exceptions which do exist to the prohibition upon the use of force, and thus both under customary international law and the law of the UN Charter, States do not have a (unilateral) right of 'armed response to acts which do not constitute an "armed attack"'.[17] Therefore, any attempts at a broad teleological interpretation of Article 2(4) are, per Brownlie and Apperley, misguided.

Regarding the legal status of humanitarian intervention, Brownlie and Apperley state that no evidence exists of such a legal right and that such a right cannot be compatible with the UN Charter. Indeed, in a number of earlier texts, Brownlie had noted the fact that while humanitarian intervention had not induced express condemnation within the Covenant of the League of Nations, nor in the Briand–Kellogg pact (and therefore its status *inter-bellum* was more discutable) it remained 'highly doubtful' that such a prohibition had survived the general interdiction regarding armed force enunciated in the UN Charter.[18] Further, as noted by Francioni, the Draft Articles on the Responsibility of States for Internationally Wrongful Acts stipulate that State responses to grave violations of international obligations owed *erga omnes* – including human rights obligations – must be lawful and consistent with the UN Charter.[19]

The argument that humanitarian intervention is without legal basis finds support from a wide selection of other authors. Akehurst, for exam-

[14] *Corfu Channel Case (UK v Albania)* (Merits) [1949] ICJ Rep 4.

[15] H Lauterpacht (ed), *Oppenheim's International Law*, vol II (London, Longman, 1952).

[16] General Assembly Resolution 3314 (XXIX) (1970), *Declaration on Principles of International Law Concerning Friendly Relations and Co-operation.*

[17] *Military and Paramilitary Activities in and against Nicaragua (Nicaragua v United States)* [1986] ICJ Rep 14, 211.

[18] See I Brownlie, *International Law and the Use of Force by States* (Oxford, Clarendon Press, 1963); I Brownlie, 'Thoughts on Kind-Hearted Gunmen' in R Lillich (ed), *Humanitarian Intervention and the United Nations* (Charlottesville, University of Virginia Press, 1973); I Brownlie, 'Humanitarian Intervention' in JN Moore (ed), *Law and Civil War in the Modern World* (Baltimore, John Hopkins University Press, 1974); I Brownlie, 'The United Nations Charter and the Use of Force, 1945–85' in A Cassese (ed), *The Current Legal Regulation of the Use of Force* (Dordrecht, Martinus Nijhoff Publishers, 1986); and I Brownlie, *The Rule of Law in International Affairs* (The Hague, Martinus Nijhoff Publishers, 1998) 206–09.

[19] F Francioni, 'Balancing the Prohibition of Force with the Need to Protect Human Rights: A Methodological Approach' in E Cannizzaro and P Palchetti (eds), *Customary International Law on the Use of Force: A Methodological Approach* (Leiden, Koninklijke Brill NV, 2005) 272.

ple, is unequivocal in stating that the evidence indicates that humanitarian intervention is 'incompatible' with international law.[20] Oscar Schachter voices a similar view, citing the probable rationale behind this:

> [G]overnments by and large (and most jurists) would not assert a right to forcible intervention to protect the nationals of another country from the atrocities carried out in that country . . .
>
> The reluctance of governments to legitimise foreign invasion in the interest of humanitarianism is understandable in the light of past abuses by powerful states. States strong enough to intervene and sufficiently interested in doing so tend to have political motives. They have a strong temptation to impose a political solution in their own national interest.[21]

However, the rationale advanced by Schachter does not stand up to scrutiny. As Rosalyn Higgins J has pointed out:

> Many writers do argue against the lawfulness of humanitarian intervention today. They make much of the fact that in the past the right has been abused. It undoubtedly has. But then so have there been countless abusive claims of the right to self-defence. This does not lead us to say that there should be no right of self-defence today . . .
>
> We delude ourselves if we think that the role of norms is to remove the possibility of abusive claims ever being made. The role of norms is the achievement of values for the common good . . .
>
> Claims which may in very restricted exceptional circumstances be regarded as lawful should not a priori be disallowed because on occasion they may be unjustly invoked.[22]

Schachter's view therefore is right insofar as most States view humanitarian intervention as illegal, but wrong inasmuch as he justifies their position with reference to the possible abuse of such a right. The illegality of humanitarian intervention was indeed upheld by the British Government, precedent to the Kosovo intervention, as evidenced by a 1986 Foreign Office Policy Document:

> [T]he best case that can be made in support of humanitarian intervention is that it cannot be said to be unambiguously illegal . . . the overwhelming majority of contemporary legal opinion comes down against the existence of a right of humanitarian intervention.[23]

[20] M Akehurst, 'Humanitarian Intervention' in H Bull (ed), *Intervention in World Politics* (Oxford, Clarendon Press, 1984). Kim agrees, stating that the consensus amongst States is still that humanitarian intervention is illegal post-Kosovo, YS Kim, 'The Responsibility to Protect, Humanitarian Intervention and North Korea' (2006) 5 *Journal of International Business and Law* 74.

[21] O Schachter, 'The Right of States to Use Armed Force' (1984) 82 *Michigan Law Review* 1620, 1629; see also O Schachter, quoted in L Henkin, 'NATO's Kosovo Intervention: Kosovo and the Law of Humanitarian Intervention' (1999) 93 *American Journal of International Law* 826.

[22] R Higgins, 'International Law and the Avoidance, Containment and Resolution of Disputes' (1991) 230 *Recueil des Cours de l'Académie de Droit International* 9, 313–16.

[23] British Foreign Office, 'Foreign Policy Document No 148' (1986) 57 *British Yearbook of International Law* 619.

The above position perhaps explains the British Government's aforementioned reticence toward adopting common parlance and dubbing the Kosovo mission 'humanitarian intervention', instead choosing to refer to a 'humanitarian catastrophe'. To do otherwise would have been to admit the illegality of the operation, as previously affirmed by their own Foreign Ministry. Coining an alternative nomenclature, as it were, at least afforded the UK the opportunity to avoid seeming openly hypocritical, and possibly to avoid appearing to be openly breaking international law.[24] In addition, the use of the word 'catastrophe', an emotive term to the ears of the masses, suggests urgency and a sense of exceptionality that makes immediate and effective action seem warranted and even indispensable to the public at large.

Based upon the above, in addition to a wide selection of further commentaries, Brownlie and Apperley are able to conclude that: (1) the careful wording of Article 2(4) was precisely intended to allay fears of smaller States in light of conduct in the inter-war period (it having been a favourite excuse of Hitler to put forward mistreatment of minorities as a rationale for military invasion). (2) The overwhelming body of legal opinion considers humanitarian intervention illegal. The authors cite 18 separate authorities, spanning 12 nationalities, and including the views of three former Presidents of the ICJ (Schwebel, Jiminez de Arechaga and Ruda). (3) Only a small minority of international lawyers have adopted the position that humanitarian intervention may be considered lawful (as distinct from excusable).

The views of Brownlie and Apperley find concurring opinion elsewhere.[25] JS Watson and Alfred Rubin, for example, both condemn humanitarian intervention (as well as attempts to enforce human rights norms through the operation of international criminal tribunals) as illegal acts

[24] Of course, this is hardly a new tactic. States have always been wont to call one thing another in order to render it more legally or politically palatable. Prominent past examples include the United States' usage of the term 'quarantine' rather than 'blockade' during the Cuban Missile Crisis and the same country's dubbing of the Vietnam War as a 'police action'.

[25] JS Watson, 'A Realistic Jurisprudence of International Law' (1980) *Yearbook of World Affairs* 265; JI Charney, 'Anticipatory Humanitarian Intervention in Kosovo' (1999) 93 *American Journal of International Law* 834, 841; S Chesterman, *Just War or Just Peace? Humanitarian Intervention and International Law* (Oxford, Oxford University Press, 2001); R Falk, 'Humanitarian Intervention After Kosovo' in L Boisson de Chazournes and V Gowlland-Debbas (eds), *L'Ordre Juridique International, Un Système en Quête d'Équité, Liber Amicorum Georges Abi-Saab* (The Hague, Martinus Nijhoff, 2001); L Hannikainen, 'The World After 11 September 2001: Is the Prohibition on the Use of Force Disintegrating?' in J Petman and J Klabbers, *Nordic Cosmopolitanism: Essays in International Law for Martti Koskenniemi* (Leiden, Martinus Nijhoff, 2003) 446; RB Bilder, 'The Implications of Kosovo for International Human Rights Law' in P Alston and E MacDonald, *Human Rights, Intervention and the Use of Force: The Collected Courses of the Academy of European Law* (Oxford, Oxford University Press, 2008). See also S Mohamed, 'Restructuring the Debate on Unauthorised Humanitarian Intervention' (2010) 88 *North Carolina Law Review* 1275, who argues that illegal humanitarian intervention does too much systemic damage to be legal or legitimate.

masquerading under the guise of legality.[26] Scholtz stresses the importance of Article 2(4), without which, he argues, international relations would be governed by the use of force, and worries that illegal humanitarian intervention may pose a risk to it.[27] O'Connell is quite unequivocal on this point, stating that 'There really is no normative basis for non-compliance'.[28]

However, not all international lawyers are in accord with Brownlie and Apperley's views. It is, I feel, particularly germane to note that many of the sources quoted in support of their position predate the invasion of Kosovo.[29] Only one cited source, that of Bruno Simma[30] is contemporaneous with the initial threats of force (undoubtedly as illegal as the use of force itself) made by NATO Member States against the FRY, and of the cited sources, Simma's is perhaps the most equivocal and least convincing, holding that 'only a thin red line separates NATO's action on Kosovo from international legality'.[31] The position adopted by Simma represented a portent of things to come. A move away from a strict legal analysis was in the offing in the wake of the Kosovo operation. Brownlie was to find his positivistic posture was no longer *en vogue*.

I shall now discuss how in the aftermath of the NATO intervention in Kosovo, a new discourse, or rather several new discourses, developed regarding the concept of humanitarian intervention.

IV. 'A THIN RED LINE' – THE ARGUMENT OF 'NEAR-LEGALITY'

Professor Bruno Simma, while admitting the illegality of humanitarian intervention, adds a caveat to this assessment, making the seemingly innocuous proposal that the NATO operation in Kosovo was not far away from being legal, and therefore 'almost legal', as it were. Simma is the leading proponent of such a position, and hence, his shall be the principal analysis referred to in this section. Simma's contention, while superficially

[26] AP Rubin, *Ethics and Authority in International Law* (Cambridge, Cambridge Univesrsity Press, 1997) 70–206.

[27] W Scholtz, 'The Changing Rules of Ius ad Bellum: Conflicts in Kosovo, Iraq and Afghanistan' (2004) 7 *Potchefstroomse Elektroniese Regsblad* 1.

[28] ME O'Connell, 'Taking Opinio Juris Seriously, A Classical Approach to International Law on the Use of Force' in E Cannizzaro and P Palchetti (eds), *Customary International Law on the Use of Force: A Methodological Approach* (Leiden, Koninklijke Brill NV, 2005) 29.

[29] This is not to say, of course that no anti-humanitarian scholarship exists in the twenty-first century. Indeed, some of the most virulent criticism has been penned since 1999. Murphy, eg states that humanitarian intervention must be understood as an international crime, falling under the scope of aggression and any future definition of aggression in the ICC must include it. SD Murphy, 'Criminalizing Humanitarian Intervention' (2009) 41 *Case Western Reserve Journal of International Law* 341.

[30] B Simma, 'NATO, the UN and the Use of Force: Legal Aspects' (1999) 10 *European Journal of International Law* 1.

[31] ibid, 22.

innocent looking, was to serve as a starting point for many scholars who used this pretended 'proximity' to legality to introduce philosophical theses to excuse or legitimise the Kosovo intervention. I shall examine these efforts later, but for the moment it is germane to assess the import of Simma's own position, which has itself been subsequently mirrored by other scholars.

Simma begins by reminding us that the obligation weighing upon States to respect and protect human rights is owed *erga omnes.*[32] Hence, in case of material breaches of such obligations, any other State has *locus standi* to consider itself injured and may therefore resort to countermeasures (not involving force) against the perpetrator. The fact that no forcible countermeasures may be adopted in such cases is further apparent due to the comprehensive nature of Article 2(4), which Simma admits is intended to be 'watertight',[33] and that such countermeasures would not fall under either of the exceptions to the general prohibition allowed under the Charter.

Simma further states that Article 2(4) represents a peremptory norm of international law, having acquired *ius cogens* status. It can therefore only be modified by another norm of a similar status. Surprisingly, having made this observation, Simma fails to expand upon it. It seems unusual that when wishing to express a contention that the NATO operation in Kosovo was proximate to legality that one would not observe that at least a minimum modicum of human rights norms are themselves *ius cogens*, and may therefore themselves conceivably alter other *ius cogens* norms, such as Article 2(4).[34] However, Simma does note the ICJ position, albeit one predating the end of the Cold War, concerning the relationship between the two: 'the use of force could not be the appropriate method to monitor or ensure . . . respect [for human rights]'.[35]

However, Simma argues that humanitarian interventions undertaken in the spirit of preventing recurrence of past atrocities ought to meet a friendlier reaction. Such interventions may breach international law. 'But such a general statement cannot be the last word'.[36] Rather, argues Simma, one must weigh concrete circumstances against the relative illegality of any operation, taking into account the efforts of the interveners to get 'as close to the law' as possible. Per Simma, such analyses will influence both legal and moral judgments. It is on the basis of this test that Simma contends that only a thin red line separates the Kosovo intervention from legality. A similar position, citing a 'trend', epitomised by the Kosovo

[32] ibid, 2.

[33] ibid, 3.

[34] See T Meron, 'On a Hierarchy of International Human Rights' (1986) 80 *American Journal of International Law* 1.

[35] *Military and Paramilitary Activities in and against Nicaragua (Nicaragua v United States)* (Merits) [1986] ICJ Rep 14 [268].

[36] Simma (1999) (n 30) 6.

intervention, which pushes humanitarian intervention into the domain of international legitimacy and 'close' to international legality is proposed by Paolo Picone.[37]

Simma notes Security Council Resolutions 1160 and 1199 of 1998, adopted under Chapter VII, which determined that 'Kosovo' represented a threat to peace and security in the region and which promised consideration of additional measures if a political solution was not found. The knowledge that Russia would veto any Resolution authorising force precluded any pursuant actions. 'At this point', Simma tells us, 'NATO took over, as it were . . . The principal legal basis for such action was to be the concept of "humanitarian intervention", linked as closely as possible under the circumstances to the UN Charter in order to further gain legitimacy'.[38] This is a curious contention, outlining the principal legal basis for an operation which Simma himself admits was illegal, and bringing to mind Truepenny CJ's contradictory dictum on adherence to law.[39] Further, the confusion of the terms 'legality' and 'legitimacy' is not a technique limited to Simma. In fact, Simma borrows this terminology from NATO Secretary-General Javier Solana, who determined that the concrete circumstances – the non-compliance of the Federal Republic of Yugoslavia (FRY) with Security Council Resolutions; the impending humanitarian catastrophe; the impossibility of procuring Security Council authorisation to use force; and Council's determination that a threat to the peace existed – constituted 'legitimate grounds for the Alliance to threaten, and if necessary, to use force'.[40] Of course, it is worth mentioning the fact that 'legitimacy' is a far more flexible and far less precise notion than law, precisely because there is no undisputed authority mandated to evaluate legitimacy, and no agreed procedure for doing so.[41] Perhaps it is for this reason that it was to become a key term in the humanitarian intervention debate.

According to Simma, citing the Resolution on Recasting Euro-Atlantic Security, adopted by the North Atlantic (Parliamentary) Assembly,[42] NATO sources acquired a clear message from the Kosovo crisis, namely that if it transpires that Security Council authorisation for future NATO non-self-defensive missions involving armed force is unobtainable, NATO must still be able to push ahead with such enforcement. Simma parallels

[37] P Picone, 'La "Guerra del Kosovo" e il Diritto Internazionale Generale' (2000) 2 *Rivista di diritto internazionale* 309, 342–46. Picone cites Kosovo as evidence of a move in this direction, also referring to interventions in Haiti and Iraq (1990) for contextual purposes.

[38] Simma (1999) (n 30) 7.

[39] This dictum runs thus: 'One of the most ancient bits of legal wisdom is the saying that a man may break the letter of the law without breaking the law itself', opinion of Truepenny CJ in L Fuller, 'The Case of the Speluncean Explorers' (1949) 62 *Harvard Law Review* 3.

[40] Letter from Secretary-General Solana, addressed to the permanent representatives to the North Atlantic Council, 9 October 1998.

[41] Danish Institute of Foreign Affairs, *Humanitarian Intervention: Legal and Political Aspects* (Copenhagen, Danish Institute of Foreign Affairs, 1999) 24.

[42] NATO Doc AR 295 SA (1998).

the language used in the Resolution with that contained in the 'Uniting for Peace' UN General Assembly Resolution of 3 November 1970, but points out that 'Uniting for Peace' was an effort to fill gaps in the Charter during the darkest era of the Cold War. He admits 'such *ersatz* constructs might have had a certain legitimacy at the time. But today, things are different: since the end of the Cold War, the Security Council is functioning precisely in the manner envisaged in 1945'.[43] The language of legitimacy creeps into Simma's rhetoric again here, and since he fails to define the concept, we are left to wonder as to what he means. However, as to the legality of the operation, we are left in no doubt. Simma affirms the primacy of the UN Charter over the Washington Treaty, adding that the 'status of the Charter should not be prejudiced by NATO',[44] (except, of course, by the circumlocution tactics that he himself proposes).

Nonetheless, it is evident that Simma reaches this conclusion with a heavy heart. His 'legitimacy' criterion, based loosely around that proposed by Javier Solana is never completely explained. Perhaps it is as well that this is so, as it can only clash with the law. Simma finishes by dubbing Kosovo a 'hard case', which it undoubtedly is, which involves terrible dilemmas, which may 'appear to leave no choice but to act outside the law'.[45] He argues for a singular interpretation of the circumstances that led to the Kosovo intervention, and that such actions should be examined *ad hoc* and case-by-case, in order to reduce their power to erode the tenets of international law. This may be done by indicating the concrete circumstances which led to the decision, and in this regard, he commends NATO for proffering a convincing case. Resort to illegality may be permissible in such circumstances, but not as an instrument of general policy. It is for this reason that only a thin red line separates the Kosovo operation from legality.

Simma's idea of relative legality, or near-legality represents a valiant attempt to wrestle with the unyielding prohibition of Article 2(4).[46] However,

[43] Simma (1999) (n 30) 17. Michael Reisman disagrees, citing the regular 'paralysing' of the Security Council by use of the veto, and argues that 'Uniting for Peace' should be built upon. WM Reisman, 'Kosovo's Antimonies' (1999) 93 *American Journal of International Law* 860.

[44] Simma (1999) (n 30) 18.

[45] Simma (1999) (n 30) 22. In employing this phrase, which echoes that of Secretary Webster's letter pursuant to the *Caroline Affair* of 1841, it is perhaps a shame that Simma fails to explore the genesis of the customary rule on self-defence and to parallel this with his own conclusions on the use of force in humanitarian catastrophes. See H Jones, *To the Webster-Ashburton Treaty: A Study in Anglo-American Relations, 1783–1843* (Chapel Hill, North Carolina, University of North Carolina Press, 1977). There are also echoes of Gustav Radbruch's contention that positive law must be set aside when it is totally incompatible with basic principles of morality and justice. G Radbruch, *Rechtsphilosophie* (Stuttgart, Koehler, 1950). However, as Francioni notes, it is somewhat 'difficult to conceive of the issue of the use of force as being beyond the reach of international law'.

[46] It is worth noting that Simma was not the first to come up with such a position. Similar ideas have been espoused and criticised by, inter alia, David Scheffer, Jim Whitman and Oliver Ramsbotham: D Scheffer, 'Toward a Modern Doctrine of Humanitarian Intervention'

problems remain with Simma's thesis. For one thing, as Francesco Francioni has pointed out, describing such a massive use of force as the two months of bombardment which took place in Kosovo as a 'minor' breach is hardly accurate.[47] While Simma does finish by avowing the legal worth of Article 2(4), which serves to render humanitarian intervention illegal, his usage of the legal/legitimate dichotomy and his avowal that interventions such as that undertaken in Kosovo may be excusable so long as not undertaken as an instrument of general policy is curious. If anything, the NATO position makes a great deal more sense. At least the NATO position, while also couched in illegality, creates a set of concrete guidelines for circumstances under which NATO may act even in the absence of Security Council authorisation. It is plain that Simma does not like this idea, as it weakens international law,[48] but surely, if 'another Kosovo' rears its head tomorrow, NATO should act again. Nehal Bhuta echoes this proposition, stating that 'one way of understanding humanitarian intervention is not so much as a "right", but as illegal conduct which is tolerated by the international community in extreme circumstances'.[49] What is the sense in an *ad hoc* decision, based upon 'concrete circumstances', if similar circumstances will always lead to a similar result (as would be the case for my hypothetical 'another Kosovo') then surely we are in the process of creating a rule-based system.[50] Further, considering the role of State practice in developing international law, consistent similar action without broad condemnation must surely lead to the gradual emergence of a legal rule. As Anthea Roberts has pointed out, Simma's approach, shifting the focus away from legality can undermine the coherence of international law, and raises the risk of any 'legitimacy test' being manipulated.[51]

If Simma's ideas will inevitably lead to a rule-based system (inside or outside the strictures of international law), it merely rests to design such rules. Antonio Cassese is amongst those who have attempted to do so,

(1991–92) 23 *University of Toledo Law Review* 253. J Whitman, 'A Cautionary Note on Humanitarian Intervention' (1994) 34 *GeoJournal* 167; O Ramsbotham, 'Humanitarian Intervention 1990–95: A Need to Reconceptualise?' (1997) 23 *Review of International Studies* 445.

[47] F Francioni, 'Of War, Humanity and Justice: International Law after Kosovo' in JA Frowein and R Wolfrum (eds), *Max Planck Yearbook of UN Law*, vol 4 (2000) 107.

[48] That is to say, it weakens the rules governing the use of force by States vis-à-vis regional security structures, which are, of course, themselves part of international law.

[49] N Bhuta, 'Paved with Good Intentions – Humanitarian War, the New Interventionism and Legal Regulation of the Use of Force, Review Essay' (2001) 25 *Melbourne University Law Review* 843.

[50] Other authors have noted that a quicker development of such a rule, preferably inside the law, could have been used to prevent many recent atrocities. P Williams and M Stewart, 'Humanitarian Intervention: The New Missing Link in the Fight to Prevent Crimes against Humanity and Genocide' (2008) *Case Western Reserve Journal of International Law* 97.

[51] A Roberts, 'Legality Verses Legitimacy: Can Uses of Force be Illegal but Justified?' in P Alston and E MacDonald, *Human Rights, Intervention and the Use of Force: The Collected Courses of the Academy of European Law* (Oxford, Oxford University Press, 2008) 180.

and I shall deal with his contribution, devised as a direct response to the arguments of Professor Simma.

V. 'CONTEMPORARY TRENDS' AND THE REFORM OF CUSTOMARY INTERNATIONAL LAW

Cassese agrees with Simma that the NATO intervention falls outside the scope of the UN Charter and is, ergo, illegal, but goes on to note that 'My agreement with Simma ends, however, when he contends that "only a thin red line separates NATO's action in Kosovo from international legality"'.[52] Per Cassese, the breach cannot be termed minor. Also, the simple fact that the Security Council had determined that a threat to the peace existed does not constitute a legal ground for an attack on a foreign State. Cassese seems therefore to adopt a trenchant position that such breaches are not merely the 'borderline' affairs that Simma attempts to dub them. Furthermore, Cassese notes that 'once a group of powerful states has realised that it can freely escape the strictures of the UN Charter and resort to force without any censure, except for that of public opinion, a Pandora's box may be opened'.[53]

It seems from the above formulation that Cassese is not prepared to adopt the same apologist undertone to his illegality argument that Simma proposes before him. However, after the bullish rhetoric initially apparent in his article, Cassese goes on to adopt a vastly more equivocal position.

Cassese affirms that in the current international community framework, three sets of values underpin inter-State relations, these being peace, human rights, and self-determination. Cassese expands upon this, opining that when tension arises between these three core values, peace must be given precedence. Such an affirmation – regardless of the fact that it is over-simplistic in that it ignores sovereignty – lends further credence to the contention that humanitarian intervention has no legal basis. Human rights, we are told, must *ceder place* to peace.

Cassese then proposes that while it is true that it is difficult to sit idly by while thousands are massacred, this shall only serve to justify the Kosovo intervention from an ethical viewpoint, not a legal one. This represents a precursor of a large-scale 'turn to ethics' which has been treated by Martti Koskenniemi, and to which I shall myself devote attention in due course. However, one may at this point make the preliminary observation that in a legal discussion, it is of dubious merit to have recourse to moral and ethical considerations in order to change one's perceptions of the *legal* validity of a

[52] A Cassese, 'Ex iniuria ius oritur: Are We Moving towards International Legitimation of Forcible Humanitarian Countermeasures in the World Community' (1999) 10 *European Journal of International Law* 23, 24.

[53] ibid, 25.

legal proposition. Above all, the question must be posed as to which barometer of morality we should use, as no morality is all-ensconcing and objective.

Despite his moralising, however, Cassese still admits that he 'cannot avoid observing in the same breath that this moral action *is contrary to current international law*' (emphasis added).[54] The use of the word 'current' is paralleled by a trend amongst international lawyers to avoid discussing the strict legality of the Kosovo operation, instead prefixing their frame of reference as 'common perceptions of international law', 'traditional international law', or, as Cassese would have it, 'current international law'.[55] The explanations for this trend are plain, allowing the discourse to also take extra-legal factors into account, but such an approach serves only to devalue international law, insofar as it plainly implies that one may take a broad range of interpretations thereof. Surely 'traditional' and 'modern' international law must be different. If not, why bother affixing the prefix in the first place?

Nonetheless, Cassese broadly concedes the illegality of the NATO operation. He goes on to contend, however, 'that as legal scholars, we must stretch our minds further and ask ourselves two questions'.[56] These are: (1) whether the action was partially rooted in contemporary trends of the international community; and (2) whether parameters were set in this operation that might lead to gradual legitimisation of forcible humanitarian countermeasures by a group of States outside any Security Council authorisation.

In order to answer the above questions, Cassese commences by examining the 'basic premise or root' of the NATO intervention. He makes six points: first, it is a 'truism' that human rights are no longer the sole concern of the State where infringed. Secondly, obligations to respect human rights are owed *erga omnes*. Any State may take non-forcible steps to ensure respect. Thirdly, an idea is emerging that large-scale atrocities may give rise to aggravated State responsibility, entailing increased countermeasures. Fourthly, the international community is increasingly intervening through international bodies when human rights are in jeopardy. Fifthly, peaceful dispute settlement measures are increasingly regarded as crucial, and the idea is firmly rooted that these must take precedence. Finally, it has been claimed by some NGOs and governmental officials that under exceptional circumstances, 'where atrocities reach such a large scale as to shock the conscience of all human beings and indeed jeopardise international

[54] ibid, 25.

[55] See M Byers and S Chesterman, 'Changing the Rules about Rules? Unilateral Humanitarian Intervention and the Future of International Law' in JL Holzgrefe and RO Keohane (eds), *Humanitarian Intervention: Ethical, Legal and Political Dilemmas* (Cambridge, Cambridge University Press, 2003) 177.

[56] Cassese (1999) (n 52) 25.

stability, forcible protection of human rights may need to outweigh the necessity to avoid friction and armed conflict'.[57]

As Cassese puts it, 'positive peace', that is the realisation of justice, should prevail over 'negative peace', that is the absence of armed conflict.[58] Anne-Sophie Massa is fervently against such a contention, arguing that the substantive provisions of Charter law clearly privilege peace over justice, and that the *travaux préparatoires* demonstrate that this was a conscious choice, fuelled indeed to some degree by a belief that allowing a right of humanitarian intervention might not be the best way to protect human rights, owing to the gap that this would create in the prohibition upon the use of force and the inevitable deaths and human rights abuses which would result from the further wars generated by this exception.[59] This rather sensible conclusion is shared by other commentators.[60]

It is clear, then, that 'negative peace', as Cassese dubs it, represents the UN Charter position (the primacy of peaceful international relations over subjective justice), and is therefore the international legal position. An appeal to a 'positive peace' based on justice represents the effective transposition of the old justice versus law conundrum – or the natural law (represented here by 'positive peace') – versus positivism (represented here by 'negative peace', that is the UN Charter) debate – onto the international sphere. Cassese's formula is all very superficially attractive, but the problem is, it has no legal basis. Cassese's 'negative peace' ought to properly be called peace *simpliciter*. His 'positive peace' is effectively a euphemism for effective (and presumably forcible) enforcement of human rights.[61] This would represent an about-face of Cassese's earlier 'values' formula, with human rights taking precedence over peace. Giving the same concepts different names does not mean they have different levels of value. Either peace is paramount or it is not, *tout court*.

[57] ibid, 26.

[58] This logic is seized upon by both Reisman and Greenwood, who go so far as to argue that international human rights law *required* the use of force. WM Reisman, 'Kosovo's Antimonies' (1999) 93 *American Journal of International Law* 860, 861; C Greenwood, 'Humanitarian Intervention: The Case of Kosovo' (1999) 10 *Finnish Yearbook of International Law* 141.

[59] AS Massa, 'Does Humanitarian Intervention Serve Human Rights? The Case of Kosovo' (2009) 1 *Amsterdam Law Forum* 50.

[60] See, eg S Murphy, *Humanitarian Intervention: The United Nations in an Evolving World Order* (Philadelphia, Univeristy of Pennsylvania Press, 1996) 70. Jarna Petman disputes this position, however, positing that the paradigm has changed, and that the fact that NATO's Kosovo intervention did not fit into the international law use of force model reflects that important changes have occurred since the Charter's entry into force. J Petman, 'The Problem of Evil and International Law' in J Petman and J Klabbers, *Nordic Cosmopolitanism: Essays in International Law for Martti Koskenniemi* (Leiden, Martinus Nijhoff, 2003) 115.

[61] Rostow employs a similar logic, albeit in a broader form, arguing that in times of stress, international law can and must change to accommodate changing global realities. N Rostow, 'International Law and the Use of Force: A Plea for Realism' (2009) 34 *Yale International Law Journal* 557.

Cassese is not alone in employing such a formula, however. Kok-Chor Tan notes with reference to liberal cosmopolitan views that 'the more demanding a conception of global justice is with respect to how states treat their own citizens, the more readily a rationale is provided for states to intervene against each other in the name of upholding justice'.[62]

Furthermore, it is questionable whether all of Cassese's six points stand up to in-depth scrutiny. It is perhaps telling that concerning the increasing trend of the international community to intervene via international bodies where human rights are in jeopardy, Cassese furnishes a generous list of examples, whereas for points three and six, which cite the emergence of opinion trends, he fails to furnish any authority whatsoever to buttress his argument. I do not for a moment contend that none exists, but rather wish to highlight the fact that Cassese deliberately chooses not to use what authority there is in this area, perhaps due to the fact that the arguments evinced by such authority may not be convincing.

In any case, 'Based on these nascent trends in the world community', Cassese contends that under strict conditions, resort to armed force may become justified absent Security Council justification (although this has yet to happen).[63] These strict conditions are: (1) gross egregious human rights breaches, thousands of innocents killed and crimes against humanity; (2) the central authorities are unwilling/unable to put an end to the abuses; (3) the Security Council is unable to act due to discord or use of a veto; (4) all peaceful avenues which may be explored consistent with the urgency of the situation have been exhausted; (5) a group of States (not one power) decides to halt the atrocities with the support or non-opposition of a majority of UN members; and (5) armed force is used exclusively to stop the atrocities.

Cassese's test, while substantially based upon 'nascent trends' and other criteria he fails to adequately justify, contains some elements which are commendable, including the 'last resort' condition, meaning that such a test may only be contemplated when the usual legal avenues – namely Security Council action – have been effectively exhausted. It is perhaps worth mentioning here that my own test for legal humanitarian intervention based upon equity and general principles of law, which will be set out in detail in chapter five, contains many similar or analogous elements to that of Cassese. It is not with the logic of his test that I wish to quibble, therefore, but rather the fact that it is insufficiently justified, and is effectively grounded in legal nothingness.

[62] K-C Tan, 'Enforcing Global Justice: The Problem of Intervention' in R Pierik and W Werner (eds), *Cosmopolitanism in Context: Perspectives from International Law and Political Theory* (Cambridge, Cambridge University Press, 2009), see www.rolandpierik.nl/theory/Downloads/GJ_IL.pdf (accessed 27 May 2011).

[63] Cassese (1999) (n 52) 27.

Cassese contends that Kosovo broadly fits into the criteria proposed by his test. This is hardly surprising given that the embryonic customary norm to which he alludes is itself a product of the Kosovo operation. However, the intervention remains unlawful, as no new customary norm has yet developed. Such a customary rule would constitute an exception to the UN Charter system of collective enforcement, similar to that encapsulated in Article 51.[64] This formulation is echoed by Olivier Corten, who, unlike Cassese argues for a straightforward and orthodox reading of the UN Charter. Corten, however, admits that Kosovo and subsequent events may yet serve as precedents which could engender a change in customary international law, effectively forming a third exception to Article 2(4) in the future. Per Corten, 'Doit-on . . . conclure que le droit international n'est pas susceptible de s'adapter aux évolutions de la société dans laquelle il s'inscrit? Certainement pas'.[65]

Cassese refines his stance in a 'follow-up' article published in the same edition of the *European Journal of International Law*,[66] in which he effectively admits to having been premature in drafting parameters for the emergence of a new customary norm, admitting it may be more sensible to await repetition of such actions under the same conditions and exigencies. However, a customary rule of international law also requires a second element in addition to conduct – the *mens rea* equivalent of statist international law – *opinio iuris*, that is, the belief that the conduct was legal. To this, Cassese devotes renewed attention.

Cassese opines that States have stopped short of viewing the Kosovo action as lawful per se. However, a phenomenon known as *opinio necessitatis* has been widespread and appears to be crystallising. Cassese makes reference to the relative paucity of persistent objectors, and the overwhelming feeling in the international community that while the intervention itself was not legal, it was felt to be 'justified'. The idea that the action was necessary and proper does not yet render it legal, however. Cassese holds that it is premature to speak of the emergence of a customary rule as the element of

[64] A nuanced take on the above is adopted by BM Benjamin, who argues that while humanitarian intervention remains illegal, it should be 'temporarily legalised' until normative change comes about, preferably through the Security Council taking a greater interest in human rights when deciding upon enforcement measures. See BM Benjamin, 'Unilateral Humanitarian Intervention: Legalizing the Use of Force to Prevent Human Rights Atrocities' (1992) 16 *Fordham International Law Journal* 120. Another similar perspective, drawing on the work of Lon Fuller is proposed by Daniel Warner: D Warner, 'Ethics, Law and Unethical Compassion in the Kosovo Intervention' in L Boisson de Chazournes and V Gowlland-Debbas (eds), *L'Ordre Juridique International, Un Système en Quête d'Équité, Liber Amicorum Georges Abi-Saab* (The Hague, Martinus Nijhoff, 2001).

[65] O Corten, 'Vers une "Déterritorialisation" de l'Interdiction du Recours à la Force dans les Relations Internationales?' (2009) 5 *Annuário Brasileiro de Direito Internacional* 207. See also O Corten and P Klein, 'L'autorisation de recourir à la force à des fins humanitaires: droit d'ingérence ou retour aux sources?' (1993) 4 *European Journal of International Law* 506.

[66] A Cassese, 'A Follow-Up: Forcible Humanitarian Countermeasures and Opinio Necessitatis' (1999) 10 *European Journal of International Law* 791.

usus or *diuturnitas* is clearly lacking.[67] Cassese posits that while there may indeed be instances where a single episode of some magnitude combined with the reactions of other States may suffice to form an 'instant custom' (the Truman Declaration and the laws of Outer Space are perhaps prime examples);[68] more is required in the case of Kosovo.[69]

VI. LEGAL INADEQUACY AND 'SOLIDARIST INTERVENTION'

Cassese's position is broadly reflective of one of the major trends of opinion concerning Kosovo. There seems to be little prospect of terming humanitarian intervention legal in the short term, and yet, most feel reticent about condemning those who endeavoured to do what they thought was right. As Habermas put it, this was 'A war on the border between legality and morality'.[70] How far to move away from the law in this regard in order to achieve the desired result was, however, a hotly debated topic, and one which brought international lawyers into competition with political scientists and ethical philosophers. Nicholas J Wheeler is at the forefront of those from outside the legal discipline who have exercised an influence upon the debate and it is to his influential ideas that I now turn.

Wheeler, in his acclaimed work, *Saving Strangers*, puts forward what he dubs 'a Solidarist theory of humanitarian intervention'. Wheeler bases his argument upon the notion that the United Nations legal model governing the use of force is manifestly inadequate to deal with the issue of humanitarian intervention, and places the debate firmly into the domain of political theory, founding his thesis (again) upon notions of international legitimacy. Rejecting the classic dictum of EH Carr that notions of international

[67] Others have, however, been more forthright about the emergence of a new norm. Leclerc-Gagné and Byers argue that if agreement for the framing of the crime of aggression can be found for the purposes of the ICC Statute, then an exception must be drafted in favour of humanitarian intervention. E Leclerc-Gagné and M Byers, 'A Question of Intent: The Crime of Aggression and Unilateral Intervention' (2009) 41 *Case Western Reserve Journal of International Law* 379. See also CP De Nicola, 'Shield for the Knights of Humanity: The ICC Should Adopt a Humanitarian Necessity Defence to the Crime of Aggression' (2008–09) 30 *University of Pennsylvania Journal of International Law* 641.

[68] The notion of 'instant custom' was introduced by Cheng B Cheng, 'Custom: The Future of General State Practice in a Divided World' in RStJ Macdonald and DM Johnston (eds), *The Structure and Process of International Law. Essays in Legal Philosophy Doctrine and Theory* (Dordrecht, Martinus Nijhoff, 1983) 513. See also B Cheng, 'United Nations Resolutions on Outer Space: "Instant" International Customary Law?' (1965) 5 *Indian Journal of International Law* 23.

[69] Hafkin argues that the more recent case of South Ossetia is legally similar to Kosovo, but that a new customary rule is not emerging due to strong objections against both operations. However, he does not exclude the appearance of such a rule in the future. G Hafkin, 'The Russo-Georgian War of 2008: Developing the Law of Unauthorized Humanitarian Intervention after Kosovo' (2010) 28 *Boston University International Law Journal* 219.

[70] J Habermas, 'Bestiality and Humanity: A War on the Border between Legality and Morality' (1999) 6 *Constellations* 263, 263.

morality or legitimacy are merely manifestations of the interests of dominant groups of nations at a particular time,[71] Wheeler posits that the 'key point of notions of international legitimacy is that they are not within the control of individual agents'.[72] This is perhaps a good point, but Wheeler fails to take stock of the fact that the logical consequence of such a statement is that measuring humanitarian intervention against the yardstick of legitimacy rather than that of legality gives every actor the right to shape his yardstick differently.[73]

Per Wheeler, humanitarian intervention exposes the conflict between order – that is, international law – and justice at its starkest. He adjudges that the Charter's prioritisation of these two values must be inverted, and hence, sees fit to move outside the realm of law.

Wheeler looks approvingly upon Michael Walzer's definition of humanitarian intervention as a justified response with a reasonable prospect of success to acts that shock the moral conscience of mankind.[74] He echoes Walzer's sentiment that States should be denied the protection of sovereignty in the extraordinary circumstances where their governments are guilty of crimes against humanity.[75] However, it is not without hesitation that Wheeler decides to depart from international law, citing Hedley Bull's assertion that any institutional order which is provided by international law forms a necessary condition for the protection and promotion of individual well-being.[76] He is highly cognisant of the fact that international law (as it stands) is in and of itself a bulwark against human rights atrocities. Nonetheless, as regards the use of force by States, Wheeler is of the view that the problem of abuse of Article 51 of the Charter confirms the Realist school of international relations' assertion that talk is cheap, a public disguise which masks the true rationales for States' actions, which they will find a way to accomplish in any case.[77] In this

[71] EH Carr, *The 20 Years Crisis 1919–39* (London, Macmillan, 1939) 111.

[72] N Wheeler, *Saving Strangers: Humanitarian Intervention in International Society* (Oxford, Oxford University Press, 2000) 6.

[73] This may be paralleled with the critiques of early English equity penned by John Selden, discussed in ch 3.

[74] Wheeler (2000) (n 72) 28.

[75] See M Walzer, *Just and Unjust Wars – A Moral Argument with Historical Illustrations* (New York, Basic Books, 1992) 107.

[76] See H Bull, *The Anarchical Society – A Study of Order in World Politics* (New York, Columbia University Press, 2001) 22.

[77] Wheeler (2000) (n 72) 30. He is supported in this opinion by Simon Chesterman, albeit with Chesterman arguing that States use the fact that there is no right of unilateral humanitarian intervention to engage in 'cheap talk' about why they cannot intervene based on international law, when in reality their motivations lie elsewhere, but that this legal prohibition does not prevent them from intervening when it is in their selfish interest to do so. See Chesterman (2001) (n 4) 231. Thomas Franck has also given examples of the abuse of Art 51 in a downcast appraisal of the continuing relevance of prohibition upon the use of force. See T Franck, 'Who Killed Article 2(4)?' (1970) 64 *American Journal of International Law* 809, 811–12. However, Mark Weisburd disputes the complete irrelevance of altruism and rejects a complete adoption of the 'cheap talk' position, citing Vietnam's invasion of Kampuchea and

way, he is able to dismiss Franck and Rodley's contention that adding another 'escape clause' covering humanitarian intervention alongside that of Article 51 will only increase opportunities for the unscrupulous to exploit.[78]

Although clearly concerned with balancing order and justice, Wheeler is convinced that selfish State interests will prevail over notions of altruism in humanitarian emergencies, and therefore *rejects* the assertion that any test for the legality or legitimacy of humanitarian intervention must rest upon the primacy of humanitarian motives for said intervention. Wheeler takes cognisance of the Realist objection that States have no business risking their soldiers' lives to save strangers, but notes that pushed to its logical extreme, 'the implication of the statist paradigm is that governments should not risk the life of even one soldier to save hundreds of thousands, or even millions of non-nationals'.[79] Perhaps this may be dubbed a *reductio ad absurdum*, but his sentiments find favour amongst other commentators, especially relating to the relative chances of intervention by democratic politics.[80] It is also worth noting the comments of Walden Bello in this regard, who remains highly sceptical about the purportedly humanitarian rationale underlying the Kosovo operation. Per Bello, while the humanitarian rationale was undoubtedly the purpose of some advocates of the Kosovo intervention, particularly those in the academic community and those holding positions in human rights NGOs, NATO's execution of the operation itself did not prioritise such concerns and merely furthered Washington's geopolitical designs (as well as, to some extent, the fear that refugee flows might destabilise other European States). 'The lasting result of the Kosovo air war was not a stable and secure network of Balkan States but NATO expansion'.[81] This sceptical position as regards the position of human rights in NATO's planning is shared by Mient Jan Faber,[82] and is borne out by the comments of one NATO spokesman, who, paraphrasing Otto von Bismarck,[83] admitted

the stated humanitarian rationales as support for his argument. AM Wesiburd, 'Consistency, Universality, and the Customary Law of Interstate Force' in E Cannizzaro and P Palchetti (eds), *Customary International Law on the Use of Force: A Methodological Approach* (Leiden, Koninklijke Brill NV, 2005) 74.

[78] T Franck and N Rodley, 'After Bangladesh: The Law of Humanitarian Intervention by Military Force' (1973) 67 *American Journal of International Law* 290.

[79] Wheeler (2000) (n 72) 31.

[80] DC Hendrickson, 'In Defence of Realism: A Commentary on Just and Unjust Wars' (1997) 11 *Ethics and International Affairs* 46.

[81] W Bello, 'Humanitarian Intervention: Evolution of a Dangerous Doctrine' (speech at the Conference on Globalisation, War and Intervention sponsored by the International Physicians for the Prevention of Nuclear War, German Chapter, Frankfurt-am-Main, 14–15 January 2006).

[82] MJ Faber, 'R2P, Humanitarian Intervention and Independence: The Proof of the Pudding is in the Eating' (2009) 1 *Amsterdam Law Forum* 4.

[83] Bismarck had famously remarked: 'Ich würde zu irgendeiner aktiven Beteiligung Deutschlands an diesen Dingen nicht raten, so lange ich in dem Ganzen für Deutschland kein Interesse sehen, welches ach nur – entschuldigen Sie die Derbheit des Ausdruckes – die

that he did not consider the arrests of senior commanders in Bosnia-Herzegovina for war crimes to be 'worth the blood of one NATO soldier'.[84]

Therefore, per Wheeler, since there is virtually no chance of States acting entirely unselfishly, a test for the legitimacy of humanitarian intervention must rest upon other criteria, these being: (1) just cause, constituting a 'supreme humanitarian emergency'; (2) that the intervention be undertaken as the last possible resort; (3) that the means used be proportionate as regards the ends to be achieved; and (4) that there be a high probability of a positive humanitarian outcome.

Leaving aside the clumsy use of the superlative ('supreme humanitarian emergency'), Wheeler's test is primarily concerned with practicality rather than normativity, and in this respect makes for interesting reading. It certainly addresses Anthea Roberts' concerns that in legal discourse surrounding humanitarian intervention there has been 'a consistent failure to address the question of the methods used in such interventions'.[85] This would seem logical, since the separation between *ius ad bellum* and *ius in bello* is hardly a new phenomenon. Wheeler's is not the only model which calls this separation into question, but it is worth recalling that the parity and equality of the parties in the conflict is hugely undermined if they are not governed by the same norms of international humanitarian law, and if one side must accept additional obligations in this regard in order to legitimise their conduct. Were Wheeler to have his way, such conduct would even serve to render humanitarian interventions legal as well as legitimate. Disagreeing with Franck and Rodley's assertion that humanitarian intervention, while morally permissible, should not be legalised,[86] Wheeler posits that accepting such moral incompatibility with the law fatally weakens the international legal regime. As Verwey has pointed out, such a position 'would imply the recognition – no more, no less – that international law is incapable of ensuring respect for socially indispensible standards of morality'.[87] As a result, according to Wheeler, human rights should rank alongside peace and security in the hierarchy of UN Charter principles. In adopting this 'counter-restrictionist' viewpoint, he posits that the logical consequence should be the eventual

gesunden Knochen eines einzigen pommerschen Musketiers wert wäre'. (I am opposed to the notion of any sort of active participation of Germany in these matters [the trouble in the Balkans], so long as I can see no reason to suppose that German interests are involved, no interests on behalf of which it is worth our risking – excuse my plain speaking – the healthy bones of one of our Pomeranian musketeers). See E Ludwig, *Bismarck. Ungekürzte Neuausgabe* (Munich, Herbig, 1975).

[84] G Robertson, 'War in Europe: The Milosevic Indictment', *The Independent,* London, 30 May 1999.

[85] A Roberts, 'NATO's Humanitarian War Over Kosovo' (1999) 41 *Survival* 110.

[86] Franck and Rodley (1973) (n 78) 304.

[87] W Verwey, 'Humanitarian Intervention in the 1990s and Beyond: An International Law Perspective' in JN Pieterse (ed), *World Orders in the Making: Humanitarian Intervention and Beyond* (London, Macmillan, 1998) 200.

recognition in international law of a unilateral right of humanitarian intervention.[88]

Wheeler's assertion of the position of human rights alongside international peace and security in the Charter purposes is undermined somewhat by an examination of the *travaux préparatoires*. These make it clear that the Charter could have potentially allowed for sanctions for gross human rights violations, but deliberately chose not to do so.[89] Therefore Wheeler's argument that human rights *should* or *ought to* be accorded hierarchical parity with international peace and security takes on an aspirational tone, the call of one arguing for future law reform, rather than one arguing for a new, so-called 'counter-restrictionist' interpretation of the positive law at hand. Further, I am not convinced by his argument that States will voice whatever justification they can to act in a way which suits their selfish interests and that opening the door to a possible legal right of humanitarian intervention would not herald a new series of abuses of such a right. One need only examine the justifications proffered by the Bush administration in retrospective defence of the Iraq war to see how, even over a short space of time, a vague notion of legitimate intervention may be stretched out of all proportion. A new legal *casus belli* that does not require primacy of humanitarian motives could be extremely dangerous in the hands of unscrupulous governments, a point which has been raised by Noam Chomsky and to which I shall return shortly.[90]

VII. 'A CUSTOM MORE HONOUR'D IN THE BREACH THAN IN THE OBSERVANCE' – THE TURN TO ETHICS

Simma, Cassese and Wheeler are indicative of the broad trends within international scholarship in the years following 1999. Dissatisfaction with Charter law was palpable. The differences in approaches reflected different tacks on how to deal with the difficulties created by the Kosovo conundrum, but all resorted to justificatory techniques based upon a moral examination of an apparently illegal act.

The essential question here was: whether the legally prudent option (abstention from the use of force), or the option which involved illegal means (humanitarian intervention) was the 'right' choice.

Of course, moral philosophers will be quick to highlight that there exists no objective 'right'. However, certain situations provoke strong feeling in the majority of the populace, including international lawyers.

[88] Wheeler (2000) (n 72) 42.

[89] R Higgins, *Problems and Process: International Law and How We Use It* (Oxford, Oxford University Press, 1994) 255.

[90] N Chomsky, *The New Military Humanism: Lessons from Kosovo* (Monroe, ME, Common Courage Press, 1999).

The efforts to justify a plainly illegal action provoked a 'turn to ethics', which has been stylishly discussed by Martti Koskenniemi.[91] The title of Koskenniemi's article, 'The Lady Doth Protest Too Much', is an allusion to William Shakespeare's *Hamlet* (1601), to which Koskenniemi repeatedly refers. The line in question describes the attempts of a piece of staged theatre within the play to prick the conscience of its audience in order to engender a desired response from the murderous King Claudius – 'the play's the thing, wherein I'll catch the conscience of the King'. However, Koskenniemi's choice of *Hamlet* as a descriptive analogy is useful on more than this level. Indeed the central theme of the play – whether to continue to tolerate an injustice or to take action although this may be dangerous and plainly illegal – mirrors perfectly the Kosovo conundrum.

The essential question here was: whether the legally prudent option (abstention from the use of force), or the option which involved illegal means (killing the murderous King) was the 'right' choice.

> To be, or not to be, – that is the question: –
> Whether 'tis nobler in the mind to suffer
> The slings and arrows of outrageous fortune,
> Or to take arms against a sea of troubles,
> And by opposing end them?[92]

As Freud has noted, throughout *Hamlet*, 'the play is built up on Hamlet's hesitations over fulfilling the task of revenge that is assigned to him'.[93] However, the role that Freud holds to be assigned to Hamlet, that of an avenger – or at the very least, of someone who can bring a murderer to justice – is not the role of a Crown Prince of Denmark, but rather that of magistrates and police. It is the audience and its moral conscience that dictate that someone must do something, since Claudius appears invulnerable to official powers. This person seems to be Hamlet. So too with humanitarian intervention. Since a deadlocked Security Council is unable to act to quell an unstable situation in Kosovo, it falls to NATO. Why Hamlet? Why NATO? It seems that the simple answer is because they can. 'Who can, should', as Michael Walzer puts it.[94]

However, such reasoning plainly takes us into a sphere, which, although doubtless interesting, lies outside the law. Reconciling moral intuitions with professional competences has therefore been a difficult endeavour for international lawyers. Koskenniemi makes reference to this, in addition to the fact that reconciling international law with cold political realities, particularly involving the use of force. Indeed, Koskenniemi opines,

[91] M Koskenniemi, '"The Lady Doth Protest Too Much" Kosovo, and the Turn to Ethics in International Law' (2002) 6 *MLR* 159.

[92] W Shakespeare, *Hamlet*, Act III, Scene I (1601).

[93] S Freud, *The Interpretation of Dreams* (New York, Avon Press, 1980) 60.

[94] M Walzer, 'The Argument about Humanitarian Intervention' (2002) *Dissent* 29, 33.

in the *Nuclear Weapons* Opinion (1996), the ICJ came very close to conceding that no law could govern self-defence when the State's very existence is at stake.[95] This has led to disputes over whether a 'closing rule' may be held to exist in international law, and whether there may be instances that are so far outside positive international law that the law may simply be indifferent to them.[96]

Koskenniemi is firmly in favour of such a 'closing rule' as regards the use of force, and is blunt in stating that 'NATO was either entitled to bomb Serbia or it was not. *Tertium non datur*. Surely it is an essential part of the Rule of Law that society contains no corner of outside-the-law?' Yet he admits shortly thereafter that 'most lawyers – including myself – have taken the ambivalent position that it was both formally illegal and morally necessary . . . Kosovo has invited international lawyers to throw away dry professionalism and imagine themselves as moral agents on a *mission civilicatrice*'.[97]

Koskenniemi outlines an intricate and relatively cogent process, in eight steps, through which international lawyers are transformed into moralists by the logic of the argument for humanitarian intervention, passing from (1) formal law *stricto sensu*, to (2) formal law *lato sensu*, to (3) instrumentalism (international law being an activity oriented toward a particular human purpose), to (4) utilitarianism, to (5) rights as trumps (per Dworkin), to (6) legislative discourse, to (7) law as procedure, and finally to (8) the turn to ethics, as Koskenniemi brands it.

To recapitulate the full logic of Koskenniemi's discourse would be overburdensome in a work of this length. In addition, I have a problem with it. The analogies with *Hamlet* which I have attempted above were inspired by parallels drawn by Koskenniemi himself. The central lesson of the play is that one should tackle problems, even if the consequences entailed in doing so may be difficult to countenance. If not, and if one procrastinates, so much the worse. One does not need to be a literary critic to garner this lesson from *Hamlet*. Similarly, one does not need to be an international lawyer to feel one's conscience pricked by the Kosovo crisis and to decide that someone must do something to ameliorate the situation, whatever it takes. Koskenniemi's eight steps are effectively unnecessary. The turn to ethics occurred due to an 'instinctive' reaction from States and commentators and a decision that in this decision, justice was paramount over law and human rights needed to be upheld by force. Koskenniemi's reasoning reads like a judicial opinion justifying a verdict which the judge reached

[95] *Legality of the Threat or Use of Nuclear Weapons* (Advisory Opinion) [1996] ICJ Rep 226 [90]–[97] and [105E] (*dispositif*).

[96] See I Dekker and W Werner, 'The Completeness of International Law and Hamlet's Dilemma (Non Liquet, The Nuclear Weapons Case and Legal Theory)' (1999) 68 *Nordic Journal of International Law* 225.

[97] Koskenniemi (2002) (n 91) 161–62.

instinctively. However, if one treats it as such, it becomes vastly more useful, demonstrating why so many theories on the Kosovo intervention read differently and yet reach the same result. The feeling evoked by the action was instinctive. The turn to ethics was a mask to shield the fact that for many, the impossibility of reconciling their consciences with the law was something that needed to be overcome.

In any case, regardless of how the turn to ethics is reached, Koskenniemi continues to describe its *mise en oeuvre*. Per Koskenniemi, even if law is not just formal texts, its informality cannot be reduced to utilitarian calculations, absolute rights, or procedural techniques either. A decision has to be made, and, as Carl Schmitt would opine, this decision is borne out of legal nothingness.[98] Per Koskenniemi, 'what counts are the experience of the decision-maker and his or her sensitivity to the demands of the situation. The problem is not about criteria or process, but about something that might be called "wisdom"'.[99] The merit of this approach is clearly that it discounts Kosovo as a precedent. However, this is cancelled out by the subjectivity of the decision-makers, that is, the intervening powers. Here we come full circle in our circumvention of the Security Council. After all, its Permanent Members are also subjective decision-makers. Neo-Realism, the anathema of international lawyers, rears its head.

Therefore, the turn to ethics may also be a turn to politics, a politics by those who have the means to control others. The Kosovar Albanian is worthy of support as long as he remains a helpless victim, but woe betide him if he attempts to liberate himself from NATO guardianship.

Morality and ethics clearly play a role in legal reasoning within the Kosovo debate, as does politics. Koskenniemi is correct in this respect, but the question remains, (how) can ethics aid in resolving the legal problems brought up by the Kosovo crisis?

VIII. ILLEGAL INTERNATIONAL LAW REFORM: ETHICS IN ACTION

Allen Buchanan is a prominent example of those scholars who have attempted to chart a practical application for the use of ethics in reforming international law. Buchanan posits that the law surrounding humanitarian intervention is in need of reform, citing the deficiencies of existing international law to support this contention.[100] He poses the question as to under what circumstances it may be morally defensible (and *ergo* excusa-

[98] G Schwab (tr), C Schmitt, *Political Theology* (Cambridge, MA, MIT Press, 1985) 31–32.

[99] Koskenniemi (2002) (n 91) 170–71.

[100] A Buchanan, 'Reforming the International Law of Humanitarian Intervention' in JL Holzgrefe and RO Keohane (eds), *Humanitarian Intervention: Ethical, Legal and Political Dilemmas* (Cambridge, Cambridge University Press, 2003) 131.

ble) to violate international law in an effort to reform it.[101] As D'Amato has stated, if we live in a system of immoral laws, 'we will spend our time thinking of ways to act illegally and subvert the system so as to establish a new system where the new laws will be entitled to respect'.[102] Noting that the Kosovo operation was justified on two bases – primarily as a necessary response to an impending humanitarian disaster but also in the opinion of some leaders as an important first step toward establishing a new norm of customary international law[103] – Buchanan assesses whether the latter contention is valid. Investigating whether such an operation, which violated international law as it then existed, was justified in order to initiate an improvement in the international legal system, Buchanan devises a series of rules to be used in determining the moral justifiability of illegal acts of reform. He is not alone in such ideas.[104]

Buchanan tells us that these guidelines are not intended to provide comprehensive conditions for the justification of humanitarian intervention, but rather are to be applied to proposals for armed interventions once the 'familiar and widely acknowledged'[105] conditions for justified intervention are already satisfied. Amongst the most important of these, Buchanan tells us, is proportionality. Unfortunately, he neglects to enumerate the others. Given that he dispenses some 20 pages previous to this discussing moral justifiability and subjectivity, failing to let the reader know what basic conditions 'justify' (objectively, one would presume) intervention as a precursor to his 'guidelines' seems a glaring omission. Leaving this lacuna aside, however, Buchanan tells us that eight guidelines may provide help in assessing the justifiability of illegal action directed towards system reform.

Very briefly, Buchanan's guidelines run thus: (1) the closer the system approximates the ideal of the rule of law, the greater the burden of justification for illegal acts; (2) the less seriously defective the system is in terms of justice, the greater the burden of justification; (3) the closer the system is to legitimacy, the greater the burden. Buchanan opines further that (4) illegal acts that violate fundamental morally defensible principles of the system carry a greater burden, and that (5) the greater the improvement that would result from reform, the stronger the case for carrying it out. Further, (6) illegal acts likely to improve system legitimacy are more easily justified; (7) illegal acts likely to improve substantive justice are more easily justified; and (8) illegal acts likely to make the system more

[101] A Buchanan, 'From Nuremburg to Kosovo: The Morality of Illegal International Legal Reform' (2001) 111 *Ethics* 673.

[102] A D'Amato, 'What Counts as International Law?' in A D'Amato, *International Law Sources. Collected Papers*, vol III (Leiden, Martinus Nijhoff, 2004) 1.

[103] Buchanan cites US Secretary of State Madeleine Albright as an example.

[104] See, eg T Bruha, 'Use of Force, Prohibition of' in R Wolfrum (ed), *United Nations: Law, Policies and Practice*, vol 2 (1995) 1387 *et seq*.

[105] Buchanan (2001) (n 101) 697.

consistent with its most morally defensible fundamental principles are more easily justified.

Buchanan's rationale for the guidelines is twofold. First, they provide a means of weighing whether any illegal acts can be accurately described as being directed toward system reform, and secondly, if this is the case, whether committing said act is compatible with a sincere commitment of bringing international relations under the rule of law.

Buchanan's guidelines appear unnecessarily complicated to my mind. Effectively, he cites four *desiderata*, namely 'the rule of law', 'substantive justice', 'legitimacy' and 'morally defensible fundamental principles', and opines that legal system reform should tend toward these, not away from them. This in itself is a simple contention, apart from the fact that he fails to define these terms. Indeed, Buchanan himself admits that 'different agents may have different views about what justice requires. Thus the guidelines are intended to provide concrete guidance without presupposing a particular theory of justice'.[106] This is where Buchanan's thesis ceases to be of any practical use. Although he brands his guidelines 'concrete', they are far from it, and are in fact merely nebulous. 'The rule of law' may, I suppose, find an adequate definition upon which lawyers, philosophers and States can broadly agree. However, the other *desiderata* are, I fear, far from clear. Their content is open to a broad range of interpretations, and this being the case, even supposing that States were to take cognisance of Buchanan's guidelines in regulating their illegal conduct, one State's interpretation of what is simultaneously an improvement in the fields of 'legitimacy', 'substantive justice', and 'morally defensible fundamental principles' may differ wildly from that of its neighbour. Francioni has further noted that such models too quickly translate the 'exigencies' of justice into positive exceptions to the UN Charter system.[107] This is so, even discounting bad faith on the part of one State and the potential for such – abusing the vagueness of the operative terminology to attain a selfish end – is clear. Buchanan as much as admits this himself:

> The guidelines proceed on the assumption that content can be given to the idea of improving the system morally and they employ the notion of justice. However, they are not intended to provide a comprehensive moral theory nor to supply content for the notion of justice.[108]

The question remains, however, without a frame of reference as regards terminology, how can these guidelines become practically useful? Buchanan attempts to demonstrate their potential utility in examining the NATO intervention in Kosovo as a 'test case'.

[106] ibid, 698.

[107] Francioni (2000) (n 47) 112. Francioni notes elsewhere that there exists no central authority entrusted with such law reform. Francioni (2005) (n 19) 280.

[108] Buchanan (2001) (n 101) 700.

Buchanan begins by dubbing the NATO intervention illegal. Moreover, he describes it as clearly meeting the threshold of an illegal act directed at international legal reform. While this claim is dubious (as it was not claimed by all intervening parties that this was an element of the rationale for launching the operation), Buchanan continues to test how this intervention fares when judged against his guidelines. In light of the deficiencies inherent in the international legal system concerning the rule of law, justice and legitimacy, Buchanan notes that the burden of justification for such an attempt at reform is not overly demanding. However, since such interventions as that in Kosovo infringe the fundamental principle of sovereignty, as articulated in Articles 2(4) and 2(7) of the UN Charter, expressly forbidding such armed interventions, the burden would appear to be much higher in this regard. Nonetheless, Buchanan informs us, it is only morally defensible fundamental norms which are to be protected, and in this respect, he adjudges that State sovereignty need not necessarily provide a definitive barrier to reform if the reform is carried out in the name of human rights.

However, Buchanan finishes by concluding that humanitarian intervention *à la* Kosovo does not qualify under his guidelines. Such a practice would be too much of a destabilising influence to the rule of law, and would not constitute a moral improvement to the international legal system. In his own words,

> [a] military alliance such as NATO is not the sort of entity that would be a plausible candidate for having a right under international law to intervene without UN authorisation. The chief difficulty is that such a norm would be too liable to abuse.[109]

Buchanan's contention seems to be that while the current rule is inadequate, the manner in which the NATO intervention was carried out cannot be held to represent a template for future actions, as this would not represent a moral improvement in the legal system.

Thus, Buchanan's 'ethics in action' failed to meet its billing, it seems. In providing us with guidelines couched in nebulous terminology, he is unable to tell us anything concrete beyond the fact that the manner in which the Kosovo intervention was undertaken is outside the realms of his *desiderata*. Perhaps here I am being harsh on Buchanan. His utopian vision of law reform via illegal action tending to buttress commendable goals such as legitimacy and the rule of law is doubtless a noble cause. However, what is required in this context is more than a utopian philosophy. Concrete criteria, rooted if possible in the law itself, are required, allowing us to distinguish the justified/legitimate/legal (depending on which discourse one follows) interventions from the abusive ones. Finally, it is perhaps germane to note the opinion of the World Court in the *Nicaragua*

[109] ibid, 703.

case, which stated that where a breach of a legal rule is accompanied by a justification of said breach referring to the rule in question, 'the significance of that attitude is to confirm rather than to weaken the rule'.[110] Hence, it is dubious whether illegal international law reform as conceived of by Buchanan is even possible. This sentiment is echoed by Corten, who explicitly states that 'A breach of international law, as such, cannot generate an evolution of the rule prohibiting force'.[111]

IX. NECESSITY AS THE MOTHER OF INVENTION

Buchanan's analysis is by no means unique. However, it is indicative of just how far away from international law the debate on humanitarian intervention has managed to travel in a remarkably short time, and it somewhat bears out Koskenniemi's theory of a 'turn to ethics'. However, this tendency was not universal. Moving so far away from the law, and vesting judgment of the legitimacy and permissibility of conduct in international relations in uncertain notions of ethics opens the door for abusive expansion of whatever framework one uses to define such legitimacy. This was realised by some scholars who attempted to couch their analyses in something more concrete, and more akin to the law itself. Thomas M Franck is a member of this group.

Franck adopts an honest, direct approach and reduces the debate on humanitarian intervention to one concerning the conflict between peace and justice, rather than legality versus legitimacy. This alternative branding of the relative positions represents somewhat more than a cosmetic readjustment of the same debate, as Franck displays a strong predisposition toward working with the positive law rather than trying to circumvent it.[112] He quotes with approval Lauterpacht's dictum that 'It is impossible, in the scheme of things devised to secure the reign of law, to provide machinery calculated to disregard the law'.[113] Franck's position in this regard certainly sets him apart from the bulk of those scholars attempting to separate the legality of humanitarian intervention from the ethics of the action. Branding humanitarian intervention as a legal exception to the prohibition on the use of force will necessarily require legal justifications, as distinct from the moral, political, linguistic and ethical

[110] *Military and Paramilitary Activities in and against Nicaragua (Nicaragua v United States)* (Merits) [1986] ICJ Rep 14, 98.

[111] O Corten, 'Breach and Evolution of Customary International Law on the Use of Force' in E Cannizzaro and P Palchetti (eds), *Customary International Law on the Use of Force: A Methodological Approach* (Leiden, Koninklijke Brill NV, 2005) 42.

[112] T Franck, *Recourse to Force – State Actions Against Threats and Armed Attacks (Hersch Lauterpacht Memorial Lectures)* (Cambridge, Cambridge University Press, 2002).

[113] H Lauterpacht, *The Function of Law in the International Community* (London, Longman, Green & Co, 1933) 372–73.

justifications proffered in defence of 'legitimacy' theories.[114] He begins with a discussion of the idea of legal 'loopholes', lacunae within the law allowing one to circumvent the general everyday rule. His view toward such phenomena is ambiguous, stating that loopholes can be bad, but can also help to 'save the law from itself'.[115] As to the current state of positive international law, Franck wonders whether the drafters of the UN Charter tried to 'plug' too many loopholes, and in attempting to forge a just international society unintentionally created situations of grave injustice.

In undertaking a teleological analysis of the Charter regime, Franck begins by examining its origins, beginning with the Covenant of the League of Nations and the 1928 Briand–Kellogg Pact. Upon examination of the Charter itself, Franck notes the peripheral role accorded to human rights provisions, particularly when compared with the overriding importance attached to the provisions outlawing the use of force. Peace, therefore, Franck concludes, has definitively been prioritised over justice.[116] Nonetheless, he notes that the historical context surrounding the Charter had also demonstrated the need 'to guard against the sacrifice of justice for peace, as in the craven Anglo–French surrender to Hitler's "humanitarian" demands on Czechoslovakia in the name of the Sudeten-Germans'.[117] With this in mind, the French, amongst others, had attempted to amend the Charter; legitimising intervention when clear violations of human rights rose to the level where they themselves could be perceived as a threat to the peace. However, such proposals were rejected.[118] Despite such failures, Franck maintains that the drafters of the Charter realised that 'To preserve peace . . . would also require an effective response to massive injustices of the kind perpetrated by Nazi and Fascist governments against their own and other populations'.[119] Here, Franck's reasoning begins to come unstuck somewhat. It is clear that a right of humanitarian intervention – which transpires to be Franck's 'effective response' of choice – was discussed at the San Francisco conference and was rejected, as were the French proposals linking human rights with a 'threat to the peace'. While such a nexus has arguably, at least to some limited degree, been established by the custom and usages of the Security Council since then,[120] to suggest that the Charter's drafters believed that

[114] Roberts (2008) (n 51) 202, see above n 40.
[115] Franck (2002) (n 112) 1.
[116] ibid, 14–17.
[117] ibid, 17.
[118] UN Conference on International Organization, Commission III, Committee 2 (10 May 1945), UN Doc No 207, III/2/A/3, 12 UNCIO 179, 191.
[119] Franck (2002) (n 112) 19.
[120] The Security Council has invoked Ch VII powers to cover situations occurring exclusively within one State, or lacking an inter-State element, eg against Rhodesia in 1966, South Africa in 1977, Haiti in 1994, the Federal Republic of Yugoslavia in 1998, and has further, with Resolution 2001/28/9, extended its powers against terrorist groups, thereby covering non-State actors.

that a *sine qua non* of the preservation of peace would entail meddling in the internal affairs of a foreign State is utopian and unrealistic. Such a position would have been anathema to any State that set high stock by its own sovereignty, and would have caused a seismic shift in international law. Further, it is perhaps worth noting that the drafting process of the Charter was contemporaneous, not subsequent, to the evidence gathering activities for the war crimes trials at Nuremberg. The full extent of Nazi atrocities was not yet completely clear. Even had it been, it is perhaps doubtful that the attitudes of many States would have been different. The numbers exterminated by Nazi genocide reached shocking proportions, but they themselves were dwarfed by the numbers killed as a result of the Second World War itself. In such circumstances, prioritising peace over justice might well have been seen as rational.

This somewhat skewed account of the drafting process aside, Franck's analysis of the international legal regime on the use of force is quite thorough. He comes to the same conclusion as Oscar Schachter in holding that the chief deficiency of international law is its lack of effective enforcement, particularly as regards the absence of compulsory jurisdiction and the limited ability of any international institution to impose effective sanctions upon a violator.[121] Per Franck, this may force recourse to self-help on the part of disgruntled States. Franck opines that if the wrong being perpetrated within a State against a portion of its own population is of a kind specifically prohibited by international agreement, then 'humanitarian intervention against those prohibited acts may be thought of as a subspecies of self-help'.[122] This is an interesting position, but raises the question as to the limits of such self-help. What about other international agreements which do not have a human rights component? Only allowing humanitarian intervention and not other intervention as a means of self-help to enforce other types of international accords presupposes a normative hierarchy of sorts with human rights sitting atop the pyramid of norms. Since nothing of the sort exists in international law (unless we take fundamental human rights norms to be *ius cogens*, in which case it is highly salient to point out that the prohibition on the use of force is also *ius cogens*) the hierarchy must be of a moral, rather than a legal nature. This brings us a long way from self-help as a mooted legal doctrine, and into the realms of moral, rather than legal, remedies.

Despite such problems, Franck makes a conscious effort to make use of the law, to stretch it rather than disregard it, and to base his model for humanitarian intervention on something more concrete than subjective conceptions of 'legitimacy'. He notes the discussion of the possible extension of any right of intervention by the ICJ in the *Nicaragua* (Merits)

[121] O Schachter, *International Law in Theory and Practice* (Netherlands, Martinus Nijhoff, 1991) 184; see also Franck (2002) (n 112) 111.

[122] Franck (2002) (n 112) 135.

judgment, which stated that 'Reliance by a State on a novel right or an unprecedented exception to the principle might, if shared in principle by other States, tend towards modification of customary international law'.[123] While Franck notes that practice itself cannot amend a treaty per se, the Court has stated in the past that the practice of a UN organ may be seen to interpret the text and thereby shape our understanding thereof.[124] Franck makes the oft-repeated observation that hard cases may make bad law, and that there is a strong tension between legal consistency on the one hand, and justice on the other. However, Franck argues, slavish adherence to a rule which is unjust in the circumstances can also undermine law's legitimacy, albeit in a different way. In order to resolve this problem, Franck proposes the transposition of the concept of necessity and the plea of mitigation from domestic law to international law.

Franck draws attention to the two most celebrated of the 'lifeboat' cases, namely *R v Dudley and Stephens*[125] and *United States v Holmes*.[126] In both cases, the defendants were convicted of murder on foot of acts of cannibalism. However, due to extreme mitigating circumstances, whereby the defendants acted in the reasonable belief that they had no other choice and that their actions were in the last resort, sentencing was significantly lighter than would otherwise have been the case. In the former case, the two defendants were sentenced to death, but Lord Coleridge, for the unanimous Court, commended them 'most earnestly to the mercy of the crown', which duly commuted their sentence to six months imprisonment, most of which had already been served. In the latter case, the penalty of six months imprisonment was subsequently remitted. Franck notes that in neither case was necessity treated as an exculpatory defence to the charge of murder, claiming that the judges 'went out of their way to ensure that murder remained a crime, even in circumstances of extreme necessity'. However, these circumstances were not ignored, and mitigated the penalties imposed upon those whose acts 'were found to have been illegal but, in the extreme circumstances, justifiable'.[127] Per Franck, there may be differences separating one national system from another as to whether necessity mitigates the consequences of a crime or excuses it completely, but all systems recognise the obligation of the law to do one or the other. It is perhaps worth noting that international law is not

[123] *Military and Paramilitary Activities in and against Nicaragua (Nicaragua v United States)* (Merits) [1986] ICJ Rep 14, 109 [207].

[124] *Legal Consequences for States of the Continued Presence of South Africa in Namibia (South West Africa) notwithstanding Security Council Resolution 276 (1970)* (Advisory Opinion) [1971] ICJ Rep 16, 22 [22], which decided that the practice of regarding the use of an abstention from voting by one of the five Permanent Members of the Security Council as a concurring vote for the motion being proposed rather than a veto thereto was a valid interpretation of the Charter.

[125] [1884] 14 QB 273.

[126] (1842) 26 Fed Cas 360; 1 Wall St J 1.

[127] Franck (2002) (n 112) 179.

completely unfamiliar with the concept of *ius neccesitatis*, but that it, perhaps justifiably, has long enjoyed a 'bad reputation' in the international legal sphere.[128] However, it is not without precedent and has been pronounced upon by international tribunals. In the early case of *The Neptune*, settled in 1797 by the international arbitral tribunal established by the 1794 Jay Treaty, the court held that a situation of necessity might allow for the setting aside of all written and customary law in certain circumstances, but that such necessity 'must be absolute and irresistible', thus establishing a very high threshold to be met, but nonetheless allowing for the possible operation of the principles of *ius necessitatis contra legem strictum*.[129] This case was partly followed by an individual opinion of Anzilotti J in the Permanent Court of International Justice (PCIJ), where he noted that 'necessity may excuse the non-observance of international obligations', though it was clear that this was to be interpreted very restrictively and that necessity was to be understood as analogous to *force majeure*.[130] The doctrine is rarely invoked by States. *Ius necessitatis* has the potential to open a 'Pandora's box' of subjective invocations of such a doctrine, and therefore any invocation of necessity doctrine is regarded with utmost suspicion by States, and its normative status – beyond certain limited situations such as the doctrine of military necessity in international humanitarian law – is dubious, and is certainly not strongly-rooted enough to tamper with the UN Charter regime.[131]

Franck argues for the transposition of the criminal law plea of necessity into the international legal system, arguing that this 'is not merely a summons to temper the law with considerations of moral legitimacy, but . . . also a reminder to consider the facts of a case before applying general normative principles'.[132] The essence of mitigation, according to Franck, is that the law recognises the continuing force and validity of a given rule, such as the prohibition upon the use of force, while also accepting that in extraordinary extenuating circumstances, condoning a justifiable violation may do more to justify the law's legitimacy than would its rigorous implementation. A similar model is proposed by Byers and Chesterman, as well as by De Nicola.[133] As Roberts points out, the language in both cases is confusing. Franck in particular argues that interventions may be

[128] P Weidenbaum, 'Necessity in International Law' (1938) 24 *Grotius Transactions* 105.

[129] *The Neptune* (1797) 4 *International Adjudication Manuscripts* 372, 433. See also G Williams, 'The Defence of Necessity' (1953) *Crim LR* 216, and *Cas Louise Ménard* (1898) Correctional Court of Chateau-Thierry in H Legret, *Les jugements du Président Magnaud*, vol 1 (Paris, 1900) 14–15.

[130] *Oscar Chinn Case* PCIJ Rep Series A/B No 63, individual opinion of Anzilotti J, 113.

[131] See MN Schmitt, 'Military Necessity and Humanity in International Humanitarian Law: Preserving the Delicate Balance' (2010) 50 *Virginia Journal of International Law* 795.

[132] ibid, 185.

[133] Byers and Chesterman (2003) (n 1) 198–201; CP De Nicola, 'Shield for the Knights of Humanity: The ICC should adopt a Humanitarian Necessity Defence to the Crime of Aggression' (2008–09) 30 *University of Pennsylvania Journal of International Law* 641.

'justified', but rather than using the tort defence of 'justification', employs the criminal law model of 'mitigation', which affirms that the intervention can never be (entirely) justified.[134] The reason for this would seem to be the fear that Kosovo could otherwise be used as a precedent.

As to the inherent subjectivity of permitting a rule which allows States to disregard the law where they may judge it 'necessary' to do so, Franck argues for a novel system of 'international jurying', whereby the political organs of the United Nations may sit in joint judgment of the legitimacy of any given employment of the necessity 'defence'. This would guard against unilateralist abuse of the necessity doctrine, as well as adding a Fuller-esque 'social dimension' to legal positivism.[135] Franck argues that, to a degree, this is already happening, with the Security Council's '*post hoc* approval of ECOMOG military action in Liberia, and implicitly, of NATO's humanitarian intervention in Kosovo'.[136] He acknowledges that he is, in reality, stretching the law quite some distance from its original intended purpose, but argues that 'necessity' and 'international jurying' are, in reality, simply examples of legal fictions, and that such legal fictions play a key role in any legal system, including the international legal system. He cites as an example the justification of the use of force by the Security Council to oust the Haitian military junta, where 'it contrived the fiction that, by causing a flow of refugees, the junta was causing a threat to international peace and security' such as to justify action under Chapter VII.[137]

Franck's analysis has much to commend it on the face of it. Unlike many of his counterparts, he only resorts to stage three (instrumentalism) of Koskenniemi's 'turn to ethics' model. In doing so, he remains firmly rooted in legal discourse. Nonetheless, Franck's ideas reveal several unforgivable flaws which render his thesis wholly inadequate for dealing with the problem of humanitarian intervention. First, the aforementioned 'moral hierarchy', permitting intervention in furtherance of human rights obligations, but not in furtherance of other State obligations, is insufficiently rooted in law, and is a construct of Franck's own devising. Secondly, Franck's reading of the UN Charter and of other international legal instruments reflects a utopian bias. Thirdly, in repeatedly refusing to allow Kosovo to be used as a precedent, he fails to distinguish between act-utilitarianism and rule-utilitarianism. Fourthly, and importantly, his 'international jurying' model, while not without its merits, effectively completely unbalances the power structure within the United Nations system. A Security Council that fails to support armed intervention in a given State due to a split in voting is likely to be equally split when a post-hoc motion of censure for the action is tabled, as was the case in Kosovo.

134 Roberts (2008) (n 51) 190–95, see above n 40.
135 If indeed this may still be termed positivism. See Warner (2001) (n 64) 209.
136 ibid, 187.
137 ibid, 188.

Furthermore, the General Assembly has no competence in this area. Awarding it such competence, as a post-hoc 'jury' would render the original power structures conceived by the drafters of the Charter defunct. The fact that Franck should feel the need to do so is also slightly surprising, given that he remains convinced that the Charter's drafters were in any case aware of the need to protect human rights in order to ensure peace. In addition, 'international jurying' is unlikely to produce consistent results in consistent circumstances, due to the fact that the 'jurors' may have selfish interests in the outcome of any given crisis. Furthermore, public opinion is highly emotional and capricious, and completely lacks any evidentiary safeguards, necessary to ensure fair legal procedure, which also forms part of the human rights *corpus*.

Franck himself admits that 'law derives part of its legitimacy from its consistent and equal application: the treating alike of like cases',[138] but admits this is unlikely using his model. He attempts to circumvent this problem by conceiving of humanitarian intervention 'not as a new legal right . . . but as a mitigating circumstance that does not create law and which is recognised as purely circumstantial and discretionary relief'.[139] He is not the only scholar to have toyed with such an idea, with Byers, Chesterman and even Ian Brownlie (many years earlier) having shown sympathy for such an approach.[140] So Franck, despite purporting to stay within the law, nonetheless feels that legitimacy and due process requirements of a legal system cannot be applied to his remedy. This is to say nothing, of course, of the incongruity of transposing a necessity model shaped in common law criminal jurisdictions into an international system of inter-State obligations which more closely resembles tort law and which knows no such concept. Even were the concept less cumbersome to transpose into international law, it is worth recalling that within common law, in cases such as *R v Dudley and Stephens* and *United States v Holmes*, a plea in mitigation is but one of five ways in which a man may escape punishment for a given act which seems prima facie to be illegal, the others being: (1) determination by a judge that he did not commit a crime; (2) decision by a prosecutor not to seek an indictment; (3) acquittal by a jury; and (4) pardon or commutation of the sentence by the executive. Although none of the final three are held within a rigid formal framework of due process that prevents factual error, excludes emotional and personal factors and guarantees that all the formalities of legal procedure will be observed, the necessity defence grew up organically in an environment which knew these other phenomena, and it may well be germane to note that inter-State international law does not particularly mirror such a

[138] ibid, 190.
[139] ibid.
[140] Brownlie (1973) (n 18) 146.

structure to any great degree, lacking, as it does, a proper prosecutor and executive.[141] It is worth perhaps reminding ourselves of the difficulties which were involved in the admission by the Appeals Chamber of the International Criminal Tribunal for the Former Yugoslavia that a related defence of duress could exist in international criminal law when contemplating how complicated transposing the similar doctrine of necessity as a defence into general international law might be.[142] One is also left wondering whether Franck could have chosen a slightly different case law based approach, resting upon the lenient punishment (a mere declaration of illegality with no sanctions) meted out to the United Kingdom by the ICJ in the *Corfu Channel* case, itself not a giant leap from the 'illegal but justified' model proposed by Franck, and resting upon much more contiguous jurisprudence.

In the end, then, Franck's necessity/jurying model, after promising much, delivers little. While resisting the urge to veer away from law and into ethics and philosophy is commendable, it does not excuse the serious deficiencies inherent in Franck's reasoning, which, much like the legality/legitimacy model, eventually loses its way by moving too far away from positive law.

Paolo Picone is representative of a select group of other scholars who attempt to root their analyses in or as close to the law as possible. Picone argues in a somewhat different vein for a case-by-case analysis, based upon what he dubs 'alcuni parametri o principi di carattere più generale'.[143] However, his parameters, although more general – bona fides; *ius necessitatis* or human catastrophe; proportionality; respect for *ius in bello*; and *'effet utile'*, while expressed somewhat differently, mirror those of Franck (and to an extent Cassese) and others, certainly as regards the approximate threshold test. Again, Picone finds himself lost somewhere between legality and legitimacy, although it is worth commending the fact that Picone – almost uniquely – makes at least fleeting reference to general principles of law, practically the sole author in this field to do so thus far. However, as shall be discussed in subsequent chapters, Picone's analysis underestimates their importance for the debate. It is further interesting that, per Picone, NATO's Kosovo does not stand up to his own test.[144]

[141] I am indebted to the opinion of Lon Fuller's Handy J for this point. Opinion of Handy J in L Fuller, 'The Case of the Speluncean Explorers' (1949) 62 *Harvard Law Review* 3, 15.

[142] *Prosecutor v Drazen Erdemovic* (Sentencing Judgment) ICTY IT-96-22-T (29 November 1996). See also LC Green, 'Drazen Erdemovic: The ICTY in Action' (1997) 10 *Leiden Journal of International Law* 363; R Cryer, 'One Appeal, Two Philosophies, Four Opinions and a Remittal: The Erdemovic Case at the ICTY Appeals Chamber' (1997) 2 *Journal of Armed Conflict* 193.

[143] P Picone, 'La "Guerra del Kosovo" e il Diritto Internazionale Generale' (2000) 2 *Rivista di diritto internazionale* 309, 345–46.

[144] ibid.

X. TAKING HUMAN RIGHTS SERIOUSLY? FROM JUST WAR TO NEO-IMPERIALISM

Overall, the direction which the humanitarian intervention discourse has taken is symptomatic of a definite regression in terms of international legal thinking, away from the regulation of the UN Charter and inter-State relations based upon sovereign equality and toward the rehabilitation of the Just War doctrine. This has been expanded upon over time, and has led to the arguments associated with the humanitarian intervention debate being used to justify other interventions on the basis of a broad conception of 'justice' – the very circumstance that those who justified the Kosovo intervention as exceptional wished to avoid. Chesterman noted this trend in his book, but failed adequately to explore its consequences and underlying causes.[145] As Wouter Werner has pointed out, in classical international law, 'the ideal typical image of a war was a duel between equal states, represented as *magni homines*'. This reasoning allowed the genesis of *ius in bello*, culminating with the Geneva Conventions and their Additional Protocols, protecting combatants and civilians and regulating conduct whatever the legal status of the war. However, this classical image has given way to a twenty-first century conception of the use of force, 'increasingly defined as enforcement or a preventive action against wrong-doers, risks to international peace and security or against "rogues"'.[146] This 'turn to the past' has been reflected by the entry into fashion of terminology strikingly similar to that of the Just War doctrine. Indeed, certain commentators have gone so far as to dub the recent conflicts in the Persian Gulf, Bosnia, Kosovo and Afghanistan 'virtuous wars'.[147] As Werner has pointed out, the increasing enthusiasm for wars conducted in the name of humanity raises fundamental questions regarding three related elements of international law, namely sovereign equality, the concept of war itself and how to define it, and the concept of the public enemy.[148] While Werner embarks upon the onerous task of examining the evolution of the concept of the public enemy in international legal thought, I shall confine myself principally to discussing the impact of the other two and their effects upon the humanitarian intervention discourse. In order to do so, it shall be necessary to offer a brief historical sketch of the two competing paradigms which have shaped Western legal thought concerning war, namely the Just War doctrine and war as an institution in law.

[145] S Chesterman, *Just War or Just Peace? Humanitarian Intervention and International Law* (Oxford, Oxford University Press, 2001).

[146] W Werner, 'From Justus Hostis to Rogue State: The Concept of the Enemy in International Legal Thinking' (2004) 17 *International Review for the Semiotics of Law* 155.

[147] J Der Derian, *Virtuous Wars, Mapping the Military-Industrial-Media-Entertainment Network* (Westview Press, 2001).

[148] Werner (2004) (n 146) 156.

a. Just War

In his *chef d'oeuvre* on bellicose jurisprudential theory, *War and the Law of Nations*, Stephen C Neff undertakes a comparative analysis of the two classical legal conceptions of warfare mentioned above.[149] Just War theory represents a moralistic justification of war's very existence. Chiefly sculpted by theologians to reconcile the opposing realities of war and the law of God, it represents a solution designed for a world that is far behind us, but the moralistic notions upon which it is grounded have known a renaissance in recent years. It is predicated upon five tenets, namely *auctoritas, justa causa, animus, persona* and *res.*

In Just War theory, a sovereign, vested with *auctoritas,* represents the collective. Individuals may be punished individually, but the war retains its collective character and a common cause. To justify belligerent acts within a just war, an *animus* of each individual is required as well as that of the sovereign. Each individual must know for what he is fighting, believe it is the right thing to do, and be prepared to die for it. This reflects an individualistic element as well as the collective aspect posited by Neff. The question as to why this is so in Just War theory may be answered with reference to the historical context. The earliest legal scholars were theologians, chiefly clerics. These men were pacifists, and as such required a means of justifying war somehow in accordance with morality. The Just War theory did just that. Some may argue that these early scholars dehumanised warfare somewhat by collectivising it. It is likely that this was carried out with the needs of the sovereign in mind. The burden of responsibility being rested upon the shoulders of one man was deemed too much to bear, so a collective construct was erected in order to collectivise responsibility and to circumvent the natural blame apportionment upon the leader.

The earliest just wars were based upon the idea of a Christian fraternity (brotherhood of man) defending itself against an outside threat, as was outlined by the Spanish Salamanca school. A common good should be defended in common, that is collectively. The *Bible* also emphasises this, with its focus on man's duties (to act, for the good of all) over and above rights. Every right-thinking individual is obliged to fight for the good of the world. The duty is placed upon all, not merely upon sovereigns, hence the collective character. Here we see a clear parallel with the rhetoric of humanitarian intervention. The 'brotherhood of man' model has been expanded beyond Christendom, of course, but otherwise the rationale – saving our brothers from unjust oppression – remains constant. Furthermore, Christian theology, while no longer *en vogue,* is largely reflected by Western liberal political theory. This transformation of international law and international affairs to

[149] S Neff, *War and the Law of Nations* (Cambridge, Cambridge University Press, 2005).

re-accommodate such notions has been dubbed as just another step in the inevitable rise and rise of liberalism.[150]

b. A Game with Few Rules

Just War tradition, Neff holds, is based upon the principle of necessity (to uphold a cause),[151] but it has few rules, particularly as regards *ius in bello.* There are exceptions to this – for example, The Second Lateran Council (1139) outlined a rule which outlawed the killing of bishops and other non-combatant classes and the banning of the use of archers and cross-bowmen in wars within Christendom – but generally rules are thin on the ground. A preliminary rule is that the unjust side did not require *justa causa* to wage war. Also worth noting is the absence of any rules governing third party States – for example neutrality. This is because neutrality or any other non-committed stance was impossible. All (Christian) States and peoples must support the justice of the cause and participate in the war. There is no element of choice. As to why the doctrine is not rule-based, again, history plays a key explicatory role. The theological argument at the time was that justice was paramount vis-à-vis the law. It was held that in order to achieve justice, one could use whatever means necessary. Positivism was sacrificed at the naturalist altar.

The return towards this element of the Just War doctrine is also pronounced when one follows the history of recent events. Concerning NATO's Kosovo intervention, for example, the fact that the American bombers flew at high altitudes in order to protect the 'just interveners' in their cockpits represented a choice hardly in line with the spirit of the Geneva Conventions. Terms such as 'targeted killings' and 'enemy combatants' have cropped up, which fly in the face of traditional conceptions of *ius in bello*. *Ius ad Bellum* has fared little better, with the Security Council's authority bypassed and rendered redundant. Here, again, the argument ran that justice must necessarily trump the law where the conscience of mankind demanded it. The arguments associated with the intervention undermined many basic rules, including that of neutrality, for not to be seen to support intervention was to be seen to be indifferent to human suffering.

c. War as an Institution in Law

The idea of war as an institution in law replaced that of the Just War as a prime component of the international order that developed in the seventeenth century. Carl Schmitt was a passionate supporter of the idea of war

[150] F Fukuyama, 'The End of History?' (1989) *National Interest* 3.
[151] Neff (2005) (n 149) 65.

as an ordered, rule-based discipline in which sovereign equality would govern relations between States and that *ius in bello* would ensure equal treatment for all combatants, regardless of the merits of their cause.[152] This paradigm 'transformed the Medieval problem of the *justa causa* for intervention into the institution of war between formally equal states: the *justi et aequales hostes*'.[153] This rule-based paradigm was reinforced by the limitations placed upon the use of force by the League of Nations (which formally recognised war as an institution in law) and the United Nations (which recognised war, but limited its legality). Schmitt, however, was worried by the changes which were already taking place in the first half of the twentieth century, whereby the justice of the *casus belli* was again assuming increasing importance. Schmitt identified two important changes in the concept of the enemy that were the result of this new appraisal of war in international legal thinking, namely a distinction between types of States and a de-nationalization of the enemy.[154] As Gerry Simpson and Wouter Werner have pointed out, the distinction between types of States led to the re-introduction of the 'rogue state' nomenclature,[155] 'a concept used to denote that a certain state behaves in such a way that it should be regarded as *hostis generis humani*'.[156] This concept was already being used (again) during the First World War, and nowadays is increasingly being chosen as a tool by Western governments seeking to justify interventions. This is little surprise, given how far some liberal theorists have taken the paradigm. John Rawls, for example, distinguishes 'decent states' from 'outlaw states' and proposes different legal regimes for both.[157] Schmitt feared that such trends would lead to wars taking the form of international enforcement actions in which the enemy would lack equal status and be regarded as a rogue and a gangster.[158] Morgenthau echoed these sentiments, predicting many wars of 're-civilization' of the enemy State by re-education, democratisation and the imposition of liberal values.[159] Writing somewhat later, Wellmer agreed that Schmitt's vision was indeed coming to pass, and that liberalism's warlike march was indeed on its way, but that the *justa causa* required to justify such

[152] C Schmitt, *Der Nomos der Erde im Völkerrecht des Jus Publicum Europaeum* (Berlin, Duncker & Humblot, 1960).

[153] Werner (2004) (n 146) 158.

[154] C Schmitt, *Die wendìng zum diskriminierenden Kriegsbegriff* (Berlin, Duncker & Humblot, 1988) 41–53.

[155] G Simpson, *Great Powers and Outlaw States: Unequal Sovereigns in the International Legal Order,* Cambridge Studies in International and Comparative Law (Cambridge, Cambridge University Press, 2004).

[156] Werner (2004) (n 146) 165.

[157] J Rawls, *The Law of Peoples, with the Law of Public Reason Revisited* (Cambridge, MA, Harvard University Press, 1999).

[158] Schmitt (1988) (n 154) 43.

[159] H Morgenthau, *In Defence of National Interest: A Critical Examination of American Foreign Policy* (Washington DC, University Press of America, 1982) 88–103.

're-civilization wars' would necessarily have to involve human rights violations in order to find a public pretext for intervention.[160]

d. Stretching Justice – From Wartime Inequality to Imperial Apology

The move towards an unequal conception of warfare has been taken still further by Fernando Tesón, who posits that 'if a war is unjust, each and every injury caused by the unjust warrior is a criminal act. There are no morally justified killings by those who fight unjust wars'.[161] The obvious problem with this is that 'justice' is necessarily a subjective notion, and that in certain cases, such as the Iraq war, humanitarian rationales are not advanced until after the fighting has commenced. Tesón makes a grievous error in employing the word 'criminal' in describing something which is contrary to his own conception of morality rather than something contrary to law. How can the individual soldier, supposedly committing criminal act after criminal act in executing an unjust war, know that he is doing so? It is not as if the Serbian or Iraqi troops (or at least those who conformed with *ius in bello*) would have been instructed that the operations which they were to carry out were inherently unjust. On the contrary, they would have been convinced that they were acting in defence of their respective governments' interests. Furthermore, when the Iraqi troops took to the battlefield, they would have been acting in self-defence, a recognised exception to the prohibition on the use of force under Article 51 of the UN Charter, in attempting to repel a force which was acting without a Security Council mandate. However, such an argument is unlikely to find favour with those, such as Tesón, who prioritise 'justice' *simpliciter* over the international rule of law and international order.

Indeed, the Iraq war is perhaps a prime example of just how far the subjective notions of justice and legitimacy may be stretched by a return to Just War thinking, and Fernando Tesón is an equally good example of someone who has worked hard to stretch such notions in order to allow interventions on wider grounds than merely those of an immediate overriding humanitarian emergency.

e. Rights as Trumps in the International Arena

In 1977, Ronald Dworkin published his acclaimed work *Taking Rights Seriously*. In this *chef d'oeuvre*, Dworkin argued that rights act as 'trumps', which people may use to defend themselves against the government and against their peers. Dworkin rightly asserts that it is due to the rights of

[160] A Wellmer, *Revolution und Interpretation, Demokratie ohne Letztbegründung* (Assen, Van Garam, 1998) 42.

[161] F Tesón, 'Self-Defence in International Law and Rights of Persons' (2004) 18 *Ethics and International Affairs* 87.

sometimes inconvenient minorities (for example political protesters) that the majority of the populace of any State, and even more so, the government, is not entitled to *carte blanche*.[162] This was a 'hot topic' in the United States in the 1970s, particularly in the context of opposition to the Vietnam War, and is again becoming controversial there, particularly with reference to draconian measures adopted as part of the 'war on terror'. Dworkin contended that if a government was not prepared to take rights, particularly important rights, held individually by its citizens, seriously, then it was not taking the law seriously either.

Tesón advances a similar thesis in favour of a right of humanitarian intervention. Tesón argues that humanitarian intervention is morally justified in appropriate cases. Per Tesón, the major purpose of States and governments is to secure human rights. Those governments that violate human rights undermine the one reason justifying their political power and should therefore not be protected by international law. Sovereignty, for Tesón, is an instrumental, and not an intrinsic, value. The two extremes of tyranny and anarchy cause the moral collapse of sovereignty.[163]

Tesón argues that persons are (human) right holders, and that these rights entail normative consequences for others, including governments. These include: (1) the obligation to respect these human rights; (2) the obligation to promote the respect of these human rights; and (3) the obligation to rescue victims who are being persecuted in violation of these human rights if the costs to the rescuer(s) are reasonable. The final obligation of this triumvirate entails the right to rescue victims encapsulated in the doctrine of humanitarian intervention, argues Tesón. Failure to intervene can render parties morally culpable.

Tesón espouses the liberal argument that extreme cruelty perpetrated as a result of a state of tyranny or anarchy is a serious form of injustice, States have a responsibility instead to strive for the Kantian 'centre'.[164] External intervention, subject to certain constraints, is morally permissible to end such injustice. Tesón denies that such a doctrine will lead to a world of many wars, and further notes that critics of humanitarian intervention are not pacifists, but that they generally support the two recognised exceptions to Article 2(4) of the UN Charter, one of which is the Article 51 (inherent) right to self-defence.

Tesón portrays victims of such a situation as trapped and impotent to help themselves, and deems them deserving of rescue. He affirms a duty to assist others in times of peril if it is at reasonable cost to ourselves. The

[162] R Dworkin, *Taking Rights Seriously* (Cambridge, MA, Harvard University Press, 1977).

[163] F Tesón, 'The Liberal Case for Humanitarian Intervention' in JL Holzgrefe and RO Keohane (eds), *Humanitarian Intervention: Ethical, Legal and Political Dilemmas* (Cambridge, Cambridge University Press, 2003).

[164] I Kant, *Zum ewigen Frieden. Ein philosophischer Entwurf* (Königsberg, erste Auflage, 1795).

right to intervene therefore stems from a more general *duty* to assist victims of grievous injustice. For Tesón, collapse of Rawlsian State legitimacy is a necessary, but not a sufficient precondition for humanitarian intervention. Some, but not all, illegitimate States shall be candidates for intervention, which must be reserved for the most serious cases only, namely tyranny and anarchy. Per Tesón, sovereignty must never be used as a shield, and can never, of itself, be a reason not to intervene, being itself contingent upon the government's fulfilments of its obligations vis-à-vis human rights.[165] Furthermore, he posits, opponents of humanitarian intervention must necessarily find themselves hoist by their own moral petard. In Tesón's opinion, the forcible defence of States permitted in Article 51 of the UN Charter is itself justified *qua* defence of persons, namely the persons within the State. If this is so, there can be no moral distinction drawn between the doctrines of self-defence and humanitarian intervention, since both are undertaken for the same reason. This argument, while clearly in line with Koskenniemi's eight steps away from law and toward ethics, employing as it does both the 'rights as trumps' and teleological approaches, is nonetheless of some value, if only for the reason that it demonstrates the harsh reality that international law is concerned primarily with the interests of States themselves, and not with the equality or rights of human beings.

Tesón rejects the notion that humanitarian concerns represent a subjective Western conception of justice, holding that certain situations are abhorrent under any plausible ethical theory, and that such situations may sometimes justify humanitarian intervention under a liberal conception of politics. This contention does not hold up to scrutiny, however, as plainly the use of the words 'any plausible ethical theory' is itself subjective. What does Tesón mean by plausible? Is this a contention that the National Socialist regime in Germany was devoid of plausible ethics? *Au contraire.* In order to gain and hold power in a democracy such as Weimar Germany, one must present a political programme built on ethics that are plausible to the populace. So too in Rwanda and Serbia. In order to encourage public participation in ethnic cleansing, surely it is necessary to formulate a reason for doing so. This reason must logically be, at the very least, plausible.

Making use of terminology such as 'plausible' and 'objective' constitutes Tesón's means of shielding the reader from divining one fatal flaw in his argumentative technique: its glaring lack of objectivity. In his 1988 volume, *Humanitarian Intervention: An Inquiry into Law and Morality,* Tesón argues that legal reasoning necessarily involves moral reasoning.[166] Therefore, it seems, one must choose a theory, a 'lens', as it were, through which to view

[165] Tesón (2003) (n 163) 97.

[166] F Tesón, *Humanitarian Intervention: An Inquiry into Law and Morality,* 1st edn (Dobbs Ferry, NY, Transnational, 1988) 10.

international law. Here, Tesón places himself squarely on the side of contractarians and rights theorists among contemporary social philosophers, and in opposition to positivists in international law. However, it is purely by virtue of this 'lens' that Tesón is able to draw the conclusions which he does – that the rights of States are derivative from those of individuals, that sovereignty is contingent upon respect for human rights and that these human rights sit atop the normative pyramid of international law. He argues that governments 'are constrained by moral principles in their international behaviour, just as they are constrained by moral principles in their domestic behaviour'.[167] However, Tesón fails to grasp the fact that he is imposing a subjective conception of what international law represents.

Tesón is critical of anti-interventionist scholars, claiming that they attempt to sever domestic from international legitimacy. 'For them, national borders mysteriously operate a change in the description of the act of humanitarian rescue; it is no longer humanitarian rescue, but war' but goes on to opine that 'national borders can hardly have a moral significance *in this context*.'[168] Per Tesón, there are two principal reasons to respect national borders: (1) the legitimacy of the social contract which is the result of free consent of autonomous individuals in civil society; and (2) the fact that national borders may help to secure the *stability* of social interaction at international level, analogous to property rights at domestic level.

Tesón notes the position of Michael Walzer, who opines that simply because a State is illegitimate internally, this is not sufficient cause for foreign armies to intervene. This is in accordance with what Walzer calls 'communal integrity', the idea that nations have histories and loyalties that define their political process, and that process should be protected as such, even if some of its outcomes are repulsive to liberal philosophers.[169] Tesón notes, however, that dictators themselves come from the societies which they eventually tyrannise. Are the people therefore (partly) responsible for the tyranny which they suffer? As David Luban put it, himself paraphrasing George Orwell,[170] 'The government fits the people the way the sole of a boot fits a human face: After a while the patterns of indentation fit with uncanny precision'.[171] Per John Stuart Mill, interveners have a right to expect at least a modicum of cooperation from those being rescued. Mill held that people cannot really be free if outsiders do all the fighting for them.[172] Tesón disagrees with this assertion, pointing out that

[167] ibid, 16.

[168] Tesón (2003) (n 163) 103.

[169] M Walzer, 'The Moral Standing of States: A Resposnse to Four Critics' (1980) 9 *Philosophy and Public Affairs* 209.

[170] G Orwell, *Nineteen Eighty-Four* (London, Secker and Warburg, 1949).

[171] D Luban, 'The Romance of the Nation-State' (1980) 9 *Philosophy and Public Affairs* 395.

[172] JS Mill, 'A Few Words on Non-Intervention' in JS Mill, *Dissertations and Discussions*, vol III (Boston, MA, Spencer, 1867) 171–76.

it is possible that the majority of the population may be complicit in the human rights violations. In such circumstances, simply because the situation grew up organically due to 'communal integrity' should not mean that it is shielded from intervention.

As regards the 'stability of social interaction' argument, Tesón notes that the purpose of international law in general, and not simply national borders, is to ensure stability in international relations. However, he points out that there is nothing important about the sovereignty of any one State itself; what is important is the preservation of the system of sovereign States to ensure continued stability, meaning that an unjust order is preferable to chaos. However, per Tesón,

> [t]yranny and anarchy are at least as likely to generate instability and chaos as interventions . . . The death of a state is never bad in itself (think of the demise of the Soviet Union or East Germany). Only the deaths of its citizens.[173]

Based upon the above considerations, which, for Tesón, outweigh the two root causes for respecting national frontiers, 'The goal of saving lives and restoring Human Rights and justice is compelling enough to authorise humanitarian intervention, even at the cost of innocent lives'.[174] A categorical non-interventionist position cannot be justified by a general abhorrence of violence, since the non-interventionist is taking a position that permits the perpetration of the atrocities. 'That position is part of a general view that killing is morally worse than letting die'.[175] Tesón clearly disapproves of this position, and yet he fails to consider the repercussions of adopting a stance which equates killing and failure to prevent death, rendering people culpable for their omissions as well as their actions at international level. The consequences of such an approach are clear: everyone who can act to prevent something bad from happening must do so. If not, they are partially responsible for any resultant loss or death. Tesón's position necessarily entails the classification of humanitarian intervention not as a right, but as an obligation owed by everyone (who is in a position to help in any way) to everyone else. This is completely at odds with jurisprudential theories of responsibility, and it seems little short of ridiculous to suppose that States would ever accept the reception of such a theory into the international legal sphere, rendering them, at least in part, responsible for how any madman dictator treats his citizens.

Furthermore, Tesón's liberal 'lens' is once again evident in his discussion of the balancing act which must be performed in order to justify an intervention. Tesón argues that the costs of an intervention must be measured against the magnitude of the evil combated.[176] This suggests that in

[173] Tesón (2003) (n 163) 112–14.
[174] ibid, 117.
[175] ibid, 119.
[176] Tesón (1988) (n 166) 116.

the first place, the priority is to stamp out evil, not necessarily to save the innocent per se and it becomes unclear how many innocent people one is prepared to sacrifice if one's estimate of the magnitude of the evil is great enough.

In short, one may state that Tesón's theory, while attractive insofar as it 'takes Human Rights seriously', and attempts to place them atop the pyramid of norms, drifts too far into the ethical sphere to be useful in the real world. The fact that his proposals would require a radical reformulation of State and individual responsibility at international level renders it little short of fanciful. Furthermore, Tesón's entire thesis, while based on assertions which he claims no 'plausible' ethical theory can deny, are inherently subjective. Placing human rights above other *ius cogens* norms has not provoked widespread approval; nor has holding State actors responsible for omissions. The idea of a 'responsibility to protect' has yet to develop proper normative roots, and while Tesón's discourse commences with an examination of concepts familiar to international lawyers – human rights and State sovereignty – it drifts toward notions which are clearly dear to the author's own heart, but which know no basis in international law.

However objectionable the above may be, worse was to come from the same author. Time and a new reading of international affairs have turned Tesón, the erstwhile ethical theorist, into a fervent apologist for American neo-imperialism, stretching and perverting the language of humanitarian intervention into an apology for US foreign policy.

f. The New Empire

Tesón has stated that NATO's Kosovo intervention established 'The most important precedent supporting the legitimacy of humanitarian intervention', holding that it may have expanded rather than breached international law, rather in the style of the Truman Declaration on the Continental Shelf rights.[177] Tesón's logic, however, has moved with the times, as it were. In addition to his earlier-enunciated principles that governments, as agents, derive rights from the people; that tyrannical governments forfeit their protection under international law, and that governments have a duty to uphold international law, Tesón, in a 2006 article adds five further criteria as thresholds for permissible humanitarian intervention.[178] Amongst these is the controversial claim that a justifiable intervention must be intended to end either tyranny or anarchy, that is, that forcible regime change must necessarily take place on foot of the intervention, and as a direct and intended result thereof, to ensure a return to the 'Kantian centre'. This is somewhat

[177] F Tesón, 'Kosovo: A Powerful Precedent for the Doctrine of Humanitarian Intervention' (2009) 1 *Amsterdam Law Forum* 42.

[178] F Tesón, 'Eight Principles of Humanitarian Intervention' (2006) 5 *Journal of Military Ethics* 93.

akin to Bernard Kouchner's '4th stage of humanitarianism', and assumes a predilection for democratic governance in the US mould which has little place in international legal norms.[179] Furthermore, it would seem that the intention to effect regime change upon the enemy State being a necessary precondition of the intervention, then the intervention can never be truly humanitarian in nature, since the intervener's intent must be regime change and the imposition of a stable government in the democratic mould. Not so, protests Tesón, who separates the 'intention' and the 'motive' of the intervention. Per Tesón, while an intervention must be *motivated* by humanitarian concerns, it must also be *intended* to effect regime change. Therefore, according to Tesón, regime change becomes a *conditio sine qua non* of permissible humanitarian intervention. Here, Tesón displays a poor understanding of international law, as well as popular conceptions of legitimacy of humanitarian intervention, few of which would stretch so far. His bias also pervades his view of history, often somewhat at odds with reality, for instance commenting that 'Even if (contrary to fact) the US' motive in 1941 was to become a dominant superpower, it did the right thing in fighting and defeating the axis',[180] implying that the United States voluntarily joined the war, motivated by some sort of *justa causa*, and omitting to mention that it had been pursuing a policy of neutrality until the bombing of Pearl Harbour and that it was Hitler who subsequently chose to declare war on the United States, and not the reverse.[181]

Tesón takes his ideas further, opining that even the killing of innocent civilians may be justified if the overall intention of the intervention is just and if the consequences thereof are equally just – that is ending tyranny.[182] However, the logic of allowing for the killing of civilians in order to effect regime change brings Tesón a long way from his supposedly cherished Kantian centre. This is particularly true when one contemplates a case like the Iraq war, which Tesón has defended as a permissible humanitarian intervention. According to Ken Roth of Human Rights Watch, brutal as the Hussein regime was, the scope of its killing in 2003 was not of an exceptional and dire magnitude so as to justify humanitarian intervention. '"Better late than never" is not a justification for humanitarian intervention, which should be countenanced only to stop mass murder, not to punish its perpetrators'.[183]

[179] B Kouchner and L Bettati (eds), *Le Devoir d'Ingerence* (Paris, Denoël, 1987). Slaughter has used a similar model to justify the US-led invasion of Iraq as unlawful but legitimate. A-M Slaughter, 'An American Vision of International Law?' (2003) 97 *American Society of International Law Proceedings* 125.

[180] Tesón (2006) (n 178) 100.

[181] See W Shirer, *The Rise and Fall of the Third Reich*, 1st Touchstone edn (London, Simon & Schuster, 1990).

[182] Tesón (2006) (n 178) 103.

[183] K Roth, 'War in Iraq: Not a Humanitarian Intervention' (2005) *Human Rights Watch* 6. Available at www.unhcr.org/refworld/pdfid/401ba99f4.pdf.

Tesón seems to draw back from imposing an overly far-reaching model by adding three limiting conditions to his test for legitimate humanitarian intervention, namely that generally only severe cases of tyranny and anarchy qualify for intervention; that the victims of tyranny or anarchy must welcome such intervention; and that any intervention should preferably receive the approval or support of the community of democratic States. However, on closer examination, these three limitation clauses actually serve more as further pretexts to intervene than any real restriction upon State action. Regarding the stipulation that only severe cases of tyranny and anarchy will qualify, Tesón adds that 'while cases like Saddam Hussein's Iraq . . . are to my mind, easy candidates for humanitarian intervention, lesser cases may also qualify'.[184] Tesón then, sets the bar so low that operations such as that in Iraq the humanitarian element of which was dubious, and which arguably did more harm than good, are 'easy candidates', and, further, would be open to stretching the permissibility test still more in order to accommodate 'lesser cases', wherever they may be. Tesón goes on to argue that even interventions purely engineered to restore democracy may be justified. As to the second criterion, he makes it plain that the test is not whether the populace as a whole, or even the broad majority, welcomes intervention, but merely those whose rights are being most severely violated. This is obviously no real limitation either, since it is difficult to think of a torture victim who would not welcome his deliverance.

Finally, the consideration that humanitarian intervention should preferably receive the approval or support of democratic States is also of little value in limiting such actions. 'Preferably' does not indicate a necessity, merely a preference, and small democratic States are likely to engage in band-wagoning when a hegemonic power engages in military action and seeks brothers in arms. However, Tesón is not alone in voicing a preference for democratic approval of acquiescence to intervention. Henry Shue has also made similar arguments, thus reproducing yet another component of the Just War doctrine, that of *auctoritas* based upon an ingrained beliefs system.[185] In Just War theory, States were expected to obtain the authority of the papacy for their wars, since the wars were partly about spreading Christendom and the Western values of the day. Similarly, a body composed of democratic States heavily ingrained with liberal values would be the appropriate body for wars which seek to spread modern Western values, namely liberal democracy.

Tesón seems to have moved in the last 20 years from a liberal viewpoint permitting humanitarian intervention in limited circumstances to

[184] Tesón (2006) (n 178) 105.

[185] H Shue, 'The Shortcomings of the "New Humanitarianism"' in A Paolini, A Jarvis and C Reus-Smit (eds), *Between Sovereignty and Global Governance: The United Nations, the State and Civil Society* (London, Macmillan, 1998) 73.

an apology for any action which the US administration has chosen to undertake. He is far from alone in this regard, and his views are merely indicative of a broader trend.[186] He has been roundly rebuked for his views on the Iraq war in particular by Terry Nardin.[187] Nardin notes that Tesón offers two particular 'humanitarian rationales' for the war in Iraq, namely the overthrow of Saddam Hussein and the defence of the United States via the promotion of democracy in the Middle-East.[188] As Nardin points out, neither of these is even remotely humanitarian in nature, and any claims that Saddam Hussein had, in the past, perpetrated gross human rights abuses against his own citizens are irrelevant, since such abuses must be on-going or imminent to qualify as a humanitarian rationale.

Nardin suggests that Tesón's viewpoint no longer belongs in the realm of the humanitarian intervention debate, but instead has encroached into the debate on empire. Bricmont holds a similar view, arguing that many theories justifying humanitarian intervention may merely serve as imperial apologies.[189] As Nardin makes clear,

> [l]ike the ideas of State sovereignty and nonintervention, the idea of humanitarian intervention makes sense only if we understand the international order to be a normative system based on the coexistence of independent states, each enjoying rights of political sovereignty and territorial integrity defined by international law.[190]

Humanitarian intervention cannot make sense, however if we understand a global order à la Tesón, since in this order 'only morally legitimate States have rights'[191] and therefore the same moral, legal and political quandaries do not arise. Skordas goes further, rooting legitimacy in hegemony itself, rather than the values it embodies, arguing for the legitimacy and eventual legality of 'hegemonic intervention', though admitting that acceptance of such a norm (which would need to override

[186] See, eg A-M Slaughter, 'Good Reasons for Going around the UN', *New York Times*, 18 March 2003, who opined that the invasion of Iraq could be 'justified' under the Kosovo 'precedent' if weapons of mass destruction were found or if a portion of the Iraqi population welcomed the intervention. An interesting alternative perspective is voiced by NN Petro, who, with reference to Abkhazia and South Ossetia, states that Western scholars must give Russia's humanitarian motives due consideration. Not doing so risks undermining the commitment of the West to international legal principles and illustrates double standards, undermining the potential for eventual normative stability. NN Petro, 'Legal Case for Russian Intervention in Georgia' (2008) 32 *Fordham International Law Journal* 1524.

[187] T Nardin, 'Humanitarian Imperialism' (2005) 19 *Ethics and International Affairs* 21.

[188] F Tesón, 'Ending Tyranny in Iraq' (2005) 19 *Ethics and International Affairs* 1.

[189] O Bricmont, *Impérialisme Humanitaire* (Brussels, Arden, 2005). See also D Rodogno, 'Réflexions liminaires à propos des interventions humanitaires des Puissances européens au XIXème siècle' (2007) 131 *Relations Internationales* 22.

[190] Nardin (2005) (n 187) 22–23.

[191] ibid, 23.

sovereign equality) is 'not [yet] in sight'.[192] Weisburd also sees such a situation as a future possibility, adding that 'Even the concept of *ius cogens* is no bar to change'.[193]

Nardin notes that the failure to provide security in the wake of the Iraq invasion and the disastrous humanitarian consequences of the disbandment of the police and security forces are glossed over by Tesón, showing again his failure to engage with the real historical facts and instead providing his own narrative. Ken Roth has pointed out that the way the invasion itself was carried out reflected the fact that a humanitarian purpose was not amongst the war goals. According to Roth, this 'is not simply an academic point; it affected the way the invasion was carried out, to the detriment of the Iraqi people'.[194] It is worth noting the parallels which Nardin finds striking between Tesón's vision of legitimate humanitarian intervention and the old literature of empire. In the latter, humanitarianism was employed to justify involvement by Western powers in the margins of the civilized world in order to uphold standards of civilized morality and suppress barbarism through international tutelage and colonialism. Tesón's account of humanitarian intervention is little different, constantly expanding to justify the US involvement in far-away places on the basis of 'protection from tyranny' and 'regime change' to effect democratic governance.[195] The US may not acquire colonies, but it does garner military bases, friendly governments and lucrative trade links. Tesón's argument amounts to imperial apology, and may not be qualified as advocacy of humanitarian intervention under any traditional guise.[196]

XI. OBSCURING THE LAW

The conclusion which one is drawn to by all of the above models, and indeed by the broad mass of the discourse on humanitarian intervention is that the illegality of humanitarian intervention is still irrefutable. The various attempts to equate the concept with legality, to bring it 'close' to the law, or to appeal to broad principles of justice in order to appeal for its permissibility are misguided, are easily exposed as transparent and are

[192] A Skordas, 'Hegemonic Intervention as Legitimate Use of Force' (2007) 16 *Minnesota Law Journal* 407.

[193] Wesiburd in Cannizzaro and Palchetti (2005) (n 77) 75.

[194] Roth (2005) (n 183) 9. Francioni similarly notes that the Iraq invasion was only retroactively justified on humanitarian grounds following the failure to find weapons of mass destruction. Francioni (2005) (n 19) 270.

[195] See N Tsagourias, 'The Inevitable Independence of Kosovo' (2009) 1 *Amsterdam Law Forum* 39.

[196] Despite concerns about abuse of humanitarian intervention, however, Goodman, inter alia, argues that such objections are not important enough to stop the push for legal intervention to protect human rights. See R Goodman, 'Humanitarian Intervention and Pretexts for War' (2006) 100 *American Journal of International Law* 107.

open to abuse. However, the fact that these efforts will continue is clear, as is the implication of such discourse upon international law. A 'blurring of the lines' between legality and illegality is occurring. Terminology such as 'traditional international law', 'emerging customary norms', and 'current trends' serve to obscure the true import of what should be a clear legal rule.[197] This obscuring process is further compounded by the efforts of many respected scholars and public figures to encourage greater human rights awareness and protection, even when such initiatives clash with the prohibition on the use of force enshrined in the UN Charter.

In a 1999 article, the then UN Secretary-General Kofi Annan described the dilemma involved in the humanitarian intervention debate:

> On the one hand, is it legitimate for a regional organisation to use force without a UN mandate? On the other, is it permissible to let gross and systematic violations of Human Rights, with grave humanitarian consequences, continue unchecked?[198]

Annan's language here is telling. His dry assessment of NATO intervening in Kosovo without Security Council backing daubs the action as a breach of a legal rule (and nothing more) without exploring its consequences. On the other hand, judging by his description of the 'grave humanitarian consequences' of 'gross and systematic' rights breaches, it is clear that for Annan, no real dilemma exists. Indeed, Annan affirms: 'the world cannot stand aside when gross and systematic violations of Human Rights are taking place . . . intervention must be based on legitimate and universal principles'.[199]

It is again obvious from Annan's vocabulary that respect for international law is not his highest priority. Principles which are 'legitimate and universal' need not necessarily be legal. Indeed, if the principles to which Annan is alluding do form part of the *corpus* of international law, why not be explicit about this? According to Annan: what the Charter does say is that 'armed force shall not be used, save in the common interest'. But what is the common interest; who shall define it; who shall defend it; under whose authority; and with what means of intervention?[200]

Annan's attempts to deliberately obscure what amounts to a fairly clear legal issue are obvious. The Charter does not confine itself to the simple statement that 'armed force shall not be used, save in the common interest'. It instead stipulates that it shall only be used in cases of self-defence or when the Security Council determines that it is warranted as a response

[197] The same may be said of the Responsibility to Protect initiative and the Human Security terminology, which have also become popular in the wake of this debate. See H Thierry, 'Réflexions sur le "Droit d'Ingérence Humanitaire"' in L Boisson de Chazournes and V Gowlland-Debbas (eds), *L'Ordre Juridique International, Un Système en Quête d'Équité, Liber Amicorum Georges Abi-Saab* (The Hague, Martinus Nijhoff, 2001) 224.

[198] K Annan, 'Two Concepts of Sovereignty', *The Economist*, London, 18 September 1999.

[199] ibid.

[200] ibid.

to a threat to international peace and security, and that outside of these two narrow exceptions, a general prohibition on force exists. As for the questions which Annan poses, there exist easy answers: the common interest is whatever the UN Security Council says it is (save in cases of self-defence which are clearly outside the discussion here); the Security Council shall define it; States or regional organisations authorised by the Security Council shall defend it; under the authority of the Security Council; and with whatever means the Security Council determines are appropriate in the circumstances.

The answers which I have provided to the questions posed by the Secretary-General are not difficult to find. All that one is required to do is to peruse the UN Charter. I do not believe for a moment that the Secretary-General's knowledge of the aforementioned document is so lacking that he proffered the above questions in earnest. Instead, his discourse was part of a concerted effort of various political, philosophical and, as we have seen, even legal scholars, to adopt an apologetic position toward the Kosovo operation, by hook or by crook. Obscuring the legal question at hand by resort to perspicacity, resulting in a reformulation of the issues in terms which are more easily manipulated is a common device, as is appealing to general principles of justice and legitimacy in lieu of referring to the law itself. This technique is also visible in the work of the recently-established Canadian-sponsored International Commission on Intervention and State Sovereignty and its December 2001 report entitled *The Responsibility to Protect*, which also proposes guidelines for permissible humanitarian intervention.

It was in the context of establishing criteria for intervention and putting the bedevilled debate on thresholds to bed, that the Canadian Government established an independent, impartial authority, the International Commission on Intervention and State Sovereignty (ICISS) which it charged with the delicate task of shaping a framework for permissible humanitarian intervention.

XII. THE RESPONSIBILITY TO PROTECT

A. Explaining the Responsibility to Protect

In order for any discussion of the humanitarian intervention debate to be complete, the Responsibility to Protect initiative cannot be ignored. In this section, I shall first set out the ideas explored by the ICISS in its report, including the threshold criteria for humanitarian intervention and their relation to international law. I shall follow this with a critique of the report's findings and its implementation, chiefly from a legal perspective but also discussing associated political, social and economic problems, while also placing the debate in its historical context. Finally, I shall conclude with an assessment of the relative successes and failures of the ICISS, evaluating its prospects for the future and asking whether alternative initiatives might be better placed to deal with the humanitarian intervention conundrum.

The ICISS was charged (and partially funded) by the Canadian Government with the mandate 'to build a broader understanding of the problem of reconciling intervention for humanitarian protection purposes and sovereignty', and more specifically 'to try to develop a global political consensus on how to move from polemics . . . towards action'.[201] Its report, entitled *The Responsibility to Protect* was delivered in 2001, along with a longer document, *Research, Bibliography, Background* explaining the ancillary points of the report. Jack Donnelly has called the report 'a watershed event on international discussions of humanitarian intervention'.[202]

i. The R2P Report

The *Responsibility to Protect Report* (also styled as the *R2P Report*) built on earlier work by Francis M Deng.[203] Its opening lines contain its central conclusion:

> State sovereignty implies responsibility, and the primary responsibility for the protection of its people lies with the State itself. Where a population is suffering serious harm as a result of internal war, insurgency, repression, or state failure and the State in question is unwilling or unable to halt or avert it, the principle of non-intervention yields to the international responsibility to protect.[204]

The report purports to 'turn the debate on its head', following Deng's model of sovereignty interpreted as responsibility. Gareth Evans and Mohamed Sahnoun, the chief figures behind the report contend that 'the whole issue must be reframed not as an argument about the "right to intervene" but about the "responsibility to protect" . . . using this alternative language will help shake up the policy debate, getting governments in particular to think afresh about what the real issues are'.[205]

The *Responsibility to Protect Report* stresses certain concepts: first, evaluations of situations are to be made from the point of view of those persons in need of support. Secondly, the primary Responsibility to Protect rests with

[201] ICISS, *The Responsibility to Protect (Report)* (2001) 2.

[202] J Donnelly, *Universal Human Rights in Theory and Practice,* 2nd edn (Ithaca, NY, Cornell University Press, 2003) 251.

[203] FM Deng, 'Frontiers of Sovereignty' (1995) 8 *Leiden Journal of Internationl Law* 249; FM Deng et al, *Sovereignty as Responsibility: Conflict Management in Africa* (Washington, DC, Brookings Institution, 1996).

[204] ICISS, *The Responsibility to Protect (Report)* (2001) xi.

[205] G Evans and M Sahnoun 'The Responsibility to Protect' (2002) 81 (6) *Foreign Affairs* 101, 99–110.

the State in question. It is only in cases where the State is unwilling or unable to protect its citizens, or when the State is sponsoring egregious human rights abuses, that other States or regional organisations garner the ability to intervene. Thirdly, the Responsibility to Protect incorporates three key sub-elements, namely the Responsibility to React, the Responsibility to Prevent, and the Responsibility to Rebuild.

Throughout, the report represents a shift in thinking about the essence of sovereignty, from a concept of control over the population to a concept of responsibility for their welfare. 'The Responsibility to Protect implies a duty to react to situations in which there is a compelling need for human protection'.[206] This is the underlying justification advanced by the ICISS for military intervention. Evans and Sahnoun admit the departure from the classic Westphalian conception of international relations, where 'the defining characteristic of sovereignty has always been the State's capacity to make authoritative decisions regarding the people and resources within its territory'. In their view, this position has shifted, to a modern 'broad consensus' opining that 'sovereignty as responsibility has become the minimum content of good international citizenship'.[207]

ii. Humanitarian Intervention à la Canadienne

The *R2P Report* stresses – repeatedly – that the primary responsibility for the welfare of the persons present on the territory of a State rests with the State itself. However, this is far from the end of the matter. This default responsibility vested in the State may be forfeited, and may be taken up by other authorities, if certain threshold criteria are fulfilled. These criteria represent the basis for a potential humanitarian intervention against the State in question.

Per the ICISS, in order to justify a potential intervention, there must first be a just cause, comprising (anticipated) loss of life on a large scale or large-scale ethnic cleansing. This being the case, there are four further checks as to whether an armed intervention may go ahead, namely: right intention; last resort; the use of proportional means; and that the operation has a reasonable prospect of success.

The above represent 'precautionary principles', and seem strikingly similar to the criteria of Just War theory of *animus, justa causa, persona,* and *res*. They are joined by the final and most controversial principle which represents the *R2P* equivalent of the Just War criterion of *auctoritas*,[208] namely right or legitimate authority.

[206] J Donnelly, *Universal Human Rights in Theory and Practice*, 2nd edn (Ithaca, NY, Cornell University Press, 2003) 251.
[207] Evans and Sahnoun (2001) (n 205) 101–02.
[208] See S Neff, *War and the Law of Nations. A General History* (Cambridge, Cambridge University Press, 2005) 14–20.

This final principle is not controversial without good reason. In a major departure from Just War theory, where *auctoritas* is the reserve of the sovereign, and the sovereign alone, the ICISS report takes a more nuanced view. The report avows that the UN Security Council should undoubtedly be the first port of call when it comes to authorising military intervention. 'The difficult question – starkly raised by the Kosovo war – is whether it should be the last'.[209] Of course, as the report notes, those who challenge or evade UN authority run the risk of eroding its authority in general and undermining the principle of a world order based on international law and universal norms. However, in effect, the report goes on to do just that, deciding very definitely that the UN Security Council should not be the final arbiter in this regard.

The report's authors, however, disavow that their intention is to lessen the primacy of the Security Council in matters relating to the use of force. 'The task', they argue,

> is not to find alternatives to the Security Council as a source of authority, but to make the council work better than it has. Security Council authorisation should, in all cases, be sought prior to any military intervention being carried out.[210]

The drafters may have missed the subtle point that this requirement would mean that the Kosovo intervention, in the wake of which the report was commissioned, would in any case be adjudged as impermissible under this criterion.

The ICISS argues that the five Permanent Members of the UN Security Council should agree not to exercise their veto power in matters where vital State interests are not involved, to defeat Resolutions authorising collective military action for humanitarian protection purposes for which there otherwise exists majority support. Evans and Sahnoun claim to know of one Permanent Member who will agree to do so. However, even if this is so, the phrase 'vital State interests' can be construed rather broadly. The five Permanent Members are powerful States with many global interests, a great deal of which they may consider 'vital', and since this term is not defined, it is difficult to ensure that it would not be used abusively.

Per the ICISS, two institutional-based solutions exist, even in the face of a blocked Security Council. The first of these comes from the General Assembly, acting under the 1950 'Uniting for Peace' Resolution, which may address a majority recommendation for urgent action to the Security Council, as was the case in Korea (1950), Egypt (1956), and Congo (1960). The other option advanced is that of regional organisations acting under Chapter VIII of the Charter, subject to seeking *subsequent* Security Council

209 ibid, 106.
210 ibid.

authorisation, as was the case with the ECOWAS (Economic Community of West African States) involvement in Sierra Leone and Liberia.

'But what if the Security Council fails to discharge its own responsibility to protect?'[211] ask Evans and Sahnoun. '[W]hich of the two evils is the worse: the damage to the international order if the Security Council is bypassed, or the damage to that order if human beings are slaughtered while the Security Council stands by?' The ICISS position is that in such cases, the need to intervene becomes the greater need and must therefore be accorded priority, but that such situations are undesirable, because such interventions may be undertaken without respect for precautionary principles, and by self-interested states for selfish reasons. Therefore, the ICISS only allows intervention as an undesirable – but better than laissez-faire – last resort.

In practical terms, regarding the political will, the ICISS accepts that it may be difficult to find States to intervene, and that while complete disinterestedness in selfish gain as a result of humanitarian intervention is the ideal, as Michael Walzer has pointed out, this is unlikely in the extreme.[212] Nonetheless, Evans and Sahnoun opine that altruistic 'right intention' as per the criteria for intervention outlined above is possible, as:

> These days, good international citizenship is a matter of national self-interest. With the world as interdependent as it now is, and with crises as capable as they now are of generating major problems elsewhere (such as terrorism, refugee outflows, health pandemics, narcotics trafficking, and organised crime), it is in every country's interest to resolve such problems, quite apart from the humanitarian imperative.[213]

iii. The R2P *in the International Arena*

While the content of the *Responsibility to Protect Report* was certainly novel, it enjoyed a mixed reception. The reasons for this are perhaps due in part at least to the fact that it was published in the direct aftermath of the 11 September terrorist attacks in the United States, and that the preoccupation with humanitarianism amongst Western commentators was ceding to an emerging stream of rhetoric dealing with the 'war on terror', 'rogue States' and the 'axis of evil'. While these events were clearly not foreseeable to the drafters of the report, they nonetheless impacted heavily upon the willingness of States and non-State actors to engage with the *R2P* concept. The problems experienced by the ICISS in attempting to incorporate the report's ideals into the international legal framework are testament to this. These efforts shall be discussed later in my critique of the report.

[211] ibid, 104

[212] M Walzer, 'The Argument about Humanitarian Intervention' (2002) 49 *Dissent* 29.

[213] Evans and Sahnoun (2001) (n 205) 108–09.

Aside from the above, when the report was issued, it still surprised many, and may have 'missed the boat', as it were. It failed to sufficiently affirm the *ius cogens* nature of human rights, presumably for fear of the obvious answer that the Article 2(4) prohibition is also a peremptory norm.[214] As David Chandler noted, it uses the criticism of many non-Western States to argue that the Security Council is in need of reform and is undemocratic and unrepresentative.[215] However, it explicitly argues against making the final authority for decisions on humanitarian intervention more democratic.[216] It rejects the idea that where the Security Council is deadlocked, the General Assembly should gain (final) authority,[217] citing the problems of obtaining a two-thirds majority.[218]

As a result of the aforementioned choices on the part of the report's drafters, combined with the political climate, as well as 'the disagreements and the divisiveness of the debate about the Iraq war', it is hard not to agree with Alex Bellamy that, 'it is remarkable that a consensus was produced at the 2005 [United Nations] World Summit [in favour of the Responsibility to Protect]'.[219] The fact that this was the case can be attributed to a number of factors, discussed by Bellamy:

First, the Canadian Government insisted that intervention should be authorised by the Security Council, brushing aside the question of the 'unreasonable veto' (and effectively brushing away the issue of authorisation by another authority), 'going as far as to articulate the pluralist view that if humanitarianism can only be "undertaken at the cost of undermining the stability of the state-based international order", then sovereignty should trump humanitarian action'.[220] This would seem, however, to be the opposite conclusion of the report, which had incorporated mechanisms to supplement the current international order owing to its inherent inadequacy as regards responding to humanitarian crises.

Secondly, the HLP (The United Nations Secretary-General's High-Level Panel on Threats, Challenges and Change) added serious breaches of international humanitarian law to the 'just cause' thresholds. It also added a preventive component to the just cause criterion, 'insisting that the criteria would be satisfied if the threat was actual or "imminently

[214] See: *Military and Paramilitary Activities in and against Nicaragua (Nicaragua v United States)* (Jurisdiction and Admissibility) [1984] ICJ Rep 392.

[215] ICISS, *The Responsibility to Protect (Report)* (2001), 51.

[216] ibid, 54.

[217] ICISS, *Research, Bibliography, Background (to the R2P Report)* (2001), 129.

[218] D Chandler, 'The Responsibility to Protect? Imposing the Liberal Peace: A Critique' (paper presented to the British International Studies Association annual conference at the London School of Economics, 16–18 December 2002 (amended version)).

[219] AJ Bellamy, 'Whither the Responsibility to Protect? Humanitarian Intervention and the 2005 World Summit' (2006) 20 *Ethics and International Affairs* 143, 153.

[220] ibid.

apprehended"'.[221] Further, like the Canadian Government, it dropped the insistence on limiting the use of the Permanent Members' vetoes.

Thirdly, Bellamy suggests that the African Union Constitutive Act, in force since 2003, helped to ensure that African States were more amenable to the concept of a right to humanitarian intervention. The Constitutive Act awarded the African Union such a right, though mitigated by the principle of non-interference. In doing so, the Union 'created an institutional mechanism that permits the regional arrangements foreseen by "The Responsibility to Protect"'. Technically, intervention within the African Union does not require Security Council authorisation, 'because through binding themselves to the Constitutive Act, members have consented to making themselves subject to intervention should the African Union Assembly see fit'.[222]

Fourthly, the willingness of the ICISS and the General Assembly to dilute the *R2P* concept somewhat proved decisive in accommodating the demands of the United States. The Bush administration's National Security Strategy of 2002 had also made a concerted effort to erode sovereignty, albeit in other ways to the *Responsibility to Protect Report*. It also took account of internal factors in order to determine whether a State should be acted against, particularly with its three tests for a 'rogue state', namely support for terrorism, the proliferation of weapons of mass destruction, and regimes that 'brutalise their own people and squander their natural resources for the personal gains of their rulers'. The US, having shown some willingness to engage with the *R2P Report*, argued that the nature of the responsibility of the host State – legal responsibility – was different to that of the international community, which could only be held to have a moral obligation. The General Assembly thus hardened the test for transferring responsibility to international society, and weakened the nature of international responsibility, in line with the US argument.

In order to satisfy anti-interventionists, the draft outcome document placed the international Responsibility to Protect squarely in the Security Council's domain. However, Bellamy argues that the precise wording of the relevant sentence leaves open the possibility of unauthorised intervention: 'We are prepared to take collective action, in a timely and decisive manner, through the Security Council, in accordance with the Charter [should peaceful means fail].'[223]

According to Bellamy, the wording (in particular the phrase 'we are prepared') falls short of insisting upon Security Council approbation, and could be interpreted as suggesting that concerned States *may* work under the Council's rubric but *may also* choose to operate via alternative

[221] ibid, 156.
[222] ibid, 158–59.
[223] 2005 World Summit Outcome A/60/L, 15 September 2005, para 139.

arrangement. Per Bellamy, this small window of opportunity was reinforced by the outcome document's brief section on the use of force.[224] This is a courageous interpretation by Bellamy, since the 'window' of opportunity noted (the use of the phrase 'we are prepared' as a less than unequivocal statement) is tiny, if it exists at all, and, it would seem that sterner stuff is required to undo the general prohibition on unauthorised force enshrined in the UN Charter.

Having discussed the content of the *R2P Report*, as well as its *mise en oeuvre*, I shall now proceed to offer a critique of what I perceive to be the major problems with the initiative.

B. Deconstructing the Responsibility to Protect

In this section, I shall first offer a critique of the shortcomings of the *R2P Report* itself, before moving on to assess the problems with the way in which it was implemented. Finally, I shall evaluate the effects of the Iraq war and the 'war on terror' on the Responsibility to Protect concept, enquiring as to whether the idea has a future and whether there may be more constructive means to move the agenda of humanitarian action ahead.

i. The Responsibility to Protect: A Flawed Concept

a. A High Bar

The Responsibility to Protect, while superficially attractive, is in my opinion, an inherently flawed concept, serving not to create a framework for permissible humanitarian intervention while guarding against abuse, but instead clouding the debate in this area and in fact creating criteria which may easily be turned to other less altruistic ends by the unscrupulous. I am not, however, the first to criticise its principles. Thomas G Weiss, in an article in *Security Dialogue*, makes reference to the fact that the six criteria set the bar very high for humanitarian intervention, and that two other 'obvious' causal factors for humanitarian intervention have been omitted from 'just cause', namely: the overthrow of democratically-elected regimes; and massive abuses of human rights.[225]

Furthermore, Weiss notes that the fact the thresholds do not include systematic racial discrimination and gross human rights abuses indicates an aversion toward international law in general on the part of the ICISS, as these represent *ius cogens* principles to most international lawyers.[226]

[224] Bellamy (2006) (n 219) 166.

[225] TG Weiss, 'The Sunset of Humanitarian Intervention? The Responsibility to Protect in a Unipolar Era' (2004) 35 *Security Dialogue* 135, 139.

[226] ibid, 139–40.

b. Terminology

However, in addition to the issues addressed by Weiss, I feel it is important to mention other faults with the Responsibility to Protect. The first of these is with the ICISS effort to change the terminology of the humanitarian intervention debate from 'intervention' to 'protection'. I fail to see how opting for an alternative nomenclature changes the issues at hand in any way whatsoever. Using different names cannot and will not affect the legitimacy, legality, or justifiability of the act in question. In my opinion the debate remains constant, and it is better to tackle the issues head on and call a spade a spade. Furthermore, it is worth noting that the report, like any text with purported normative value, once published, is out of the Commission's control, as it were. The ultimate content of the report is indeterminate, as the interpretation of its provisions is left to the States which may use (and/or abuse) it as they choose. In this way, the substantive content of the report, in particular the six threshold criteria, may even be used by the anti-interventionist lobby rather than as a *casus belli*.

This view is supported by Alex Bellamy, who notes that in the case of the Security Council debates concerning possible intervention in Darfur, the *R2P acquis* 'allowed traditional opponents of intervention to replace largely discredited "sovereignty-as-absolute" – type arguments against intervention in supreme humanitarian emergencies with arguments about who had the primary responsibility to protect Darfur's civilians'.[227] Thus, the novel language of the report can make it a tool which can constrain as well as enable intervention.

c. Good International Citizenship

The discourse on the Responsibility to Protect advances dubious claims. The idea of 'good international citizenship', affirming that it is in the interest of every State to intervene anywhere in the world when serious crises emerge, due to the interdependence of the world community, and that this may counterbalance fears of opportunistic interventions by neighbouring States looking for selfish gains from the action, is fanciful at best. As Martti Koskenniemi points out, 'it is never Algeria that will intervene in France, or Finland in Chechnya'.[228] This simple fact, further, makes the idea that the five Permanent Members of the Security Council not exercise their veto unless a matter concerns them directly in cases of humanitarian crisis effectively worthless. It is almost always the large, powerful States which intervene, and therefore, almost every crisis worldwide is connected to the

[227] AJ Bellamy, 'Responsibility to Protect or Trojan Horse? The Crisis in Darfur and Humanitarian Intervention after Iraq' (2005) 19 *Ethics and International Affairs* 31, 52.

[228] M Koskenniemi, 'The Lady Doth Protest Too Much: Kosovo, and the Turn to Ethics in International Law' (2002) 65 *MLR* 159, 172.

Permanent Members. 'The Commission argues that their perspective is not based on power or *Realpolitik* but morality. The "Responsibility to Protect" implies a duty on the state to act as a moral agent'.[229]

In the above affirmation, the Commission reveals a worrying bias against (neo-) Realist international relations theory and in favour of a liberal, quasi-utopian view of a world of cooperative, interdependent States, each of which has some level of interest in every conflict, everywhere, at every time, due to the desire of all for a stable world environment as a basis for further cooperation. This vision is roundly refuted by Realists, who point to the fact that unless States' vital interests are at stake, they will not intervene if this risks soldiers' lives or incurs serious economic costs. Per such a position, the best we can hope for is a 'happy coincidence' where the promotion of national security also defends human rights. The strength of this position is that it is recognisant the reality of State interests and power. However, as Wheeler notes, 'its weakness is that it makes humanitarianism dependent upon shifting geopolitical and strategic considerations'.[230] It is due to their recognition of this reality that some alternative formulae for permissible humanitarian intervention do not posit primacy of humanitarian motives as a *conditio sine qua non* of intervention.[231] As Thomas G Weiss notes, the importance of State interests, or a lack thereof, particularly with regard to Western States that have the military capacity to tackle such situations, is plain for all to see in the case of the Congo, where 3.5 million people have died since 1998, which demonstrates sparse *R2P* and plenty of humanitarian non-intervention.[232]

The above problems are admitted by the ICISS, which candidly admits that if the risks and costs of intervention are high and State interests are not directly involved, it is unlikely that States will be disposed toward intervening. 'Those who advocate action to protect human rights must inevitably come to grips with the nature of political self-interest to achieve good ends'.[233] Nonetheless, the report fails to adequately address such questions, attributing too much weight to 'good international citizenship' and paying little heed to the inherent conflict arising from the fact that while, by the ICISS's own admission, States are unlikely to intervene unless vital interests are involved, the primacy of humanitarian motives is the crux of the precautionary principle of 'right intention', one of the six threshold criteria for intervention.

[229] ICISS, *Research, Bibliography, Background (to the R2P Report)* (2001), 136.

[230] NJ Wheeler, '*Saving Strangers: Humanitarian Intervention in International Society*' (Oxford, Oxford University Press, 2000) 30.

[231] ibid, 33–34.

[232] Weiss (2004) (n 225)153.

[233] ICISS, *Research, Bibliography, Background (to the R2P Report)* (2001), 140.

d. Expansion of the *R2P* Discourse – A Duty to Prevent

It is worth underlining the fact that the Responsibility to Protect is a recent concept, and the direction of the discourse concerning its operation is uncertain. Indeed, one may already observe the inherent dangers of the terminology used by the ICISS in the writings of Fenstein and Slaughter, who have used the Responsibility to Protect to develop a corollary – the 'Duty to Prevent' acquisition of weapons of mass destruction by States without internal checks on their power – which can plainly be used as a pretext for American neo-imperialist designs.[234] Per Fenstein and Slaughter, this 'Duty to Prevent' 'extrapolates from recent developments in the law of intervention for humanitarian purposes', namely the Responsibility to Protect.[235]

Fenstein and Slaughter's idea stems from the idea that the international community has a duty to prevent security disasters as well as humanitarian ones, even at the price of violating sovereignty. 'Like the responsibility to protect, the duty to prevent begins from the premise that the rules now governing the use of force devised in 1945 . . . are inadequate'.[236] The Duty to Prevent – like the *R2P* – lifts the veil of sovereignty and examines the internal workings of the State machinery. While the first threshold criterion for the *R2P* is ethnic cleansing or mass murder, for the Duty to Prevent, it is the lack of internal checks on the power of the government of a State. Per Fenstein and Slaughter, many such States are currently pursuing WMD (weapons of mass destruction) proliferation, even without breaking international law. These States may also be involved in supplying WMD to terrorist groups.

Fenstein and Slaughter's model is worth examining more closely, as it makes many of the same base-line assumptions as that of the ICISS, but enunciates them more explicitly and takes them further. In this manner, it is easier to understand and to criticise the flaws in its logic. The idea that a State without internal checks on its power must be prevented from supplying terrorists with weapons implies that the same duty to prevent does not weigh on the international community with regard to States with a proper system of checks and balances. Why is this value judgement made? Is it reasonable to confer a right on some States and not on others? The contention that States with internal checks on their power are highly unlikely to supply arms to terrorist movements is clearly falsified by the Irish experience, where collusion between the Irish Government and the

[234] Olivier Corten has discussed such trends in detail, positing that post-9/11, pre-emptive self-defence became the biggest issue in international law and that such concerns have lent credence to corollaries such as the 'Duty to Prevent'. O Corten, *Le retour des guerres preventives* (Brussels, Labor, 2003).

[235] L Fenstein and A-M Slaughter, 'A Duty to Prevent' (2004) 83 *Foreign Affairs* 136, 149.

[236] ibid, 138 (This would suggest that the entire international legal regime on the use of force is contained in the UN Charter, which represents a fundamental misunderstanding, notably, of the rule on self-defence).

IRA (Irish Republican Army) and the Northern Irish administration and the loyalist paramilitaries, including supply of arms, was widespread. Fenstein and Slaughter justify this separation, affirming that 'the behaviour of open societies [not necessarily democratic societies] is subject to scrutiny, criticism and countermeasures by opponents'.[237] However, the fact that 'checks on internal power' and 'terrorism' remain undefined leaves many questions to be answered. For example, it is worth noting that the UK Prime Minister has at least theoretically almost unlimited power due to the unwritten nature of the UK Constitution. Other matters are also puzzling, not least where the legal basis of the 'duty' lies. In fact, the doctrine varies between a statement of a positive duty and an aspirational framework for future law reform based around a condemnation of the law 'as is' with a strong pro-American bias:

> Aiming at the weapons themselves rather than the states or regimes that develop or acquire them has been judged to be a more objective basis for international action. The problem with this approach is to treat North Korea as if it were Norway. This flaw has exposed the non-proliferation regime to abuse by determined and defiant regimes, especially those headed by dictatorial rulers . . .
>
> Just as effective gun control in the United States requires both outlawing the most dangerous weapons and ammunition and applying more stringent controls on citizens with criminal records and other risk factors, an effective international non-proliferation campaign must target both WMD and international actors with suspect intentions.[238]

The above resonates with pro-Western, and above all, pro-American sentiment.[239] However, the inherent bias is unable to abide by its own flawed logic. Identifying dangerous States by 'risk factors' and by past criminal activity as is done at domestic level is all very well, but if one is to do so, one may well ask whether the United States of America or North Korea has been involved in more illegal military operations in the last 20 years.[240]

The malleable structure of the *R2P* and the attempts to expand upon its premises are regrettable, insofar as they may damage any goodwill the report had engendered, and render the initiative ripe for abuse.[241] *R2P* rhetoric has abounded since the report's publication, and, as Jean-Marie Crouzatier, inter alia, has noted, is often used in such a way that it seems to cloud the initial responsibility of States – namely to react peaceably and

[237] ibid.

[238] ibid.

[239] See EA Heinze, 'Humanitarian Intervention and the War in Iraq: Norms, Discourse and Practice' (2006) 36 *Parameters* 20, who notes the post-factum attribution of humanitarian concerns to the Iraq war.

[240] G Molier, 'Humanitarian Intervention and the Responsibility to Protect after 9/11' (2006) 53 *Netherlands International Law Review* 37.

[241] S Sur, 'Quelle légalité pour le conflit armé en droit international?' (2005) 24 *Cités* 103.

look for non-violent solutions to such situations.[242] It also shows the dangerous consequences of any departure from the positive structure of the international legal regime on the use of force, a matter to which I shall now turn.

e. The *R2P*: A Bastard Son

I turn now to perhaps the most important criticism of the ICISS report, the fact that it is rooted in legal nothingness. Despite efforts to gain support for the concept, neither State practice, nor major treaties have included affirmative references to the concept, and while UN Security Council Resolution 1674 (28 April 2006) 'Reaffirm[ed] the provisions of paragraphs 138 and 139 of the 2005 World Summit Outcome Document regarding the responsibility to protect populations from genocide, war crimes, ethnic cleansing and crimes against humanity', this did not entail legal incorporation of the Responsibility to Protect, nor is it to serve as any sort of future guideline for Security Council activities. This is the most fundamental problem with the Responsibility to Protect.

Clearly, the ICISS was attempting to engage with the palpable cleavage between popular sentiment and the majority interpretation of international law's position on humanitarian intervention. However, in doing so, it has strayed too far from the essence of international law, and has no legal basis.[243] The question must be posed as to why this is the case. Perhaps the fact that, as noted earlier, the general prohibition on the use of force represents a norm of *ius cogens* meant that the ICISS were unwilling to challenge it, as any normative framework built in contravention of this general prohibition would surely founder. However, if this was the case, it was surely worth noting that many of the most basic human rights norms are also popularly accorded *ius cogens* status,[244] and that the (exclusive) means of effecting change upon a peremptory norm is by use of another peremptory norm.

Furthermore, it is perhaps also worth noting that such *cogentes* human rights norms are necessarily obligations *erga omnes*, as 'obligations *erga omnes* constitute a wider ensemble encompassing all peremptory norms but not necessarily coinciding with them'.[245] The *erga omnes* nature of the

[242] J-M Crouzatier, 'Le Principe de la Responsabilité de Protéger: Avancée de la Solidarité Internationale ou Ultime Avatar de L'Impérialisme?' (2008) 2 *Revue Aspects* 13. Crouzatier further notes the potential for *R2P* doctrine or indeed any doctrine justifying humanitarian intervention to be abused to justify neo-imperialist projects. See also O Bricmont, *Impérialisme Humanitaire* (Brussels, Arden, 2005).

[243] D Janssen, 'Humanitarian Intervention and the Prevention of Genocide' (2008) 10 *Journal of Genocide Research* 289.

[244] O Quirico, 'A Formal Prescriptive Approach to General Principles of (International) Law' (2007) 19 *European University Institute Working Papers: Law* 20.

[245] ibid, 21.

obligation to protect such rights could, at least theoretically, have been used as a starting point on which to base the interest of all States and/or the international community as a whole, since 'even the consent or acquiescence of the state directly injured does not prevent other states from judging the breach' in cases of breaches of *erga omnes* obligations.[246] Perhaps the ICISS 'missed a trick' here.

In fact, the flight from traditional terminology and traditional international law, so that States' prerogatives may not be asserted as overriding human rights is only half the story. The rhetoric employed is inherently Janus-faced, as David Chandler notes:

> While the traditional terminology of 'rights' is removed from the debate . . . 'rights' are smuggled back in and given to the individuals who have the 'right to protection'. Despite the protestations of the Commission, the Report overtly argues that individual human rights 'trump' the rights of sovereignty . . .
>
> The Commission does not start from the UN Charter rules on whether intervention is permissible, but theorises the legitimacy of intervention from the starting point of the 'protection' of the potential victim. This enables the Commission to come up with a set of moral criteria for military intervention which are held to exist independently of international law or any particular political decision or consensus in the Security Council.[247]

The ICISS initiative can thus be viewed as part of a broad trend on the part of those who support an extensive right, or even a duty, or humanitarian intervention to remove the question from the realm of law and place it squarely in the domain of political theory. As Francesco Francioni has noted, such theories tend to underestimate the fact that the international rule of law is a value in and of itself, and there is no doubt that the rule governing the use of force in international relations remains one of the fundamental principles of the international legal system.[248]

The Responsibility to Protect, while attempting to herald a new departure in the international use of force, may thus be described as a bastard son, insofar as it deliberately disassociates itself from the regime which governs this area, namely international law, rather than using its *acquis* to argue for law reform or a broader interpretation of the existing rules.[249] Rooted in legal nothingness, until it is formally embraced by the international community, and in particular the Security Council, it will remain 'pie in the sky' – a theory, but nothing more.

Having offered a critique of the *R2P* doctrine itself on several fronts, I shall now assess whether the attempts to put theory into practice, and thus overcome to some degree the contention that the doctrine has no

[246] ibid, 23.

[247] Chandler (2002, amended) (n 218) 9, 15.

[248] Francioni (2005) (n 19) 276–77.

[249] It is perhaps hardly worth noting that the *R2P* principles have no precedent in State practice.

basis in international law by incorporating it into international legal instruments and State practice, have been successful.

ii. R2P *in Action: A Failing Initiative*

The virtually contemporary occurrence of the terrorist attacks in the United States with the publication of the ICISS's report was to prove a major drag factor on the impact of the *R2P* doctrine worldwide. In a matter of months, the world political climate was to change significantly as the Bush administration announced its 'war on terror' and invaded Afghanistan. However, even before the true implications of these events became clear, there was recognition on the part of the report's drafters that political will would be an important obstacle to be overcome before the Responsibility to Protect could garner universal acceptance. Nonetheless, Evans and Sahnoun struck a positive tone, noting that

> [t]oo often, more time is spent lamenting the absence of political will than on analysing its ingredients and how to mobilise them . . . Moral appeals inspire and legitimise in almost any political environment: political leaders often underestimate the sheer sense of decency and compassion that prevails among their electorates.[250]

The means employed to mobilise opinion amongst State leaders and to further the moral concerns underlying the *R2P Report* were, however, questionable, and one might even argue, counterproductive. As outlined earlier, in attempting to reach a consensus at the 2005 World Summit, and thus include as many States as possible in an affirmation of the *R2P*'s principles, its supporters showed a willingness to compromise which ultimately led to a significant dilution of its original aims, to say the least. This was undertaken in the main to accommodate the United States, taking cognisance of the stark reality of US military hegemony and the need to have their active participation in any solution. It is indeed worth observing that the term 'primacy' 'fails to capture the fact that Washington's military expenditures are more than the rest of the world combined'.[251] The ICISS took the view that some progress under a banner of consensus is better than none. As Nicholas Wheeler has noted, 'once established, norms will serve to constrain even the most powerful states'.[252]

However, as EH Carr astutely observed, theories of international morality or legitimacy, particularly those which obtain normative force are always 'the product of dominant nations or groups of nations', and therefore 'supposedly absolute and universal principles . . . [are] not principles

[250] Evans and Sahnoun (2001) (n 205) 109.

[251] SN MacFarlane, CJ Thielking and TG Weiss, 'The Responsibility to Protect: Is Anyone Interested in Humanitarian Intervention?' (2004) 25 *Third World Quarterly* 977, 985.

[252] Wheeler (2000) (n 72) 7.

at all, but the unconscious reflections of national policy based on a particular interpretation of national interest at a particular time'.[253] In essence, this meant that if any conception of the Responsibility to Protect were to gain normative force, it would need to suit the agendum of each of the most powerful States.

It was clear from the outset that the five Permanent Members of the UN Security Council 'were unwilling to give up the practice of case-by-case decision-making about whether to intervene for humanitarian or any other reasons'.[254] Hence the Canadian Government, the HLP and even the ICISS resigning themselves to the effective removal of the 'unreasonable veto' component from the *R2P* package. Furthermore, the paragraphs eventually adopted awarded the role of final arbiter conclusively to the Security Council, despite Alex Bellamy's contention that the words 'we are prepared to take collective action' means that the international community may also be prepared to act in another manner. This was a massive blow, as it effectively rendered a 'future Kosovo' both illegal and illegitimate under the *R2P* framework to be adopted.

Despite some optimistic rhetoric emerging from proponents of the *R2P* in the wake of the 2005 World Summit Outcome Document and UN Security Council Resolution 1674 of 2006, the fact is that both of these texts endorsed a version of the Responsibility to Protect doctrine scarcely recognisable when compared with that in the 2001 *R2P Report*. Even Alex Bellamy, while striking a positive tone, concedes that 'Perhaps the most worrying development is that in attempting to forge a consensus, the ICISS and its supporters sacrificed almost all of the key elements of their twin strategies'.[255] This makes depressing reading for supporters of the *R2P*, but it demonstrates the extent of the diplomatic jiggery-pokery that was necessary to get the United States and China on board.

In addition, the legal effect of the World Summit Outcome Document is dubious, with much of its rhetoric striking an aspirational note, and no provision for definitive and meaningful commitments by States. Resolution 1674, which notably was not adopted under Chapter VII of the UN Charter, is little better. It is worth recalling the fact that any Resolution adopted by the Security Council outside of this Chapter lacks the 'teeth' to impact upon the Security Council's unfettered discretion to decide upon issues concerning the use of force in any way whatsoever.

iii. Effects of the 'War on Terror' and the Iraq War on the Responsibility to Protect

A recurrent theme in any debate on shaping criteria for justifiable humanitarian intervention is the question of abuse. Such criteria, it is felt, must

[253] EH Carr, *The Twenty Years Crisis 1919–39* (London, Macmillan, 1939) 111.
[254] MacFarlane, Thielking and Weiss (2004) (n 251) 983.
[255] Bellamy (2006) (n 219) 169.

be copper-fastened to humanitarian, and only humanitarian, missions. Otherwise, they may become a 'Trojan horse', as it were, a *casus belli* for interventions which are anything but humanitarian.

In 2004, Thomas G Weiss was wont to dismiss such concerns about the Responsibility to Protect, arguing that the purported danger of the concept being used as an excuse for non-humanitarian interventions is fundamentally incorrect, and rather that intervention by the United States in its pre-emptive or preventive war mode is *the* pressing concern.[256] However, after the failure to find the much-vaunted weapons of mass destruction in Iraq, humanitarian rationales, borrowing language strikingly similar to that of the *R2P*, were retrospectively put forward by the alliance as having been essential in the decision to act against Saddam Hussein's regime.

The consequences of this avowal have proven to be far-reaching, not because it has bolstered the status of the Responsibility to Protect and a right of humanitarian intervention in general in the international legal sphere, but because, quite simply, the American rationale was not believed. Bellamy notes that if 'a norm is undermined by the perceptions that [unscrupulous states] have abused it or raised it for primarily self-serving purposes, the process of normative change is likely to be slowed or reversed'.[257] Perhaps this explains why in studies of past examples of humanitarian intervention, Hitler's 'intervention' in the Sudetenland is so rarely discussed.

Ostensibly, the US–UK action in Iraq has fundamentally undermined their standing as norm carriers.[258] As David Chandler pointed out, it was

> apparent that the arguments developed by the Commission in support of the liberal peace thesis appear to have been fully appropriated by the Conservative 'hawks' in the Washington establishment who are seen to be guided by the principles of *Realpolitik* and US power rather than any desire to 'refocus the discussion on the victims' . . . military intervention [in Iraq] was clearly posed in the terminology of the 'Responsibility to Protect' rather than traditional warfighting, as George Bush stated to the world's press.[259]

The above conclusion does not augur well for the immediate future. It is true, for example, that Security Council debates on the crisis in Darfur have been peppered with Responsibility to Protect terminology. The meaning attributed to such language, however, has been hotly contested. Such defiance and disbelief lends credence to the thesis that the US and UK's usage of *R2P* language to justify their actions in the past has damaged not only their status as norm carriers, but also the concept's prospects for the future. German Bundeskanzler Gerhard Schröder – a prominent proponent of the

[256] Weiss (2004) (n 225) 137.
[257] Bellamy (2005) (n 227) 33.
[258] ibid, 32.
[259] Chandler (2002, amended) (n 218) 22, 24.

Responsibility to Protect – reportedly rejected a UK communiqué supporting the idea that the *R2P* ought to override State sovereignty in supreme humanitarian emergencies because he feared that any doctrine of unauthorised humanitarian intervention would be used by the US and the UK to justify the Iraq war.[260]

Concerns surrounding the potential hijacking of altruistic humanitarianism as a front for Anglo-American foreign policy designs extends beyond the Iraq war, however.[261] The 'Bush doctrine' of preventive self-defence is viewed by many States as a genuine threat to the current international order. This has led to calls for a renewed commitment to the non-intervention rule. As a result, according to some commentators, 'there is likely to be more pressure to return to classic Westphalian notions of sovereignty that underpin international society than to pursue vigorously criteria that justify humanitarian intervention'.[262]

The Darfur experience, and the lack of appetite amongst Western States for real and effective action to save lives, suggests that concerns about increased interventionism in the wake of Kosovo and 9/11 are misplaced. The changes wrought on the (potential) normative status of humanitarian intervention and particularly the Responsibility to Protect criteria are more subtle. Two trends in particular may be identified: first, the UK and the US appeared to recognise the fact that their diminished credibility as norm carriers would make it harder for them in building a Security Council consensus on action – just at the moment when they were too overstretched militarily to contemplate unilateralism. Secondly, Darfur supports the contention that the *R2P* criteria could constrain as well as enable intervention.[263]

On an official visit to Rwanda in late January 2008, a State which had been ravaged by genocide 15 years previously, UN Secretary-General Ban Ki-Moon spoke of the continuing need 'to translate the concept of the Responsibility to Protect from words to deeds'.[264] It is a damning indictment of the progress of the Responsibility to Protect that six and a half years after the report's publication, so little headway had been made on the *R2P* initiative, an initiative intended to prevent future 'Rwandas', that the Secretary-General felt the need to refer to it as a bare 'concept' still in need of effective transposition to the international sphere.

260 Bellamy (2005) (n 227) 39.

261 There are, however, commentators who posit that while abuse is inevitable, that this should not serve as an excuse for anything less than the full legal adoption of the *R2P*, since it will still do more good than harm, and since abusers will find a way to circumvent the law in any case. See M Bettati, 'Du droit d'ingérence à la responsabilité de protéger' (2007) 20 *Outre-terre* 381.

262 MacFarlane, Thielking and Weiss (2004) (n 251) 984.

263 Bellamy (2005) (n 227) 50–52.

264 'In Rwanda, Ban Ki-moon says world must protect civilians from genocide', 29 January 2008, available at www.un.org/apps/news/story.asp?NewsID=25441&Cr=rwanda&Cr1.

The challenges facing the drafters of the ICISS report were not inconsiderable. The UN Charter, seen by many as the ultimate guarantor of inter-State harmony, would seem to prioritise peace over human rights. Furthermore, to call for humanitarian intervention is necessarily to 'open a can of worms', as it were. The ICISS needed to take cognisance of the fact that 'the West's conception of humanitarian intervention is [perceived as] so ideologically biased that the "silent genocide" of death through poverty is rendered natural and inevitable'[265] and therefore any supposed altruistic military action is viewed with extreme suspicion by a large section of the world community. The *R2P Report* indeed took such concerns on board, rejecting Wheeler's pragmatic (and realistic) utilitarian test for humanitarian intervention and imposing a utopian formula firmly founded upon the primacy of humanitarian motives.[266] Nonetheless, the changing political climate, particularly in the wake of Iraq and the 'war on terror', increased international scepticism about humanitarian intervention still further, proving a bridge too far for the Responsibility to Protect.

However, even absent 9/11 and subsequent events, it is hard to convince oneself of the merits of the Responsibility to Protect. Clearly, the Canadian initiative was undertaken with the best intentions, but, as I have outlined above, the doctrine that emerged from it leaves a great deal to be desired *qua* theory. It fails to justify itself with reference to international law and finds no support in State practice. The initiative – to find a means to craft a third exception to the Charter prohibition on the use of force in favour of humanitarian intervention – is a commendable one. However, the twin dangers of abuse of the doctrine and the damage it could do to the credibility of international law – in addition to the problems outlined above both in its substantive theory and its *mise en oeuvre* – mean that that the *R2P* is ill-suited to accomplish the delicate task of allowing for forcible protection against the worst human rights abuses. Wherever the solution to this conundrum is to be found, it is not here.

XIII. CONCLUSION

What is obvious from the above discourse is that dissatisfaction exists in many quarters regarding the compatibility of the international legal norms concerning the use of force with commonly held conceptions of justice. However, resort to philosophy, ethics, politics, fantasy norms and deliberately obscure terminology is not the way to tackle such incompatibility, and, as noted elsewhere, merely serves to further complicate the

[265] Wheeler (2000) (n 72) 308.
[266] ICISS, *Research, Bibliography, Background (to the R2P Report)* (2001), 363.

issue.[267] As Anthea Roberts has pointed out, the notion that the use of force, even for a good cause, may be 'technically' or 'formally' illegal is highly suspect.[268] Ideas of 'necessity' are equally inadequate. Tony Blair portrayed Kosovo as the choice between doing something and doing nothing.[269] However, his represents a false dichotomy. Unilateral intervention in the form of air strikes was by no means the only option. Thomas Franck, who has dealt with the *ius necessitatis* question in detail, as noted above, writes of '[acting] off the Charter, while leaving the Charter norms "intact"',[270] while Bruno Simma writes of having no choice but to 'act outside the law' in exceptional circumstances.[271] However, it is clear that such phrases are weasel words, euphemisms for lawbreaking. Like 'formal' illegality and 'classical' international law, such language aids in clouding the importance of breaches of perhaps the fundamental Charter provision – the prohibition on the use of force. After all, as Francioni notes, it is somewhat 'difficult to conceive of the issue of the use of force as being beyond the reach of international law'.[272] Moreover, as Roberts has affirmed 'acting off the Charter does not leave the Charter norms "intact" . . . by acting off the Charter, these norms are broken rather than bent'.[273] Such rules further underestimate the worth of the rule of law as a value unto itself.

It is telling when the Secretary-General of the United Nations, a body which more than any other embodies international law and which should ideally promote its worth, resorts to such tactics. Secretary-General Annan should not lose sight of the fact that the effectiveness of the United Nations is contingent upon its ability to regulate, at least to some degree, State conduct. In no area is this more important than concerning the use of force. More than in any other area of international relations, the upholding of international law, namely the prohibition of 'war', knowing only two narrow exceptions, would seem paramount. After all, it was the ineffectiveness of the League of Nations, the UN's predecessor, to control such situations and its consequential failure to avert the commencement of the Second World War that led to the League's dissolution and its subsequent replacement by the UN. Indeed, it was during the League's heyday that 'rights talk', based on the then-important international legal principles of minority rights and international tutelage, was used as

[267] P Picone, 'La "Guerra del Kosovo" e il Diritto Internazionale Generale' (2000) 2 *Rivista di diritto internazionale* 309, 344; J Zajadlo, 'Legality and Legitimization of Humanitarian Intervention: New Challenges in the Age of the War on Terrorism' (2005) 8 *American Behavioral Scientist* 653.

[268] Roberts (2008) (n 51) 185.

[269] See Chesterman (2001) (n 4) 220.

[270] Franck (2002) (n 112) 190.

[271] Simma (1999) (n 30) 22.

[272] Francioni (2005) (n 19) 270.

[273] Roberts (2008) (n 51) 188.

a pretext for the disregarding of the legal regime on the use of force and the interventions in the Sudetenland and Abyssinia.[274]

The UN was intended to succeed where the League failed. However, language such as that espoused by Kofi Annan weakens the image of international law. A supposedly neutral figure, representing an organisation which is supposed to represent and defend international law using such reasoning as that employed by the Secretary-General can only weaken the general aura of respectability surrounding international law. For Walden Bello, the use, and partial acceptance amongst commentators, of humanitarian rationales by the Bush administration to retrospectively legitimise the invasion of Iraq represented the 'dead end' for humanitarian intervention, but it was a death which had become imminent ever since the broadly tolerant reaction to NATO's 1999 adventure in Serbia amongst leading commentators and representatives.[275] Talk was perhaps not as cheap as some had suggested.[276] The Kosovo intervention 'contributed mightily to the erosion of the credibility of the United Nations', because the United States chose to use NATO to circumvent the UN as a means of legitimising its actions, and the UN tolerated it. NATO, in turn, 'was a fig-leaf for a war 95 per cent of which was carried out by US forces'.[277] This mirrors the ECOWAS intervention in Liberia, where a similar proportion of troops were of Nigerian origin and raises the problem of regional security organisations or 'grand alliances' being used as a collective construct to mask de facto unilateralism.

One can easily condemn justificatory discourse, particularly when it emanates from figures such as Annan and from renowned international legal scholars.[278] This is doubly the case due to the fact that in international law, the publicist, uniquely, enjoys a role somewhere between a subsidiary lawgiver and a judge per Article 38(1) of the ICJ Statute. This renders the efforts of the various scholars discussed not only misguided but dangerous as they may serve to obscure legal certainty.[279] However, it is important not to ignore the motivation underlying such justifications. The inability of the UN to do enough, or to do anything, to avert Srebrenica,

[274] N Berman, 'Intervention in a Divided World: Axes of Legitimacy' in P Alston and E MacDonald, *Human Rights, Intervention and the Use of Force: The Collected Courses of the Academy of European Law* (Oxford, Oxford University Press, 2008) 215–42, 226–27.

[275] W Bello, 'Humanitarian Intervention: Evolution of a Dangerous Doctrine' (speech delivered at the Conference on Globalisation, War and Intervention sponsored by the International Physicians for the Prevention of Nuclear War, German Chapter, Frankfurt-am-Main, 14–15 January 2006).

[276] See Wheeler (2000) (n 72) generally.

[277] ibid, 56.

[278] This opinion has also been expressed by Peter Hilpold, who hopes for better reasoning from the ICJ in the *Kosovo* case. P Hilpold, 'The Kosovo Case and International Law: Looking for Applicable Theories' (2009) 8 *Chinese Journal of International Law* 47.

[279] See A D'Amato, 'Is the Publicist a Subsidiary Source?' in A D'Amato, *International Law Sources. Collected Papers,* vol III (Leiden, Martinus Nijhoff, 2004) 213–14.

Somalia and Rwanda led to a feeling that 'enough is enough'. The conscience of many was affected to such a degree that they refused to stand by and watch another parallel situation develop without a possible remedy upon which to call. The feeling again echoes Hamlet's resolution at the end of the play:

> How stand I then,
> That have a father kill'd, a mother stain'd,
> Excitements of my reason and my blood,
> And let all sleep? while, to my shame, I see
> The imminent death of twenty thousand men,
> That, for a fantasy and trick of fame,
> Go to their graves like beds, fight for a plot
> Whereon the numbers cannot try the cause,
> Which is not tomb enough and continent
> To hide the slain? O, from this time forth,
> My thoughts be bloody, or be nothing worth![280]

Regarding the two accepted legal exceptions to the prohibition on the use of force, it is clear, inter alia, from a recent resolution of the Institut de Droit International, that the foremost minds in legal scholarship are still wary of the abuse that anything but a strict reading of Security Council Resolutions which authorise recourse to force under Chapter VII would entail. Here, the Institut trenchantly stated that any Security Council Resolution authorising the use of force must be interpreted strictly, and that the absence of condemnation or reaction from the Security Council on foot of ultra vires usage of any such resolution should never be viewed as constituting an implicit or ex post facto approbation of such usages of force.[281] This is certainly a sensible position, seeing as any abusive usage of such a Resolution by a State or coalition of States including a Permanent Member of the Security Council would presumably never be condemned, given that the Permanent Member would almost certainly veto any such condemnation.[282] The wariness of abuse is further evident from how carefully Security Council Resolutions are usually drafted, and how sceptical the world became when the Bush Jr and Blair administrations attempted to justify intervention in Iraq by virtue of Resolutions which had not explicitly authorised recourse to armed force. The modalities of operation of recourse to force under the auspices of Security Council Resolutions are occasionally exceeded, but their surgical regulatory language serves to restrict States, and the border between legal usage and illegal ultra vires utilisation of such Resolutions is usually easy to demarcate. A classic

[280] W Shakespeare, *Hamlet* (1601) Act IV, Scene IV.

[281] *L'autorisation du recours à la force par les Nations Unies*, Institut de Droit International, 10ème Commission, Session de Rhodes, 2011 Plenière (9 Septembre 2011)

[282] See C Scott, 'Interpreting Intervention' (2001) *Annuaire Canadien de Droit International* 360.

example of this is the Bush Sr administration's defence of Kuwait against Iraq. Under Resolution 678 (1990), Iraq was given until 15 January 1991 to withdraw from Kuwait. It thereafter empowered states to use 'all necessary means' to force Iraq out of Kuwait after the deadline. Coalition forces (France, the UK and the US, plus a plethora of other States contributing in small numbers) engaged the Iraqi army militarily, forcing them from Kuwaiti territory, and back into Iraq. However, they did not press home their advantage and march to Baghdad, since this was beyond the terms of the Resolution and the United States would not have had the support of its allies in doing so.

Self-defence is a little less clear-cut. The right exists *inherently*, that is, it would seem to be inherent in the essence of a State that it disposes of the right to defend itself when attacked. States may also respond collectively to defend their allies. However, this right only applies until such time as 'the Security Council has taken measures necessary to maintain international peace and security'.[283] Nonetheless, the traditional reading of Article 51 is of a right that predates the Charter itself, entailing that the 'customary international law of necessity and proportionality would dictate the degree of permissible defensive force'.[284] It is telling that the 1837 *Caroline* affair is still the starting point for self-defence in most international law textbooks.[285] The *Caroline* criteria state that the necessity of self-defence must be 'instant, overwhelming, leaving no choice of means, and no moment of deliberation', and that the response must be proportionate and not excessive. While the 'instant' element is now somewhat dubious, the remainder of the test is largely still applicable. However, as Rostow notes, the right is significantly circumscribed, both temporally and substantively by Article 51, which fits self-defence into a broader framework and delegates 'primary' responsibility for international peace and security to the Security Council. Therefore, 'When, and if, the circumstances creating the right of self-defence no longer exist, whether because of Security Council action or otherwise, the right may not be exercised'.[286] Further, as demonstrated by the ICJ's *Nicaragua* judgment, a restrictive interpretation will be applied to any of the narrow exceptions which do exist to the prohibition upon the use of force, and thus both under customary international law and the law of the UN Charter, States do not have a (unilateral) right of 'armed response to acts which do not constitute an "armed attack"'.[287]

[283] Article 51, Charter of the United Nations.

[284] N Rostow, 'The International Use of Force after the Cold War' (1991) 32 *Harvard Journal of International Law* 416.

[285] See, eg DJ Harris, *Cases and Materials on International Law* (London, Thomson, Sweet and Maxwell, 2004).

[286] Rostow (1991) (n 284) 416.

[287] *Military and Paramilitary Activities in and against Nicaragua (Nicaragua v United States)* (Merits) [1986] ICJ Rep 16 [211].

Therefore, any attempts at a broad teleological interpretation of Article 2(4) are, quite clearly, misguided.

Respect for the Article 2(4) regime amongst States and commentators is also clearly borne out by the arguments presented to justify illegal acts. States that might have justified their actions with reference to notions of 'humanitarian intervention' or something of its ilk in the past have shied away from doing so. States defended their actions on the basis of traditional self-defence (India, in Pakistan and Tanzania in Uganda); the rescue of nationals abroad (Entebbe, the three interventions in the Congo / Zaïre); because of previous colonial issues and alleged requests from post-coup governments (France in the Central African Empire) but rarely with reference to humanitarian motives. As discussed in greater detail below, leading scholars have concluded that no norm of intervention is emerging and that States tend to cling to the Article 2(4) regime in order to justify their actions.[288] The ICJ has further stated that it

> can only regard the alleged right of intervention as a policy of force, such as has, in the past, given rise to the most serious abuses and such as cannot, whatever be the present defects in international organisation, find a place in international law.[289]

Perhaps the best indicator for the general concurrence upon the complete or closed nature of the Article 2(4) regime, however, is found in the post-Kosovo humanitarian intervention debate itself. Scholars such as Koskenniemi and Massa have catalogued and criticised the turn away from law and towards ethics and politics by great swathes of the international legal community in the wake of NATO's Kosovo intervention. As Craig Scott has noted, 'No single provision in any single Security Council resolution can be pointed to as the textual location for inferring either a prior resolution or an *ex-post facto* validation'.[290] That international lawyers were persuaded to move away from the law by their consciences is not the key issue here. Rather, the point of note is that international lawyers were forced to sidestep their own discipline because the regime on the use of force as it stood, as they saw it, was so tightly knitted together, and no skewing of past practice or creative interpretation of treaty law could bring them to a point where humanitarian intervention might be permissible.

There is widespread discomfort with the impotence of international law to allow a *modus operandi* to deal with situations where people are suffering gross human rights abuses, and where a deadlocked Security Council pre-

[288] See Chesterman (2001) (n 4). Many other authors have used similar past examples and have drawn similar conclusions. See, eg F Abiew, *The Evolution of the Doctrine and Practice of Humanitarian Intervention* (The Hague, Kluwer Law International, 1999); M Kanade, 'Article 2(4) of the UN Charter: Alive and Well', *Peace and Conflict Monitor*, 7 July 2009.

[289] *Corfu Channel Case* (*UK v Albania*) (Merits) [1949] ICJ Rep 4, 35.

[290] Scott (2001) (n 282).

vents collective action under Chapter VII. However, a resort to international illegality, or philosophy, or ethics, or politics is not the answer. Those who argue that uses of force such as that against Serbia should be judged by a higher moral standard than the law ignore the fact that the rules on the use of force reflect the moral beliefs of the community that formed them.[291] Human rights norms are, after all, part of international law. How can one argue that we must uphold such norms by breaking an even more fundamental – or at least equally fundamental – norm? Although I have undertaken an examination in this chapter of various efforts to solve this crisis of conscience by several authors, using a variety of means, I confess that I have barely scratched the surface of the debate. Many other models have also been proposed, and although they are, in the main, somewhat similar to those described above, they all reflect a preoccupation with reconciling the doctrine of humanitarian intervention with international law, or at least with justifying its operability even outside of the law.

There is, however, a potential solution to this puzzle which has, to my knowledge, yet to be considered by international legal scholars. This solution rests on the operation of the third source of international law – namely 'the general principles of law recognised by civilised nations'[292] – and particularly the principles of equity, which have been affirmed by past judgments of the World Court to form part of this *corpus*. This legal source has been almost completely overlooked during the recent debate on humanitarian intervention.[293] Due to the deficiencies and potential for abuse of the solutions outlined above, I feel that an examination of the operability of such principles may be invaluable in shedding new light upon the humanitarian intervention debate as a whole and as a possible means of permitting humanitarian intervention with a firm legal footing. It is to this possibility that I shall turn in conducting the forthcoming chapters.

However, before turning to the crux of this work, namely equity's impact upon – and interplay with – the rules governing humanitarian intervention, it is perhaps germane to acknowledge what this work does not do, which is to explore the previous patterns of State practice and *opinio iuris* in situations where the UN Charter regime on the use of force has failed to function, and which have been defended by States and by scholars as 'humanitarian' in nature.

A chapter treating such past examples briefly constituted part of the plan for this work, but was ultimately discarded. The reason for this is simple: this work aims to present an original perspective on humanitarian

[291] O'Connell (2005) (n 28) 11–12.

[292] Statute of the International Court of Justice, Art 38(1)(c); Statute of the Permanent Court of International Justice, Art 38(I)(iii).

[293] Aside, perhaps from some fleeting but interesting references by Paolo Picone. See Picone (2000) (n 37) 309–60.

intervention rooted in legal norms, namely general principles of law and equity. While customary international law is also an important legal source, and while it is normally to customary law that one would be expected to look when treaty rules run out,[294] or when they fail to function, a number of authors have already undertaken quite exhaustive studies on past examples of State practice which might be classed as 'humanitarian intervention' in the broadest sense. Recalling their conclusions in detail would have been overly burdensome and only of tangential relevance to the arguments presented here. However, a few paragraphs outlining the main points regarding customary international law in this area are warranted.

Post-Kosovo, one of the leading studies on this subject was penned by Simon Chesterman.[295] Chesterman, a student of Brownlie at Oxford, devotes much of his excellent book to a historical synopsis and legal evaluation of past cases, including the Belgian intervention in the Congo (Léopoldville) (1960); the Belgian/US intervention in the Congo (Stanleyville) (1964); the US intervention in the Dominican Republic (1965); the Indian intervention in East Pakistan/Bangladesh (1971); the Israeli Entebbe operation in Uganda (1976); the Franco-Belgian intervention in Zaïre (1978); the Tanzanian intervention in Uganda (1978–79); the Vietnamese intervention in Kampuchea (1978–79); the French intervention in the Central African Empire (1979); the US intervention in Panama (1989); the ECOWAS intervention in Liberia (1990); the UK/US/French imposition of 'no-fly zones' in Iraq (1991–2003); the ECOWAS intervention in Sierra Leone (1997–98); and, perhaps most obviously the NATO intervention in the Federal Republic of Yugoslavia (1999) itself.[296] This lengthy work is undertaken in order to determine whether a norm of customary international law in favour of humanitarian intervention may be emerging. It certainly represents an area worth investigating, especially in light of the observation of the ICJ in the *Nicaragua* case that the UN Charter does not cover the entire area of the use of force in international relations.[297] This, along with the prescription in

[294] This is not to suggest that customary international law in some way 'outranks' general principles in hierarchical terms. However, the fact is that in normal international legal analysis, custom is generally more likely to be turned to in lieu of treaty norms than general principles The *procès-verbaux* of the Advisory Commission of Jurists which composed the PCIJ Statute enumerated the sources of law set out in Art 38(1) and stated that they *shall* all be considered in all cases before the Court. This formulation implies that they should also (all) be considered in the resolution of any legal dispute, though in practice, the specificities of treaty and/or customary norms render resort to general principles a rare occurrence. See PCIJ/Advisory Committee of Jurists (ACJ), *Procès-verbaux of the Proceedings of the Committee*, 16–24 June 1920 (The Hague, van Langhuysen, 1920). See also the section in ch 2 entitled, 'General Principles by the Front Door: An Unpopular Source of Law?'.

[295] S Chesterman, *Just War or Just Peace? Humanitarian Intervention and International Law* (Oxford, Oxford University Press, 2001). Many other authors have used similar past examples and have drawn similar conclusions. See, eg Abiew (1999) (n 12).

[296] Chesterman (2001) (n 4) 53–87.

[297] *Military and Paramilitary Activities in and against Nicaragua (Nicaragua v United States)* (Merits) [1986] ICJ Rep 16 [176].

Article 51 of the Charter itself that the right of self-defence is 'inherent' to States, that it inheres naturally in them by virtue of their essence, would certainly lend weight to the arguments of those who posit that the rules on the use of force do not begin and end with the UN Charter. Therefore, searching for wisdom in this regard via the norms of customary law (or indeed, general principles) would not seem misguided.

However, Chesterman and others have concluded that no norm of customary law in favour of humanitarian intervention exists or is emerging.[298] This is hardly surprising, for a variety of reasons. The *Corfu Channel* case clearly demonstrates that when mechanisms for conflict resolution (inter alia, the UN Charter provisions prohibiting the resort to armed force by States) fail to operate, that no right to 'self-help' may exist. It is perhaps worth re-emphasising the ICJ's position that it

> can only regard the alleged right of intervention as a policy of force, such as has, in the past, given rise to the most serious abuses and such as cannot, whatever be the present defects in international organisation, find a place in international law.[299]

Lauterpacht labelled the judgment an 'emphatic rejection' of any putative right of intervention.[300] In *Nicaragua*, the *Corfu Channel* judgment was further cited in support of a general principle of non-intervention.[301] While Tesón, inter alia, argues in favour of a customary right, his argument falls down when examined in detail and has been roundly criticised earlier in this work for ignoring the *opinio iuris* requirement and for adopting a definition of customary law which, while suiting his own ends, is quite at odds with its actual status in international law.

The idea that a new customary right may have emerged since the Charter's inception is also refuted. The examples listed above have been cited by certain authors as constituting practice of humanitarian intervention, but in truth, such incidents fell far short of satisfying the practice plus *opinio iuris* test. States were quick to hold up the flag of self-defence, that of the rescue of nationals, or a variety of other grounds, as discussed above, in order to excuse military incursion, but rarely took the opportunity to invoke humanitarian motives as legal justification for their actions. Indeed, practice in many of these cases was far from humanitarian, but rather involved regime change, the weakening of enemies and the rescue of State nationals abroad, all falling far outside the realm of humanitarian intervention. Chesterman notes that the East Pakistan, Uganda, and

[298] A Orford, *Reading Humanitarian Intervention: Human Rights and the Use of Force in International Law* (Cambridge, Cambridge University Press, 2003).

[299] *Corfu Channel Case* (*UK v Albania*) (Merits) [1949] ICJ Rep 4, 35.

[300] H Lauterpacht, *The Development of International Law by the International Court* (London, Stevens and Sons, 1958) 90, 317.

[301] *Military and Paramilitary Activities in and against Nicaragua (Nicaragua v United States)* (Merits) [1986] ICJ Rep 16, 106–07 [202].

Kampuchea examples are regarded somewhat more favourably in the international community, but that in none of these cases were humanitarian concerns invoked in order to justify the use of force.[302]

Those authors who have sought to justify humanitarian intervention by portraying it as a norm of customary international law have studiously ignored the *opinio iuris* element in such cases, and have occasionally even been guilty of bending the factual narrative to support their position. Tesón, in particular, is guilty of the above, attacking customary law itself and stating that

> [a] theory of law devoid of any moral underpinnings, one whose only currency is the sanctimonious language of government officials, is hardly deserving of the name. It matters little that the Tanzanians (wrongly) thought that they were acting in self-defence . . . The logic of the situation tells a different story.[303]

Per Tesón, the *opinio iuris* requirement is effectively redundant and instead, we must apply the doctrine of *res ipsa loquitur*, that is, that the thing speaks for itself. However, the judgment that such a situation speaks for itself and negates the stated rationale of the State in question – which is 'wrong' – runs contrary to the doctrine of State sovereignty, which underpins the formation of customary international law. Furthermore, Tesón's *res ipsa loquitur* argument does not hold water when held up against the facts. With reference to the Tanzanian intervention in Idi Amin's Uganda, it is far from clear that humanitarian reasons played the principal role in Julius Nyere's decision to intervene, with Uganda having annexed Tanzanian territory north of the Kagera river. While the ICJ has shown itself willing to countenance assuming the presence of *opinio iuris* where a strong general consensus exists amongst States, supported by continuous practice, and where the logic of the situation merits such a conclusion.[304] However, it is clear that such a conclusion could never have been reached in the Tanzanian case, nor in the case of humanitarian intervention in general, since a strong consensus and evidence of continuous generalised practice are lacking. It is clear then that no such right had emerged in customary international law pre-Kosovo.

The final issue regarding customary international law is the idea that NATO's 1999 adventure in Serbia was the beginning of a 'new departure' in international law, which would furnish forth a new customary norm in favour of unilateral humanitarian intervention. As discussed earlier, Cassese is amongst those who have spoken of 'nascent trends' in the world community leading to the 'justifiability' of humanitarian intervention, though he found it premature to speak of its 'legality', since the element of *usus* or *diuturnitas* was lacking immediately post-Kosovo. The

[302] Chesterman (2001) (n 4) 84.
[303] Tesón (1997) (n 12) 193.
[304] *Delimitation of the Maritime Boundary in the Gulf of Maine Area* [1984] ICJ Rep 246, 293–94.

question is whether perhaps this has changed, with certain authors opining that it has.[305] Buchanan, as noted above, favoured reforming customary international law by breaking it. However, Kosovo alone is not enough for this. Few authors have argued that the Kosovo intervention may be used as an example of so-called 'instant custom', a rare occurrence in international legal history.[306] Even Cassese did not go this far. A paucity of analogous examples post-Kosovo of what could be termed 'humanitarian intervention' does not lead one to the conclusion that Kosovo set a legal precedent which will henceforth be followed in analogous situations and will be tolerated and approved of by the community of States at large. Fenstein and Slaughter, inter alia, have attempted to use rhetoric justifying humanitarian intervention, notably the *R2P* doctrine, to cast the US-led 2003 invasion as a humanitarian operation.[307] This mirrored token attempts by the Bush administration, which advanced humanitarian rationales amidst a myriad of other reasons to legally justify the attack. However, such arguments were given short shrift by most legal commentators, who viewed the war as patently illegal and nothing akin to humanitarian intervention.[308] Equally, while humanitarian motives were advanced by the Russian Government to justify the 2008 interventions in South Ossetia and Abkhazia, few States lent credence to these claims.[309] This is particularly evidenced by the fact that the newly-independent (though highly Russian reliant) Republics of South Ossetia and Abkhazia have, to date, been recognised only by a handful of States.[310] With respect to the 2011 crisis in Libya, it is telling that force was only employed to protect civilians after the UN Security Council adopted Resolution 1973 (2011), authorising the use of 'all necessary means' to protect civilians. In the run-up to the Resolution's adoption, numerous States, including those

[305] M Stanulova, 'Has Humanitarian Intervention Become an Exception to the Prohibition on the Use of Force in Article 2(4) of the UN Charter?' (2010) *Atlantic Community* 1, available at www.atlantic-community.org/app/webroot/files/articlepdf/Stanulova_Humanitarian%20Intervention.pdf.

[306] A Roberts, 'Traditional and Modern Approaches to Customary International Law: A Reconciliation' (2001) 95 *American Journal of International Law* 757.

[307] See Slaughter (2003) (n 179), who opined that the invasion of Iraq could be 'justified' under the Kosovo 'precedent' if weapons of mass destruction were found or if a portion of the Iraqi population welcomed the intervention. See also Fenstein and Slaughter (2004) (n 235) 136–50.

[308] Roth (2005) (n 183) 6.

[309] Faber (2009) (n 82). Hafkin, however, argues that the more recent case of South Ossetia is legally similar to Kosovo, but that a new customary rule is not emerging due to strong objections against both operations. However, he does not exclude the appearance of such a rule in the future. Hafkin (2010) (n 69). An alternative perspective is voiced by NN Petro, who, with reference to Abkhazia and South Ossetia, states that Western scholars must give Russia's humanitarian motives due consideration. Not doing so risks undermining the commitment of the West to international legal principles and illustrates double standards, undermining the potential for eventual normative stability. See Petro (2008) (n 186).

[310] To date, the Russian Federation, Nauru, Nicaragua, Venezuela and Vanuatu are the only UN Member States that have recognised the two Republics.

that were eventually to intervene, underlined the need for Security Council approbation before force could be contemplated.

It would seem, then, that the idea of an existing – or emerging – customary norm of humanitarian intervention is not supported by much real evidence. If not based upon a 'reinterpretation' of the UN Charter, or a separation of the legality of the intervention from its legitimacy, as some apologists for intervention have suggested, then a conception of intervention under customary international law would seem the next logical port of call. However, when cast as an exception to the general prohibition upon the use of force, which has achieved *ius cogens* status, the new customary exception would need to achieve the same status, making those requirements necessary for its emergence still more exacting than for an ordinary rule of customary international law. As noted, our present examination of such a notion is far from exhaustive, constituting a mere perusal of research which has been adequately completed by others. Clearly, one must take into account that customary international law is in constant flux, and undergoes a constant evolution under the pressure of the plurality of political and economic actors and under the ex post control of *opinio iuris*.[311] Hence, acts contrary to existing law do have the potential to become 'practice', and thereby create new law, subject to the requirement of *opinio iuris*. As Bianchi notes, 'The need to consider the emergence of values which enjoy an ever-increasing recognition in international society seems compelling, particularly in hard cases'.[312] However, there seems to be so little real evidence of either consistent practice or of *opinio iuris* in favour of a customary norm permitting humanitarian intervention that one can state with real confidence that no such customary norm exists.

While clearly, custom ought to be the first port of call when treaty norms fail to function, it should not be the last. In lieu of a customary norm permitting humanitarian intervention, study in this area must turn to the third principal source of international law. The problems cited with the potential emergence of a customary norm permitting humanitarian intervention would not arise in the case of humanitarian intervention based on the 'general principles' normative source. General principles of law derive from the national legal systems of States, and as such do not require evidence of State practice or *opinio iuris* to confirm their normative status. Rather, their normative status is confirmed by evidence of their adoption by a broad majority of developed legal traditions and, where possible, confirmation, either by way of State practice or their explicit enunciation in widely-adopted treaties, or, more likely, by means of pronouncements by the highest international tribunals. General principles are unlike the

[311] See MH Mendelson, 'The Formation of Customary International Law' (1998) 272 *Hague Academy Collected Courses* 155.

[312] A Bianchi, 'Human Rights and the Magic of Jus Cogens' (2008) 19 *European Journal of International Law* 504.

other principal sources of international law – treaty and custom – insofar as they are not rooted exclusively in pure voluntarism on the part of States. Hence, a series of equitable general principles allowing for a right of humanitarian intervention in limited circumstances could exist without the need for the demonstration of precedents in State practice. The lack of attention which the 'general principles' source has received in the humanitarian intervention debate until now is an unfortunate oversight in this context, and it is one which the remainder of this work shall seek to rectify.

2

The Third Source of International Law

I. INTRODUCTION

AS OUTLINED IN the previous chapter, there has been a marked reluctance amongst international legal scholars treating the area of humanitarian intervention, and indeed the use of force in general, to deal with the third source of international law, namely general principles, and of any equitable gap-filling or correctional mechanisms contained therein. The following chapters will focus upon a detailed examination of the 'general principles' category, outlining its content and extent, and to what degree an international law equivalent of the common law notion of 'equity' may have presented itself as a subset of this source.

This chapter shall commence with an examination of Article 38(1) of the Statute of the International Court of Justice (ICJ) and shall examine the merits of its claim to represent an accurate description of the sources of international law. I shall look at how the current formulation of Article 38 was arrived at, and in particular, how the 'general principles' clause was formulated, including an analysis of the legal landscape in which it was formulated. Thereafter, I will examine the still more important matter of subsequent practice. In doing so, I shall look at how Article 38(1) has been applied, based upon the practice of the World Court, and shall ask whether it has represented a departure from the previous formulation of international legal sources.

II. ARTICLE 38(1) AS THE WELLSPRING OF INTERNATIONAL LEGAL SOURCES

Article 38(1) of the ICJ Statute prescribes that the Court, whose function it is to decide in accordance with international law such disputes as are submitted to it, shall apply: (a) international treaties; (b) customary international law; (c) the general principles of law recognised by civilised nations; and (d) judicial decisions and the teachings of leading scholars as a subsidiary means for determination of rules of law.[1] The order in which

[1] The words 'rules of law' would seem, necessarily, also to encompass principles of law.

the first three component parts of international law are enumerated is not intended to denote a juridical hierarchy, but merely to indicate the order in which they would normally present themselves to the mind of the international judge.[2] While there remains a limited amount of debate as to the scope of Article 38(1), it is now nonetheless widely accepted that the Article may be treated as the authoritative representation of the sources of general international law and their state.[3] Further testimony to the declaratory nature of Article 38(1) may be found in a memorandum of the UN Secretary-General, who, when speaking of the sources of international law stated that 'The codification of this aspect of international law has been successfully accomplished by the definition of the sources of international law as given in Article 38 . . . That definition has been repeatedly treated as authoritative by international arbitral tribunals'.[4] This position is further supported by the fact that in pleadings before the ICJ and its predecessor the Permanent Court of International Justice (PCIJ), no party has ever attempted to argue that the sources of law to be applied by either court were not precisely representative of general international law as a whole. Hence, one may state that there is a general concurrence amongst States that Article 38(1) represents the standard encapsulation of the sources of international law. It is also germane to note that Article 92 of the UN Charter prescribes that the ICJ Statute forms an integral part of the Charter text.

The inclusion of international treaties and customary international law as primary sources of international law was a relatively uncontroversial decision. The inclusion of judicial decisions and the teachings of leading publicists also caused little upset, given that such decisions and teachings do not of themselves give rise to or create legal rules, but merely serve as a means of determining such rules, and as such, may also be denoted as law-determining agencies rather than subsidiary sources.[5] However, the

[2] B Cheng, *General Principles of Law as Applied by International Courts and Tribunals* (Cambridge, Grotius, 1987) 22.

[3] See A D'Amato,*The Concept of Custom in International Law* (Ithaca, New York, Cornell University Press, 1971) 88; H Thirlway, *International Customary Law and its Codification* (Leiden, AW Sijthoff, 1972) 58; O Schachter, 'The Evolving International Law of Development' (1976) 15 *Columbia Journal of Transnational Law* 20; Cheng (1987) (n 2) 21–27; P Dallier and A Pellet, *Droit International Public*, 7th edn (Paris, Librairie Générale de Droit et Jurisprudence, 2002) 114; P Kooijmans, *Internationaal publiekrecht in vogelvlucht*, 9th edn (Deventer, Netherlands, Kluwer, 2002); D Ruzié, *Droit international public*, 17th edn (Paris, Dalloz, 2004) 15; M Karg,*IGH vs ISGH. Die Beziehung zwischen zwei völkerrechtlichen Streitbeilegungsorganen* (Baden-Baden, Nomos, 2005); A Zimmermann (ed),*The Statute of the International Court of Justice: A Commentary* (Oxford, Oxford University Press, 2006); FO Raimondo, *General Principles of Law in the Decisions of International Criminal Courts and Tribunals* (Leiden, Martinus Nijhoff, 2008) 20–21.

[4] UN, 'Survey of International Law in Relation to the Work of Codification of the International Law Commission', Memorandum submitted by the Secretary-General (1949) A/CN. 4/1/Rev 1, 22.

[5] Cheng (1987) (n 2) 23.

inclusion of 'the general principles of law recognised by civilised nations' caused somewhat rather more of a stir. In the following sections, I shall attempt to explain how this phrase was arrived at, and what precisely it may be held to denote.

Article 38 of the ICJ Statute mirrors that of the Statute of the PCIJ – its predecessor, except for superficial alterations to the numbering of the paragraphs and sub-paragraphs, and the addition of a few words of no significant practical consequence in the introductory stanza. When the PCIJ Statute was first published, the phrase 'les principes généraux de droit reconnus par les nations civilisées' and its insertion as part of the law to be examined by the PCIJ generated considerable discussion amongst international legal scholars.

Lauterpacht places general principles and analogies from municipal law at the centre of his understanding of the international legal order, identifying them with natural law, and stating that:

> [W]ith the Statute of the Permanent Court of International Justice, which declared 'general principles of law recognised by civilised nations' – in some ways a modern version of the law of nature – to be one of the primary sources of international law, what was of the essence of the law of nature, namely its conformity with the actual legal experience of mankind, came once more into its own.[6]

The substantive aspect of Lauterpacht's thesis is based in natural law, but the explanation of its operation is rooted in the relative indeterminacy of law as expressed in the doctrine of gradual concretisation. He states that the ambivalence inherent in natural law ideology is 'only slightly relevant in the field of international law'. There, he argues, 'it has acted as a lever of progress . . . the uncertainty of the "higher law" is preferable to the arbitrariness and insolence of naked force'.[7] Lauterpacht wrote most of the above in the context of *praeter legem* application of general principles and/or natural law, in a series of discussions related to *non liquet* situations. He argued that avoiding *non liquet* was the principal reason why Article 38(1)(c) had been drafted in the manner that it was, and that such general principles and/or natural law also helped to render treaties more effective as a supplemental means of regulating their applicability.[8] Lauterpacht further stated that gaps in the law were something unavoidable, and that in international law, 'in a sense they are the rule rather than the exception'.[9] Dealing with these gaps was to be achieved by reference

[6] H Lauterpacht 'Some Observations on the Prohibition of "Non Liquet" and the Completeness of the Law' in *Symbolae Verzijl. Présentées au Professor JHW Verzijl à l'occasion de son LXX-ième anniversaire* (The Hague, Martinus Nijhoff, 1958) 115.

[7] H Lauterpacht, 'The Grotian Tradition in International Law' (1946) 23 *British Yearbook of International Law* 48, 48–49.

[8] IGM Scobbie, 'The Theorist as Judge: Hersch Lauterpacht's Concept of the International Judicial Function' (1997) 2 *European Journal of International Law* 274.

[9] Lauterpacht (1958) (n 6) 204.

to the 'adversarial principle', demanding that a decision be made possible in every case; and by recourse to general principles of law (incorporating, per Lauterpacht, natural law doctrine) under Article 38(1)(c). This two-prong mechanism would make 'certain that there would always be at hand, if necessary, a legal rule or principle for the legal solution of any controversy'.[10] Per Lauterpacht, lacunae arise in cases where 'there is no clear rule of international law in existence', but in such situations, tribunals may fill the gaps through resort to general principles. Ergo, the international legal system is complete, there are no real gaps (since principles fill all lacunae which arise), and 'the principle affirming the completeness of the international legal order . . . is the positive formulation of the prohibition of non liquet'.[11]

Julius Stone presented what has been termed the 'paradigmatic counter-thesis' to Lauterpacht.[12] Stone's position is that the prohibition of *non liquet* does not arise from application of general principles; that recourse to municipal analogies is unwarranted and dangerous given the differences in the exercise of international judicial powers; and that there is no residual 'closing rule' in international law,[13] leading to the completeness of the system. Stone argues instead that if *non liquet* is to be avoided, then international tribunals must be (and are) endowed with lawmaking power in this regard. Therefore, they may fill gaps *praeter legem* if and when such a need arises. Karl Engisch has suggested that a *Rechtsfreier Raum* exists in international law, as well as in domestic law, related to acts about which the law says nothing, and that therefore there may exist a space that is simply devoid of law.[14] Stone seizes upon this reasoning, arguing that 'gap-filling' general principles and/or natural law constituting a residual closing rule 'would directly provide . . . a substantive rule in contentious cases . . . any absence of prohibition would, under this application, constitute the presence of a legal permission. The "no-laws land" of *non liquet* would be occupied by permissive legal rules'.[15] While even Lauterpacht occasionally cast doubt on the existence of such a 'residual principle',[16] Stone was more sceptical still, opining that 'There may be conduct . . . about which the norms say nothing at all'.[17]

[10] ibid, 205.

[11] ibid, 199

[12] ibid, 286.

[13] J Stone, *Non Liquet and the Function of Law in the International Community* (Oxford, Oxford University Press, 1960) 127–59.

[14] K Engisch, 'Der Rechtsfreie Raum' (1952) 108 *Zeitschrift für die Gesamte Staatwissenschaft* 385.

[15] J Stone, *Non Liquet and the International Judicial Function* in C Perelman (ed), *Le problem des lacunes en droit* (Brussels, Bruylant, 1968) 305.

[16] J Kammerhofer, 'Gaps, the Nuclear Weapons Advisory Opinion and the Structure of International Legal Argument between Theory and Practice' (2009) 80 *British Yearbook of International Law* 337.

[17] Stone (1968) (n 15) 308–09.

This position on gaps within the law was fundamentally at odds with Kelsen, who argued that 'real gaps do not exist, in the sense that it would [somehow] not be possible to solve a legal dispute in accordance with the valid norms, because the law . . . cannot be applied due to a lack of rules'.[18] Kelsen holds firm to the adage that what is not legally prohibited to the subjects of the law is legally permitted to them, describing this as a 'fundamental principle'.[19] This leads him to categorically disavow the possibility of gaps within the law.

The debate about gaps in the law may thus be summarised as follows: in order to prevent a *non liquet*, Lauterpacht argued for the completeness of the international legal system through use of the adversarial principle and general principles, incorporating natural law. Stone, *a contrario*, posited that gaps were inherent and unavoidable in international law, and that international courts and tribunals must therefore necessarily be endowed with law-making powers.

For the purposes of this volume, the above debate is certainly highly relevant. The case law of the ICJ and PCIJ is leant upon heavily in subsequent chapters in order to give an accurate representation of what content the principal judicial organ of the United Nations has assigned to the 'general principles of law recognised by civilised nations' as a normative category. For the purposes of this discussion, the assumption is made that the Court is not itself a legislator, as Stone would suggest, but rather that it interprets the provisions of international law and applies them to the case at hand. In cases where the norms themselves are obscure or in dispute (as is undoubtedly the case with much of the general principles corpus) ICJ/PCIJ judgments are relied upon as a subsidiary means of determining or clarifying their context and extent. Such an interpretation is in accordance with Article 38(1)(d) of the ICJ Statute, which establishes the pronouncements of international tribunals and the teachings of leading scholars as a subsidiary source of international law for interpretation purposes.

Of course, it would also have been possible to examine the opinions of leading scholars on general principles of law for guidance in this regard. However, a detailed examination would perhaps not have been a fruitful endeavour, bringing forth little clarity. The initial debate regarding the normative content of the 'general principles of law recognised by civilised nations' category enunciated in the PCIJ Statute brought forth three schools of thought. A first school, led by Morelli,[20] Castberg[21] and

[18] H Kelsen, 'Zur Theorie der Interpretation' (1934) 8 *Revue internationale de la theorie du droit* 9.

[19] H Kelsen, *Principles of International Law* (New York, Rinehart, 1952) 306.

[20] G Morelli, 'La théorie générale du procès international' (1937) 61 *Recueil La Haye* 253, 344 *et seq*.

[21] J Castberg, 'La méthodologie du droit international public' (1933) 43 *Recueil La Haye* 313, 370 *et seq*.

Anzilotti,[22] held that the expression referred primarily to general principles of international law, and only to a subsidiary degree, to principles found in the municipal law of domestic legal systems.[23] A second school held, *a contrario*, that the expression entailed principles obtaining in municipal law, more than principles of international law.[24] A third school, represented by Lauterpacht[25] and Ripert[26] believed particularly that the phrase referred to principles of private law from domestic legal systems that had been transposed to the international legal sphere.[27] However, much of the debate which ensued during the years immediately subsequent to the initial enactment of the PCIJ Statute was conducted without the benefit of having examined the *travaux préparatoires* of the Statute and paid only scant attention to what international legal practice had termed 'general principles' prior to the Statute's drafting. Therefore, interesting though the content of this debate may be, it is obviously more germane to examine the rival theories in light of these additional sources of information, in order to decide what, in fact, constituted the intention of the drafters of the Statute.

It would seem that in the decades since these early debates, little has changed, and that the doctrinal position amongst legal scholars is still the subject of some debate. A recent article by Jaye Ellis in the *European Journal of International Law*[28] gave rise to immediate criticism as to the author's conception of the general principles category, and the methods by which such principles may be identified.[29] Since the teachings of leading scholars were and still are far from uniform on the matter of general principles, the judgments of the PCIJ/ICJ seem an obvious place to look for guidance in this area.[30] I would however make a number of observations. First, whether or

[22] D Anzilotti, *Cours de Droit International* (Paris, Recueil Sirey, 1929) 117.

[23] See also MO Hudson, *The Permanent Court of International Justice 1920–42* (New York, Macmillan, 1943) 611.

[24] K Strupp, 'Le droit du juge international de statuer selon l'équité' (1930) 33 *Recueil La Haye* 357, 474–75; M Scerni, *I principi generali di diritto riconosciuti dalle nazioni civili nella giurisprudenza della Corte Permanente di Giustizia Internazionale* (Rome, Cedam, 1932) 13 *et seq*.

[25] H Lauterpacht, *Private Law Sources and Analogies of International Law (with special reference to international arbitration)* (London, Longman, Green and Co, 1927) 71, 85.

[26] G Ripert, 'Règles du droit civil applicables aux rapports internationaux' (1933) 44 *Recueil La Haye* 569.

[27] See also P Grapin, *Valeur internationale des principes généraux du droit* (Paris, Domat-Montchrestien, 1934) 64–66.

[28] J Ellis, 'General Principles and Comparative Law' (2011) 22 *European Journal of International Law* 949.

[29] AZ Borda, 'Comparative Law and the Ad Hoc Tribunals: A Reply to Jaye Ellis' *EJIL Talk! – The Blog of the European Journal of International Law* (1 June 2012), available at www.ejiltalk.org/comparative-law-and-the-ad-hoc-tribunals-a-reply-to-jaye-ellis-2/.

[30] It is worth noting that relatively little attention has been paid to other international courts and tribunals in this work. This is regrettable, but lamentably inevitable in a work of this scale. Embarking upon an analysis of disputes in other international judicial fora would, most certainly, have raised the question of contradictory or diverging interpretations of a single principle in different international courts. Much is currently being written about the fragmentation of international law into so-called 'self-contained regimes', each of which may or may not have

not general principles of law constitute a 'closing rule' in international law (ie whether we adopt Lauterpacht or Stone's position[31]), the fact is that such principles do enjoy normative force, and normative parity with treaty and custom, per Article 38(1) of the ICJ Statute. They *must* therefore be considered when questions arise as to the legality of acts, not just before the ICJ, but throughout international law in general. Courts, and more particularly the ICJ and PCIJ before it, are not legislating when they apply such principles, they are merely applying a universally acknowledged source. The fact that the content of this normative source is somewhat vague and flexible is another matter. It is precisely for this reason that Article 38(1)(d) prescribes that the judgments of international courts and tribunals may be used as a subsidiary means of determining the content of certain norms. In some cases, norms (including treaty and customary norms, and not merely general principles) are unclear. The value of international judgments in this regard is that they often serve to frame such norms in a clearer manner. It is for this reason that I have made such willing use of the ICJ and PCIJ jurisprudence.

A. Some Preliminary Remarks on Treaty Interpretation

The current chapter of this volume adopts an historical perspective on Article 38(1) of the ICJ Statute. It is argued herein that this Article encapsulates a reflection of the sources of international law as they stand. However, since the main thrust of this book will concentrate upon the relationship between general principles and the way in which they impact upon the regime governing the use of force by States, it would appear germane to insert here some brief comments upon the dynamics which govern such rapports generally. Since the United Nations Charter is an international treaty, it is governed by the customary international law rules relating to international treaties. Such rules have, in the main, been

special rules and principles applicable within it. However, to embark upon such a discussion in the middle of this work could well have compromised the focus of the discussion, and would certainly have confused it. As Brownlie has noted, 'The assumption is made that there are discrete subjects such as "international human rights law", or "international law and development". As a consequence, the quality and coherence of international law as a whole are threatened'. I Brownlie, 'The Rights of Peoples in Modern International Law' in J Crawford (ed), *The Rights of Peoples* (Oxford, Clarendon Press, 1988) 15. Since the regime on the use of force by States is chiefly governed by the UN, and since the principal judicial organ of that body is the ICJ, I chose, in the main, to limit the study to the judgments of that Court and its predecessor, the PCIJ, the judgments of which are frequently relied upon by the ICJ itself, using the term 'World Court' as a term of art to describe them both.

[31] I would tend, for the record, to agree with Koskenniemi that something should either be legal or illegal, particularly in the international legal sphere: 'NATO was either entitled to bomb Serbia or it was not. *Tertium non datur*. Surely it is an essential part of the Rule of Law that society contains no corner of outside-the-law?' M Koskenniemi, 'The Lady Doth Protest Too Much: Kosovo, and the Turn to Ethics in International Law' (2002) 65 *MLR* 159, 161–62.

codified by the 1969 Vienna Convention on the Law of Treaties (VCLT[32]), and a number of these rules merit examination here.[33]

Particularly for the present purposes, it is necessary to examine under what circumstances the World Court, or any international tribunal, may wish to move beyond the primary text of a treaty document to determine its correct meaning, by reference to extraneous legal sources such as customary international law, other treaties, and for our particular purposes, general principles of law. Such a study is especially necessary due to the prevalent view that the UN Charter provides the principal rules of guidance relating to the use of force by States and that general principles have little or nothing to do with the area.

Article 31(3)(c) VCLT prescribes that

> There shall be taken into account, together with the context: . . . (c) any relevant rules of international law applicable in the relations between the parties.

As an aspect of the interpretative process, it must be taken into account alongside, and integral to: Article 31(1), the 'basic rule' of treaty interpretation – that is, that a treaty is to be interpreted in good faith, with the ordinary meaning given to the terms of the treaty in the light of its object and purpose; Article 31(2), the treaty's context; Article 31(3)(a) and (b), subsequent agreements and subsequent practice; Article 31(4), any relevant special meaning; and Article 32, dealing with supplementary means of interpretation. However, as French notes, 'as a feature of treaty interpretation, it has long since been marginalised and ignored',[34] while Sands comments that

> what it actually means in practice is difficult to know since it appears to have been expressly relied upon only very occasionally in judicial practice. It also seems to have attracted little academic comment. There appears to be a general reluctance to refer to Article 31(3)(c).[35]

This is a common complaint regarding legal provisions with a nexus to the general principles category, as has already been noted. Nonetheless, it is important to note that the 2004 Report of the International Law Commission (ILC) stated that the fact 'that article 31(3)(c) was rarely expressly cited should not obscure its importance as a rule of treaty

[32] Vienna Convention on the Law of Treaties, done at Vienna on 23 May 1969, entered into force on 27 January 1980, 1155 UNTS 33.

[33] For the relationship between customary international law on treaty interpretation and the VCLT regime, see *Libya v Chad* [1994] ICJ Rep 6, 21; and 'United States – Standards for Reformulated and Conventional Gasoline', Report of the WTO Appellate Body (AB-1996-1) (29 April 1996) (WT/DS2/AB/R).

[34] D French, 'Treaty Interpretation and the Incorporation of Extraneous Legal Rules' (2006) 55 *ICLQ* 281, 300.

[35] P Sands, 'Sustainable Development: Treaty, Custom, and the Cross-fertilization of International Law' in A Boyle and D Freestone (eds), *International Law and Sustainable Development – Past Achievements and Future Challenges* (Oxford, Oxford University Press, 1999) 49–50, cited by French (n 34).

interpretation'.[36] It is further worth noting that Article 31 in its entirety is entitled the 'general rule of interpretation', and not the basic rule in Article 31(1) as is sometimes stated in legal treatises. It is of course true that not all elements of Article 31 will be relevant in all cases. However, when they are, to whatever extent, they *must* be utilised. Article 31(2) and (3) are not merely discretionary appendages, but rather prescriptive and mandatory components of the general rule of treaty interpretation. Article 31(3) is unambiguous about this, stating 'There shall be taken into account' and leaving no room for judicial discretion in this regard. As French notes, while the above rules on treaty interpretation are incumbent upon judges in international tribunals, they are equally so upon States who wish to interpret international treaties in accordance with the rules established in international law. However, lamentably, practice demonstrates that there is perhaps a lack of awareness of the scope of these rules, though this has not prevented tribunals from occasionally employing general principles and other extraneous norms in interpreting treaties.[37]

However, while the legal possibility to look to, inter alia, general principles in treaty interpretation is clearly confirmed by Article 31 VCLT, the question remains as to under what circumstances such considerations may be taken into account and how they may impact upon treaty norms. Tribunals may simply wish to refer to extraneous norms to provide support to an interpretation which was already reached through analysis of a treaty alone. Such an approach is relatively uncontroversial. However, in cases where recourse to other rules in order to clarify the meaning of an ambiguous provision is merited, the controversy may be said to begin, since 'clarification' may itself be construed rather broadly. Going still further, the idea of employing extraneous norms to 'read into' a treaty additional rights or obligations, while a fairly common procedure in domestic fora, may be viewed with some scepticism at international level, at least by those who conceive of international law from a purely voluntarist point of view. Further, legal certainty and judicial self-restraint remain fundamental to the operation of a viable and trusted international legal system. Hence, somewhat scant use of the reasoning laid down in Article 31(3)(c) is perhaps unsurprising.

Nonetheless, it remains the case, as noted by Koroma J that 'the application of general international law on [treaty norms] forms part of the interpretation process which [the World Court] has been entrusted to carry out'.[38] Simma J agrees, citing the importance of 'the rules of general international law "surrounding" the treaty'.[39] Such a position seems com-

[36] 'Report of the Group Established by the ILC on the Fragmentation of International Law', Report of the 56th Session (2004) (A/59/10) 301.

[37] French (2006) (n 34) 301.

[38] *Oil Platforms (Iran v United States)* [2003] ICJ Rep 161, declaration of Koroma J.

[39] ibid, separate opinion of Simma J, [9].

pletely logical, since a contrary interpretation would render Article 31(3)(c) a dead letter. Orakhelashvili notes that the purpose of referring to such extraneous rules is, 'normally, not to defer the provisions . . . but to clarify the content', but nonetheless leaves open the possibility of treaty provisions being deferred by extraneous norms in limited circumstances.[40] This is certainly the case, for example where the extraneous rules in question constitute norms of *ius cogens*, and even the *lex specialis* principle will not operate to the exclusion of such norms.[41] As noted in the *Iron Rhine Railway* arbitration, such extraneous principles, particularly those capable of evolving interpretations, are considered particularly important when the treaty in question 'was not intended as a treaty of limited or fixed duration'. This would certainly be the case when discussing the UN Charter.[42] The matter of treaty interpretation is a well-travelled road in international legal scholarship, and I do not intend to make it the principal focus of this work. However, it is as well to be clear that the general rule on treaty interpretation does allow for the employment of extraneous norms, including general principles of law, in interpreting international treaties.

B. Use and Development of General Principles in Early International Arbitral Practice

Despite the above, it is clear that the application of general principles of law in one form or another was both frequent and prevalent in international arbitral practice before the advent of the PCIJ.[43] This was perhaps even more so the case then than in modern times, since as international law has continued to develop its other sources, principally in the form of a veritable explosion of multilateral treaty law, but also in terms of new forms of custom, the need for resort to general principles within well-developed branches of international law has decreased.[44] As explained above, judges are slow to refer to general principles to read new rights and obligations into treaties. However, this is not to say that the need for resort to general principles has disappeared, as recent judicial opinion makes clear.[45]

[40] A Orakhelashvili, 'Restrictive Interpretation of Human Rights Treaties in the Recent Jurisprudence of the European Court of Human Rights' (2003) 14 *European Journal of International Law* 537.

[41] *Oil Platforms* [2003] ICJ Rep 161, separate opinion of Simma J, [3]; and dissenting opinion of Al-Khasawneh J, [9].

[42] *Award in the Arbitration regarding the Iron Rhine ('Ijzeren Rijn') Railway between Belgium and the Netherlands* (2005) 27 RIAA 35, [80].

[43] See Lauterpacht (1927) (n 25); Cheng (1987) (n 2) 20.

[44] M Sorensen, 'Principes de droit international public, Cours Général' (1960) 101 *Recueil des Cours* 18.

[45] *Oil Platforms (Iran v United States)* (Judgment) [2003] ICJ Rep 161, separate opinion of Simma J, [65]–[74].

From the end of the eighteenth century to the 1920s, there occurred a proliferation of arbitral courts and tribunals, established to settle disputes between States. While the treaties covered by the jurisdiction of such tribunals inevitably varied, there was nonetheless a broad recourse to general principles, particularly in order to settle questions which were not satisfactorily covered either by the terms of the treaties in question or by the customary international law of the day. This occurred in three broad ways, which may be termed *infra legem, praeter legem* and, occasionally, *contra legem*. The use of general principles *infra legem* involves a situation where there are two possible solutions presented by the law at hand. In such cases, general principles may be used as a tool to decide which of the two possible legal solutions ought to be applied in a given case. General principles *praeter legem* supposes that there are lacunae within a legal system, and that general principles may be used to fill gaps in order to supplement the law and thus obviate the necessity of pronouncing a *non liquet*. General principles *contra legem* represents the most controversial and least well-known category in international law, namely the idea that in extreme circumstances, general principles may be employed to overturn or reject the application of laws based on the circumstances of the case at hand. This category is particularly controversial because it requires the judge or arbitrator to meet head-on the question of whether a law is just under the circumstances.[46]

In the early phases of international arbitration, frequent recourse was had to general principles of Roman law.[47] Later, when statutes were adopted, States laid down applicable law for tribunals, but the formulations for the law to be applied have varied, with phrases such as 'justice, equity and the law of nations';[48] 'the principles of justice, the law of nations and the stipulations of the treaty';[49] and proceeding upon 'the basis of respect of law',[50] amongst a myriad of others, being employed. Such broad terminology suggests that a strictly positivist construction of international law provided an insufficient legal basis for the settlement of all international legal disputes, and that the need was had for recourse to a further source of international law in addition to custom and treaty. It was clear that terminology such as 'general principles of law', 'principles of justice' and 'principles of equity' was employed in such treaties as denoting a legal source, in contradistinction to decisions taken *'ex aequo et bono'*, a

[46] C Rossi, *Equity and International Law: A Legal Realist Approach to International Decision Making* (Irvington, New York, Transnational, 1993) 9–10.

[47] Sorensen (1960) (n 44) 16.

[48] Article 7, Treaty of Amity, Commerce and Navigation between his Britannic Majesty and the United States of America, 19 November 1794.

[49] Article 4, Convention for the Adjustment of Claims of Citizens of the United States of America against Mexico, 11 April 1839.

[50] Article 15, Hague Convention of 1899 for the Pacific Settlement of International Disputes; Article 37, Hague Convention of 1907 for the Pacific Settlement of Disputes.

situation reflected exactly by the two successive Statutes of the World Court.[51] I shall now embark upon a brief examination of how such principles were applied in such tribunals prior to, and briefly, contemporaneously with, the establishment of the World Court, and what their content entailed in this period. It is evident that such a treatment must necessarily be illustrative rather than exhaustive in a study of this size. Bearing this in mind, I shall restrict myself to demonstrating that such a practice of resort to general principles did indeed exist, with the aid of a number of examples.

i. General Principles Infra Legem

Reasoning *infra legem* is without a doubt the most easily applicable and least controversial employment of general principles in international law. Despite the *desiderata* that the law be clear and not contradict itself, it occurs on an occasional basis that legal systems provide two competing possible solutions for a legal conundrum. When this happens, it frequently falls to judges or arbitrators to decide which course to choose. As well as canons of interpretation, the treatment of which lies outside the ambit of this chapter, the judge or arbitrator may be guided in his decision by the general principles of law. This theory fits in well with the image of general principles as a subsidiary source of international law

An important example of the above at international level is the principle of good faith, this principle being inherent in all domestic legal systems to some degree or another and having thus been carried into the international sphere. In the *Metzger and Co* case, it was held that 'It cannot be that good faith is less obligatory upon nations than upon individuals in carrying out agreements'.[52] In the *Venezuelan Preferential Claims* case, it was held that the principle of good faith 'ought to govern international relations'.[53]

ii. General Principles Praeter Legem

The application of general principles *praeter legem* is based upon the idea that the written or customary law may be incomplete in certain cases, and that in such cases – which the lawmaker failed to account for – the risk of a *non liquet* or the finding of a lacuna within the legal system may be avoided by resort to general principles. This device also fits well with the idea that general principles may be treated as a subsidiary source of international law.

[51] Raimondo (2008) (n 3) 10. See also M Akehurst, 'Equity and The General Principles of Law' (1976) 25 *ICLQ* 801, 801–02.

[52] *Metzger and Co (United States v Haiti)* [1901] USFR 262, 271.

[53] *Venezuelan Preferential Claims (Germany, United Kingdom and Italy v Venezuela et al)* (1904) Scott Hague Court Rep 55, 60.

A good example of the above device was demonstrated in *The Russian Indemnity Case*. Here, the Permanent Court of Arbitration denied that States have a right to assert a privileged status with respect to monetary debts due to their sovereign character. The Court drew a broad analogy with legal relations between private individuals and concluded that 'the general principle of the responsibility of States implies a special responsibility in the matter of delay of payment . . . unless the existence of a contrary custom is proven'.[54] Lauterpacht points out that since positive international law was silent upon this point, this was an exercise by the Court in gap-filling.[55]

The *Eastern Extension* case is another good example of an arbitral tribunal condoning the use of general principles as a gap-filling device. Here, the tribunal expressly condoned the use of equity for such purposes.[56]

iii. General Principles Contra Legem

As noted earlier, the employment of general principles as a motive for disregarding strictly positive law was and remains a controversial idea.[57] Nonetheless, the early arbitral awards make it clear that such a notion was not alien to the fledgling system of international justice. For example, in the case of *The Neptune*, settled as early as 1797 by the international arbitral tribunal established by the 1794 Jay Treaty, the court held that under the (now defunct) general principle of self-preservation belonging to States, a situation of necessity might allow for the setting aside of all written and customary law in certain circumstances, but that such necessity 'must be absolute and irresistible', thus establishing a very high threshold to be met, but nonetheless allowing for the possible operation of general principles of international law *contra legem strictum*.[58] This case was partly followed by an individual opinion of Anzilotti J in the PCIJ, where he noted that 'necessity may excuse the non-observance of international obligations'.[59] Such an approach is controversial in part because it strongly contradicts the idea that general principles are a subsidiary source of international law, and rather leans toward the suggestion that

[54] *The Russian Indemnity Case (Russia v Turkey)* (1912) 11 RIAA 421. See Raimondo (2008) (n 3) 14.

[55] Lauterpacht (1927) (n 25) 257–58.

[56] *Eastern Extension, Australia and China Telegraph Co Ltd (United Kingdom v United States)* (1923) 6 RIAA 112.

[57] See F Francioni, 'Equity in International Law' in R Wolfrum (ed), *The Max Planck Encyclopedia of Public International Law* (Oxford, Oxford University Press, 2008) paras 1–10.

[58] *The Neptune* (1797) 4 *International Adjudication Manuscripts* 372, 433. See also G Williams, 'The Defence of Necessity' (1953) *Crim LR* 216; and *Cas Louise Ménard* (1898) Correctional Court of Chateau-Thierry in H Legret, *Les jugements du Président Magnaud*, vol 1 (Paris, 1900) 14–15.

[59] *Oscar Chinn Case* PCIJ Rep Series A/B No 63, individual opinion of Anzilotti J, 113.

in certain instances they may have normative priority or hierarchy over positive law.

However, to what extent a case of necessity will allow for the setting aside of other law will depend heavily upon the underlying circumstances. In the *Faber* case, the German–Venezuelan Mixed Claims Commission set a rather high bar for the application of such a principle, which seems at odds with *The Neptune*. In a case concerning the shared use of an adjacent river, claimed by Germany as a right, the Commission held that

> [t]he rights of an individual are not created or determined by his wants or even his necessities. The starving man who takes the bread of another is nonetheless a thief, legally, although the morality of the act is so slight as to justify it.

The Commission concluded that, generally, the wants or necessities of one party cannot create legal rights for them, or infringe upon the existing rights of others.[60]

A general principle was held to alter the terms of a treaty in the *Affaire Yuille, Shortridge et Cie* in 1861. Here, the arbitral tribunal recognised restrictions to exist upon usurious interest rates by virtue of what it referred to as *'droit commun'*, since there was no applicable treaty or custom preventing such rates being charged at international level. Here, in filling the gap in international law *praeter legem*, the principle which was used to remedy this lacuna was applied *contra legem*, that is against the terms of the agreement in question.[61]

This judgment was reflected in the *Angola* case, heard before the Portugo-German Arbitral Tribunal, settled as late as 1928, which justified the notion of reprisals in international law in limited circumstances, on the basis of the same general principle of self-preservation, with the effect being one of

> self-help [*Selbsthilfehandlung*] . . . to suspend temporarily the observance of a particular rule of the law of nations in the relations between the two States . . . limited by the experiences of humanity and by the rules of good faith [*Treu und Glauben*], applicable in International Relations.[62]

Here it is germane to note that the setting aside of legal rules is tempered by the application of general principles such as good faith which continue to apply, even when the written law has been set aside. This suggests that general principles function *en bloc* and should not be separated from one another.

[60] *Faber case,* German-Venezuelan Mixed Claims Commission, [1903] Reports of International Arbitral Awards, vol 10 438–67.

[61] *Affaire Yuille, Shortridge et Cie* [1861] Arbitrage de la Commission designée par le Sénat libre de Hambourg, sentence du 21 octobre 1861. See also Raimondo (2008) (n 3) 11, who refers to this as a case of general principles *praeter legem* only.

[62] *Angola* (1928) 2 RIAA 1011, 1025–26. The translation is my own.

Further, in the *Georges Pinson* case, the presiding commissioner, JHW Verzijl, interpreted the role of the general principles associated with equity as rendering inapplicable the ordinary rules of international law regarding State responsibility and the exhaustion of remedies in certain circumstances.[63] A similar outcome had transpired in the earlier *Montijo* case, where the principle *nullus comodum capere de sua iniuria propria* (no one may profit from his own wrong) was applied.[64]

General principles have even been used to overturn other general rules in certain circumstances. In the *Finnish Vessels* case, the rule that one must exhaust local domestic remedies before resorting to international justice was held to be 'trumped' by the rule that States must carry out their obligations in good faith and that fraudulent fulfilment of such obligations corrupts the act in question. The respondent State must do real justice and must allow access to effective remedies, otherwise the rule will be set aside, and cannot be used as a shield.[65]

iv. General Principles, Generally

Verdross notes that arbitral awards before the advent of the PCIJ were broadly reflective of one another, and that the understanding of general principles in the various international courts and tribunals was consistent.[66] Even decisions which failed to uphold the existence of general principles often noted, obiter dictum or otherwise, that were such principles to exist in a given case, they could operate to fill gaps in, and temper the law, even going so far as to render otherwise permissible acts illegal.[67] The fact that resort to such principles was relatively widespread and that such principles were relatively consistently applied is little short of remarkable, insofar as the various arbitral courts and tribunals were located in different parts of the world, operating in different languages and in different areas of international law. Knowledge of comparative law as a discipline was in its infancy, and yet references to the fact that certain principles were part of 'universal jurisprudence', recognised by 'the legislation of all nations' were often used to justify the resort to particular general principles.[68] The adoption of common principles – such as the ultra vires doctrine for acts of State officials – were justified on the basis of 'logic' and 'justice'.[69]

[63] *Georges Pinson (France v United Mexican States)* (1928) 5 RIAA 327.

[64] *The Montijo* (1875) 2 Moore Intl Arbitrations 1421, 1437.

[65] *Finnish Vessels* (1934) 3 RIAA 1479, 1501.

[66] A Verdross, 'Les principes généraux du droit dans la jurisprudence internationale' (1935) 52 *Recueil des Cours* 207. Raimondo (2008) (n 3) 16 agrees with this.

[67] *Affaire du Capitaine Thomas Melville White* [1864] Décision de la Commission chargée, par le Sénat de la ville libre hanséatique de Hambourg, de prononcer dans la cause du Capitaine Thomas Melville White, date de Hambourg du 13 avril 1864. See also Raimondo (2008) (n 3) 12.

[68] See, eg the *Affaire du Queen, cf* Cheng (1987) (n 2) 327–28.

[69] Italian-Venezuelan Mixed Claims Commission, *Venezuelan Arbitration* [1903] 666, 680.

The normative nature of such general principles seems to have been a rather confused issue in these early awards. While the *infra legem* and *praeter legem* usage of general principles indicated something between a canon of judicial interpretation and a subsidiary source of law to be applied when the other rules 'ran out', the occasional applications *contra legem* ran very much contrary to this theory and pointed instead to normative hierarchy, albeit one which would only be applied in exceptional circumstances, usually in the interests of either necessity or a just outcome to the case. Also, successive judgments on the basis of general principles held that there was no distinction between the types of responsibility arising in international law depending on what source of international law has been breached in a particular case.[70] This would tend, if anything, to indicate normative equality between the various sources. There may be no doubt, however, that judges and arbitrators of this period were aware of the existence of general principles in the international legal order and were far from shy when applying them

a. The Drafting of the PCIJ Statute

It was with this legal landscape that the Advisory Committee of Jurists – assembled by the League of Nations to draft a statute for a new Permanent World Court – was faced. It was a landscape in which general principles had played a key role in the limited history of international adjudication, but where their normative value was disputable. It is therefore highly germane to examine the arguments advanced by these jurists as regards the sources of law to be applied by the new court, how they would be described in the 'sources' Article of the Statute and what would be the position as regards normative hierarchy, having already acquainted ourselves with the legal landscape of the day.

The debate as to the applicable sources of law began with the President of the Committee, Baron Descamps of Belgium, suggesting that the new Permanent Court ought to apply conventional law, international custom, and 'the rules of international law as recognised by the legal conscience of civilised nations', and 'international jurisprudence' (case law), in that order.[71] It is not entirely clear as to whether the phrase 'in that order' entailed normative hierarchy or suggested that if the judge were satisfied that the treaty in question was clear enough to apply directly, he ought not consider the import of customary international law or general principles on the case at hand.

[70] *Goldenberg Case (Germany v Romania)* (1928) 2 RIAA 901, 908. See also *Interpretation of the Treaty of Neuilly* PCIJ Rep Series A No 3, 8 (decision taken by the Chamber of Summary Procedure relating to Art 38(1) of the PCIJ Statute).

[71] PCIJ/Advisory Committee of Jurists (ACJ), *Procès-verbaux of the Proceedings of the Committee*, 16–24 June 1920 (The Hague, van Langhuysen, 1920) 306–18. (Hereinafter *Procès-verbaux*).

Elihu Root, of the United States, while not objecting to the inclusion of treaty and customary international law, said that he could not understand the exact meaning of Clause 3 ('the rules of international law as recognised by the legal conscience of civilised nations'). He wondered, based on the traditional voluntarist conception of international law, whether it was possible to compel States to submit their disputes to a court 'which would administer not merely law, but also what it deems to be the conscience of civilised peoples'.[72] However, Descamps countered that formulation reflected the fact that, as evidenced by earlier arbitral case law, such principles were already part of the international legal order, and this fact had not been met with widespread revolt by States. He termed them 'rules of objective justice', citing the principle of *res iudicata,* as upheld in the *Pious Fund Case*[73] by the Permanent Court of Arbitration as an example.[74] Lord Phillimore of the United Kingdom broadly agreed with this formulation, stating that 'generally speaking, all the principles of the Common Law are applicable to international relations. They are in fact part of international law'.[75] This was very much in tune with earlier arbitral awards, which had found many of the common law principles, including estoppel and equity, to have taken root in international law via the general principles category.

All of the members of the Advisory Committee were of the view that the position of the international judge ought to be the same as that of a national judge.[76] However, differences manifested themselves between the common law and civil law conceptions of the judge's office and role. Root argued that in accordance with a strict separation of powers, the PCIJ ought not possess the power to legislate. Therefore, a broad conception of what general principles might entail could not be entertained as it might lead to judicial prevarication bordering on legislative powers.[77] Phillimore broadly concurred.[78] However, Hagerup of Norway raised the spectre of a *non liquet* – the court being unable to pronounce upon a given question (and therefore denying justice to the parties to the case) by reason of a lack of applicable law – something which would be unthinkable for continental jurists.[79] He therefore proposed a broad understanding of general principles, in order to act as a 'catch-all' category, at least insofar as was necessary to fill in gaps which were left by custom and treaties. His

[72] *Procès-verbaux,* 293–94.
[73] *Pious Fund Case (United States v Mexico)* (1902) 9 RIAA 1.
[74] *Procès-verbaux*, 310, 318, 322–25.
[75] ibid, 316.
[76] ibid, 312–17, 333, 346. See Cheng (1987) (n 2) 16.
[77] *Procès-verbaux*, 309.
[78] ibid, 295, 311.
[79] ibid, 296.

position was, unsurprisingly, supported by fellow continental jurists Descamps,[80] Loder and de la Pradelle.[81]

As Cheng has noted, these divergences between the continental and Anglo-Saxon jurists reflect exactly the relative powers of the judge within each system. Within continental legal systems, strict limitations are, at the outset, placed upon judges, but then, through fear of restricting them to too great a degree, they are given complete and unabridged freedom to act within these limits. The common law system is different; the judge takes an oath 'to do justice according to law'.[82] In light of the ensuing debate, Root proposed as a compromise formulation 'the general principles of law recognised by civilised nations'. This was eventually accepted by all members of the Committee.[83] When pushed as to what such principles might entail, Phillimore said that by general principles of law, he understood 'maxims of law', which are part of international law and which are accepted *in foro domestico*, such as good faith, *res iudicata*, certain principles of procedure, et cetera.[84] No member objected to this formulation.[85]

It was stated that the application of such general principles had hitherto been a consistent practice of the international tribunals of the day, and although in doing so, such courts had occasionally brought 'latent' legal rules to light, they had never 'created' new rules: the members of the Committee were unequivocal in stating that a judge must never legislate. Furthermore, in answer to the objection that the application of such principles would be contrary to the purely voluntarist conception of international law, it was agreed that if a State consented to the settlement of its disputes in accordance with international law, it could not then complain if general principles were employed as part of that international law, since it had long been clear that general principles formed part of the *corpus* of international law.[86]

As regards the question of a hierarchy of sources, Ricci-Busatti of Italy said that the phrase *'dans l'ordre successif'* which had been part of Descamps' original proposal ought to be deleted. Ricci-Busatti took strong exception to the hierarchical arrangement of Descamps' original proposal. Much of his critique related to the notion of hierarchy itself, while another tenet argued

[80] ibid, 310–11, 324.

[81] ibid, 312.

[82] Cheng (1987) (n 2) 16.

[83] *Procès-verbaux*, 344.

[84] ibid, 316, 335.

[85] L Phillimore, 'Scheme for the Permanent Court of International Justice' (1920) 6 *Grotius Transactions* 89, 94.

[86] This line of reasoning was confirmed by the discussion of Art 38 by the Committees of the First Assembly of the League of Nations, where it was confirmed that the application of 'pure equity' (decisions taken *ex aequo et bono*) could not be placed upon the same footing as the application of such general principles, hence the separate formulation in Art 38(2), which requires special consent of both parties to be operable.

against Descamps' inclusion of 'international jurisprudence' as a source of law. Ricci-Busatti argued that the judge ought to consider the various sources simultaneously in relation to one another. Per Ricci-Busatti, the impression that the judge could not consider general principles till he had considered treaty and then custom was misleading, and if construed in such a way 'would be a misrepresentation of the committee's intentions'. He therefore argued that general principles should be placed upon an equal footing with custom and treaties, but was unable to purge the troublesome notion of hierarchy completely from the draft, despite the strong support of Hagerup.[87]

However, the Ricci-Busatti/Hagerup position was eventually to win the day. Their position was affirmed during the discussions in the Committees of the First Assembly of the League of Nations, where the delegates were strongly opposed to retention of the phrase *'dans l'ordre successif'*. It is debatable as to whether, even in Descamps' original formulation, a strict hierarchy existed at all, or at least whether this was what Descamps intended, but if it did, or if indeed an ambiguity existed, the formulation was transformed to allow for three principal sources of international law with normative parity, with decisions of international courts and teachings of leading scholars as a fourth, subsidiary, source.

It is worth noting that this decision was engineered by the League of Nations itself, by handing the duty of ratifying and streamlining the Draft Statute proposed by the Advisory Committee to its own Third Assembly Committee, which had been carefully composed of five of the original members of the Advisory Committee, but which was shorn of those who had argued to some degree for a reference to some sort of formal hierarchy, namely Descamps, Root and Phillimore.[88] With Hagerup as its chair and Ricci-Busatti as his deputy, the question of hierarchy was quickly resolved and all references to it removed.[89] This reflected the fact that the members of the League had chosen particularly those jurists who were plainly in favour of a rejection of the hierarchical model, and had therefore voluntarily and consciously abandoned the possibility of something more closely approaching a strictly voluntarist conception of the sources

[87] *Procès-verbaux*, 337–38.

[88] Root had, in particular, argued strongly against a prominent role for general principles in the Court's Statute, stating that 'The beginning must be modest; before conferring broad powers on the Court, it must first be permitted to justify the confidence in it which would warrant such an extension [of powers]'. *Procès-verbaux*, 308–09. Root was following the reasoning of John Salmond who had devised a theory of common law which divided legal sources into two parts, namely material and formal sources. Formal sources at international level would be constituted by treaty and custom. Material sources would be equivalent to the 'wellspring' from which these sources derive, a part of which would be general principles. See J Salmond, *Jurisprudence, or, the Theory of the Law* (London, Stevens and Haynes, 1902) 99–112. See also Rossi (1993) (n 46) 100–01.

[89] Rossi (1993) (n 46) 98.

of international law, and, in doing so had allowed general principles an equal footing.

Therefore, the mood amongst States at the time seems to have been that it was better to continue to apply international law as it had been applied by the international arbitral tribunals, assigning a prominent role to general principles. Indeed, subsequent arbitral tribunals referred to the PCIJ Statute as a means of justifying their resort to general principles, further reinforcing the idea that the PCIJ Statute did not merely reflect the sources of international law to be applied by the Permanent Court itself, but the sources of international law in general.[90] This may be interpreted as reflecting a broad contentment with the way in which general principles had been employed by the arbitral tribunals in the years preceding the enactment of the Statute and a wish that international judgments proceed in the same vein. Thus, the consent of the members of the League was given to a system of international norms a subset of which was out of their direct control when compared with customary and conventional law. It was on the basis of this law that the PCIJ would decide cases, with the final wording of Article 38 reading:

> The Court shall apply:
>
> 1. International conventions, whether general or particular, establishing rules expressly recognized by the contesting States;
> 2. International custom, as evidence of a general practice accepted as law;
> 3. The general principles of law recognized by civilized nations;
> 4. Subject to the provisions of Article 59, judicial decisions and the teachings of the most highly qualified publicists of the various nations, as subsidiary means for the determination of rules of law. This provision shall not prejudice the power of the Court to decide a case ex aequo et bono, if the parties agree thereto.[91]

b. The ICJ Statute

The PCIJ Statute was amended once, by the Protocol of 14 September 1929, but the changes to the text were largely superficial and affected in no way the content of the 'sources of law' clauses in Article 38.[92] While the machinery of the League of Nations was exposed as faulty by Mussolini's invasion of Abyssinia, Japan's incursions into Manchuria, and above all by its failure to prevent or contain the Second World War, the Permanent

[90] See, eg *Goldenberg Case (Germany v Romania)* (1928) 2 RIAA 901.

[91] Art 38, Statute of the Permanent Court of Justice, done 16 December 1920 at Geneva. Text available online at www.worldcourts.com/pcij/eng/documents/1920.12.16_statute.htm#_Toc160729737.

[92] Protocol for the Revision of the Statute of the Permanent Court of International Justice, done 14 September 1929 at Geneva. In force from 1 February 1936. Text available online at www.worldcourts.com/pcij/eng/documents/1929.09.14_protocol.htm.

Court was seen as the only organ which had fulfilled its mandate in an adequate manner and which ought to be retained with its powers and Statute largely unchanged.[93] As the war was drawing to a close, the Allied Powers began to make arrangements for a new international organisation to supersede and replace the League. This would eventually become the United Nations. A committee was established to give recommendations on the future of the PCIJ. As regards the sources of law to be applied by any court replacing the PCIJ, the committee commented that

> [t]he Law to be applied by the Court is set out in Article 38 of the Statute, and, although the wording of this provision is open to certain criticisms, it has worked well in practice and its retention is recommended.[94]

Thus, Article 38 was adopted once again, with the mere addition in the introductory stanza of the words 'whose function it is to decide in accordance with international law such disputes as are submitted to it'.[95] No new element was thus introduced to the sources of law Article, nor any deleted. The only change brought forth by the new words was an increased emphasis on the fact that the various rules and principles enumerated in Article 38(1) in fact constituted the sources of international law.[96] Also, the newly-enacted United Nations Charter prescribed, in its Article 92, that the ICJ Statute formed an integral part of the Charter itself, meaning that it applied to all Member States of the UN.

A position had thus been arrived at – with the approval of the PCIJ Statute – and had twice been confirmed – during the amendment of the PCIJ Statute and the approval of the ICJ Statute – by the international community, whereby 'the general principles of law recognised by civilised nations' would serve as one of the three sources of international law, on a foot of normative equality with international treaties and custom. However, the content of what this phrase might entail was not entirely clear. True, prior to, and for a time contemporaneously with, the PCIJ's existence, there had been frequent references to this category by the various arbitral courts and tribunals in existence at the time, and true, their interpretation of what was contained within this category was largely quite uniform. However, the advent of the League of Nations marked the beginning of a proliferation of new international treaties, and a period of rapid development of international law. Particularly in the years immediately subsequent to the Second World War, the diversification of inter-

[93] MO Hudson, 'The Succession of the International Court of Justice to the Permanent Court of International Justice' (1957) 51 *American Journal of International Law* 569.

[94] UN, 'Report of the Informal Inter-Allied Committee on the Future of the Permanent Court of International Justice' (10 February 1944) *British Parliamentary Papers Miscellaneous No 2* (Cmd 6531, 1944) 36, para 140.

[95] Article 38, Statute of the International Court of Justice (1945). Text available online at www.icj-cij.org/documents/index.php?p1=4&p2=2&p3=0.

[96] Cheng (1987) (n 2) 22 agrees with this position.

national law led to significant changes in the legal landscape, with international criminal law and international human rights law, to name but two branches, becoming integral and important elements of the international legal order. Therefore, rather than base any analysis of what the 'general principles' category entails purely upon pre-PCIJ arbitral judgments alone, it is certainly more useful to examine the judgments of the two incarnations of the World Court, and the opinions of leading scholars on their import, to establish what elements of this category are known to us.

III. GENERAL PRINCIPLES OF LAW IN THE WORLD COURT

The *procès-verbaux* of the Advisory Committee of Jurists agreed on certain principles as being exemplary of the 'general principles' category. These included *res iudicata*, the principle of good faith, certain principles relating to procedure,[97] the principle that what is not forbidden is allowed, the principle proscribing the abuse of rights, and the principle *lex specialis generalibus derogat*.[98] However, the conclusions of the Advisory Committee, while not irrelevant, and while largely founded upon the practice of the arbitral tribunals, cannot be cited in and of themselves as positive confirmation that such principles are part of the third source of international law. However, when searching for ICJ judgments that make explicit references to general principles as a source of law, the legal scholar has little material to go on.

A. General Principles by the Front Door: An Unpopular Source of Law?

While the World Court has had cause to utilise customary international law as an extraneous source in the interpretation of treaties,[99] the ICJ has only ever referred explicitly to general principles once in its judgments, and this was to rule out the application of a particular legal principle in the circumstances rather than to apply a general principle of law.[100] General principles have, however, been referred to rather more frequently in separate and dissenting opinions and in *ad hoc* judgments.[101] Nonetheless,

[97] *Procès-verbaux*, 335.

[98] ibid, 314–15, 337.

[99] See, inter alia, *Legal Consequences for States of the Continued Presence of South Africa in Namibia (South West Africa) notwithstanding Security Council Resolution 276 (1970)* (Advisory Opinion) [1971] ICJ Rep 16, 31, and *Case Concerning Gabčíkovo-Nagymaros Project (Hungary v Slovakia)* [1997] ICJ Rep 7, 67.

[100] *South West Africa* (Judgment) [1966] ICJ Rep 6, 47.

[101] Examples include: *Lighthouses in Crete and Samos* (Judgment) PCIJ Rep Series A/B No 71,

a distinctive break may be drawn between the frequent overt recourse to general principles by the arbitral tribunals and the visible reluctance on the part of the judges of the World Court to utilise general principles as a source of law, at least overtly.

The above trend is remarkable, insofar as leading scholars agree that there exists no normative hierarchy between treaty, custom and general principles. This being the case, and there being three distinctive sources of international law, one might expect each to be represented, if not equally throughout international judgments, then at least somewhat proportionately. That this is not the case leads one to pose the question as to why. Why were the PCIJ and ICJ so reluctant to explicitly refer to general principles? After all, 'interpreting a treaty through reference to other law permits a tribunal to ensure that the narrow application of a rule is not allowed to overcome broader notions of justice'.[102] This question is particularly interesting due to the fact that this reluctance has only come about since the advent of the World Court, and also because, as I shall illustrate later, the PCIJ and ICJ have in fact reached many important conclusions on the basis of general principles reasoning, but have disguised this fact through use of deceptive terminology and legal jargon, and have rarely been willing to admit that what they were doing had anything to do with the third source described in Article 38. However, legal scholars who have written past treatises upon the subject of general principles in the international legal order have failed to demonstrate why this was the case. The reason for this may be that there is no one obvious answer, and that any possible reasons which may be proffered are virtually impossible to prove. A number of possibilities present themselves, and the likelihood is that the reason why the Court has been so reticent in employing general principles as a base for its judgments is a *Gestalt* composed of all of them.

First amongst these is the unprecedented and rapid increase in the number of treaties concluded between States since the end of the First World War. The fact that these treaties were concluded between States, which themselves would have had to reconcile the treaties to the principles familiar to their own legal systems increases the likelihood that much of the spirit of 'the general principles of law recognised by civilised

separate judgment by Séfériadès J, 137–38; *International Status of South West Africa* (Advisory Opinion) [1950] ICJ Rep 128, separate opinion by Sir McNair, 148; *Anglo-Iranian Oil Co* (Preliminary Objection) [1952] ICJ Rep 93, dissenting opinion of Levi Carneiro J, 161; *Application of the Convention of 1902 Governing the Guardianship of Infants (Netherlands v Sweden)* (Judgment) [1958] ICJ Rep 55, separate opinion of Moreno Quintana J, 107; *Right of Passage Over Indian Territory* (Merits) [1960] ICJ Rep 6, separate opinion of Wellington Koo J, 66–67; *Temple of Preah Vihear (Cambodia v Thailand)* (Merits) [1962] ICJ Rep 6, dissenting opinion of Alfaro J, 42–43; *Legality of the Treat or Use of Nuclear Weapons* (Advisory Opinion) [1996] ICJ Rep 226, declaration of Fleischhauer J, 308–09; *Oil Platforms (Iran v United States)* (Merits) [2003] ICJ Rep 161, separate opinion of Simma J, 66–74.

[102] French (2006) (n 34) 286.

nations' would already be encapsulated in the treaty texts themselves. This proliferation of positive law also lessened the possibility of legal lacunae requiring resort to general principles *praeter legem*. So too, to an extent, with custom. It is unlikely (though not impossible) that States would develop an international custom with broad acceptance that was repugnant to general principles of law which were accepted by the vast majority of States. This being the case, resort to reasoning on the basis of general principles became less and less necessary, as particularly the increased codification of international law meant that legal questions which arose could increasingly frequently be settled by simple recourse to treaty law, occasionally with the aid of custom, and that since such norms were in broad accordance with the underlying general principle, there was no need to resort to the third source of international law in the circumstances.

The second reason why the World Court may have been reluctant to explicitly refer to general principles in its reasoning is the reaction which frequent resort to such a legal source might have provoked. While the arbitral tribunals had been established to deal with specific legal problems set around defined time periods and usually between only a small number of States in each case, and while even the Permanent Court of Arbitration required the specific consent of States to settle any matter referred to it, the World Court was equipped with an Optional Protocol, allowing for compulsory jurisdiction, to which it was hoped a good number of States would eventually accede. It would have been a strong disincentive to States to accede to the Optional Protocol if frequent instances occurred whereby, despite States having adopted what they interpreted to be a clear and firm stance regarding a given legal matter via the enactment of an international treaty or their participation in an international custom, the Court might see fit to apply a general principle in the matter, either instead of the treaty or custom, or in tandem with it, to reach a different result from that which the States had anticipated. The fall-out from the *Nicaragua* case, with the United States withdrawing their assent to the Optional Protocol in protest at the Court's somewhat 'original' interpretation of the reciprocity requirement contained therein demonstrates that State consent to the Optional Protocol – an important tenet of the Court's machinery – may be vulnerable when judgments are based upon grounds with which States do not agree.[103] It is obviously far less likely that a State will object to a custom or treaty in which it has actively participated than a general principle which goes against it.

The third reason for the World Court's trepidation is the palpable sense of conservatism which has pervaded the judgments of the PCIJ and ICJ

[103] *Military and Paramilitary Activities in and against Nicaragua (Nicaragua v United States)* (Jurisdiction and Admissibility) [1984] ICJ Rep 392.

since the foundation of the institution, and which has arguably become still more evident in recent years. By this, I mean the general reluctance of the Court to refer to any areas of international law or concepts contained therein which might be termed as 'controversial' in some way or another.[104] It has been noted elsewhere that the Court has been singularly reluctant to utter the words 'human rights'[105] or *'ius cogens'*[106] in its judgments, and it has been suggested that such conservatism has had political motives, owing to the sensitivity of the two concepts, their lack of universal acceptance (or at the very least universal accord as to their content), and the damage that a negative reception to their employment by the World Court in its decisions could do to the ICJ itself and international order in general. If this is true as regards *ius cogens* and human rights, there is no reason to suppose why it may not be so as regards general principles of law, since the same concerns may be levelled against this category of international legal norms as against the two aforementioned categories.

A final explanation may be proffered by reference to the German Historical School of jurisprudence. The basic premise of the German Historical School is that law is not to be regarded as an arbitrary group of regulations laid down by some authority. Rather, those regulations are to be seen as the historical expression of the convictions of the people, in the same manner as language, customs and practices are expressions of the people. The law is grounded in a form of popular consciousness called the *Volksgeist*.[107] This model may be seen to have parallels with regard to international law. Traditional international law is largely customary in nature, emerging from collective practice, and grounded in a shared consciousness expressed in 'the general principles of law recognised by civilised nations'. That this is so is due to the entire lack of a higher authority or lawgiver. International collective practice reflected the 'popular consciousness' of the States and their leaders. However, the *Volksgeist* theory, as pioneered by Friedrich Carl von Savigny, the most renowned author of the German Historical School, knew one major complication. There was, besides this old *Gewohnheitsrecht*, a great deal of German law which had not developed in this way. Aside from positive law, there was a significant

[104] This discounts the few obvious exceptions, such as the interpretation of reciprocity applied in the *Nicaragua* judgment, discussed above.

[105] JR Crook, 'The International Court of Justice and Human Rights' (2003) 1 *Northwestern University Journal of International Human Rights* 2; SM Schwebel, 'The Seminal Contributions of the World Court to the Law of Human Rights' (address to the International Bioethics Committee of UNESCO, Fifth Session, Proceedings December 1998); R Higgins, 'Human Rights in the International Court of Justice' (2007) 20 *Leiden Journal of International Law* 745.

[106] A Verdross, 'Jus Dispositivum and Jus Cogens in International Law' (1966) 60 *American Journal of International Law* 55; GA Christenson, 'The World Court and Jus Cogens' (1987) 81 *American Journal of International Law* 93.

[107] FC von Savigny, *Vom Beruf unserer Zeit für Gesetzgebung und Rechtswissenschaft* (Goldbach, Germany, Keip, 1814 reprinted 1997).

amount of modern Roman law, or *Pandektenlehre*, which could not be said to have grown out of German consciousness or to reflect their peculiar national character. 'Germanists' such as Otto von Gierke disputed the influence of such law, but 'Romanists' such as Savigny embraced it, arguing it played a pivotal role in shaping the historical development of law, inhering in the very nature of German historicism.[108] Savigny held that while law grew with the popular consciousness, a point arrived in each nation's history where a professional legal class emerges, which may use other sources to complement traditional laws, and which may move away from and re-shape the *Volksgeist*.[109] Here again, one may trace parallels with the international sphere. Written laws – other than bilateral treaties – represent a comparatively recent phenomenon on the international stage. However, this codification has only served to complement customary international law, not to supersede it. Indeed, customary international law continues to evolve, in accordance with the collective will of the States. The *Volksgeist* lives on, even if it has been complicated by this new wave of written law. The cleavage described above between the frequent resort to general principles by the early arbitral judgments and the opposite trend noticeable in the judgments of the World Court stems from the dilution of customary international *Gewohnheitsrecht* via the increased influence of new sources. The job of the ICJ is rendered more difficult by the fact that new forces are effecting a re-shaping of the global *Volksgeist*. This *Volksgeist* (or *Weltgeist*) – which may be treated as an approximate translation of a shared legal spirit, coming very close to 'the general principles of law recognised by civilised nations' – at international level is not a static phenomenon, and is not as easily accessible to the judges of international courts as previously, precisely because of the influence of international *Pandektenlehre*, which has diluted and diverted the *Weltgeist*, and which has rendered the job of accessing it all the more difficult.

As mentioned earlier, proving any of the proposed hypotheses – and there may be more – as to why the World Court has shied away from using general principles in its judgments would be near-impossible, since the Court has never publicly explained its reasoning in this regard. It may also be the case that the Court simply views general principles as a marginal source of law, which only rarely warrants application. However, such a theory would seem odd, given that general principles enjoy normative parity with treaty and customary law. Further, this position does not resonate with the practice of the Court itself, which has in fact had quite frequent recourse to general principles, but on an implicit rather than an overt basis.

[108] FC von Savigny, *Das Recht des Besitzes: Eine civilistische Abhandlung* (Giessen, Germnay, Heyer, 1803).

[109] FC von Savigny and OL Heuser, *System des heutigen römischen Rechts* (1840) Text available online at www.archive.org/stream/systemdesheutige01saviuoft#page/n3/mode/2up

B. General Principles by the Back Door

As Georg Schwarzenberger has noted, 'International courts and tribunals fight shy of laying bare the equitable and common-sense reasons on which, in fact, their interpretative work is based'.[110] While this aversion to outright candour has persisted through time, the World Court resorting to general principles by implicit means has constituted a regular feature of its practice almost since the PCIJ began to hear cases. This is hardly surprising. While concerns regarding consensualism preclude frank invocation of Article 31(3)(c) VCLT and through it, consideration of Article 38(1)(c) of the ICJ Statute, it was always clear that while interpreting treaties,

> by referring to other rules of law, a tribunal can seek to provide for a more just answer than one that a restricted interpretation might otherwise give. Of course this is most clear when the Court refers to notions of equity.[111]

Over the years, the PCIJ and ICJ have extensively referred to various general principles, including elements of equity in their judgments, albeit in a rather quiet manner. This has caused some disquiet in the World Court, with Buergenthal J in a separate opinion, critically opining that 'rules of international law cannot be brought [into legal disputes] through the back door'.[112]

In this section, I shall furnish a few brief examples of cases which have included references to principles included in this category, and how they have been applied. As French notes, 'there are numerous examples of where a tribunal relies upon "other" law, but without any clear attempt to clarify what it is doing or why it has done so'.[113] The study below is therefore not intended to be exhaustive, but merely to furnish a brief overview of certain principles which have been exposed by the World Court in its judgments and opinions. A more thorough treatment will be furnished in later chapters, relating principally to the principles of equity. However, the purpose of the examples outlined below is merely to illustrate that the PCIJ and ICJ, despite their noted reluctance to explicitly refer to 'the general principles of law recognised by civilised nations' by name, have been wont to refer nonetheless to general principles on a not infrequent basis, to use them as a legal source, and to base certain judgments upon them.

[110] G Schwarzenberger, *A Manual of International Law,* vol 1, 4th edn (London, Stevens and Sons, 1960) 153.

[111] French (2006) (n 34) 286.

[112] *Oil Platforms (Iran v United States)* (Merits) [2003] ICJ Rep 161, separate opinion of Buergenthal J, [28].

[113] French (2006) (n 34) 292.

i. Textual Interpretation

In the *Jaworzina* Advisory Opinion, the PCIJ interpreted a decision of the Conference of Ambassadors, which had been established to settle an on-going frontier dispute between Poland and Czechoslovakia in accordance with the principle of textual interpretation, referring repeatedly to the 'plain language' of the decision, and not according to the *eius est interpretare legem cuius condere* principle, which secondary documents had been produced to argue for. The decision was seen as being plain and clear (*acte claire* doctrine), and therefore secondary documents, which contradicted this account, were legally irrelevant.[114]

ii. The Principle of Self-Preservation

In *The Wimbledon*, before the PCIJ, the principle of self-preservation was discussed. While not upheld by the majority in the circumstances of the case, a dissenting opinion by Huber and Anzilotti JJ treated the principle in detail as a classic embodiment of State sovereignty.[115] While plainly the principle's ambits in international law have been limited somewhat since 1923 by the Briand–Kellogg Pact and the United Nations Charter, it is germane to note that the existence of this principle as part of the general principles *corpus* was acknowledged here. This was echoed by the classic dictum in *The Lotus* case, 'Restrictions upon the independence of States cannot therefore be presumed'.[116] Further, in the *Austro-German Customs Union* Advisory Opinion, Anzilotti in an individual opinion applied a necessary corollary of the principle, stating that according to ordinary international law, every State 'is free to renounce its independence and even its existence'.[117] Limits were placed upon such State rights stemming from sovereignty, however, with the PCIJ in the *Chevreau* case recognising that such rights, discretionary though they may be, 'must be exercised in good faith'.[118] In the same case, the Court noted that such discretion must not be exercised in an arbitrary manner[119] and that it must not be accompanied by unnecessary hardship or indignity to anyone it may affect.[120]

[114] *Question of Jaworzina (Polish–Czechoslovakian Frontier)* (Advisory Opinion) PCIJ Rep Series B No 8, 28, 30, 36. See also Raimondo (2008) (n 3) 23.

[115] 'The right of a State to adopt the course which it considers best suited to the exigencies of its security and to the maintenance of its integrity, is so essential a right that, in case of doubt, treaty stipulations cannot be interpreted as limiting it, even though these stipulations do not conflict with such an interpretation . . . This right possessed by all nations, which is based on generally accepted usage, cannot lose it's 'raison d'être simply because it may in some cases have been abused'. *The SS Wimbledon* PCIJ Rep Series A No 1, dissenting opinion of Anzilotti and Huber JJ, 36–37.

[116] *Case of the SS Lotus* PCIJ Rep Series A No 10, 18.

[117] *Customs Regime between Germany and Austria* (Advisory Opinion) PCIJ Rep Series A/B No 41, individual opinion by Anzilotti J, 59.

[118] *Chevreau Case (France v United Kingdom)* (1923) 2 RIAA 1113.

[119] ibid, 1123.

[120] ibid, 1123–24.

iii. Nemo Iudex in Re Sua

In the *Interpretation of the Treaty of Lausanne* Advisory Opinion, regarding the determination of the Southern frontier of Turkey with Iraq, the PCIJ utilised the principle of *nemo iudex in re sua* (no one may be judge in his own case) to interpret Article 5(1) of the Covenant of the League of Nations, since the instrument itself was silent as to whether the representatives of the interested parties could participate in the vote.[121] Further, as Raimondo has noted,[122] the application of the *nemo iudex in re sua* principle to settle the legal dispute before the World Court in this instance reflects a large degree of malleability and flexibility of the content, scope and applicability of general principles of law. This is so, because, although the purpose of this particular rule is to ensure the impartiality of the judiciary, the PCIJ saw fit to apply it in connection with a dispute before the Council of the League of Nations, a political organ of an international organisation.[123]

iv. Nullus Commodum Capere de Sua Iniuria Propria

In the *Chorzów Factory* judgment, reparations were due from Poland to Germany. Poland lodged an objection to the PCIJ's jurisdiction, amongst other reasons, because there were other courts in which the injured companies which were represented by Germany could assert their right to an indemnity.[124] The Permanent Court considered Poland's request in light of the Geneva Convention concerning Upper Silesia. Based upon this convention, the Court considered that it had jurisdiction in the case. It also invoked the *nullus commodum capere de sua iniuria propria* (no one may profit by his own misdeeds) principle in order to confirm the decision based upon Article 23 of the Convention.[125] This case shows that general principles may be used in tandem with other legal sources to reach a result.[126]

In the *Jurisdiction of the Danzig Courts* Advisory Opinion, the principle *nullus commodum capere de sua iniuria propria* was again applied. Here, a

[121] *Art 3(2) of the Treaty of Lausanne (Frontier between Turkey and Iraq)* (Advisory Opinion) PCIJ Rep Series B No 12, 27–32.

[122] Raimondo (2008) (n 3) 26.

[123] Since the UN Security Council is the closest organ to a direct successor to the League Council, this Advisory Opinion also raises the interesting question as to whether in international legal terms the Security Council may be deemed a sort of quasi-court, or at least a body possessing some degree of judicial functions. If the answer to this question is yes, then one may also ask whether it must abide by general principles of law concerning due process, etc.

[124] *Case concerning the Factory at Chorzów (Claim for Indemnity)* (Jurisdiction) PCIJ Rep Series A No 9, 25 *et seq*.

[125] ibid, 31.

[126] See also G Kaeckenbeeck, 'Upper Silesia and the League of Nations' (1946) 243 *Annals of the American Academy of Political and Social Science* 129.

treaty entitled the *Beamtenabkommen* regulated the employment conditions of Danzig railway employees who had, after the First World War, passed into the service of the Polish Railways Administration. Poland's contention that this treaty only created inter-State rights was rejected. The Court said that 'it cannot be disputed that the very object of an international agreement, according to the intention of the contracting Parties, may be the adoption by the Parties of some definite rules creating individual rights and enforceable by the national courts'. This being the case, Poland could not claim that the courts of the Free City of Danzig were not entitled to apply the provisions of the *Beamtenabkommen* simply due to its own failure to transpose the relevant provisions of the treaty into its national law. The Court therefore held that States may not make a profit from their own misdeeds.[127] This case was followed by Reed J of the ICJ in his dissenting opinion in the *Interpretation of Peace Treaties* Advisory Opinion. According to Reed, no government ought to be allowed to raise such legal objections which would 'let such a government profit from its own wrong'. Reed also raised the common law principle of estoppel, as a general principle of international law, to bolster his argument.[128] A similar principle, *ex turpi causa/delicto non oritur acto* – an unlawful action cannot serve as the basis for an action in law – had been applied by Anzilotti in a dissenting opinion in the *Eastern Greenland* case.[129]

v. Ubi Ius, Ubi Remedium

The *Chorzów Factory* affair did not end with the dispute over jurisdiction. In the judgment on the merits of the complaint, Poland argued that the convention in question did not provide for reparations, or indeed any remedy, in the event of non-fulfilment by one party of its obligations, and that therefore the Court could not impose such a remedy. The Court based its ruling in this matter on the principle *ubi ius, ubi remedium,* that is, that equity (justice) will not suffer a wrong to be without a remedy. The Court stated that

> [r]eparation is the indispensable complement of a failure to apply a convention, and there is no necessity for this to be stated in the convention itself . . . [it is] a general conception of law that any breach of an engagement involves an obligation to make reparation.[130]

[127] *Jurisdiction of the Courts of Danzig (Pecuniary Claims of Danzig Railway Officials who have Passed into the Polish Service, against the Polish Railways Administration)* (Advisory Opinion) PCIJ Rep Series B No 15, 26–27.

[128] *Interpretation of Peace Treaties* (Advisory Opinion) (Second Phase) [1950] ICJ Rep 221, dissenting opinion of Reed J, 244.

[129] *Legal Status of Eastern Greenland (Denmark v Norway)* PCIJ Rep Series A/B No 53, dissenting opinion by Anzilotti J, 95.

[130] *Case Concerning the Factory at Chorzów* (*Germany v Poland*) (Merits) PCIJ Rep Series A No 17, 29. The Court here repeatedly stated its preference for full and adequate restitution

The existence of this principle in international law may be held to have far-reaching consequences, as shall be discussed in later chapters.

vi. Ex Re Sed non ex Nomine

The *Chorzów Factory* (Merits) case is also notable for the dissenting opinion of Ehrlich J, who, commenting on the principle of good faith in international law, held that the principle *ex re sed non ex nomine* is a component of the good faith principle.[131] This maxim states that the law will look to the real state of affairs and not merely the legal form underlying it to determine the responsibility in each case. This principle is equivalent to the English common law dictum that 'equity looks to the substance rather than the form', and may also be held to have far-reaching consequences.

vii. Ius Necessitatis

The principle of *ius necessitatis* (the equivalent of the French *l'état de nécessité,* the German *Notstand,* and the Italian and Swiss *lo stato di necessità,* all of which are now codified, and the common law defence of necessity[132]), which had been recognised as early as 1797 by the arbitral tribunals, was upheld by Anzilotti in an individual opinion in the *Oscar Chinn* case,[133] but was refined by the *Serbian and Brazilian Loans* cases, which set rather a higher bar than the earlier arbitral award, almost equating the concept with the conditions necessary for a plea of *force majeure* rendering performance of the obligation to be set aside by reason of the *ius necessitatis* impossible.[134] While this principle does possess normative force at international level, then, its limits are extremely circumscribed and it may only be invoked when there is no other reasonable course of action. This mirrors the position in many national legal systems.

viii. Bona Fides

The principle of good faith was outlined again by Anzilotti in the PCIJ in the *Electricity Company of Sofia and Bulgaria* case. Relating to the denunciation of a treaty, Anzilotti held that 'While a party is free to denounce a treaty at any time, it should not do so immediately on learning that the

wherever possible – *restitutio in integrum* – but warned that measures needed to be taken to avoid compensating twice for any one wrong, echoing the English common law maxim that 'equity guards against double portions'.

[131] ibid, dissenting opinion of Ehrlich J, 87.

[132] See also G Williams, 'The Defence of Necessity' (1953) *Crim LR* 216.

[133] *Oscar Chinn Case* PCIJ Rep Series A/B No 63, individual opinion of Anzilotti J, 113.

[134] *Case Concerning the Payment of Various Serbian Loans Issued in France (Documents Relating to Judgment No 14)* PCIJ Rep Series C No 16-III, 306 (text in French).

other party wishes to invoke the treaty . . . otherwise it loses all practical effect'.[135] This is indicative of a broader trend toward the recognition of good faith generally in international law. As Cheng has pointed out, *pacta sunt servanda* 'is but an expression of good faith . . . without this rule, international law . . . would be a mere mockery'. Every right is the legal protection of some legitimate interest.[136] The recognition of good faith as a general principle was reinforced by the *Anglo-Norwegian Fisheries Case*, where the ICJ recognised the theory of abuse of rights (*abus de droit*) as part of the broader conception of good faith.[137] This was very much in the same vein as previous arbitral awards, where the Franco-Venezuelan Mixed Claims Commission had defined a treaty as 'a solemn compact between nations . . . [with] the same essential qualities as a contract . . . enhanced by the weightier quality of the parties . . . To be valid, it imports a mutual assent'.[138]

ix. The Acceptance of Indirect Evidence

In the *Corfu Channel* case, due to the extreme difficulties in gathering direct or first-hand evidence, the ICJ accepted indirect evidence. This was deemed acceptable because such practice 'is admitted in all systems of law', provided that it leaves 'no room for reasonable doubt'. On this basis, the Court saw fit to admit evidence by way of factual inference or circumstantial evidence.[139] This was a clear example of general principles *praeter legem*, since the Court saw fit to fill the gap in the relevant provisions in its Rules of Procedure with general principles. This judgment is of further relevance since it shows that the World Court conceives of general principles not belonging exclusively to national legal systems, but as common to 'all systems of law', although it is less clear exactly what this entails or how the ICJ reached this conclusion.

x. Res Iudicata

In the *Awards of Compensation by an Administrative Tribunal* case, the World Court ruled that the United Nations General Assembly did not possess the right to refuse to give effect to an award of compensation which had been decided upon by the United Nations Administrative Tribunal, since the Tribunal's Statute plainly stated that the award was final and could

[135] *Electricity Co of Sofia and Bulgaria* (Preliminary Objection) PCIJ Rep Series A/B No 77, dissenting opinion by Anzilotti J, 97–98.
[136] Cheng (1987) (n 2) 113, 122.
[137] *Anglo-Norwegian Fisheries Case (United Kingdom v Norway)* [1951] ICJ Rep 116, 142.
[138] *Maninat Case* (1902) Franco-Venezuelan Mixed Claims Commission [1905] Ralston's Report 44, 73.
[139] *Corfu Channel Case (United Kingdom v Albania)* (Merits) [1949] ICJ Rep 4, 18.

not be appealed against.[140] The Court stated that in accordance with 'a well-established and generally recognised principle of law', a judgment passed by a judicial body is *res iudicata* and is therefore binding upon the parties to the dispute.[141] This opinion closely followed those of the early arbitral tribunals related to cases of *res iudicata*.

xi. Lex Specialis Derogat Legi Generali

In the *Right of Passage* case, the ICJ discussed India's obligation to allow Portugal – or rather more accurately, the agents of Portugal – through its territory. Portugal founded its claim on a bilateral custom, general customary international law, and subsidiarily on general principles of law relating to rights of passage over the territory of another, presenting a detailed comparative law research project, covering 64 different domestic legal systems from different legal families encompassing a variety of similar general principles at national level.[142] The ICJ decided not to examine the general principles argument in this instance, or indeed general custom, given that a special bilateral custom regulated this area in the past. Raimondo argues that this case is particularly important, since it shows that general principles as a legal source may be held to be subsidiary insofar as *lex specialis derogat legi generali* – itself a general principle – applies.[143] This may well be the case in the majority of circumstances, but it is in fact the nature of certain general principles (in particular certain principles of equity insofar as they apply in international law) that they – despite being classified as general principles – may in fact derogate specific provisions of law in certain circumstances. This will be discussed in depth in later chapters, so it is as well not to dwell on it here. One further point may be made about the *Right of Passage* case, and that is that despite the fact that the majority of the judges chose not to dwell on the general principle of a right of passage over the territory of another for the reasons outlined above, one judge, Wellington Koo J did so, in a dissenting opinion, and saw no difficulties in transposing the principle into international law.[144]

xii. Actio Popularis

In the 1966 *South West Africa* judgment, the legal principle at stake was the Roman law idea of *actio popularis*, the ancient idea that any (male) member

[140] *Effect of Awards of Compensation made by the United Nations Administrative Tribunal* (Advisory Opinion) [1954] ICJ Rep 47.

[141] ibid, 53.

[142] *Right of Passage over Indian Territory* (Merits) [1960] ICJ Rep 6.

[143] Raimondo (2008) (n 3) 30.

[144] *Right of Passage over Indian Territory* (Merits) [1960] ICJ Rep 6, dissenting opinion of Wellingtom Koo J, 66.

of society could bring an action relating to any legal matter, provided it was in the interest of public welfare. The ICJ examined the argument that, as a safeguard for the performance of the mandates which had been conferred by the League of Nations that each Member State of the League, and later of the United Nations, could have a stake in the matter, and that ultimately this would confer the right upon each State to take action *pro bono publico* in the matter before the Court. The ICJ rejected this argument, on the basis that the *actio popularis* principle was only accepted in a limited number of domestic legal jurisdictions.[145] This case demonstrates that a broad plurality of States must recognise a general principle before the World Court will consider it as a candidate for 'the general principles of law recognised by civilised nations', one of the few concrete elements of a 'test' for general principles that the Court has explicitly set out.

IV. CONCLUSION

From a cursory examination of past case law of the World Court, one may proffer certain tentative conclusions. First, it is difficult to find examples of clear usage of general principles in *dispositif* judgments in recent years. One is more likely to find them in dissenting or separate opinions. This, however, still indicates that they are being factored into judicial reasoning, or at least that of certain judges. Secondly, it is far from clear in reading the judgments how the PCIJ and ICJ have identified general principles. There seems to be no clear formula, or if such a formula does indeed exist, it is one which has never been made public. Thirdly, there has been a marked reluctance to refer to 'general principles of law recognised by civilised nations' by their proper name. Instead the Court has resorted to numerous euphemistic terms in order to communicate the same concept. Examples include 'traditional principle' (*Jaworzina*); 'principles generally accepted' (*Chorzów Factory*, Jurisdiction); 'a general conception of law' (*Chorzów Factory*, Merits); 'the well-known rule' (*Interpretation of the Treaty of Lausanne*); and 'a well-established and generally recognised principle of law' (*Awards of Compensation by an Administrative Tribunal*). However, in the *Right of Passage* case, the Court did refer to 'general principles of law recognised by civilised nations', although it did not base its judgment on such principles. Similarly, in the *South West Africa* (Second Phase) judgment, the Court referred to 'general principles of law' but failed to uphold such principles in the circumstances. If one may draw a tentative conclusion from such practice, it is that the recognition of the existence of the general principles category by the Court in its judgments is, of itself, uncontroversial, but the usage of such general principles as a legal basis

[145] *South West Africa* (Second Phase) (Judgment) [1966] ICJ Rep 6, 46–47.

on which to found a judgment is something which the Court is far more reluctant to do. Cheng and Raimondo have both noted a strong willingness by the Court to uphold principles already used by arbitral tribunals in their judgments.[146] No one reason can aptly explain the relative paucity of references to general principles in recent years in ICJ judgments and opinions, but one may be certain that simply because general principles have not been *en vogue* of late is not to say that they have lost any normative force. Rather, it is clear that in the absence of a re-conceptualisation of the sources of international law, general principles will continue to retain their normative equality with treaties and custom.

However, despite having shown the existence of general principles as a normative source and their suitability for use by the World Court, the limited explanations proffered by the Court fail to adequately explain how such principles are arrived at, where they come from, and what the phrase 'the general principles of law recognised by civilised nations' actually means, leaves the extent and potential usefulness of an important source of international law at least partially unclear. This lack of clarity is disappointing insofar as it is difficult to reach any broad conclusions about how general principles may be employed in the tackling of difficult legal issues.

It is worth reiterating that treaty interpretation is as much a matter for States as it is for courts. States are also under an obligation to interpret their rights and duties in light of extraneous legal sources such as general principles of law. If one would expect States to understand their treaty obligations in terms of subsequent agreement and practice (Articles 31(3)(a) and (b)), then there would seem to be no reason why the same should not apply re 'any relevant rules of international law', qua Article 31(3)(c). Even the principal critiques of the usage of extraneous legal sources in the interpretation of treaties before the World Court have focussed upon the fact that doing so exceeded the Court's jurisdiction, arising from individual treaties.[147] Such arguments, whether right or wrong, can and should not hamper States in interpreting treaties for determining the legality of acts.

From the point of view of this study, it is worth recalling that any proposed solution to the humanitarian intervention debate must be based upon solid legal foundations, since this is precisely where past proposals have foundered. Clearly the humanitarian intervention conundrum cannot be solved by reference to principles such as good faith, *pacta sunt servanda* et cetera *in abstracto*. It is necessary to demonstrate how such principles have actively been dynamically employed to tackle complex

[146] Cheng (1987) (n 2) 29–394; Raimondo (2008) (n 3) 35.

[147] *Oil Platforms (Iran v United States)* [2003] ICJ Rep 161, separate opinion of Buergenthal J, [22]–[24].

legal issues, how far they may be stretched, and for what reasons the principles came into being in the first place, before one can build upon them.

The crux of the humanitarian intervention debacle in legal terms is one of legal rigidity. The rigidity of the United Nations Charter, insusceptible to reform, is ill-adjusted to take account of gross human rights violations and its machinery is inconsistent with the effective protection of human rights when such effective protection requires the use of force by States, and when the Security Council will not sanction such action. The following chapter will set about examining a series of general legal principles, many of which originate in the common law legal system, and which were devised specifically to deal with legal rigidity. I will take a close look at these principles – the principles of equity – and ask whether and to what extent these principles have been applied across the world's legal systems, so that they may themselves be qualified as 'general principles of law recognised by civilised nations' and may thus be effective at international level.

3

Equity as 'General Principles' in the Legal Systems of 'Civilised Nations'

I. INTRODUCTION: A BAYONET TO PRICK THE CONSCIENCE

AS OUTLINED EARLIER, the 1999 NATO intervention in Kosovo was contemporaneously accompanied by a period of reticence from many international lawyers, who were reluctant to discuss the *strict* legality of the operation.[1] As discussed in chapter one, many of those who proffered comment upon the matter couched their analyses in terms of 'classical international law'[2] or 'traditional international law'.[3] This characterisation was accompanied to a 'turn to ethics' and various other attempts to advance apologist theories based on morality, politics, or near-legality. The rationale which explains this phenomenon is that it is clear from the UN Charter that any affirmation of the strict legality of NATO's activities could be disproved by any lawyer with consummate ease.

When attempting to decide upon the legal status of humanitarian intervention, the legal provisions to which international lawyers had recourse were, naturally enough, the general prohibition on the use of force enshrined in Article 2(4) of the UN Charter and its two widely accepted derogations, the inherent right to self-defence under Article 51, and collective action under Chapter VII of the Charter. Since humanitarian intervention *qua* Kosovo could not fall under either of these two explicit exceptions, it was, seemingly, abundantly clear that the UN Charter prohibited humanitarian intervention.

Why therefore the notable reluctance on the part of international lawyers at the time of the Kosovo crisis to avow this easily comprehensible state of affairs? The answer, as noted in chapter one, is the unpalatable results that stem from such an avowal. In case of a Security Council veto

[1] M Byers and S Chesterman, 'Changing the Rules about Rules? Unilateral Humanitarian Intervention and the Future of International Law' in JL Holzgrefe and RO Keohane (eds) *Humanitarian Intervention: Ethical, Legal and Political Dilemmas* (Cambridge, Cambridge University Press, 2003) 177.

[2] See, eg C Greenwood, 'Yes, but is the war legal?', *Observer*, London, 28 March 1999.

[3] See J Habermas, 'Bestiality and Humanity: A War on the Border between Legality and Morality' (1999) 6 *Constellations* 263, 264, who uses the term 'classical international law'.

by one of the five Permanent Members, blocking any prospect of a Resolution permitting action under Chapter VII, an adherence to the central tenets of the modern international legal regime, namely respect for State sovereignty, non-interference and the prohibition on the use of force will in fact serve to prevent action which most people would believe to be warranted and which could result in the saving of a great many lives. Being an apologist for unobstructed ethnic slaughter leaves a bitter taste in the mouth.

The particular temporal context of the Kosovo intervention may also play a part. The 1990s had witnessed gross human rights abuses, including the genocides in Rwanda and at Srebrenica. Mass media had made the world aware of the inaction or inadequate action of the UN Security Council, and the consequences which had resulted from this. International lawyers were, therefore, reluctant to adhere to a positivist interpretation of the legal framework on the use of force and, in doing so, condemn an action, which, while prima facie illegal, was perceived as having saved lives. To borrow the words of Bruno Simma, 'could it not be that "humanitarian interventions" now undertaken in the spirit of ensuring that Srebrenica does not happen again, as it were, deserve a friendlier reaction on the part of international lawyers?'.[4] The age-old *Kulturkampf* between morality and law was transferred to the international scene.

This battle is not a new phenomenon. It may be described as the central continuing argument of legal philosophy. Positivists such as Jeremy Bentham, John Austin and HLA Hart have long since argued for the rejection of any confusion of 'what is' and 'what ought to be'.[5] Conversely, natural lawyers, such as St Thomas Aquinas, Hugh Kennedy and Lon Fuller argue, in varying degrees, that a higher law or morality must regulate the lawmaker in his draughtsmanship, and those laws and legal regimes which fall too far foul of this basic morality are void – *lex iniusta non es lex*.[6]

International law is a phenomenon which is heavily criticised by several schools of international relations theory, notably Neo-Realism. Neo-Realists claim that the influence exerted upon international affairs by the United Nations, and indeed, international law in general, is a minimal one, itself a

[4] B Simma, 'NATO, the UN and the Use of Force: Legal Aspects' (1999) 10 *European Journal of International Law* 1, 5.

[5] See J Austin, *The Province of Jurisprudence Determined* (London, J Murray, 1832) (text available online at www.worldcat.org/oclc/58975674); J Bentham, *The Limits of Jurisprudence Defined* (New York, Columbia University Press, 1945); HLA Hart, *The Concept of Law* (London, Clarendon, 1961).

[6] See T McDermott (ed and tr) and T Aquinas, *Summa Theologiae – A Concise Translation* (Westminster, Maryland, USA, Christian Classics, 1989, originally published in 1274); L Fuller, *The Morality of Law*, revised edn (Cambridge, Yale University Press, 1964); and H Kennedy, in his opinion as Chief Justice in *State (Ryan) v Lennon* [1935] IR 1, and his introduction to L Kohn, *Die Verfassung des Irischen Freistaats* (Tübingen, Archiv des öffentlichen Rechts, 1928) 1–16.

mere by-product of State power games, the ultimate goal of which is to improve one's own position at the expense of one's neighbour. Therefore, it has fallen to international lawyers to defend their discipline in recent decades, to reinforce its inherent value and worth, as it were, in the face of Realist assertions that States will only obey international law when it is in their selfish self-interest to do so. This affirmative role is predicated upon being able to point to written stipulations or interdictions to enforce rights and obligations upon States and other parties. Customary law may also be used as a source, but it is certainly relatively unpopular to appeal to sources outside those enunciated by Article 38(I) of the ICJ, such as the 'law of God' or the 'law of reason'. This is perhaps also due to the fact that such conceptions suggest an inherent subjectivity, perhaps commonly held within each culture, and perhaps even within whole regions – a national *Volksgeist* as Savigny would have it – but surely no common worldwide connotation beyond the most cursory and abstract principles.

Nonetheless, despite the above trends, and despite the fact that the NATO Member States effectively did as they pleased in Kosovo, paying scant heed to their international legal obligations, either in terms of general international law or international humanitarian law, few international lawyers were wont to condemn their actions as downright illegal. The affirmative positivist trend did not extend this far. Perhaps this is a lesson from history. Gustav Radbruch fervently believed that a too-strict adherence to positivistic philosophy in pre-National Socialist Germany enabled a smoother route to dictatorship and the gross levels of abuses which followed.[7] It is open to debate whether Radbuch was justified, but Allen Buchanan echoed Radbruch's sentiments nearly 60 years later in his rejection of 'legal absolutism', the view that 'it is virtually never justifiable to violate international law or at least not the most basic norms of international law, even for the sake of protecting Human Rights'.[8] However, given the leaning toward affirmative positivist rhetoric amongst the international legal community in the face of the taunts of international relations scholars, it required in both historical contexts a show of armed force combined with human suffering to prick the conscience of legal scholars. Pre-war, Radbruch had been a revered German positivist. Similarly it is germane to note how in the aftermath of the NATO operations in Kosovo, pricked consciences have transformed erstwhile positivists into fervent apologists for humanitarian intervention. This was achieved by a myriad of means, including attempting to separate the legality of the operation from its 'legitimacy' (Kosovo Report); attempting to brand it legal *simpliciter* (Robin Cook and Jeremy Greenstock); exploring 'the exception' in international law (Martti

[7] G Radbruch, 'Die Erneuerung des Rechts' (1947) 2 *Die Wandlung* 8, 8–10.
[8] A Buchanan, *Justice, Legitimacy, and Self-Determination: Moral Foundations for International Law* (Oxford, Oxford University Press, 2004) 441.

Koskenniemi); or formulating morally acceptable ways to disobey, and in time hopefully reform, international law (Allen Buchanan). I could go on.

II. LEGAL RIGIDITY AS THE CRUX OF THE PROBLEM

All of the formulae described above attempted to resolve the same problem, namely that international lawyers wished to find a solution which would broadly accommodate respect for international law, and at the same time ensure adequate – and above all effective – respect for human rights. It was a futile attempt to 'eat one's cake and have it too', in my opinion, since none of the authors of these theories achieved their goal and reconciled the commands of their consciences with the letter of the law. The law just could not be stretched that far, and in moving away from law and into other domains, they opened the door for abuse of their formulae by the unscrupulous. It remains to propose an alternative formulation which might better deal with the situation. I propose to look to the law itself, and above all to its past efforts in dealing with such problems, in order to chart a way forward.

The foundation of the humanitarian intervention debate may be summarised in the following form:

The rigidity of the statutory instrument (the UN Charter, governing the use of force by States, and the *ius cogens* nature of the norms involved) *and the factual likelihood that it will not soon be reformed* (due to the interests of powerful States in preserving the status quo) *result in a situation where a recognisably unjust result may occur* (gross human rights violations) *without the possibility of an effective solution which exists being legally achievable* (this being humanitarian intervention).

It strikes me in examining this formulation that the kernel of the problem rests in the rigidity, inflexibility and stagnation of the statutory instrument at hand. The United Nations Charter was drafted at a time when human rights occupied a distinctly peripheral role in international law. This situation has known significant change in the past 60 years, to the extent that the human rights domain now constitutes one of the most important tenets of the international legal system. However, the inadaptability of the United Nations Charter, and, in particular, the impossibility of any concord amongst the Member States on reforms to the regime governing the use of force by States means that an impasse has been reached.

Legal rigidity is not a new problem. It has been dealt with in the past in various domestic legal systems. What surprises me is that the assortment of solutions proposed by the various international lawyers and politicians above discussed did not touch upon a solution which had proved effective in a variety of disparate legal regimes across the world in resolving problems wrought by legal rigidity impinging upon the achievement of just results. The solution to which I refer is equity.

In national legal systems throughout the world, equity in one form or another has served to soften the rigour of strict law. I propose to examine whether systemic trends may be traced between different national legal orders, and whether analogous equitable general principles may be observed in a broad plurality of legal systems. If such principles do indeed exist, it may be the case that they can be qualified as 'general principles of law recognised by civilised nations', which, per Article 38(1), constitute the third principal source of international law. If this indeed is the case, then such equitable general principles may be used in an analogous manner in the international legal arena to that in which they are used in national legal systems. If such principles are indeed identified as having normative life at international level, they could potentially play a key role as a tool to deal with legal rigidity in international law. However, before using this tool, it will be necessary to determine its existence, in the first instance via a detailed examination of equity in national law. It is to this analysis that I now turn.

A. Equity as a Panacea: The History of Equity in the Common Law

In sixteenth-century Tudor England, a long drawn-out process began to solve a problem which had beset the English judiciary system for some time. In order to undertake legal proceedings, any plaintiff was required to submit a 'writ'. Writs were only available for certain offences (trespass, trespass to the person and battery being examples), while for other wrongs committed, no writs were procurable. Judges had attempted to create new writs, but had been prohibited from doing so by the 1258 Provisions of Oxford and subsequent orders from the monarch, who was ill-disposed towards legal reform.[9] A common practice of lawyers was to attempt to 'shoehorn' wrongs committed into standard writs, but since the writs prescribed the elements necessary for such wrongs to be committed, such actions were usually defeated; resulting in disappointed parties who were unable to recover any compensation for wrongs suffered. This situation was compounded by the fact that the monetary damages which were generally payable as compensation were often insufficient (as the level of such damages would be determined by statute rather than by the judge himself), or completely unsuitable (when the owner would have preferred the return of a stolen object which was precious to him, for example). The legislative and executive were indisposed toward legal reform, thus the system of writs persisted. In essence:

[9] C Rossi, *Equity and International Law: A Legal Realist Approach to International Decision Making* (Irvington, New York, Transnational Publishers Inc, 1993) 36.

The rigidity of the statutory instrument (the laws of England and in particular the writs system) *and the factual likelihood that it will not soon be reformed* (due to the interests of the Crown in preserving the status quo) *result in a situation where a recognisably unjust result may occur* (uncompensated damage) *without the possibility of an effective solution which exists being legally achievable* (specific performance of the legal obligations defaulted upon or restitution to remedy the wrong committed).

Due to dissatisfaction with the justice furnished by the common law courts of England, legal historians have cited fears in England of a reception of the Roman law to supplement, or even oust, the common law.[10] Scholars at the pinnacle of the English legal profession at the time, including Starkey, debated the issue, Starkey being in favour of the reception as he did not feel the common law represented purely enough common conceptions of morality at the time – namely divine and natural law – specifically complaining that the English principles of guardianship and primogeniture were unreasonable.

The increasing importance of the need to find a solution to the inflexibility and inadequacy of the common law statutes was highlighted by the near-anarchy which resulted in the wake of the War of the Roses, due to the urgent need to restore law and order unencumbered by common law procedures and unreliable juries.[11]

In the end, the solution came from within the system itself. There had long existed the possibility of a special appeal to the King (or, as it was called, to the conscience of the King), via an individual petition in the wake of a result at common law that was manifestly unjust. The King would then proceed to decide on the basis of justice, whether to entertain the submission of the plaintiff, and if such submission might succeed, what remedy to award or impose. The remedy awarded by the King would not be limited by statute and could also take the form of specific restitution or performance of an obligation, and not merely the payment of monetary damages, as was the case with the regular common law courts. This system was predicated upon the medieval notion that the Prince, who is not subject to positive law, retains power to intervene to enforce a natural obligation for which the positive law is unable to provide a remedy.

Due to the instability discussed above, combined with the patent failure of the common law to meet the needs of an increasingly commercial economy, dissatisfaction with justice at common law grew amongst the population and resort to individual appeals to the monarch grew in popularity exponentially. Since such activities were encroaching too severely upon

[10] S Prall, 'The Development of Equity in Tudor England' (1964) 8 *American Journal of Legal History* 9.

[11] ibid, 12.

the King's time, he delegated the responsibility for dealing with such pleas to the Lord Chancellor. In time, this also became too much work for the Lord Chancellor and his assistant the Master of the Rolls, and a separate system of courts of conscience, the Courts of Chancery, were created. They functioned separately as an alternative to common law courts for three centuries,[12] until the Union of Judicature Acts 1873 and 1875, combined the two jurisdictions.[13] The central tenet of the Acts was that in a situation of conflict between equity and the law, equity would prevail. Ever since, equity has functioned as a 'softening' influence on legal rigidity, both in England and other common law jurisdictions.

i. The Nature of Common Law Equity

It is important to realise that while equitable jurisdiction developed as a means of mitigating the harshness of the common law, one must nonetheless stress that equity's functioning was dependent upon the framework which the common law provided. In the words of Lord Denning, 'Equity comes in, true to form, to mitigate the rigours of strict law'.[14] Furthermore, one of the hallmarks of the remedies which equity creates is that they are discretionary in nature, and will only come into operation when the justice and circumstances of the case in question demand it. As Greene MR pointed out, in common law, if such injustice leading to a claim in equity exists, 'it must be shown to have an ancestry, founded in history and in the practice and precedents of courts administering equity jurisdiction'.[15] Such a formulation, rooted in law and legal practice, was undoubtedly necessary to guard against wanton subjectivity on the part of judges when dealing with the flexible doctrines of equity. After all, it is clear that principles of certainty and consistency form an integral part of the fair administration of justice. While it is doubtless true that the precise circumstances in which equity may be permitted to intervene may well evolve as time goes by, the underlying rationale for its intervention – rectifying injustices arising from the strictures of the law – remains the same.[16]

[12] See the *Earl of Oxford's Case* [1615] 1 Rep Ch 1.

[13] These acts were mirrored by similar provisions in other common law jurisdictions. For example, S 28(11) of the Supreme Court of Judicature (Ireland) Act 1877 stipulated that where any conflict arose between the principles of equity and those of the common law, the equitable rule was to prevail.

[14] Lord Denning MR in *Crabb v Arun DC* [1976] Ch 179, 187, [1975] 3 All ER 865.

[15] Lord Greene MR, in *Re Diplock* [1948] Ch 465, 481–82.

[16] H Delany, *Equity and the Law of Trusts in Ireland,* 3rd edn (Dublin, Thomson Roundhall, 2003) 2. Millett agrees: 'The traditional objects of equity have not changed: to relieve against mistake, fraud, accident and surprise; to protect the weak from exploitation and trust and confidence from betrayal; to prevent the unconscionable assertion of legal rights; and to give relief against every kind of unconscionable conduct. It demands not merely honesty and a willingness to meet one's commitments, but integrity, good conscience and fidelity'. P Millet, 'Equity – The Road Ahead' (1995) 9 *Trust Law International* 35, 36–37.

The fusion that was accomplished by the 1873 and 1875 Acts between the common law and equity led to a certain level of confusion within the legal community of the day as to whether the fusion was purely of a procedural nature, or whether one might genuinely speak of a combined system. Historically, equitable remedies had been discretionary, and applied *in personam,* whereas common law remedies were prescribed by statute, and acted *in rem*. For a time, Lord Ashburner's classic statement on the situation represented the standard position: 'The two streams of jurisdiction, though they run in the same channel, run side by side and do not mingle their waters'.[17] However, Ashburner's position has been changed somewhat by the continuous evolution within the common law, which was expressed by Lord Diplock in the case of *United Scientific Holdings Ltd v Burnley Borough Council.*[18] Diplock's view was that the distinctions between common law and equitable duties had ceased to matter 'a jot', and were no longer of any great consequence.

However, while it is undoubtedly true that the *in personam* versus *in rem* distinction has become so blurred as to matter little anymore, it is worth remembering,[19] as Hilary Delany points out, that the distinction between legal and equitable rights and remedies has not been completely washed away, since, for example 'to obtain an equitable remedy, a litigant must rely upon the court's discretion, whereas if he seeks a common law remedy, once he has established that a right existing at common law has been breached, a remedy will be granted'.[20] However, not merely in England, but throughout the common law sphere, there have been signs in recent judgments that courts are increasingly sceptical of any suggestion of a separation of the two concepts. In England, Lord Diplock damned Asburner's dictum as 'both mischievous and deceptive', stating that if the 'fluvial metaphor is to be retained at all, the waters of the confluent streams of law and equity have surely mingled now'. In his view, since the Judicature Acts of the 1870s, 'the two systems of substantive and adjectival law formerly administered by courts of law and courts of equity . . . were fused'.[21] This view has found favour, inter alia, in New Zealand,[22] and in Ireland, where O'Higgins CJ reaffirmed the 'fusion of the common law and equitable rules'.[23]

[17] W Ashburner, *Principles of Equity,* 2nd edn (London, Butterworths, 1933) 18.

[18] *United Scientific Holdings Ltd v Burnley BC* [1978] AC 904.

[19] J Martin, *Hanbury and Martin: Modern Equity,* 16th edn (London, Sweet and Maxwell, 2001) 10–23.

[20] Delany (2003) (n 16) 8.

[21] *United Scientific Holdings Ltd v Burnley BC* [1978] AC 904, 904–25.

[22] 'As law and equity are now mingled . . . it does not seem to me to matter whether the duty be classified as equitable or not. The full range of remedies deriving historically from either common law or equity should be available' – per Cooke P in *Attorney-General for the United Kingdom of Great Britain and Northern Ireland v Wellington Newspapers Ltd* [1988] NZLR 129, 172.

[23] *Hynes v Independent Newspapers Ltd* [1980] IR 204, 221.

However, while the basic purpose of equity – to compensate for the strictures of law and put right injustices – had not changed over time, its *modus operandi* had, even before the Judicature Acts, changed considerably. Equity had come under fire from critics who attacked the lack of legal certainty inherent in a system which dispensed justice based upon an unarticulated conception of right and wrong, known only to the judge (at this time the Chancellor), and which could obviously vary from one judge to the next. John Selden is perhaps the most celebrated of equity's critics in this period, branding equity 'a roguish thing . . . for law we have a measure . . . equity is according to the conscience of him that is chancellor . . .'Tis all one as if they should make the standard for the measure we call a foot, a chancellor's foot'.[24] Selden's pronouncement has become a byword for the classic critique of equity and its inherent subjectivity.

With, and to some degree even before, procedural fusion, however, came the influence of the common law doctrine of stare decisis, the legal principle by which judges are obliged to obey the precedents established by prior decisions.[25] Its development was instrumental in transforming equity from a mere corrective agency to a hardened system of jurisprudence. Uniform and consistent application of law provided the subjects of the common law with proper constructive notice of the permissions and prohibitions of the society in which they lived. Furthermore, stare decisis highlighted the belief that a significant proportion of law was rooted in human experience and could somehow be understood and placed within a system of substantive jurisprudence.[26]

ii. Maxims of Equity

As equitable jurisprudence developed, aided by the stare decisis rule, certain general principles of law began to emerge. Too broad to be steadfast legal rules, these principles were rather encapsulated by 'maxims', which emerged over time to establish a sort of guiding quasi-precedent on which future equitable decisions might be based. These maxims would establish the legal principles according to which equity was to be applied. However, some element of flexibility in the exercise of such principles would be retained, since, after all, equity hinged upon the justice of the case. Nonetheless, the charge of the Chancellor's conscience being measured according to the Chancellor's foot was duly answered. A maxim is described as 'a conclusion of reason; a proposition to be of all men confessed and granted without proof, argument or discourse'.[27]

[24] J Selden, *The Table Talk of John Selden (with notes by David Irving)* (Edinburgh, Constable, 1854) 62–63.

[25] From the Latin *Stare decisis et non quieta movere* (maintain what has been decided and do not alter that which has been established).

[26] See Rossi (1993) (n 9) 35.

[27] E Coke, 'Preface' in *Black's Law Dictionary*, 3rd edn (St Paul, Minnesota, West, 1933).

Once it is understood that the function of maxims is to furnish general principles as points of departure and not to encapsulate solutions to specific problems per se, their inherent worth reveals itself. Few have survived across all common law jurisdictions, and have adapted to a varied legal landscape over the past centuries, but those which have done so have acclimatised and survived in 'mixed' legal systems and have survived transplantations of law.[28] This suggests their potential compatibility with other legal systems outside the common law sphere and their possible qualification as 'general principles of law recognised by civilised nations' within the international legal sphere.[29] I shall now proceed to explain some of the most prominent equitable maxims of the common law and how they function.

a. *Ubi ius, ubi remedium*

An equitable maxim is 'a summary statement of a broad theme which underlies equitable concepts and principles'.[30] None are more important than the maxim *ubi ius, ubi remedium*, or 'equity will not suffer a wrong to be without a remedy'. This is a truly fundamental maxim, and represents the basis of equity's 'gap-filling' in particular. For example, the right of the government to inspect a corporation's records may be clear, but its method of enforcement unstipulated. Equity will cure this defect of law.[31] This is equally so when a right is conferred by statute upon an individual, but without an adequate remedy for breaches of this right.[32] This characteristic is, in effect the very basis of equitable jurisdiction.[33]

However, the ambit of this maxim has been limited in certain ways. In the first place, it has not found favour in the criminal law as a means of setting aside rules regarding admissibility of evidence when justice demands it. Secondly, and more importantly, in order to invoke the maxim, one must demonstrate that a legal wrong – and not merely a moral wrong – exists. The word 'wrong' refers therefore to conduct contrary to the law rather than simply morally reprehensible behaviour. Other notable illustrations of the operation of this maxim may be found in relation to the development of equitable remedies. The concept of an injunction developed as a route to justice where the remedy of damages – traditionally available at common law – could not provide an adequate recompense. Nowadays, such injunctions, which restrain the behaviour of one of the parties, may be issued to

[28] HL Oleck, 'Maxims of Equity Reappraised' (1952) 6 *Rutgers Law Review* 528.

[29] M White, 'Equity – A General Principle of Law Recognised by Civilised Nations?' (2003) 4 *Queensland Law Journal* 103, 115–16.

[30] Mason CJ in *Corin v Patton* (1990) 169 CLR 540, 557 (Australia).

[31] *Engelhart's Estate v Larimer* (1936) 211 Ind 218, 5 NE 2d 304.

[32] HL Oleck, *Creditor's Rights and Remedies* (Oxford, Oxford University Press, 1949) 10.

[33] J Pomeroy, *Equity Jurisprudence and Equitable Remedies*, 5th edn (London, General Books, 1941) sub-s 423,4

prevent an on-going nuisance or in *quia timet* (as a preventive measure) to prevent a wrong from occurring.[34]

Injunctions are not the only example of remedies which have been devised in the spirit of this maxim. Another example has been the notion of the constructive trust, originally devised in 1972 by Lord Denning in the case of *Hussey v Palmer*, to be imposed 'whenever justice and good conscience require it'.[35] This resort to new remedies in the interests of justice and conscience comes dangerously close to judicial prevarication, however, and has been roundly criticised by some, including Maudsley, who said that it was possible to infer from decisions involving constructive trusts the principle that 'in cases in which the plaintiff ought to win, but has no legal doctrine or authority to support him, a constructive trust in his favour will do the trick'.[36] This has led to constructive trusts being deemed 'a bridge too far' for equity in some jurisdictions, such as Australia.[37] Nonetheless, the very existence of remedies such as specific performance, constructive trusts, and injunctions, demonstrates equity's flexibility in ensuring that when legal interests are unprotected, and that this lack of protection amounts to a serious injustice in the circumstances, a solution will be found.

b. Equity Follows the Law

The ambit of the maxim *ubi ius, ubi remedium* is tempered somewhat further by another maxim, *aequitas sequitur legem* – equity follows the law. This maxim is intended to place limits on the ambit of the preceding maxim, so that equity can no longer be seen as a 'roguish thing', as Selden one dubbed it, steeped in subjectivity. Rather, this maxim ensures that equity will not tamper with a situation when a sound, strict and indisputable rule of law already exists regarding a settled area of the law. Howard Oleck has pointed out that this maxim may be qualified as 'minor', since it will not generally prevent equity's operation *infra legem*, or *praeter legem*, but merely limits equity *contra legem* where the rules are so clear as to leave no room for doubt.[38] However, it is clear that this maxim is designed specifically to prevent widespread invocation of *contra legem* doctrine and to keep Pandora's proverbial box firmly closed.

[34] Delany (2003) (n 16) 14.
[35] *Hussey v Palmer* [1972] 1 WLR 1286, 1290.
[36] RH Maudsley, 'Constructive Trusts' (1977) 28 *Northern Ireland Law Quarterly* 123.
[37] *Muschinski v Dodds* (1985) 160 CLR 583, 615.
[38] Oleck (1952) (n 28) 530.

c. Equity Acts *in Personam*

Equity acts personally and not *in rem*. 'Equity cannot presume to interfere with or to control the action of the common law courts. It acts upon the person who is inequitably suing in those courts'.[39] This maxim effectively designates equity as a mandate ordering an individual party to do or not to do a specific act, upon punishment for contempt of court in the event of disobedience. This demonstrates that equity will not overrule judgments *stricto sensu* via the power of the government, but will constrain the parties to overrule the effects of such judgments themselves (*in personam*). It was said that the power of this maxim was over a man's conscience, not his estate.[40]

However, the meaning and extent of this maxim have long been disputed. It has been commented that of all equitable maxims, this was perhaps 'historically of the greatest importance, theoretically the most elusive, and practically of the most dubious significance',[41] while Delany has commented that 'this maxim must increasingly be treated with some degree of caution'.[42] Perhaps, given the confusion over how this principle operates, it is enlightening to furnish a concrete example in the form of the famous case of *Penn v Lord Baltimore*.[43] Here, the English Chancery Courts decreed specific performance of an agreement between the proprietary governors concerning the boundaries of the American colonies of Maryland and Pennsylvania. This, despite the fact that the English courts did not have jurisdiction over land disputes in this area. The specific performance order was upon the parties, not an order for redistribution of the land itself. The idea is that the parties being within the law's jurisdiction, even if the property was not, this maxim could be operated against their persons rather than their estates to achieve the same result. The order was not that the land be transferred per se. The order was that the party in question was to transfer the land. The order was against the party, not regarding the property.[44] As time has progressed, however, this maxim has ceased to be of particular significance, but it further illustrates equity's predisposition to going the extra mile to achieve justice.

[39] FW Maitland, *Equity – A Course of Lectures*, 2nd edn (Cambridge, Cambridge University Press, 1936) 258.

[40] *Arglasse v Muschamp* (1682) 23 ER 322.

[41] RP Meagher, WMC Gummow and JRF Lehane, *Equity: Doctrines and Remedies*, 3rd edn (London, Butterworths, 1992) 96.

[42] Delany (2003) (n 16) 37.

[43] *Penn v Lord Baltimore* (1750) 1 Vesey Sr 444.

[44] See also Lord Selbourne in *Ewing v Orr Ewing (No1)* (1883) 9 App Cas 34, 40.

d. Equity Looks to the Substance Rather than the Form – *ex re sed non ex nomine*

Equity abhors formalism and will not allow a shroud of legality to protect wrongdoers. Therefore, intended transactions that do not fulfil formal requirements will be enforced where the justice of the circumstances requires it.[45] Furthermore, of tremendous importance is the fact that equity will not be constrained by the formal technical nature of a corporation or association if that vehicle is used as a shield for an improper or illicit purpose.[46] The extent of this maxim is unclear, and will vary from case to case, but, as Delany notes, while this does not mean that legal formalities will not be required by equity, 'it looks to the substance rather than the form of a transaction and does not require "unnecessary formalities" to be observed'.[47] Ergo contracts may be created without observing all formalities and trusts may be created without even using the word 'trust'; intention to create a binding instrument combined with some precatory language is sufficient.

e. Equity Regards as Done that which Ought to Have Been Done

This maxim is very much in the same vein as the preceding principle. The point of this maxim is that within a legal relationship, even if the formalities have not been observed throughout, equity will regard as done such acts as should have been accomplished had the contract been properly executed. Therefore, a specifically enforceable contract for a lease is treated as being equivalent to a lease, and all rights and duties belonging to the parties are treated as being equal to what they would have been, had the lease actually been executed. However, this maxim is again limited, as was outlined by Lindley LJ in *Re Anstis*: 'The obligation to do what ought to be done is not an absolute duty, but only an obligation arising from contract . . . in favour of some person entitled to enforce the contract as against the person liable to perform it'.[48] This case demonstrates that equity will generally not assist a volunteer in such circumstances, and that the obligation may only be carried out in favour of those persons who are entitled to specifically enforce the contract.

f. *Vigilantibus et Non Dormientibus Aequitas Subvenit*

Equity aids the vigilant and not those who sleep on their rights. This maxim constitutes equity's equivalent of the Statute of Limitations and is

[45] *Horn v Keteltas* (1871) 46 NY 605; *Rochester Savings Bank v Stoeltzen and Tapper* (1941) 176 Misc 140.

[46] *Brown County Bank v Freie Presse Printing Co* (1928) 174 Minnesota 143, 218 NW 557.

[47] Delany (2003) (n 16) 34.

[48] *Re Anstis* (1886) 31 Ch 595, 605.

intended to discourage unreasonable delays regarding presentation of claims and enforcement of rights.[49] What is unreasonable will be determined with reference to specific circumstances.[50] This principle may be divided into two separate but related categories, laches – those who neglect the upholding of their rights for so long that they may become extinguished – and acquiescence – those who fail to object or give implied assent when another party infringes their rights. However, it has been noted that such principles are only likely to apply to a relatively small number of cases within domestic legal systems, since usually such areas are adequately dealt with by statute law.[51]

The application of this maxim has seen divergences between the various common law jurisdictions in modern years, however. In Ireland, 'Mere delay will not of itself disentitle a plaintiff to an injunction in aid of his legal rights' unless statutory restrictions are breached.[52] However, in a later case, Keane J held that lapse of time coupled with circumstances making it inequitable to enforce the claim was sufficient to bar the plaintiff's action.[53] In England, the position is slightly different, with *Habib Bank Ltd v Habib Bank Aktiengesellschaft Zürich* holding that laches is always relevant when equitable relief is sought and that no distinction ought to be made between cases where such relief is sought to give effect to legal as opposed to equitable rights.[54] Delany notes that in deciding whether a defence of laches may be upheld, a court must consider in the first place whether the plaintiff has delayed unreasonably in bringing his claim to court, and in the second place whether prejudice or detriment has been suffered by the defendant as a result. Delay alone is insufficient. Such an approach means that acquiescence and laches are to an increasing extent dealt with in the same manner before the courts.[55]

g. *Non Concedit Venire contra Factum Proprium* (Estoppel)

The 'bar' of laches and acquiescence is paralleled by the bar of estoppel, which serves as an extension of the previous maxim.[56] If a party may not sleep on his rights, then he equally may not make a representation that he intends not to uphold them, only to renege upon the assurance given at a later date. In order for one to claim estoppel, there must exist: (1) an assurance given by one party; (2) reliance thereupon by the other party; and

[49] *Luellen v City of Aberdeen*, 20 Wash 2d 594, 148 P 2d (1944), 849.
[50] *United States v National Rockland Bank*, 35 F Supp (D Mass 1940) 912.
[51] R Keane, *Equity and the Law of Trusts in the Republic of Ireland* (Dublin, Butterworths, 1988) 35–36.
[52] Budd J in *Cahill v Irish Motor Traders Association* [1966] IR 430, 449.
[53] *JH v WJH* (1977) (Irish High Court, no 5831 P, 20 December 1979).
[54] *Habib Bank Ltd v Habib Bank Aktiengesellschaft Zürich* [1981] WLR 1265.
[55] Delany (2003) (n 16) 29.
[56] T Pospishil, 'Equitable Estoppel' (1940) 19 *Nebraska Law Bulletin* 222.

(3) detriment resulting to the second party on foot of, and resulting from, this reliance. If this three-stage test is satisfied, then the first party will be held to be 'estopped' from denying his original assurance, and must fulfil whatever promise he made to the second party.[57] As Lord Cranworth put it, 'If a person makes any false representation to another, and that other acts upon that false representation, the person who has made it shall not afterwards be allowed to set up that what he said was false'.[58]

Although the concept of estoppel by representation is relatively simple at its core, with the three-stage test an easy barometer, in practice, it has been complicated by court judgments over time. Nineteenth-century English cases already added the element of 'unconscionability', that is that equity would only give relief where the truth or accuracy of a future representation had been denied in an unconscionable manner.[59] Further, initially, cases were limited to dealing with interests in property, that is proprietary estoppel. However, this was extended in 1947 by Lord Denning in the famous *High Trees* case, giving rise to the idea of promissory estoppel, that is any promise made which is 'intended to create legal relations and which, to the knowledge of the person making the promise, was going to be acted on by the person to whom it was made and was in fact so acted upon', thus bringing the doctrine outside the boundaries of proprietary interests.[60]

The operability of estoppel outside of proprietary interests has, however, continued to be of some controversy, since the 1951 case of *Coombe v Coombe* declared that the doctrine might only be used 'as a shield, not a sword', that is as a defence, but not as grounds for a legal action.[61] However, reaction to this position has diverged throughout the common law world. For instance, the position was rejected outright in Australia, with Mason CJ stating that he saw no reason why promissory estoppel might not be used as a sword as well as a shield.[62] Indeed, in an earlier English case, Templeman J had adopted much the same position, rejecting the argument that promissory estoppel could not confer a cause of action, and said that it applies whenever 'the promissor knows and intends that the promisee will irretrievably alter his position on the promise'.[63] In Ireland, Costello J held that promissory estoppel could indeed give rise to a cause of action, and was also capable of creating proprietary rights.[64] This has given rise to the further doctrine of legitimate expectation,

[57] *Ackerman v True*, 175 NY (1903), 353.

[58] *Jorden v Money* (1854) 5 HLC 185, 210.

[59] *Hughes v Metropolitan Railway Co* [1877] 2 AC 489; *Birmingham and District Land Co v London and Northwestern Railway Co* (1888) 40 Ch 268.

[60] *Central London Property Trust Ltd v High Trees House Ltd* [1947] 1 KB 130, 134.

[61] *Coombe v Coombe* [1951] 2 KB 215, 224.

[62] *Walton Stores (Interstate) v Maher* (1988) 164 CLR 387, 400.

[63] *Re Wyvern Developments Ltd* [1974] 2 All ER 535, [1974] 1 WLR 1097, 1104.

[64] *Re JR* [1993] ILRM 657.

whereby one may rely on promises which are believed to be made in good faith by an appropriate agent, who may not then recant his promises. Finlay CJ described legitimate expectation doctrine as 'but an aspect of the well-recognised equitable concept of promissory estoppel'.[65] It would now seem that the *Coombe v Coombe* position has been altered sufficiently throughout much of the common law sphere for there to be 'but one doctrine of estoppel'.[66]

Another aspect of the doctrine which has provoked a certain degree of debate is the boundary limits of the three-stage test. As regards the furnishing of an assurance, with the intention that this be relied upon, it is now accepted that a conscious silence may suffice in certain circumstances.[67] Concerning the element of reliance, it must be shown that the representation of the promissor 'was calculated to influence the judgment of a reasonable man'.[68] As to the element of detriment, it is for the party who has suffered the loss to demonstrate the detriment, and the causal link with his reliance upon the assurance given.[69] Per Balcombe LJ in *Wayling v Jones*,

> [o]nce it has been established that promises were made and that there has been conduct by the plaintiff of such a nature that inducement may be inferred, then the burden of proof shifts to the defendant to establish that he did not rely on the promises.[70]

The detriment may take any form, and need not concern an interest in land.[71] However, even if detriment is established, it 'must be approached as part of a broad inquiry as to whether repudiation of an assurance is or is not unconscionable in all the circumstances'.[72]

As regards the remedy available in cases of estoppel, the value of the equity in question will depend on the underlying circumstances. 'The task of the court is to do justice. The most essential requirement is that there must be proportionality between the expectation and the detriment'.[73] This was echoed in Australia by Mason CJ, who stressed that there must be proportionality between the remedy and the detriment which it is designed to avoid.[74] While it might be the natural response of a court to seek to satiate the claimant's responses if they are well-founded, if they are disproportionate or extravagant, the court will satisfy the equity in a

65 *Webb v Ireland* [1988] IR 353.
66 *Australia v Verwayen* (1990) 170 CLR 394, 412.
67 Delany (2003) (n 16) 638.
68 Lord Denning MR in *Brikom Investments v Carr* [1979] QB 467, 483.
69 *Industrial Yarns Ltd v Greene* [1984] ILRM 15.
70 *Wayling v Jones* (1993) 69 P & CR 170, 173.
71 *Re Basham* [1986] WLR 1498, 1509.
72 Robert Walker LJ in *Gillet v Holt* [2001] Ch 211.
73 Aldous LJ in *Jennings v Rice* [2002] EWCA Civ 159.
74 *Australia v Verwayen* (1990) 170 CLR 394, 413.

more limited way. As Delany has noted, the question of whether the court's task ought to be the compensation of a claimant for detriment suffered, or the fulfilment of his expectations is one which has provoked considerable academic debate, and no clear winner seems to have emerged, with – typically for equity – prudence, proportionality, and the justice of the case being determining factors.[75]

h. He Who Comes to Equity Must Come with Clean Hands

This maxim is highly indicative of equity's moral origins. In order to benefit from equity, one must be free of iniquity. Therefore, any person seeking equitable relief must refrain from fraud, misrepresentation, or any other form of dishonest or disreputable comportment if this person wishes to be granted access to a remedy.[76] This principle is paralleled in the civil law system by the requirement of *bonne foi,* for example in French contract law, which requires fair and open dealing by parties in order to qualify for fair and open treatment in court.[77] In order to be entitled to the application of justice, one must have acted justly in past dealings. It is also somewhat comparable to the legal principle of reciprocity, which requires adherence to a contract on one side to allow a party to complain of his partner's non-adherence to his obligations under the contract. However, here again, there is a caveat, as the dishonest conduct 'must have an immediate and necessary relation to the equity sued for; it must be a depravity in a legal as well as a moral sense'.[78] This restriction guards against over-extending equity's judgmental effect to a situation where a party has been morally despicable but has no legal turpitude to answer for. It is, however, important to note that it is not necessary for the dishonest conduct of the plaintiff to have prejudiced the defendant in any way for him to be barred from action.[79]

i. He Who Seeks Equity Must Do Equity

The corollary of the 'clean hands' principle is that when one applies for equitable relief, one must equally be prepared to act in an equitable manner. One may not derive undue benefit from equity's application, only what is due and no more. One may further be constrained, as a condition of receiving equity's aid, to do or not to do, something which would not

[75] Delany (2003) (n 16) 654–67.

[76] LJH, 'Clean Hands Doctrine' (1939) 18 *Texas Law Review* 506.

[77] J Bell, S Boyron and S Whittaker, *Principles of French Law* (Oxford, Oxford University Press, 1998) 105–61.

[78] Lord Eyre CB in *Dering v Earl of Winchelsea* (1787) 1 Cox Eq Cas 318, 319–20.

[79] Costello J in *Parkes v Parkes* [1980] ILRM 137, 144. Here, although the husband's dishonest conduct had in no way prejudiced his wife in this instance, it was nonetheless sufficient to disentitle him to the equitable relief which he sought before the court.

otherwise be necessary.[80] This criterion prohibits unjust enrichment, and represents a truly fundamental maxim. In order to be entitled to the application of justice, one must be prepared to act justly in the future.[81]

This is one of the few maxims that can be interpreted fairly literally.[82] It has also been noted that there are many illustrations of, and almost no exceptions to, this principle.[83] A common example of the operation of this principle is that an interlocutory injunction will generally not be granted without an 'undertaking' (sum) in damages to ensure that the defendant will be compensated if the plaintiff fails at trial. This principle is also the basis for the doctrine of election, which often attaches to wills, stipulating that one may not approbate and reprobate, that is, that one cannot take a benefit while rejecting an associated burden.[84] As Lord Denning pronounced, referring to this maxim, 'if one party seeks relief, he must be ready and willing to do his part in it'.[85]

j. Where Equities on Both Sides are Equal, the Law Prevails

This maxim represents the intrinsic impartiality and neutrality of equity. As between equal moral rights, equitable jurisprudence is not in fact brought into play at all; the balance of moral rights being equally balanced, the legal rules may apply in isolation, without equitable considerations.[86]

A further minor maxim – *Qui prior est tempore, potior est jure, ie aequitate* – may be appended here.[87] This stipulates that where equities are equal, the one which is prior in time will prevail. It is, however, a minor maxim, and not as authoritative as that which stipulates that where equities are equal, the law shall prevail.[88]

k. Equity Delights in Equality

This is an important maxim, also sometimes formulated as 'equality is equity'. It operates chiefly where there are more than two parties participating in a given litigation, for example in the distribution of the assets of an insolvent debtor amongst his creditors *pro rata*.[89] This basic doctrine applies in the absence of any clearly stated rule of law. It does not necessarily lead to precisely equal distribution of assets, but rather an equitable

[80] *Semidey v Central Aguirre Co* (1st Cir, 1917), 239 Fed P630.
[81] HL Oleck, 'Historical Nature of Equity Jurisprudence' (1951) 20 *Fordham Law Review* 27.
[82] Delany (2003) (n 16) 17.
[83] Meagher, Gummow and Lehane (1992) (n 41) 77.
[84] See Chitty J in *Re Lord Chesham* (1886) 31 Ch D 466, 473.
[85] *Chappell v Times Newspapers Ltd* [1975] WLR 482, 502.
[86] *Frink v Commercial Bank*, 195 Iowa 1011, 191 NW (1923) 513.
[87] *Oppenheim Collins & Co v Beir*, 187 NY Misc (1946) 428.
[88] Oleck (1952) (n 28) 543.
[89] *Des Moines Joint Stock Land Bank v Allen* (1935) 220 Iowa 448.

distribution defining 'equality' as is equitable given the specific circumstances of the case, as Waite J noted in the English courts: 'This is not an area where the maxim that equality is equity falls to be applied unwittingly'.[90]

l. Equity Acts Specifically

The medieval common law relating to torts and contractual obligations showed a strong predisposition towards monetary damages. The idea was not to correct the wrong, but rather to compensate the wronged party. However, this was not always sufficient in the circumstances. Preferring specific performance of an obligation over the payment of damages for non-compliance as a better remedy (to put the wronged party back into the position he ought to have been in) is a central characteristic of equity's operation.[91] Since specific performance of an obligation or an injunction (eg to prevent the continuing recurrence of a nuisance) is highly preferable to damages in some instances, as it confers a worthwhile remedy to the wronged party, equity has shown its preference for this method, even *contra legem* in the face of statutes which have limited available remedies to fixed sums of pecuniary compensation.[92]

This trend may be used to describe equity's flexibility in terms of remedies, but such flexibility is not limited to specific performance. In reality, equitable jurisprudence has demonstrated remarkable creativity in devising new remedies to do justice in the circumstances. A prime example of this is seen in the notion of an injunction. An injunction is an order restraining the party to whom it is addressed from carrying out a specific act or requiring him to perform such an act, thus imposing either positive or negative obligations depending on the circumstances.[93] However, in deciding to grant such an injunction, the court shall exercise its discretion and will be wary of not unduly prejudicing the rights of third parties.[94] However, it is clear that this will not always be the deciding factor, and that the defendant himself may not be held accountable for the acts of third parties.[95] Although injunctions are generally awarded on the basis of a past infringement to regulate future conduct, *quia timet* injunctions may also be granted, before any injury or damage has been suffered, in circumstances where the plaintiff's injury is merely apprehended or threatened. This is necessary 'to prevent the jurisdiction of the courts being stultified',

[90] *Hammond v Mitchell* [1991] 1 WLR 1127, 1137.

[91] *Dr David Kennedy Corp v David Kennedy* (1901) 165 NY 353.

[92] Oleck (1952) (n 28) 545.

[93] *Bellew v Cement Ltd* [1948] IR 61; Delany (2003) (n 16) 448–59.

[94] *Miller v Jackson* [1977] QB 966. Here, the plaintiff was granted a remedy confined to damages alone, since the injunction he requested would have reduced the enjoyment of an amenity (a cricket club) for the local residents had it been awarded.

[95] *Phonographic Performance (Ireland) Ltd v Chariot Inns* (Irish High Court, no 4673 P, 1992).

that is to fill lacunae in the system of justice which would result if such a remedy were not available.[96] However, it is for the plaintiff to show that there exists 'a strong case of probability that such apprehended mischief will, in fact, arise'.[97]

The above maxim is supplemented by the minor maxim that 'equity delights to do justice, and not by halves'. This principle affirms that equity will still give traditional remedies such as damages if this will result in a more just result.[98] In short, equity looks at the best medium to place the parties back into the positions they should have occupied had there been no wrong committed, and implements this medium. This is further evidence of equity's flexible nature, and its inventiveness with regards to new remedies.

m. Equity will not Stoop to Pick Up Pins

Equity deals only with serious injustices and does not concern itself with trifles. If the amount of injury suffered is seen to be so small as to be trivial, equity will not meddle with it. This has been described as a 'minor maxim',[99] but its importance must not be underestimated. Equity will not concern itself with the minor injustices 'which beset the everyday existence of every righteous man'.[100] Rather it confines its ambit to remedying the grosser injustices, which have the potential to seriously affect people. This allows equity to claim a certain *gravitas*, in that it only enters the fray when important matters are at stake.[101]

n. Equity will not Decree a Vain Thing

Equity deals with making a practical and real contribution to substantive justice, not with making legal decrees or judgments which cannot or will not be carried out.[102] Equity, in short, is designed to help people attain justice. If it cannot, it will not get involved.

o. 'Equity's Darling'

To temper the application of the list of the maxims above, equity in the common law system has also produced one last innovation which merits a brief description, this being the category known as 'equity's darling'.

[96] Lord Upjohn in *Redland Bricks v Morris* [1970] AC 652, 664.
[97] Chitty J in *Attorney-General v Manchester Corp* [1893] 2 Ch 87, 92.
[98] *Wheeler v Standard Oil Co of New York* 263 NY 34 (1933).
[99] Oleck (1952) (n 28) 546.
[100] Ezekiel, Ch 15, verse 17, *Holy Bible*.
[101] *United States v Causby* 328 US 256 (1946).
[102] *Kennedy v Hazelton* 128 US 667 (1888).

Over time, a rule developed whereby a bona fide purchaser for a fair valuation of a property, without notice of a legal estate or equitable interest being held in the land which he was buying belonging to another, would take the land free of any equitable interest of which he had no notice. This device again demonstrates equity's concern with being fair, assuming that if someone was genuine, honest, and paid the full price, having made adequate inquiries about the property he was buying, he would not later be penalised by any 'surprises' which might be sprung upon him by parties unknown after the transaction had been completed. This purchaser was nicknamed 'equity's darling', since equity would not be applied to deprive him of his interests.

However, the above position was tempered somewhat by the doctrine of notice. If the purchaser had notice of the interest, then such a position would not apply. This was equally the case if he failed to make all enquiries and inspections which he ought reasonably to have made, judged with reference to standard conveyancing procedures. In this instance, even if he was not actually aware of the interest, it would be deemed that he should have been aware, via the doctrine of constructive notice. Also, any information which an agent of the purchaser is aware of, or should have been aware of via the doctrine of constructive notice, will be imputed to the purchaser himself via the doctrine of imputed notice.[103] This again demonstrates that equity will aid those who are of good faith from suffering wrongs, provided that their own negligence is not a contributory factor in such wrong being suffered.

B. Common Law Equity and Legal Rigidity

The value of the historical precedent of equity in the common law cannot be overstated. Here we have an example of a system of general principles, developed organically and over time by the courts, which dealt successfully with not one but a series of manifest injustices which arose in the common law legal system. Furthermore, this system was not merely adopted in England alone, but throughout the various common law jurisdictions of the world, including well-developed legal systems such as those of Ireland, Australia and New Zealand. Moreover, these general principles developed from a system which at first was dubbed too loose to administer objective justice to something else entirely – a system of principles, which while flexible, were nonetheless sufficiently concrete to not be used over-extensively, and to result in a justice which became increasingly predictable and uniform. In reality, in England, as elsewhere, while the import of general principles and maxims of equity has remained, their

[103] See Delany (2003) (n 16) 40–47.

explicit invocation has waned. This is largely due to the increasing complexity of the law and the fact that multiple series of court precedents invoking equity to temper the law's letter improved legislative finesse. Lawmakers wished to see the letter of their laws respected, and to do so required coherence with equitable principles, ergo laws were drafted with such principles in mind. However, when clashes occur, as they still do, equitable principles are still imbued with the same normative force.

Clearly, such principles are adept at solving a myriad of individual problems stemming from legal rigidity. However, from the point of view of the humanitarian intervention debate, we must not take too much from this precedent. While the common law tradition represents one of the world's most widely-used and respected legal systems, the judgments of the World Court have already demonstrated that, approval by one major legal system does not merit a principle's adoption as one of the 'general principles of law recognised by civilised nations'.[104] Therefore, wholesale transposition of the maxims of equity would be a bridge too far. However, the cases discussed in the preceding chapter show that, while the test for what constitutes a general principle in the eyes of the World Court is not entirely clear, evidence that principles are 'generally accepted' amongst major legal systems may be important in determining whether they qualify as a component part of the third source of international law.[105] Bearing this in mind, it seems appropriate to dedicate the remainder of this chapter to an examination of whether such principles of equity *à l'anglaise* – or something approximately equivalent to them – exist in other systems of law. If, indeed, other legal systems have crafted an equivalent set of principles to deal with legal rigidity and injustices in specific cases, it may well be that such generally accepted principles constitute 'general principles of law recognised by civilised nations'. If this indeed transpires to be the case, then the third source of international law may yet shed unexpected light on the humanitarian intervention conundrum.

III. EQUITY OUTSIDE THE ENGLISH COMMON LAW MODEL

In order to undertake an examination of equity outside of the common law, it is insufficient merely to take the maxims and remedies devised by equity within the common law system and examine whether these same devices exist elsewhere. The system of equity which developed in England and spread throughout the common law world developed organically according to the legal landscape and historical period with which it was

[104] *South West Africa (Second Phase)* (Judgment) [1966] ICJ Rep 6, 46–47.
[105] *Effect of Awards of Compensation made by the United Nations Administrative Tribunal* (Advisory Opinion) [1954] ICJ Rep 47.

faced. All things being equal, things may have developed in the same manner outside of the common law realm. All things, however, are, and never were, equal. The principles which grew up in the English law cannot expect to find carbon copies in other legal systems. As Francioni notes, 'Equity is a polymorphous concept even in the narrow confines of legal language',[106] though the same author does go on to posit the existence of 'a common sense of fairness and equity among the different peoples of the world'.[107] Our search, then, rather than seeking identical principles to those furnished by the English case, will be for principles that are broadly equivalent, which tackle legal rigidity, which display the hallmarks of equity, and which are used to render justice in circumstances when the written law is insufficiently equipped to do so.

The purpose of the remainder of this chapter, then, shall be to examine the origins of equity, and to look at how it has developed, and how it has been translated into general principles in legal systems outside of the common law. While a completely exhaustive study of every legal system worldwide would be excessively demanding for a study of this size, I shall nonetheless furnish a cross-section of a wide variety of major legal systems, many of which have known transplantation to other States. For this chapter section, I am deeply indebted to – and shall draw heavily upon – Ralph A Newman's 1973 work *Equity in the World's Legal Systems*.[108] This book, edited by Newman, consists of a compendium of essays comparing the import of equity in a variety of legal systems. It has served as a starting point for research on a number of systems with which I was largely unfamiliar, and much of the wisdom contained in this volume has been reproduced in the following pages, accompanied by a large number of other sources. Sources on comparative equity are so rare as to be almost a non-category. Without this collection of essays, therefore, structuring the following section would have been overly burdensome, and perhaps near-impossible to complete in an adequate manner. I feel it is therefore appropriate to acknowledge my debt to its various authors in this regard.

However, the forthcoming section seeks not merely to reproduce the research of others, but to build upon it. In comparing the various legal regimes in the selected countries, it is my hope to discover common trends, which may help to identify 'general principles of law recognised by civilised nations'. International normative consequences may be divined from an in-depth comparative analysis. If a legal principle is prevalent throughout the systems examined, there may be sufficient cause for supposing that it has known transposition to international law. Subsequent chapters will deal with whether any such principles have

[106] F Francioni, 'Equity in International Law' in R Wolfrum (ed), *The Max Planck Encyclopedia of Public International Law* (Oxford, Oxford University Press, 2008) para 1.

[107] ibid, para 3.

[108] RA Newman (ed) *Equity in the World's Legal Systems* (Brussels, Bruylant, 1973)

been used by the World Court as further evidence of their existence as international legal norms.

A. The History of Equity outside the English Common Law

In recounting a history of the conception and development of equity as a legal concept outside the common law, one is forced to paint with a fairly broad brush. In reality, equity has been a notoriously difficult term even to define, with different descriptions in each legal culture, and with one commentator noting that 'The only common element is a term whose connotations are famous for their generality, vagueness and ambiguity'.[109] Rossi comments that its history 'has not produced an accepted definition of its constitutive elements, its function, or its application. In both theory and practice, equity is shrouded in mystery'.[110] However, perhaps it is as well to heed the advice of Richard Falk, who counselled that equity is better discussed than defined.[111]

The history of equity is a disputable one, according to Rossi, revealing two disparate interpretations. A first school indeed considers equity in terms of a corrective utilised principally by judges to mitigate unnecessary hardship caused by the application of general principles or specific rules, but this interpretation is disputed by a second school which considers equity within the framework of the natural law, and imparts to it the character of a source of law, while viewing equity as an inseparable component of the process of adjudication. In reality, it is probably somewhere between the two. Certainly the ancestry of the concept cannot distil to a single legal system, with the concept of equity being expressed, inter alia, in the legal systems of Ancient Greece (*epieikeia* – clemency); Ancient Rome (*aequitas* – equality); traditional Chinese law (*Ch'ing* – compassion); and the Hindu tradition (*Dharma* – righteousness).[112] However, the links with natural law must be addressed before proceeding further, for fear of confusing the two concepts.

i. Natural Law and Equity

The links between the classical conception of equity and that of the natural law spring largely from the notion of conscience. While natural law is traditionally portrayed as a compelling force decreed by a higher power

[109] T Opsahl, 'Struggling with Equity in the Modern World' (1975) 42/43 *Annuairede l'Association des auditeurs et anciens auditeurs de l'Academie de droitinternational de la Haye, 1972–73*, 72, 77.

[110] Rossi (1993) (n 9) 21.

[111] R Falk, 'Foreword' in Rossi (1993) (n 9) 9.

[112] RA Newman, '*The Principle of Equity as a Source of World Law*' (1966) 1 *Israel Law Review* 616, 616–18. See also Rossi (1993) (n 9) 22.

or higher morality which may override incompatible man-made laws, the truth is that many of the best-known examples of natural law being invoked have sprung from the demands of the consciences of those who sought to invoke it. I am not the first to note this. R Neil Snyder points out that Antigone's famous resolution of her dilemma 'is a dramatic example of the capacity of men [or in this case, women] to rise to the impelling demands of conscience, recognise an unjust element in the hierarchy of normative commands, and refuse such elements'.[113] Snyder also notes that Martin Luther's famous declaration that 'Ich kann nicht anders tun' (is the assertion of conscience in consonance with a 'higher law').[114] These examples show that, while natural law was conceived of as a higher law being invoked by reference to a higher authority – namely God – it was a fundamental objection of the complainant's conscience that called him or her to refer to such law. Parallels may be drawn with equity, *qua* common law at least, where a fundamental injustice in the domestic legal system cause the plaintiff to appeal to the conscience of a higher authority – namely the King. While natural law was not limited in its extent by the conscience of any person in particular, resort to its content would be pre-empted by the demands of one's conscience. In order for such a demand to be well received, it would, at the very least, be necessary for any such 'commands of conscience' to be in accordance with common conceptions of moral conduct at the time. Likewise, as equity evolved, its association with the power of the King faded, and it became associated with the notion of 'unconscionability' – that is, a result arising from the law which would so offend the moral conscience of a reasonable man at that time and place that resort to equity would be called for.

If one understands equity and natural law in the manner described above, it may seem that there is little enough to distinguish them. Indeed, Rossi has described Aristotle's conception of equity as 'an extension of natural justice [ie natural law]'.[115] However, while this may be the case, Aristotle's conception of equity spoke of equity as a concept somewhat at odds with that of the natural law, not as a hierarchical legal source, a sort of natural peremptory normative *bloc*, but rather as a corrective mechanism. He argued that in any situation in which the law may speak universally, but in which the issue at hand happens to fall outside the universal formula, 'it is correct to rectify the shortcoming, in other words the omission and mistake of a lawgiver due to the generality of his statement'.[116] Per Aristotle, such a rectification in fact corresponds to how the lawgiver himself would have legislated, had he foreseen the possibility of such a

[113] RN Snyder, 'Natural Law and Equity' in Newman (n108) 33.
[114] ibid.
[115] Rossi (1993) (n 9) 23.
[116] Aristotle and M Ostwald (tr), *The Nicomachean Ethics* (Washington, The Library of Liberal Arts, 1962) 141–42.

situation arising. 'That [therefore] is why the equitable [solution] is both just and also better than the law in one sense'.[117] Rather than being an extension of natural law theory, in expounding equity as a corrective, Aristotle instead 'provided the theory which integrated equity into the spheres of legal justice [ie law *stricto sensu*]'.[118] As Snyder notes, a legal system which is predicated purely upon positive law alone tends to substitute order for order's sake in the place of order as a means of achieving justice. This construction tends to forbid judicial innovation when judicial innovation may be warranted and even essential in a given context. Furthermore, it may result in the upholding of rules and regulations where to do so is both unjust and impracticable.[119] Without resorting to the disputed normative category of natural law, equity as a corrective mechanism, as described by Aristotle, enables the general rule to be modified with reference to specific (and presumably unusual) circumstances which could not have been foreseen by the legislator at the outset.

Of course, while the employment of equity as a corrective mechanism sounds attractive on the face of it, particularly as an alternative to the notion of a hierarchically superior 'natural law' which may make rubbish of our own norms at a stroke, the fact is that it will always be difficult to define what the 'demands of one's conscience' or the 'demands of the conscience of a reasonable man' actually constitute. Roscoe Pound brands equity 'a universal element in that it aims to indicate a standard in the maintenance of which the administration of law corresponds to a man's best social nature'.[120] Per Pound, such universal elements are within social control, insofar as society (ie people) has been able 'to discover by experience and test by reason. In essence, these are what Duguit describes as the principles of social solidarity; those principles which maximise cooperative tendencies and forestall social disintegration'.[121] As such, the corrective may in turn lead to law reform, either by means of the use of equitable precedents, or by actual legislative correction, to fill the lacunae which equity seeks to address. Thus equity may serve 'as the bridge between the world of strict law, precedent and custom, to the realisation of the perfectibility of legal rules'.[122] This formulation is certainly attractive, although the problems as to equity's somewhat indeterminate content remain.

[117] ibid. See also EJ Weinrib, 'Legal Formalism, on the Immanent Reality of Law' in D Patterson, *Philosophy of Law and Legal Theory: An Anthology* (Malden, Massachusetts, Blackwell, 2003) 370–74.

[118] Y Makkonen, 'Western Attitudes to International Equity' (1975) 42/43 *Annuairede l'Association des auditeurs et anciens auditeurs de l'Academie de droitinternational de la Haye* 86.

[119] Snyder in Newman (1973) (n 112) 37.

[120] R Pound, 'Comparative Law and History as Bases for Chinese Law' (1948) 61 *Harvard Law Review* 749, 749, 753.

[121] ibid.

[122] Snyder in Newman (1973) (n 112) 40.

A further problem, and one that can certainly be keenly felt as regards international law, is the distinction between the usefulness of equity as a palliative to inherently unjust solutions, and the damage that a somewhat indeterminate corrective may do to the established order within any legal system. This is certainly also a point which equity shares with the natural law, and it is a concern that shall be further discussed in later chapters. For the present, it is sufficient to note the fact that as regards equity, this is not a new concern. As early as 1765, Blackstone, in his renowned *Commentaries*, stated that, for the sake of the order of the legal system, the freedom to consider cases in an equitable light should not be pushed too far, 'lest thereby we destroy all law'.[123] The test that Blackstone proposed was whether a specific application of an equitable principle would lead to an essential realisation of justice in the circumstances, while conforming to a moderate sense of 'fairness', or whether in securing the plaintiff's wants, it would be done so at the cost of others. Snyder broadens this concept, arguing that an act-utilitarian analysis of equity must be balanced by the rule-utilitarian consequences which would ensue were any such corrective device to obtain a permanent position within the legal *corpus*. Thus,

> occasionally, the immanent cry for 'justice' in a particular case must be unanswered because of broader social reasons; an occasional individual injustice being part of the price of the broader justice enjoyed by all if social order is to be preserved.[124]

ii. Equity and Roman Law

Having thus distinguished the *métier* of equity from that of natural law, we are free to proceed with our exploration of equitable principles outside the common law sphere. The obvious point of departure for this purpose would seem to be in the Roman law, it being the antecedent of many of the modern legal systems of the world. It is particularly true that the bulk of those legal systems which have not known the influence of the common law of England have received, to some degree or another, key elements of the Roman law and have incorporated them as cornerstones of their legal systems. Exploring the impact of equitable principles within the Roman law, then, is necessarily of singular importance if we are to admit that they form part of the 'general principles of law recognised by civilised nations'.

Sir Henry Maine has noted that equity gained currency at an early stage of the development of the Roman law system, as indeed had been the case

[123] W Blackstone with HG St George Tucker, *Blackstone's Commentaries: With Notes of Reference to the Constitution and Laws, of the Federal Government of the United States, and of the Commonwealth of Virginia: In Five*, 1996 reprint of 1765 edn (Philadelphia, Birch and Small, 1996) S 1, sub-ss 61–62, 67.

[124] Snyder in Newman (1973) (n 112) 40–41.

in the common law. He defined equity as 'a set of legal principles, entitled by their intrinsic superiority to supersede the older law'.[125] This reference to 'intrinsic superiority' may be contrasted with the concept of normative superiority. To Maine, then, it was not the normative source of equity, but rather the nature of equity's intrinsic content, which allowed it in certain circumstances to supersede the positive statute law. However, whether this represented the legal position in Roman times is less clear.

Early Roman law was characterised, much like common law prior to the advent of equity, by legal rigidity. The Twelve Tables were enacted in the mid-fifth century BC, and contained the principles of the *ius civile* – the civil law. Those principles which came to supersede such law were regarded as *ius gentium* – that is, principles 'common to all civilised people, because they appeared to be dictated by the common sense shared by all such people'.[126] This represented a sort of rights-based *corpus*, which was unfettered by the notion of citizenship, and applied equally to all people, regardless of whether they were Roman citizens or not, which was not the case with the *ius civile.* Justinian's *Corpus Iuris Civilis* of 529–34 AD offers an excellent understanding of the development of Roman law over a period of almost 1,000 years dating from the adoption of the Twelve Tables, and charting the interaction between the *ius gentium* and the *ius civile.*[127] The *Corpus Iuris Civilis* (also known as *Justinian's Digest*) and subsequent commentaries make clear that, over time, the *ius civile* became increasingly refined, and began to afford particular protection of rights to the Roman *publicus.* Rossi notes that through this process of refinement at municipal level, the equitable element in the *ius civile* began to expand from a vague notion of the comportment of a good citizen – roughly equivalent to the 'reasonable man' *qua* common law – to a set of small, albeit inconsistently applied, procedural remedies, largely affecting the areas of proprietary rights and contract law.[128] However, Rossi notes that such rights were only applicable to Roman citizens, and such equitable expansion did not take place in dealings with foreigners.[129]

Nonetheless, the *ius gentium* was also experiencing a process of change, although this began somewhat later than the *ius civile*. As the parallel universal system matured, it began to incorporate what had become fundamental principles of Roman civil law into its own free-standing legal structure. Of these principles, good faith (bona fides) was the most important as it served as the bedrock of many key tenets of the Roman legal structure. It is noteworthy by way of example to cite the fact that virtually

[125] H Maine, *Ancient Law* (London, Dent and Sons, 1861) 36.
[126] P Stein, 'Equitable Principles in Roman Law' in Newman (1973) (n 112) 75.
[127] We are fortunate enough to have access in the modern age to an electronic version, translated into English and elegantly annotated by Fred H Blume, and supported by the University of Wyoming. See uwacadweb.uwyo.edu/blume&justinian/.
[128] Rossi (1993) (n 9) 28.
[129] ibid, 29.

all actions arising from consensual or real (proprietary) contracts (*pacta sunt servanda*), *rei uxoriae*, quasi-contract and the protection of the interests of third parties (*negotiorum gestorum*) and fiduciary guardianship (*tutela fiduciaria*) were guided by this principle of good faith.[130]

However, despite the development of rights within both the *ius civile* and *ius gentium*, the legal system had remained relatively rigid as regards both remedies and statute law. This resulted in not infrequent denials of justice, even in cases where recognised rights had been infringed. It therefore fell to the praetor urbanus – the chief city magistrate – to issue remedies, which were termed *ius honorarium*. Such remedies were proclaimed by way of praetorian edicts (an approximation of something between civil regulations and public judgments), which built up into a *corpus* of binding precedents. While technically the praetor was forbidden from making use of such powers to legislate (and could be tried for treason if he did so), in reality, the fact that such precedents were binding gave them the force of law and regulated the conduct of citizens. In this respect, the praetor's powers were both legislative and judicial, and he possessed power to issue edicts (*ius edicendi*) to aid, supplement, or correct the existing law, that is *infra, praeter,* or *contra legem*.[131] Through the use of such edicts, successive praetors created alongside the narrow, formalistic civil law a body of flexible, adaptable law more sensitive to the demands of justice. This *ius honorarium* gave 'better' remedies to right-holders, and even created new rights where none had previously existed in the interests of justice.[132]

Commentaries on the praetors' activities show that practices developed over time to keep the impact of the subjectivity of the personal judgment of any one praetor to a minimum, much as common law equity responded to John Selden's taunt regarding the Chancellor's foot. It became clear that if the praetor used his power too enthusiastically, he would undermine public confidence in the law and its forms. Nonetheless, principles of remarkable similarity to those teased out by equity's practice in the common law may be observed in the *ius honorarium*. For example, the praetor was concerned to apply the principle that parties who had seriously and earnestly entered into a transaction with honest intentions of completing a bargain ought to have such intentions fulfilled, even in cases where they had failed to adhere to the particular formalities laid down by the law. Such tendencies were exemplified by the development of the idea of 'bonitary ownership' (roughly equivalent to an equitable interest) in Roman law, and parallel the development of the common law principle that 'equity looks to the substance rather than the form'.[133]

[130] ibid, 30.
[131] See ch 2 for a definition of such application of equitable doctines.
[132] WW Buckland, 'Praetor and Chancellor' (1939) 13 *Tulane Law Review* 163.
[133] Stein in Newman (1973) (n 125) 78.

Further, the *ius honorarium* could correct the civil law by conferring a remedy upon one person, where someone else may have been equally or more entitled at civil law, because the praetor considered the grantee more worthy of protection, often due to having behaved himself equitably and in good faith throughout. This parallels the common law doctrine that equity will not prejudice the interests of a bona fide purchaser for value without notice of any wrongdoing. It was also notable that the praetor was often prepared to go outside the boundaries of the statue law in conferring remedies upon individuals. For example, where only damages were provided for, but where *restitutio in integrum* would provide a more adequate compensation, this is what the praetor would ordain.[134] This was in strict contrast to the traditional *ius civile*, which, akin to the statutory common law, 'aimed not at making a party carry out his contract, but at making him pay for not doing so'.[135]

The principle prohibiting unjust enrichment was set out clearly by the praetors, and was incorporated into *Justinian's Digest*.[136] Furthermore, another principle consecrated by the *ius honorarium* stated that no one may take advantage of his own wrong. This was in contrast to the position regarding fundamental error, which vitiated the transaction *ab initio*, whether it was bona fides or *stricti iuris*.[137]

A further point of note is the palpable protection that the *ius honorarium* afforded to those parties who found themselves disadvantaged for whatever reason. Stein devotes considerable attention to this area, noting that praetors were not wont to apply legal rules to the prejudice of those who, for any reason for which they are not themselves to blame, are incapable of amply safeguarding their own interests. For example, where a man had been disenfranchised of some rights, particularly property rights, through lapse of time (prescription) or through non-appearance in court to contest his rights, because he was absent on State affairs or had been captured as a prisoner of war, he could later obtain *restitutio in integrum* and be restored to the position he would have occupied, had the prejudicial event never occurred.[138]

Another example of the above is the position concerning persons who have reached their majority – that is who are adults and who have attained full legal capacity – but who are at a distinct disadvantage by reason of their circumstances. For example, in Roman times, it was the custom that at the age of 14, a young man would quit his tutor, and was therefore considered to all intents and purposes to have become an adult. However, it

[134] ibid, 82.

[135] WW Buckland and AD McNair, *Roman Law and Canon Law: A Comparison in Outline*, 2nd edn, revised by FH Lawson (Cambridge, Cambridge University Press, 1965) 412, fn 1.

[136] D.50.17.206, see Stein in Newman (1973) (n 125) 87.

[137] Stein in Newman (1973) (n 125) 83.

[138] ibid, 88.

is clear that a young man of 14 is hardly capable of looking after his own interests when he partakes in commercial transactions, and already in the third century BC, a statute entitled the *Lex Laetoria* provided him with a defence if he was sued by one who had deliberately taken advantage of his greenness. Later, the praetor was to grant him *restitutio in integrum* of a transaction where he had suffered loss, harm or damage through his own inexperience or through the fraudulent machinations of the other party. The result of these successive measures was that persons would not transact with young adults between 14 and 25 years of age, unless they were accompanied by an independent adult to advise them, and the appointment of such a person, known as a *curator*, became standard practice.[139] This final example is of particular note, as it mirrors the position which the modern common law has adopted in most jurisdictions relative to those persons who are at risk of making a bad bargain by reason of exploitation by another who may be in a stronger position. Such has developed into the doctrine of undue influence, and while the age of legal majority is higher now – 18 in most jurisdictions – there remain categories of persons for which the modern law retains a special level of concern. A prominent example is when a wife makes a transaction with a bank which may not be in her best interest, the bank is obliged, when negotiating with the wife, to take note of the fact that her husband may exercise influence over her, and that the transaction may therefore either be entered into either with faulty information on the part of the wife, or to some extent *à contre-coeur*. Such is the regularity with which such manipulation of wives by their husbands in transactions of this kind occurs that the bank is obliged to ensure that the wife has taken independent legal and financial advice, either from a solicitor, a financial advisor, or another informed and independent person before the transaction is carried out. If this is not accomplished, the bank risks the annulment of the transaction *ab initio* for undue influence, of which it was constructively notified by the circumstances of the transaction.[140]

Overall, then, the Roman *ius honorarium* displays many of the tenets associated with equity *qua* common law. A preoccupation with standards of reasonableness and good faith is evident throughout, as is the careful balance between occasionally setting aside the rigid letter of the law in the name of justice and an awareness of the damage it could do if the legisla-

[139] ibid, 89.

[140] In truth, the modern common law position in this regard is vastly more nuanced than I have time to recount here. A fuller account of the position may be gleaned from the seminal cases of *Barclay's Bank v O'Brien* [1994] 1 AC 180, [1993] 4 All ER 417 and *Royal Bank of Scotland v Etridge* [2001] UKHL 44, [1998] 4 All ER 705 (CA); text available at www.publications.parliament.uk/pa/ld200102/ldjudgmt/jd011011/etridg-1.htm. See also M Beaumont, *Barclay's Bank: An Exercise in the Happily Illogical*, text available at www.windsorchambers.com/assets/article.pdf; and P Giliker, 'Barclay's Bank v O'Brien Revisited: What a Difference Five Years Can Make' (1999) 62 *MLR* 609.

tor's powers were seen to be usurped by the judiciary. Over the course of the period catalogued by *Justinian's Digest*, aside from the edicts of the praetors, there are many further examples of imperial interference with the application of the classical rules of Roman law 'in the course of efforts to protect the weak against the strong'.[141] Judges were also instructed to apply the law 'benevolently' or 'equitably'. Equity's stamp on the Roman legal system, then, is unmistakable.

iii. Equity in Muslim Law

The idea of a religion – and more particularly religious dogma – influencing a legal system is not an alien one to Western scholars. On the contrary, the influence of canon law upon Western legal systems has been significant. However, while others have endeavoured to chart the influence of equitable principles and equitable doctrine on canon law,[142] I consider it beyond the ambit of the current study to do so. The reason for this is that we are presently attempting to undertake a study of the impact of equity as an element of 'the general principles of law recognised by civilised nations', a particularly distinct category. The profound influence which equity in the Roman law and common law models have had upon modern legal systems merits their inclusion and examination in such a study. However, the influence of equity in canon law has been restricted by the Church, and since such a position does not seem to reflect any of the modern predominantly Christian States around the world – save perhaps the Holy See – a detailed analysis of equity's place in canon law seems superfluous here. It will suffice to say that despite the initial reluctance of the Church to concede a role to equity, such a berth was eventually created for a limited number of principles, and canon law is not therefore devoid of equitable considerations. Van Hove notes that written and unwritten sources of equity may be employed in such circumstances,[143] while Lefebve recalls the judicial rule of Pope Leo XIII that 'in extreme cases, equity shall prevail'.[144]

The same peripheral role accorded to canon law may not be accorded to Muslim law, however. The permeation of religion into political and legal systems throughout the Islamic world is such that religious principles

[141] Stein in Newman (1973) (n 125) 91–92.

[142] See, eg E Wohlhaupter, *Aequitas Canonica* (Paderborn, Germany, Schöningh, 1931); A Stiegler, *Der kirchliche Rechtsbegriff, Elemente und Phasen seiner Erkenntnisgeschichte* (Munich, Schnell and Steiner, 1958); F Elsener, 'Gesetz, Billigkeit und Gnade im Kanonischen Recht' in *Summum Ius, Summa Iniuria* (Tübingen, Mohr, 1963) 168–90; A McCoy, 'Canonical Equity Versus the Proliferation of Dispensations and Privileges' (1966) 23 *The Jurist* 95; and C Lefebvre, 'Equity in Canon Law' in Newman (1973) (n 112).

[143] A Van Hove, *De legibus ecclesiasticis* (Mechelen, Belgium, Dessain, 1930) 290.

[144] Lefebvre in Newman (1973) (n 141) 94. See also CJ Hering, 'Die Billigkeit im kanonischen Recht' in E Wolff, *Deutsche Landesreferate zum III. Internationalen Kongreß für Rechtsvergleichung in London* (Berlin, de Gruyter, 1950).

dominate many national legal systems.[145] While certain predominantly Muslim countries have modernised their legal systems, and have adopted a secularist model based upon Western values,[146] the majority of such States have remained true to the commands of their religion in many aspects of their legal systems. Such positions have been eroded in recent years by the human rights movement to some extent, but the civil law position remains broadly constant.

The *Koran*, the Sunnat, the Idjmaa and the following of the rites – these being analogy (*Ghyas*) and reason (*Aghl*) – are the four principal sources of Islamic law, while usage, custom and doctrine play a less important role.[147] According to Islamic ideals, God is the one 'true' legislator. Justice in Islamic law is described as a search for the truth rather than a balancing of competing legal interests. The *Sourat* stipulates that the Islamic faith, and therefore Islamic law, has been perfected, and legislators must therefore not diverge from it.[148] As Afchar has noted, 'the role of Equity in a juridical system in which the legislator no longer makes laws is and must be enormous'.[149] This would seem to be reflected by legal–religious texts, particularly the *Sourat*, which states that equity must rule in Muslim society, and encouraging followers not to follow passion to the detriment of equity.[150] There are further references to the Prophet ordaining that equity must rule amongst the faithful,[151] and that God himself has ordered equity.[152]

However, the precise content of Islamic equity remains to be examined. There are two words which find common usage in Muslim law, both of which can be considered to be a translation of the concept of equity. These are *Adle* and *Insaf*. Afchar notes that certain Islamic schools, amongst them Matazala and the Chiites, consider equity to be one of the Divine attributes, for iniquity – and by extension a complete absence of equity whereby unjust results cannot be corrected – is irreconcilable with the power and infinite wisdom of the God of the *Koran*, the lawgiver of Islam.[153]

As to how these equitable principles are realised in practice, the great rule that no one may cause unjust harm to another (*Lazaar*) underlies all dealings in Islamic law and which may never be surpassed. Two principal sub-rules may be derived from this, namely that God will require of no

[145] See FE Vogel, *Islamic Law and Legal System, Studies of Saudi Arabia* (Leiden, Brill, 2000).

[146] Turkey is a prime example of this, where the Civil Code is strongly influenced by that of Switzerland, and where the Kemalist tradition has ensured that Islamic principles have known little impact in the civil law since the collapse of the Ottoman Empire. See C Morris, *The New Turkey: The Quiet Revolution on the Edge of Europe* (London, Granta Books, 2005); and C Rumpf, *Recht und Wirtschaft der Türkei* (Stuttgart, Local Global, 2007).

[147] H Afchar, 'Equity in Musulman Law' in Newman (1973) (n 112) 111.

[148] *Sourat*, Book V, Verse 3: 'today, I have made your religion perfect'.

[149] Afchar in Newman (1973) (n 146) 111–12.

[150] *Sourat*, Book IV, Verse 135.

[151] *Sourat*, Book XLII, Verse 15.

[152] *Sourat*, Book XVI, Verse 90.

[153] Afchar in Newman (1973) (n 146) 112.

man more than he himself can accomplish.[154] This may be translated as the beginnings of a standard of reasonableness in conduct, which is certainly a common equitable principle in various legal systems. The second sub-rule is that bad faith will never receive protection by legal means. This stipulation finds a parallel in the Western conception of bona fides and the theory of the prevention of the abuse of one's rights. Further, Afchar notes that 18 separate verses of the *Koran* affirm that each man shall be rewarded only according to what he has accomplished (and not further).[155] This is clearly an approximation of the common and civil law doctrine of the prohibition of unjust enrichment.

Far from being a legal system in which equity is an alien element as one might have imagined at the outset, Islamic law, being strongly underpinned by ethics, has long been a system which protected the rights of those who were wronged but for whom the law was ill-adapted, this being the very role that equity was intended to play. What is perhaps interesting is that it was not merely Islamic judges who were expected to employ equitable formulations in their decisions, but rather every individual was formally required by law to act in an equitable manner toward his neighbour. What this entailed *in concreto* was more than merely refraining from encroaching upon others' rights, but rather for each person to be somewhat indulgent toward his neighbour and not exercise his rights in violation of his neighbour's interests unless it was completely necessary. This could extend to suspending journeys to help sick travellers (which may be paralleled with the French 'duty to rescue'), a duty to help hungry neighbours and a variety of other such rules.[156] The role of ethics seems to be significantly stronger in Islamic law than either the Romano-Germanic of common law systems. It is worth recalling, for example, that the common law duty of care model, based upon Lord Atkin's famous 'neighbour principle', which gave birth to the entire law of tort (non-contractual) negligence liability only came into being after the celebrated case of *Donoghue v Stevenson* in 1932.[157] It would seem clear that a similar extensive duty of care towards those with whom one had contact but no actual contractual links, existed in Islamic law many centuries before this date.

Afchar notes that in contractual relations, while equitable conduct is required throughout dealings for the party's conduct to be valid, equity itself is reducible to a series of maxims. These include: that one must not overreach one's co-contractor by way of lesion; that one must suffer the loss resulting from the contract if one's co-contractor is economically weak; that one must not be obdurate in demanding performance; that one

[154] *Sourat*, Book II, Verse 286 and Book VII, Verse 42.
[155] Afchar in Newman (1973) (n 146) 111.
[156] ibid, 117.
[157] *Donoghue v Stevenson* [1932] AC 562, [1932] All ER 1.

must pay readily one's debts without waiting for money to be demanded or legal action to be taken to extort it; that one must agree readily to prior rescission of the contract if the other party requests it; and that if one makes a contract with a person who is in an economically weak or otherwise disadvantageous position, one must do so having taken all relevant precautions, and with the knowledge that one may be required to relieve the other party of their obligations if they are unable to carry them out by reason of their disadvantage, economic or otherwise.[158]

This inexhaustive list of maxims does not precisely parallel that of the common law, or indeed the model furnished forth by the Roman law, though it would be foolish to say that they do not have a great deal in common. In the end, it seems, that, as elsewhere, equity in Islamic law is a device which is renowned above all for its flexibility and which may adapt to given situations as they come before it. If injustice or an unsatisfactory result is forthcoming due to inherent inadequacies of the statute law, 'the walls of the statutory rules, sooner or later, yield before the assaults of this eternally vital element'.[159]

iv. Equity in French Law

Having focused our attention thus far more on legal history rather than contemporary legal principles, we must now turn our attention to modern legal systems to gauge the applicability of equitable principles in systems outside of, and partially within, the common law. It is, as I have already had cause to outline, beyond the scope of the present study to examine minutely every legal system of every State in the world. In any case, such a study might well be pointless, seeing as various transplantations of law have taken place, and that the majority of modern States have adopted slightly adapted versions of one of several popular European models. There are important exceptions to this, such as Chinese law, which we shall have cause to examine later, and of course the now-defunct Soviet system had its idiosyncrasies also, but since we are dealing with 'the general principles of law recognised by civilised nations' as they stand nowadays, it is perhaps appropriate to turn our attention rather to the legal systems of States which are either highly typical of a large number of national legal systems, or which have influenced the composition of a great number of legal systems in foreign States. France is certainly possessed of such a legal system. Indeed, the French system, along with that of England, has been that which perhaps has been the most influential worldwide in recent centuries, largely due to the French colonial empire

[158] Afchar in Newman (1973) (n 146) 121.
[159] ibid, 122.

and the intelligent composition of the *Code Napoléon* which found admirers and imitators throughout the world.[160]

The position of equity within the French legal system, seems, at the first glance, to be a peripheral one. Despite the French passion for codification and clarity, equity is not set down as a source of law. There have been few exhaustive studies into its influence, and only incidentally is it referred to by the legislator. Courts rarely use the word, and positively avoid it most of the time. Even administrative judges, who are afforded far more freedom in their dealings, practically never mention equity.[161] Explaining this phenomenon is not particularly difficult however, and may be traced to French history, and a conception of law which finds its genome in the 1789 Revolution.[162] Even pre-Revolution, Montesquieu had identified the reason for this silence, stating that the nation's judges are simply the mouthpiece which pronounces the words of the law, and (should) lack power to moderate its force, its rigidity, or its interpretation; automatons rather than arbiters.[163] This position was attenuated somewhat by the Civil Code of the Project of the Year VIII which stated that in civil matters, in the absence of a specific statute, the judge should be considered a minister of equity, and might return to custom or natural law, but Benoit Jeanneau has noted that this did not prevent the resurgence of legalism and of constraining of judges.[164] Nonetheless, per Jeanneau, in spite of this, a certain latitude remains for the judges. While equity may not be employed by the French judge as openly as in systems where its presence as a formal source of law is more openly acknowledged, judges have, 'indirectly by devious processes' managed to incorporate many equitable principles into French law.[165]

The beginnings of such a process of incorporation are to be found in the *Code Civil* itself. While notorious for its exactitude and attention to detail, particularly when compared with common law statutes, the French Civil Code is nonetheless replete with a considerable number of rules or ideas, which, by the suppleness of their formulation, permit to the judge a margin of appreciation of their application, thus allowing him to adapt the abstract norm to concrete situations, rendering its application significantly

[160] Originally, *Code Civil des Français* (1804). See RB Holtman, *The Napoleonic Revolution* (Baton Rouge, Louisiana State University Press, 1981).

[161] R Chapuis, *Droit du contentieux administrative* (Paris, Montchrestien, 2006); J-C Bonichot, P Cassia and B Poujade,*Les Grands Arrêts du contentieux administrative* (Paris, Dalloz, 2006); M Long, P Weil, G Braibant, P Delvové and B Genevois,*Les Grands Arrêts de la jurisprudence administrative* (Paris, Dalloz, 2007).

[162] See E Burke, *Reflections on the Revolution in France and on the Proceedings in Certain Societies in London Relative to that Event* (London, Dodsley, 1790).

[163] Montesquieu, *Défense de l'esprit des loix* (Genève, Barillot, 1748) (known nowadays as *L'esprit des lois*).

[164] B Jeanneau, 'The Reception of Equity in French Public and Private Law' in Newman (1973) (n 112) 223–24.

[165] ibid.

more equitable. A frequent example of this is the tendency of judges to attempt to protect the party who was weaker in a given transaction. While Article 1116 of the Civil Code, dealing with fraud, requires the *manoeuvres* undertaken by the fraudulent party to have been deliberate, the courts have frequently softened this requirement, imposing in the name of equity upon the more powerful contractor a duty to divulge information to the other party *in contrahendo*. This is particularly the case where the more powerful party is a professional or *connoisseur*, and reflects the position in Roman law regarding young adults who enter contracts, and in the common law in cases of undue influence as discussed earlier in this chapter. The position of matrimonial acquisitions and undue influence concerning wives in French law is certainly somewhat similar to that prevalent in common law jurisdictions, as outlined in Article 1576, *alinéa* 2.

The need for equity in French law has been outlined by several legal scholars. As George L Clark has pointed out, the reason for equity's advent in common law was due to the defects inherent within the system, principally legal rigidity, but also the fact that it could only deal with two-sided cases, its inability to enforce judgments specifically, and the exclusively contentious nature of the law.[166] As Jacques Duffaux succinctly noted, French law – and indeed all civil law – is hardly immune to such defects.[167] However, the remedies devised for such problems – particularly as regards legal rigidity – are somewhat different in the French system. Some of the solutions come from within the *Code civil* itself, and were thus designed by its drafters. For example, the provisions of Articles 6, 900 and 1133 concerning *'ordre public'* confer upon judges a wide discretion to define and shape the ambit of such a concept of public order and security in whichever way best fits the circumstances before them. This is broadened still further by the lack of a rule of concrete stare decisis, which means that judges are not formally bound by past decisions (although the doctrine of *jurisprudence constante* affirms that they may not diverge from past consistent case law without due cause). The drafters of the Code also prescribed that the courts must clarify legal provisions in case of 'silence, obscurity or insufficiency', binding them under pain of prosecution for denial of justice.[168] This has led to creative solutions to problems from judges who are very aware of their duty to do justice by the parties. This has extended in various ways, including interpreting the silence of the *Code civil* was implying the maintenance of solutions which were valid under old French law, despite the general abrogation thereof by the Code. This was the case, for example, with the rule *'nemo auditor propriam turpidudinem allegans'*.[169]

[166] GL Clark, *Principles of Equity* (Mississippi, Columbia Press, 1919) 5–22.
[167] J Duffaux, 'Equity and French Private Law' in Newman (1973) (n 112) 245.
[168] Art 4, *Code civil*; Art 505 *Code de procédure civile*; Art 185 *Code pénal*.
[169] Req 1 février 1910, (1912) Recueil Dalloz I 65.

Equity may also play a role, not so much in interpreting the statute law as making it suppler and more pliable in and of itself (*inflexion juris stricti*).[170] An example of this is the granting of delay in the execution of a party's obligations. Article 1244 of the Civil Code confers this power upon judges, and they may exercise a broad discretion in how to employ it, depending upon circumstances and taking account of the position of the debtor. Articles 1184, *alinéa* 3 and 1655 contain similar provisions.

Good faith – *l'obligation de bonne foi* – is also a key element of the equitable apparatus in French law. Under Article 1134, *alinéa* 3 of the Civil Code, parties are under a duty to exercise their contractual obligations in good faith. This extends far beyond a bare conception of good faith into the prohibition of the abuse of one's rights (*théorie de l'abus du droit*), which was partly elaborated by judicial 'stretching' of the various *Code civil* provisions, stipulating that rights may be abused if used not for their owner's interest, but as a means of harming others. As early as 1913, Perreau had noted the development of a procedural technique by judges for softening the rigours of the positive law,[171] which Jeanneau has dubbed 'a form, hardly disguised, of equity'.[172] Further, the doctrine of *détournement de pouvoir* (the employment of power for a purpose other than that for which it was originally intended) – another manifestation of the good faith principle – has, for many years, permitted the Conseil d'État to push its investigations beyond the prima facie assessment of legality of the administrative action being examined.[173]

Equity's *modus operandi*, then, is quite different in French law to that which exists in common law jurisdictions. Despite the stereotypical impression of French law as a restrictive, rigid system, the civil law system, in certain circumstances, renders the judge 'a veritable minister of equity', in allowing him or her to determine every aspect of a number of comprehensive ideas which occupy important places in the French legal system. Amongst these are the concepts of *bon père de famille, diligence professionnelle normale* and *besoins* (roughly corresponding to 'diligent father/guardian of the family', 'normal professional diligence', and 'needs', respectively).[174] Through the interpretation of such concepts according to circumstances, the judge may exercise a very wide discretion indeed.

[170] ibid, 226.

[171] EH Perreau, 'Origine et développement de la théorie de l'abus du droit' (1913) *Revue génerale du droit* 481.

[172] Jeanneau in Newman (1973) (n 163) 229.

[173] ibid, 231.

[174] ibid, 227. See also A Boureau, 'Droit naturel et abstraction judiciaire: Hypothèses sur la nature du droit médiéval' (2002) 6 *Annales. Histoire, Sciences Sociales* 1463, available at www.cairn.info/article.php?ID_ARTICLE=ANNA_576_1463. Duffaux also disputes the veracity of the 'minister of equity' formulation, pointing out that such wording was removed from an early draft of the *Code civil* in the 8th year of the First Republic. J Duffaux in Newman (1973) (n 166) 248. The Cour de Cassation also had cause to reject this formulation: Cour de Cassation, Chambre Sociale, 23 Janvier 1948, JCP (1948) II 4229.

More striking still is the so-called 'theory of exceptional circumstances', originally conceived by the Conseil d'État for periods of 'trouble and upheaval', whereby the courts may give relief against the effect of what they would consider to be a too strict exercise of administrative regulations which were formulated for normal times. In the celebrated case of *Dame de la Murette*, the Tribunal des Conflits established by its authority this power of the judge to 'modify' the demands of the strictures of the law, in accordance with the circumstances of the case.[175] This power has since been extended significantly and is applied broadly by the administrative courts, although it is worth noting that administrative law allows the judge a greater modicum of freedom than in normal civil cases.

The above does not mean that the law of civil responsibility has not been strongly influenced by equity, however. French civil law has, on the contrary, felt equity's influence quite strongly. It is simply the case that the judge who pronounces in a civil court may not call equity by its name. Nonetheless, equity's progress in the last century or so has been unmistakable, and is acknowledged by leading scholars.[176] A well-known example of this progression has been the increasingly flexible interpretation of Article 1384, *alinéa* 1, which covers *'les choses qu'on a sous sa garde'*, approximately translated as things which are within the stewardship of a person. This article, while relatively unimportant on the face of it, has been construed over time by the courts to adapt civil responsibility to the rapidly advancing consequences of mechanisation and technological progress and to permit compensation for traffic and industrial accidents which would otherwise have been uncompensated and thus resulted in a denial of justice.[177] It has been further extended by the courts to cover the area of responsibility for any dangerous object that one may have in one's possession.[178] However, such advances were not without limits, and in order to prevent financial chaos on foot of such rapid systemic change, the Government saw fit to enact legislation in favour of insurance companies, which placed some limits upon liability.[179]

[175] *Dame de la Murette*, Tribunal des Conflits, 21 March 1952, (1954) Recueil Dalloz 291, note C Eisenmann.

[176] Jeanneau in Newman (1973) (n 163) 233–34.

[177] In traffic accidents, this was established by the Cour de Cassation in a celebrated Decree of 13 February 1930, establishing the complete responsibility of the 'owner' of the inanimate object (the vehicle), 'ownership' for such purposes being determined not by mere proprietary rights, which had previously been the case but which could clearly result in injustice, but rather upon the three-fold test established and concretised in subsequent cases of determining who had 'le pouvoir, la direction et le contrôle' of the vehicle. See: Chambres Réunies, 13 February 1930, (1930) Recueil Dalloz I.57, rapport Le Marchadour, conclusion Matter, note Ripert.

[178] This was extended in a case involving a fire which began in a barrel of resin which had been left unattended: Chambre Civil, 16 Novembre 1920, DI 169, note R Savatier.

[179] Loi du 7 Novembre 1922.

The development of Article 1384 in this manner 'assuredly ingenious, although tardily discovered, is actually equity'.[180] If indeed we may admit that it is, as Jeanneau has posited, a manifestation of equity, it again demonstrates equity's inherent adaptability to the time, place, and setting in which it finds itself. In England, equity came to the fore by reason of the necessity of tackling the inflexibility of the writs system and its unsuitability for the evolving sixteenth-century world in which it was operating. In France, again by reason of the necessity of the circumstances, equity appeared to render the *Code civil* somewhat more malleable in order to take account of the newly-mechanised world which was evolving and the injustices which would arise if the outdated Articles of the Code were inflexibly applied. This being the case, one is struck by the possibility that equity may have certain points in common with the doctrine of *ius necessitatis*. It is a point to which we shall be careful to return in later chapters.

The French civil law was to know more of equity's manifestations. This was certainly the case of the doctrine of strict liability (*responsabilité sans faute*) which was developed over time and which is set out in Article 1382 of the Code. Despite the principle established under Article 1384 that one was responsible for accidents caused by those inanimate things which one had under one's own stewardship, there was an evident necessity to attach a 'rider' clause, stipulating that if, for example, an employee was injured by a machine at which he was working but which belonged to his employer, and if he had committed no fault or had not misused the machine in any way, then the employer, and not he, was responsible for his injuries. This, again, demonstrates equity's aversion to fixed rules. Advocate-General Schmelck said as much before the Cour de Cassation: 'Equity does not accept without resistance abstract and absolute formulae. It demands a permanent adaptation to pressing necessities of life and to changing needs of human relations'.[181]

It is clear that the particular structure of French law – with three organs (namely the Cour de Cassation, the Conseil Constitutionnel and the Conseil d'État) all of which display some of the characteristics of a supreme court – generally makes the drawing of broad principles difficult. The differences between the civil law and administrative law are particularly notable in this regard. However, what is remarkable about equity to the extent that it has found a footing in the French system is that despite the differences between the various legal sub-systems in France, equitable principles have pervaded them all to some degree or another, often in a very similar manner from one sub-system to the next. We see a prime example of this in the fact that the above-discussed principle of *responsabilité sans faute* was consecrated by the

[180] Jeanneau in Newman (1973) (n 163) 235.
[181] Pronouncement of Advocate-General Schmelck, Cour de Cassation, 20 December 1968.

Conseil d'État into French administrative law as early as 1895 in the *Cames* case. Here, Commissoner Romieu stated that

> it is the function of the administrative judge to examine directly, according to his own lights, according to his conscience and in conformity with the principles of equity, the reciprocal rights of the State and its workers in the execution of public service.[182]

The process of equity's transcendence of the civil law / administrative law boundary may be used as evidence that equity *as a corrective* possesses the attributes of a general principle, or a series of general principles. This is significant not only because this chapter deals with assessing general principles of law, but because the normative worth of general principles is formally recognised in the French legal system. In fact, certain general principles are held to be part of the French *bloc de constitutionalité*, the collection of legal sources, which, together, form the law of the Constitution of France.[183] Further, within the civil law, explicit reference is made to the operability of the 'principles of natural equity' in Article 535 of the Civil Code, which seem to be largely inspired by Roman *ius honorarium*. Amongst these are classic equitable rules such as *nemo auditor propriam turpitudinem allegans;* the rule according to which he who has profited must bear the burden (*ubi emolumentum, ibi onus*, incorporating the prohibition of unjust enrichment[184]); and the rule according to which a man who was not in a position to defend his rights may not be divested of them (*contra non volentem agree non curit prescriptio*, incorporating equality of arms).[185]

Equitable, flexible remedies have also found favour in French civil law. The Cour de Cassation has stated that wherever the performance of an obligation depends upon the debtor's necessary initiative or requires certain personal qualities or actions on his behalf, the judge is possessed of discretionary power to substitute payment of damages for specific performance.[186] The opposite – specific performance in lieu of damages may also apply if the circumstances thus merit it. Furthermore, as regards receiving a remedy at all from equity, it is noteworthy that one's own conscience must be clear in order to do so. Duffaux notes that in France, analogous to common law, 'he who comes to equity must come with clean hands' and that this maxim 'is always considered by the French courts . . . in . . . serious cases'.[187]

[182] Pronouncement of Commissioner Romieu, Conseil d'État, 21 June 1895, (1897) S.3.33. Recueil 509, note M Hauriou.

[183] The other sources being the 1958 Constitution of the 5th Republic, the Preamble to the 1946 Constitution of the 4th Republic and the 1789 *Déclaration des droits de l'homme et du citoyen*.

[184] See: *Moniava v Beguiachvili*, Cour de Cassation, 2 July 1961.

[185] See: P Le Tourneau, *La règle 'nemo auditur'* (Paris, Librairie générale de droit et de jurisprudence, 1970).

[186] Cour de Cassation, 31 October 1906, Recueil, DP (1907) I 135.

[187] Duffaux in Newman (1973) (n 166) 258.

Due to the weight of French history discouraging judicial prevarication, instances of explicit decisions in the civil courts based solely on general principles (particularly *contra legem*) are extremely rare. However, such cases do occur.[188] In administrative law, the traditional judicial conservatism is less pronounced due to the less restrictive legislation, and this led the Conseil d'État, from 1945 onwards, to recognise an entire *corpus* of administrative general principles, applicable even in the absence of text, to mirror those recognised in the *bloc de constitutionalité,* and in French civil law forming, in effect, a new source of French public (administrative) law. The modalities of the *mise en oeuvre* of this source transpired to be remarkably similar to those of the civil law. For example in 1966, the principle providing for the prohibition of unjust enrichment, even in the absence of a textual provision to this effect, was upheld in French administrative law.[189] This followed the incorporation of the *recours pour excès de pouvoir* (an extended notion of the abuse of rights) into the administrative law in a similar manner some years earlier, having been justified, even without a textual provision, as a necessary principle which 'assumes the function of assuring, in conformity with the general principles of law, respect for legality'.[190] Jeanneau has noted that throughout the three branches of the French legal system, the general principles of law 'correspond in reality to superior values considered essential to a liberal and individualistic civilisation. So regarded, they are in a certain manner a manifestation of equity in the English sense'.[191]

French law, arguably the most influential of the civil law systems, may be held out as an excellent example of equity's operation in the civil law sphere. Those of the remaining sections which touch upon civil law systems will therefore endeavour to avoid repeating observations which have already been made regarding the intricacies of the civil law in general, and shall focus in the main upon their own distinctive characteristics. We shall continue our examination of comparative equity with a look at the German legal system.

v. Equity in German Law

We now turn our attention to the role of equity in the legal system of the German Federal Republic. The choice of Germany – another European

[188] See, eg Cour de Cassation, 15 June 1892, S (1893) I 283, note Labbé, which was decided upon the general principle prohibiting unjust enrichment, and which was later confirmed in two further cases: Cour de Cassation, 12 May 1914, S (1918) I 41, note E Naquet; Cour de Cassation, 11 December 1928, DH (1929) 18.

[189] *Ministère de la Construction c/ Ville de Bordeaux*, Conseil d'État, 14 October 1966, RDP (1967) 167.

[190] *Ministère de l'Agriculture c/ Dame Lamotte*, Conseil d'État, 17 February 1950, RDP (1951) 478, conclusion Devolvé, note Waline.

[191] Jeanneau in Newman (1973) (n 163) 240–41.

legal system – might seem somewhat Euro-centric on the face of it. However, this is by no means the case. On the contrary, the German legal system, while it has perhaps not met with the same degree of global reception and transposition of its French and English counterparts, it is nonetheless an important legal system, representing the epitome of the Germanic strand of the modern Romano-Germanic (civil law) tradition, and serving as the basis for many transplantations of law. For example, the legal systems of Japan, the Republic of Korea, and to some extent the People's Republic of China have all been strongly influenced by German law.[192]

German law, like French law, is a 'unified' system, that is, law and equity have never been separate autonomous entities. Nonetheless, it is clear that, as in France, a broad conception of equity may be found in the German legal order. EJ Cohn notes that it was certainly the intention of the drafters of the *Bürgerliches Gesetzbuch* (BGB, the German Civil Code) to find an equitable compromise for every conflict of interest, and thus to make equity a positive element of the Code.[193] The BGB regularly articulates flexible equitable concepts (adequate price, adequate damage, etc). However, in German legal theory, 'equity' is conceived of somewhat differently – as a means to counteract certain legalisms and as a way to achieve a level of relativity towards certain legal statuses.

Integral to German legal thought post-enlightenment was the view that 'fairness' assumed the nature of an integrated requirement of justice according to a law which unites *'was billig und recht ist'*.[194] However, due to the 'slight' nature of the integration of standards of fairness into the German Civil Code,[195] it became necessary to lessen the rigours of the application of strict law by way of corrective mechanisms. Therefore, like the common law before it, twentieth-century German law experienced a 'cross-pollenisation' between law and equity, albeit without the two diverging into separate streams of jurisprudence.[196] Nonetheless, equity is playing its own role 'as the defender of individual justice against the rigidities of the law, but without building up its own system of procedure, rules, or cases'.[197] The reason for this, presumably, is the absence of the stare decisis principle in German law.

Section 242 of the *Bürgerliches Gesetzbuch* has transpired to be the key rule where equity is concerned. A veritable *ius aequum* has been derived,

[192] See C Choi, 'On the Reception of Western Law in Korea' (1981) 9 *Korean Journal of Comparative Law* 141.

[193] EJ Cohn (ed), *Manual of German Law: General Introduction and Civil Law*, vol I (London, British Institute of International and ComparativeLaw, 1968).

[194] 'What is fair and lawful'.

[195] J Esser, 'The Inflitration of Aequitas into the German Civil Law' in Newman (1973) (n 112) 300.

[196] ibid, 299.

[197] ibid.

by way of doctrine as well as legal decisions, from this rule, which correct and modify the *ius strictum*. The rule runs thus:

> Der Schuldner ist verpflichtet, die Leistung so zu bewirken, wie Treu und Glauben mit Rücksicht auf die Verkehrssitte es erfordern.[198]

This Section would seem rather an innocuous and common good faith clause, which one might expect to find in any Civil Code. However, the German courts have made rather more of its content. Courts in fact often use Section 242 as an 'escape clause' from the rigidity of the written law, combining Section 242 with the notion of *Unzumutbarkeit* (disproportionate burden, unreasonableness). Section 242's good faith principle may influence obligations in three ways: by expanding obligations through the creation of additional duties to those laid down by contract or law; by limiting the exercise of legal rights; and by providing extraordinary remedies for the treatment of the problem of changed or unforeseen circumstances.[199] Diedrichsen posits that the second of these functions – the limitation of the exercise of rights – is probably its most important and most comprehensive role, insofar as it incorporates such important principles as the prohibition of the abuse of rights.[200] Also incorporated into the 'good faith' provision has been the prohibition of *venire contra factum proprium*, which is a close parallel of the English doctrine of estoppel, prohibiting contradictory conduct.[201]

Still further principles have been teased out of Section 242. A subcategory of *venire contra factum proprium* is the principle of 'laches' (*Verwirkung*) – similar to the doctrine of laches and acquiescence *qua* common law – which is always treated separately in textbooks due to its considerable importance.[202] This concept is applicable throughout the field of private law, and also in public law. Another principle which has derived from Section 242 is the idea of dishonest acquisition of rights, corresponding to the Roman law principle of *exceptio doli praeteriti*. This stipulates that the exercise of a right will be considered unlawful if the right-holder has acquired it by way of dishonest conduct or contrary to an agreement.

198 Literally translated as: 'The debtor is bound to effect performance of his debt according to the requirements of good faith, ordinary usage being taken into consideration'.

199 U Diedrichsen, 'Principles of Equity in German Civil Law' in Newman (1973) (n 112) 279.

200 ibid, 281. This principle finds a parallel in other provisions of earlier versions of the *Bürgerliches Gesetzbuch*, eg in the now-defunct S 361, which prohibits the making use of a formal right in a manner which is inconsistent with the purpose of the rule of law or contract for which it was derived.

201 W Weber, 'S 242 BGB' in J von Staudinger, *Kommentar zum Bürgerlichen Gesetzbuch, mit Einführungsgesetz und Nebengesetzen*, 2nd edn, vol II (Berlin, de Gruyter, 1954/1961 as amended) pt Ib, 323–94.

202 G Boehmer, *Grundlagen der bürgerlichen Rechtsordnung: Praxis der Richterlichen Rechtsschöpfung*, vol II (Tübingen, Archiv des Öffentlichen Rechts, 1952) s 2, 100–18; J Esser, *Schuldrecht: Allgemeiner Teil*, 4th edn, vol I (Karlsruhe, Müller, 1970) s 6 III 2.

However, in German law, the applicability of this principle is restricted by a number of other provisions in the BGB reflecting similar considerations.[203] Similarly, the exercise of a right will be considered unlawful if done so in an inconsiderate and excessively self-interested manner. That is, if such exercise of a right is grossly inequitable and inconsiderate as regards the interests of the other party. This flexible equitable standard is for the judge to decide upon, and, with its strong regard for the circumstances of each case, is undoubtedly a highly equitable principle.[204] A further example of this idea of flexible equity is the domain of *contrats d'adhésion* (standard service contracts where one party may not negotiate terms – must just 'take it or leave it'). Judicial decisions have traditionally restricted the content of such contracts by reference either to immorality (*Sittenwidrigkeit*) per Section 138, especially in the case of monopolies, or to good faith (*Treu und Glauben*) per Section 242. This in itself is equitable, reflecting concern for the interests of the weaker party, but a modern tendency has been to look for recourse to an equitable control mechanism (*Billigkeitskontrolle*) on the basis of Section 315, wherever one party is deprived to some degree of his autonomy in a contractual situation. This is especially the case regarding wills.[205]

Outside of Section 242, there are a number of further Sections of the German Civil Code, the interpretation of which, has followed the logic of common law equity. A prominent example is Section 125 – *Nichtigkeit wegen Formmangels* – which stipulates that any contract made without due regard to the proper rules of form is void.[206] However, the German courts soon set aside such a rigid rule, as they recognised that the strict application of Section 125 could lead to results which were manifestly unjust.[207] A rule was instead adopted that prioritised the substance of the transaction over the fulfilment of any formal requirements. In German law, this position developed at an early stage, with the former Reichsgericht applying the principle that recourse to nullity for non-compliance with rules of form was to be denied if – in consideration of all relevant circumstances

[203] eg S 123 (*Anfechtbarkeit wegen Täuschung oder Drohung*); S 138 (*Sittenwidriges Rechtsgeschäft; Wucher*); S 162 (*Verhinderung oder Herbeiführung des Bedingungseintritts*). See: F Wieacker, *Zur rechtstheoretischen Präzisierung des§242 BGB* (Tübingen, Archiv des öffentlichen Rechts, 1956) 30–33; and G Knopp, 'Schuldrecht (vol II)' in HT Soergel and W Siebert, *Bürgerliches Gesetzbuch, ein Kommentar,* 10th edn (Stuttgart, Kohlhammer, 1967) 193–208.

[204] See Knopp in Soergel (1967) (n 202) 262–67; and Diedrichsen in Newman (1973) (n 198) 285.

[205] B Dutoit, 'Good Faith and Equity in Swiss Law' in Newman (1973) (n 112) 315.

[206] The exact text reads: 'Ein Rechtsgeschäft, welches der durch Gesetz vorgeschriebenen Form ermangelt, ist nichtig. Der Mangel der durch Rechtsgeschäft bestimmten Form hat im Zweifel gleichfalls Nichtigkeit zur Folge'. (A legal transaction that lacks the form prescribed by statute is void. In case of doubt, lack of the form specified by legal transaction also results in invalidity).

[207] See Knopp in Soergel (1967) (n 202) 338–61; Diedrichsen in Newman (1973) (n 198) 286–87; Esser (1970) (n 201) 3.

– such recourse would be incompatible with the principle of bona fides.[208] The Bundesgerichtshof, in due course, adopted a similar formula.[209] However, this approach has been criticised by some German legal scholars as too vague and not sufficiently concrete, though clearly the search for a balance between legal certainty and individual substantive justice is a recurring problem which besets equitable principles.[210] Diedrichsen notes that neither court decisions nor legal scholars in Germany reflect a great deal of consensus on this issue.[211] Often, courts in particular have struggled to formulate principled approaches which may be consistently applied in areas where equitable principles frequently intervene. This has certainly been the case in decisions regarding the abuse of rules of form, and more particularly the 'lifting of the corporate veil' – that is, the disregarding of legal personality.[212]

It is clear that judicial decisions in regard to Section 242 BGB 'have increased in the form of a flood' in the twentieth century.[213] This reflected the relatively late, but extremely rapid, entry of equity into the German legal consciousness, pushed most likely by the drive away from strict positivism which occurred in the aftermath of the Second World War. Already in 1961, Weber's commentary on Section 242 in von Staudiger's treatise had reached 1,388 pages in length, longer than the text on all 240 Sections of the *Allgemeine Teil* of the BGB combined.[214] The extensive interpretation of Section 242 has permitted the courts to 'apply the codified law with astonishing flexibility, to modify it wherever its strict application would lead to inequitable results and to adapt it to the more and more rapidly changing conditions of our time'.[215] In this manner, the courts have incorporated the concept of equity into German law.

The permeation of equity into the German legal system is very much in keeping with what Esser describes as a 'world-wide recognition of the principles of a "minimum ethic" opposing the rigor iuris, ranging from the condemnation of fraud and deceit to the recognition of bona fides'.[216] Esser connects this 'minimum ethic' with Article 38(1) of the Statute of the

[208] *Amtliche Sammlung der Entscheidungen des Reichsgerichts in Zivilsachen* (1960) vol 157, 207–09; vol 170, 203–05.

[209] *Entscheidungen des Bundesgerichthofes in Zivilsachen* (1967) vol 16, 334–39.

[210] D Reinicke, *Rechtsfolgen formwidrig abgeschlossener Verträge* (Bad Homburg, Gehlen, 1969) 34.

[211] Diedrichsen in Newman (1973) (n 198) 287.

[212] See L Enneccerus and H Lehmann, *Recht der Schuldverhältnisse*, 15th edn (Tübingen, Mohr, 1958); and L Enneccerus and G Nipperdey, *Allgemeiner Teil des BGB*, vol I (1959) s 103 III.

[213] The quote is Diedrichsen's, and was made as early as 1973. His sentiments are still correct, perhaps even more so today. Diedrichsen in Newman (1973) (n 198) 296.

[214] W Weber, 'S 242 BGB' in J von Staudiger, *Kommentar zum Bürgerlichen Gesetzbuch, mit Einführungsgesetz und Nebengesetzen*, 2nd edn (Berlin, de Gruyter, 1954).

[215] Diedrichsen in Newman (1973) (n 198) 296.

[216] Esser in Newman (1973) (n 194) 305.

World Court and its recognition of 'general principles of law recognised by civilised nations', positing that the former must necessarily be a sub-category of the latter.[217] He mentions that he has been strengthened in his confidence in this respect by the parallels between the principles of equity in the common law and *Zumutbarkeit* (imputability) in the German legal system, adding that 'It is not only their maxims, but also concrete remedies which correspond'.[218] While Esser notes that the legal system of each State is different, the parallels may be found in the strict letter of the law being set aside on the basis of 'material considerations of justice and imputability'.[219] He describes it as the 'ethicisation' of the law, by means of resort to pre-dogmatic formulations of solutions, and the transformation of the conception of the purpose of law to that of 'a protector of society' with the judge interpreting his task in light of this ideal.[220]

vi. Equity in Dutch Law

Civil law in the Netherlands is an interesting case for the purposes of our study, since it combines elements of several of the systems already examined. Prior to the nineteenth century, the various legal systems which had been established in various regions of the Netherlands were heavily influenced by Roman law. The *Code Napoléon* maintained a short-lived existence in Holland under French rule, and finally, in 1838, some 25 years after the Dutch had re-attained independence, a Code was enacted by Parliament – the *Burgerlijk Wetboek* – which was to stand the test of time, and which was a curious mix of Roman, Dutch and French law.[221] Despite various and prolonged calls for substantive revision to this Code, especially in the decades immediately subsequent to the end of the Second World War, it was 1992 before the Dutch Code experienced a thorough overhaul. This reformed text was heavily influenced by the German *Bürgerliches Gesetzbuch* model, and represented a move toward a more equitable legal system, introducing new remedies and affording judges a far wider ambit of discretion in their decisions.[222]

The new Code merged the domains of commercial and civil law into a single regime, and thus was able to apply common standards throughout Dutch private law. With this being the case, and taking into account the German influence, it is not surprising to see that a significant place in the Code has been accorded to general principles of an equitable nature.

[217] ibid, 304.
[218] ibid, 305.
[219] ibid, 306.
[220] ibid.
[221] G Meijer, 'The Influence of the Code Civil in the Netherlands' (2002) 14 *European Journal of Law and Economics* 227, 228–32.
[222] M Hesselink, *The Harmonisation of European Contract Law* (London, Hart, 2006) 40–41.

Throughout the Code are frequent restatements of the general requirement of good faith, while Articles 1 and 2 of Book 6 state that both parties in a legal relationship must behave equitably and reasonably toward one another.[223] Actions are also available for unjust enrichment – Book 6, Article 212[224] – and abuse of rights or circumstances.[225]

Despite the fact that the new Code has functioned well and has resulted in increased levels of equity in Dutch law, it has come under criticism for too-closely resembling the German model, for representing a break with Dutch legal traditions, and above all for affording judges excessive levels of discretion.[226] While this may be, to an extent, justified, it is worth noting that Dutch legal tradition – that is, the Dutch legal tradition which followed the adoption of the original *Burgerlijk Wetboek* in 1838 – was already both familiar and comfortable with the concept of equity.[227] The previous Dutch Code had a lengthy and relatively settled existence. In the twentieth century, it served as a partial inspiration for certain transplantations of law to newly-independent States, including former Dutch colonies,[228] and was itself a sort of *Gestalt* of Roman, French, and indigenous Dutch legal

[223] 'Verbintenissen kunnen slechts ontstaan, indien dit uit de wet voortvloeit . . . Schuldeiser en schuldenaar zijn verplicht zich jegens elkaar te gedragen overeenkomstig de eisen van redelijkheid en billijkheid. Een tussen hen krachtens wet, gewoonte of rechtshandeling geldende regel is niet van toepassing, voor zover dit in de gegeven omstandigheden naar maatstaven van redelijkheid en billijkheid onaanvaardbaar zou zijn'.(Obligations can only arise if this results from law . . . The creditor and debtor must act towards one another in accordance with the standards of reasonableness and fairness. A rule in force between a creditor and his debtor by virtue of law, common practice (custom) or a juridical (legal) act does not apply as far as, in the given circumstances, this would be unacceptable by standards of reasonableness and fairness.

[224] '1.Hij die ongerechtvaardigd is verrijkt ten koste van een ander, is verplicht, voor zover dit redelijk is, diens schade te vergoeden tot het bedrag van zijn verrijking. 2.Voor zover de verrijking is verminderd als gevolg van een omstandigheid die niet aan de verrijkte kan worden toegerekend, blijft zij buiten beschouwing. 3. Is de verrijking verminderd in de periode waarin de verrijkte redelijkerwijze met een verplichting tot vergoeding van de schade geen rekening behoefde te houden, dan wordt hem dit niet toegerekend. Bij de vaststelling van deze vermindering wordt mede rekening gehouden met uitgaven die zonder de verrijking zouden zijn uitgebleven'.(1. A person who has been unjustifiably enriched at the expense of another person, has the obligation towards that other person to repair the damage up to the amount of his enrichment, as far as this is reasonable. 2. As far as the enrichment has been decreased as a result of an event which cannot be attributed to the enriched person, this decrease will not be taken into consideration in determining the amount of the enrichment that has to be rectified. 3. In case the enrichment has been decreased during a period in which the enriched person reasonably should not have been aware of the existence of an obligation to repair the damage, this decrease is not attributable to him. In determining this decrease, expenditures which the enriched person would not have made in the absence of the enrichment are taken into account)

[225] CJH Brunner, 'Abuse of Rights in Dutch Law' (1976–77) 37 *Louisiana Law Review* 729.

[226] A Hartkamp, 'Judicial Discretion under the New Civil Code of the Netherlands' (2002) 40 *American Journal of Comparative Law* 551.

[227] See H Warendorf, R Thomas and I Curry-Summer, *The Civil Code of the Netherlands* (Leiden, Kluwer, 2009).

[228] D Berkowitz, K Pistor and J-F Richard, 'The Transplant Effect' (2003) 51 *American Journal of Comparative Law* 163.

thinking. With this in mind, a brief examination of the previous Civil Code's development of equity is warranted.

While Section 11 of the Law Providing General Provisions Concerning the Legislation of the Kingdom of the Netherlands of 1829 provided that the judge must decide purely according to the law, and may not judge about the value or equity of the law, in practice a broader interpretative power was applied, especially post-Second World War. Until then, positivism's influence had been significant, but with the drafting of the preliminary statute of a revised Code in 1955, this began to change. Furthermore, what equitable advances there had been in Dutch courts – via equitable flexibility and interpretation et cetera – began to be codified.[229] Section 1374(3) of the pre-1992 Civil Code provided that contracts must be performed in good faith, while Section 1375 provided that contracts create obligations not only according to their own terms, but also according to everything which is demanded by the nature of the contract, custom and equity. Many areas of Dutch law were, even pre-1992 'characterised by the compulsory balancing of the interests and the protection of the weaker party'.[230]

The evidence of equity's influence was not merely confined to statute law, however. Judicial decisions also established the existence of equitable principles, sometimes in the absence of, or even against the strict provisions of, legislation. The Hoge Raad (Dutch Supreme Court) has, on occasion, not been shy about establishing rights and remedies in such circumstances when it sees fit. For example, in 1936, there existed no general provision in Dutch law outlawing the abuse of rights. Nonetheless, in a case where a landowner had constructed a tower in his garden purely to impair the view of his neighbour, the Hoge Raad held that such a doctrine could exist in certain circumstances.[231] This was confirmed and expanded by later decisions.[232] Such judicial activity also expanded the notion and effectiveness of good faith[233] and amended undue influence standards to make them more stringent for banks and stronger parties, much like in Roman law and common law.[234] The prioritisation of the substance of a transaction over the fulfilment of legal formalities was also set established.[235] In the renowned *Lindebaum v Cohen* case, standards of care in one's conduct which previously had only applied in contractual relations were broadened to encompass a standard of negligence in tort law, quite

[229] JLM Elders, 'Equity in Dutch Law' in Newman (1973) (n 112) 355.
[230] ibid, 357.
[231] Hoge Raad, 13 March 1936, (1936) *Nederlandse Jurisprudentie* 705.
[232] See (1961) *Nederlandse Jurisprudentie* 553.
[233] Hoge Raad, 29 January 1931, (1931) *Nederlandse Jurisprudentie* 1317.
[234] Hoge Raad, 11 January 1957, (1959) *Nederlandse Jurisprudentie* 37; and Hoge Raad, 19 January 1967, (1967) *Nederlandse Jurisprudentie* 261.
[235] Hoge Raad, 20 February 1933, (1933) *Nederlandse Jurisprudentie* 918.

akin to *Donoghue v Stevenson* in England.[236] The *Lindebaum* case in particular represented a landmark, since it represented the beginning of equitable standards of decency, reasonableness and good faith pervading into judgments on a not infrequent basis in the Dutch legal system and thus consecrating a significant role for equity in Dutch law.[237]

The fact that equity has played such an important role in Dutch law throughout the years demonstrates that Dutch civil law, much like other civil law systems, has had a propensity to adopt a system of *ius honorarium* to soften the rigours of the statute law. This was the case even before the 1992 reform which brought the system closer to Germany, and in doing so increased the level of equitable influence. In fact, the reforms accomplished in 1992 largely served only to alter those areas of the law which had been least touched by equity's influence, leaving the equitable *acquis* in other areas intact.[238] The notable role of equitable principles in the Dutch legal culture is further evidence of their claim to be counted as 'general principles of law recognised by civilised nations'. This is further borne out by the fact that the Dutch legal system has itself had a significant influence on the legal cultures of its former colonies, and occasionally neighbours of former colonies. South Africa,[239] Namibia, Lesotho, Swaziland, Zimbabwe, Sri Lanka and Guyana have all felt significant Dutch influences upon their respective legal systems. This is true in all areas of law, including that of equity and general principles.[240]

vii. Equity in Swiss Law

The Swiss Civil Code of 10 December 1907 (German: *Zivilgesetzbuch*; French: *Code civil*; Italian: *Codice civile*; Romansh: *Cudesch civil*, ZGB) represents the codified civil law of Switzerland, which regulates relationships between individuals. It has been in force since 1912. It was largely influenced by the German Civil Code, and partly influenced by the French Civil Code, but the majority of comparative law scholars argue that the Swiss Code derives from a distinct paradigm of civil law.[241] This renders it

[236] *Lindenbaum v Cohen*, Hoge Raad, 31 January 1919, (1919) *Nederlandse Jurisprudentie* 161.
[237] See Elders in Newman (1973) (n 228) 361.
[238] JM Milo, 'General Principles' in D Busch and HN Schnelhaas (eds), *The Principles of European Contract Law (Pt III) and Dutch Law*, vol II (The Hague, Kluwer, 2006) 77.
[239] As a general rule, South Africa follows English law in the areas of procedural law, company law and the law of evidence; while Roman–Dutch common law is followed in South African contract law, tort, law of persons, law of real property, and family law.
[240] See R Feenstra and R Zimmermann (eds),*Das romisch-holländische Recht. Fortschritte des Zivilrechts im 17. und 18. Jahrhundert* (Berlin, Duncker and Humblot, 1992); R Zimmermann, *The Law of Obligations* (Cape Town, 1990).
[241] R Sacco, 'Codificare: Modo Superato di Legiferare?' (1983) 5 *Rivista di Diritto Civile* 117; K Zweigert and H Kötz, *Einführung in die Rechtsvergleichung auf dem Gebiete des Privatrechts*, 3rd edn (Tübingen, Mohr, 1996) 165–76.

instructive and interesting for a comparative study. Furthermore, the Swiss Civil Code system has been exported and transplanted elsewhere, most prominently in the Turkish Republic, with the Civil Code of Turkey representing a largely unmodified version of the Swiss Code, adopted in 1926 during the Kemalist Government's period of secularisation. However, despite being considered the embodiment of a distinct legal paradigm by many scholars, in practice, the Swiss conception of equity is very similar to that of its neighbour Germany.

Much as in Germany, the concepts of good faith and equity can be considered to be the two traditional methods of adapting abstract and rigid legal rules to the eventualities of everyday life: good faith being directed to 'the measure of contractual obligation'; whereas equity functions as a praetorian law complementing the written law.[242] Article 1.2 of the Civil Code stipulates that equity has a role in filling gaps in the law, since the judge is directed, where lacunae appear, to act according to custom, and where no custom exists, as he would imagine the legislator to wish.[243] Furthermore, Article 2.1 establishes the principle of good faith as the criterion of interpreting and completing juridical and legal acts. Article 2.2 complements this by prohibiting the abuse of rights.[244] Importantly, Article 4 explicitly provides the judge with the power to make decrees on the basis of equity, taking into account all necessary surrounding circumstances, where the law permits him a margin of appreciation.[245]

In addition to the provisions of the Civil Code, case law in Switzerland displays frequent interpretation of legal rules with reference to equity, often without any reference to any of the above provisions.[246] Particularly

[242] H Deschenaux, 'Le traitement de l'equité en droit suisse' in M Bridel (ed), *Recueil de travaux suisses présentés au VIIIème Congrès international de droit comparé* (Basel, Helbing and Lichtenhahn, 1970) 29.

[243] Art 1.2 stipulates: 'Kann dem Gesetz keine Vorschrift entnommen werden so soll das Gericht, nach Gewohnheitsrecht und, wo auch ein solchesfehlt, nach der Regel entscheiden, die es als Gesetzgeber aufstellen würde'. (In the absence of a provision, the court shall decide in accordance with customary law and, in the absence of customary law, in accordance with the rule that it would make as legislator.)

[244] 'Jedermann hat in der Ausübung seiner Rechte und in der Erfüllung seiner Pflichten nach Treu und Glauben zu handeln . . . Der offenbare Missbrauch eines Rechtes findet keinen Rechtsschutz'. (Every person must act in good faith in the exercise of his or her rights and in the performance of his or her obligations . . . The manifest abuse of a right is not protected by law.)

[245] Art 4 states: 'Wo das Gesetz das Gericht auf sein Ermessen oder auf die Würdigung der Umstände oder auf wichtige Gründe verweist, hat es seine Entscheidung nach Recht und Billigkeit zu treffen'.(Where the law confers discretion on the court or makes reference to an assessment of the circumstances or to good cause, the court must reach its decision in accordance with the principles of justice and equity.) The French text, also authoritative, is seemingly even more explicit on this point, making reference to *équité* (equity) rather than the German *Billigkeit*, which is ambiguous and can also mean fairness: 'Le juge applique les règles du droit et de l'équité, lorsque la loi réserve son pouvoir d'appréciation ou qu'elle le charge de prononcer en tenant compte soit des circonstances, soit de justes motifs'.

[246] Dutoit in Newman (1973) (n 204) 308.

due to Article 1.2, however, the road is wide open for the Swiss judge to create 'an "equitable law" in the sense of Roman equity of the classical period or of equity in the Anglo-Saxon system, conceived of less as a means of correcting than of completing the existing law'.[247] Deschenaux notes that within the scope of Article 1.2, the judge is called upon 'to forge a rule out of nothing beyond the law, but within the scope of a given juridical regime and the general principles which support it'.[248] As to the ambit of the good faith provision, it has been described as being a means of reconciling law with social reality.[249] It is clear that the actual will of the parties must be established as a starting point for contractual interpretation, according to Article 20 of the *Code des Obligations*. However, if such a subjective interpretation fails to disclose the intentions of the parties, the judge must examine their actions and declarations in deciding by means of a so-called objective interpretation of the facts at hand. Such examination presupposes and is governed by the principle of good faith.[250] However, unlike in Germany, the courts have not pronounced upon the matter of *contrats d'adhésion* as of yet. Nonetheless, it would seem that a similar line to that prevalent in Germany (where care is taken to protect the weaker party) would also apply here. This is in no small part due to the fact that the Federal Tribunal has made clear that the provisions of Article 2 of the Zivilgesetzbuch (ZGB) represent a *'Bestandteil der allgemeinen Rechtslehre'* (constitutive element of the common juridical doctrine), which implies that the duty of good faith and the prohibition of the abuse of rights apply in all legal spheres within Swiss law, that is, in cantonal and public law as well as in civil and federal law.[251] Intent to abuse is not necessary for an abuse of a right to occur, so long as one is exerting one's right in a way that is harmful to another in furtherance of an interest that is not entitled to protection. This goes marginally further than the French position.[252]

Analogous to the French legal position regarding strict liability for dangerous objects in one's possession, an obligation of protection and due diligence is imposed upon any person who has created a dangerous situation. If such a danger, however, is inherent within the contract's execution, it becomes an explicit accessory object to the contract, as the other party was made aware of, and accepted, the danger.[253] A further extension

[247] ibid.

[248] Deschenaux (1970) (n 241) 32.

[249] Dutoit in Newman (1973) (n 204) 311–13.

[250] H Merz, 'Einleitung: Art 1-10 ZGB' in M Gmür, et al, *Berner Kommentar zum Schweizerischen Zivilgesetzbuch* (Berne, Stämpfli, 1962) 258.

[251] *Recueil officiel des arrêts du Tribunal Fédéral Suisse*, vol 83, no 2, 349.

[252] D Manaï, *Le juge entre la loi et l'équité: essai sur le pouvoir d'appréciation du juge en droit Suisse* (Lausanne, Payot, 1985) 188–204.

[253] *Recueil officiel des arrêts du Tribunal Fédéral Suisse*, vol 79, no 2, 69, vol 71, no 2, 107.

of the good faith doctrine surrounds the unfair acquisition of rights. While in Swiss law there is no rule according to which only an honest person may exercise his rights, the acquisition of a right in bad faith will still preclude its owner from utilising it by reason of the maxims *'nemo auditor propriam turpitudinem allegans'* and 'he who seeks equity must do equity'.[254] In the field of contract law, this principle finds a precise illustration in the duty imposed upon any party who seeks the enforcement of a bilateral contract to have performed – or offered to perform – his own obligations, as well as the detailed rules relative to the effects of failure to perform one's obligations.[255]

There is no fast and firm rule of estoppel or *venire contra factum proprium* in Swiss law, but such conduct will nonetheless be seen to violate the principle of good faith if it is blatant.[256] It can also constitute an abuse of right, for example in the case of the usage of prescription periods governing rights, when one had given assurances that one would not do so.[257] However, the idea of *Verwirkung* (laches), which entails the loss of rights by reason of delay in enforcing them, applies in a similar manner to German law. As regards rules of form, a 'middle road' is taken. Dutoit notes that although modern Swiss law has progressed from the consideration of form as constituting the very origin of the results of a juridical act (*Wirkform*) to the sole function of form as an element in assuring the security of transactions (*Zweckform*) – and thus adopting a purposive approach – form in fact has almost no connection with the purpose to be attained, and thus should be relatively unimportant. However, he goes on to note that generally speaking, one party could not employ the abuse of right doctrine against the other party who seeks to annul his obligation by reason of defect of formal rules, even if the plaintiff had on his part already executed his obligation, although an obvious exception to this would occur in cases of utilisation of a formal rule in a manner so as to defeat its particular purpose.[258]

As regards the power of the Swiss judge to decide on the basis of equity, as set out in Article 4 of the ZGB, it would seem, from the text of the Article at least, to be a situation of gap-filling (*praeter legem*) rather than any possible *contra legem* panacea. Although stare decisis is alien to the Swiss system, the judge 'must try to work up criteria of interpretation sufficiently objective to lend themselves to a certain degree of generalisation and to enable him to reach identical solutions for identical cases'.[259] However, quite aside from the powers conferred in Article 4 in this regard, it would seem that the judge is conferred with another implicit power to

[254] Dutoit in Newman (1973) (n 204) 332.
[255] ibid. See also Arts 82 and 97, *Code des Obligations*.
[256] Merz (1962) (n 249) 333–45.
[257] *Recueil officiel des arrêts du Tribunal Fédéral Suisse*, vol 42, no 2, 682.
[258] Dutoit in Newman (1973) (n 204) 335, 339.
[259] ibid, 342.

use equity as an auxiliary canon of interpretation. Dutoit points out that quite apart from good faith or the provisions of Article 4, equity or unwritten law plays a 'by no means negligible' further role in Swiss law, which has been demonstrated by several cases in which the Swiss Federal Tribunal has rendered a judgment clearly in contradiction to the express text of the statute, because the statute 'is not adapted to new social realities or to the requirements of equity'.[260]

Thus it would seem from our study of the European civil law systems that equity, while quite a different beast from that of the common law, plays a role which is in some respects very similar to that of its Anglo-Saxon counterpart. It functions as a softener of legal rigidity, an occasional corrective, and a means for justice to be done where the rules either run out or are insufficiently clear or poorly drafted. The main distinction would seem to be that while most of what equity provides at common law has been teased out of case law over the centuries, the equitable principles of the civil law systems find their basis, in the main, within the Codes themselves, and have merely been expanded upon by the courts. However, it remains to examine whether this neat similarity is followed in systems outside of Europe, whether they base their legal principles on common law, civil law, both or neither.

viii. Equity in the Legal System of the United States of America

No study of the legal systems of the 'civilised nations' of the modern world would be complete without a perspective on that of the United States. The hegemonic position which the United States occupies in international politics has dictated that a number of other States have imitated elements of its legal system, including its particular take on the common law.[261] The American legal system was predictably affected by that of its former colonial masters, and the developments which were experienced in English equity until the late eighteenth century were, by and large, replicated by the 13 original British colonies in their local courts until independence, and for a period thereafter.[262] However, with the 1776 Declaration of Independence and subsequent revolution, a decentralised system predicated strongly upon the autonomy of each State (that is, each

[260] ibid, 344. A few examples of this doctrine are to be found: *Recueil officiel des arrêts du Tribunal Fédéral Suisse*, vol 43, no 2, 225, vol 51, no 2, 171, vol 55, no 2, 23, and vol 80, no 2, 311.

[261] SeeJ-M Crouzatier, 'Le Régime Présidentiel: Les Etats-Unis d'Amerique' in, *Introduction au droit public et droit Constitutionnel* (Lectures Series, Université des Sciences Sociales Toulouse-I, 2004) w3.univ-tlse1.fr/CERCP/CrouzatierConstit%201%B0%20ann%E9e%20Cours.htm; see also R Séroussi, *Introduction au Droit Comparé (IV: Le Droit Américain)*, 3rd edn (Paris, Dunod, 2008) 73–126.

[262] The 13 original colonies being: Delaware, Pennsylvania, New Jersey, New York, Georgia, Connecticut, Massachusetts, Rhode Island, Virginia, Maryland South Carolina, North Carolina and New Hampshire.

former colony) was to emerge. The Articles of Confederation and Perpetual Union, drafted during the revolution and ratified by all States in 1881 formed the newly-independent former colonies into a loose confederation which would cooperate for the purposes of trade, defence and foreign affairs. While technically the United States of America's first Constitution, the Articles of Confederation kept the powers of the central government to a minimum. While the Confederation's Parliament (Congress) could make decisions, unanimous approval of State legislatures was required to ratify any major decisions.[263] In the formative years of the United States, the confederated structure resulted in a strong conception of State rights, which led to some divergences in legal cultures.

With the advent of the United States Constitution of 1787, and its ratification in 1788, a federal government with real and effective legislative, executive and judicial powers was established. However, supposing that this hierarchy had been adopted voluntarily by the 13 former colonies would be misleading. While the 1785 Mount Vernon Conference and the 1786 Annapolis Convention are cited by some as moves toward an effective federal Constitution, the reality is that these measures were undertaken in order to regulate trade and to divide the resources of the Potomac River.[264] The reality is that, much like the Articles of Confederation, the Constitution was foisted upon the putative Confederation of States by necessity, the necessity being to quell civil unrest and form a centralised government with effective police powers. The 'Shays' Rebellion' of 1786–87 was the largest manifestation of a restless populace unhappy with the fact that taxes and debt had actually increased since independence. The fear wrought upon the governing classes by the Shays' Rebellion and others like it represented the motivation which won the day for the federalist camp at the Philadelphia Congress, resulting in the relatively powerful federal governmental structure which is still in place today.[265]

The preceding historical note is necessary to demonstrate the complexities of the United States' various legal systems – at federal and State levels, and the fact that many States have historically been unwilling to 'toe the line' and follow federal instructions where there is no clear rule requiring such conduct. A good modern example of this is the fallout from the celebrated *La Grand* case before the International Court of Justice.[266] The *Kulturkampf* between the rights of individual States and the federal gov-

[263] DS Lutz, 'The Articles of Confederation' in SL Schechter, *Roots of the Republic: American Founding Documents Interpreted* (Oxford, Madison House, 1990).

[264] L Richards, *Shays' Rebellion: The American Revolution's Final Battle* (Philadelphia, University of Pennsylvania Press, 2002) 1–4, 129–30.

[265] For an instructive note on this process from a constitutional law point of view, see Crouzatier (2004) (n 260).

[266] *La Grand (Germany v United States)* (Judgment) [2001] ICJ Rep 466; see also: *Germany v United States*, 526 US (1999) 111.

ernment can also be traced as being the root cause of the civil war, with the secessionist Confederate States of America originally conceived of as a nineteenth-century equivalent of the original Confederation of States, with the powers of central government strongly curtailed.[267]

The dynamic tension between State and federal law which has persistently beset the legal system of the United States, has, however, not had as negative an impact upon equity's incorporation into the American legal sphere to as great a degree as one might imagine. While it is beyond the scope of this study to examine each federal State's individual take on equity in isolation, a few remarks may be made.

The dual courts system which was in place in England prior to the Judicature Acts of the 1870s was retained in 11 of the 13 colonies post-independence, with Pennsylvania and Massachusetts the exceptions, although during the nineteenth century, both these States conferred power upon their courts to administer equitable relief.[268] From the beginning of the nineteenth century, it became clear, as in England, that two systems of justice in two parallel systems of courts at State level was a deficient model, and rendered the already complicated federal–State legal dichotomy still more complex. However, reform in the United States was different to that in England, 'due to the formalism of a positivist type of legal philosophy, which attempted to combine common law and equitable remedies into a single system of procedure'.[269] Under this doctrine, there was to be but one form of action in private law, that being a civil lawsuit. The process of conversion to this model began in 1848 with the State of New York, and was followed by the majority of other States so that at this time, of the 46 States and 4 Commonwealths, 33 have such a combined 'civil' system. This differed somewhat from the conception in England, where the Judicature Act of 1873, although also embodying a positivist philosophy, accepted the premise that while the distinction between law and equity had been artificially created, it was at the time so embedded so as to be insusceptible to outright abolition.[270] In practice, however, the systems have given rise to almost identical results, and despite the 'insusceptibility' toward fusion of common law and equity in England in the 1870s – Ashburner's famous 'fluvial metaphor' stating this position – it is worth recalling Lord Diplock's damning of the fluvial metaphor as 'both mischievous and deceptive', stating that if the 'fluvial metaphor is to be retained at all, the waters of the confluent streams of law and equity have

[267] PD Escott, *After Secession: Jefferson Davis and the Failure of Confederate Nationalism* (Baton Rouge, Louisiana State University Press, 1992) 55–112.

[268] G Glenn and K Redden, 'Equity – A Visit to the Founding Fathers' (1945) 31 *Virginia Law Review* 757, fn 13.

[269] BF Brown, 'Equity in the Law of the United States of America' in Newman (1973) (n 112) 213.

[270] ibid.

surely mingled now'.[271] Thus, the differential between the traditional common law model and the preponderant position in the majority of the US State systems as regards equity is relatively insignificant.

Obviously, the above is not to say that all US States enjoy a comparatively homogenous legal ethos as regards private law, loosely based upon the common law tradition. Important differences do exist, with Louisiana representing, perhaps, the prime example of an anomalistic case. Nonetheless, the civil law of Louisiana is strongly influenced by the French Civil Code, and thus is not immune to equitable influence itself. The now-abolished Article 21 of the Louisiana Civil Code, for example, stated that

> [i]n all matters where there is no express law, the judge is bound to proceed and decide according to equity.

The reason for the abolition of this Article – which is both in tune with considerations of equity and the civil law need to avoid situations of *non liquet* – was the adoption of new provisions into the Code that to a large degree replicate the common law conception of equity as a corrective mechanism employed in the interests of justice, even within a civil law legal system.[272] This is indicative of a slow process of harmonisation of private law in the United States that has been taking place in recent decades.[273]

US federal law also experienced a merger of common law and equity into a single system of procedure, with the adoption by congressional statute of the Federal Rules of Civil Procedure in 1938. However, equitable justice played and is continuing to play an important role in US federal law. For example, in the case of *Isle Royale Mining Company v Hertin*, it was held that the doctrine of unjust enrichment, originating from equity, had not been given adequate effect by the legal formula of quasi-contract so as to protect the rights of weaker parties. Therefore it was held not to apply in the case in question.[274] Equity further developed the *in personam* remedies of rescission and reformation[275] in American law.[276] In doing so, equity 'moved away from the formalism of the law, which protected rights of personality only if a property right was involved'.[277] It was therefore no longer necessary to 'fictionalise' a property right as was famously done by Lord

[271] *United Scientific Holdings Ltd v Burnley BC* [1978] AC 904, 925.

[272] AN Yiannopoulous, 'Louisiana Civil Law: A Lost Cause?' (1980) 54 *Tulane Law Review* 830.

[273] ibid.

[274] *Isle Royale Mining CovHertin* 37 Mich 332 (1877) (Sup Ct of Michigan).

[275] 'Reformation' meaning that the words of a written instrument are modified or changed so as to express the true intent of the parties. This gives expression to the equitable maxim 'equity looks to the substance rather than the form'.

[276] See *Costello v Sykes* 143 Minn 109 (1919), 172 NW 907.

[277] L Eames, 'The Protection of Personal Rights in Equity since 1946' (1952) 32 *Boston University Law Review* 419, 427.

Eldon in *Gee v Pritchard* in 1818.[278] Equity also gave rise to remedies such as injunctions, which proved invaluable in achieving justice.[279]

In sum, in spite of the complications created by the tension between State and federal law, equity's influence has, in the interests of justice, been seen to pervade deeply into the American legal system, and has functioned in a deeply similar manner to English equity. Equity has been indispensable in dealing with the various problems created by the emergence of new forms of property, mechanisation and has proven itself highly adaptable to changing economic and social conditions throughout the country.[280]

ix. Equity in Chinese Law

One could not attempt to trace an understanding of general principles of law in major legal systems without taking cognisance of the unique legal tradition of China. The Chinese legal system is a complex one, and exhibits characteristics which set it apart and make it unique. Historically, China has a history of having very little written law, with community-based decision and disciplinary procedures supplanting and supplementing the central legal system. Therefore, as Victor H Li has pointed out, any Western lawyer attempting to grapple with the historical development of Chinese law would find very little law to work with.[281] Over the past 2,000 years, China developed an enormous, relatively effective bureaucratic system. However, there was no contemporaneous development of an effective centralised legal system. Despite the existence for several centuries of Codes of law and a State courts system, 'law' itself did not play a particularly important part in regulating the conduct of private individuals – or even State organs – until recent times.[282] Furthermore, the use of law was permeated with the Confucian philosophical tradition, whereby the imposition of sanctions for transgressions of the law was seen as far from ideal. Individuals were supposed to internalise moral and legal norms, and resort to the courts was frowned upon, as this showed the parties were unreasonable men who were unable to settle their differences in an amicable manner.[283] The impact of law

[278] *Gee v Pritchard* (1818) ER 670.

[279] R Moreland, 'Injunctive Control of Family Relations' (1930) 18 *Kentucky Law Journal* 207. See also de WQ Funiak, 'Equitable Protection of Personal or Individual Rights' (1947) 36 *Kentucky Law Journal* 7.

[280] Brown in Newman (1973) (n 268) 220.

[281] VH Li, 'The Legal System of the People's Republic of China and Problems of Equity' in Newman (1973) (n 112) 522.

[282] See T-T Chü, *Law and Society in Traditional China* (The Hague, Mouton, 1961); D Bodde and C Morris, *Law in Imperial China* (Cambridge, Mass, Harvard University Press, 1967).

[283] BI Schwartz, 'On Attitudes Toward Law in China' in JA Cohen, *The Criminal Process in the People's Republic of China 1949–63; An Introduction* (Cambridge, Mass, Harvard University Press, 1967).

until the twentieth century began was therefore far less profound in China than elsewhere.

However, from 1911 onwards, with the overthrow of the Qing dynasty, great efforts were undertaken by the then-leaders of the various regions of China to install Western legal systems. By 1927, Chiang Kai-shek's Kuomintang forces were able totake control from the various warring factions within China and gain control of most of the country. Established in Nanjing, the Kuomintang Government attempted to develop Western-style legal and penal systems. Few of the Kuomintang Codes, however, were implemented nationwide. Although government leaders strove for a Western-inspired system of codified law, the traditional Chinese preference for collective social sanctions over impersonal legalism hindered constitutional and legal development. A new system of laws was promulgated based on the German legal system. The spirit of the new laws never penetrated to the grass-roots level or provided hoped-for stability. Ideally, individuals were to be equal before the law, but this premise proved to be more rhetorical than substantive. In the end, most of the new laws were discarded as the Kuomintang became preoccupied with fighting the Chinese Communists and the invading Japanese.

Post-Second World War and following the Chinese civil war, China – and consequently the Chinese legal system – was split into two, with the Republic of China (Taiwan) occupying a tiny fraction of the territory and continuing the existence of the previous State, while the People's Republic of China (PRC) occupied the majority of the Chinese territory and founded a Communist Republic largely based on the Soviet model. While the Taiwan Government has steadily proceeded with the modernisation of their legal system, based strongly upon the French system of codification per civil law, their Communist neighbours have had a somewhat more complicated history.

The People's Republic of China inherited a system in 1949 which had already been based largely on the continental European model, but which in practice had hardly been implemented. The widespread sentiment of the powers-that-be was that this position was intolerable, and there was a push for change in this regard. The PRC therefore swiftly moved to establish a system based upon that of the Soviet Union, with the promulgation of a new Constitution and related laws and codes in 1954. However, this was not such a radical change, since the Soviet system itself owed much to continental European law.[284] However, an important distinction separated Communist China from the USSR: while many of the early leaders of the Soviet Union were lawyers – Lenin, Krylenko and Krestinsky to name but three – the early leaders of the People's Republic of China were by enlarge

[284] TT Hsia, *Guide to Selected Legal Sources of Mainland China* (Washington DC, Library of Congress, 1967).

writers, teachers and men of letters.[285] This hardly contributed to a legal system which rectified the defects of local non-compliance which had beset earlier Chinese law. Nor did the purging of the professional legal classes which occurred in the 1960s and their replacement with political officers.

However, it was remarkable during this period that equity came to play a significant role in Chinese law. Since compliance with the courts system had historically been reluctant and scattered at best, an extraordinary level of power and influence was left in the hands of local institutions, including power to diverge from the strictures of statute in certain circumstances in the interests of justice. Furthermore, decision-makers and judges were formally instructed 'not to be "mechanical and inflexible" in their application of the law'.[286] Laws were stated in very broad terms to ensure flexibility and avoid injustice arising from legal rigidity, illustrating that legislators were wholly in touch with the need for equity. Many laws were susceptible to myriad interpretations, and judges were instructed to examine each case upon its own merits to decide how a rule ought to be applied, or even whether it should be applied at all.[287]

The above system, while it gave judges great freedom and made excellent provision for equitable outcomes, was also reflective of the Communist Party's wish to maintain a flexible legal structure so as not to constrain its own activities. However, a significant problem throughout this period for Chinese lawmakers was their inability to enforce any sort of central law upon local communities.[288] This approach was to change from 1979 onwards, as, following the end of the Cultural Revolution, concrete steps were taken to impose a system of civil law inspired by the German model. In private law, codes similar to the *Bürgerliches Gesetzbuch* (BGB) were enacted. However, the development of law during the PRC was incrementally achieved over the space of several decades from 1980 onwards and has led to accusations of incoherence.[289] Nonetheless, the good faith and equity provisions of the BGB have been largely followed, and have resulted in a *jurisprudence constante* position whereby equity plays a similar role to that which it does in Germany. The only exception to this is in the Hong Kong Special Administrative Region, where a close conception of British common law is still applied, and which, based on stare decisis doctrine, incorporates a large *corpus* of equitable decisions and dicta, virtually identical with those applicable in Britain.

[285] Li in Newman (1973) (n 280) 526. See also Union Researchers Institute, *Who's Who in Communist China* (Hong Kong, Union Researchers Institute, 1966).
[286] ibid, 533.
[287] ibid.
[288] ibid, 536.
[289] Séroussi (2008) (n 260) 159–72.

x. *Equity in Japanese Law*

We turn now to the legal system of Japan. Japanese law was historically highly influenced by the Chinese system, and by Confucianism and Buddhism. Various immature legal systems were put in place, with one replacing another, and there is strong evidence that few of these systems were either effective or widely respected. However, from the nineteenth century onwards, this was to change significantly, as an increasingly influential role was given to principles of civil law systems transplanted from Western Europe. This modernisation of Japanese law began after the Meiji Restoration in 1868, in which the Japanese Emperor was restored to political power.[290] The first major legislation enacted in Japan was the Criminal Code of 1880, followed by the Constitution of the Empire of Japan in 1889, the Commercial Code, Criminal Procedure Act and Civil Procedure Act in 1890 and the Civil Code in 1896 and 1898.These were called the *roppo* (Six Codes) and the term began to be used to denote the entirety of Japan's statute law.The *roppo* thus included administrative law of both central and local government and international law in the treaties and agreements of the new government under the emperor. The Meiji Constitution was wholly replaced by the new Constitution of Japan in 1947 following Japan's capitulation in the Second World War. There then followed a thorough revision of the whole legal system to bring it into accordance with the new constitutional principles. The new Constitution is characterised by three basic traits: first, it was a transplantation of the American common law system, second, it overturned the former divine authority of the Emperor to found a legal system based on democracy in accordance with modern civil liberties and, third, its Ninth Article renounced war and the military, with Japan effectively becoming a US protectorate for defence purposes.[291]

However, despite the significant constitutional reforms which took place in Japan subsequent to the Second World War, the Civil Code and other instruments regulating the private law sphere remained substantially unchanged (apart from sections regulating family law and succession). This 1896 Code, entitled the 民法 (*Minpō*), was heavily influenced by the French *Code Napoléon*, and still more so by early drafts (notably that of 1888) of the German *Bürgerliches Gesetzbuch*. The *Minpō* itself was later to have a significant role in the development of civil law in several other East Asian States including the Republic of Korea and the Republic of China (Taiwan).

But what of equity in this land which combines a common law constitutional framework with a civil law code? It seems that, as one might

[290] M Chiba, 'Japan' in P-L Tan, *Asian Legal Systems* (London, Butterworths, 1997).

[291] R David and JEC Brierley, *Legal Systems in the World Today, An Introduction to the Comparative Study of Law*, 2nd edn (London, Stevens and Sons, 1978) 479–505.

expect, the fact that private law is regulated within the civil law framework has resulted in an approach that is more analogous to civil law systems than that of the common law. However, this is nuanced somewhat by the 'middle road' which Japanese law charts as regards judicial precedent, which is somewhat stronger than the *jurisprudence constante* doctrine of civil law, but is still not equal to stare decisis in the English or American mould. This ensures that when courts make equitable gains, it is very difficult for subsequent judgments to revert back to the previous position where such gains did not exist.[292] As with most civil law systems, however, Japanese law makes no real and firm distinction between law and equity. All civil law in Japan is based upon the Civil Code or other enacted laws. However, it is notable that 'The principles of equity have been completely absorbed into the norms of Japanese law'.[293] This is due to the Japanese legal and societal tradition, according to Koshikawa, who argues that Japanese people see in the body of the law a statement of morality, with law being an attempt to effect a realisation of substantive justice. This is the very essence of equity.[294]

The principles of equity may be characterised as a source of law in Japan. As in France, judges are obliged to decide cases even in the absence of written law. The Dakojan (National Council of State) Decree 103 of 1875 provides that in civil law, those areas for which no written legal stipulation exists are governed by custom, and those areas for which there is no clear custom shall be decided in accordance with inference on the basis of reason by the judge. This mirrors to a large degree the systems of France, Germany and Switzerland.[295] Further, the obligation of good faith plays a sizeable role analogous to that in Germany, and mirroring Article 157 BGB, equitable principles are also received, as in the case of the acceptance of the principles of trustworthiness (*Treu und Glauben*) in synallagmatic contracts. Articles 703, 705, 706, and 707 of the Japanese Civil Code set out much of the civil law doctrine of abuse of rights and unjust enrichment. Also, analogous to the common law, an action *de in rem verso* may be incompetent by reason of the equitable principle 'he who comes to equity must come with clean hands'. The plaintiff must show not only that his act is reasonable at the time of action, but also that his past actions have not been illegal. The illegal/illicit act is to be adjudged in accordance with its relevance to the relief sought.[296] Strict liability may also be imposed in certain circumstances, analogous to the regime of Article 1341 *alinéa* 1 of the French *Code civil.*

[292] R Pekkanen, *Japan's Dual Civil Society: Members Without Advocates*, Contemporary Issues in Asia and Pacific (Standford, California, Stanford University Press, 2006) 49.

[293] J Koshikawa, 'Equity in Japanese Law' in Newman (1973) (n 112) 425.

[294] ibid.

[295] See RA Newman, 'The Hidden Equity' (1967) 19 *Hastings Law Journal* 48.

[296] Koshikawa in Newman (1973) (n 292) 431. See also RA Newman, 'The Place and Function of Pure Equity in the Structure of Law' (1965) 16 *Hastings Law Journal* 401, 402–05.

Equity has also adapted certain principles to the particularities of Japanese life. The institution of 'informal marriage' – a ceremonial marriage without civil registration – for example, was relatively popular in Japan, at least until the 1940s, but found no legal regulation and no corresponding institution in European law. However, in the famous case of *Takinawa v Nozawa*, the Great Court of Judicature held that the breach of an informal marriage constituted nonetheless the breach of an obligation in law, indicating a flexible equitable interpretation of the Code, and transposing the principle 'equity looks to the substance rather than the form' into an area of law which it would never have encountered in Europe.[297] Here again, equity demonstrates its flexibility and its ability to adapt to new situations.

xi. Equity in the Legal System of the Republic of South Africa

The South African legal system is remarkable, insofar as it draws both on uncodified Roman–Dutch *ius commune* and the English common law for inspiration. It may thus be classified as a modern 'mixed' legal system, and it is therefore interesting to examine general principles of law and equity in the South African legal system, since any such principles must necessarily function in a *Gestalt* environment.[298] It is further worth mentioning that South Africa is traditionally viewed as a 'leader' amongst many post-colonial sub-Saharan African countries in terms of its legal system, and hence the influence of the South African system on the broader African continent has been significant. While the history of South African law is long and rich, devoting undue attention to its development and particularly to the impact of the *apartheid* regime would divert attention from the main focus of this chapter, so I shall resist the temptation to delve into the human rights discourse, so dominant in textbooks on South African law, and shall focus on the incorporation of equity and general principles into the legal system.

Since the South African legal system is effectively uncodified (apart from large-scale codifications in specific areas such as company law), common law and precedent play a significant role in legal regulation. Of course, no one area of modern South African law is solely dependent upon principles of law, but it is nonetheless a 'cardinal feature' of South African law that the rules and principles of large swathes of law, particularly the law of obligations and property law, are not contained in

[297] *Takinawa v Nozawa* (1915) 21 *Record of Great Court of Judicature Civil Judgments* 49 (Great Court of Judicature, United Civil Departments, 26 January 1915).

[298] F Du Bois and DP Visser, 'Der Einfluss des europäischen Rechts in Südafrika' (2001) 2 *Jahrbuch für Europäische Geschichte* 47.

legislation.[299] As a general rule, South Africa follows English law in the areas of procedural law, company law and the law of evidence; while Roman–Dutch common law is followed in South African contract law, tort, law of persons, law of real property, and family law. However, there exists a certain degree of intermixing in each category. Nonetheless, for the purpose of analysis of general principles of law and equity, it is probably true to say that the South African system is closer to the traditional Dutch model than its English equivalent. Thus, South African lawyers speak of the 'law of things', and distinguish between personal and real rights, between 'moveables' and 'immoveables' and between personal and praedial servitudes that would resonate with an eighteenth-century Dutch jurist.[300] As such, South African law may be described as an adaptation of Roman–Dutch law.

However, it is certainly true that English common law provided the catalyst for a certain process of adaptation. During the nineteenth and twentieth centuries, English laws and doctrines, including general principles and elements of equity were imported into the South African legal sphere. These included trusts,[301] the doctrine of estoppel, innocent misrepresentation and the doctrine of the undisclosed principal.[302] This is not to say that the earlier Dutch law had not unearthed its fair share of equitable doctrines and remedies, such as *restitutio in integrum* and the *mandament van spolie*.[303] The principle of good faith is highly developed within South African law, as is that of general social morality, to the extent that superior courts are constitutionally recognised to dispose of the power to overrule horizontal precedents when they no longer concur with prevailing *boni mores*, or social morality. This may be paralleled with the idea of *bonnes moeurs* in French law.[304]

South African law is deeply embedded with a variety of equitable principles. The prioritisation of substance over form is a recurring theme in case law.[305] Implicit contract terms incorporating conceptions of good faith and the equitable distribution of responsibility for fault or breach, called *naturalia* and *incidentalia*, are routinely applied.[306] Relief for *mora*

[299] F Du Bois, 'Introduction: History, System and Sources' in CG van der Merwe and JE du Plessis, *Introduction to the Law of South Africa* (The Hague, Kluwer, 2004) 40.

[300] ibid, 42.

[301] E Cameron, 'Constructive Trusts in South African Law: The Legacy Refused' (1999) 3 *Edinburgh Law Review* 341.

[302] See, generally R Zimmerman and DP Visser (eds), *Southern Cross: Civil Law and Common Law in South Africa* (Oxford, Clarendon, 1996); VV Palmer (ed), *Mixed Jurisdictions Worldwide: The Third Legal Family* (Cambridge, Cambridge University Press, 2001).

[303] Du Bois in van der Merwe and du Plessis (2004) (n 298) 42.

[304] ibid, 44.

[305] *Goldblatt v Freemantle* (1920) All Dominion Law Rep 123.

[306] G Lubbe and J du Plessis, 'Law of Contract' in van der Merwe and du Plessis (2004) (n 298) 256–58.

debitoris (delay) and positive malperformance are also upheld.[307] Flexible equitable conceptions of remedy have been crafted, including specific performance, which is, in fact, regarded as the 'natural' contractual remedy under South African contract law.[308] Cancellation and damages, however, are also widely available. The doctrine of *exception non adimpleti contractus*, embodying the power of one party to an agreement to withhold performance on account of the failure of his opposite number to perform, is also in use.[309] The determination of wrongfulness by application of the general principle of reasonableness – rooted in public policy – plays a key role in fixing and limiting liability and aids in the protection of weaker parties, in many cases replacing the traditional focus on the foreseeability of harm.[310] Balancing of interests, hardship doctrine and strict liability are all also known to the South African system.[311]

xii. Equity in Other Legal Systems

At this point in our study, we begin to notice a series of common trends running through the equitable provisions of the various legal systems. However, there remain legal systems with distinct histories, which warrant at least cursory examination in this study. Clearly, to be completely exhaustive is impossible here, but this should not discourage us from making some elementary observations on a limited number of further systems which display distinctive traits.

a. The Edges of the Common Law – Scotland

While a certain distinction remains perceptible between common law and civil law as systems, the common law systems discussed in detail – England and the United States – display relatively comparable takes on equity. It is scarcely necessary to mention States such as Canada, Ireland or Australia, further bastions of the common law, since these countries remained within the British Commonwealth till well after the Judicature Acts of the 1870s, and thus had an appeal of last resort to the House of Lords well into the twentieth century. In this way, equity has developed in an extremely similar way in these jurisdictions, to the extent that for many equitable affairs, Irish cases may be used as persuasive authority before British courts, and vice versa, with the same applying for Canada and Australia, and to a large extent Hong Kong prior to its reunification with China.

[307] ibid, 260.

[308] *Benson v SA Mutual Life Assurance Society* (1986) 1 SA 776 A.

[309] *BK Tooling (Edms) Bpk v Scope Precision Engineering (Edms)* (1979) 1 SA 391 A.

[310] M Loubser, 'Law of Delict' in van der Merwe and du Plessis (2004) (n 298) 277.

[311] See, eg the Nuclear Energy Act 92 (1982), s 41(1); and the Post Office Act 44 (1958), s 108.

The case as regards Scots law – that is, the law of Scotland – is somewhat more complicated. Although Scotland became part of Great Britain in 1707 and the United Kingdom in 1800, with a common legislature and court of ultimate appeal shared with England, Wales, Northern Ireland, and certain Commonwealth States, the 1707 Treaty of Union maintained the independent existence of Scots law and the Scottish courts. This legal system, although it has been vastly altered by House of Lords judgments and UK legislation, continues to exist today, and is significantly different from that of England. This legal system was influenced by indigenous custom, Dutch, Roman, Canon and North German law, although the Canon influence waned after the Scottish Reformation. Also, relations with Europe, which had caused this mix of legal influences, began to die off after the Crowns of England and Scotland became held by the same line post-1603. Nonetheless, even today, Scots law remains a sort of common law–civil law *Gestalt* entity.[312]

While the Courts of Chancery developed equity in England due to a prematurely rigid common law, in Scotland, the common law which did pervade the Scots law *corpus* developed more slowly and used a formless approach, coming under the influence of the Roman *ius honorarium* doctrine, which developed the flexible approach that the aim was to find a remedy where there appeared to have been an interest infringed.[313] Thus Scotland remained without a separate jurisdiction for equity as had evolved in England, for the simple reason that there was no need for one to develop. Walker notes that while equity in England 'was, and to some extent is, a body of rules and principles which form an appendage or gloss to the general rules of law', equity in Scotland 'is undoubtedly the idea of actual justice and fairness' which 'explains and justifies a number of principles and rules which are among the general rules of law'.[314] He goes on to note that it is 'utterly and completely wrong' to think that Scots law has adopted or copied English equity, since the equity which is found in Scots law was either inherent in the Scottish customary understanding of law or was received from the Roman law.[315] This would seem to provide further evidence that equity is by its very nature something organic in all legal systems, a point to which I shall shortly return.

[312] VV Palmer, *Mixed Jurisdictions Worldwide: The Third Legal Family* (Cambridge, Cambridge University Press, 2001) 400.

[313] DM Walker, 'Equity in Scots Law' in Newman (1973) (n 112) 201.

[314] ibid, 191, 201.

[315] ibid, 202.

b. Other Legal Systems

Italy

The remainder of the civil law systems frequently display characteristics that are quite similar to those already discussed as regards equity. For example, the Italian Civil Code is heavily influenced by both the French system and Roman law,[316] both of which have already received significant treatment here, and since Italian colonial efforts were largely unsuccessful, resulting in a less significant impact of the Italian legal system worldwide, a relatively brief discussion will suffice to sketch the influence of equity in the Italian legal sphere.

The standard position as regards the hierarchy of norms in Italian law is that statute law enjoys superiority over other sources (save, evidently, constitutional norms and certain norms of the international and European Union legal orders), which may only come into play when a statute specifically refers to them. This has the effect of limiting equity's role in Italian law somewhat. Equity in Italy is described by a leading author as 'a feeling or a concept, sometimes individual, sometimes of a general character, requiring that a given legal relationship or a category of relationship be settled in a certain way'.[317] The same expert goes on to say that as long as equity remains an aspiration, it may not be assimilated and assume the place of a rule in decisions: to do so, it must become law, and this will only happen when the aspiration becomes a conviction of the general populace, which will demand its enactment as law. However, this position is somewhat misleading, as it implies that not a great deal of equity has been incorporated into Italian law in this manner. On the contrary, a significant equitable *acquis* exists. For example, Articles 1341 and 1342 of the *Codice civile* provide expressly for the protection of the weaker party in *contrats d'adhésion* by validating only the clauses of which the diligent co-contractor had, or should have had, knowledge, and by demanding that certain clauses dangerous to the buyer must expressly be approved by him in writing. Article 1664 of the Code parallels the French model of *l'hardship*, stipulating that where in the course of work some unforeseen difficulties arise owing to acts outside the parties control or natural causes making the burden considerably greater on one party, that party may claim an equitable compensation.

In the judicial sphere, the idea that the law may be defective by reason of its generality is still alive and well in Italy.[318] A decision in equity has

[316] CG Cecioni, 'La Traducibilità del linguaggio giuridico inglese' in G Cortese (ed), *Tradurre i linguaggi settoriali. Atti del seminario di Anglistica nell'ambito del progetto strategico CNR 'I problemi della traduzione nell'Italia dell'Europa': Università degli studi di Torino, Facoltà di Scienze Politiche, 27–28 maggio 1993* (Turin, Libreria Cortina, 1996) 155–73.

[317] V Scialoja, 'Del diritto positive e dell'equità' in V Scialoja and L Trompeo, *Studi giuridici* (Roma, Anonima Romana, 1932) 35.

[318] M Matteucci, 'Equity in Italian Law' in Newman (1973) (n 112) 371–72.

been defined as one that is awarded by the court on the basis of criteria that aim at attenuating the strict law by harmonising it with the morality arising from the specific circumstances of the case.[319] Equity has also been defined as a benevolent interpretation of the legal rule which may be made in any case where, by reason of events or specific circumstances which were unforeseen by the legislator, a strict appliance of the legal rule would lead to an unjust and vexing solution.[320] Therefore we see that equity – both in the form of principles which ensure substantive justice and in the form of a corrective to deal with injustice arising from legal rigidity – plays an important role in the Italian legal system.[321]

Spain

In the Spanish legal system, *equidad* (equity) is not evident as a juridical element, properly speaking. The Spanish Civil Code, true to the atmosphere of nineteenth-century positivism in which it was devised, holds up the legal norm as the supreme, and it would seem, sole juridical source. However, while such a legal architecture might point to a system completely out of kilter with those systems already examined, in reality, Spain actually shares a great deal of common ground with those civil law systems already examined. As noted by Andres Ollero, the 'closing' of the juridical system is guaranteed by 'general principles of law', representing 'the skeleton of a dogma abstracted from the legal standards'.[322] Nonetheless, it is perhaps the case that Spanish law makes less provision for the use of equitable principles than other systems. For example, the Civil Code fails to provide for the doctrine of *abus de droit*.

However, this seeming defect has been remedied to some degree both by judicial activism and by subsequent legislative action. For example, a 1944 decision of the Supreme Court discarded the unfettered usage of subjective rights, partly on the basis that they violate 'the borders imposed by equity and good faith'.[323] Such equitable norms have acquired a greater foothold in the Spanish legal *corpus* since the inception of the Civil Code, helping to underpin principles of material justice and 'express the basic values of a juridical system'.[324] However, some commentators have noted the potential for such principles to open the door to extra-judicial functions on the part of the judge, resulting in the advent of doctrines such as *abus de droit* without written foundation, reflecting a general reticence to

[319] Italian Court of Cassation, 28 April 1960, no 943.

[320] Court of Appeal of Naples, 30 October 1951.

[321] For a more general take on equity in Italian law, see R Calvo, '*L'equitá nel diritto privato. Individualitá, valori e regole nel prisma della contemporaneitá* (Milan, Giuffrè, 2010).

[322] A Ollero, 'Equity in Spanish Law?' in Newman (1973) (n 112) 381–82.

[323] Spanish Supreme Court, Decision II 14 (1944)

[324] E Garcia Enterria, *Legislación delegada, potestad reglamentaria y control judicial* (Madrid, Tecnos, 1970) 32.

acknowledge equity's import in the Spanish legal order.[325] Puig Brutau has insisted upon a similarity between common law and Spanish law in respect of the operation of equity, noting that the rigidity and limited understanding of general principles in the Civil Code has forced the hand of the Supreme Court in using often unwritten equitable principles to supplement its judgments to achieve substantive justice in the cases before it.[326]

While it is clear that the Spanish legal tradition is not one which ordinarily expressly recognises the power of judges to use equitable notions in their judgments, certain clauses have been written which take account of equitable notions. For example, Article 1154 of the Civil Code holds that the judge will 'equitably modify' the applicable penalty in case of partial fulfilment of an obligation. In a similar vein, Article 1103 states that statutory liability for negligence may be moderated by the courts depending upon the particulars of the case at hand when executing sentences for the annulment of marriages. Nonetheless, the Spanish legal tradition's understanding of equity is certainly one of the most restrictive, setting it apart to some degree from the legal mainstream.[327]

Argentina

Argentina's legal order is representative of much of Latin America, in that it is heavily influenced by the Spanish legal tradition, but equally owes a certain amount to the French civil law system.[328] This French influence is felt in Article 15 of the Argentine Civil Code, which replicates Article 4 of the French Code Civil, stating that the judge cannot refuse to decide upon the case before him. This stated impossibility of *non liquet* creates a necessity for the *praeter legem* employment of general principles of law and equity to fill gaps in the legal system when they arise. Gény has noted that this reflects a long-standing necessity in Argentinian law to minimise legal rigidity 'with the more or less sincere conviction that Equity can always be found, at least in a germinal state and inductively in the law itself'.[329] More specific measures are prescribed in Article 16, which states that if a civil question cannot be resolved

[325] E Garcia Enterria, 'Reflexiones sobre la ley y los principios generales del derecho en el Derecho Administrativo' (1963) 40 *Revista de Administración Publica* 211.

[326] J Puig Brutau, *La Jurisprudencia como fuente del derecho (Interpretación creadora y arbitrio judicial)* (Barcelona, Bosch, 1954) 236.

[327] JL de los Mozos, 'Derecho y equidad' in JL de los Mozos, *Metodología y ciencia en el Derecho Privado contemporáneo* (Madrid, Editorial de derecho privado, 1977).

[328] An exhaustive run-down of the influence of equity on seven different Latin American legal systems (all of which have yielded similar results) is provided by a volume edited by José Thompson: J Thompson, *Acceso a la justicia y equidad: estudio en siete países de América Latina* (San José, Costa Rica, Instituto Interamericano de Derechos Humanos, 2000).

[329] F Gény, *Método de interpretación y Fuentes en Derecho Privado Positivo* (Madrid, Hijos de Reus, 1902) 36.

either by the words or the spirit of the law, principles of analogous laws shall be considered, and if the question were still in doubt, it will be resolved by the law's general principles.

This is particularly significant, since 'the spirit of the law' can be broadly interpreted in favour of teleology and general principles, meaning that such principles may derogate the written law even in cases where it is not necessary to resort to principles of analogous laws.

While general principles *praeter legem* have thus always had a significant role in Argentinean law, the broader role of equity in the system has historically been less evident. However, this situation was amended by Law 17.711, which brought substantial reforms to the Civil Code. This law stressed that in exceptional circumstances, 'the judge must use subjective and personal interpretation to provide a framework for the recognition of conduct in exceptional circumstances'.[330] This law also conferred upon the judge the right to prioritise substance over form, and gave them the ability 'to order compensation in favour of the victim founded in reasons of equity'. Argentina, therefore, affords a significant role for equitable principles, explicitly allowing the judge a wide margin of appreciation and making several written references to the fact that the judge may take account of equity and general principles in deciding cases.

Sweden

The Swedish legal system represents an example of the Scandinavian legal system, which branched off from the Germanic tradition of the civil law in medieval times, but which retains much of its structure. Swedish law has been influential due to its position as the most populous and powerful of the Scandinavian countries, being a superpower of sorts until 1648. Further, it is germane to note that Sweden was home to a pre-Napoleonic codification in 1734. The place of equity in Swedish law is difficult to explain, partly because the word finds no accurate translation in Swedish legal texts.[331] Stig Stromhölm points out that while equity serves principally as a corrective elsewhere, in Sweden, the function of equity is somewhat different. While sixteenth-century common law was characterised by rigidity, creating an impetus for recourse to equity, Stromhölm's proposition is that in a system where the legislator is promptly responsive to the needs of all parties, particularly the vulnerable, and where judges are aware of this, there will be less need for equity as a corrective. He points out that the same legislative *naïveté* that beset

[330] EE Borga, 'Equity in Argentine's Judicial Order' in Newman (1973) (n 112) 403.

[331] *Måttlig* has been suggested as an approximate translation. However, this is complicated by the presence in many Swedish instruments of words such as *skälig* (reasonable) and *tillbörlig* (due). Also worth considering in this context are *god sed* (acceptable custom); *god tro* (good faith); and *tro och heder* (faith and honesty), all of which pop up frequently in Swedish statutes.

many foreign legal systems – whereby the legislators never doubted the finality or perfectibility of their laws, which would therefore never require correction – has never applied in Sweden. He posits that much equity in Swedish law is accomplished by what he dubs 'equity by legislative reform', whereby the legislator steps in to 'repair' legislation which has been proved to be defective by reason of its generality, rather than leaving this role to the judge.[332] This model, while unusual, is certainly more in keeping with a strict separation of powers.[333]

However, this model has served to ensure the incorporation of a great number of equitable principles into the positive law of Sweden, a prominent example being the prioritisation of substance over form throughout the rules.[334] The caution with which Swedish courts have applied equitable rules in the absence of statute was one of the key reasons for the enactment of so many rules to protect consumers in the 1970s, and perhaps paradoxically, the Swedish has resultantly become one of the most equitable legal systems in Europe, with weaker parties specially protected in a myriad of situations against unscrupulous or exploitative co-contractors.

IV. THE COMMON CORE OF EQUITY

It would be possible to continue our study further, comparing various other legal systems and the equitable principles contained therein. However, it is my confident belief that the trends which have been displayed above would be replicated. There is certainly good reason for such confidence. Many of the States examined have had part or all of their legal systems replicated by transplantations of law, often in former colonies or fallen empires or theocracies. Furthermore, there is evidence that other systems which have not been examined closely in this discussion display broadly similar traits to those discussed. Examples of systems displaying a limited number of similar traits include Greece,[335] Belgium[336] and Finland.[337] There is a strong sense that equity pervades a good majority of modern legal systems, particularly those that are more developed. A

[332] S Stromhölm, 'Equity in Swedish Law' in Newman (1973) (n 112) 444–49.

[333] See *Nytt Juridiskt Arkiv* (1957) 279 for a Swedish Supreme Court case which embodies this doctrine.

[334] eg in the 1949 Freedom of the Press Act, Ch 1, S 4.

[335] PJ Zepos, 'Equity in Greek Law' in Newman (1973) (n 112).

[336] J Renauld, 'Reflections on the Concept of Equity in Belgian Law' in Newman (1973) (n 112).

[337] See, eg the 1929 Finnish Contract Act, as amended by Law 956/1982, which states that contract terms which lead to an unjust result may be set aside, depending on the circumstances of the parties and the contract itself. In determining what is unfair, regard is to be had to the entire contents of the contract, the positions of the parties, the circumstances prevailing at and after the conclusion of the contract, and to 'other factors'. In circumstances where the setting aside of such a term renders the contract unfair, the remainder of the contract may be either adjusted or terminated.

developed legal system must surely be a hallmark of the archetypal 'civilised nation' that the drafters of the PCIJ and ICJ Statutes had in mind. It would seem, then, that equity has a strong claim to be represented as a key component of the general principles category represented by these civilised nations.

However, the above statement only represents a first step. It is evident even from those inferences that may be drawn from our doubtless incomplete – though wide-ranging – study that equity has manifested itself in vastly different ways throughout many legal systems. One distinction is particularly evident: while similar principles may have evolved in various systems, they have evolved for different reasons and involving different modalities; some being judge-led precedential models, while others have involved strategic positions for such principles in legislation and codes. Nonetheless, there would seem to be a common core of principles of equity which are common to the vast majority of developed legal systems. Several principles, such as good faith and the prioritisation of substance over form in limited circumstances crop up in virtually every legal system. Where they did not exist in the past, they have been added to the normative framework, either by way of judicial creativity and precedent, or by enactment of the legislator. The practice over time in this regard would tend toward a rather startling conclusion, namely that legal systems based upon a liberal and civilised conception of social interaction simply cannot function without equity. How else may we explain the repeated reception into law, 'by hook or by crook', as it were, in so many legal systems worldwide, of virtually identical principles?

The above position is borne out somewhat by the empirical evidence which has been brought together here. Equitable principles can and do develop by various different means depending on the type of legal system that is in place, and depending on to what extent equitable considerations have been taken into account by the legislative branch of government. However, whatever differences inhere in legal systems, equity finds a way to make its presence felt. This is perhaps best exemplified by our original case study of the common law. Here, the legislator – the King – felt no impulsion toward imbuing the legal sphere of sixteenth-century England with flexible equitable remedies that could protect the weak, especially when their rights had been infringed. However, it was beyond even his conscience to countenance condemning wronged individuals to such a fate by his laws when they appealed to him directly. Nonetheless, he was ill-disposed toward legal reform, but equity still managed to craft a way – through judicial precedent over time, and the slow development of principles – of securing a place in the English legal architecture. The table below demonstrates the fact that in the relatively broad spectrum of legal systems here examined, the same equitable principles keep cropping up again and again.

Table: Comparing Reception of Equitable Principles ('Yes' Denotes Reception to Significant Degree)

	EN	Muslim	FR	DE	NL
Substance>form	yes	yes	yes	yes	yes
Good faith	yes	yes	yes	yes	yes
Unjust enrichment	yes		yes	yes	yes
Damage mitigation	yes			yes	yes
Relief for mistake	yes		yes		
Reasonable expectation/estoppel	yes		yes	yes	yes
Denial of relief to unscrupulous	yes	yes	yes	yes	yes
Abuse of right	yes	yes	yes	yes	yes
Specific enforcement/*Reparation En nature*	yes		yes	yes	yes
Frustration doctrine	yes		yes	yes	yes
Protection of weaker party	yes	yes	yes	yes	yes
Strict liability/burden-sharing	yes		yes		
Relief for failure in performance of essential obligations	yes		yes	yes	yes
Relief for delay			yes	yes	yes
Application of statutory policy to situations outside statute		yes			
Doctrine of balancing interests/hardship	yes		yes		

CH	USA	CN	JAP	SA	SC	IT	ES	AR	SE
yes	yes	yes	yes	yes	yes	yes	yes	yes	yes
yes	yes	yes	yes	yes	yes	yes	yes	yes	yes
yes	yes	yes	yes	yes	yes	yes	yes	yes	yes
		yes	yes	yes	yes		yes	yes	yes
yes	yes	yes		yes	yes	yes			yes
yes	yes	yes		yes	yes	yes	yes	yes	yes
yes	yes	yes	yes	yes	yes	yes	yes	yes	yes
yes	yes	yes	yes	yes	yes	yes	yes	yes	yes
yes	yes	yes	yes	yes	yes				
	yes	yes		yes	yes	yes			yes
yes	yes	yes		yes	yes		yes	yes	yes
	yes		yes	yes	yes	yes	yes	yes	yes
yes	yes	yes	yes	yes	yes	yes	yes	yes	yes
yes	yes	yes		yes	yes				
	yes			yes	yes		yes	yes	
yes	yes			yes	yes	yes	yes	yes	yes

The evidence gathered in the sources examined in this chapter and demonstrated by the table above furnishes a fairly compelling case for the general reception of a number of equitable principles in the legal systems of civilised nations. It is clear that reception of general principles may only be talked of on a general, rather than a universal level. It will always be possible to find a certain exception as regards one element of the equitable conception of law, but one must admit that the case for the admission of quasi-universal acceptance of certain doctrines, such as good faith, substance over form, and the doctrine of the abuse of rights, is very strong indeed. Other principles of equity are less common or are difficult to compare. The definition of the application of statutory policy outside the statute itself, for example, is difficult to measure, since it is evident that judges engage in such practice in many jurisdictions, but without explicit reference to what they are doing. In such circumstances, comparing one jurisdiction to another and evaluating whether such practice is present in one, the other, neither or both, becomes extremely difficult, and proffering concrete opinions on such areas is beyond the scope of this chapter. This explains partly why I have left blank spaces on the table above; since in certain circumstances I could not say for certain whether the practice was positive or negative within a certain legal system as regards the recognition of a given equitable principle. In fact, this type of ambiguity was frequently encountered. Therefore, I have not placed any 'no' indicators into the grid to counterpoint the many 'yes' indicators that are visible. For our purposes, that is, for the purpose of ascertaining general recognition of general principles, whether there is a majority of 'yes' indicators in any one row is our primary concern, with our secondary concern being how strong such a majority is. Whether the reception of such a principle in other jurisdictions is limited, circumvented, ambiguous or non-existent, is a tangential question.

V. CONCLUSION: EQUITY AS A HALLMARK OF 'CIVILISED' LEGAL SYSTEMS

The obvious question that poses itself at this point is whether equity – whether we can define it or whether we adopt a flexible definition as we have done up until this point – is a universal element of legal systems. Such a conclusion would certainly add weight to any arguments founded upon equitable general principles in the area of humanitarian intervention, since universality implies a presence in international law also. Personally, I would be loath to adopt a trenchant position in favour of equity's universality, though others have certainly done so, with Weil stating with particular reference to international law that 'Le Droit (avec un grand D), le droit *largo sensu,* c'est le droit proprement dit plus l'équité'.[338] I, however, would rather describe equity in terms of its overwhelming acceptance in domestic legal systems, and its universal existence in some form or another amongst 'civilised', or developed, legal systems.

The words 'civilised' and 'developed' are somewhat dangerous ones for any commentator to use, particularly in the context in which I am writing, implying as they do a certain modicum of subjectivity. I began this volume by being bitterly critical of some of the foremost legal scholars international academia has to offer for what I deemed to be their unfounded and over-hasty opinions on humanitarian intervention proffered in the aftermath of NATO's Kosovo operation. I argued that their justificatory theories were largely based upon poorly-defined criteria that were not normatively rooted and which, as such, might be subjectively re-interpreted by unscrupulous actors wishing to cover future illegal operations under a veil of legitimacy. I disputed their right to make value judgments about the normative ambit and value of international law. It would seem mildly hypocritical of me, then, to myself embark upon value judgements regarding the level of development of certain legal systems. Nonetheless, I hope to differentiate my own conclusions from those of the authors whom I criticised in the first chapter.

The story of the development of legal systems is inequal and piecemeal. Differences abound, and tracing common strands in the comparative histories of the various jurisdictions in their putative states is by no means an easy task. The civil law, the common law, and the Muslim legal systems, to take but three prominent examples, all began in very different geographical settings, with their early rules corresponding to the important interests in each society. These early systems of rules represented three extremely diverse models of legal systems. However, in recent centuries, a marked convergence has occurred. As outlined in this chapter, despite tracing their origins from extremely different and varied sources, domestic legal systems have developed analogous principles throughout the world. These general legal principles of an equitable nature arose in response to the harm that occurred – or that potentially could occur – when the bare application of a specific legal rule resulted in an unjust result in a particular set of circumstances. That such a situation should arise in any legal system founded upon a series of strict rules is predictable. What is perhaps slightly more surprising is the fact that such principles developed in an analogous and highly comparable manner in such diverse legal systems.

Legal history has shown that equitable general principles will arise at a certain point in the development of a legal system. A legal system may be

[338] P Weil, 'L'équité dans la jurisprudence de la Cour Internationale de Justice: Un mystère en voie de dissipation?' in V Lowe and M Fitzmaurice, *Fifty Years of the International Court of Justice* (Cambridge, Cambridge University Press, 1996) 138.

water-tight, with no room for judicial prevarication whatsoever, but equity will find cracks and seep through. The Norwegians, for example, formerly a society boasting a legal system with a scant regard for equity – a 'zero-sum', winner-takes-all approach – reformed this model in less than 100 years into one that is exceedingly equitable, with emphases on compromise and problem-solving techniques.[339] If a legal system of a civilised nation resists equity's influence, respect for the legal system will, in the long term, diminish and collapse, and it will cease to be a legal system, or the citizens will revolt against it. If a legal system in the modern age fails to develop the principles of good faith and the abuse of rights, how is one supposed to carry out business? When the law will not rescue plaintiffs from the shenanigans of unscrupulous charlatans, then vigilante justice increases in attraction.[340]

Perhaps, as such, equity may be held to be one of the quintessential notions which may be covered under the 'general principles of law recognised by civilised nations', since it is one of the few common strata which unites them. Either legislators are far-sighted enough to imbue laws and codes with equitable provisions – particularly to combat legal rigidity and the defects in legislation which emerge due to its generality – or equity will develop organically via jurisprudence and practice as a corrective to such defects. *Tertium non datur*. If neither happens within a legal system, then it can hardly be held to be 'civilised' (or, if the modern scholar prefers, 'developed'), since injustice and the abuse of rights are allowed to flourish.

It has been argued by some that the phrase 'civilised nations' was, even at the drafting of the PCIJ Statute, a somewhat antiquated and possibly prejudicial formulation, in that the use of the word 'civilised' as distinct from 'nations' *simpliciter* denoted a hierarchy of States, some of which were developed enough to lend legal doctrine to the international sphere, others of which were not.[341] This was seen as a Western, pro-colonialist stance, differentiating the developed elite from the barbarians, the haves from the have-nots. However, it could also be argued that the word 'civilised' was a reference to the sophistication and development of the legal system. The fact that the word is used to prefix 'nations' lends itself to a nexus between the two, and suggests some sort of test for the 'civilisation', or development, of domestic legal systems. Clearly, legal principles from States that did not share a basic conception of good faith could find no place in a system of international law underpinned by the value of State sovereignty,

[339] W Aubert, 'Law as a Way of Resolving Conflicts: The Case of a Small Industrialised Society' in L Nader (ed), *Law in Culture and Society* (Chicago, Aldine, 1969).

[340] This is not intended to be a direct reference to the Kosovo case, although it does spring to mind.

[341] FT Jalet, 'The Quest for the General Principles of Law Recognized by Civilized Nations – A Study' (1962–63) 10 *University of California at Los Angeles Law Review* 1041.

where honest dealing was necessary for the upkeep of international order. If one accepts such an interpretation – and one may argue that such an interpretation is compelling – it invites the conclusion that only State systems possessing a sufficiently developed conception of general principles of law may lend such a conception to the international legal system. Equity is necessarily a significant part of this general principles *corpus*. While equitable principles are relatively thin on the ground in international legal documents (and where they are found they necessarily come under the banner of treaty law as a source rather than general principles) it is clear from an examination of the case law of the World Court that a shortfall in positive textual provisions reflecting equity would not prevent judges from taking equitable principles into account, either tacitly or explicitly, in their judgments. In fact, the judges of the World Court have had cause to apply equity as an auxiliary canon of interpretation, as a gap-filling corrective, and even, in limited and controversial circumstances, *contra legem*. A study of the practice of the PCIJ and ICJ in this regard and the implications that this practice may have for the humanitarian intervention conundrum shall constitute the subject of the next chapter.

4

Equity in International Legal Practice

I. INTRODUCTION

THE PRECEDING CHAPTER demonstrated that while equity as a concept is difficult to define in a manner that describes its operability in every legal system in which it is found, some conception of equity is clearly detectable in a broad majority of national legal systems. Since equity is generally a flexible notion, and is comprised more of principles than of strict rules – its function in many instances being indeed to soften the rigour of strict rules – one would suppose that the equitable *corpus* has a strong claim to be considered as part of the 'general principles of law recognised by civilised nations', that is the third source of international law (though there are those who have posited that the source of international equity may equally reside in customary international law[1]), and therefore a veritable wellspring of international legal norms. However, before reaching such a bold conclusion, we must first determine whether and to what extent such an interpretation of the role of equity has found favour with the judges of the International Court of Justice and its predecessor, the Permanent Court of International Justice. The reason that I have chosen the practice of the international courts system as a barometer for equity's reception into international law is relatively simple, namely that it represents the only practical means of determining whether equity occupies a place in the international legal system, in the absence of an accepted test for the existence of general principles. In treaty law, references to equity – outside certain specialised domains such as the law of maritime delimitation[2] – are scarce, and certainly have little effect upon general international law concerning the use of force, which is the topic upon which we are attempting to shed some new light. As regards international custom, it would seem that attempting to distinguish whether States had in fact had the *opinio iuris* that they were acting in accordance with the general principles of equity rather than on the basis of any other

[1] P Weil, 'L'équité dans la jurisprudence de la Cour Internationale de Justice: Un mystère en voie de dissipation?' in V Lowe and M Fitzmaurice, *Fifty Years of the International Court of Justice* (Cambridge, Cambridge University Press, 1996) 126.

[2] The 1982 UN Convention on the Law of the Sea, UNTS 1833, for example, contains explicit references to equity.

international legal norms would be a difficult thing to determine. States are not in the habit of affirming such actions. This may well be because equity, and indeed the entire general principles category, is something which is shrouded in uncertainty. There is no doubt that it represents an international legal source, but it is one that is viewed as somewhat obscure, somewhat indeterminate and certainly somewhat difficult to accurately define. Therefore, where there is an option, States will attempt to place themselves upon surer ground, as it were, by referring to treaty or customary international law in order to justify their actions, since the grounds for determining the validity of treaty and custom are clear and precise.

Indeed, the test for determining the validity of general principles has never been made entirely clear. While it is evident that there must be some acceptance of such principles by a plurality of States for them to be considered, it is unclear how large a number of States must accept such principles, and to what extent such an acceptance must be uniform. If two States recognise the doctrine of abuse of rights as a general principle, for example, but do so to different extents and through different legal modalities, can this be used as evidence of widespread acceptance of the same principle? This difficult situation has been compounded by the failure of the International Court of Justice to furnish forth a concrete test for the susceptibility to transposition and applicability of domestic general principles in international law. However, the Court has made some vague pronouncements, as noted in chapter two, as to the suitability of well-known, long-standing principles for reception into international law. While this does not provide us with a concrete test per se, it does offer a certain modicum of guidance, a road sign to our final destination, if you will. In addition, a limited number of PCIJ and ICJ cases feature specific pronouncements by judges, either in judgments proper or in dissenting or separate opinions, affirming the existence and reception of certain general principles, including principles of equity, in the international legal order. Having examined the comparative reception of equitable principles in domestic legal systems in the preceding chapter, it now remains to determine the extent of their existence in the international legal sphere.

In conducting this examination, it is wise to remind ourselves of the conclusions reached in chapter two, namely that international courts are slow to make explicit reference to any general principles, and that such reference is likely to be found in dissenting or separate opinions. Furthermore, even when judges do refer to general principles, they avoid speaking concretely of the general principles category consecrated in Article 38(1) of the ICJ Statute, rather couching such references in similar terminology, speaking of well accepted rules and so forth. This reflects a trend within the Court's judgments to avoid grappling with the general principles category, as well as an aversion to a non-purely voluntaristic conception of international law, and further suggests that when judges can solve a problem in a satisfactory manner without reference to this particular source of law, they will probably do so. Recognition of the existence of the general principles category by the Court in its judgments is, of itself, uncontroversial, but the usage of such general principles as a legal basis on which to found a judgment is something that the Court is far more reluctant to do. Nonetheless, having examined the comparative modalities of equitable reception in national legal systems, spotting equitable principles creeping into the Court's reasoning, even by the back door, as it were, should be considerably easier.

Since reference to general principles is so rare from the ICJ, reference to equitable general principles, a sub-set of the former, will be even rarer. Not all general principles are equitable in nature. Nonetheless, many are 'borderline', that is, while they are not traditionally associated with equity *stricto sensu*, they have a net effect that leads to the realisation of substantive justice by rendering the positive law more flexible. The individual effect of any one principle in isolation may be minor, but the potential for application of a series of equitable principles together certainly exists. Despite the relative paucity of references to general principles of law (and their frequent couching in terminology which does not make direct reference to Article 38(I) of the ICJ Statute), it is nonetheless essential to our present study to undertake a thorough examination of all ICJ and PCIJ cases which make reference to the third source of international law, however obliquely.[3] This chapter will, in effect, be dedicated to determining the number, size and strength of the 'building blocks', as it were, upon which any 'equitable theory of humanitarian intervention' must necessarily be grounded.

II. EQUITABLE GENERAL PRINCIPLES IN THE JUDGMENTS OF THE WORLD COURT

For expediency's sake, since the same, or similar, principles have arisen before the Permanent Court of International Justice and before the ICJ, I shall dispense with the division of this study into two time periods. As I have already discussed, the World Court was the sole organ of the League of Nations that was left substantially unchanged during the changeover to the United Nations framework. This may be held up as evidence of broad satisfaction with the Court's machinery. It is further germane to highlight once again that Article 38, the sources of law clause in the Statute, was left basically unaltered. Therefore, the principal sources to which the Court was to refer remained international treaties, customary

[3] I have covered the potential rationales underlying this endemic obliqueness in ch 2.

international law and, once again, 'the general principles of law recognised by civilised nations'. While it is evident that the advent of the United Nations Charter brought with it a seismic effect upon the *corpus* of international treaty law, and to some extent customary international law (particularly as regards the use of force by States), it is also clear that the effect which the new machinery had upon the third source of international law – general principles – was minimal. Aside from a curtailing of the principle of self-preservation, the collection of general principles existing as international norms remained broadly constant. If we consider the evidence presented in chapters two and three on the origin of these general principles, such a position makes complete sense. General principles as an international legal source derive from general principles that are found in a broad plurality of developed legal systems of States. They apply generally, that is regardless of the treaties or contracts, or indeed of the other sources of law, around them. Therefore, while reference to a pre-UN Charter era might seem, on the face of it, mildly illogical when trying to devise solutions to problems arising from the structure and rules of the UN Charter itself, this is not the case. In fact it is both highly logical and absolutely necessary to take cognisance of any and all references to equitable general principles contained in the judgments of the Permanent Court, particularly since, pre-Second World War, there seemed to be, on the part of the Court, a somewhat less marked aversion to at least quasi-openly dealing with the general principles category in pronouncing upon legal disputes. Therefore, our study shall focus upon the 'World Court', used as a general term to denote the PCIJ and ICJ together.

When examining the deliberations of the Advisory Committee of Jurists established to draft a Statute for the Permanent Court, it became evident that some broad conception of equitable principles had been generally agreed upon by the members, although the extent to which equity could be relied upon in and of itself to decide legal problems was a source of some dispute, and the question was left open, with the 'general principles' formulation used instead, with equity a presumed sub-category of general principles.[4] Nonetheless, it became evident that, although certainly not coterminus with its role in any one national jurisdiction, equity had then been somewhat consecrated as a composite element of one of the sources of international law.[5] This was shown to be no hollow sop to common lawyers, when in the following years the Courts, first the PCIJ and later the ICJ, developed their interpretation of the conception of equity to be applied in concrete cases. According to Article 38 of the ICJ Statute, such international judgments are themselves a subsidiary source of international

[4] See ch 2.

[5] S Rosenne, 'The Position of the International Court of Justice on the Foundations of the Principle of Equity in International Law' in A Bloed and P van Dijk (eds), *Forty Years of the International Court of Justice* (Utrecht. Europa-Instituut, 1988) 85.

law, making them particularly useful for the purpose of determining the boundaries of a category as uncertain as general principles.

Such determination of the normative content of equity was both a necessary and a difficult task for the Court. As we have seen, resort to general principles was generally accomplished 'by the back door', meaning that any reference to equity would have to be somewhat less than overt, for fear of charges of judicial prevarication, amongst other things. This was clearly an important consideration for the Court, and also for many leading authors. Elihu Lauterpacht, for example, attempted to distinguish legally legitimate and illegitimate uses of the terms 'equity' and 'equitable principles', terming impermissible usages as 'elements in the legal decision which have no objectively identifiable normative content. They are . . . virtually synonymous with "fair" or "reasonable"'. Lauterpacht insisted that such (illegitimate) usages of equitable terminology must be firmly distinguished from (legitimate and normatively sound) equity and equitable principles as part of international law. This was important for the purposes of clarity as regards legal scholarship and textbooks, but obviously still more so as regards the judgments of the ICJ, given that the relative paucity of judgments meant that any slip-ups in the usage of equitable terminology could have significant repercussions regarding the interpretation of the normative content of general principles of law.[6] Lauterpacht's fears of subjective and inconsistent application of equity in international fora were well founded. While such poorly-grounded usages of equity have not frequently surfaced in the World Court, it is perhaps germane to draw attention to the perils of judicial prevarication in other fora. A celebrated example of this occurred in the *Sheik of Abu Dhabi* case of 1951.[7] Here, the arbitrator, Lord Asquith claimed he could not address the choice of law conflict which arose in the case, since

> no such law [of Abu Dhabi] can reasonably be said to exist . . . the Sheik administers a purely discretionary justice with the assistance of the Koran; and it would be fanciful to suggest that in this very primitive region there is any settled body of legal principles applicable to the construction of modern commercial instruments.[8]

Therefore, having circumvented his own unfamiliarity with the local law, and perhaps to avoid a *non liquet*, Asquith applied his own law, this being the system he was most familiar with, namely the common law, and with it a broad conception of all the equitable principles contained therein. Although he admitted that English municipal law could not possibly be applicable in the case, he held that 'some of its rules [were] so firmly

[6] E Lauterpacht, 'Equity, Evasion, Equivocation and Evolution in International Law' (1977–78) *American Branch International Law Association Procedure and Commission Report* 34.

[7] *Sheik of Abu Dhabi v Petroleum Development (Trucial Coast) Ltd* (1951) 18 ILR 144.

[8] ibid, 148–49.

grounded in reason as to form part of this broad body of jurisprudence, this "modern law of nature"'.[9]

Judgments such as that proposed by Asquith were rare, but they were enough to render many international lawyers distrustful of equity and general principles. The problem of the variation of notions of justice and morality throughout different jurisdictions was well documented.[10] Resort to anything beyond the black letter was viewed with suspicion, and it was therefore necessary for the World Court to carefully buttress many of its references to equity in a broadly-based recapitulation of comparative legal history to avoid charges of partiality or subjectivity. Indeed, such buttressed argumentation was what the Court resorted to on its 'good days'. In other instances, the Court, in less bullish mood, but needing nonetheless to use equitable principles, would resort to such principles without discussion of what they were and would attempt to justify its decision on the basis of some other normative source. As Weil notes, throughout its history, 'la cour a eu la sagesse de ne pas s'aventurer dans de savants dissertations sur la distinction entre droit, justice et équité' (the court had the wisdom not to venture into scholarly essays on the distinction between law, justice and equity),[11] since a profound discussion of such relationships would require a degree of subjective assessment ill-at-ease with a consensualist conception of international law.

A. Good Faith, Clean Hands and Equitable Maxims – The Meuse Case

The case that came before the PCIJ in 1937 involving the diversion of water from the river Meuse (in French, or Maas in Dutch) is often cited as an important moment for equity in the history of international legal practice.[12] The facts of the dispute are perhaps relevant in order to understand the disputed legal issues, so I shall proffer a brief summary.

The Meuse is an international waterway, which rises in the mountains of North-Eastern France and which flows through Belgium, into the Netherlands, into the North Sea, forming a common delta with the Rhine. Two sections of the river form the boundary between Belgium and the Netherlands. Since the Meuse is a rain-fed river, river discharges may vary considerably, and periodic water shortage has long been considered

[9] ibid, 149.

[10] G von Glahn, *Law Among Nations: An Introduction to Public International Law*, 4th edn (New York, Macmillan, 1981) 24–25.

[11] Weil (1996) (n 1) 123.

[12] *Diversion of Water from the Meuse* PCIJ Rep Series A/B No 70, PCIJ Rep Series C No 81. See CW Jenks, *The Prospects of International Adjudication* (London, Stevens and Sons, 1964) 320–24; E McWhinney, 'Equity in International Law' in RA Newman, *Equity in the World's Legal Systems* (Brussels, Établissements Émile Bruylant, 1973) 581; MW Janis, 'Equity and International Law: The Comment in the Tentative Draft' (1982) 57 *Tulane Law Review* 80, 80, 86.

an important international issue. In the mid-nineteenth century, various conflicts over the distribution of the river's water arose between Belgium and the Netherlands. These conflicts were caused by the construction of a system of irrigation canals in the district of Campine in Belgium, which were linked to the (already existing) Zuid-Willemsvaart canal. Since the Zuid-Willemsvaart canal was fed by the water from the Meuse, these new canals also took water from the river.[13] The construction of the new canals caused detriment to the Netherlands in three discernible ways. First, the large volume of water which was required to continuously feed the new canals caused an excessive current in the Zuid-Willemsvaart canal, which hindered navigation. Secondly, the reduced water level in the Meuse – an immediate impact of the new canals' construction – rendered the Meuse itself significantly less navigable, and finally, the irrigation projects within the Campine district caused flooding in some parts of the southern Netherlands. Belgium and the Netherlands made various attempts to resolve the problems, and in 1863 concluded a Treaty, which established a legal regime governing the extraction and usage of water from the Meuse by the riparian States.[14] Importantly, this Treaty in its first Article provided for the construction of a new intake near Maastricht, on Dutch territory, which would constitute 'the feeding conduct for all canals situated below that town and for irrigation in the Campine and in the Netherlands'. The Treaty also provided for the raising of the water level in the Zuid-Willemsvaart canal so as to decrease the speed of currents, and the completion of some infrastructural improvements aimed at ameliorating the navigability of the joint section of the Meuse. Finally, the Treaty regulated the volume of water to be taken at the feeders governed by the Treaty depending on both the time of the year and the water level in the river.[15] This Treaty kept things relatively stable between the two States until 1921 when they both embarked upon further canal-building projects. In 1925, the two States signed a new agreement, designed to settle all differences concerning the construction or the enlargement of new canals. The Netherlands First Chamber (Parliament), however, refused to ratify the agreement. Following this, the Netherlands began construction of the Juliana canal, the Bosscheveld lock and the Borgharen barrage, while Belgium began to construct the Albert canal, a barrage at Monsin and a lock at Neerhaeren. The Netherlands seized the Permanent Court of International Justice with a unilateral application under Article 36(2) of the Court's Statute (compulsory jurisdiction).

[13] N Bouwman, 'A New Regime for the Meuse' (1996) 5 *Review of European Community and International Environmental Law* 161.

[14] Belgium–Netherlands, Treaty Regulating the Diversion of Water from the Meuse, The Hague, 12 May 1863.

[15] C Robb, *International Environmental Law Papers: Early Decisions,* vol 1 (Cambridge, Cambridge University Press, 1999) 159.

The Netherlands asked the Court to declare that the construction of the new canals by Belgium was contrary to the Treaty of 1863, and to order Belgium: (a) to discontinue all the works and to restore to a condition consistent with the Treaty of 1863 all works constructed in breach of that Treaty; and (b) to discontinue any feeding held to be contrary to the said Treaty and to refrain from any further feeding. Belgium asked the Court to declare that the Netherlands' submission was ill-founded, that the Borgharen barrage had been constructed in breach of the Treaty of 1863 and that the Juliana canal too, was subject to the provisions of that same Treaty.[16]

The Netherlands sought relief in the form of an injunction – a classic equitable remedy – and argued that the selection of the site for the feeder line in its territory (at Maastricht) had, from the signing of the Treaty, placed the parties in a position of legal inequality. However, the court quickly rejected this contention. Both Graver and Rossi have noted that in doing so, the Court was upholding the equitable principle that 'equity delights in equality' or 'equality is equity'.[17] Anzilotti J went still further in a dissenting opinion, stating that the principle of *inadimplenti non est inadimplentum (aequitas est equalitas)* is 'so just, so equitable, so universally recognised that it must be applied in international relations . . . [and is] one of the general principles of law recognised by civilised nations'. As Schwebel J noted in the *Nicaragua* case, Anzilotti's opinion on this score has never been juridically contested.[18]

When the problem was presented in purely equal terms, it fell to Manley Hudson J, in a separate opinion, to formulate the crux of the problem in equitable terms. Where two parties have assumed an identical or reciprocal obligation, should one party that is engaged in a continuing non-performance of that obligation be permitted to take advantage of a similar non-performance by the other? In deciding that such conduct should not be permitted, Hudson relied upon rationally-based extrapolations of equitable principles transposed from various municipal systems of law.[19] A wide-ranging examination of doctrine, common law, Roman law, as well as uses of equity in arbitral history led him to state that 'principles of equity have long been considered to constitute a part of international law and as such they have often been applied by international tribunals'.[20] He

[16] *Diversion of Water from the Meuse* (n 12).

[17] C Graver, 'The Role of Equity in the Jurisprudence of the World Court' (1979) 37 *University of Toronto Faculty of Law Review* 101, 103; C Rossi, *Equity and International Law: A Legal Realist Approach to International Decision Making* (Irvington, New York, Transnational Publishers Inc, 1993) 156–57.

[18] *Military and Paramilitary Activities in and against Nicaragua (Nicaragua v United States)* (Jurisdiction and Admissibility) [1984] ICJ Rep 392, 392–94.

[19] Rossi (1993) (n 17) 159.

[20] *Diversion of Water from the Meuse* PCIJ Rep Series A / B No 70, individual opinion of Manley Hudson J, 76.

made it clear that he was speaking of the power of the Court to decide in law, while applying equitable principles, rather than a judgment *ex aequo et bono*, as provided for in Article 38(2) of the PCIJ Statute, stating that 'The Court's recognition of equity as a part of international law is in no way restrained by the special power conferred upon it to decide a case ex aequo et bono if the parties agree thereto'.[21] In this way, he made it clear that equity in terms of general principles was a different beast to the 'equitable power of judgment' which could be agreed upon as an alternative to judgment at law by the parties according to the PCIJ (and later the ICJ) Statute. Hudson's reading of the Statute is clearly in tune with the *travaux préparatoires*, noting that 'under Article 38 of the Statute, if not independently of that Article, the Court has some freedom to consider principles of equity as part of the international law which it must apply'.[22] Hudson went on to note:

> It would seem to be an important principle of equity that where two parties have assumed an identical or reciprocal obligation, one party which is engaged in a continuing non-performance of that obligation should not be permitted to take advantage of a similar non-performance of that obligation by the other party. The principle finds expression in the so-called maxims of equity which exercised great influence in the creative period of the Anglo-American law. Some of these maxims are, 'equality is equity', 'he who seeks equity must do equity' . . . a very similar principle was received into Roman Law.[23]

As Rossi notes, in fundamental ways, Hudson J's opinion provided the gateway through which classical equitable and general principles doctrine, which had been fairly prevalent in international adjudication, became linked to the modern World Court sphere.[24] Hudson believed, however, that international judges must make 'a very sparing application' of general principles of law, and have 'scrupulous regard for the limitations which are necessary' when using them.[25]

However, Hudson's was a separate opinion, and the majority of the Court was at odds with his position. The Court, by 10 votes to 3 decided that there were not enough grounds to involve general international law and that the Treaty was, for the most part, specific enough to cover the dispute at hand.

The majority of the Court rejected the claim of the Netherlands that the construction of a canal that would render it possible for Belgium to feed canals situated below Maastricht with water taken from the Meuse at another place than at the Treaty feeder was inconsistent with the Treaty.

[21] ibid.
[22] ibid, 77.
[23] ibid.
[24] Rossi (1993) (n 17) 162.
[25] *Diversion of Water from the Meuse* PCIJ Rep Series A / B No 70, individual opinion of Manley Hudson J, 77.

According to the Court, the fact that the Treaty feeder was situated on Dutch territory gave the Netherlands, as territorial sovereign, a right of supervision which Belgium could not possess.[26] However, such a right did not impose an obligation on Belgium not to construct works which could be used to feed canals below Maastricht with water diverted from the Meuse elsewhere than at the Treaty feeder, whereas there was no such obligation for the Netherlands. The Court was of the opinion that such a right 'would presumably have been granted on a reciprocal basis'.[27] If the objective of the Treaty was to create inequality between the contracting parties, this should have been expressed clearly in the text of the Treaty. In absence of such a provision, both States should be treated equally, because the Treaty was 'an agreement freely concluded between two States seeking to reconcile their practical interests with a view to improving an existing situation rather than to settle a legal dispute concerning mutually contested rights'.[28]

Rossi criticises the majority opinion as a thinly-disguised *non liquet*, arguing that Hudson's approach provided a more satisfactory route to the same conclusion, namely: why should the Court countenance a claim and lend its authority to a final judgment favouring one State over another when both States are clearly engaged in the same type of illegal behaviour?[29] In Hudson's judgment, we see a general principle analogous to the common law maxim 'he who comes to equity must come with clean hands'.[30] Rossi notes that this principle has gained a certain acceptance in the World Court, having also been referred to in the *Chorzów Factory* and *Nicaragua* cases.[31]

The importance of Manley Hudson J's separate opinion in the *Meuse* case must be measured extremely carefully. First, we must not fail to remember that this was a separate opinion, and therefore did not form part of the judgment of the Court. Nonetheless, given the relative paucity of international judgments by the World Court, it is clear that dissenting and separate opinions, if they are not consistently expressly overruled by later judgments, are significant for forging an understanding of the normative extent of parts of the legal *corpus* which are comparatively obscure, and which have not been adequately discussed in the *dispositif* of ICJ or PCIJ judgments. They are certainly important for understanding equity and general principles of law. This is a point to which I shall return later,

[26] Robb (1999) (n 15) 163.

[27] O Spiermann, *International Legal Argument in the Permanent Court of International Justice, The Rise of the International Judiciary*, Cambridge Studies in International and Comparative Law (New York, Cambridge University Press, 2005) 374.

[28] *Meuse* PCIJ Rep Series A/B No 70, 20.

[29] Rossi (1993) (n 17) 163.

[30] However, it is also germane to note that the other judge who defended this principle was Anzilotti, a civil law judge, showing that it is not merely a bald transposition of the common law as in the *Sheik of Abu Dhabi* case.

[31] Rossi (1993) (n 17) 164.

but for now it shall suffice to note that it is common and accepted practice amongst leading scholars on the subject of general principles of law to make frequent reference to dissenting and separate opinions to support their conclusions.[32]

Bearing the above consideration in mind, we can fully appreciate the import of Manley Hudson J's pronouncements in the *Meuse* case, which have yet to be refuted by any subsequent international judgment, and which have found support in several subsequent opinions of the ICJ. Hudson had no qualms about applying equitable principles to solve a legal problem, even when this problem was rooted in a fairly specific treaty. Indeed, it is notable that Hudson's fellow judges refrained from criticising his usage of such principles as a source of law. Had the feeling amongst his colleagues been that such principles had no place in the international normative *corpus*, it would have been a great sin – and indeed a great mistake – to apply them in the solution of a legal problem, irrespective of the presence of other norms which might be used in the solution of the dispute at hand. The fact that neither Hudson's fellow judges in the *Meuse* case nor the judges of the ICJ in the plethora of disputes which have come before it since then have voiced vociferous and trenchant objections to Hudson's usage of equitable principles in his reasoning suggests that there is indeed a general acceptance amongst the international judiciary that equitable principles may be employed in the solution of legal problems. Such principles must necessarily be understood as a subcategory of the general principles referenced in Article 38(I), therefore enjoying normative parity with treaty and customary law.

While we may feel relatively comfortable in assuming that Hudson's fellow judges were not shocked and appalled by the learned judge's usage of equity as a legal source since they did not object to its normative power per se, a further question must be posed before leaving the *Meuse* dispute aside: why was Hudson – apart, to some extent from Anzilotti – alone in his usage of equity as a source of law to help settle this dispute? The answer, I feel, must necessarily lie in the (equitable) maxim *aequitus sequitur legem*, or 'equity follows the law', which itself is, in international law at least, a corollary of the general principle *lex specialis generalibus derogat*, which had been agreed upon as a general principle of law by the PCIJ Advisory Committee of Jurists.[33] This principle states, as a general – but not universal – rule that where a conflict arises between a sound and settled norm of a specific nature and a more general norm covering a wider area of law, *ceteris paribus*, the specific rule shall prevail, and as

[32] Bin Cheng and Christopher Rossi's works are replete with frequent references to such opinions.

[33] PCIJ/Advisory Committee of Jurists (ACJ), *Procès-verbaux of the Proceedings of the Committee, 16 June–24 June* (den Haag, van Langhuysen Brothers, 1920) 314–15, 337. (Hereinafter *Procès-verbaux*).

noted earlier, is designed to prevent excessive invocation of equitable principles *contra legem*. It is clear from the argumentation employed by the majority of the judges in the *Meuse* case that they felt that resort to general principles in this case was unnecessary, since the 1863 Treaty concerning the extraction and diversion of water from the river Meuse was found to be of a specific and comprehensive enough nature to provide a solution to the dispute in question without resorting to more general sources of law such as custom and general principles.

The *Meuse* case may well be international equity's '*locus classicus*', as one leading scholar has termed it.[34] The fact that Hudson's conclusions have stood the test of time without being roundly denounced, either by his fellow judges or by the vast majority of international legal scholarship on the subject,[35] is tremendously important in and of itself. However, the fact that the other judges in the case were not tempted to follow Hudson's reasoning demonstrates to us the weight associated with the *lex specialis generalibus derogat* principle. Treaty is more specific than custom; custom (generally) more specific than general principles. This state of affairs, combined with the *lex specialis generalibus derogat* principle partly explains why the scholar searching international judgments for regular guidance on the content of the 'general principles' category set out in the sources of law clause in the ICJ Statute will be left disappointed. It is a rare move indeed for judges to apply general principles, particularly *contra legem*, which they must effectively do if they are to supersede the *lex specialis* rule. Such a course of action is called for exceedingly infrequently, especially since disputes tend to arise over areas of international law that are covered by international instruments, or at least by custom. Further, even when it is called for, judges may tend to stray on the side of conservatism and attempt to apply a less controversial and more 'mainstream' law source, for fear of charges of prevarication or partiality.[36] Hence the lamentable paucity with which international judgments throw up references to general principles and equity.

B. *Ubi ius, ubi remedium*

The 1970 *Barcelona Traction, Light and Power Company Limited* case[37] was a dispute which arose between Belgium and Spain and which was notable for our purposes not only because it raised equitable considerations, but

34 Jenks (1964) (n 12) 322.

35 See TM Franck and DM Sugrue, 'The International Role of Equity-as-Fairness' (1992–93) 81 *Georgetown Law Journal* 563.

36 Rossi notes: 'It is impossible to keep separate the notions of prevarication and equity . . . [however] To treat them as indistinguishable is to misunderstand fundamentally the law as it is and the law as it should be'. Rossi (1993) (n 17) 173.

37 *Barcelona Traction, Light and Power Co Ltd (Belgium v Spain)* [1970] ICJ Rep 3.

because it dealt, albeit inferentially, with an extremely potent equitable principle, namely *ubi ius, ubi remedium*. This principle stipulates that for every wrong committed, there must be a remedy, but while it may seem an elegant legal transposition of Newton's Third Law of Motion,[38] the experienced lawyer is aware that such a principle may be applied *contra legem* only rarely, if ever. Therefore, even inferential reference to such a principle merits close examination.

The facts of the case run thus: the Barcelona Traction, Light and Power Company was a utilities provider which had been incorporated in Canada in 1911, where its headquarters was located. It later formed a series of subsidiary entities for the purpose of creating and developing electricity in Catalonia, some of which were incorporated in Spain, some in Canada. Some years later, the share capital of the company came to be largely held by Belgian nationals. In the fallout from the Spanish Civil War, the Franco Government and judiciary made it difficult for foreigners to do business in Spain. New shares were issued, and then sold and resold by the Spanish courts. The company was later declared bankrupt, despite the fact that the company itself was not informed of the bankruptcy proceedings in time to enter a plea of opposition to them. The shareholders, backed initially by the British, Canadian, US and Belgian Governments, argued that the proceedings had been fundamentally unfair and made representations to the Spanish Government in this regard. However, importantly, the Canadian Government ceased its interposition in 1955, and eventually it was Belgium alone which, faced with intransigence from the Spanish Government, brought the case before the ICJ.

Problematic in this case was the fact that Belgium was representing the shareholders, but the company itself was incorporated in Canada. Belgium effectively wished to exercise a right of diplomatic protection over the company on behalf of its shareholders. Given that the right of diplomatic protection was originally conceived as a means to protect natural persons rather than legal entities such as corporations, the idea of stretching the notion still further so that the State of the shareholders, as well as the State of the company's incorporation, might have the right to exercise diplomatic protection over corporate entities in such cases proved a bridge too far for the ICJ. The Court ruled that only the Canadian Government could sue in this case, and that therefore, Belgium lacked the requisite *locus standi* to bring such an action.

The *Barcelona Traction* case is important from an international legal perspective for a number of reasons, not least because it definitively demonstrates that diplomatic protection may be exercised in favour of corporate

[38] Newton's Third Law of Motion states that for every action, there must be an equal and opposite reaction. See I Newton, IB Cohen (tr), A Whitman (tr) and J Budenz (tr), *The Principia: Mathematical Principles of Natural Philosophy* (Berkeley, California, University of California Press, 1999).

entities as well as natural persons, something which had been in some dispute before the judgment. However, from an equitable perspective, it is interesting for a number of reasons. First, the extension of the right of diplomatic protection to States over legal entities represented a breakthrough, where the Court felt bold enough to extend an accepted right in the interests of justice. The norm (*ius*) existed; ergo there must be a remedy (*remedium*), since there was no sufficiently specific legal barrier prohibiting the extension of such a right to legal as well as natural persons. This move by the Court demonstrates an – albeit limited – usage of two equitable doctrines, namely *ubi ius, ubi remedium* and the prioritisation of substance over form (in the interests of justice). Rossi notes that this 'bolder' expression by the Court 'marks a relatively rare occurrence in international jurisprudence. Normally the Court is loath to break new juridical ground if it can limit its decision to more narrowly circumscribed issues'.[39] Such a stance is clearly in keeping with what is a fundamental precept of judicial restraint. To stray too frequently outside this precept may bring forth charges of prevarication. However, it is perhaps worth noting the earlier *Chorzów Factory* case to gain some perspective here. In the *Chorzów Factory* case, the PCIJ had already extolled the equitable principle '*ubi ius, ubi remedium*'. The Court held that

> reparation is the indispensible complement of a failure to apply a convention, and there is no necessity for this to be stated in the convention itself . . . [it is] a general conception of law that any breach of an engagement involves an obligation to make reparation.[40]

This was a far-reaching statement indeed, as it assumed an implied power of the Court – and indeed perhaps a broader power at law, not necessarily vesting exclusively in the Court – to create a remedy where none was explicitly provided for. This case was expanded upon somewhat by a 1949 Advisory Opinion of the ICJ, where instead of interpreting the silence of a UN Charter provision restrictively, the World Court again felt compelled in general interests of justice to take a teleological approach to what consequences the legal personality of UN organs must necessarily entail.[41] Here, as Rossi has noted, the Court 'naturally assumed it had a legal entitlement to interpret the terms of the Charter [and other international instruments]' and took this very broad teleological reading despite the silence of the provisions 'to avoid the manifestly unreasonable result that otherwise would have obtained'.[42] Both of the above cases represent examples of equity *praeter legem*, possibly bordering on *contra legem*. Therefore,

[39] Rossi (1993) (n 17) 173–74.

[40] *Case Concerning the Factory at Chorzów (Germany v Poland)* (Merits) PCIJ Rep Series A No 17.

[41] *Reparation for Injuries Suffered in the Service of the United Nations* (Advisory Opinion) [1949] ICJ Rep 174.

[42] Rossi (1993) (n 17) 131–32.

Barcelona Traction may not be quite as groundbreaking as it may seem at the first glance.

However, from an equitable perspective, *Barcelona Traction* may be considered just as important because of the ground it does not break as because of that which it does. Having demonstrated a predisposition towards a flexible equitable interpretation of legal rules, the Court nonetheless ruled against Belgium, holding that, despite the fairly firmly established close nexus between Belgium and the company, Belgium could not exercise diplomatic protection in this case since the company was incorporated in Canada. The Court, however, took the time in its judgment to weigh the arguments on behalf of Belgium, asking whether 'considerations of equity do not require that [Belgium] be held to possess a right of protection'.[43] The Court went on to state that

> in view of the discretionary nature of diplomatic protection, considerations of equity cannot require more than the possibility for some protector state to intervene, whether it be the state of the company by virtue of the general rule [which the Court had just established] . . . or, in a secondary capacity, the national state of the shareholders who claim protection.[44]

However, despite recognising the equity of the notion of diplomatic protection of shareholders to prevent potential abuses such as those apparently committed by the Spanish Government against Barcelona Traction, the Court recognised that to do so would open the door to competing claims on the part of different States, which could create an atmosphere of insecurity in international economic relations. Therefore, the Court was not willing to extend the right of *ius standi* to Belgium in this case.

The fact that the ICJ was unwilling to extend the right of diplomatic protection to shareholders is in complete concord with equity's role in national legal systems. Equity seeks to do justice, to do more harm than good, and here, therefore would not act, as to do so would have 'opened the door to legal anarchy'.[45] This explains the failure to extend *ubi ius, ubi remedium* to this case. In national legal systems, equity's limits are more frequently reached when they clash with a sound and settled rule of law which ensures an ordered and predictable state of affairs in a given area, giving rise to the maxim *aequitus sequitur legem* – equity follows the law. However, at international level, it would seem, judges are wont to take account of international order and stability itself as an important value, in order to ensure the coherence of the *corpus* of international law and forestay legal anarchy. Such an approach, while vaguely unsatisfying for Belgium in this instance, is a sensible and, moreover, an equitable approach.

[43] *Barcelona Traction, Light and Power Co Ltd (Belgium v Spain)* [1970] ICJ Rep 3, 48.
[44] ibid.
[45] Rosenne (1988) (n 5) 102.

Barcelona Traction, therefore, gives the legal scholar a prime example of the exercise, but also of the limits, of the equitable principle that for every wrong there must be a remedy in the international legal arena. However the extent of the principle is clouded somewhat by the fact that, for certain judges of the ICJ, it was felt that the Court had been too conservative. Sir Gerald Fitzmaurice, in a separate opinion noted the deficiencies of international law, and recognised the ever-increasing need for the implementation by the Court of 'a body of rules which can play some sort of part internationally as the English system of equity does, or at least originally did, in the common law countries that adopted it'.[46] Fitzmaurice went on to note that 'Deciding a case on the rules of equity, that are part of the general system of law applicable, is something quite different from giving a decision *ex aequo et bono*'.[47] Fitzmaurice was of the opinion, therefore, that the ICJ had not been firm enough in implementing a conception of equity analogous to that which had taken root in common law systems, and that its reticence to extend the principle *ubi ius ubi remedium* a little further (without necessarily awarding *locus standi* to Belgium) may have been misguided, and that certainly, on a broader level, equity needs more of a foothold in international law.

C. 'Substance Over Form' and Equitable Flexibility

The 1986 *Case Concerning Military and Paramilitary Activities in and against Nicaragua* represented another instance in which equitable principles, albeit 'by the back door', as it were, played a role. Here, the ICJ held that the US had breached international law by supporting the Contra guerrillas in their rebellion against the left-leaning Nicaraguan Government and by mining Nicaragua's harbours. The Court found in its verdict that the United States was 'in breach of its obligations under customary international law not to use force against another State', 'not to intervene in its affairs', 'not to violate its sovereignty', 'not to interrupt peaceful maritime commerce', and 'in breach of its obligations under Article XIX of the Treaty of Friendship, Commerce and Navigation between the Parties signed at Managua on 21 January 1956'.[48]

However, more important for our purposes than how the Court arrived at its decision is how the Court actually came to the conclusion that it had jurisdiction to hear the case. The United States contended, as part of its defence, that the ICJ did not have jurisdiction to hear the action in the first place. The purported jurisdiction in this case arose from a combination of

[46] *Barcelona Traction, Light and Power Co Ltd (Belgium v Spain)* [1970] ICJ Rep 3, separate opinion of Fitzmaurice, 85.

[47] ibid.

[48] *Military and Paramilitary Activities in and against Nicaragua (Nicaragua v United States)* (Judgment) [1986] ICJ Rep 16.

Articles 36(1), 36(2) and 36(5) of the Statute of the ICJ. Article 36(1) allows States to make declarations accepting the Court's jurisdiction as compulsory regarding specific matters arising from treaties concluded between them; Article 36(2) allows States to make declarations accepting the Court's jurisdiction as compulsory regarding all cases which are brought involving them; while Article 36(5) provides for jurisdiction on the basis of declarations made under the Statute of the Permanent Court of International Justice.[49] However, all the above are tempered by the principle of reciprocity in international law, which allows one party to take advantage of any weakness in the declaration of adherence to the Court on the part of the other party to a dispute, in order to ensure parity of arms and a fair judicial process. The United States sought to rely upon this principle in order to expose a weakness on the part of Nicaragua.

Despite several entreaties from the League of Nations, Nicaragua never formally completed the process of ratification of its adherence to the PCIJ Statute, and in one famous instance actually relied upon this imperfection in order to excuse itself from the jurisdiction of the Permanent Court.[50] To the five dissenting judges, it was manifestly unreasonable that Nicaragua could 'eat its cake and have it too', that is, seek to rely upon its non-conformity with the formal requirements at one point and then seek to rely upon its effective adherence to the same requirements later. The majority of the Court were, however, of another mind, pointing to Article 36(5), which preserved declarations made during the tenure of the PCIJ which were still in force.[51] The Court concluded that Nicaragua should be treated as having met the juridical requirements of the optional clause of compulsory jurisdiction. This was the case, despite the fact that Nicaragua in fact admitted that it had never deposited its Protocol of Signature with the relevant League of Nations bureau, and despite the Court having found that 'Nicaragua, having failed to deposit its instrument of ratification of the Protocol of Signature to the Permanent Court, was not a party to that treaty'.[52]

This decision constituted a massive step for the ICJ, and was seen by many as prevarication writ large. The perception of bias created by this piece of reasoning from the Court undoubtedly played a key role in the subsequent decision of the US to take no further part in proceedings and to block the enforcement of the Court's judgment via the Security Council.[53]

[49] Art 37 of the ICJ's Statute similarly transfers jurisdiction under any compromissory clause in a treaty that gave jurisdiction to the PCIJ.

[50] See detailed account in the dissenting opinion of Oda J in *Nicaragua* (Judgment) [1986] ICJ Rep 16, 472–89.

[51] *Nicaragua* (Jurisdiction and Admissibility) [1984] ICJ Rep 392, 406.

[52] ibid, 404.

[53] C Schulte, *Compliance with Decisions of the International Court of Justice* (New York, Oxford University Press, 2004) 282–85.

Rossi notes that, absent the application of what he calls 'pure' equity (ie reasoning purely in terms of what is just and without taking the legal framework into account),

> it is indeed difficult to conceive of a basis for the court's prevarication from the procedural requirements of due process. It could be argued that Nicaragua did indeed manifest an intention to be bound by the optional protocol by virtue of the simple fact that it initiated the suit.[54]

However, such a theory of immediate perfection of consent is ill-conceived, since to allow for such *ad hoc* availing of what is intended to be a permanent clause of jurisdiction within the ICJ Statute is to defeat the purpose of the Article itself. Nicaragua put forward the argument that it had effectively acquiesced to the jurisdiction of the Court in failing to object to a series of United Nations publications which listed Nicaragua as a State party to the Court's jurisdiction. However, these books contained legal disclaimers which removed any authoritative basis upon which any such argument could prevail and thus the Court dismissed this from its reasoning.

So why did the ICJ take this huge and uncharacteristic step? Rossi cites 'extra-legal considerations . . . militating toward the conclusion that it would simply be unjust to dismiss the Nicaraguan complaint due to such a technical deficiency'.[55] However, I am loath to accept such a position. That the majority of a World Court composed of learned judges of various nationalities would prioritise what Rossi seems to describe as public sentiment over international law appears unlikely to me. This is particularly true when one reminds one's self of the inherent conservatism detectable in so many ICJ judgments, which has been discussed both here and in chapter two. Rather, it is my contention that general principles of law, albeit primitively expressed and poorly explained by the judiciary – again, perhaps for fear of opening themselves to charges of prevarication, which ironically happened in any case – played a key role. The alternative – that judges simply dismissed the law because they did not like it – is both too frightening and too far-fetched to contemplate.

It remains, however, to determine, what 'general principles of law recognised by civilised nations', or variations thereof, were applied by the Court in this instance. In order to decipher which principles were applied, we must look at the pure legal substance of the judgment, rather than the text itself, since the wording provides virtually no clues as to what the Court's reasoning must have been in this regard. In brief, the Court determined that a technical defect, the importance of which was in some dispute, should not be held to vitiate the consent of the Nicaraguan Government to the optional clause of compulsory jurisdiction under Article 36(1) and (5)

[54] Rossi (1993) (n 17) 187.
[55] ibid.

of the ICJ Statute. This, despite the fact that, on the face of it, such a technical defect rendered the purported consent of the Nicaraguan Government imperfect and incomplete.[56] Hence, the condition of reciprocity had not been satisfied and the US should not have been bound. However, it is a strongly consecrated principle of equity that *ex re sed non ex nomine*, or equity will look to the substance of a transaction rather than to its form. As repeatedly noted in chapter three, equity abhors formalism and will not allow a shroud of legality to protect wrongdoers. Therefore, intended transactions which do not fulfil formal requirements will be enforced. This principle was noted as early as the sixteenth century in English courts, and has been used to reach conclusions in a number of famous judgments.[57] The extent of this maxim is not completely understood, and will certainly vary from case to case, but, as Hilary Delany notes, while this does not mean that legal formalities will not be required by equity, equity will not require the observance of 'unnecessary formalities'.[58] Such a principle is not specific to the common law system, but as is evident from the conclusions drawn in chapter three, it is perhaps the sole principle – along with the doctrine of the abuse of rights – which exists in every legal system examined. Therefore, there is no doubt that it can be classified without reservation as a general principle of law recognised by civilised nations. It is perhaps further germane to note that recourse to a formal defect by a wrongdoer is also classified as an abuse of right in certain jurisdictions. The fact that both of these principles are so deeply embedded into the legal systems of civilised nations, combined with the Court's long history of introducing general principles 'by the back door' (ie without duly acknowledging them for what they are) gives – I would contend, justified – cause to argue that the *Nicaragua* jurisdiction decision was based upon the principle of the prioritisation of substance over form and, perhaps to a limited extent, the doctrine of the abuse of rights. Some weight is added to the above theory by the ICJ's own (deeply unspecific) pronouncement that 'The Court cannot regard Nicaragua's reliance on the optional clause as in any way contrary to good faith or equity'.[59] This case can only add weight to the arguments of those who opine that equity plays a shadowy – but important – role in international law.

[56] Indeed, the Nicaraguan Government had previously relied upon this defect in consent to excuse itself from jurisdiction in a previous case.

[57] See, eg *Horn v Keteltas* 46 NY 605 (1871); *Rochester Savings Bank v Stoeltzen & Tapper* (1941) 176 Misc 140.

[58] H Delany, *Equity and the Law of Trusts in Ireland*, 3rd edn (Dublin, Thomson Roundhall, 2003) 34.

[59] *Military and Paramilitary Activities in and against Nicaragua (Nicaragua v United States)* (Jurisdiction and Admissibility) [1984] ICJ Rep 392, 415.

D. Estoppel – The Temple of Preah Vihear and Other Stories

One of equity's most potent doctrines is that of estoppel. Also known as *non concedit venire contra factum proprium,* the doctrine holds that a party may not make a serious representation as to his future conduct, which is relied upon by the other party, only to renege upon the assurance given at a later date. In order for one to claim estoppel, there must exist: (1) an assurance given by one party; (2) reliance thereupon by the other party; and (3) detriment resulting to the second party on foot of, and resulting from, this reliance. If this three-stage test is satisfied, then the first party will be held to be 'estopped' from denying his original assurance, and must fulfil whatever promise he made to the second party.[60] While a thorough transposition of this principle into international law would be impossible, given the complex manner in which it is exercised within national legal systems, the case law of the World Court has thrown up a number of interesting references to the doctrine, which suggest a limited reception of estoppel doctrine in the international legal system.

When the Permanent Court of International Justice came into being, leading scholars noted that estoppel had thus far received little attention in the international legal discourse.[61] This was despite the contention that 'the principle underlying estoppel is recognised by all systems of private law, not only with regard to estoppel by record . . . but also, under different names, with regard to estoppel by conduct and deed', and the logical conclusion that, given that this was the case, it is 'not easy to adduce why those general principles underlying estoppel should be disregarded in the relations between States'.[62] However, by the 1950s, it had become clear that there was some constancy in conceptions of the doctrine in international law. Particularly, States were required to be consistent in their attitudes to given factual or legal situations. MacGibbon notes that such a demand 'may be rooted in the continuing need for at least a modicum of stability and for some measure of predictability in the pattern of State conduct'.[63] Such predictability further explains bona fides as a general principle of law, and it is not uncommon to find estoppel discussed as a particular manifestation of the broader principle.[64] Lauterpacht agrees, positing that 'A State cannot be allowed to avail itself of the advantages of the treaty when it suits it to do so and repudiate it when its performance

[60] *Ackerman v True* 175 NY 353 (1903).

[61] A McNair, 'The Legality of the Occupation of the Ruhr' (1924) 5 *British Yearbook of International Law* 17, 34. Also noted by IC MacGibbon, 'Estoppel in International Law' (1958) 7 *ICLQ* 468.

[62] H Lauterpacht, *Private Law Sources and Analogies of International Law (With Special Reference to International Arbitration)* (London, Longman, Green & Co, 1927) 204–05.

[63] MacGibbon (1958) (n 61) 469.

[64] ibid, 471.

becomes onerous'.[65] Schwarzenberger points out that every breach of a treaty involves a breach of the principle of good faith, and opines that estoppel doctrine may be expressed 'in more specialised terms which are congenial to the realm of good faith such as the prohibition of fraud or *venire contra factum proprium* in treaty relations'.[66] The same author goes on to say that 'the legal effect of every act of recognition is to create an estoppel'.[67] Strongly linked to the idea of acquiescence, it is also clear that an estoppel may arise by virtue of a State's knowing acquiescence to a situation rather than a specific assurance, that is that passive, as well as active assurances, which are later relied upon by the other party, are possible. Previous recognition or admission bars subsequent challenge.[68]

The fact that leading scholars had paid little attention to the doctrine until the 1950s had not discouraged international courts and tribunals from using it. Indeed, already at the time of the foundation of the PCIJ, McNair was forced to admit that 'international jurisprudence has a place for some recognition of the principle that a State cannot blow hot and cold – *allegans contraria non audiendus est*'.[69] Lauterpacht was more emphatic 10 years later, stating that the PCIJ's early case law had shown a practice 'reminiscent of some of the elements of estoppel in English law',[70] citing the *Polish Nationals in Danzig*,[71] *Free Zones of Upper Savoy and the District of Gex*[72] and *Greco-Bulgarian Communities*[73] cases as examples. Since then, the PCIJ and ICJ have made repeated and explicit reference to the doctrine of estoppel, albeit without a completely consistent conception of what that doctrine entails or of how far it may be extended in international law. For this reason, it shall be necessary to refer to a large number of cases to examine its applicability in international fora.

Early references to the principle included the *Chorzów Factory* case, where it was held that a State party was estopped from pleading that the Court lacked jurisdiction in the case on the grounds that

65 H Lauterpacht (acting as Special Rapporteur to the International Law Commission on the Law of Treaties), 'Report on the Law of Treaties' UN Doc A/CN 4/63, (24 March 1953) 157, 166.

66 G Schwarzenberger, 'The Fundamental Principles of International Law' (1955) 87 *Recueil de la Haye* 303.

67 ibid, 353.

68 MacGibbon (1958) (n 61) 482.

69 McNair (1924) (n 61) 35. A note of caution must be sounded here, however, since such a pronouncement seems somewhat at odds with the already discussed *Nicaragua* judgment.

70 H Lauterpacht, 'Some Observations on the Prohibition of "Non Liquet" and the Completeness of the Law' in *Symbolae Verzijl. Présentées au Prof JHW Verzijl à l'occasion de son LXX-ième anniversaire* (The Hague, Martinus Nijhoff, 1958).

71 *Treatment of Polish Nationals and Other Persons of Polish Origin or Speech in the Danzig Territory* PCIJ Rep Series A/B No 44.

72 *Case of the Free Zones of Upper Savoy and the District of Gex* PCIJ Rep Series A No 22.

73 *The Greco-Bulgarian 'Communities'* (Advisory Opinion) PCIJ Rep Series B No17.

> it is . . . a principle generally accepted in the jurisprudence of international arbitration, as well as by municipal courts, that one party cannot avail itself of the fact that the other has not fulfilled some obligation, or has not had recourse to some means of redress, if the former party has, by some illegal act, prevented the latter from fulfilling the obligation in question, or from having recourse to the tribunal which would have been open to him.[74]

If one State had failed to appoint a commissioner, the same State could not later complain that the commission was unfair due to the absence of its commissioner. It was thereby estopped by virtue of its own acquiescence.

In the *Serbian and Brazilian Loans* case, the PCIJ approved of the principle of estoppel by implication, but held that in the facts of this case, insufficient grounds existed for its application, stating that there was a lack of a 'clear and unequivocal representation by the bondholders' upon which the debtor State was entitled to rely, and further a lack of evidence of a change of position by the debtor State.[75] Therefore, the Court held that 'when the requirements of the principle of estoppel to establish a loss of right are considered, it is quite clear that no sufficient basis has been shown for applying the principle in this case'.[76] However, here again the World Court showed no compulsions about applying the doctrine, provided the prerequisite conditions underlying its operability were met.

A similar position was maintained by the PCIJ in the *Eastern Greenland* case.[77] Here, Norway argued that the rather eager stance maintained by the Danish Government when seeking recognition of its position in the Greenlandic territory as regards third States from 1915–21 was wholly inconsistent with the possession of sovereignty at that time, and that as a result, Denmark was estopped from alleging a long-held sovereignty over the entirety of the island.[78] The Court, however, disagreed, finding that such circumstances were insufficient grounds to hold Denmark to be thus precluded from making its claim.[79] The Court further observed that by accepting as binding several international treaties regarding Danish territorial possessions, 'Norway reaffirmed that she recognised the whole of Greenland as Danish; and therefore has debarred herself from contesting Danish sovereignty'.[80] It is perhaps worth noting that the words 'debarred' and 'estopped' are synonymous, but the Court, in typical fashion, chose to

[74] *Case Concerning the Factory at Chorzów* (Claim for Indemnity) (Jurisdiction) PCIJ Rep Series A No 9, 31. This passage was also quoted in the pleadings of the *Interpretation of the Peace Treaties Case* before the ICJ. See also MacGibbon (1958) (n 61) 480.

[75] *Case Concernjng the Payment of Various Serbian Loans Issued in France and Case Concerning the Payment in Gold of the Brazilian Federal Loans Issued in France* PCIJ Rep Series A No 20/21, 38–39.

[76] ibid, 5.

[77] *Legal Status of Eastern Greenland (Denmark v Norway)* PCIJ Rep Series A/B No 53.

[78] ibid, 45.

[79] ibid, 62.

[80] ibid, 68–69.

couch its judgment in terminology which gave as little explicit recognition to general principles as possible, while nonetheless using them to decide the case. The judgment of the PCIJ held that due to the understanding reached in the famous declaration by Norwegian Foreign Minister, Nils Claus Ihlen,[81] on 22 July 1919, Norway was under an obligation not to contest Danish sovereignty over Greenland as a whole.[82] The judgment has frequently been cited by authors as proof that States must keep their promises to one another.[83] However, the *Eastern Commission of the Danube* Advisory Opinion made it clear that if such promises contain explicit disclaimers, the situation may be somewhat different, and that 'Any representation that carries a condition not later materialised akin to "without prejudice" representation common in the course of negotiation, cannot give rise to estoppel'.[84] Furthermore, the representation made must be a voluntary one, and duress or fraud will nullify a plea of estoppel (showing again the nexus with the principle of good faith).[85]

An example of estoppel by acquiescence – or 'sleeping on one's rights' arose in the *Anglo-Norwegian Fisheries* case. Here, the Court held that the method of coastal measurement by means of straight lines for bays and fjords, which had been adopted by Norway, 'had been consolidated by a constant and sufficiently long practice', and that the attitude adopted by the various State Governments in reaction to this – namely their failure to protest – 'bears witness to the fact that they did not consider it to be contrary to international law'.[86] Waldock has described the conclusion of the ICJ in this regard as 'amongst the boldest and most important judgments pronounced by any international tribunal',[87] though frankly it is difficult to see why, since the *Anglo-Norwegian Fisheries* judgment seems to be in complete accord with the earlier case law, both of the PCIJ (above), and of a significant number of earlier arbitral awards.[88]

[81] The relevant clause of the declaration stated that 'the plans of the Royal [Danish] Government respecting Danish sovereignty over the whole of Greenland . . . would be met with no difficulties on the part of Norway'.

[82] *Legal Status of Eastern Greenland (Denmark v Norway)* PCIJ Rep Series A/B No 53, 73. See also B Cheng, *General Principles of Law as Applied by International Courts and Tribunals* (Cambridge, Grotius, 1987) 198 *et seq.* Cheng deals with the Ihlen Declaration and much of the concept of estoppel under the heading of 'responsibility' as a general principle of law.

[83] See M Fitzmaurice and O Elias, *Contemporary Issues in the Law of Treaties* (Utrecht, Eleven International Publishing, 2005) 13.

[84] *Advisory Opinion on the Eastern Commission of the Danube between Galatz and Braila* (1927) PCIJ Series B No 14, 6.

[85] DW Bowett, 'Estoppel before International Tribunals and its Relation to Acquiescence' (1957) 33 *British Yearbook of International Law* 176, 190.

[86] *Anglo-Norwegian Fisheries (United Kingdom and Northern Ireland v Norway)* [1951] ICJ Rep 116, 139.

[87] CHM Waldock, 'The Anglo-Norwegian Fisheries Case' (1951) 28 *British Yearbook of International Law* 114.

[88] Lauterpacht has noted the frequency with which estoppel and acquiescence had arisen prior to – and contemporaneously with – the PCIJ in a wide variety of early arbitral cases. Amongst those cited by Lauterpacht are the *Pious Fund of the Californias* case, the *Venezuelan*

In the *Gulf of Maine* case, contested by Canada and the US, the ICJ discussed the differences between acquiescence and estoppel. The Court noted that the two concepts 'are . . . based on different legal reasoning, since acquiescence is equivalent to tacit recognition manifested by unilateral conduct which the other party may interpret as consent, while estoppel is linked to the idea of preclusion'.[89] However, it is perhaps lamentable that the Court did not discuss this point in greater detail, since the two concepts have appeared to be analogous in the previous case law of the Court, with the sole discernible difference being that estoppel rests on the basis of an active assurance, whereas acquiescence is founded on its passive equivalent. This would seem an important point in international law, particularly as regards customary international law, since persistent objection during the formative period of a norm seems to be the only means of ensuring that a State is not bound by that norm (unless the norm is part of the *corpus cogentes*). States are effectively precluded (or estopped, if you will) from later objecting to the norm if they do not do so *ab initio*. The doctrinal difference between this and an estoppel based on an active representation seems difficult to grasp. Their acquiescence, even to general norms of customary international law, ties their hands. MacGibbon draws attention to an excellent, albeit rather old, example of both estoppel and acquiescence working in tandem, which arose in the context of the American Civil War. He cites a legal objection drafted by the British Law Officers as regards the United States Government's failure to recognise the Prize Court established by the Confederate States Government. MacGibbon gives a rather long citation, but I feel it is both colourful and useful to re-cite the better part of it:

> [T]he United States government, having demanded from all Neutral States the particular rights incident during a state of war only, and to a belligerent only, and having exercised these rights to the great annoyance and distress of neutral commerce, now declare that they will not discharge the corresponding duties of a belligerent; now deny that their enemy has any right to a Prize Court . . . though it be a title universally recognised by all civilised States, and although neutral States have the right to insist on the existence of such a court in the territory de facto occupied by the Confederate States. Upon these principles, it is manifest that the maintenance of a blockade, the search and visit and condemnation of neutral ships, put in practice by the United States, instead of being lawful acts, are so many acts of unjustifiable violence, insult and wrong. We think that upon this point, there should be sent without delay

Preferential Claims case, the *Russian Indemnity* case, the *Croft Case*, the *Mechanic* case, the *Cantons of Thurgau and St Gallen* case, the *Chamizal Arbitration*, the *Alaskan Boundary Dispute*, the *Corvaia* case, the *Island of Palmas* arbitration, the *Tinoco* arbitration, the *Landreau* claim and the *Shufeldt* claim. See Lauterpacht (1927) (n 62) 205–09.

[89] *Delimitation of the Maritime Boundary of the Gulf of Maine Area* (*Canada v United States*) [1984] ICJ Rep 246, 305.

> to the United States government as strong and full a remonstrance as can be framed.[90]

The above example shows that failure to object to norms such as those governing the conduct of wars binds States, but equally that by upholding one part of a combined and connected body of norms which change the position of several parties (in this case both belligerents as well as neutral trading partner States) estops a State party from denying the validity of any other part thereof, unless perhaps, this State had been a persistent objector in the past. It also shows the strength of estoppel arising from acquiescence vis-à-vis general norms of international law, and not merely from bilateral or multilateral treaties. This would seem to render the Court's pronouncement in the *Gulf of Maine* case either anomalous or cryptic. However, given that no further elucidation was offered by the Chamber, we shall leave it aside for the moment and shall examine perhaps the most frequently cited example of a case involving estoppel before the World Court, namely the *Temple of Preah Vihear* case.[91]

In *Temple of Preah Vihear*, the ICJ applied a conception of estoppel and acquiescence. The Court ruled that Thailand (then Siam) should be estopped from denying the validity of a 1907 map, known as the Annex I map, which had originally been drawn up for a prior Franco-Siamese boundary delimitation settlement in 1904, and which covered the Preah Vihear region. The 1907 acceptance as accurate by Thailand of a map, and 50 years of accepting the benefits of a stable frontier that came as a direct result of a treaty concluded using this map, constituted an abstention from protest, an acquiescence. The Thai royal family had even visited the temple with the French flag flying (Cambodia was then a French colony). To then, 50 years later, begin to dispute the status quo, was impermissible. Thailand was thereby precluded from asserting that it had not accepted the boundary.

The *Temple of Preah Vihear* case is doubly important because the facts of the case are not as clear-cut as they may at first appear. First, the Court ignored a 'material error' that had occurred in the drafting of the map, which placed it in Cambodia, then under the French Protectorate.[92] Secondly, as noted by Wellington Koo J in his dissenting opinion, Prince Damrong, the representative of the Thai royal family had visited the temple in the capacity of a private individual, and his visit did not entail any official endorsement on the part of the Siamese Government. He also requested that the receiving French officer 'get out of his uniform', and

[90] Report of the Law Officers to Lord Russell, 16 September 1863. Quoted by MacGibbon (1958) (n 61) 496.

[91] *Case Concerning the Temple of Preah Vihear (Cambodia v Thailand)* [1962] ICJ Rep 6.

[92] PCW Chan, 'Acquiescence/Estoppel in International Boundaries: Temple of Preah Vihear Revisited' (2004) 3 *Chinese Journal of International Law* 421, 425.

held no material governmental ranks at the relevant times.[93] Chan also notes that Siam was a relatively weak, non-colonised Asiatic State and had to protect herself and avoid aggravating France with what it felt were needless protests.[94]

Despite these imperfections in Thai consent, however, the majority of the ICJ concluded that sufficient acts had been carried out by Thailand – in accepting the map and approving the royal visit – and that there was a sufficient level of abstention – insofar as the matter had not been submitted to the Court at an earlier juncture – for an estoppel to arise. Thailand was therefore precluded from asserting that Cambodia had no right to claim the Temple of Preah Vihear as part of its sovereign territory. However, there is a *caveat* to be appended to any reading of this case, since, characteristically, the ICJ shied away from a thorough engagement with general principles, failing to refer to the principle of estoppel or preclusion *eo nomine* and instead stating the principle that *qui tacet consentire videtur si loqui debuisset ac potuisset* (he who is silent appears to consent if he should, and could, have spoken).[95] Substantially the result in the case was the same regardless of the application of the principle, but the fact that the Court avoided the overtly normative language of estoppel and instead relied on a narrower and altogether less renowned incarnation of the principle is deeply instructive. It is also interesting to note the dissenting opinion of Percy Spencer J, who referred to preclusion doctrine *eo nomine* and who criticised the main judgment for treating the principle as a 'formless . . . maxim' rather than a substantive instrument of international law.[96]

References to estoppel have continued with a relatively constant frequency throughout ICJ judgments, albeit not always contained in the *dispositif* and not always stated entirely explicitly. In a dissenting opinion in the 1997 *Gabčíkovo – Nagymaros Project* case, Vice-President Weeramantry made express reference to estoppel doctrine in his separate concurring opinion. Here, Hungary and Czechoslovakia had entered a Treaty to implement an investment project on the Danube in 1977. Neither party performed its obligations under the Treaty, but Vice-President Weeramantry found that Hungary's conduct precluded their asserting that their obligations were no longer binding. Hungary had allowed Czechoslovakia, and later Slovakia, to believe that it was the intent of the Hungarian administration to fulfil the terms of the Treaty.[97] In the *ELSI* case, the limits of acquiescence doctrine were noted when the ICJ stated that

[93] *Case Concerning the Temple of Preah Vihear (Cambodia v Thailand)* [1962] ICJ Rep 6, dissenting opinion of Wellington Koo J, 90.

[94] Chan (2004) (n 92) 432.

[95] *Temple of Preah Vihear* (n 93) 23.

[96] ibid, dissenting opinion of Percy Spencer J, 143.

[97] *Case Concerning the Gabčíkovo – Nagymaros Project (Hungary v Slovakia)* [1997] ICJ Rep 7.

> although it cannot be excluded that an estoppel could in certain circumstances arise from a silence when something ought to have been said, there are obvious difficulties in constructing an estoppel from a mere failure to mention a matter at a particular point in somewhat desultory diplomatic exchanges.[98]

All in all, references to estoppel in the World Court have been both frequent, and, uncharacteristically for the general principles of law category, quite often explicit. The World Court has not shied away from using the terms 'estoppel' or its French equivalent, *'préclusion'*. This illustrates that the principles underlying estoppel, as an extension of the principle of good faith, are deeply ingrained into the architecture of international law. This is important for the purposes of our discussion, since estoppel is such a potent doctrine. Indeed, the simplicity with which it functions at international level, while reflecting a level of generality which is doubtless necessary to take due account of the various legal systems from which it has evolved, renders it significantly stronger at international level than in domestic law. In the common law, for example, the discourse on estoppel is beset by the vexed questions of whether promissory estoppel may be used as a sword as well as a shield, that is, as a cause of action as well as a defence, as well as technical distinctions between the ideas of promissory and proprietary estoppel. The international legal system, being altogether more rudimentary in nature, has no need to take account of such technicalities. At international level, estoppel doctrine arises as an extension of the general principle of good faith, a principle common to all legal systems, all of which have (admittedly varying) mechanisms to ensure that parties exercise their obligations in good faith and keep their promises when a serious representation has been made. The principle of estoppel therefore supplements *pacta sunt servanda* – 'the cornerstone of international law'.[99] It is worth concluding by noting the pronouncement of the Judicial Committee of the Privy Council in dubbing the principle of estoppel as 'perhaps the most powerful and flexible instrument to be found in any system of court jurisprudence'.[100]

E. Equity, General Principles and Human Rights

The cases examined illustrate the readiness of the World Court to give equity a broad base in international law. Strong equitable principles such as *ubi ius, ubi remedium* and estoppel have been enunciated by the Court, enough for Margaret White J of the Supreme Court of Queensland to proclaim equity itself as a general principle of law recognised by civilised

[98] *Case Concerning Elettronica Sicula SPA (ELSI) (United States v Italy)* [1989] ICJ Rep 15, 44.

[99] IC MacGibbon, 'The Scope of Acquiescence in International Law' (1954) 31 *British Yearbook of International Law* 143, 181–82.

[100] *Canada and Dominion Sugar Co v Canadian National (West Indies) Steamships* [1947] AC 46, 55.

nations.[101] However, there is evidence that when straying too far from broad conceptions of equity based fairly exactly on a transposition of theory from national legal systems to the international legal system, things begin to become a lot less clear. Two areas are of particular interest in this regard, first that of obligations arising from individual rights and humanitarian issues and secondly that of maritime delimitation.

The area of human rights, although evidently covered by general principles of law, does not derive its source from general principles as norms. International human rights instruments provided the catalyst for the conferring of individual rights in international law, and a number of these rights now enjoy the status of customary norms, with a select few having risen to the status of *ius cogens*. At national level, such rights are usually protected in State constitutions or via statutory instruments, so there would seem, on the face of it, to be few general principles of law generally recognised by the majority of States to transpose to the international level in this regard.

Nonetheless, the International Court of Justice has had cause to refer to a curious category of principle in this regard, ill-defined and of dubious origin. The seminal case here is that of the *Corfu Channel*, contested by the United Kingdom and Albania.[102] This case concerned damage incurred to British warships when they struck mines in the Albanian-controlled Corfu Channel, the British later conducting a mine-sweeping exercise in these waters. Having failed in an attempt to involve the Security Council in the matter, the British Government addressed itself to the ICJ. This was the first case the ICJ adjudicated. In December 1949 the Court awarded the UK the sum of £843,947, having determined that irrespective of who was responsible for planting the mines, the Albanian Government should have observed any such action, since the minefield was directly contiguous to their coastline, and they failed to discharge their duty to inform the UK of this danger. According to the Court, such a duty arose, inter alia, due to 'elementary considerations of humanity', which the Court held were 'even more exacting in peace than in war'.[103] From what basis such elementary considerations are held to derive is unclear, but Rossi places them under the aegis of equitable principles in international law, while noting that the fact that the Court

> did not pause to spell out the legal basis of this obligation is unfortunate because such an explanation could have provided fertile ground for the further explanation of both the international minimum standards of protection for individuals under international law and the law of state responsibility.[104]

[101] M White, 'Equity – A General Principle of Law Recognised by Civilised Nations?' (2003) 4 *Queensland Law Journal* 103.

[102] *Corfu Channel Case* (*United Kingdom v Albania*) (Merits) [1949] ICJ Rep 4.

[103] ibid, 22.

[104] Rossi (1993) (n 17) 180.

The unearthing of such 'elementary considerations of humanity' by the ICJ in its very first case was a momentous juncture indeed, for it showed that general principles of law comprehended a certain (quasi-) human rights component. The scope of this component had not been explained by the Court, nor indeed the precise legal principles upon which such rights are grounded. If we are to understand that such elementary considerations of humanity derive from general principles of law recognised by the majority of States with developed legal systems, then their basis is murky indeed. It is clear that in a wide variety of legal systems, basic considerations of justice, due process and a certain portion of the human rights *corpus* have been held to derive from unwritten – or 'implicit' or 'unenunciated' – principles of law, held to constitute norms either of legal or of constitutional value.[105] However, it is far beyond the scope of this present study to attempt to distil a common understanding of such principles from the broad variety of legal interpretations of the notion which have been adopted at national level, which, to be exhaustive, would be a considerable undertaking in its own right.

The issue received further attention in – and was further complicated by – the *South West Africa* case in 1966. In 1960, Ethiopia and Liberia had brought a case before the ICJ against South Africa, claiming that South Africa had failed in its duties as a mandatory power assuming responsibility for South West Africa under the League of Nations' Guidelines.[106] The ICJ held that the two African States in question did not have the requisite *locus standi* to bring such a suit. Ethiopia and Liberia had sought to rely upon the 'elementary considerations of humanity' principle invoked in the *Corfu Channel* case to support their claim. In its reasoning for this decision, the Court held, inter alia, that the suggestion 'that humanitarian principles are sufficient in themselves to generate legal rights and obligations' was incorrect and that the Court '[could] take account of moral principles only insofar as these are given a sufficient expression in legal form'.[107] This position seemed wholly inconsistent with the position adopted in the *Corfu Channel* case, since that judgment had cited 'elementary considerations of humanity' amongst indisputably legal reasons for reaching the conclusion that Albania had a duty to warn the British ships

[105] An excellent legal debate on the virtues of such principles is to be found in the dissenting opinion of Kennedy CJ, in *The State (at the prosecution of Jeremiah Ryan and Others) v Captain Michael Lennon, Governor of the Military Detention Barracks, Arbour Hill, Dublin, Colonel Frank Bennett and Others, The Members of the Constitution (Special Powers) Tribunal; and in the Matter of the Courts of Justice Act 1924 and in the Matter of the Constitution of Saorstát na hÉireann* [1935] IR 1.

[106] South Africa had earlier refused to switch the status of South-West Africa from a League of Nations mandate to a UN trust territory. The ICJ had held that this was permissible, but that the UN General Assembly would have a supervisory in lieu of the Assembly of the League.

[107] *South West Africa (Liberia and Ethiopia v South Africa)* [1966] ICJ Rep 6, 34.

of their proximity to peril. For the same organ to come out and say that such considerations were insufficient 'in themselves to generate legal rights and obligations' was fairly incredible. As Rossi notes, it was also wholly unnecessary on the part of the ICJ, since it ruled that the two applicant States lacked the requisite standing to bring the suit in the first place, rendering it superfluous to examine the merits of their claim further. 'Consequently, the discussion about the humanitarian provisions – as important yet nonsensical as it was – was never really at the forefront of the case',[108] though, this being said, it is clear that its import must nonetheless be taken into account in our present study. It is perhaps further worth noting here that Tanaka and Jessup JJ penned vitriolic and expansive dissents to the majority line in this case, emphasising human rights norms, general principles of law, and even *ius cogens* and natural law.[109]

The discussion in the *Corfu Channel* and *South West Africa* cases indicates an area of unwritten general principles that may at best be loosely grouped with equity. However, it would be an exaggeration to say that a joint reading of these two cases draws any light to the subject. The judgment in the *Corfu Channel* case is wholly inconsistent with the – effectively obiter dictum – conclusions in the *South West Africa* case. This is a great shame, particularly for the scholar who wishes to study the fields of human rights and general principles in tandem. Nonetheless, it would be folly to use any detail gleaned from these two cases in this regard in our prospective study of humanitarian intervention and equity in the coming chapter, and I do not intend to do so.

One final note is perhaps necessary before leaving the *South West Africa* case. It involves a further general principle and I am indebted to Rossi for his delicate understanding of the principle in question. In the judgment on the question of *locus standi*, the Court noted the separation of the mandatory agreement into 'conduct provisions' and 'special interest provisions', noting that individuals had no rights against conduct provisions and therefore no actions which were effectively on behalf of individuals (although brought forward in this instance by two States) could be upheld. As Rossi notes, 'This holding was astounding because it overturned the jurisdictional decision of the 1962 [South West Africa] Case through the use of a rationale completely removed from the original bases of the Court's jurisdiction'. Per Rossi, this was an important move, since it effectively put into question the principle that *expression unis est exclusion alterius*, or that an express rule is superior to all others, which itself is an offshoot of the *lex specialis generalibus derogat* principle.[110] This is undoubtedly of huge importance for the purposes of our discussion, since the fact

[108] Rossi (1993) (n 17) 182.

[109] See, particularly, *South West Africa (Liberia and Ethiopia v South Africa)*, [1966] ICJ Rep 6, dissenting opinion of Tanaka J, 276.

[110] Rossi (1993) (n 17) 183.

that this principle is not universally applicable makes it more realistic to assert the normative equality of custom, treaty and general principles, since such parity would effectively be meaningless if it were subject to an appendix which stated that the more specific express written rules would always trump their shadier cousins in all circumstances.

F. Maritime Delimitation – Equity *Praeter Legem*

The law on maritime delimitation is a particular area of international law, and while cases involving the law of the sea are peppered with references to 'equity', it is the homonymous nature of equity that a great number of such references may have little or nothing to do with our present discussion. Hence, it is worth treating this subject carefully. The Court itself further noted the fact that while its maritime delimitation decisions are legal decisions, certain (economic and other) 'realities must be borne in mind'.[111] However, such factors must not lead to decisions on purely equitable grounds – that is *ex aequo et bono* – without State consent, which the Court came out strongly against as *contra legem* in the *Continental Shelf (Libya v Malta)* case in 1985.[112] Nonetheless, it is clear that equity has a considerable role to play in the law of maritime delimitation, as is evidenced by the relative frequency with which references to the concept occur in this area. Lamentably, however, Rossi notes that 'No succinct restatement or synthesis of equity obtains from the relatively substantial maritime jurisprudence, despite the Court's heavy reliance on equity'.[113]

The most well-known example of equity's application in relation to the law of maritime delimitation concerns the *North Sea Continental Shelf* case, disputed between the German Federal Republic and Denmark on one hand, and the German Federal Republic and the Netherlands on the other.[114] The dispute in question related to Article 6 of the 1958 Geneva Convention on the Law of the Sea Concerning the Continental Shelf.[115] The Treaty stated that if two countries are separated by a sea, then the boundary between then should be calculated as the point equidistant from both coastlines. This is known as the equidistance principle. The Netherlands, Denmark, and the German Federal Republic had all signed the Convention, but Germany had not ratified the instrument, ostensibly on the grounds that it did not consider it to be in its interest to do so. While the Netherlands and Denmark

[111] *Anglo-Norwegian Fisheries (United Kingdom and Northern Ireland v Norway)* [1951] ICJ Rep 116, 133.

[112] *Case Concerning the Continental Shelf (Libya v Malta)* [1985] ICJ Rep 13, 39.

[113] Rossi (1993) (n 17) 215.

[114] *Case Concerning the North Sea Continental Shelf (Federal Republic of Germany v Denmark; Federal Republic of Germany v Netherlands)* [1969] ICJ Rep 3.

[115] Geneva Convention on the Law of the Sea, 516 UNTS (1958) 205.

had convex strips of coastline adjacent to the German coast, the German coastline contiguous to the North Sea was concave in nature. This meant that to apply the equidistance principle in both cases would be to grant Germany only a tapering segment of continental shelf rights, which would deprive it of the possibility of exploiting the oil which was known to be abundant within the continental shelf in this region. The Netherlands and Denmark sought to argue that the Geneva Convention constituted customary international law in any case. The German representative argued otherwise, and further argued that even if this were the case, a theory of 'just and equitable share of the continental shelf' precluded its application in this case, effectively emanating from the concept of distributive justice, 'a generally recognised principle inherent in all legal principles, including the legal system of the international community'.[116]

The Court's response to the two competing interpretations was to apply a compromise solution. It first denied the presumption favouring equidistance, stating that delimitation had

> to be effected by agreement in accordance with equitable principles, and taking account of all the relevant circumstances, in such a way as to leave as much as possible to each party all those parts of the continental shelf that constitute a natural prolongation of its land territory into and under the sea.[117]

This was clearly a major step for the Court, but, as in the area of humanitarian principles, the fact that there was little or no equivalent national law to fall back on in the enunciation of equitable principles in this regard caused problems. Brownlie, for example, came out strongly against the Court's reasoning, stating that such a means of supposedly developing equitable principles 'amounts to no more than a bundle of highly impressionistic ideas about the distorting effect' of special circumstances, and that employed in such a fashion, equitable principles

> become merely faint indications of the reasoning, or of the unreasoned premises on which judicial discretion has been exercised . . . The point is a simple one: with little or no clear content, a direction to apply equitable principles is a conferment of a general discretionary power upon the decision-making body.[118]

Jennings went still further, opining that 'what the litigants get is in effect a decision *ex aequo et bono* whether they wanted it or not'.[119]

Brownlie's view is indeed a potent one. Equitable principles become highly problematic at international level when too far detached from easily

[116] *North Sea Continental Shelf* (Pleadings) [1969] ICJ Rep 3, 30.
[117] *North Sea Continental Shelf* [1969] ICJ Rep 3, 53.
[118] I Brownlie, 'Legal Status of Natural Resources in International Law (Some Aspects)' (1979) 162 *Recueil des Cours* 287.
[119] R Jennings, 'The Principles Governing Marine Boundaries' in K Hailbronner (eds), *Staat und Völkerrechtsordnung: Festschrift für Karl Doehring* (Berlin, Springer-Verlag, 1989) 401.

identifiable general principles of law which have grown up in national legal systems. Their origin is unclear and their application by international tribunals may raise charges of prevarication and subjectivity. The idea of 'natural prolongation of . . . land territory into and under the sea' is one which requires refinement over time, since clearly one definition of natural prolongation may differ from the next. Much like the 'elementary considerations of humanity' alluded to in the *Corfu Channel* judgment, such notions, being less firmly rooted in the equitable *corpus* which has emerged in national law than long-standing ideas like estoppel, are less easy to define and control, since there exist almost no parallel ideas at national levels which may be used as legal yardsticks. While basic notions of justice, fairness and flexibility, as well as taking account of special circumstances, may well play a role in the jurisprudence of the majority of developed legal systems, such notions may only really be assessed on a case-by-case basis, and are difficult to define. They may well figure as a sort of *ersatz* subcategory of general principles of law, but their potential for abuse and subjective interpretation is so evident that their use – particularly *contra legem* – must be regarded with an extremely suspicious eye. Otherwise, we risk upsetting the stability of international law as a whole.

As Rossi notes, the Court did not expend a great deal of energy explaining or justifying the move from the equidistance formula to equity. Noting that the Court had relied upon customary international law to justify its decision, and pointing out the fact that the Court had, per Ammoun J's dissenting opinion, failed duly 'to have regard to the general principles of law recognised by nations',[120] Rossi opines that the Court had potentially unearthed another possible source of equitable principles in international law, namely customary international law.[121] In doing so, the Court had effectively entangled itself in a similar web of jurisprudential problems to the one that had so confused Lapradelle and others almost 50 years beforehand in the Advisory Committee of Jurists' meetings regarding the sources of law to be applied in the PCIJ. The Court in the *North Sea Continental Shelf* case had stated that that if equidistance were to be applied as a norm of customary international law, then such a position 'would not be consistent with certain basic legal notions which . . . have from the beginning [regarding the Continental Shelf] reflected the opinio juris in the matter of delimitation'.[122] However, the Court did not stipulate the nature of the basic legal notions that reflected such an *opinio iuris*, except to state that 'delimitation must be the object of agreement by the States concerned, and that such agreement must be arrived at in accordance with equitable principles'.[123] While such an interpretation clearly

[120] *North Sea Continental Shelf* [1969] ICJ Rep 3, dissenting opinion of Ammoun J, 131.
[121] Rossi (1993) (n 17) 222–24.
[122] *North Sea Continental Shelf* [1969] ICJ Rep 3, 46.
[123] ibid.

does not preclude equitable principles from being a sub-set of the general principles of law category, the confusion between this category and *opinio iuris* in this area is evident. The Court went on to state that such rules rest 'on a foundation of very general precepts of justice and good faith',[124] attributes which Rossi notes, are historically far more connected to basic ideas of judicial administration (general principles) than to the practice (customary international law) of States in matters concerning maritime resources.[125]

In the *Tunisia v Libya Continental Shelf* case, which was also decided with reference to equitable criteria, the Court held that 'the legal concept of equity is a general principle applicable as law'.[126] Francioni has highlighted the case as a 'high water mark' for *praeter legem* application of equity, stating that the case shows it to be a self-standing source of legal principles, which does not require specific consent by the parties to be operable.[127] This finding is important, since maritime delimitation is one of the few areas of international law where major conventions contain explicit references to equity as a means of solving disputes. Francioni's assertion would tend to indicate that the explicit consent given in some international maritime treaties for equity's usage as a legal tool is unnecessary, and that equity may function in such a manner as an independent legal source. The facts of the case, perhaps too burdensome to adequately recapitulate here, would tend to buttress such a position. However, Gros J' dissent in the same case has been seized upon by Weil, inter alia, who warns of the dangers of subjectivity if such equitable principles are applied in an unrestrained manner.[128]

In the *Gulf of Maine* case,[129] the Court clarified its position in the *North Sea Continental Shelf* case further by stating that 'customary international law . . . contains a general requirement of the application of equitable criteria and the utilisation of practical methods capable of implementing them'.[130] However, this pronouncement came 10 pages after the Court had stated in relation to the same case that the delimitative criteria involved in maritime delimitation cases are 'determined in relation to each particular case . . . this precludes the possibility of those conditions arising which are necessary for the formation of principles and rules of customary law'.[131] This position would seem to state that no completely stable customary

[124] ibid.

[125] Rossi (1993) (n 17) 227.

[126] *Case Concerning the Continental Shelf (Tunisia v Libya)* [1982] ICJ Rep 18 [71].

[127] F Francioni, 'Equity in International Law' in R Wolfrum (ed), *The Max Planck Encyclopedia of Public International Law* (Oxford, Oxford University Press, 2008) para 12.

[128] Weil (1996) (n 1) 134–35.

[129] *Delimitation of the Maritime Boundary of the Gulf of Maine Area (Canada v United States)* [1984] ICJ Rep 246.

[130] ibid, 300.

[131] ibid, 290.

regime regarding maritime delimitation can exist, and in the absence of a firm set of legal rules, States must take account of the ever-present general principles, which serve to fill a gap in the law *praeter legem*. Such a position, while somewhat inconsistent with that adopted in the *North Sea Continental Shelf* case, would seem to explain why judges are so ready to resort to the language of equity in judgments concerned with maritime delimitation. In the absence of treaty law[132] and considering the effective impossibility of customary international law existing in this area per the Court's reasoning, it is only natural that general principles should be applied to fill the gap, at least to some extent. States are obliged to fulfil their obligations in good faith in any case, but the obligation assumes an increased importance when there are few other rules governing their conduct in a given situation.

The *Gulf of Maine* case was further notable for a test which was applied by the Court to ensure that the result obtained was not 'radically inequitable'.[133] It had been proposed to the Court that the effect that its judgment would have upon people's livelihoods should be taken into account. While the Court rejected this argument, it went on to say that it could nonetheless not lay down a judgment which would be radically inequitable in nature, taking account of all relevant circumstances. This language is extremely reminiscent of the idea of a 'manifest injustice', which was often the catalyst for equity's entry into the legal consideration of a given case at national level within common law jurisdictions. Such manifest injustices were intolerable in equitable terms, even if they resulted from a rigid interpretation of the statute law, and equitable principles would then be applied to 'soften' the result in the interests of substantive justice. However, in the *Gulf of Maine* case, any potential manifest injustice would be felt most harshly by the fishermen on either side of the George's Bank, rather than by the States themselves. The States were the right-holders in this dispute, and therefore any serious loss to either of them would effectively be largely economic in nature, since the Gulf was not strategically important. The Court stated that in such cases, economic considerations would be taken into account for the correction of 'only the most flagrant deviations from the standard of reasonableness', namely deviations that would 'entail catastrophic repercussions for the livelihood and economic well-being of the population of the countries concerned'.[134] While this is a very narrow test, it does however show that the rights and interests of individuals will, to some degree, play a part in cases where they are not parties to the dispute, and in fact raises the question whether

[132] It should be noted here that there exists a plethora of international treaties concerning the law of the sea. However, the interesting cases from the point of view of this study arise when treaties do not (clearly) cover the dispute between the States in question.

[133] *Gulf of Maine* [1984] ICJ Rep 246, 342.

[134] ibid.

the *Corfu Channel* case's ideas regarding 'elementary considerations of humanity' may have more legal import than they first appeared.

The evolution of equitable principles in maritime delimitation, as in the area of human rights, has been both confused and confusing. Sometimes general principles are 'barely distinguishable' from customary international law in these areas.[135] However, this should come as no surprise to the experienced student of equity. Rossi notes:

> This confusion would be of greater concern if the practice of the Court were not in keeping with well-founded examples of judicial behaviour throughout history. When faced with the inadequacies of the law, judges apply equity. And if the doctrinal attempt to synthesise the confusion is unsatisfactory, then one should recall that a little more than 20 years [now 40] has elapsed since the judicial articulation of equitable principles in the North Sea Continental Shelf cases. It took equity more than 400 years to harden into a system of common law.[136]

III. EQUITY BY ANALOGY – THE THIRD CATEGORY OF THE THIRD SOURCE

Despite equity and general principles' somewhat problematic adaptation to areas of the law which are harder to parallel with national legal systems such as the law of the sea and human rights, this study shows strong evidence that firmly established equitable principles such as estoppel, 'clean hands' doctrine, and the prioritisation of substance over form, have, at least to some degree, been transferred to the international sphere. The same is true of elementary general principles such as *res iudicata* and textual interpretation, as Cheng has elegantly demonstrated, and as we have ourselves discussed in chapter two. [137] It would seem, therefore, that the World Court is more prepared to countenance the existence of a given general principle of law in the international legal sphere if it has been firmly embedded into the legal systems of a broad spectrum of States. Other, more novel principles may also exist, but if their origin is unclear and if analogies with national law are difficult to establish, then the ambit and applicability of such principles may also be so. Such a situation should render any legal scholar extremely wary of founding arguments upon general principles of law that are not clearly paralleled by national precedents, even if they have been upheld by the ICJ or PCIJ as having international normative status. Any argument based upon the application of such principles must necessarily incorporate a strong measure of

[135] MC Bassiouni, 'A Functional Approach to "General Principles of International Law"' (1990) 11 *Michigan Journal of International Law* 768, 791.

[136] Rossi (1993) (n 17) 246. While it is true that Rossi's '20 years' has since become 40, his point nonetheless remains both valid and instructive.

[137] See Cheng (n 82).

subjectivity, since such principles are so new, so 'raw' – so to speak – and since so little about the way in which they operate has been confirmed by legal practice.

Principles such as estoppel and good faith, which find their roots in national legal systems, however, are an entirely different matter. Again, a certain amount of international case law confirms their existence in international law, but their applicability in a given situation is rendered both easier and clearer by the fact that equivalent principles have long existed in national legal systems. As a result, analogy may be had to the application of such principles in national law for at least a modicum of guidance, and determining the content of such principles, where their normative force begins and ends, and their potential usefulness – or lack thereof – in solving a given legal problem becomes, in comparative terms, quite clear.[138]

However, there is yet a third category to consider. Bassiouni makes the important observation that 'The Advisory Committee for the ICJ's Statute was in agreement that a judge did not legislate by using "General Principles" because although "applying them [brought] 'latent' rules to light, [it] did not 'create' new rules"'.[139] Since this is the case, there may exist further general principles of law, which are recognised by civilised nations, but which have never surfaced in the judgments of the World Court for one reason or another. There is indeed great reason for supposing that in the comparatively brief lifetime of the PCIJ and ICJ as international legal bodies, the Courts have heard too few cases to aptly and explicitly enunciate every norm of international law.[140] Further, it is germane to remind ourselves of an observation made in chapter two, namely that the World Court has always been reluctant to explicitly pronounce upon general principles in any case, since doing so may be viewed as unnecessarily subjective,[141] and if it does so, it is usually by 'the back door', as it were. Weil notes that this is equally the case regarding equity.[142] Taking into account the relative paucity of international cases before the World Court, along with its infrequent use of general principles, or at least its lack of candour when doing so, we are met with the intriguing prospect that perhaps there may be a significant number of the 'general principles of law recognised by civilised nations' which have yet to be 'discovered' by the Court. This is not to say that they do not already enjoy normative force in international law, however, but

[138] This is not to contend, for one moment, that the operability of estoppel doctrine at national level may be reasonably compared to its international equivalent for all practical purposes, but we would nonetheless be foolish if we did not look to the national precedents for guidance in this regard.

[139] Bassiouni (1990) (n 135) 784, part-quoting Cheng (1987) (n 82) 25.

[140] As of 10 April 2010, the PCIJ had heard 27 contentious cases, the ICJ 142. These numbers pale in significance to the number of cases tried in England alone in any one calendar year.

[141] JL Brierly, *The Law of Nations*, 6th edn (Oxford, Oxford University Press, 1963) 63.

[142] Weil (1996) (n 1) 123.

merely that the Court has not yet had the opportunity (or in some cases perhaps, the courage) to utilise such principles in its judgments.

Determining whether such a category of principles exist – and if so, what its content may be – is not an easy task. As Bassiouni has noted, the scholarly debate on general principles has principally centred not so much 'on dogmatic or doctrinal conceptions, but more pragmatically on what evidences the existence of "General Principles" [ie on Court judgments rather than the theory behind them]'.[143] This would seem rather paradoxical. Schlesinger has termed general principles as 'a core of legal ideas which are common to all civilised legal systems'.[144] If this is indeed the case – and such a definition would certainly seem to chime with the definition provided in Article 38(1)(c) and its predecessor Article 38(I)(3) – it ought to be superfluous to refer to the judgments of the World Court for guidance, since the principles should be known and accessible to any legal scholar with a broad knowledge of comparative national law. The conduct of the two Courts, however, in applying – or, to be more accurate, in usually not applying – such principles, has rendered this category somewhat less clear and somewhat more nebulous than it needs to be. The debate over the precise meaning of what 'the general principles of law recognised by civilised nations' are, or what they should be defined as, has been allowed to rage largely because the Court has been recalcitrant in taking the proverbial bit between its teeth and laying down a standard and exhaustive definition in this regard. As a result, as Bassiouni has noted,

> [w]hat is needed is a multidisciplinary approach that can bring together specialists in public and private international law, jurisprudence, philosophy of law and legal methods, and empiricists of various backgrounds. Without such an approach, we will continue to be faced with confusion in this important area of law.[145]

Clearly, it is beyond our brief discussion to meet Bassiouni's exacting standards and thus lay down a precise definition of general principles beyond what the Court has dealt with, but I shall nonetheless attempt to shed some light on the subject.

There are three tools which we may employ to aid us in this regard. First, the judgments of the World Court itself, have, as we have seen, made occasional – albeit usually implicit – reference to a number of general principles of law. Such references, and the foundations upon which their reasoning is built, may presumably be extrapolated upon. Legal logic which is sufficiently concise to unearth one general principle ought, in principle, to be sufficient to unearth another similar principle.

[143] Bassiouni (1990) (n 135) 770.

[144] R Schlesinger, 'Research on the General Principles of Law Recognised by Civilised Nations' (1957) 51 *American Journal of International Law* 734, 739.

[145] Bassiouni (1990) (n 135) 802.

Secondly, we know that the basis for general principles as a source of international law is that such principles are widely recognised in the national legal systems of 'civilised nations', for which we may read 'States with developed legal systems' in lieu of a more concise definition. It should be noted, however, that even in adopting such a position, I am – inadvertently and somewhat unwillingly – placing myself on one side of the doctrinal debate. Bassiouni, for example, makes the argument that the term 'civilised nations' can no longer have any legal validity and that the phrase 'all States' should be substituted in its place. He argues that to do otherwise would be to presuppose a primitive hierarchy of national legal orders, and that such a position is incompatible with the idea of State equality. Per Bassiouni, 'the words "recognised by civilised nations" . . . at one time . . . regarded with suspicion . . . are now a guarantee of the universality of sources of principles. Indeed all Member States of the United Nations are presumed to be "civilised nations"'.[146] However, my own position is to disagree with Bassiouni, insofar as the drafters of the PCIJ and ICJ Statutes deliberately adopted such a wording to ensure that the world's major legal families would be represented in international legal reasoning, but that primitive legal orders would be excluded.[147] States consented to such a wording, which, per Cheng, has become a part of customary international law, being aware of the *travaux préparatoires* and without lodging formal objections against the terminology employed. Therefore, I would construe the fact that any State which was a member of the League or of the United Nations, and which felt its general principles of law were not largely co-terminus with those prevalent in the major legal families, in failing to object over an extended period, is held to have acquiesced to the crystallising of customary law, and has therefore lost its right to argue otherwise. Also, the idea of sovereign equality of States was in existence long before the advent of the League of Nations, and if such a doctrine would nowadays render the words 'civilised nations' a meaningless trinket, then this was the case *ab initio* and is no new development, as Bassiouni seems to argue. I fail to understand why or how this doctrine has changed since the 1920s.

Happily, however, Bassiouni and I, though divided on the meaning of 'civilised nations', should find that our conception of general principles will nonetheless be substantially the same, at least nowadays, since the overwhelming majority of States in the United Nations system, and indeed in the world, can now be grouped under the umbrella of one of the world's major legal families. Therefore, although I stand by my point in this regard, the debate for our purposes is a purely academic one, since the principles resultant from either interpretation ought to be substantially the same.

[146] Bassiouni (1990) (n 135) 783–84.
[147] For a more detailed examination of this logic, see ch 2.

As regards the third tool which we may utilise to frame a definition of general principles of international law, our study in chapter three reveals that, in the domain of general principles, 'civilised nations', even those with very different legal and cultural histories, share much common ground with one another, and that many legal principles seem to transcend all – or almost all – developed systems of law.

Unfortunately, legal scholarship regarding 'general principles of law recognised by civilised nations' is unlikely to furnish much help in this regard. The problems in this regard are threefold. First, the amount of attention devoted to the 'general principles' category in recent times by leading scholars has been meagre, particularly since the advent of the *ius cogens* category, which seems to have distracted much attention from the area. Secondly, what scholarship there is in existence frequently confines itself to discussing general principles of international law to the principles which have been enunciated by the Court, ignoring the fact that the Court does not legislate, and is itself incapable of creating principles, merely stating those which already exist under Article 38(1)(c). Thirdly, and perhaps most importantly, of the extremely small amount of attention which has been paid to this category which does not confine itself to statements of the World Court, the doctrinal debate is inconsistent, frequently ambiguous and at times confusing. 'To that extent, it is the bane of practitioners, whether judges or advocates. Worse yet, it renders no service to . . . an exigent necessity of law; namely certainty'.[148]

Regardless of the deficiencies associated with legal scholarship in this area, we are left with the conclusion that if we can determine the 'threshold test' which has been employed by the PCIJ and ICJ to determine whether a legal principle may be held to be a general principle of law recognised by civilised nations, then we may be able to assert the existence of certain general principles as norms of international law, even in the absence of confirmation to this effect from the case law of the World Court. The elements of such a test must be determined through the usage of inductive reasoning. Unfortunately, deciphering the nature of this test is not made any easier by the conduct of the Court in its judgments, which, characteristic of its limited engagement with the general principles category, has failed to even attempt to set down what it required for a principle of this kind to acquire normative force at international level. Nonetheless, we have been left with some 'clues', as it were. While a full encapsulation of every World Court pronouncement which might be classified in this category would be too time consuming for a work of this size and on this subject, I shall attempt to furnish what I believe to be some instructive examples.

[148] Bassiouni (1990) (n 135) 802–03. See also F Lopez de Oñate, *La Certezza del Diritto* (Milan, Giuffrè, 1968).

In the *SS Lotus* case, the Permanent Court gave some basic instructions on how to ascertain if a general principle exists in international law. The Court stated that

> in the fulfilment of its task of itself ascertaining what the international law is, [the Court] has included in its researches all precedents and facts to which it had access and which might possibly have revealed the existence of one of the principles of international law.[149]

A year later, in the *Chorzów Factory* (Claim for Indemnity) judgment, the PCIJ expanded upon this somewhat in determining that the essential principle contained in the notion of an illegal act

> a principle which seems to be established by international practice and by the decisions of arbitral tribunals – is that reparation must, as far as possible, wipe out all the consequences of the illegal act and re-establish the situation which would, in all probability, have existed if that act had not been committed.[150]

These two judgments read in tandem reveal that the Court will have reference to precedents at national and international level and to doctrinal teachings, as well as any salient facts in the case. This is in accordance with Article 38(1)(d), which establishes the pronouncements of international tribunals and the teachings of leading scholars as a subsidiary source of international law for interpretation purposes. This would suggest that once the World Court (or possibly an international arbitral tribunal) has confirmed a principle as being part of the 'general principles of law recognised by civilised nations' then it is legitimate for a subsequent World Court decision to base its reasoning on the precedent this has created.

More explicit reference has also been made to the necessity for consideration to be had to national legal systems. In the *Lighthouses* case, Séfériades J, in a separate opinion, noted that 'Contracting parties are always assumed to be acting honestly and in good faith', noting that 'This is a legal principle. Which is recognised in private law, and cannot be ignored in international law'.[151] This dictum represented a simple transposition of private law principles to the international sphere. In the *Interpretation of the Greco-Turkish Agreement* case, the PCIJ made reference to the idea of *compétence de la compétence* as the 'principle that, as a general rule, any body possessing jurisdictional powers has the right in the first place itself to determine the extent of its jurisdiction'.[152] It was clear in this instance that the Court had been influenced in such a determination both

[149] *Case of the SS Lotus* PCIJ Rep Series A No10, 31.

[150] *Case Concerning the Factory at Chorzów* (*Germany v Poland*) (Merits) PCIJ Rep Series A No 17, 47.

[151] *Lighthouses Case (France v Greece)* PCIJ Rep Series A/B No 62, 34.

[152] *Interpretation of the Greco-Turkish Agreement of 1 December 1926* (Advisory Opinion) PCIJ Rep Series B No 16, 20.

by past international arbitral practice and by national legal practice. This followed the dissenting opinion of John Bassett Moore J in the *Mavrommatis Palestine Concessions* case, who had held that the requirement that a court have jurisdiction before it can act is one common to all legal systems, noting 'certain elementary conceptions common to all systems or jurisprudence', amongst which the requirement of jurisdiction was one. Interestingly, Moore J went on to call this principle 'fundamental and peremptory in the international [sphere]', language which, but for the date of the case involved, is more associated with *ius cogens* than general principles, and certainly refutes any contention that general principles are merely a subsidiary normative source.[153]

It would seem from the above cases, as well as those examined earlier in this chapter and in chapter two, that the Court will have due regard to international precedents, be they from earlier World Court opinions or judgments, or from international arbitral tribunals. Further, it will take cognisance of judgments at the national level, and any doctrinal teachings that may be of use in determining the nature and ambit of general principles of law. However, being more specific about the composite elements of any test – and logic would suggest that this test has remained unchanged throughout the history of the World Court – which the ICJ and PCIJ have used to determine their existence in international law is difficult. Using evidence garnered via World Court judgments up to and including the early 1950s, Bin Cheng suggested a draft code of general principles of international law, which he suggested as a candidate for international codification.[154] Cheng's list, though far from exhaustive, is useful, insofar as he offers some guidance as to what criteria must be fulfilled (aside from being enunciated by the World Court) in order for a principle to qualify as a general principle of law recognised by civilised nations. Cheng discards the dual origin of such principles, arguing that they are not separated into a grouping originating from national law and a grouping from international law, but rather that it is 'precisely the nature of these principles that they belong to no particular system of law, but are common to them all'.[155] Therefore, per Cheng, the test lies in identifying principles which are transcendental in nature, insofar as they pervade, to some degree or another, all developed systems of law. Cheng argues, further, that within international law, since it is a system where relatively few precisely formulated rules exist, the function of general principles of law as a directly applicable legal solution to a given case 'acquires a special significance, and has contributed greatly towards defining the legal relations between

[153] *Mavrommatis Palestine Concessions* PCIJ Rep Series A No 2, dissenting opinion of John Bassett Moore J, 57–59.

[154] Cheng (1987) (n 82) 397–98. See also B Cheng, 'General Principles of Law as a Subject for International Codification' (1951) 4 *Current Legal Problems* 35.

[155] Cheng (1987) (n 82) 390.

States'.[156] According to Cheng's study, therefore, general principles must represent something inherent in a developed legal system, something essential – he frequently uses extended notions of good faith as an example – and such principles are likely to prove more potent at international level than at national level, since there exists more scope for their employment due to the relative lack of written rules and clear customary international law. Cheng's criteria are backed by the judgment of the court in the *Abu Dhabi Oil* arbitration. In noting that general principles of law 'are rooted in the good sense and common practice of civilised nations', the court noted that such principles were those which 'civilised mankind has learned in its long experience in the municipal sphere to be those leading to justice and which it would perforce have to follow if it wished to establish Law and Justice among Nations'.[157]

There is, on the face of it at least, a good deal of sense in Cheng's argument. Principles truly need to be essential to a legal system if they are to bridge the gap between national and international law. Fabián Raimondo devotes several pages of discussion in his excellent work on general principles of criminal law to arguments that have been proffered against the transposition of general principles of national law to the international sphere. First, and perhaps most obviously, he draws attention to the doctrine of sovereignty in international law, noting that the usage of general principles strays from the voluntarist conception of international relations which has been built up between States. This is certainly an important observation, and one to which opinions offered in the World Court have also alluded.[158] Secondly, Raimondo notes that the special character of international law has frequently been invoked as an objection to employing general principles designed for national systems. Obviously international law consists of a system where the interests which are protected are vastly different to those which are protected at national level, particularly if one adopts the now somewhat outmoded model of the State as an organ with an absolute moral and legal value.[159] Even before this model became obsolete, there were already some leading scholars who argued that the interests of a State were not altogether different from those of an individual in any case.[160] Thirdly, it has been argued that the lack of an organ of central authority which can enforce sanctions renders comparisons between national and international legal systems unrealistic and unhelpful. According to this argument, principles applied by analogy to national

[156] ibid.

[157] A Bishopstone, *Award of Lord Asquith of Bishopstone* (1952) 1 ICLQ 247, 251.

[158] *Case of the Free Zones of Upper Savoy and the District of Gex* PCIJ Rep Series A No 22, opinion of Nyholm, 26–27.

[159] FO Raimondo, *General Principles of Law in the Decisions of International Criminal Courts and Tribunals* (Leiden, Martinus Nijhoff, 2008) 64.

[160] Lauterpacht (1927) (n 62) 71–73.

law should be applied only as a measure of last resort.[161] However, to this objection it is as well to counter that enforcement measures and sanctions are themselves merely a means of last resort, both in national and international law, and habitual compliance (which constitutes normal behaviour) with the stated body of rules is important in shaping the force of norms in both cases. Therefore the lack of a proper central enforcement mechanism – if we discount the various United Nations organs and their respective functions or at least deem them inadequate – at international level is less of a concern.[162]

Taking into account the three common objections to the direct transposition of general principles from national law into the international sphere, it would seem that Cheng's ideas about a principle needing to be fairly essential to the efficient and equitable functioning of a legal system for it to gain acceptance as a general principle are well-grounded. If such a threshold needs to be crossed in order for principles to be acceptable, it would go some way to explaining the reticence of the World Court in exploring the category further. States are only likely to accept principles which curb their monopoly on normative creation under the consensualist conception of international law if such principles are useful to them. Principles which are essential for the smooth and equitable functioning of a legal system will undoubtedly be viewed as useful by States as rules governing international relations, even if they may dispute their validity in certain cases in order to further their own interests. This point is well demonstrated by the adoption of the Vienna Convention on the Law of Treaties.[163] Here, a multitude of States agreed to the codification of several such utilitarian principles, further clarifying their normative power. These principles included certain rules regarding treaty interpretation and the principle of good faith. Bassiouni describes the adoption of the Vienna Convention and its subsequent acceptance as customary international law as 'The best evidence that [State-created] international law has not only accepted but relied upon "General Principles"'.[164]

It would seem, therefore, that we have the beginnings of a test. First, the principle must be common to an (undefined) majority of developed systems of law. Secondly, the principle may be unearthed with reference to analogies of national law, or to earlier international judgments or arbitral awards. Thirdly, the principle must be important enough to the just and effective functioning of the international legal system that States

[161] S Rosenne, 'The Perplexities of Modern International Law' (2001) 291 *Recueil des Cours* 63; P Weil, 'Le droit international en quête de son identité' (1992) 237 *Recueil des Cours* 147.

[162] See Raimondo (2008) (n 159) 68.

[163] Vienna Convention on the Law of Treaties, 23 May 1969, 1155 UNTS 331.

[164] Bassiouni (1990) (n 135) 786–87.

will tolerate its encroachment upon their norm-creation hegemony.[165] However, this test is, I am the first to admit, grossly inadequate. Judging whether legal principles may be qualified as 'general principles of law recognised by civilised nations' requires tools of surgical precision. The test just offered is a sledgehammer by comparison. Nonetheless, the dedicated legal scholar may well be able to refine this test further with a thorough examination of the World Court past case law. However, my own perusal in this regard is not encouraging. The World Court has shied away from even admitting that it was using general principles, let alone explaining its reasons for so doing or how the existence of such principles might be determined. Therefore, the elementary test which I propose requires an added element to be of practical use. Such an added element may perhaps be located via an examination of common elements detectable in the principles which have thus far been espoused in World Court judgments. If such common elements are identified, then other principles which share such common elements but which have not been referenced by the Court may also qualify as general principles of international law. Since these principles are 'general principles of law recognised by civilised nations', any such common elements should logically relate to their comparative level of acceptance in similar legal cultures to those principles which have already been accepted by the World Court, provided that such principles are, by their nature, easily transposable to the international context. Therefore, for example, given that our perusal of general principles in national legal systems in the previous chapter showed that the principle of denial of relief to the unscrupulous is as popularly embedded as – or even more popularly embedded than – the doctrine of estoppel, one might expect that this principle ought to exist in international law as well. However, as Margaret White J has noted, the application of general principles, particularly those which are of an equitable nature in international law will never be precisely 'co-terminus with its role in any national jurisdiction'.[166] Therefore, if the Court were to countenance transposition of such a principle, it would need to take account of the specific nature of international law, which frequently upholds the validity of acts that would be deemed unscrupulous and therefore illicit at national level. A prime example of this is the fact that agreements imposed upon the vanquished party immediately after a war are not held to be invalid for duress, as equivalent instruments might be in parallel circumstances regarding individuals in national law. Hence, while there is good cause to suppose that the denial of relief to the unscrupulous is a principle of inter-

[165] It may alternatively be formulated that States, in (tacitly or actively) accepting the unearthing of new general principles by the Court, and indeed in accepting the presence of Art 38(1)(c) as part of the sources of international law are exercising consent, and therefore their monopoly upon norm creation is intact.

[166] White (2003) (n 101) 111.

national law, its content and applicability is extremely difficult to determine without guidance from the World Court.[167] Similar cases could be made for other principles, such as *reparation en nature*, but without guidance from the Court, or a better knowledge of the test it uses, it remains frustratingly difficult to determine what is 'in' and what is 'out'.

IV. CONCLUSION

Despite the limitations imposed by the Court's inability or unwillingness to be explicit about its usage of general principles and the uncertainty surrounding the 'test' for general principles of law, it would nonetheless seem apparent that equity has gained something approaching a firm footing in international law via the general principles category. The Court has repeatedly – though often cryptically – made reference to a number of powerful principles which have had real normative consequences for the legal problems before it. Although a good percentage of these references have come through the medium of dissenting or separate opinions, the absence of a concerted backlash against such opinions, either from the majority judgment, subsequent Court judgments, or States themselves, would tend to suggest that the principles enunciated in such opinions are widely perceived as legally valid. This is an important point, and one which warrants consideration. The fact that substantive principles such as estoppel doctrine and *ubi ius, ubi remedium* enjoy any life in international law may come as a surprise to certain commentators (for instance, Realist IR scholars), since it suggests that the international society which States have built is something more than a consensualist free-for-all. Such rules limit the freedom of States to act as they wish. Their ability to individually construct specific treaties or carry out specific acts which vitiate these general principles is dubious, particularly if they have failed to consistently object to their validity in the past. Such rules suggest that States have a strong interest in an international society governed by something more profound than the specific rules which they and their allies concoct, and that there exists a fundamental interest for States in good faith and honest conduct, transgressions of which render otherwise legal and legitimate conduct illegal and impermissible. By failing to object to – and by failing to take action to rid international law of – such principles, States are effectively consenting to their normative presence in the international legal *corpus*. However, in so doing, they are allowing for occasions where such principles may frustrate their immediate intentions or render their desired conduct impermissible.

[167] Indeed, the Court may have missed a fine opportunity to explore the applicability of this principle in the *Nicaragua* jurisdiction dispute.

Equitable general principles of law are a good thing at a systemic level. As Maitland once opined, equity has not come to destroy the law, but to fulfil it. The international society of States, international relations theorists remind us, is anarchic, due to the lack of a central authority. It is not, however, chaotic, since universally assented-to 'rules of the game' keep selfish State interests in check, at least to some degree. The more layers of such rules we have, the closer we move towards an ordered society of States. The fact that some rules can be altered *ad hoc* like bilateral treaties by small numbers of States indicates that certain layers of rules are fragile and potentially impermanent. However, equitable principles such as good faith and the doctrine of *abus de droit* prevent – or at the very least render impermissible – cheating at the game and thereby letting down one's fellow States. Such rules are deeply embedded and permanent in nature, and cannot be changed without the consent of the international community of States *en masse*. The fact that there is no pressure for the abandonment of such rules proves that States view such principles as rule-utilitarian, even if individual States may be frustrated by the consequences of individual invocations of such principles in given situations. Despite the general reticence of the PCIJ and ICJ to use general principles of law, occasionally, they have strayed from this cautious approach and have allowed general principles

> to serve a 'normative function' in the regulation of State conduct whenever '[the State's] infraction cannot be looked upon as a mere incident of the proceedings'. In that sense, the two courts have overridden the presumption of freedom of action of States.[168]

Through the acceptance of such general principles, States lightly accept the erosion of their control for the sake of a stable environment in which to trade and interact with one another. Such a conclusion renders questionable the idea of a zero-sum game proposed by Realist IR scholars since such principles are to the benefit of all States and usually only restrict those States who would otherwise have the power to abuse rights – that is usually powerful States.

However, the price to be paid for general principles, and in particular, equitable general principles, is not inconsiderable. While it is possible to 'legislate around' a certain number of general principles due to the *lex specialis derogat legi generali* principle (itself, ironically enough, a general principle),[169] equitable principles do not usually function in this manner. While it may be possible with clever legal terminology and careful

[168] Bassiouni (1990) (n 135) 801, part-quoting *Temple of Preah Vihear* (n 93) 41–42.

[169] A good example of this is the *nemo iudex in re sua* principle, that no one may be the judge in his own case. States may, of course, establish judicial, or quasi-judicial bodies which allow State representatives to serve as judges in cases involving those same States. This is often the case with *ad hoc* judges before the ICJ and was discussed in the PCIJ in the *Interpretation of the Treaty of Lausanne* case. See *Article 3(2) of the Treaty of Lausanne (Frontier between Turkey and Iraq)* (Advisory Opinion) PCIJ Rep Series B No 12, 27–32.

draughtsmanship to lessen the effect of the principle that the substance of a transaction will be looked to rather than its form alone, principles such as good faith and its various manifestations such as estoppel are very difficult – perhaps even impossible – to block out completely. Such principles may function regardless of the specificity or form of the legal transaction in question. Precisely why this is so shall be discussed in the forthcoming chapter. What is clear, however, is that several potent principles have been consecrated by the World Court. The life that the Court's judgments and opinion has breathed into these principles may have major consequences for a wide variety of legal disputes, including those involving the UN Charter. Their ability to interpret, to supplement, and occasionally to bend both conventional and customary international law may provide new perspectives and potentially fresh solutions to tricky legal problems. It is to one such problem – that of humanitarian intervention – that I now, at last, return.

5

A Framework for Equitable Humanitarian Intervention

I. INTRODUCTION

THIS CHAPTER WILL be dedicated to combining the lessons learned thus far in our discussion of humanitarian intervention in international law and those learned in our discussion of equity as a sub-set of the third source of international law. If equity is truly an elemental category of general principles of law, then why is the concept so rarely upheld as a means of solving legal conundrums? In particular, in the heat of the debate surrounding NATO's Kosovo operation, when respected scholars were throwing the legal rule book out the proverbial window, why did no one reach instead for the sources of international law and outline the fact that neither equity nor the broader category of general principles had even been discussed in relation to one of the great legal disputes of recent years? Why, when the two more frequently invoked sources of international law provided such unsatisfactory answers, did scholars turn to political, ethical and moral theory, rather than invoking the third source in order to shed light on the subject? More importantly, perhaps than all of the above is the question: does this 'third source of international law' indeed have something to say about the issue of humanitarian intervention, or were Cassese, Simma et al wise not to raise general principles in their argumentation?

The above questions will be treated in detail in this chapter. Briefly, however, it is my contention that the turn to ethical theory on the part of the international legal community was the result not only of an inability to square the United Nations Charter regime on the use of force with their consciences, but also of an unfamiliarity with the import of general principles of law, and with equity as a corrective mechanism and gap-filler in particular. Perceived as a supplementary source of law by many,[1] hardly discussed in most modern treatises on international law,[2] and particularly

[1] SA Sadat-Akhavi, *Methods of Resolving Conflicts Between Treaties* (Leiden, Martinus Nijhoff, 2003) 189.

[2] See, eg DJ Harris, *Cases and Materials on International Law* (London, Thomson, Sweet and Maxwell, 2004), which, while otherwise quite exhaustive in terms of its treatment of international legal sources, devotes scant attention to general principles of law.

disregarded in scholarship since the advent of the *ius cogens* category, general principles are hardly in fashion.[3] Cheng's 1953 text remains perhaps the leading general source on the subject.[4] However, the popular perception of general principles as an afterthought, conceived to prevent a *non liquet* in the World Court, is dreadfully misguided. General principles represent a normative category with real teeth. Every international agreement is predicated upon the fundamental doctrine of good faith. Substance has been preferred over form both by the United Nations Security Council and by the World Court on multiple occasions. These are principles that are so fundamental, so elementary, that they are rarely remarked upon or discussed in any detail. However, their effect is so important that without them, international agreements would cease to have structure or binding effect. It would seem somewhere between farcical and impossible to conclude a treaty between two States which expressly excludes good faith doctrine. Such a doctrine, and indeed other general principles of law such as the doctrine of *abus de droit*, seem so inherently necessary to any bilateral or multilateral undertaking, that far from being subsidiary and a mere afterthought, they are so fundamental that dispensing with them, even if expressly convened upon by States, would seem (near-) impossible. Though perhaps not normatively superior, their fundamental nature and the necessity of considering such norms in the solution of legal disputes is undeniable, and the (quasi-) impossibility of contracting out of at least a portion of such norms renders them a curious category, but one that is undoubtedly important.

If we are indeed to craft an equitable framework for humanitarian intervention based upon general principles of law, a discussion of general principles and their relationship with other sources of international law will certainly be necessary. Therefore, the first portion of this chapter will be given over to a treatment of this relationship and its various elements. Thereafter, it is my intention to show that such general principles of law allow for the possibility of a third exception to the prohibition upon the use of force by States as prescribed by Article 2(4) of the UN Charter. This shall be discussed in the second half of this chapter.

II. THE RELATIONSHIP BETWEEN EQUITY, GENERAL PRINCIPLES AND OTHER SOURCES OF INTERNATIONAL LAW

This section will seek to clarify to some degree the rather problematic position of where general principles of law fit into the international legal

[3] MC Bassiouni, 'A Functional Approach to "General Principles of International Law"' (1990) 11 *Michigan Journal of International Law* 768.

[4] B Cheng, *General Principles of Law as Applied by International Courts and Tribunals* (Cambridge, Grotius, 1987).

system. This shall be discussed with reference first to treaty law and customary international law, and then with reference to the more complicated categories of human rights and *ius cogens*, which are of particular interest to us in relation to this study. Such an examination should provide context for how and when general principles may be applied.

Before beginning, it is, however, perhaps germane to note one area that will not be treated in detail in this chapter, namely the relationship between general principles and natural law in the international legal sphere. Whether or not general principles have much in common with natural law doctrine – as Lauterpacht and others have argued – is essentially irrelevant for the purposes of this discussion, or, at best, an interesting aside. The fact is that, natural heritage or not, the content of certain norms such as good faith, estoppel/*préclusion*, and the abuse of rights have found favour in a broad majority of legal systems in all the legal families worldwide. They have further been upheld as having normative value in judgments of the ICJ and PCIJ. It is upon these principles that I base my argument, without wishing to make subjective value judgments about whether international law is an open or closed system, or whether the general principles category represents 'natural law by the back door'. Of course, failure to discuss the connection here, despite some basic attention to the nexus between the concepts attempted in chapters two and four, lays this work open to categorisation as the work of a natural lawyer attempting to utilise formalist logic in order to import natural law reasoning – disingenuously disguised as source-based formalism – into the debate on humanitarian intervention. However, in reality, this is far from the case. In eschewing a deeper discussion of the links between natural law theory and legal sources, I am endeavouring to avoid falling into the moralist 'trap' that so many of the scholars I roundly criticise in the first chapter have seemed to find themselves in. The rules used in this chapter are general principles that have found favour across the globe in domestic law, and that have been transposed into international law, as evidenced by the pronouncements of the World Court. Deep value judgments regarding their relation to the development and doctrine of natural law would neither add to, nor take away from, their normative value, but might well distract from the central thrust of this chapter. The fact is that the treatment delivered herein endeavours to garner wisdom derived from reliable *legal* sources – rather than aspirational moral values – in order to solve a *legal* problem.

A. General Principles, Treaty and Custom

The relationship between general principles and the two other principal sources of international law is an important one, particularly since no formal hierarchy exists to distinguish the three sources. Therefore, establishing a hierarchy between individual norms is extremely difficult in practice. Although general guidelines, such as the *lex specialis* and *prior in tempore, potior in iure* principles exist as general guidelines, their application is curtailed, as Sadat-Akhavi has noted, by the largely conventional nature of international law: 'Rules of international law are set out in universal, regional and bilateral treaties. Such concepts, which do not exist at all in national laws, totally change the picture of the conflict-resolving process'.[5] The *prior in tempore, potior in iure* rule was set aside, for example in the *Mavrommatis Palestine Concessions* judgment, while the *lex specialis* rule was, in this instance, upheld.[6] It would seem that the absence of a central legislative authority renders the transposition of such rules to the international sphere tricky at best. Further, in assessing the relationship between general principles and treaty law, it is important not to forget the rules on treaty interpretation, set out in the 1969 Vienna Convention, and discussed in chapter two.

Aside from the above, it would seem that while the *lex specialis* principle may be suited for dealing with conflicts between treaties, and indeed to an extent to conflicts between treaties and customary international law, it is relatively inadequate in treating some – though not all – cases of conflicts between treaties and general principles.[7] Such a conclusion follows the position which is prevalent in national legal systems. Taking, for example the French *Code civil* as an example of the tendency in continental European legal systems toward legislating for every eventuality, it would seem that the need for general principles should have almost disappeared, or at least that their applicability would be entirely effaced by the leviathans of specific law, due to the *lex specialis legi generali derogat* principle. This, however, has not been the case. French lawyers have continued to find a place for good faith and equity in both legal arguments and judgments. Certain general principles have themselves been written into the Code, further reinforcing their continuing presence in the law.[8] Practice has shown that specific clauses in the Code will rarely, if ever, derogate from these general principles (though it is worth observing, for clarity's sake, that other general principles are frequently derogated by specific law). The same is true in common law systems, although a limited exception in both cases may exist in the case of strict liability (*responsabilité sans faute*), though both legal systems (exceptionally) justify the doctrine on the basis that one voluntarily and knowingly takes responsibility for the things which are under one's control (*sous sa garde)* and which are likely to

[5] Sadat-Akhavi (2003) (n 1) 191.

[6] *Mavrommatis Palestine Concessions* (Judgment) PCIJ Rep Series A No 2, 6–31.

[7] It is fair to say that the *lex specialis* rule still plays an important role in this area, but that it does not have the same quasi-universal ambit as it does in cases of treaty v treaty conflicts.

[8] See, eg Art 1134, *alinéa* 3.

be inherently dangerous. For example, for wild animals kept in captivity (such as lions or bears), called animals *ferae naturae*, the common law presumes the owner's *scienter* of the danger the animal represents.[9] Such a model, involving voluntary assumption of responsibility in all circumstances, effectively serves as a conscious waiver of rights on the part of the individual who is responsible for the dangerous animal, preserving the import of general principles, generally, but waiving the rights which arise from them in this instance.

Without the *lex specialis* principle as a useful aid in resolving conflicts between sources of law, we are forced to examine the nature of general principles themselves. As Sadat-Akhavi has lamented, the main problem of general principles of law vis-à-vis other legal sources lies not in their characterisation, but rather in their effectiveness, or lack thereof, in resolving conflicts between sources. He cites three main problems: first, that general principles are often 'self-effacing' insofar as they frustrate their own application; secondly, that certain ideas such as *lex specialis* and *lex posterior* often contradict one another with no obvious 'winner'; and thirdly, that they are, by their very nature, vague and not entirely concrete, making founding legal solutions upon them rather difficult.[10] Charles Rousseau has voiced similar concerns.[11] Nonetheless, if one examines national legal systems and their methods for dealing with general principles of law, and one further takes into account the practice of the PCIJ and ICJ in this regard, one may be assuaged. As Bassiouni has noted, general principles are unlike other legal rules, in that the focus should fall more upon their functions than their specific content.[12] Such principles aim for a given goal, a given solution, and are, in the main, less bound by rules of form than other legal norms.

Despite the inherent flexibility of such principles, however, it is clear from their genesis in national legal systems that they may interact with other norms in a variety of ways, either as an interpretative source for other norms, as a legislative guide for developing new law, as a supplemental source and gap-filler, or occasionally as a modifier or superseding normative category. This is also the case in international law, where general principles may be used *infra legem*, *praeter legem*, or *contra legem*, though the latter

[9] 'Scienter' is an antiquated term, meaning notice or knowledge. The term originates in legal parlance from *Applebee v Percy* (1874) LR 9 CP 647. Here, the court held: 'A distinction has always been taken between animals which are by nature fierce and untameable, such as tigers and others ferae naturae, and those which are not in their general nature ferocious . . . If a man keeps an animal of the former class, and another is injured, the owner of the animal is liable without any evidence of a scienter; but, where the animal belongs to a class which is not habitually ferocious, it is necessary to sh[o]w that its owner has notice that it has on former occasions sh[o]wn symptoms of a disposition to bite mankind'.

[10] Sadat-Akhavi (2003) (n 1) 190.

[11] C Rousseau, *Droit International Public*, Vol I (Paris, Sirey, 1970) 156.

[12] Bassiouni (1990) (n 3) 774–76.

category is controversial.[13] However, particularly as regards equitable principles, there is little reason to exclude the possibility of application of general principles in derogation of treaty or customary international law. Rossi has pointed out that such a position would represent the transposition of classical doctrine regarding equity's operation to the international sphere.[14] In the previous chapter, we demonstrated the reception of equity into international law by way of international legal practice. If such principles have been received by the World Court and are accepted by States, there is no reason to suppose that they should function any differently at international level to national level. Such a position would be inconsistent with the nature of such principles and would therefore rob them of a significant portion of their function. Furthermore, it is clear that the drafters of the PCIJ Statute were aware of notable arbitral cases such as *The Neptune*[15] and *L'Affaire Yuille, Shortridge et Cie*,[16] where general principles had been held to derogate from the written law. In drafting the PCIJ (and later the ICJ) Statute without explicitly excluding the possibility of *contra legem* application of general principles, the learned Advisory Committee of Jurists was expressing the opinion that the law had not changed in this regard. This position was reinforced by subsequent arbitral judgments,[17] and by pronouncements from within the World Court itself.[18]

The fact that *contra legem* application of general principles has not found frequent application in the judgments of the PCIJ and ICJ should not come as a surprise, however. The nature of the aforementioned arbitral awards was usually one of fairly exceptional circumstances. The cases which have come before the World Court have, in the main, been, at least relatively speaking, fairly mundane and somewhat more predictable in terms of the legal issues at stake. Further, there is the issue of judicial reluctance to explicitly make reference to general principles of law to consider. If general principles are the controversial category which may only enter 'by the

[13] ibid, 775–86. See also Cheng (1987) (n 4) 390, who argues for a more restrictive application of general principles of law, omitting the possibility of *contra legem* application in the international sphere. Rossi, C Rossi, *Equity and International Law: A Legal Realist Approach to International Decision Making* (Irvington, New York, Transnational Publishers Inc, 1993) 9–10, 119–54, advocates a somewhat more expansive interpretation, including the possibility of some *contra legem* application, particularly regarding equity. Raimondo takes a middle position, strongly affirming the equality of general principles of law as a normative source with treaty and custom, but omitting the logical consequence of this pronouncement, namely the possibility of general principles being applied instead of custom or treaty in exceptional situations: FO Raimondo, *General Principles of Law in the Decisions of International Criminal Courts and Tribunals* (Leiden, Martinus Nijhoff Publishers, 2008).

[14] Rossi (1993) (n 13) 9–10.

[15] *The Neptune* (1797) 4 *International Adjudication Manuscripts* 372, 433.

[16] *Affaire Yuille, Shortridge et Cie* (1861) *Arbitrage de la Commission désignée par le Sénat libre de Hambourg* 21 October 1861.

[17] *Georges Pinson (France v Mexico)* (1928) 5 RIAA 327; *Angola Case* (1928) 2 RIAA 1011, 1025–26.

[18] *Oscar Chinn Case* PCIJ Rep Series A/B No 63, individual opinion of Anzilotti J, 113.

back door', then *contra legem* application of such principles is the ultimate taboo. Nonetheless, neither this reluctance on the part of the World Court, nor Cheng's mistaken omission of *contra legem* applicability from his 'list of functions' of general principles is indicative of the truth of the matter. The oversight of a leading scholar and the cowardice of a court cannot be used to pervert the law. The evidence is clear, and international law has not substantially changed in terms of its conception of the sources of law and their function since the arbitral awards of the 1920s. Classical doctrine has undoubtedly been transposed to international law, particularly as regards equitable general principles, as Bassiouni and Rossi have rightly argued.

While mapping out when and where treaty and custom may feel the influence of general principles of law is extremely difficult, partly due to a recalcitrant ICJ, and partly due to a lack of detailed scholarly attention to the subject, it is sufficient for our purposes to note the normative parity which the three sources enjoy, the possibility of *infra-*, *praeter-*, and *contra legem* applicability of general principles, and the controversial, rare, and exceptional status of the latter – and to a lesser extent the second – of these categories.

B. General Principles and Human Rights Norms

If the situation regarding the relationship between general principles of law and treaty and customary international law is somewhat unclear, then the relationship between general principles and human rights norms is even more so. This is particularly the case in the context of our present discussion. The regime surrounding the use of force by States deals with the rights and obligations of States as actors in international law. Human rights, on the other hand, are primarily the preserve of individuals, and have little prima facie bearing upon the duties that States owe to one another.

To present such a picture is, however, both over-simplistic and inaccurate. Individual rights have come a long way in a short time in international law, from a position in 1924 where the PCIJ asserted that

> [i]t is an elementary principle of international law that a state is entitled to protect its subjects . . . Once a state has taken up a case on behalf of one of its subjects before an international tribunal, in the eyes of the latter the state is [the] sole claimant.[19]

Here, the PCIJ effectively held that in such cases, although the subject-matter of the claim is the individual and/or his property, the legal claim

[19] *Mavrommatis Palestine Concessions* PCIJ Rep Series A No 2, 11–12.

in international law is essentially that of the State, which may exercise its sovereign discretion as to whether to uphold such a claim against the offending State(s). While the above case concerned diplomatic protection of individuals, the principles laid down in the judgment might have been applied to any individual rights which were internationally opposable at the time. However, human rights have developed a real life of their own since the 1920s. Particularly in the aftermath of the Second World War, significant strides were made to impose real and binding obligations upon States to respect the rights of individuals.

Inspired to some degree by the 'Four Freedoms' enunciated by Franklin Roosevelt,[20] the United States pushed for the inclusion of a reference to human rights in the Charter of the United Nations, despite some resistance from the United Kingdom and the Soviet Union.[21] Eventually, the American position prevailed, and references to human rights were inserted into both the Preamble and the Purposes Clause of the Charter. This purpose was to be pursued, at least at first, by the elaboration of an international bill of rights, which President Truman promised 'will be as much a part of international life as our own Bill of Rights is part of our Constitution'.[22] This was a bold promise. The American Bill of Rights is a series of 10 amendments to the Constitution, appended to the main text in order to secure fundamental freedoms for the citizens of the United States. Forming part of constitutional law, it is superior to federal legislation and is directly opposable by individuals against other individuals as well as against the State. It creates rights and obligations, and may be used as a basis for action by any private person in court.

Truman's vision has not yet come to proper fruition, but enormous progress has nonetheless been made. The 'international bill of rights' was watered down to a declaration – the Universal Declaration of Human Rights (UDHR), due to ideological opposition between West and East over its content. Instead of a binding treaty, the international community crafted something which, 'on its own . . . represented little more than an exhalation of hot pious air'.[23] Despite this somewhat justified criticism, the UDHR transpired to be enormously important, precisely because it did not need to stand alone, as States began to adopt international treaties which protected a variety of human rights. The UDHR has served as the foundation for two binding UN human rights covenants, the International Covenant on Civil

[20] The 'Four Freedoms' are: freedom of expression; freedom of religious worship; freedom from want and freedom from fear. See SI Rosenman (ed) and FD Roosevelt, *The Public Papers and Addresses of Franklin D Roosevelt*, vol 4 (London, Macmillan, 1941) 672.

[21] J Mahoney, *The Challenge of Human Rights: Origin, Development and Significance* (Oxford, Blackwell, 2007) 44.

[22] UN Conference on International Organisation, 'Vol I: Closing Plenary Session' (26 June 1945) Doc 1209 P/16, 683.

[23] AWB Simpson, *Human Rights and the End of Empire: Britain and the Genesis of the European Convention* (Oxford, Oxford University Press, 2001) 11.

and Political Rights and the International Covenant on Economic, Social and Cultural Rights, and the principles of the Declaration are elaborated in international treaties such as the International Convention on the Elimination of All Forms of Racial Discrimination, the International Convention on the Elimination of Discrimination Against Women, the United Nations Convention on the Rights of the Child, the United Nations Convention Against Torture and others besides. Due to these more recent developments, the aspirations enshrined in the UDHR have acquired normative force, with many leading commentators contending that the vast majority of the UDHR is now part of the *corpus* of customary international law.[24] From a watered-down bagatelle, the UDHR is now an oft-cited normative powerhouse, providing a series of rights that are legally opposable by individuals against States.

The treatment of rights provided above is admittedly very brief. A more detailed history of the evolution of human rights norms can be found in any generalist public international law treatise, as well as in the myriad specialist texts on the subject. Where progress in the field has fallen short, however, is regarding enforcement mechanisms. The Universal Declaration on Human Rights provides that

> everyone has the right to an effective remedy by the competent national tribunals for acts violating the fundamental rights granted him by the constitution or by law.[25]

While national tribunals provide recourse, to varying degrees, to individuals for wrongs committed against them by the State, there exists no global 'World Court of Human Rights' to which one may appeal for relief for human rights violations occasioned by one's own State or by another State.[26] In certain regions, arrangements such as the European Convention on Human Rights and the Inter-American Convention on Human Rights have been put in place, which provide for an international human rights court to which individuals may petition. Nonetheless, such courts, while commendable in and of themselves, are of regional jurisdiction only, and do not provide a universal solution. While human rights have taken root and established themselves in the international legal sphere by way of

[24] T Meron, *Human Rights and Humanitarian Norms as Customary Law* (Oxford, Clarendon, 1989); R Lillich, 'The Growing Importance of Customary International Human Rights Law' (1995) 25 *Georgia Journal of International and Comparative Law* 1; H Hannum, 'The Status of the Universal Declaration of Human Rights in National and International Law' (1995) 25 *Georgia Journal of International and Comparative Law* 287; L Sohn, 'Sources of International Law III: The Status and Future of the Customary International Law of Human Rights' (1995) 25 *Georgia Journal of International and Comparative Law* 399; H Hannum, 'The UCHR in National and International Law' (1998) 3 *Health and Human Rights* 144.

[25] UDHR, UN General Assembly Resolution 217 A (III), UN Doc A/810 (1948) 71, Art 8.

[26] However, recent academic initiatives point to the future possible creation of such an organ. See J Kozma, M Nowak and M Scheinin, *A World Court of Human Rights – Consolidated Statute and Commentary* (Vienna, Neuer Wissenschaftlicher Verlag, 2010).

treaty and customary international law, upholding and enforcing such rights against States remains problematic.

The relationship between human rights and general principles of law is multi-layered. The *Corfu Channel* case would seem to provide evidence that general principles of law are, in and of themselves, a source of certain human rights norms, with its reference to 'elementary considerations of humanity . . . even more exacting in peace than in war' as part of the *dispositif* in its judgment.[27] The scope of this human rights component within the general principles *corpus* has not, however, been explained by the Court, nor indeed the precise legal principles upon which such rights are grounded. If we are to understand that such elementary considerations of humanity derive from general principles of law recognised by the majority of States with developed legal systems, then their basis is murky indeed, since conceptions of what constitute elementary considerations of humanity are quite varied amongst the constitutional and statute law of the world's legal systems. A comparative analysis of from whence such principles emerge, and their normative content at national level is beyond the ambit of this modest study, though happily for our purposes, a thorough examination of their import and existence is unnecessary. Simply acknowledging that the general principles of law category incorporates some limited human rights content is sufficient for now.

The second tenet of the relationship between human rights and general principles, beyond what can be stated about the relationship between general principles and any rights arising from treaties, is more important for our purposes. This is the idea that general principles may enhance the effective protection of individual rights. Such enhancement may take a variety of forms, but ultimately, the strength of general principles of law is that, by enlarge, they apply across the spectrum of general international law, and therefore principles such as good faith, *ubi ius, ubi remedium*, the doctrine of *abus de droit* and estoppel must necessarily have a role to play in human rights cases. Perhaps the best example of general principles being applied in the World Court came in the *Jurisdiction of the Danzig Courts* Advisory Opinion, where the principle *nullus commodum capere de sua iniuria propria* was applied. Here, the Permanent Court held that

> it cannot be disputed that the very object of an international agreement, according to the intention of the contracting Parties, may be the adoption by the Parties of some definite rules creating individual rights and enforceable by the national courts.

This being the case, Poland could not claim that the Danzig courts were not entitled to apply the provisions of the *Beamtenabkommen* simply due to its own failure to transpose the relevant provisions of the treaty into its

[27] *Corfu Channel Case* (*United Kingdom v Albania*) (Merits) [1949] ICJ Rep 4, 22. See also ch 4.

national law. The Court therefore held that States may not derive profit from their own misdeeds.[28] A general principle was of law providing the justification for the Court to compel a State to give effect to individual rights.

The idea that general principles may enhance the actionability or effective protection of individual rights has become both increasingly relevant and increasingly important in recent decades. As human rights have gradually acquired a firm normative footing in international law, their potential to interact with general principles of law, and particularly with equity, has increased. It is not the nature of either category to perfect imperfect rights or titles,[29] but when such rights are already properly founded in law, equity and general principles may give effect or afford protection to such rights. A treatment of how this may be relevant to the idea of humanitarian intervention will be discussed later in this chapter.

C. General Principles and *Ius Cogens*

Finally, it is necessary to turn our attention to the relationship between the 'general principles of law recognised by civilised nations' and the still-controversial category of *ius cogens.* Little attention has been paid to any potential nexus between these categories, and at first glance, this is hardly surprising. After all, *ius cogens* may be labelled as the 'hardest' normative category in the international legal sphere – a non-derogable core of peremptory norms – whereas general principles conversely represent the 'softest', since they are comparatively malleable, vague, and may be adapted to the circumstances of a given case. The two categories would seem to be poles apart, and have little to do with one another, except to note that when they conflict with one another, *ius cogens*, as a peremptory normative category, must always prevail.

However, such a simplistic conception of the relationship between the two categories is misguided at best. Bassiouni has noted a link of sorts between the two categories, but one that is not easily defined or framed. He has linked the demise of scholarship on general principles to the advent of the *ius cogens* category, which holds more promise for legal scholarship, a more enticing category, which has devoured much of the theoretical impetus that would otherwise have been directed at general principles of law.[30] The trouble with charting a clearer link in normative

[28] *Jurisdiction of the Courts of Danzig (Pecuniary Claims of Danzig Railway Officials who have Passed into the Polish Service, against the Polish Railways Administration)* (Advisory Opinion) PCIJ Rep Series B No 15, 26–27.

[29] It is one of the maxims of equity in common law that 'equity will not perfect an imperfect gift'.

[30] Bassiouni (1990) (n 3) 802–18.

terms between the two categories is that they are both substantially unclear, with their boundaries and functions, to some degree, at least, both controversial and still in dispute. As regards general principles, our study has already charted how and why this is so. Concerning *ius cogens*, however, the problems are not entirely dissimilar.

Chief amongst the problems that beset the *ius cogens* category is the doctrinal debate, which has been both ambiguous and confusing. Anthony D'Amato sarcastically branded the sheer ephemerality of *ius cogens* 'an asset', remarking that it enables 'any writer to christen any ordinary norm of his or her choice as a new ius cogens norm, thereby in one stroke investing it with magical power'.[31] Andrea Bianchi has echoed such a position, describing international lawyers as 'magicians, administering the rites of ius cogens and invoking its magical power'.[32] D'Amato notes that *ius cogens* lacks a real substantive content of its own, and that the views of publicists – which are by no means uniform – have developed an added importance in the determination of what this category entails, since States and international courts are not inclined to refer to it as often as they might. Bianchi agrees, citing the fact that the ICJ chose instead to refer to obligations *erga omnes* in the *Legal Consequences of the Construction of a Wall in the Occupied Palestinian Territory* Advisory Opinion, but noting, contrastingly that in the recent *Congo* case, an important legal issue – here the Court's jurisdiction – was settled with reference to *ius cogens*.[33] Both authors have drawn attention to the underlying issue that while international treaties, most notably Article 53 of the Vienna Convention on the Law of Treaties, have prescribed the existence of the *ius cogens* category, it has fallen to legal scholarship to devise which norms may fall within its ambit.[34]

Parker and Neylon have noted that it has become a common assertion in international legal scholarship that most (but not all) of the human rights *corpus* now holds the status of *ius cogens*.[35] The boundaries of which human rights norms do and do not fall under this heading are, however, in some dispute. However, it seems to be generally agreed that (at the very least) the prohibition of torture;[36] the prohibition of maritime piracy;[37]

[31] A D'Amato, 'It's a Bird, It's a Plane, It's Jus Cogens!' in A D'Amato, *International Law Sources, Collected Papers*, vol III (Leiden, Martinus Nijhoff, 2004) 334.

[32] A Bianchi, 'Human Rights and the Magic of Jus Cogens' (2008) 19 *European Journal of International Law* 491.

[33] ibid, 502–03.

[34] ibid, 491–94. See also G Abi-Saab, 'The Uses of Article 19' (1999) 10 *European Journal of International Law* 341.

[35] K Parker and LB Neylon, 'Jus Cogens: Compelling the Law of Human Rights' (1989) 12 *Hastings International and Comparative Law Review* 411. See also Bianchi (2008) (n 32) 491–92.

[36] *Prosecutor v Furundžija* (Judgment of the Appeals Chamber) ICTY IT-95-17/1A (21 July 2000), 121ILR 213.

[37] G Schwarzenberger, *'International Ius Cogens?'* (1964–65) 43 *Texas Law Review* 455.

the prohibition of genocide;[38] that of slavery and those of war crimes and crimes against humanity[39] all represent *cogentes* norms.

The *ius cogens* status of the prohibition upon the use of force is a slightly more complicated matter. It is certainly true that an overwhelming majority of leading scholars view the prohibition as peremptory in nature.[40] The International Law Commission (ILC) has also adopted this position.[41] While the World Court has been recalcitrant about referring to the peremptory category of norms, it did state in the *Nicaragua* judgment that the prohibition upon the use of force by States constituted 'a conspicuous example of a rule of international law having the character of *jus cogens*'.[42] However, it is important to note here, as James Green has done, that the Court in this case was merely quoting (albeit seemingly approvingly) an earlier statement of the ILC.[43] Green notes the myriad problems associated with the classification of the prohibition of the use of force as a peremptory norm, including the inherent flexibility of the law on the use of force, the variety of associated rules and sources, the debated exceptions and the uncertain scope of the regime.[44] Further, Nikolas Stürchler has noted that Article 2(4) places the prohibition of the threat of armed force on a normative par with the prohibition upon its active use by States, while further observing that this position is not borne out by the practice of the community of States.[45] In order to eschew the complicated, contradictory, and occasionally paradoxical reasoning brought about by conceiving of the prohibition upon the use of force by States – incorporating its accepted (flexible) exceptions, State practice and extraneous norms – as a norm of *ius cogens*, Orakhelashvili prefers to conclude that 'the *ius ad bellum* as a whole is peremptory'.[46] However, this approach is itself

[38] MC Bassiouni, 'International Crimes and Obligations Erga Omnes' (1996) 59 *Law and Contemporary Problems* 63.

[39] ibid.

[40] See, inter alia, D Kritsiotis, 'Reappraising Policy Objections to Humanitarian Intervention' (1998) 19 *Michigan Journal of International Law* 1005, 1042–43; N Wheeler, *Saving Strangers: Humanitarian Intervention in International Society* (Oxford, Oxford University Press, 2000) 44–45; W Scholtz, 'The Changing Rules of Jus ad Bellum: Conflicts in Kosovo, Iraq, and Afghanistan' (2004) 7 *Potchefstroom Electronic Law Journal* at http://elecper.0fees.net/NWU,%20Potchefstroom%20Electronic%20Law%20Journal%20index.htm 1, 8–10; A Orakhelashvili, *Peremptory Norms in International Law* (Oxford, Oxford University Press, 2006) 50; J Crawford, *The Creation of States in International Law*, 2nd edn (Oxford, Oxford University Press, 2006) 146; JA Frowein, 'Ius Cogens' in R Wolfrum (ed), *The Max Planck Encyclopedia of Public International Law* (online edition Oxford University Press, 2008: www.mpepil.com) para 8.

[41] UNGA, 'Report of the International Law Commission', 53rd Session (23 April–1 June 2001 and 2 July–10 August 2001) 283.

[42] *Case Concerning Military and Paramilitary Activities in and against Nicaragua (Nicaragua v United States)* (Judgment) [1986] ICJ Rep 14.

[43] J Green, 'Questioning the Peremptory Status of the Prohibition of the Use of Force' (2011) 32 *Michigan Journal of International Law* 215, 222–24.

[44] ibid, 217.

[45] See N Stürchler, *The Threat of Force in International Law* (Cambridge, Cambridge University Press, 2007).

[46] Orakhelashvili (2006) (n 40) 51.

problematic, as Green notes, since the *ius ad bellum* is not a norm, but rather a network thereof.[47] For the purposes of the present discussion, it would render any potential derogation from the general prohibition upon the use of force significantly easier to justify if one were to qualify it as anything less than a peremptory norm. However, despite the legitimate concerns voiced by Green and others as to such a classification, the overwhelming majority of legal opinion would appear to hold to the position that the prohibition is peremptory in nature, and thus it is not the intention of this work to contest its *ius cogens* standing to any significant degree.

While a certain central core of norms are rarely disputed (particularly since the collapse of the Soviet Union) as having peremptory character, 'frequent references to *ius cogens*, or in its other appellation, "peremptory norm", or the undisciplined use of such terms as "compelling", "inherent", "inalienable", "essential", "fundamental" and "overriding" does not contribute greater clarity to the concept'.[48] Yet such language is frequently used by legal scholars. Bianchi notes the pitfalls inherent in such frequent invocation of the category, stating that 'one of the major threats to the concept of *ius cogens* is the tendency by some of its most fervent supporters to see it everywhere'.[49] The dangers of emotive language and moralising in international legal scholarship have been thoroughly discussed (and condemned) in chapter one, due primarily to the subjectivity that necessarily accompanies any non-normative language in such contexts. Further dilutions of clarity may occur when standard definitions of certain terms are taken exception to by States in order to eschew clashing with *ius cogens* norms through redefining them. This has been much discussed with reference to the United States and the notorious 'torture memos' in the context of the 'war on terror', whereby a limited definition of torture was adopted in order to allow practices which would normally be outside the boundaries of law.[50] Such subjectivity – on both sides – leads to a regrettable dilution of legal certainty, which is of added importance in the international legal sphere, due to the absence of a central law-making authority, rendering any certainty which is achieved delicate and easily upset by reckless scholarship or unscrupulous governments. Loss of legal certainty may upset international order as States adopt different flexible interpretations of what was formerly a single standard rule, leading to conflict.

[47] Green (2011) (n 43) 231.

[48] Bassiouni (1990) (n 3) 802–03. See also F Lopez de Oñate, *La Certezza del Diritto* (Milan, Giuffrè, 1968).

[49] Bianchi (2008) (n 32) 506.

[50] See K Ambos, 'Prosecuting Guantanamo in Europe: Can and Shall the Masterminds of the "Torture Memos" be held Criminally Responsible on the Basis of Universal Jurisdiction?' (2009) 42 *Case Western Reserve Journal of International Law* 405.

Verdross has opined that definitions of *ius cogens* may be redundant because the idea of *ius cogens* is clear in and of itself.[51] However, Bassiouni has branded such a facile exit from a difficult conundrum as insufficient, and akin to Stewart J's statement regarding the definition of obscenity: 'perhaps I could never succeed in intelligibly doing so. But I know it when I see it'.[52] I have to agree with Bassiouni on this point, since such an approach – stating that *ius cogens* is inherently understandable and requires no further definition – seems to have been empirically disproven by subsequent literature, since such disparate conceptions of the category have emerged from various authors, meaning that the concept cannot be so clear as to require no further explanation. Bassiouni notes: 'almost all the operative terms used in describing jus cogens are value-laden and susceptible of multiple definitions based on differing concepts. They are capable of producing several outcomes, some contradictory'.[53] However, it is perhaps germane to note that the exact same thing might well be said of general principles.[54]

This is not the only characteristic that is shared between general principles and *ius cogens* norms. While general principles are normally branded as being the 'softest' of the principal norms of international law, and *ius cogens* norms the 'hardest', such a position amounts to something of an oversimplification of reality. While general principles may sometimes be more malleable, and while they will certainly be the subject of derogations on the basis of the *lex specialis* principle, for example, as discussed above with reference to treaty law, others are unlikely to bend to more specific norms. This is certainly the case with the principle of good faith, which would seem to be essentially non-derogable. Further, certain principles of equity are, by their very nature, derogatory, in that their sole function is to derogate more specific norms. This is certainly the case with estoppel, the doctrine of *abus de droit* and the prioritisation of substance over form. All of these principles may derogate specific legal provisions, be they treaty law or something else. This power derives from their nature at national level, which has been transposed to the international legal sphere, and which has been applied *in concreto* in cases before the PCIJ and ICJ, as discussed in chapter four. Therefore, despite their prima facie 'softness', general principles occasionally have the ability to stand firm against other sources. Whether this is the case as regards *ius cogens*, however, is a tricky question.

[51] A Verdross, 'Jus Dispositivum and Jus Cogens in International Law' (1966) 60 *American Journal of International Law* 55, 57.

[52] *Jacobellis v Ohio* 378 US 184 (1964) 197, Stewart J, concurring. See also Bassiouni (1990) (n 3) 803 and *Hustler Magazine, Inc v Falwell* 485 US 46 (1988).

[53] Bassiouni (1990) (n 3) 805.

[54] See M McDougal, HD Laswell and M Reisman, 'The World Constitutive Process of Authoritative Decision Making' in C Black and R Falk (eds), *The Future of the International Legal Order*, vol I (Princeton, NJ, Princeton University Press, 1969) 73.

Formal logic would suggest that there is no scope for general principles of law to derogate *ius cogens* at any level. However, it would nonetheless seem uncontroversial to suggest that general principles may be used *infra legem* as a canon of interpretation for deciding conflicts between different norms of *ius cogens* and for delimiting lines between *ius cogens* norms and norms of customary international law and treaty law. This would seem logical, since Article 54 of the Vienna Convention on the Law of Treaties stipulates that a norm of *ius cogens* may only be modified 'by a subsequent norm of general international law having the same character'.[55] However, if one is to follow the formal logic of this Article, while *infra legem* and possible *praeter legem* application of general principles with regard to *ius cogens* norms may be conceivable – assuming of course that gaps exist in such norms – derogation or *contra legem* application of general principles against peremptory norms seems inconceivable. Certainly, the World Court has never even come close to such a conception of general principles.

This may not be the end of the story, however. At domestic level, purposive interpretation of constitutional norms has led to certain judges expressing the opinion that formal legal hierarchy may be derogated from in extreme cases on the basis of abusive invocation, for example, of temporary constitutional provisions concerning emergency powers, due to its conflict with general legal precepts such as good faith and the prohibition of *abus de droit*. Whether general principles may be employed against *ius cogens* norms in international law in the same manner in which they have been employed against constitutional and other fundamental norms at national level is debatable, but such a possibility cannot be entirely excluded. In order to determine whether such an approach may be possible at international level, it is necessary for us to have due regard to at least one instance in which general principles and overriding interests have been invoked as a means to override constitutional norms at national level. The best examples of such instances are in the rare cases where the constitutionality of constitutional amendments has been put into question by national courts. By carefully examining such cases, it may be possible to understand whether the approach used in such cases may be transposed to international law or whether such an idea is misguided. There are, perhaps, three categories of such cases, which may be distinguished. The first refers to cases where certain provisions of a Constitution are specifically referred to as being 'unalterable', and are then altered. The second refers to situations where a Constitution is amended without the proper procedure, that is where amendment requires a two-thirds electoral majority, and an amendment is appended on the basis of only a simple majority. Such situations, while not entirely uninteresting, are

[55] Vienna Convention on the Law of Treaties, 23 May 1969 (Entered into force 27 January 1980), 1155 UNTS 331.

largely irrelevant for the purposes of our study. It is the third category, however, from which some guidance may be gleaned, namely the rare and controversial occasions on which the constitutionality of constitutional amendments is challenged due to their content and its incompatibility with implicit and unwritten fundamental principles of whatever nature. Such cases are few and far between, but examples of discussions in this regard do exist, and I shall proceed to furnish a brief discussion of a number of them.

D. Unconstitutional Constitutional Amendments

One recent prominent case relevant to our discussion is that of the *Anayasa Mahkemesi* (Constitutional Court of the Turkish Republic) of 5 June 2008. Here, the Court issued a decision annulling Parliament's amendments to the 1982 Constitution regarding the principle of equality and the right to education; the goal of Parliament having been to abolish the ban on headscarves in universities.[56] The Court held that such an amendment was unconstitutional, since it infringed upon the principle of secularism, which was constitutionally protected. While the idea of an unconstitutional constitutional amendment might seem in and of itself a self-contradictory concept,[57] many scholars have argued that fundamental values which constitute the embodiment of – and are essential to – the meaning and purpose of a Constitution may not be altered, at least beyond a certain point.[58]

Theoretical bases for limitations upon which constitutional provisions may be amended are too varied to be explored in full here. However, it is worth mentioning one of the more dominant and enduring arguments, presented by l'Abbé Sieyès, who distinguished the constituent power – the extraordinary power stemming from the immediate expression of the nation – from the constituted power – the power created by the Constitution. Per Sieyès, these two powers exist on different planes, and while the Constitution may grant the constituted power the ability to amend the Constitution, it may not alter the fundamentals established by the constituent power, or may not enact amendments which go so far as to overthrow

[56] *Anayasa Mahkemesi* no 2008/16, 5 June 2008 (Constitutional Court of the Turkish Republic).

[57] E Özbudun, 'Judicial Review of Constitutional Amendments in Turkey' (2009) 15 *European Public Law* 533.

[58] See, eg J Mazzone, 'Unamendments' (2004–05) 90 *Iowa Law Review* 1747; VJ Samar, 'Can a Constitutional Amendment be Unconstitutional?' (2008) 33 *Oklahoma City University Law Review* 667; R Albert, 'Nonconstitutional Amendments' (2009) 22 *Canadian Journal of Law and Jurisprudence* 5.

the fundamental aspects of the Constitution.[59] French constitutional ideals and those of the *Francophonie* have been heavily influenced by this thinking. While French and other Constitutions up until the current 1958 *Constitution de la Vème Republique* have incorporated 'unamendable' provisions (such as Article 89 of the 1958 Constitution dealing with the republican form of government[60]), Sieyès' theory has also been used to argue for the existence of implicitly unamendable constitutional provisions.[61] Carl Schmitt seized upon Sieyès' terminology, arguing that a distinction must be drawn between the constituent power and the amendment power; the former being the power to establish a new Constitution, whereas the latter is the power to amend the Constitution in force, which, like every constitutional authority, is necessarily limited in scope.[62] For Schmitt, broad amendments could be made, but not revisions to the fundamental political decisions forming the substance of the Constitution. For example, a constitutional amendment transforming a democratic State into a totalitarian monarchy would not be constitutional.[63]

From the twentieth century onwards, cases concerning unconstitutional constitutional amendments often concerned basic rights, either enshrined explicitly as unamendable or implicitly argued to have this status. Article 79(3) of the German *Grundgesetz*, for example, prohibits amendments affecting human dignity, the constitutional order, or the basic institutional principles establishing Germany as a democratic State. Other protected principles included the separation between Church and State,[64] Islam as the State religion,[65] democratic governance,[66] and the separation of powers.[67] These

[59] EJ Sieyès, *Political Writings* (London, Hackett, 2003) 136. See also A Le Pillouer, 'Pouvoir constituent originaire et pouvoir constituent derive: à propos de l'émergence d'une distinction conceptuelle' (2005–06) 25–26 *Revue d'histoire des facultés de droit et de la science juridique* 123.

[60] See, inter alia, Mexican Constitution 1824, Art 3; Venezuelan Constitution 1830, Art 228; Venezuelan Constitution 1858, Art 164; Ecuadorian Constitutions of 1843, Art 110; 1851, Art 139; 1852, Art 143; 1967, Art 258; and 2008, Art 441.

[61] See MF Mohallem, 'Immutable Clauses and Judicial Review: Social Rights and Politics in the Jurisprudence of India, Brazil and South Africa' (Westminster Graduate Conference on Law and Politics: Democracy, Human Rights and Power, 11 June 2010) 6–7.

[62] C Schmitt, *Constitutional Theory* (London, Duke University Press, 2008) 150.

[63] One may perhaps allow one's self a smile here. It is a well-known fact that Schmitt became involved with the National Socialist regime after its ascent to power in Weimar Germany. The fact that this was accomplished via the notorious 1933 *Ermächtigungsgesetz* (Enabling Act), which transformed Weimar Germany from a constitutional democracy to a totalitarian police State, and which itself effectively abrogated much of the Weimar Constitution, does not exactly sit easily with Schmitt's doctrinal position here.

[64] Portuguese Constitution 1976, Art 228; Angolan Constitution 2010, Art 236; Congan Constitution 2006, Art 220.

[65] Bahrain Constitution 1973, Art 120; Iranian Constitution 1979, Art 177; Algerian Constitution 1989, Art 178.

[66] Czech Constitution 1992, Art 9.

[67] Greek Constitution 1975, Art 110; Portuguese Constitution 1976, Art 288; Brazilian Constitution 1988, Art 60(4).

provisions rarely found themselves challenged, except in specific jurisdictions and circumstances, such as the long-running controversy in Turkey between the secular Constitution and the ruling AKP party which wishes to abrogate elements of its secularism (*laiklik*). Instead, the elevation of basic fundamental rights to potentially unamendable constitutional norms formed the centre point for much of the debate in this field. Turkey is nonetheless an interesting case, since the *Anayasa Mahkemesi* has seen fit to review the constitutionality of constitutional amendments with regards to their substance, despite the fact that the 1982 Constitution restricts such review to a review on formal grounds (Article 148(1)). This process is indicative of a broader trend amongst courts in such circumstances, which will set aside formal rules as regards procedure and jurisdiction when the values at stake in the case at hand are of such magnitude that to do otherwise would be profoundly unjust and contrary to the spirit of the law. This trend mirrors the principle that equity looks to the substance rather than the form, and is itself mirrored by the reasoning of the ICJ in the *Nicaragua* jurisdiction hearing, discussed earlier.

In recent decades, however, fundamental rights have played a leading role in cases where the constitutionality of constitutional amendments has been questioned. In the Indian Supreme Court, for example, in the celebrated *GolakNath* case, it was found – albeit obiter – that no amendment which violated the fundamental rights provisions of the Indian Constitution would be held constitutional.[68] The argument underlying the Court's reasoning ran thus: per Article 13(2), any law abridging these rights is void. The Court decided that a constitutional amendment was itself a sort of 'law', and hence must be held void if it purported to abridge said rights. Further, in *Kesavanda Bharati v State of Kerala*, the Supreme Court, although overruling *GolakNath* (holding that 'law' does not refer to a constitutional amendment), nonetheless held that 'the power to amend the constitution does not include the power to alter the basic structure, or framework of the constitution so as to change its identity'.[69] This 'basic structure' doctrine was used as a bulwark to protect, inter alia, fundamental rights. After *Kesavanda*, the Indian Supreme Court used the doctrine on four further occasions to strike down the validity of amendments to the Constitution.[70] The rationale for this continued invocation was best expressed in the *Minerva Mills* case: 'If by a constitutional amendment, Parliament were granted unlimited power of amendment, it would cease to be an authority under the Constitution, but would become supreme over it'.[71]

[68] *GolakNath v Punjab* [1967] All Ind Rep 1643 (SC).

[69] *Kesavanda Bharati v State of Kerala* [1973] All Ind Rep 1461 (SC).

[70] *Indira Nehru Gandhi v Raj Narain* [1975] All Ind Rep 2299 (SC); *Minerva Mills v India* [1980] All Ind Rep 1789 (SC); *Sambamurthy v Andhra Pradesh* [1987] AIR 663 (SC); *Chandrakumar v Union of India* [1997] All Ind Rep (SC) 1125.

[71] *Minerva Mills v India* [1980] All Ind Rep 1824 (SC).

This quotation helps to shed light on the reasoning of the Court, and underlines the importance of the basic structure doctrine. A seeming *excès de pouvoir* on the part of the Court is seemingly necessary for the preservation of normative order. A limited exception to the hierarchy of rules is justified in order to preserve and ensure the effective functioning of this hierarchy of rules.[72] After the adoption of the basic structure doctrine by the Indian Supreme Court, it was adopted in a virtually identical manner by the neighbouring Nepalese,[73] Bangladeshi[74] and Pakistani[75] legal orders. However, the doctrine failed to find favour in Malaysia, Singapore and Sri Lanka.

The idea of a limited amendment power is also prevalent in many African legal systems. Here, the influence of the French and Portuguese traditions on this subject is quite clearly evident, particularly in Francophone[76] and Lusophone[77] States. However, the theory has not been universally adopted throughout the continent[78] although the theory has been influential in South Africa. The Indian legal system was a significant source of inspiration for the drafters of the South African Constitution; ergo this should not come as a great surprise. However, the Indian basic structure doctrine has not been fully and formally incorporated into South African law by the Constitutional Court, despite positive reference to it by the judiciary.[79] A revealing statement was made by the Court in the case of *Premier of KwaZulu-Natal v President of the Republic of South Africa*. Here, Mahomed DP, with the rest of the judges concurring, stated that: 'It may be that a purported amendment to the Constitution, following the formal procedures prescribed by the Constitution, but radically and fundamentally restructuring and reorganising the fundamental premises of the constitution, might not qualify as an "amendment" at all'.[80]

This position, although case law on the subject is sparse, has received broad approval throughout a variety of African jurisdictions.

It would be possible to continue our study here, undertaking an appraisal of the various positions on unconstitutional constitutional amendments worldwide. However, such an endeavour would be over-burdensome for

[72] See S Krishnaswamy, *Democracy and Constitutionalism in India: A Study of the Basic Structure Doctrine* (Oxford, Oxford University Press, 2009).

[73] M Hutt, 'Drafting the Nepal Constitution' (1991) 31 *Asian Survey* 1020, 1028–32.

[74] *Anwar Hossain Chowdhury v Bangladesh* (1989) 41 Dominion LR 165 (App Div).

[75] *Darvesh M Arbey v Federation of Pakistan*, PLD 1980 Lah 846.

[76] Algerian Constitution 1989, Art 178; Chad Constitution 1996, Art 223, Malian Constitution 1992, Art 118; Senegalese Constitution 2001, Art 103.

[77] Angolan Constitution 1975, Art 159; Constitution of Equatorial Guinea 1991, Art 104; Mozambiquean Constitution 2004, Art 292; Burundian Constitution 2005, Art 299.

[78] See Namibian Constitution 1990, Art 131.

[79] A Sachs, 'Making Rights Work: The South African Experience' in P Smith (ed), *Making Rights Work* (Dartmouth, Ashgate, 1999) 10; See also S Terreblanche, 'Privelegie teen selfinkriminasie: 'n tyd om weer te dink' (1991) 7 *South African Journal of Criminal Justice* 177.

[80] *Premier of KwaZulu-Natal v President of the Republic of South Africa* [1995] ZACC 10.

the present purposes. The current brief overview is sufficient to raise awareness of the fact that such a doctrine exists, at least in certain jurisdictions worldwide. Whether such a 'basic structure' doctrine could ever justify derogations or exceptions to peremptory norms at international level is another story altogether, and would not necessarily be aided by further study of comparative cases. Nonetheless, it remains clear that the 'basic structure' doctrine has much to recommend it at a conceptual level. What is also interesting is that any effort via an amendment to confer to an organ – be it Parliament or the executive – rights abrogated from the Constitution to the extent that this organ becomes superior to the Constitution effectively amounts to a *détournement de pouvoir* on the part of the organ which initiated the amendment. This is little more than an extension of ultra vires doctrine – itself a manifestation of the principle of good faith – to the constitutional sphere. Where, conversely, the 'basic structure' is violated by the suspension of fundamental rights, those rights, being fundamental, may be seen as irrevocable *droits acquis*, which have been assured to citizens by the constitutional order. Abrogation of these rights necessarily constitutes a detriment to citizenry; therefore, the State effectively finds itself 'estopped' from denying these rights to its citizens via an amendment. These cases demonstrate the capacity of general principles of law and related doctrines to modify even the highest of norms in limited and extreme circumstances. While, again, cases involving these general principles applied at a constitutional level combined with fundamental rights concerns may be particularly interesting for the purposes of the present discussion, it would be premature at this stage to discuss their potential for transposition to the international legal sphere. However, an in-depth examination of such a case, and the arguments for and against the idea of unconstitutional constitutional amendments may be useful in order to garner perspective here. The case which I have chosen for examination in this regard is that of *The State (Ryan and Others) v Lennon and Others*, a 1935 decision of the Irish Supreme Court.[81]

E. *The State (Ryan) v Lennon*

The case in question centred on the 1922 Constitution of the Irish Free State. The fledgling State was still feeling the reverberations of the 1921–22 Civil War and public unrest was still rife throughout the 1920s. As a result, a number of Public Safety laws were enacted, which provided for intern-

[81] *The State (at the prosecution of Jeremiah Ryan and Others) v Captain Michael Lennon, Governor of the Military Detention Barracks, Arbour Hill, Dublin, Colonel Frank Bennett and Others, The Members of the Constitution (Special Powers) Tribunal ; and in the Matter of the Courts of Justice Act 1924 and in the Matter of the Constitution of Saorstát na hÉireann* [1935] 1 IR 170. See www.courts.ie/supremecourt/.../State%20(Ryan)%20v%20Lennon_1934.rtf (Retrieved 3 December 2010).

ment as well as for trials by military tribunal.[82] Such emergency measures did not sit easily with the guarantee of personal liberty which was enshrined in Article 6 of the Constitution and the Article 70 limitations on the power of military tribunals.[83] Such measures were made possible by an extraordinary provision which had been inserted into the Constitution, providing for its amendment by way of ordinary legislation for a period of eight years after its enactment. This power had been inserted at the 11th hour, and was justified by the document's chief draughtsman, Hugh Kennedy, the Irish Chief Justice, as useful 'so that drafting or verbal amendments, not altogether unlikely to appear necessary . . . might be made without the more elaborate process proper for the purpose of more important amendments'.[84] Kennedy was later to lament his own draughtsmanship in this regard, since such a provision was to pave the way for alterations 'far removed in principle from the ideas and ideals before the minds of the first authors of the instrument'.[85] The most striking of such alterations were achieved under the Constitution (Amendment No 16) Act of 1928 and the Constitution (Amendment No 17) Act of 1931. The former extended the period allowing for constitutional amendment by ordinary legislation from 8 to 16 years, and the latter, enacted in the extended period, introduced a new Article 2A into the Constitution. The content of this new Article was expansive, with 5 parts, 32 Sections and an Appendix, but importantly, it provided for a standing military tribunal, composed of army officers selected by the executive, which was empowered to try any offence which was referred to it (again, by the executive), from which there might be no right of appeal, and which was empowered to impose any penalty, including death, even if this contradicted ordinary law. Furthermore, Article 2A stated that all other Articles of the Constitution should be construed subject to those of Article 2A, and if irreconcilable differences arose, Article 2A should prevail.

The case involved an appeal from the High Court by several persons who had been arrested and tried under the provisions of Article 2A, and who wished to dispute its constitutionality on the basis of the unconstitutionality of the two aforementioned constitutional Amendment Acts. It has been described as a 'jurisprudential goldmine', an assessment with which I warmly concur.[86] It pits a resort to higher principles – mostly through an invocation of natural law – by the Chief Justice and drafter of

[82] O Clarke, 'The State (Ryan) v Lennon: A Victory for Man over God?' (2007) 15 *Irish Student Law Review* 136, 137.

[83] G Hogan, 'A Desert Island Case set in the Silver Sea: The State (Ryan) v Lennon (1934)' in E O'Dell (ed), *Leading Cases of the Twentieth Century* (Dublin, Roundhall Sweet and Maxwell, 2000) 81.

[84] H Kennedy (writing as Aodh Ó Cinnéide), '*Vorwort*' in L Kohn, *Die Verfassung des Irischen Freistaats* (Heidelberg, Mohr, 1928) xiii.

[85] See Clarke (2007) (n 82) 137.

[86] ibid, 138.

the Constitution, Hugh Kennedy, against a reluctant, sarcastic, but strictly positivistic reading of the two offending amendments by FitzGibbon and Murnaghan JJ, and while its relevance in a discussion of the legality of humanitarian intervention may not be entirely obvious from the outset, I would beg the patience of the reader while I attempt to explain the connection.

Hugh Kennedy's judgment is the important one for the purposes of our study, and while ultimately his renowned defence of his vision of the 1922 Constitution as a document founded on the basic principles of natural law, fundamental rights and popular sovereignty was to finish in the minority, the resultant positivist victory was to be a hollow one; Irish constitutional law was to be strongly influenced by the ideals which Kennedy enunciated right up until the present day. Kennedy's dissenting judgment is a jurisprudential *tour de force*, placing principles emanating from an overreaching conception of popular sovereignty and natural law above the text of the constitutional amendments. Kennedy's statement upholds natural law on the basis that it is irrational to conceive of certain rights as being self-evident and existing beyond the limits of legislation, and yet allowing the legislature free reign to erode and destroy such rights.[87] Kennedy argues that the basic tenets of the Constitution were agreed upon by a constituent assembly of the Irish people, and that such tenets may only be altered with the explicit and express consent of the Irish people, either by way of a referendum, or by the re-convocation of a constituent assembly, rather than via the vote of a simple parliamentary majority. Kennedy employs the language of natural law and basic principles, but there is, interestingly, a frequent invocation of such terminology in defence of individual rights. This is quite singular, since the language of human rights was yet to be fully developed in the 1930s. For example, Kennedy quotes with approval the statement of Alexander Hamilton that

> [t]he creation of crimes after the commission of the fact or, in other words, the subjecting of men to punishment for things which, when they were done, were breaches of no law, and the practice of arbitrary imprisonments, have been, in all ages, the favourite and most formidable instruments of tyranny.[88]

The idea that the creation of retrospective legislation which deprived individuals of their basic rights was reprehensible and tyrannical was not a new one, as Hamilton's statement attests, but the argument that such individual rights as those arising from due process may not be unjustly fettered by governmental or parliamentary edict is more in tune with post-Second World War ideals.

[87] ibid, 140.

[88] A Hamilton, *The Federalist,* No LXXXIV, quoted by Kennedy CJ in *State (Ryan) v Lennon* [1935] IR 1, 19. See also Henry Cabot Lodge (ed), *The Works of Alexander Hamilton* (New York, Putnam, 1904).

Kennedy's judgment makes reference to a publication by the Irish Government Stationery Office, entitled *Index to the Legislation passed by the Oireachtas in the Years 1922–32*,[89] which states that the new Article 2A 'is in the nature of a Public Safety Act'. However, while Kennedy concedes that extreme measures amounting to derogations from fundamental rights may be justified in times of emergency, he argues that Article 2A, and the amendment which rendered it a part of the Constitution, are nothing of the sort. They require no emergency and no extreme circumstances to be put into effect, merely the judgment of the executive that it is 'expedient' to do so. Such expediency extends to the sentencing of any individual to death for any crime the executive chooses, 'to be executed in such as manner as it directs, including even the most barbarous lethal process, should a particular "Tribunal" at some future time be overwhelmed by passion or be constituted of members of a perverted morality'.[90] Evidence rules are cast aside in such cases, where certain selected members of the Garda Síochána (police force) are permitted to give oral testimony, declared to be 'conclusive evidence, incapable of being rebutted or questioned by cross-examination, rebutting evidence, or otherwise'.[91] Police of any rank are also permitted to detain 'suspects', without proof of suspicion, and without charge, for up to 32 days before bringing them before the tribunal, which itself is staffed by military commanders rather than judges, specifically selected for the purpose by the executive. Kennedy is forceful about the incompatibility of Article 2A with basic notions such as due process and the rule of law: 'In general it may be said that some of the provisions to which I have been referring are the antithesis of the rule of law, and are, within their scope, the rule of anarchy'.[92]

Kennedy goes on to state that 'it is clear that the new Article 2A is no mere amendment in, but effects a radical alteration of, the basic scheme and principles of the Constitution enacted for the Saorstát by the Constituent Assembly'.[93] Kennedy notes the strict separation of powers laid down in the original Article 2, and points out that Article 2A amounts to a usurpation of effective judicial power by the executive. He goes on to say that

> it falls to the Courts of Justice of the State to stand between the citizen and the Executive . . . as the only defence of the citizen against encroachments on his rights and liberties, always in danger of such encroachments when watchfulness slackens.[94]

[89] It should be noted here that Oireachtas refers to the Irish Gaelic term for the two Houses of Parliament when referred to in tandem. Dáil and Seanad refer to the lower and upper Houses respectively.

[90] Kennedy CJ in *State (Ryan) v Lennon* [1935] IR 1, 198.

[91] ibid, 199.

[92] ibid, 198.

[93] ibid, 200. Saorstát refers to Saorstat Éireann, the official, Irish Gaelic name for the Irish Free State.

[94] Kennedy CJ in *State (Ryan) v Lennon* [1935] IR 1, 200. See also Farwell LJ in *Dyson v Attorney-General* [1911] 1 KB 410, 424.

Therefore, the disestablishment of the Irish courts' protection in such matters amounts to a disestablishment of one of the fundamental tenets of the Constitution. However, Kennedy is forceful about the role of the courts in such circumstances, stating that 'we must be watchdogs to protect against unlawful encroachment and to maintain intact . . . the principles and provisions embodied in the Constitution for the protection of the liberties of the citizens in mass and individually'.[95]

Kennedy notes the revisionist position adopted by the Government Stationery Office of the Irish Free State, which attributes the redaction and enactment of the 1922 Constitution to the Oireachtas (combined Houses of Parliament). Kennedy notes that it was rather he himself who principally drafted the document, and the Third Dáil Éireann, sitting as a Constituent Assembly, which enacted said Constitution. The Oireachtas did not come into existence until the Constitution itself had entered into force on 6 December 1922. In light of this historical clarification, he asserts that since the Constituent Assembly conferred a limited, eight-year power upon the Oireachtas to alter the content of the Constitution, such a power could only be extended or altered by re-convocation of the Constituent Assembly. In this manner, Kennedy argues that Article 50, which confers upon the Oireachtas power to amend the Constitution, is 'limited and circumscribed by a number of restrictions in respect of the manner and conditions of its exercise and of the substance of the amendments permitted'.[96]

Kennedy's outlining of the circumscription of such powers is, however, by modern standards somewhat antiquated. He refers first to the Constitution Act, the Act which establishes the 1922 Constitution as law, noting that it refers to all lawful authority flowing from God to the people, as the basis for the natural law pillar of his argument. Secondly he refers, on somewhat firmer ground, to Article 2 of the 1922 Constitution, unaltered by Article 2A, which states that 'all powers of government and all authority, legislative, executive and judicial, in Ireland, are derived from the people of Ireland'. It is in this second excerpt that he frames the popular sovereignty pillar of his discourse.

Dealing first with natural law, while Kennedy is certainly correct in his assertion that much of the brutality of Article 2A necessarily offends against natural law principles, his citation of the Constitution Act – and more particularly of one sentence of this Act – is illustrative of the shaky ground upon which he was to found his argument. The fact that Kennedy resorted to this Act is a result of the fact that the 1922 Constitution itself failed to refer to God or natural law at any point in its text. An earlier draft of the constitutional document, replete with several religious references, had been rejected. While it was plain that Kennedy felt that the most

[95] Kennedy CJ in *State (Ryan) v Lennon* [1935] IR 1, 200.
[96] ibid, 204.

recent changes were repugnant to the spirit of the Constitution, he struggled for a means of expressing this. Resort to natural law was a misguided approach, as Murnaghan and FitzGibbon JJ were quick to point out in their majority judgments. Therefore, the resort to natural law principles, while intellectually interesting, is surprisingly (for the Chief Justice and a noted academic) poorly founded in law, and we would do well to turn our attention to other aspects of his argument.

Kennedy's second qualm also relates to the Constitution Act, and seems, on the face of it, to be better founded than his appeals to the natural law. In Section 2 of that Act – which was enacted by the Constituent Assembly – it is stated that

> if any provisions of the said Constitution or of any amendment thereof or of any law made thereunder is in any respect repugnant to any of the provisions of the Scheduled Treaty, it shall, to the extent only of such repugnancy, be absolutely void and inoperative.[97]

This argument was based on the fact that the British Parliament and the Irish Constituent Assembly had passed one single Act which passed effective control of 26 counties of the island of Ireland to the Irish people, under the supervision of the British Sovereign. The 'Scheduled Treaty' referred to the Treaty between Ireland and the United Kingdom, and repugnancy with the provisions of this Treaty was impossible for the Constitution, per the provisions of the Constitution Act. However, Kennedy – again surprisingly – dismissed the potential legal consequences that Commonwealth membership could entail and failed to rely on the international treaty to any great degree.

Where Kennedy did find more purchase was the concept of popular sovereignty as a source of general principles, which the Constitution was bound to respect. Per Kennedy,

> the Constituent Assembly . . . enunciated certain propositions, containing statements of fundamental principle in the constitutional sphere so expressed as to convey clearly the intention that they are to be accepted for the purposes of the Constitution as immutable and absolute, subject only to the specific qualifications expressed in certain cases.[98]

Amongst these propositions, Kennedy holds, are the separation of powers, and the inviolability of personal liberty, per Article 6 of the Constitution, 'except in accordance with law'. In addition, the phrase 'in accordance with the law' would appear to be a limited one, since

> [a]n enactment to the general effect that a citizen may be taken and detained in custody, without being charged with an offence known to the law but just

[97] Constitution of the Irish Free State (Saorstát Eireann) Act 1922 www.irishstatutebook.ie/1922/en/act/pub/0001/index.html.

[98] Kennedy CJ in *State (Ryan) v Lennon* [1935] IR 1, 208.

> whenever and for as long as a soldier or policeman deems it expedient . . . would be invalid and void and could not be sustained under the power of amendment.[99]

Kennedy held that the same principles applied regarding Article 7 (inviolability of private dwellings), Article 8 (freedom of conscience and religion) and Article 9 (freedom of expression and freedom of assembly, subject to public morality). Per Kennedy, the Third Dáil Éireann (the Constituent Assembly) had effectively proclaimed certain general principles to be 'fundamental and absolute (except as expressly qualified) and, so, necessarily, immutable'.[100]

Kennedy's reliance upon the powers of the Constituent Assembly to implicitly render sections of the Constitution unalterable did not end there, however. Having attacked the substance of the Constitution (Amendment No 17) Act of 1931, he proceeded, using the same tools, to attack the substance of the Constitution (Amendment No 16) Act of 1928, which had extended the period during which the Oireachtas might enact ordinary legislation to amend the Constitution from 8 to 16 years. It was notable that amendments to the Constitution needed to be passed by both Houses of Parliament, then submitted to a popular referendum, requiring either a majority of registered voters or two-thirds of those who actually cast their ballots to vote in favour of an amendment. This was a rather high bar. However, for the first eight years, a special power was conferred upon the Oireachtas to amend the Constitution by way of ordinary legislation. However, Kennedy noted that amendment by way of referendum was also possible during this eight-year period, and that such a dual amendment procedure suggested that only certain kinds of amendment would be suitable for enactment under what Kennedy repeatedly refers to as a 'special power'.[101] Such a position is generally accepted in France since the Third Republic, where technical and procedural amendments may be undertaken by way of legislative enactment, but where significant and radical constitutional amendments require direct consultation of the citizens. Kennedy, however, does not refer to the French constitutional tradition in this regard, and we may ask whether he was aware of it, as there is no evidence of him having spoken French. Under the French model – which Kennedy's reasoning mimics – serious changes such as those effected via the 16th and 17th Amendments to the 1922 Constitution would be impermissible without prior consultation of the people via a referendum. This particularly applies to the former of the two amendments, since the eight-year special power was seen by Kennedy as a 'grace' bestowed upon the Oireachtas by the Constituent Assembly, and

99 ibid.
100 ibid, 209.
101 ibid, 210.

not something which the Oireachtas itself could extend, stating that if the power to amend the Constitution during the eight-year period included power to amend the length of the period itself, he would have expected this to be explicitly stated.[102] Kennedy believed that the power to make amendments was not an essential component of a Constitution, since amendment can always be effectively achieved by re-convocation of a constituent assembly in any case, which could amend the former text or simply enact a new Constitution.

For a combination of the above reasons, the Chief Justice held that the Constitution (Amendment No 16) Act, No 10 of 1929 was invalid, and the amendment of the Constitution contained therein was inoperative, null and void. By extension, the Constitution (Amendment No 17) Act, No 37 of 1931 was enacted ultra vires and without the proper procedure, and therefore never became law. Further, the Chief Justice noted that had the new Article 2A, or at least parts thereof been validly enacted, it would have been incapable of becoming part of the Constitution even if it had been amended prior to the expiration of the eight-year period, by reason of its content.

Kennedy's judgment is a fascinating one for a number of reasons. For the purposes of our discussion, however, it is germane to note that his opinion as regards the unconstitutionality of the two amendments was based, at least in part, upon their incompatibility with certain general principles of law which Kennedy, as drafter of the 1922 Constitution, regarded as fundamental. Amongst such principles were elements of the natural law *corpus* and the notion of popular sovereignty as cornerstones of the Irish constitutional order, but other principles were also involved. A close reading of the judgment reveals principles which are perhaps more familiar to private lawyers, such as the ultra vires doctrine, *excès de pouvoir*, and *abus de droit*, or at least concepts closely analogous to such principles.

Quite aside from the above, however, it is important to restate the fact that the Chief Justice found himself in a minority in the Irish Supreme Court. Murnaghan and FitzGibbon JJ both penned judgments which are almost as fascinating as that devised by Kennedy. FitzGibbon's judgment, in particular, is strongly instructive regarding the dilemma faced by the judges in the Supreme Court. In clinging to a more positivist interpretation and upholding the 1922 Constitution, as amended, FitzGibbon nonetheless did his best to expose the inadequacy of the protection afforded to individual rights, since no rights were sacrosanct unless expressly stated as such. FitzGibbon points out that the separation of powers to which Kennedy seems so attached means that it is the duty of the courts 'to ascertain and declare the law to the best of our ability and we are not

[102] ibid, 210–14.

concerned with the wisdom or propriety of the Acts of the Legislature'.[103] He points out that the potential for rights protection to be effective and immutable is removed by the *caveat* allowing for derogations in accordance with law, the content of which may be determined by the legislature. In rejecting the argument that the rights clauses in the Irish Constitution may be held to be modelled on that of France and the United States, FitzGibbon argues that

> the fact that the Constitutions of other countries prohibit such invasions of the rights of liberty and property, and such extraordinary innovations in the methods of administering justice in criminal cases as have been introduced into our Constitution by Amendment No. 17, affords no ground for condemning as unconstitutional in this country, or as contrary to any inalienable rights of an Irish citizen, an enactment which appears to have received the almost unanimous support of the *Oireachtas*.[104]

Indeed, it would seem that any kind of abuse of this kind would be valid, regardless of how repugnant it may be to the general principles which are held dear by other democratic and civilised nations.[105] FitzGibbon went on, to somewhat darkly speculate as to whether these new amendments 'more truly represent our national ideals',[106] adding, in a tone dipped in sarcasm, that

> we find the Briton's conceptions of liberty and justice set forth in his *Magna Charta* and his Bill of Rights; those of the American in his Declaration of Independence and his Constitution; while those of the Gael are enshrined in Amendment No. 17.[107]

In finding that nothing in the 'spirit' of the Constitution prevented amendments that, in essence, went so far as to rip the original text and the intent of its drafters asunder, FitzGibbon's judgment (and that of his colleague Murnaghan) should seem logically to have been the authoritative ones. Indeed, in the legal dispute at hand, this was the case. The decision of the High Court was upheld by the Supreme Court, the order of *habeus corpus* was refused, and the constitutionality of the two offending amendments was upheld. However, in the longer term, the case became massively influential, and it was to Kennedy's judgment and not those of his colleagues in the majority that most attention has been paid. Indeed, despite FitzGibbon's sarcastic pronouncements, Kennedy's judgment – rather than Amendment No 17 – is seen by some as a cornerstone of the foundation of an indigenous Irish legal *Volksgeist*, distinct from the British common law

[103] FitzGibbon J in *State (Ryan) v Lennon* [1935] IR 1, 229.
[104] ibid, 235.
[105] Clarke (2007) (n 82) 143.
[106] FitzGibbon J in *State (Ryan) v Lennon* [1935] IR 1, 235.
[107] ibid.

tradition.[108] The 'loopholes' which permitted the bastardisation of the 1922 Constitution were avoided in the drafting of the 1937 Constitution, which came into force only two years after the reporting of *State (Ryan) v Lennon*. The 1937 Constitution affords tighter and more concrete protection to fundamental rights, dedicates the document 'In the Name of the Most Holy Trinity, from Whom is all authority and to Whom, as our final end, all actions both of men and States must be referred' which gives a stronger indication of natural law influence, and also affords an important – perhaps even pre-eminent – position to popular sovereignty, as evidenced by a series of cases from the 1990s.[109] Such measures brought the protection of individual rights in Ireland into line with those in other democratic and civilised nations, surpassing that of many other jurisdictions.

A joint reading of the judgments of Kennedy and FitzGibbon JJ, combined with an awareness of the influence of *State (Ryan) v Lennon* on the Irish legal *Volksgeist* is instructive on a number of levels. FitzGibbon and Kennedy disagreed as to whether such a pronounced schism between the 1922 Constitution's original ideals and the text as amended caused its invalidity. However, both recognised the fact that certain general tenets of democratic and civilised constitutional order existed in other jurisdictions, and had existed in Ireland prior to the enactment of the offending amendments. FitzGibbon's sarcastic assertion that Amendment No 17 represented the Irishman's basic conceptions of liberty and justice are generally seen as the expression of the profound frustration that he felt at having to find in favour of the legality of such morally reprehensible constitutional amendments. In essence, the protection that certain general and fundamental principles were afforded in other jurisdictions was lacking in Irish law. That both sides of such a prominent judgment found this situation so reprehensible that it prompted vitriol and sarcasm on one side, and resort to dubious legal reasoning based upon concepts such as natural law on the other, indicates that the tenets of the constitutional amendments offended deeply against some deeply-held shared values. What these values are may be difficult to discern *in concreto*, but it is clear that the Government's actions in enacting Amendments Nos 16 and 17 amounted to acts that went deeply against the spirit of the powers entrusted to them by the 1922 Constitution, a breach of good faith and an abuse of their position. Whether such an act, interpreted according to the laws of Ireland and according to the provisions of the 1922 Constitution, was legal and legitimate (per FitzGibbon) or was not (per Kennedy), is not necessarily the most important question that this case raises. Rather, both

[108] See T Mohr, 'British Involvement in the Creation of the Constitution of the Irish Free State' (2008) 30 *Dublin University Law Journal* 166.

[109] *Re: Article 26 and the Information (Termination of Pregnancies) Bill* [1995] 1 IR 1; *Hanafin v Minister for the Environment* [1996] 2 IR 321; and *Riordan v An Taoiseach (No 1)* [1999] 4 IR 325. See Clarke (2007) (n 82) 146.

judges agreed that certain principles existed which could, in certain constitutional regimes, derogate from the letter of the law, and even perhaps invalidate constitutional amendments, which would otherwise be completely legally valid. Where they differed was whether the Irish Free State could be included into such a category, with FitzGibbon's majority judgment concluding that it could not, simply due to the legal draughtsmanship which handed the keys to unfettered amendment, and therefore, to unlimited power, to the executive. In essence, Kennedy, as drafter of the Constitution, had only himself to blame.

However, it is instructive to see that the 1937 Constitution differed so greatly from its predecessor, and that fundamental rights, equity and general principles of law – all, albeit, in different respects – enjoy a significant place in the current Irish legal architecture. It may be argued that, owing to the accepted significance of *State (Ryan) v Lennon*, and its influence upon Irish jurisprudence, that incompatibility with general principles of fundamental importance is an unsustainable model in a 'civilised', developed legal system. Such a position is borne out by Kennedy's resort to every possible means to justify voiding Amendments Nos 16 and 17, by FitzGibbon's sarcasm, and above all by the fact that the document which was soon to replace the 1922 Constitution took such careful heed of the problems of the past. Article 38 of the PCIJ and ICJ Statutes speaks of 'the general principles of law recognised by civilised nations'. It would seem clear that the word 'civilised' resonates a little more meaning than it is generally credited with nowadays when one considers the implications of a case such as *State (Ryan) v Lennon*. The fact that these principles were absent from the Irish legal framework created discomfort for Kennedy, Murnaghan and FitzGibbon, one of whom considered them so important that he desperately tried to derive them from different sources, and two of whom contented themselves with scathing sarcasm which amounted to stating that an absence of such principles was an abhorrent reflection upon the protection of rights and the separation of powers in a civilised country – a fairly astonishing moral commentary to accompany a judgment. Further, the situation helped to create the impetus for the incoming Fianna Fáil Government to replace the 1922 Constitution with a document which ensured that adequate, permanent protection would be afforded to the separation of powers, popular sovereignty, natural law and general principles.

That three such significant – albeit diverse – reactions to constitutional amendments, which were enacted according to the letter of the law, were provoked by the content of such amendments evinces the fact that a lack of protection of general principles and fundamental values in a developed legal system is a difficult situation to sustain. Such a situation – allowing governments to employ loopholes and faulty draughtsmanship to act in a manner that would otherwise be ultra vires and contrary to good faith –

does not sit well with the legal culture of a civilised and developed State. The fact that rectification via the 1937 Constitution was necessary is particularly demonstrative in this regard. The word 'civilised' employed in Article 38 of the Statute of the PCIJ and ICJ sits uneasily with modern legal commentators, who see it as an anachronistic throwback to a 1920s vision of the world, with the 'haves' of the European elite being contrasted with the 'have nots' of Asia, Africa and South and Central America.[110] However, if one closely examines the text of the *procès-verbaux* of the Advisory Committee of Jurists that drafted the PCIJ Statute, it is clear that such a position amounts to an oversimplification. 'Civilised' refers rather to the level of development of the legal systems that are to be considered in deciding which general principles will fall into this category. The fact that 'general principles' and 'civilised nations' are mentioned together in the same sentence indicates a close nexus between the two concepts. The sources of law clauses in the PCIJ and ICJ Statutes do not seek to impose a purely Westernised legal vision upon the international community of States, but rather continue the traditional international legal vision of voluntarism by and large. However, the most progressive move towards a 'shared values' approach is contained in the 'general principles' clause. Limiting 'general principles' to a category of States (or 'nations') with 'civilised' legal systems reflects a certain value judgment by the drafters of the PCIJ Statute – and, by extension, by the community of States that accepted Article 38 as a restatement of the sources of law – as regards the level of development of legal systems to be considered. The fact that *State (Ryan) v Lennon* caused such a furore due to the inability of Irish constitutional law to permit, in extreme circumstances, general principles such as good faith and the ultra vires doctrine to adequately fetter the power of the executive to abuse their own position, indicates that the Irish legal system had fallen foul of the requirement to recognise general principles of law which are necessary for 'civilised nations'. This explains FitzGibbon's allusions to other legal systems, and Kennedy's generally repugnant attitude.

If we are to argue that the failure to adequately recognise general principles of law pushes a legal system outside that group which is considered to constitute the category of 'civilised nations' – and such a position is certainly suggested by the wording of Article 38 of the ICJ Statute as well as the judgments of both FitzGibbon and Kennedy – then that legal system and its conception of general principles cease to be relevant in framing and defining the constitutive elements of the third source of international law. The Irish Free State, in the mid-1930s, was therefore no longer a State the legal system of which might be considered in deciding cases before the PCIJ which dealt with 'general principles of law recog-

[110] See ch 2.

nised by civilised nations' since it failed to adequately espouse such principles at national level. The logical consequence of such a position is that certain general principles must be, if not supra-constitutional, then at least be universally pervasive at all normative levels. Good faith, and related doctrines such as the prohibition of the abuse of rights (*détournement de procedure*), represent perhaps the best examples of these. If such principles may be derogated from at will by governments, then the system would seem to fall foul of the test enunciated in Article 38. This does not necessarily condemn the legal system as illegitimate – since such judgments are inherently value-laden – but it would seem that a legal system which does not *respect* general principles of law, or which attributes to them a lesser or residual value, cannot be considered from an international legal viewpoint when seeking to identify 'civilised nations' which *recognise* general principles of law. Hence, such a position would maintain that unless there exists the potential for general principles to be applied in an effective manner at all normative levels, then such legal systems will not be considered to exert an influence upon the international legal *corpus,* at least in this regard. This is not to say that such general principles must be given a formal status or value within domestic legal systems, particularly since the modalities of reception of such principles are so varied. However, some level of respect for such principles must exist within a developed legal system in order for it to be included within the Article 38 category.

To move a little further with this reasoning, while it is clear that international law and national law are not one and the same thing, it may be held that, in the field of general principles of law, at least, the modality of operation of selected general principles which are transposed to international law from national legal systems will mirror, as closely as is possible and practicable, that of the national legal systems from which they are derived. While it is clear that a norm of *ius cogens* may only be modified by another subsequent norm of the same standing, the modalities of how this modification may take place are somewhat unclear. General principles of law may well exert significant influence upon how, for example, peremptory human rights norms impact upon the (equally peremptory) general prohibition upon the use of force.[111] Bearing this in mind, there is good reason to argue that if legal systems in which general principles may potentially act *infra legem, praeter legem* and very occasionally *contra legem* vis-à-vis all levels of norms are those which may be considered 'civilised' for the purposes of international law, then the same modalities will be applied when using such general principles at international level. This would entail that general principles of law could have a pervasive effect not merely upon norms with which they enjoy hierarchical equality, such as treaty and custom, but also as regards peremptory norms (*ius cogens*).

[111] But see Green (2011) (n 43) for objections to this classification and a discussion thereof.

The above observations shed some light upon the strange role played by general principles of law in the international legal arena, and perhaps go some way to explaining why so few scholars have attacked the subject vigorously and analytically. It is germane to note that the bulk of texts on the sources of international law fail to adequately analyse the modalities of general principles or their origins, preferring merely to make reference to them rhetorically. This reticence mirrors that of the World Court. Norms such as good faith and the prohibition of the abuse of rights are *essential* to the proper functioning of the international legal system. For this reason, as demonstrated above, in a number of jurisdictions they have been used to derogate even constitutional norms, which are, on a hierarchical scale, superior to them. They are not, however, *peremptory,* at least not in the sense of *ius cogens*. Fitting such a category into a classical normative pyramid is not an easy task, though it would seem that there is scope for the argument that the 'basic structure' doctrine or some equivalent of it may be used at international level. Then there is the matter of voluntarist theory. General principles stray furthest from a purely voluntarist conception of international law. Per the classical dictum in the *Lotus* case, voluntarist theory basically entails that 'Restrictions upon the independence of States cannot . . . be presumed'.[112] Such a position has been quoted by many a jurist, but its importance is overblown, as demonstrated by the 2009 *Dispute regarding Navigational and Related Rights on the San Juan River* case. Here, in affording the notion of 'commerce' a (contemporarily dictionary-correct) connotation which could not have been anticipated by the States parties at the time of the Treaty's conclusion, and which was, up until the present day, disputed by Nicaragua, the ICJ effectively crafted a presumption of assent by Nicaragua to the evolution of the meaning of the word 'commerce' in accordance with its normal construction in everyday use.[113] Hence, the overbearing conception of voluntarism in international law described by most commentators may have been somewhat exaggerated.

If the content of general principles may therefore derogate – or even 'merely' regulate the applicability of – norms which follow a more strictly construed conception of voluntarism, then voluntarism – the lynchpin of how international law is justified – becomes a relative, rather than an absolute, indicator, tempered by a deeply-rooted conception of shared values reflecting a global *Volksgeist*. It is on this putative *Volksgeist* that I wish to rely in attempting to proffer a legal solution to the humanitarian intervention conundrum.

[112] *Case of the SS Lotus* PCIJ Rep Series A No 10, 18.

[113] For an excellent analysis of the importance of this case, see M Milanovic, 'The ICJ and Evolutionary Treaty Interpretation' *European Journal of International Law: Talk!* (14 July 2009).

III. THE THIRD EXCEPTION? INTERNATIONAL EQUITY AND HUMANITARIAN INTERVENTION

In the first chapter of this work, I repeatedly criticised the likes of Antonio Cassese and Bruno Simma, whose views on humanitarian intervention in the wake of NATO's Kosovo operation were not, I felt, befitting of scholars at the vanguard of the international legal profession. However, Simma and Cassese epitomised the dominant sentiment that swept through the international legal community at the turn of the century. Strict adherence to international law furnished forth solutions that were inequitable, inhumane and so unjust that it became unconscionable as well as unpalatable to maintain such a position. No one wishes to offer an apology for *genocidaires*, so a variety of solutions which may at best be described as utopian were devised. On the other side of the argument were Ian Brownlie and his associates, rather less numerous than those in the Simma/Cassese camp, who stood firm and offered an affirmatively positivist interpretation of international law, protecting the international legal order from the confusion and instability which the adoption of any of the novel models proposed by the other 'camp' would engender, but equally effectively signalling that nothing could legally be done about dictators committing gross human rights violations against their own citizens if the UN Security Council failed to act.

Apologists for a regime which left the patently culpable unpunished and able to continue their misdeeds, or utopians whose resort to novel perspectives promised to replace legal certainty with moral subjectivity and thereby upset the stability which the international legal order sustains; the humanitarian intervention debate truly seemed one that no argument could win. However, the time has come to demonstrate that there exists a third way; a third approach, based on the third source of international law, which may unlock the door to a third exception to the prohibition on the use of force by States. One may dub this an equitable framework for humanitarian intervention.

Grounding a legal doctrine largely on general principles of law in the international sphere is not a task which may be undertaken lightly. As noted earlier, their existence in international law is well established, but evidence of general principles in State practice is difficult to establish, while the World Court has been recalcitrant in applying them concretely. Nonetheless, we are not left without firm indicators of how and when such principles may be applied. After all, the World Court has, albeit reluctantly, invoked general principles as a source of law both in dissenting and separate opinions on the one hand, and occasionally in the *dispositif*, on the other. Furthermore, it should not come as any great surprise that State practice has shown little evidence of general principles, since such principles are not derived from State practice in the way that customary international law may be, but rather relate to certain internal norms within the national legal systems of States. While our knowledge of the parameters and applicability of general principles may be somewhat less refined and focussed than that regarding treaty law or customary international law, this does not preclude general principles from being useful – and even decisive – in the solution of legal conundrums. They enjoy, after all, normative equality with the other two main sources of law. Also, if we are to reach a –surely desirable – juncture where general principles may be said to be comprehensively understood and their import accurately calculated vis-à-vis other normative categories, then shying away from the study of such principles – as the international legal community has lamentably done in past decades – is hardly the way to achieve such an outcome. On the contrary, we should not be afraid to tackle general principles with enthusiasm and vigour. While studies on general principles require any scholar to be simultaneously a comparative jurist, an international legal scholar and – to an extent – a legal theorist, this area, perhaps due to the difficulty in dealing with it adequately, has received little attention. There is room for new study to be conducted here, and for new theories to be propounded. Both the science surrounding, and the literature concerning, such principles are certainly inadequate, particularly since the rarely-acknowledged confusion over the parameters of the operability of such principles and their various *mises en oeuvre* is hardly conducive to legal certainty, which must represent a key value in the international legal system if the (relative) stability of world affairs is to be preserved. General principles, being somewhat less well understood than other categories, have been overlooked time and again. However, this does nothing to denude them of their normative potency. They have become the 'elephant in the room' of international law, something which is undoubtedly important, but which most scholars choose to ignore because to deal with it would be too difficult, too controversial, or too taboo.

I do not intend to be as reticent regarding the potential that general principles hold as many of those who have gone before me. It is my contention that such principles may hold the key to the solutions to a great many legal dilemmas. That I have chosen to attempt to apply what knowledge I have garnered concerning their operability to the question of humanitarian intervention alone reflects the restrictions of what can be properly argued in a work of this length, rather than a belief that general principles do not have the potential to bestow solutions to other tricky legal problems in international law.

A. The Problem: The United Nations Charter and Human Rights

To recapitulate in brief what has been explained in detail elsewhere, the Charter of the United Nations effectively places a ban upon the use of force by State actors. Two exceptions – enforcement action sanctioned by the Security Council, and self-defence against an armed attack – exist, though the ambit of such exceptions is generally interpreted strictly, in order to prevent abuses. The problem stems from the incompatibility of the UN Charter regime with the increasingly important normative role enjoyed by human rights norms in international law. While human rights norms constituted a peripheral category in international law in the years immediately subsequent to the Second World War, they have since assumed an ever-increasing importance in the international legal order. However, no mechanism exists to effectively address situations of gross human rights abuses on a large scale committed by governments against their own citizens. When diplomatic efforts from other States fail to address such situations, and when the UN Security Council finds itself disinclined to confer the authority upon States to intervene, few meaningful options would seem to remain under such a rigid framework. The General Assembly, certain States and other international organisations may condemn the abuses, but in reality, regimes engaging in such abuses on a gross scale rarely listen to the entreaties of their neighbours. The use of force – the only effective means of putting an end to such illegal activity – is itself precluded by the rigidity of the law.

Legal rigidity, then, represents the crux of the problem. Dealing with this situation adequately – that is, finding a means to effectively put an end to gross human rights abuses committed by States against their own citizens while adhering to international legal rules on the use of force – seems impossible. However, commentators such as those treated in chapter one have addressed this problem solely with reference to custom and treaty law. Since such international law sources provided unsatisfactory conclusions – namely that there was nothing that the international community of States could do about such gross human rights abuses – many scholars turned to political and ethical theory. International law reform on a significant scale – the 'Responsibility to Protect' initiative – was also attempted. Ultimately, however, these new departures were counterproductive. Ethical and political theory, being less normatively grounded, is more easily bastardised by the unscrupulous for their own ends. Such a conclusion is borne out by the fact that many justificatory theories that had been employed to justify the legitimacy and/or legality of NATO's 1999 Kosovo operation were later used to lend a veneer of legitimacy and/or legality to the US-led invasion of Iraq in 2003. The same is true of the Responsibility to Protect, which gave rise to a supposed corollary 'Duty to Prevent', that, according to Fenstein and Slaughter, amongst others, confers a right upon States to invade their neighbours pre-emptively if they determine that ample evidence of imminent gross threats to human rights exists. This was combined with the fact that when the 'R2P' initiative was finally codified into international law – via the World Summit

Outcome Document – its tenets had little to do with the original intent of the ICISS, causing some of the founders of the concept to disown it.

As concluded in chapter one, scholarship on humanitarian intervention since Kosovo has been messy and over-idealistic. Those in the international legal community have been unable to reconcile their consciences with the *lex lata.* Upholding a legal regime which is manifestly inadequate and which acts as a shield for tyrants to butcher their citizens is an unpalatable position to have to defend. So too, however, are bold new theories, which put ethical, moral and political values above the international legal framework which has helped to maintain international stability since the Second World War. However, due to the apparently unbending rigidity of the UN Charter system, States and legal commentators were left having to nail their colours to one or other unstable mast. Endanger human rights or endanger international law. *Tertium non datur.*

However, what is evident from a thorough appraisal of the relevant literature is that the blinkered methodology that has become a central feature of much international legal scholarship in recent decades pervades significantly the discourse on humanitarian intervention since Kosovo. While treaties and custom are discussed in great detail, and while a wealth of historical examples are proffered by the likes of Chesterman and Tesón, the third principal source of international law is ignored. The final stone in the international legal apparatus is left unturned. It remains to be seen whether it may be the cornerstone.

B. The Solution? Equity and General Principles of Law as Extraneous Norms

That legal rigidity would prove to be at the focal point of an important legal problem comes as no surprise. Ever hath it been so. Legal rigidity has beset legal institutions and the systems to which they have given rise since the advent of written law, and likely even before this time. The famous code of Hammurabi – one of the most ancient examples of written law on record – was hampered by such problems, due to the warning issued by Hammurabi himself that his laws should stand for all time.[114]

It is notable, particularly in the context of the common law tradition, as has been discussed in chapter three, that when faced with problems brought about by legal rigidity, legal systems have developed general principles to interpret, soften, and occasionally even alter the written law. Such principles are generally grouped together as 'principles of equity' by scholars of

[114] JD Prince, 'Review: The Code of Hammurabi' (1904) 8 *American Journal of Theology* 601; J Flach, 'Le Code de Hammourabi et la constitution originaire de la propriété dans l'ancienne Chaldée' (1907) 5 *Revue historique* 272, v 94, a 32, 1907, II.

the common law. As I have demonstrated in chapter three, however, such principles are by no means the sole preserve of the British and post-colonial legal systems which make up the common law jurisdictions. Analogous principles have emerged – albeit by somewhat different means – in legal systems throughout the world, regardless of their historical legal traditions. That the development of such principles has transcended national borders, and even the significant chasms which occasionally separate the various legal systems does much to suggest that inherent in such principles lies something quite fundamental, and that their presence is necessary for the smooth functioning of a developed legal system.

It is further evident that general principles closely equivalent to the basic maxims of common law equity were held to be of great import across the various legal systems by the learned panel of jurists who drafted the Statute of the Permanent Court of International Justice, as outlined in chapter two. That this Statute was effectively retained for the Permanent Court's successor, the ICJ, even in the face of the sweeping systemic reform which was being undertaken on the rest of the defunct League's machinery, indicates that the judgments made by the Advisory Committee of Jurists in the early 1920s were still valid in the new international legal order which had been created post-Second World War. While such principles have failed to take root in international legal discourse to any significant degree,[115] the World Court has, in a series of judgments and Advisory Opinions, made repeated reference to this category. However, as illustrated in chapter four, that such references have often been somewhat less than explicit and have avoided using the accepted normative terminology is perhaps illustrative of the fact that the non-voluntarist general principles category – and particularly concepts like equity which have the power to (potentially) derogate voluntarily convened-upon norms such as treaty and custom – remains highly controversial and that its usage shall be restricted to extreme cases. The stakes involved in international law are simply too high for it to be otherwise.

While general principles and equity may have suffered from the obscurity of the references by the World Court to such concepts and the general ignorance/indifference of international legal scholarship in recent decades, the myopia which has affected the international legal community during the debate which NATO's Kosovo intervention began is quite singular. While it was evident even to the most inexperienced international lawyers that legal rigidity stood out as the crux of the problem, and while it is generally acknowledged that Article 38(1) of the ICJ Statute represents the definitive encapsulation of the sources of international law, few grasped the extraordinarily simple premise that a problem of legal rigid-

[115] It is perhaps illustrative of this point that the present work refers to so few works on the topic of general principles and equity in international law. The reason for this is that few (worthy) dedicated works exist.

ity might be resolved by the usage of a normative source which had developed in national legal systems – in some areas, at least – as a means of dealing with the problems of legal rigidity. Equity, needless to say, is the aforementioned normative source, and its presence as a sub-set of the third source of international law (general principles) has been exhaustively demonstrated in chapter two, so there is little need to revisit it here. Sufficeth to say that within the international law tool-kit, there existed an implement which had proven useful for dealing with similar problems in other legal systems. That the international legal community chose to ignore it in this context is, quite frankly, astonishing.

However, possessing a tool and knowing how to use it are different things indeed. While basic notions of equity have helped to rectify legal problems in various national jurisdictions, such notions developed there organically and of necessity. In the international context, equity was transposed into the system, and its functioning is certainly 'not co-terminus with its role in any one national jurisdiction'.[116] It remains to be seen whether the tool which proved effective in the domestic context will transpire to be equally useful in international law.

A further observation might be made at this juncture, namely that any potential impact of equity and general principles upon the UN Charter regime on the use of force by States would not be a unique example of extraneous legal sources impacting upon this area of the law. It is quite clear that the Charter machinery has never worked as it was envisaged, particularly with regard to enforcement actions under Chapter VII. Frowein and Krisch note that

> [d]ue to the advent of the Cold War, the broad powers under Chapter VII lay mostly dormant during the first decades of the Security Council's work. Military measures were impossible, partly because the agreements foreseen in Article 43 were not arrived at. Only in the Korean conflict could the SC agree on the use of force, but it mostly encouraged states to act in collective self-defence and did not take actual measures of collective security.[117]

Randelzhofer agrees, noting that it was not on the basis of Articles 39 and 42 that force was employed in many enforcement actions from the Korean War onwards. In the Korean case, in the absence of the Soviet representative, the Security Council characterised North Korea's invasion of South Korea as a breach of the peace, and recommended that members assist the South Koreans. However, further resolutions under Article 42

[116] S Rosenne, 'The Position of the International Court of Justice on the Foundations of the Principle of Equity in International Law' in A Bloed and P van Dijk (eds), *Forty Years of the International Court of Justice* (Utrecht, Europa-Instituut, 1988) 85.

[117] JA Frowein and N Krisch, 'Chapter VII: Action with Respect to Threats to the Peace, Breaches of the Peace, and Acts of Aggression' in B Simma (ed), *The Charter of the United Nations: A Commentary*, 2nd edn (Oxford, Oxford University Press, 2002) 704.

were vetoed by the Soviet representative, who had since returned to fill the 'empty chair'.[118]

The Korean War illustrates how far the UN had strayed from the Charter, even in its infancy. Security Council Resolutions call for the concurring opinions of all five Permanent Members of the Council, but the 'empty chair' policy of the Soviet Union resulted in the adoption of resolutions by the other members, treating the effective abstention of the Soviet Union as a concurring vote.[119] This has resulted in a practice whereby the Council has since treated abstentions as constituting concurring opinions for the purposes of validating Resolutions. Further, the machinery of Articles 39–43 was inoperable in this instance, and has been ever since, due to the inability of the international community of States to put together the regional collective security arrangements envisaged in the Charter text. As a result, the Security Council has been relying on State armies, assembled on an *ad hoc* basis, the famous 'coalition of the willing', rather than calling upon a force put at its disposal on a permanent basis. Again, the Charter text was departed from due to the exigencies of reality. Despite the 'global policeman' role of the Security Council, it ultimately falls to States to provide their own troops and resources in such operations. State interests will therefore determine if and how the Security Council will be able to send an effective force into a troubled region, and will determine the parameters of such action.

Clearly the above factors, combined with the nuclear arms race and the Cold War, meant that the Security Council's functions as regards the maintenance of international peace and security never operated as originally envisaged. This caused Undersecretary-General Brian Urquhart, amongst others, to demand Charter reform and the instigation of a Security Council-directed Rapid Reaction Force, a standing army for the Council, sourced from all corners of the globe.[120] However, this vision was utopian, as the Council members, particularly the Permanent Members, had gained power individually (although they had arguably collectively lost legitimacy) from the new interpretations/constructions/practice (delete as necessary) of the relevant Charter provisions that allowed abstentions to count as votes and removed any obligation of solidarity or participation in armed forces consigned for enforcement action missions. This situation resulted in a world where the Security Council functioned in a manner very different from that originally planned by the Charter's drafters. This opens the intriguing possibility that a lacuna, or lacunae, may have appeared in situations where the Council ought to have been

[118] A Randelzhofer, 'Article 2(4)' in Simma (2002) (n 117) 127.

[119] This is in addition to the fact that Nationalist China, rather than Communist China, was represented on the Council at this time.

[120] J Levitt, 'Rapid Deployment Requires a Permanent UN Force' (2012) *UN Association of the USA World Bulletin:* www.unausa.org/worldbulletin/012010/levitt.

empowered to act, but was unable or unwilling to do so by virtue of the new 'rules of the game' which had been imposed by virtue of the circumstances of the early years of the Cold War.

When one considers the above, one is left with a somewhat more nuanced picture of the Charter text regarding the use of force by States. The Council is acting in a manner which amounts, at the very least, to a creative interpretation of the text, and certainly a diversion from an interpretation of the Charter in accordance with the 'basic rule' of treaty interpretation – that is, that a treaty is to be interpreted in good faith, with the ordinary meaning given to the terms of the treaty in the light of its object and purpose. This rule is laid down in Article 31(1) of the 1969 Vienna Convention on the Law of Treaties (VCLT), and while this treaty was not in force at the time of the Korean War, it is nonetheless germane to note that the Convention was devised by States as a means of codifying the previous customary position.[121] However, the Convention rules do state that the 'basic rule' is merely the principal component of the general rule, comprising Article 31 VCLT in its entirety. It is of course true that not all elements of Article 31 will be relevant in all cases. However, when they are, to whatever extent, they must be utilised. Article 31(2) and (3) are not merely discretionary appendages, but rather prescriptive and mandatory components of the general rule of treaty interpretation. Article 31(2) makes reference to the treaty's context, and Article 31(3)(c) VCLT prescribes that

> [t]here shall be taken into account, together with the context: . . . (c) any relevant rules of international law applicable in the relations between the parties.

Explaining the Council's actions during the Korean War becomes somewhat simpler with the broader remit that the entirety of Article 31 allows in terms of treaty interpretation.

In the particular context of the United Nations Charter, the Security Council is responsible for the maintenance of international peace and security, and per Article 31(3)(c) VCLT, extraneous legal norms may be taken into account in interpreting the modalities of this remit. This is particularly important when the written rules on international peace and security have been diverged from. Clearly, the practice of States, combined with *opinio iuris,* has emerged in favour of an interpretation – a divergence – from the 'basic rule' in this instance. The practice of treating abstentions as concurring votes amongst Security Council members significantly alters the threshold for enforcement action, as does the failure to put the regional arrangements envisaged in the Charter into place, resulting in another unforeseen 'usage', namely the employment of *ad hoc* forces. These facts demonstrate that customary international law may

[121] See M Villiger, *Commentary on the 1969 Vienna Convention on the Law of Treaties* (Leiden, Martinus Nijhoff, 2009).

impact upon the operability and interpretation of international treaties in certain circumstances. This is important for the purposes of our current discussion, because it suggests that extraneous legal norms may indeed play an important role in interpreting the operation of the UN Charter, particularly in circumstances where the natural meaning of the Charter provisions is not being followed.

A further customary derogation to the general prohibition beyond the two most commonly acknowledged exceptions further exists within the domain of the law of the sea. Per Articles 104–10 of the UN Convention on the Law of the Sea, warships are entitled to stop, search and seize a ship engaging in piracy or the slave trade on the high seas.[122] As Randelzhofer notes,

> [t]o do so successfully will eventually require threat or use of military force . . . It is true that these types of force are not directed against the territorial integrity or political independence of any State. Nor are they in any other manner inconsistent with the purposes of the United Nations, as it is not arguable that the Charter of the United Nations is directed against well-established rules of the Law of the Sea.[123]

However, while Randelzhofer uses the Article 2(4) formulation 'against the territorial integrity or political independence of any state' to eschew conflict with the law of the sea provisions, I do not fully agree with his treatment. Brownlie and Apperley note that the Charter's *travaux préparatoires* indicate that this phrase ought to be afforded a strict interpretation, and that the phrase 'against the territorial integrity and political independence of any state' may not be construed to refer to a particular threshold which must be reached by threats and uses of force in order to render them illegal.[124] As Massa has pointed out, far from restricting the scope of

[122] This replicates the provisions of Arts 14–22 of the 1958 Geneva Convention on the High Seas. Further, as noted by Tullio Treves, some States, such as the US, Israel, Switzerland and Venezuala, while not bound by the UNCLOS, are bound by the 1958 Convention. Treves notes that the UNCLOS provisions reflect the (customary) law currently in force. See T Treves, 'Piracy, Law of the Sea, and the Use of Force: Developments off the Coast of Somalia' (2009) 20 *European Journal of International Law* 399, 401. It is also germane to note that the *ratione loci* and *ratione materiae* of the provisions concerning piracy have been extended by the Security Council via SC Resolutions 1816, 1846 and 1851 (all 2008), allowing for similar action in the territorial waters of Somalia (and authorising 'all necessary means', common Security Council parlance for 'the use of force'). However, this Resolution is both temporally (12-month time period) and geographically (specific reference to Somalia) limited, and further explicitly states that it shall not give rise to customary law.

[123] Randelshofer in Simma (2002) (n 118) 124. Treves concurs. See Treves (2009) (n 122) 412.

[124] I Brownlie and CJ Apperley, 'Kosovo Crisis Inquiry: Memorandum on the International Law Aspects' (2000) 49 *ICLQ* 878. A contrary interpretation is argued by, amongst others, A D'Amato, *International Law: Process and Prospects* (New York, Transnational Publishers, 1987) 57–73; F Tesón, F, *Humanitarian Intervention: An Inquiry into Peace, Law and Morality*, 2nd edn (New York, Transnational Publishers, 1997) 150–51; and F Abiew, *The Evolution of the Doctrine and Practice of Humanitarian Intervention* (The Hague, London, Boston, Kluwer Law International, 1999) 94–95.

the prohibition, these words 'were inserted as a guarantee for small states to reinforce the impermissible character of recourses to force against a state'.[125] This is further evidenced by the rejection of a more supple interpretation of this phrase by the ICJ in the *Corfu Channel* case (1949).[126]

Further evidence of the legality of the use of force by States on the high seas in such circumstances may be garnered from the 1995 UN Fish Stocks Agreement.[127] This Treaty permits certain non-flag States to board and inspect fishing vessels on the high seas. Such activities should not, in principle, require the use of force, since the flag State is 'bound to accept and facilitate the prompt and sage boarding by the inspectors', and must sanction the master of the vessel if he refuses to acquiesce.[128] However, the possibility of the use of force is nonetheless provided for in Article 22(1)(f), which prescribes that the inspecting State shall

> avoid the use of force except when and to the degree necessary to ensure the safety of the inspectors and where the inspectors are obstructed in the execution of their duties . . . The degree of force used shall not exceed that required in the circumstances.

Commenting on the above provisions, Treves links them to the UN Convention on the Law of the Sea (UNCLOS) (which the UN Fish Stocks Agreement is intended to help the implementation of), commenting that

> [g]eneral international law, in authorising stopping or boarding for the purpose of exercising the right of visit under Article 110 of UNCLOS or the seizure of a pirate ship under Article 105, presupposes that force may be used to reach these objectives.[129]

This position would seem to be confirmed by *MV Saiga No 2* judgment of the International Tribunal for the Law of the Sea, where, rather than proscribing the use of force, the tribunal delineated its limits, stating that 'international law requires that the use of force must be avoided as far as possible and, where force is inevitable, it must not go beyond what is reasonable and necessary in the circumstances'.[130] A 2007 arbitral award deciding a maritime border between Guyana and Surinam expanded upon this statement, also considering the distinction drawn by the ICJ in the *Nicaragua* case between uses of force that constitute an armed attack and 'other less grave

[125] AS Massa, 'Does Humanitarian Intervention Serve Human Rights? The Case of Kosovo' (2009) 1 *Amsterdam Law Forum* 50, 52.

[126] *Corfu Channel Case (United Kingdom v Albania)*[1949] ICJ Rep 4.

[127] Agreement for the Implementation of Provisions of the UN Convention on the Law of the Sea of 10 December 1982 Relating to the Conservation and Management of Straddling Fish Stocks and Highly Migratory Fish Stock, opened to signature in New York on 4 December 1995, (1995) 34 ILM 1547.

[128] Ibid, Art 22(3) and (4). See also Treves (2009) (n 122) 413.

[129] Treves (2009) (n 122) 413.

[130] *MV Saiga No2* [1999] ITLOS Reports 10 [155].

forms'.[131] The Arbitral Tribunal accepted 'the argument that in international law force may be used in law enforcement activities provided that such force is unavoidable, reasonable, and necessary'.[132]

Since ships on the high seas constitute an extension of the jurisdiction of the flag State, any use of force employed against such ships necessarily imputes use of force against the flag State. It is clear from past practice that such uses of force are viewed as perfectly legal in the circumstances prescribed by the Law of the Sea Convention. While the Convention merely codifies pre-existing customary law, it nonetheless constitutes further proof that extraneous legal norms may impact upon the prohibition upon the use of force set out in the UN Charter, in this case customary norms existent before the Charter's inception. This further demonstrates that previously existing extraneous norms, as well as new custom (though perhaps not treaty law, due to the 'supremacy clause' of Article 103 of the Charter) may impact upon the Charter regime on the use of force.

As an aside to the above, one must not discount the progressions in international law that have been experienced since the era of the Korean War. A succession of international human rights treaties has conferred an important position to individual rights within the international legal framework. International human rights treaties such as the International Covenant on Civil and Political Rights (ICCPR), International Covenant on Economic, Social and Cultural Rights (ICESCR) and the UN Convention Against Torture have been widely ratified, with many norms codified therein also forming part of customary international law, and certain norms having attained peremptory status as *ius cogens*. While the literature on humanitarian intervention has made reference to such norms, this has not been done in the context of 'extraneous norms' impacting upon the UN Charter as an international treaty. Perhaps this is understandable. Despite the fact that the Charter machinery has not functioned in the manner originally envisaged, opposing individual rights alone against one of the most fundamental provisions of the international legal apparatus is a difficult proposition. It is understandable that no scholars were able to find within this category a *modus operandi* for the derogation of the prohibition on the use of force.

The examples briefly discussed above demonstrate, to various degrees, the interaction of extraneous legal norms with the UN Charter regime governing the use of force by States. This may be particularly illuminating when discussing disputed areas such as the legality and legitimacy of humanitarian intervention. Nonetheless, none of the above – alone or in tandem – point to a solution, within the law, which would permit non-

[131] *Militarv and Puramilitary Activities in and against Nicaragua (Nicaragua v United States)* [1986] ICJ Rep 14 [191].

[132] *Guyana v Surinam* (2008) 47 ILM 66 [445] (Arbitral Tribunal constituted under Annex VII of UNCLOS).

Security Council sanctioned interventions to protect human rights. However, while most scholars seeking clarity in this area end their analysis of the international legal system at this point and look for a moral solution to a legal problem, I will not do so, and shall instead turn my attention to the largely-ignored general principles of law category.

C. A Framework for Equitable Humanitarian Intervention

In commencing to draft a framework for how equity and general principles may impact upon the legal regime governing the use of force and more particularly with reference to humanitarian intervention, it is, first of all, useful to be aware of the dangers inherent in such an examination. An over-enthusiastic employment of equity and general principles could amount to picking principles out of thin air, as it were, and would be worse, even, than ignoring such principles completely. Hence, in framing our discussion, I shall employ only those principles that have shown evidence of reception in international law. These are, for the most part, those principles which have manifested themselves in the judgments and opinions of the World Court as discussed in chapter four. While it is undoubtedly the case that general principles exist other than those which been received and enunciated by the PCIJ and ICJ in their jurisprudence, lamentably neither court possessed the courage to set forth a definitive threshold test of what constitutes a principle which may be held up as one of the 'general principles of law recognised by civilised nations'. In chapter four, I tentatively proposed the elements necessary for a test which would determine further general principles by analogy first to those principles which are already accepted as forming part of the international legal apparatus, and secondly to those present in national legal systems. However, I criticised my own conclusions as being on shaky ground, pointing out that it remains virtually impossible to conclusively divine what constitutes a general principle of international law without guidance from the World Court. While certain elements of a test are discernible, the general principles elixir remains elusive. With this in mind, I will not employ any principles that would be applicable by analogy under any plausible test, but which are – frustratingly – effectively impossible to confirm or unconfirm as general principles of international law.

Bearing the above in mind, we must again return to the World Court. In addition to the three principal sources of international law, Article 38(1) of the ICJ Statute stipulates that 'judicial decisions and the teachings of the most highly qualified publicists of the various nations' may be used 'as subsidiary means for the determination of rules of law'. These means are to be interpreted 'Subject to the provisions of Article 59 [ICJ]'. Article 59 states that 'The decision of the Court has no binding force except between the parties and in respect of that particular case'. Read in tandem, Articles 38(1) and 59 give us insight into the means which we may employ to determine the existence of general principles. Since general principles are often obscure and unclear, recourse may be had to judicial decisions and the teachings of publicists as a supplementary source of law to determine the content of the primary rules. However, the latter of these subsidiary sources may, at least in the case of general principles of law, be almost entirely discounted. While academic scholarship has shown itself to be of enormous use in shedding light on the content and modalities of treaties and customary law, the relative paucity of study in this area means that it is difficult to rely upon it. This is in addition to the fact that most authors hold contradictory opinions on what constitutes a general principle of law and how it may be applied. We are left, then, with 'judicial teachings'. While the World Court is by no means the only international tribunal of respected standing, I have chosen to examine its judgments alone – with a few contextualised exceptions – for the purposes of this study. To do otherwise would have been impossible in a work of this scale, and would have necessarily required an in-depth examination of the much-discussed topic of fragmentation of international law. I do not contend that such a discussion is not, in and of itself, worthwhile, but to embark upon such a course now would be ill-advised. Furthermore, there are significant merits in the lone selection of the World Court as a barometer of the import of general principles. First, few other courts have dealt with such principles in the area of inter-State relations. While the International Criminal Tribunals have, as Raimondo has elegantly exposed, been developing a dynamic set of general principles of international criminal law, such principles are hardly relevant to inter-State rules governing the use of force. Secondly, the PCIJ/ICJ has a wealth of experience unparalleled by other global judicial fora due to the age of the World Court as an institution, having been in almost continuous existence for 90 years. Thirdly, the World Court is one of the principal organs of the United Nations, and, absent any formal and convened hierarchy between the various international courts and tribunals, it must be to the ICJ that we look for guidance on tricky over-arching areas such as general principles of law. As regards the stipulation in Article 59 that the Court's decision is only binding *inter partes*, this provision was only inserted to exclude the liability of States which were not party to the dispute or which might not have signed the Statute. The idea that a statement by the Court that a certain rule possesses normative force in international law generally could be interpreted in a manner which would make such a statement apply to that case only is, frankly, preposterous. If a rule possesses normative force in international law in one situation, it possesses normative force in international law in all analogous situations. The only question is whether it will apply to a given set of facts in a given situation or whether another norm will be applied in its stead. Hence, the decision to use the history of the World Court's treatment of general principles, as described in chapter four, would appear the best – and safest – base upon which to ground any notion of an equitable theory of humanitarian intervention. Therefore, our study will proceed using those principles alone that have been concretely referenced by judgments and opinions given by the World Court in its case law.

i. Good Faith

The principle of good faith is perhaps the most fundamental general principle of law. Its existence is indisputable in international law, being present in all developed domestic legal systems[133] as well as being accepted by States in a variety of international treaties.[134] In fact, the very conclusion of a treaty implies an understanding of the principle of good faith in the form of the doctrine of *pacta sunt servanda*,[135] without which, 'international law, as well as civil law, would be a mere mockery'.[136] In addition, its validity has been upheld by a number of significant international judgments. In the *Metzger & Co* case, it was held that 'It cannot be that good faith is less obligatory upon nations than upon individuals in carrying out agreements'.[137] In the *Venezuelan Preferential Claims* case, it was held that the principle of good faith 'ought to govern international relations'.[138] In the *Lighthouses* case, Séfériades J, in a separate opinion, noted that 'Contracting parties are always assumed to be acting honestly and in good faith', noting that 'This is a legal principle which is recognised in private law, and cannot be ignored in international law'.[139] In the *North Sea Continental Shelf* case, the ICJ noted that international legal relations rest 'on a foundation of very general precepts of justice and good faith'.[140] In addition, the existence or validity of this principle has never been put into question by a litigant State before the World Court. Its existence is so fundamental in ensuring an international legal system which

[133] See ch 3.

[134] See, eg the Vienna Convention on the Law of Treaties, 23 May 1969, 1155 UNTS 331, Preamble, Arts 31, 46 and 69, all of which refer to the universal acceptance of the principle of good faith.

[135] See *Marinat's Case* [1905] Ralston's Report 44 (Franco-Venezuelan Mixed Claims Commission) 73: 'A treaty is a solemn compact between nations. It possesses in ordinary the same essential qualities as a contract between individuals, enhanced by the weightier quality of the parties and by the greater magnitude of the subject matter. To be valid, it imports a mutual assent'.

[136] Cheng (1987) (n 4) 113.

[137] *Metzger & Co (United States v Haiti)* [1901] USFR 262, 271.

[138] *Venezuelan Preferential Claims (German Empire, United Kingdom and Italy v Venezuela et al)* [1904] Scott Hague Court Rep 55, 60.

[139] *Lighthouses Case (France v Greece)* PCIJ Rep Series A/B No 62, 34

[140] *Case Concerning the North Sea Continental Shelf (Federal Republic of Germany v Denmark; Federal Republic of Germany v Netherlands)* [1969] ICJ Rep 46

States can reasonably interact with one another, can conclude contractual (treaty) agreements and can trust that promises made will be kept that to argue with its normative importance is, frankly, preposterous.

The nexus between the principle of bona fides and the humanitarian intervention discourse ought to be fairly obvious. Whenever a State acts in violation of a norm to which it has voluntarily assented – either a treaty or a customary norm – it is acting *mala fides*, given the fact that it had previously engaged itself – or had taken a position tantamount to engaging itself – to respect this norm.[141] Hence, when customary and treaty law on human rights such as the prohibitions upon genocide and torture – as well as individual rights such as the right to life – are violated, their violation is not merely a violation of customary and treaty law, but is also an infraction upon the general principle of good faith. As Cheng surmises, 'In short, good faith requires that one party should be able to place confidence in the words of the other'.[142] Every right must be seen as the protection of a legal interest. Further, any alleged exercise of such a right 'not in furtherance of such interest, but with the malicious purpose of injuring others can no longer claim the protection of the law. *Malitiis non est indulgendum*'.[143] The ideas behind good faith have given rise to stronger and more direct doctrines in international law such as estoppel and *ubi ius, ubi remedium*, which shall be discussed with reference to humanitarian intervention anon, but good faith is, in and of itself a powerful doctrine. The fact that a State may (ab)use the doctrine of sovereignty and the general prohibition upon the use of force by States as a cloak to shield its own abuses against its citizens in violation of international law may be effectively permitted (though hardly intended) by the UN Charter apparatus, but according to Cheng – who is, as far as this author can ascertain, unchallenged on the point – the bad faith exercised by the offending State is a breach of a general principle of law. This is interesting in particular if we consider the UN Charter as an international treaty. In the *Electricity Company of Sofia and Bulgaria* case, Anzilotti J stated that: 'While a party is free to denounce a treaty [or part thereof] at any time, it should not do so immediately on learning that the other party wishes to invoke the treaty . . . otherwise it loses all practical effect'.[144] This pronouncement is demonstrative of the fact that any usage of a treaty *mala fides* may be held to be tantamount to a breach of said treaty, since the nexus between the good faith implied in the conclusion of the treaty and the treaty itself is extremely close. What many commentators on the legal regime surround-

[141] In this manner, the good faith principle enjoys a complemetarity with the principles of *pacta sunt servanda* and *rebus sic standibus*.

[142] Cheng (1987) (n 4) 108.

[143] ibid, 122.

[144] *Electricity Co of Sofia and Bulgaria* (Preliminary Objection) PCIJ Series A/B No 77, dissenting opinion of Anzilotti J, 97–98.

ing humanitarian intervention have overlooked is the fact that gross abuses of human rights norms committed against their own citizens by States are not merely illegal under international human rights treaties and customary international law, but also amount to a breach of the principle of good faith relating to the UN Charter, including its regime relating to the use of force by States. In employing the inability of the community of States to effectively uphold international human rights law (presuming the Security Council is deadlocked), the offending State is acting in defiance of its obligations entered into vis-à-vis other States. This amounts to a breach of good faith, having given assurances that it would not do so. As Cheng notes, 'by infusing such qualities as honesty, sincerity, reasonableness and moderation into the exercise of rights, [good faith] promotes the smooth and proper functioning of the [international] legal system'.[145] I would go somewhat further than Cheng, and would argue that it is in fact both *essential* and *indispensable* to the smooth and proper functioning of the international legal system. One can hardly imagine a treaty including a stipulation that the instrument in question is to be interpreted in bad faith. The very idea borders on the ludicrous. The good faith principle represents a systemically essential norm. This being the case, any manoeuvre that seeks to undermine an element of an international agreement or customary arrangement through bad faith amounts to a breach of good faith relating to the agreement in question, which, as noted, is tantamount to a breach *stricto sensu* of said agreement. Any State, therefore, which knowingly uses the UN Charter regime governing the use of force by States as a shield to protect itself from the consequences of gross violations of human rights is acting *mala fides* vis-à-vis the Charter, and is therefore acting in a manner which is tantamount to an effective and material breach of the Charter. Such an action may also be construed as *abus de droit*.

Hence, States which commit gross human rights violations against their own citizens breach the normative principle of good faith in a number of manners. First, in denying their own previous position as regards the observance of human rights norms, they commit a breach of faith concerning the assurances they previously offered. Secondly, they act in bad faith vis-à-vis the UN Charter, since they seek to use the strictness of its regime on the use of force as a cloak to shield themselves against any serious consequences arising from their own actions. However, it is a long-standing principle of international law that *nullus comodum capere de sua iniuria propria* (that no one may be allowed to profit by his own wrongdoing[146]), as was amply demonstrated, for example, in the *Jurisdiction of*

[145] Cheng (1987) (n 4) 136.
[146] See *The Montijo Case* (1875) 2 Moore Intl Arbitrations 1421, 1437.

the Danzig Courts Advisory Opinion.[147] The recognition of good faith as a general principle was reinforced by the *Anglo-Norwegian Fisheries* case, where the ICJ recognised the theory of abuse of rights (*abus de droit*) as part of the broader conception of good faith.[148] A breach of (good) faith cannot be permitted to benefit the perpetrator. This is an embedded principle of international law, which has, like domestic fora, adopted rules such as estoppel and the doctrine of the abuse of rights to deal with it.

ii. Ubi ius, ubi remedium

The breach of good faith relating to the UN Charter regime on the use of force represents, then, a discernible and identifiable legal wrong; a breach by the transgressor State of its obligations owed to other States. This is quite apart from the fact that the transgressor State is also committing further legal wrongs by perpetrating gross and systematic human rights abuses against its own citizens, thereby breaching fundamental human rights norms – both in terms of treaties and customary international law, as well as 'elementary considerations of humanity'[149] – some of which may possess peremptory character. However, in both cases, remedies to these legal wrongs would not seem to be immediately obvious.

The principle that for every wrong committed there must be an adequate remedy is integral to the logic underlying equity. As noted in chapter four, it would seem to represent an elegant legal transposition of Newton's Third Law of Motion to the legal sphere. The ambit of this principle is not easily defined, even within domestic legal fora, since a blind application of the maxim would seem to entail automatic *restitutio in integrum* for every wrong committed. It is evident that, even within the common law sphere, where this principle has been most comprehensively expanded upon, this is not – and has never been – the case. Rather, *ubi ius remedium* is the epitome of equity's gap-filling (*praeter legem*) function, dealing with situations where the law is incomplete, usually in terms of remedies. A classic example comes from the case of *Engelhart's Estate v Larimer.* Here, the right of the Government to inspect a company's records was clearly set out, but its method of enforcement was not stipulated. Equity has the power to cure this defect of law through its gap-filling mechanism, in creating an enforcement mechanism regardless of the lack of statutory provision.[150] This also applies when a right is conferred by

[147] *Jurisdiction of the Courts of Danzig (Pecuniary Claims of Danzig Railway Officials who have Passed into the Polish Service, against the Polish Railways Administration)* (Advisory Opinion) PCIJ Rep Series B No 15, 26–27.

[148] *Anglo-Norwegian Fisheries Case (United Kingdom of Great Britain and Northern Ireland v Norway)* [1951] ICJ Rep 116, 142.

[149] *Corfu Channel Case* (*United Kingdom v Albania*) (Merits) [1949] ICJ Rep 4, 22.

[150] *Engelhart's Estate v Larimer*, 211 Ind 218, 5 NE 2d (1936) 304.

statute upon an individual, but without an adequate remedy for breaches of this right, a fact that quite evidently may have major repercussions for human rights law and humanitarian intervention.[151] This characteristic has been described by Pomeroy as the very basis of equitable jurisdiction.[152]

If the status of this principle is somewhat cloudy in the various national jurisdictions, however, its position in international law is still more obscure. As ever, the paucity of international judgments that have expressly referred to the principle renders framing its ambit a difficult task. Nonetheless, as noted in chapters two and four, there have been some references to the idea in past cases. In the *Chorzów Factory* case, the Court stated that

> [r]eparation is the indispensable complement of a failure to apply a convention, and there is no necessity for this to be stated in the convention itself . . . [it is] a general conception of law that any breach of an engagement involves an obligation to make reparation.[153]

Here, mirroring the doctrine expressed in *Engelhart's Estate v Larimer*, the PCIJ gave effect to the gap-filling role for which this principle was crafted. Later, the ICJ followed its predecessor in recognising the potential applicability of this principle in the *Reparation for Injuries* case, where the lack of an effective remedy for a legal wrong committed did not preclude the Court from 'creating' one in the interests of justice.[154] Its applicability in international law was further suggested in the *Barcelona Traction* case, where the Court felt bold enough to extend an accepted right in the interests of justice. The norm (*ius*) existed; ergo there must be a remedy (*remedium*), since there was no sufficiently specific legal barrier prohibiting the extension of such a right to legal as well as natural persons.[155]

It remains a fact, of course, that the World Court does not 'create' norms or remedies. They exist independently of its judgments and opinions, which may merely serve as a guide to the international lawyer to determine the existence and extent of norms the existence and ambit of which are not sufficiently clear, due either to their unwritten nature, their rare invocation, or their uncertain modalities of operation. This is an important point, upon which one should pause a moment. As noted in chapter four, there is good reason to suppose the existence of a number of general

[151] HL Oleck, *Creditor's Rights and Remedies* (Oxford, Oxford University Press, 1949) 10.

[152] J Pomeroy, *Equity Jurisprudence and Equitable Remedies*, 5th edn (London, General Books, 1941) sub-ss 423, 424

[153] *Factory at Chorzów (Germany v Poland)* (Merits) PCIJ Rep Series A No 17, 29. The Court here repeatedly stated its preference for full and adequate restitution wherever possible – *restitutio in integrum* – but warned that measures needed to be taken to avoid compensating twice for any one wrong, echoing the English common law maxim that 'equity guards against double portions'.

[154] *Reparation for Injuries Suffered in the Service of the United Nations* (Advisory Opinion) [1949] ICJ Rep 174.

[155] *Barcelona Traction, Light and Power Co Ltd (Belgium v Spain)* [1970] ICJ Rep 3. See also ch 4

principles within the sphere of international law, which the World Court has never had occasion to pronounce upon. Though uncertainty over their precise content has prevented this author from having the courage to use them in this particular work, their normativity remains unaffected. Equally, the fact that the principle *ubi ius, ubi remedium* has normative value in international law entails that it may be applicable in situations to which the Court has never had occasion to apply it. The fact that the Court has never done so is irrelevant vis-à-vis the normative strength of the principle wherever it may be applied. It is my contention that the operability of this principle has been rendered sufficiently clear by the previously-referenced judgments of the World Court – as well as the seminal *Barcelona Traction* case – for us to attempt to use it in situations with regard to which the World Court has never had occasion to do so, namely with regard to human rights and humanitarian intervention.

Since the end of the Second World War, and subsequent to the adoption of the UN Charter, human rights norms have developed significant normative standing in the international legal sphere. While the Charter itself makes fleeting references to human rights as being amongst the purposes of the United Nations and in its Preamble, such references are without real normative effect. Indeed, Charter-era efforts to list basic rights in the style of the French Revolution such as the Universal Declaration of Human Rights were dismissed as representing 'little more than an exhalation of pious hot air'.[156] However, subsequent initiatives such as the International Covenant on Civil and Political Rights and the respective European and American Conventions on Human Rights gave normative 'teeth' to these early declarations, with many States voluntarily signing and ratifying such treaties, indicating a firm willingness to be bound. In addition, a number of conventions prohibiting specific gross human rights abuses were drawn up, some of which attracted the popular support of a broad plurality of States.[157] The weight of this body of treaty law would seem to be substantial, with a broad consensus having emerged that a number of human rights norms have now attained the status of customary law, and perhaps even that of *ius cogens*.[158] Such status has, in the main been suggested by scholarly opinion rather than by the jurisprudence of the World Court, but it is worth recalling that, particularly in cases such as this where a broad consensus in scholarly opinion exists, such discourse may itself be a subsidiary source used for the determination of primary rules of international law.

[156] AWB Simpson, *Human Rights and the End of Empire: Britain and the Genesis of the European Convention* (Oxford, Oxford University Press, 2001) 11.

[157] eg the Convention on the Prevention and Punishment of the Crime of Genocide, adopted by the UN Assembly in 1948, in force since 1951.

[158] The respective prohibitions on slavery, genocide and crimes against humanity may be examples. See M Janis and J Noyes, *International Law: Cases and Commentary*, 3rd edn (St Paul, Minnesota, Thomson, 2006) 148.

Despite the growth of human rights law at international level in recent decades into a considerable body of norms, effective protection of such rights remains substantially inadequate. The remedies available to rectify damage, compensate victims, alleviate suffering and punish wrongdoers are insufficient to deal with the vast bulk of the human rights abuses that occur in the world today. This is above all illustrated by the humanitarian intervention discourse. The fact that, when gross human rights abuses are perpetrated by a State against its own citizens, the international community would often seem bereft of the right to react, has spurred a debate which shows no sign of abating. The problem, as ever, is the UN Charter. Drafted long before human rights came to be centrally important to the international legal framework, it would now seem evident that the Charter sports a gaping lacuna. State sovereignty and the idea that States should not interfere in the internal affairs of their neighbours represent the Charter position on international affairs. A limited right of self-defence is provided for under Article 51, broadly reflecting the classical international legal position in this regard. Aside from this, the only permitted recourse to force is set out under Chapter VII, according to which the Security Council may confer authority upon a State, groups of States, or regional defence organisations, to engage in armed force in a given State or region in order to preserve or restore 'international peace and security'. In theory, based upon the most cursory examination, the Chapter VII apparatus should go a long way toward protecting against gross human rights abuses, since it is within the context of armed conflicts and international strife that the most egregious human rights atrocities are wont to occur.[159] However, in reality, the effectiveness of the Security Council's mandate is constricted by three factors: namely, the subjectivity of the Council's judgment; the use of the veto by one of the Permanent Members; and the fact that 'international peace and security' is not synonymous with 'human rights'.

The fact that the Security Council is composed of State actors renders any judgment upon whether to authorise any armed force distinctly subjective. While this is not the place to discuss in depth the rival international relations theories which attempt to explain why States act the way they do, it suffices to say that each State shall cast its vote in the Council in accordance with its narrow self-interests (which may, however, include the preservation of international order) rather than altruistic sentiments. Such a state of affairs renders the Security Council an organ which may be ineffective in fulfilling its role in assessing objectively whether a breach of international peace and security, or threat thereof, has occurred, and whether to take action against it. Furthermore, the fact that, even when a broad consensus is reached that a breach of the peace is in progress, and

[159] M Walzer, 'The Argument about Humanitarian Intervention' (2002) *Dissent* 29.

that action ought to be taken to put a halt to such a breach, one of the five Permanent Members of the Security Council may, without obligation to furnish a reason for its action, veto the Resolution as agreed by the rest of the members provides a further check upon the effectiveness of the Security Council in any possible human rights protection role. Finally, and perhaps most importantly, one must remind one's self that the Security Council does not (necessarily) dispose of a human rights protection role in the first place. The Council's role in ensuring international peace and security is not necessarily co-terminus with a role as a human rights protection agent. After all, international peace and security may be secured in a region where States enjoy friendly relations with their neighbours, but where within individual States, torture and genocide are rampant. The non-identical nature of 'human rights' and 'international peace and security' means that protecting the latter may theoretically be accomplished effectively without unduly concerning oneself with the former.

The inherent limitations which are visible in the UN Charter system of rules governing the use of force by States have given rise to a situation whereby, de facto, when gross human rights abuses are perpetrated by a State against its own citizens, there is very little the international community can do in the absence of Security Council action. From this, we may infer that no effective remedy exists in such circumstances. However, as shown by the previous jurisprudence of the World Court, and notably the *Chorzów Factory, Reparation for Injuries* and *Barcelona Traction* cases, in limited circumstances, when an established right is violated, but when a concomitant remedy is absent the World Court will see fit to 'create' one. However, as noted above, the Court does not in fact 'create' such remedies. They exist as invisible corollaries to the rights upon which they are founded by virtue of the general principle that equity will not suffer a wrong to be without a remedy – *ubi ius, ubi remedium*. Equity exists in such circumstances to fill the gaps (*praeter legem*) which exist within the legal structure in order to rectify manifest injustices that would otherwise occur. Few would argue that unpunished gross and systematic human rights abuses on a large scale constitute a manifest injustice. There is good reason to suspect that, therefore, such a situation may qualify for the limited invocation of the maxim *ubi ius, ubi remedium* in international law. What this would entail is the recognition of the existence of an implied remedy to deal with violations of human rights norms on a gross scale where no other effective remedy exists. In the case being treated by this study, this would amount to armed humanitarian intervention by a State or coalition of States in order to put an end to such abuses. Such equitable humanitarian intervention would be rendered legal by equity's operation in the international legal system.

However, there remains one issue which must not be forgotten before we may begin to spread our equitable balm over the humanitarian intervention debate, namely that of *ius cogens*. Per the Vienna Convention on the Law of Treaties:

> A treaty is void if, at the time of its conclusion, it conflicts with a peremptory norm of general international law. For the purposes of the present Convention, a peremptory norm of general international law is a norm accepted and recognized by the international community of states as a whole as a norm from which no derogation is permitted and which can be modified only by a subsequent norm of general international law having the same character.[160]

The Vienna Convention does not outline any specific examples of peremptory norms, but does afford the UN Charter regime on the use of force an analogous treatment to that of *ius cogens* vis-à-vis its effect upon treaty norms.[161] This goes some way toward suggesting that the UN Charter's general prohibition upon the use of force by States constitutes a peremptory norm. The issue of the potential *ius cogens* status of the prohibition of the use of force – and the problems inherent in such an affirmation – have been discussed earlier in this chapter. It is clear that a contrary position may also be argued.[162] However, as noted above, such an interpretation, while it might render an argument for a legal framework derogating the prohibition somewhat easier, is not concordant with the majority of scholarly opinion on the subject. The *ius cogens* status of the prohibition upon the use of force has been buttressed by the opinions of a wide array of leading scholars, and the Charter regime constitutes one of the relatively few international legal norms that are rarely contested as being peremptory in nature.[163]

Any recognition of the Charter's prohibition as peremptory in nature would seem to suggest that even if an equitable remedy of a right to humanitarian intervention may be advanced then such a remedy, while existing at a theoretical level, will never be applicable, since it will always clash with the peremptory prohibition upon such activities. Such a position would seem to preclude the recognition of the equitable remedy of humanitarian intervention in the international legal system. However, such a position is only half the story. Indeed, as noted above, certain norms connected – to a greater or lesser degree – with the human rights *corpus* have also been recognised as being *cogentes* norms. Amongst these are: the prohibition of torture;[164] the prohibition of maritime piracy;[165] the

[160] Vienna Convention on the Law of Treaties, 23 May 1969, 1155 UNTS 331, (1969) 8 ILM 679, Art 53.

[161] ibid, Art 52.

[162] See Green (2011) (n 43) 215–57.

[163] M Bossuyt and J Wouters, *Grondlijnen van internationaal recht* (Antwerp, Intersentia, 2005) 92.

[164] *Prosecutor v Furundžija* (Judgment of the Appeals Chamber) ICTY IT-95-17/1A, 121 ILR 213 (21 July 2000).

[165] C Schwarzenberger, *'International Ius Cogens?'* (1964–65) 43 *Texas Law Review* 455.

prohibition of genocide;[166] that of slavery and those of war crimes and crimes against humanity.[167] Suggestions have even been made that the entirety of the human rights *corpus* is moving towards being incorporated into the *ius cogens* bloc, due to its ever-increasing importance to international law as a whole, though such a view remains controversial.[168]

Even if we adopt a conservative assessment of the inroads that human rights have made into the peremptory category, we are left with a significant assortment of peremptory norms pertaining to human rights, many of which have acquired this status since the advent of the UN Charter. According to Article 53 of the Vienna Convention on the Law of Treaties, a norm of *ius cogens* 'can be modified only by a subsequent norm of general international law having the same character'. Such an assessment changes the picture of a rigid, inflexible, peremptory rule governing the use of force by States somewhat. Human rights norms of a peremptory nature, being at the same normative level as the general rule prohibiting the use of force by States, and having acquired such status subsequent to its acquisition by the UN Charter rule, would seem to be ideally positioned to derogate the Charter rule. However, it is important here to note the word of caution sound by Bianchi, himself paraphrasing the separate opinion of Dugard J in the *Congo* case, that *ius cogens*

> may not be applied regardless of context and policy. There must be limits. And yet, it would be a defeat for the international community to get rid of the concept altogether, reneging on the difficult but ultimately successful building up of communitarian values.[169]

While peremptory human rights do not, in and of themselves, contain sufficient specificity concerning their enforcement and modalities of operation, such lacunae are remedied by the maxim *ubi ius, ubi remedium*. Any remedy which flows from a given peremptory human right – even if it is not explicitly stated and needs to be divined through the use of equity, either by a Court or by another actor – must also, of necessity, have peremptory status, since otherwise the *effet utile* of the norm's peremptory nature would be lost. The fact that such remedies may need to be ascertained through the use of an equitable (non-peremptory) general principle of law does not entail that they acquire themselves the same normative force as this general principle. Rather, such an implied remedy will have the same normative status as the right from which it flows. Ergo, if the human right upon which a given remedy is based is of a peremptory nature, then the remedy itself will also be peremptory.

[166] MC Bassiouni, 'International Crimes and Obligations Erga Omnes' (1996) 59 *Law and Contemporary Problems* 63.

[167] ibid.

[168] K Parker and LB Neylon, 'Jus Cogens: Compelling the Law of Human Rights' (1989) 12 *Hastings International and Comparative Law Review* 411, 451.

[169] Bianchi (2008) (n 32) 503.

Considering the above, if a situation arises where a State is in the process of committing gross human rights abuses against its own citizens, and the international community is unable to effectively respond due to an intransigent Security Council, the implied remedies which are attached to violations of peremptory human rights norms by virtue of the maxim *ubi ius, ubi remedium* may create the possibility that the UN Charter regime on the use of force may be derogated from in favour of humanitarian intervention in order to put an end to the atrocities. For this to be the case, of course, the violations in question would need to be very grave indeed, constituting either genocide, crimes against humanity, war crimes, or widespread use of torture. Of course, the question as to which State or international body may determine whether such offences are occurring is a thorny one. Allowing States to make individual determinations in this regard is a dangerous position, as it opens the door to potential abuse of the doctrine. However, the World Court, perhaps the best judge in this regard, is unlikely to pronounce adequately, clearly, or in due time, even if requested to do so by the General Assembly. Further, it is by no means certain that the General Assembly would refer such a question to the Court. Hence, the various United Nations – and perhaps Red Cross – human rights and international humanitarian law bodies should be the preferred barometer.

Ubi ius, ubi remedium is not, of course, a catch-all principle. It will apply only in limited circumstances, where a sufficiently clear lacuna exists in the international legal framework to create a situation whereby a clearly-established right is left without a remedy. While I would argue that the international human rights *corpus* is a perfect example of such a phenomenon, it is worth reminding ourselves of the fact that when we refer to humanitarian intervention, we may conceivably be discussing something more than 'merely' *aequitas praeter legem*. In derogating an already established rule, and particularly a structurally important norm of *ius cogens*, albeit with the support of other *ius cogens* norms – as shall be discussed anon – it is possible that we may also venture into the realm of *aequitas contra legem*. As mentioned in our discussion of equitable general principles in earlier chapters, it was noted that for such principles to act against an established rule of law, exceptional circumstances are necessary, and such *contra legem* operability will only rarely be allowed (though our discussion of unconstitutional constitutional amendments does demonstrate that there is a possibility of general principles operating against the written rules even at the highest normative level). In view of this fact, it would seem premature to argue at this juncture that *ubi ius, ubi remedium* may be applied on its own to derogate from the UN Charter regime on the use of force, particularly since there are other equitable principles of international law to be considered, which may influence any tentative conclusions in this discussion. Chief amongst these principles is the doctrine of estoppel in international law.

iii. Estoppel (non venire contra factum proprium)

The doctrine of estoppel represents the idea that actors must be held accountable for the promises which they make. In national legal systems, its operability – as estoppel, preclusion *à la française,* or the maxim *non venire contra factum proprium* – is extremely varied, despite certain core elements. In the international legal system, as discussed in chapter four, the potent doctrine of estoppel has experienced, at the very least, a partial reception into international law. This was an entirely logical development. As Lauterpacht has observed, since estoppel is recognised 'in all systems of private law', it is not easy to disregard the logic underlying estoppel in inter-State relations.[170] States, like private actors in national legal systems, were required to be consistent in their attitudes to given factual or legal situations. MacGibbon notes that such a demand 'may be rooted in the continuing need for at least a modicum of stability and for some measure of predictability in the pattern of State conduct'.[171] While good faith is the primary embodiment of the 'rules of the game' which are necessary for States to be able to communicate and interact with one another in a stable and predictable environment, mechanisms must be built upon the idea of good faith which ensure that transgressions of such bona fides such as the breaking of promises are not without normative consequences.

Perhaps the epitome of equitable doctrines crafted to ensure adherence to the idea of good faith and honourable conduct *inter partes* is the doctrine of estoppel. To recapitulate, the tripartite test for estoppel is founded upon: (1) an assurance given by one party; (2) reliance thereupon by the other party; and (3) detriment resulting to the second party on foot of, and resulting from, this reliance. Its development in the international legal sphere is hardly a recent phenomenon, with the early case law of the Permanent Court displaying tendencies 'reminiscent of some of the elements of estoppel in English law',[172] with Lauterpacht citing the *Polish Nationals in Danzig,*[173] *Free Zones of Upper Savoy and the District of Gex*[174] and *Greco-Bulgarian Communities*[175] cases as early examples. In more recent times, the World Court has made repeated and explicit reference to the doctrine of estoppel. However, somewhat lamentably for our present purposes, as noted in chapter four, such references have not been entirely consistent with one another, and do not serve to clarify the ambit of estop-

[170] H Lauterpacht, *Private Law Sources and Analogies of International Law (With Special Reference to International Arbitration)* (London, Longman, Green and Co, 1927) 204–05.

[171] IC MacGibbon, 'Estoppel in International Law' (1958) 7 *ICLQ* 468.

[172] H Lauterpacht, *The Development of International Law by the Permanent Court of International Justice* (London, Longmans, Green and Co, 1934) 83.

[173] *Treatment of Polish Nationals and Other Persons of Polish Origin or Speech in the Danzig Territory* PCIJ Rep Series A/B No 44.

[174] *Case of the Free Zones of Upper Savoy and the District of Gex* PCIJ Rep Series A No 22.

[175] *The Greco-Bulgarian 'Communities'* (Advisory Opinion) PCIJ Rep Series B No 17.

pel doctrine in international law. In the *Chorzów Factory* case, where it was held that a State party was estopped from pleading that the Court lacked jurisdiction in the case on the grounds that

> it is . . . a principle generally accepted in the jurisprudence of international arbitration . . . that one party cannot avail itself of the fact that the other has not fulfilled some obligation, or has not had recourse to some means of redress, if the former party has, by some illegal act, prevented the latter from fulfilling the obligation in question, or from having recourse to the tribunal which would have been open to him.[176]

This was followed by an implicit recognition of something analogous to estoppel doctrine in the *Eastern Greenland* case, where the Court, typically avoiding the terminology of the general principle, utilised the term 'debarred' in lieu of 'estopped', though ultimately the judgment amounted to the same thing.[177] In the *Gulf of Maine* case, the related notion of acquiescence (creating a situation of preclusion), also known as 'sleeping on one's rights' was discussed.[178] The *Anglo-Norwegian Fisheries* case had earlier set out this principle in international law, with Waldock describing the ICJ's reasoning in the case as 'amongst the boldest and most important judgments pronounced by any international tribunal'.[179] The *Temple of Preah Vihear* case is perhaps the quintessential modern example of international estoppel and acquiescence doctrine being applied by the World Court.[180] It is certainly treated as such by most leading authors, despite imperfections in the consent given by the parties and the fact that the classical doctrine of estoppel was not the principle which was applied, but rather the analogous *qui tacet consentire videtur si loqui debuisset ac potuisset* (he who is silent appears to consent if he should, and could, have spoken).[181] Further references to estoppel were made in the *Gabcíkovo – Nagymaros Project* case in Vice-President Weeramantry's separate concurring opinion.[182]

Despite somewhat varying conceptions of the conditions necessary to establish an estoppel, either by acquiescence or by virtue of a specific and explicit assurance, there can be little doubt that the doctrine exists in

[176] *Case Concerning the Factory at Chorzów* (Claim for Indemnity) (Jurisdiction) PCIJ Rep Series A No 9, 31. This passage was also quoted in the pleadings of the *Interpretation of the Peace Treaties Case* before the ICJ. See also MacGibbon (1958) (n 171) 480.

[177] The principle laid down in the case lies somewhere between the doctrines of legitimate expectation and estoppel. Both doctrines require the keeping of promises based upon assurances earlier received. *Legal Status of Eastern Greenland (Denmark v Norway)* PCIJ Rep Series A/B No 53, 62.

[178] *Delimitation of the Maritime Boundary of the Gulf of Maine Area (Canada v United States)* [1984] ICJ Rep 246, 305.

[179] CHM Waldock, '*The Anglo-Norwegian Fisheries Case*' (1951) 28 *British Yearbook of International Law* 114.

[180] *Case Concerning the Temple of Preah Vihear (Cambodia v Thailand)* [1962] ICJ Rep 6.

[181] ibid, 23. See also the dissenting opinion of Percy Spencer J in this regard, 143.

[182] *Case Concerning the Gabčíkovo – Nagymaros Project (Hungary v Slovakia)* [1997] ICJ Rep 7.

international law. References to estoppel by the PCIJ and ICJ have been both frequent, and, uncharacteristically for general principles, quite often explicit. The World Court has not always shied away from using the terms 'estoppel' or its French equivalent, *'préclusion'*. As noted in chapter four, this is illustrative of the fact that the principles underlying estoppel, embodying the essence of good faith, are deeply ingrained into the architecture of international law, and that their existence is relatively unchallenged.[183] This is particularly significant for the purposes of this discussion due to the inherent potency of estoppel doctrine. Indeed, despite the wavering conceptions of estoppel applied by the World Court in its judgments, it is worth noting that estoppel does tend to apply in a simpler, more cogent manner at international level than in some national legal systems. In the common law, by way of example, the separation between promissory and proprietary estoppel has caused confusion and cleavages between the various common law jurisdictions. At international level, estoppel is far simpler, with MacGibbon dubbing it as the natural and necessary complement to *pacta sunt servanda*, which he notes constitutes the cornerstone of the international legal system.[184]

Relating the doctrine of estoppel and acquiescence to humanitarian intervention might not seem an obvious course of action. However, it is my opinion that the doctrine may indeed be relevant to our discussion. It is the nature of human rights norms, and particularly those which reach the threshold of *ius cogens*, that they are owed *erga omnes*, entailing that they are owed to the international community as a whole. According to the International Court of Justice in *Barcelona Traction*, 'all States can be held to have a legal interest in their protection'.[185] Breaches of *erga omnes* obligations such as those human rights norms which constitute *ius cogens* constitute breaches of obligations vis-à-vis the international community as a whole, and against all States. Hence, any State – or combination of States – may consider itself to have suffered a wrong when a neighbouring State acts in breach of a pre-convened obligation which is owed *erga omnes*.

We may consider the signature of human rights instruments – or indeed any acquiescence to the development of customary international human rights norms without persistent objection – by a State as constituting an assurance *erga omnes* that any obligations incumbent upon the State by virtue of such norms will be respected. This assurance extends in international law to other States, and in national law to its citizens, that those

[183] Of course, this is not to say that the extent and operability of their ambit is universally agreed. On the contrary, this is an area where more clarity would certainly be welcomed.

[184] IC MacGibbon, 'The Scope of Acquiescence in International Law' (1954) 31 *British Yearbook of International Law* 143, 181–82.

[185] *Barcelona Traction, Light and Power Co Ltd (Belgium v Spain)* (Second Phase) [1970] ICJ Rep 3 [33]–[34].

persons resident on its territory will be guaranteed a certain level of protection. Reliance upon this assurance is clearly visible from the citizens of the State, who live free from fear, largely due to the fact that such an assurance has been given. More importantly, though less obviously, reliance upon this assurance by other States may also be held to exist. The State in question has, in effect, promised to respect certain norms, a promise upon which other States rely in their dealings with this State. For example, the European Union has continuously delayed Turkey's consideration for eventual accession to the Union due to its questionable human rights record. It is clear that Turkey's possible admission to the EU will be partially predicated upon specific assurances that human rights norms will be respected. Reliance upon the human rights record of a given State is clearly visible from the way in which certain other States – notably developed States which themselves boast a good human rights record – engage with a State. Particularly for democratic States in modern times, significant engagement with States who commit serious human rights abuses against their own citizens is seen as repugnant by the populace. This is, for example, evidenced by the increasing public distaste in Western Europe and North America for the maintenance of friendly relations with the apartheid regime in South Africa, which led to an eventual souring of relations between South Africa and the West during the 1980s, despite the country's obvious usefulness as a potentially friendly ally and bulwark against communism.

A detriment is incurred by other States on foot of the reliance upon a State's human rights obligations when such obligations are reneged upon. These States have adopted a position toward the transgressor State by virtue of previous assurances that the transgressor State would abide by human rights norms. This position may entail trade links, aid, co-membership of international organisations, diplomatic missions et cetera. When the transgressor State then engages in gross human rights abuses against its own citizens in contravention of international law, detriment is caused to other States which changed their position towards the transgressor, since they would not have done so had they known that the transgressor was planning to run roughshod over human rights norms. Such supportive positions and trade links to States which engage in such abuses may damage the international reputation of States, may damage the popularity of State governments, and may damage their prospects for engagement with other States which view respect for human rights and international law as paramount priorities. Establishing a sufficient nexus between the human rights based assurance and the detriment suffered by other States in changing their position may be a difficult, but by no means impossible, proposition. Since assurance, reliance and detriment constitute the three prerequisite elements necessary for the establishment of an international estoppel, it would seem that such an estoppel could indeed arise in such circumstances. In such circumstances, the transgressor State may be held to be legally precluded from denying the original assurance given.

Determining the existence of an estoppel is generally a job for the courts. However, here again the ICJ is hardly ideally poised to make such a determination, given the limits imposed upon its jurisdiction by the justiciability of issues before it. States are unlikely to refer such cases to the Court. Also problematic is the question of what appropriate remedy may be proffered to enforce the estoppel. The World Court discussed the possibility that it itself might issue an international injunction preventing the transgressor State from further acting in breach of the estoppel in the *Serbian Loans* case.[186] However, the jurisdiction of the ICJ renders the prospect of such injunctions extremely unlikely. In addition, there is the problem that while injunctions at national level were devised as a powerful instrument to supplement court orders (and notably equitable orders in the common law), international injunctions cannot expect to carry the same power. At common law, for example, failure to comply with an injunction is backed by the sanction of contempt of court, usually accompanied by significant fines and/or a custodial sentence. International law lacks the same means to enforce such injunctions.

As discussed earlier, while a court may determine the existence of an estoppel, and may order an appropriate remedy, the fact that a court lacks the opportunity to pronounce upon a given situation does not mean that the law does not apply. If the circumstances are sufficiently clear, then a determination by the World Court that an international estoppel arises may not be necessary (though of course, such a determination, even via an Advisory Opinion, would be highly desirable). In a situation where a State is held to be estopped from denying its previous human rights assurances by other States, and where diplomatic remedies are clearly inadequate to engender compliance from the transgressor State, one must have recourse again to the principle *ubi ius, ubi remedium*. To do otherwise would be to allow the fact that international law has a lacuna regarding enforcement measures to act as an effective permission for States to act in violation of international estoppel at will, effectively robbing the doctrine of any meaningful use. Such a conclusion adds weight to the proposition that in such circumstances, as is its nature, equity will allow for the devising of an effective remedy in the circumstances. In situations such as those discussed above, it would seem that States which themselves have a clean human rights record, and which are therefore entitled to feel aggrieved that the assurances proffered toward the international community by the transgressor State have been reneged upon, may be permitted to act by

[186] *Case Concerning the Payment of Various Serbian Loans Issued in France* PCIJ Rep Series A No 20/21, 38–39.

any means necessary to enforce the international estoppel. This may – potentially – include usage of armed force via an intervention.

iv. 'Clean Hands' Doctrine

Adding further to the idea that some – rather than all – States may be in a position to claim a right to intervene in limited circumstances is the double-edged notion of clean hands doctrine. This doctrine is perhaps best described by the maxim that 'he who comes to equity must comes with clean hands', or that 'he who seeks equity's assistance must himself be free of iniquity'. However, the doctrine also works prospectively, meaning that one who seeks equity's assistance must also be prepared to act in an equitable manner. While such a principle is not universally acknowledged throughout the various national legal systems examined earlier, it has known reception into the international legal system. This was first apparent in Manley Hudson J's oft-discussed opinion in the *Diversion of Water from the River Meuse* case. The Netherlands had complained that Belgium, through its erection of a lock on the River Meuse had violated an agreement *inter partes* that they would only extract water from the river under certain conditions. However, during this period, the Netherlands had also constructed and operated a similarly unlawful lock. Manley Hudson affirmed that one unlawful lock could not be treated differently from the next:

> It would seem to be an important principle of equity that where two parties have assumed an identical or reciprocal obligation, one party which is engaged in a continuing non-performance of that obligation should not be permitted to take advantage of a similar non-performance of that obligation by the other party. The principle finds expression in the so-called maxims of equity which exercised great influence in the creative period of the Anglo-American law. Some of these maxims are, 'equality is equity', 'he who seeks equity must do equity' . . . a very similar principle was received into Roman Law.[187]

Per Hudson, it would be illegitimate to give voice to the concerns of the Netherlands when they themselves were acting in a way which was contrary to the rule they purported to be upholding. The Netherlands' hands were not clean, as it were, and therefore, they were not entitled to relief in this instance.

While Hudson's opinion in the *Meuse* case was a separate (though concurring) one, other cases before the World Court have given additional credence to the clean hands principle at international level. Rossi notes that this principle has gained a certain acceptance in the World Court, having also been referred to, inter alia, in the *Chorzów Factory* and *Nicaragua*

[187] *Diversion of Water from the Meuse* PCIJ Rep Series A/B No 70, individual opinion of Manley Hudson J, 77.

cases.[188] It is clear from the above cases that this principle is also to be interpreted prospectively, that is, when equitable relief is granted to one party, this party may not then act in an inequitable manner vis-à-vis his neighbour, and must not do more than is necessary to repair the damage incurred. Such cases would indicate that if an exception to the general prohibition on the use of force may be crafted in favour of an equitable doctrine of humanitarian intervention, then, despite the *erga omnes* nature of many human rights norms, it will not be the case that all States dispose of an equal right to intervene. Hypocrisy as regards enforcement of similar norms will not be tolerated in international law. For law to permit one State which engages in gross human rights violations to intervene in another to put an end to similar human rights violations is, quite simply, absurd. In order for a State to dispose of any rights arising from a breach of an *erga omnes* human rights norm by its neighbour, it must itself respect this norm. This would seem to create both a threshold requirement for potential intervention and a prospective 'code of conduct', quite separate from international humanitarian law, whereby States may not themselves become serious transgressors of human rights norms in carrying out the intervention itself, traversing the usual threshold distinction between *ius ad bellum* and *ius in bello.* If international humanitarian law alone cannot constrain intervening States to act humanely and with caution and respect for the lives of civilians, then perhaps the maxims of equity may lend fresh perspective on the need to avoid hypocrisy – purporting to save civilians while killing civilians – in the conduct of such operations.

It is, perhaps, necessary to expand somewhat further upon the 'clean hands' principle in relation to humanitarian intervention. Intervening to protect and uphold human rights cannot be permitted with bayonets still wet with the blood of one's own civilians. It is notable that the United States, inter alia, has been a willing intervening power in recent decades in several States where human rights and humanitarian concerns were cited as being amongst the justifications for intervention. This was certainly the case in Northern Iraq and in Kosovo. However, it is clear that the United States' own human rights and international humanitarian law record is far from exemplary. In recent years, the waterboarding of terrorism suspects, the execution of foreign criminals without according them their right to consular protection,[189] the practice of illegal rendition flights, the detention conditions of detainees at Guantanamo and other detention centres and the use of drones and other methods for targeted killings which fall foul of the laws and customs of warfare are amongst some of the better-known and more egregious examples of the United

[188] Rossi (1993) (n 13) 164.

[189] *La Grand (Germany v United States)* (Judgment) [2001] ICJ Rep 466; *Case Concerning Avena and Other Mexican Nationals (Mexico v United States)* (Judgment) [2004] ICJ Rep 1.

States' transgressions against international human rights law. The question, again, is necessarily one of subjectivity. Where do we draw the line? There is no easy answer to this question. It is clear that, while States like the US have committed serious human rights abuses in and of themselves, and while such abuses should not be taken lightly, they do not qualify as gross and systematic human rights abuses on a large scale, which must represent our threshold criterion in determining the cleanliness of the hands of any potential intervening State. Such a formulation does not entirely eschew questions of subjectivity, but it does add the requirement that a discernible systematic pattern must be identifiable, and that isolated incidents of human rights abuses by States may not be used as a pretext for abusive and disingenuous invocation of the equitable model, or, *a contrario*, the debarring of would-be interveners on the basis of isolated elements of their own human rights record. No State is entirely free of human rights transgressions to a greater or lesser extent. The idea of 'clean hands' doctrine is to prevent the worst transgressors against human rights from being able to opportunistically and hypocritically intervene against their neighbours. It is not to create a threshold that no State could meet.

As Manley Hudson J pointed out, in the context of the *Meuse* case, it would have been illegitimate to give voice to the concerns of the Netherlands when they themselves were acting in a way which was contrary to the rule they purported to be upholding. Equally, a law to permit one State which engages in gross human rights violations to intervene in another to put an end to similar human rights violations is, quite simply, absurd. Human rights are owed *erga omnes*, but despite this, not all States will dispose of an equal right to intervene. In order for a State to dispose of any rights arising from a breach of an *erga omnes* human right norm by its neighbour, it must itself respect this norm. This is not to say that the intervening States' hands must be freshly washed, but nor may they be dripping with blood.

v. Substance over Form

The prioritisation of the substance of a legal instrument or regime over its form is, as demonstrated in chapter three, a principle that has found reception in all national systems and regional legal traditions examined. From the English common law, to its American cousin, to the French civil law, to the Islamic legal culture, to that of China, Japan and beyond, receipt of this principle has been as close to universal as any within the broad equitable *corpus*. The extent and modality of the principle, also commonly referred to as *ex re sed non ex nomine*, varies from case-to-case, but, as Delany notes, while this does not mean that legal formalities will not be required by equity, 'it looks to the substance rather than the form of a transaction and does not require "unnecessary formalities" to be observed'.[190] For example, this device has been used by courts to go beyond formal rules for dealing with corporations and their directors when such corporations were being used as a shield for an improper or illicit purpose.[191] Much like estoppel doctrine, 'clean hands' derives from notions of good faith, and is closely linked to the principles of ultra vires and *abus de droit*.

Within international law, perhaps unsurprisingly, there has also been an – admittedly limited – reception of this doctrine. As discussed in chapter four, the *Barcelona Traction* case presents perhaps the best example here. The extension of the right of diplomatic protection to States over legal entities represented a significant juncture, where the Court felt bold enough to extend an accepted right – namely diplomatic protection – in the interests of justice. Of particular importance in this case is the fact that it demonstrates the dynamic and flexible interaction of multiple equitable principles in order to achieve a just result. The norm (*ius*) of diplomatic protection was undisputed; ergo there must be a remedy (*remedium*), since there was no overbearing legal barrier prohibiting the extension of such a right to legal as well as natural persons. This move by the Court demonstrates an – albeit limited – usage of two equitable doctrines, namely *ubi ius, ubi remedium* and the prioritisation of substance over form (in the interests of justice) in tandem. Rossi notes that this 'bolder' expression by the Court 'marks a relatively rare occurrence in international jurisprudence. Normally the Court is loath to break new juridical ground if it can limit its decision to more narrowly circumscribed issues'.[192] It was also noted in chapter four that in the *Nicaragua* case, the decision to 'perfect' the consent of Nicaragua as regards the optional clause of compulsory jurisdiction of the ICJ owes much to the doctrine of *ex re sed non ex nomine*. There were clear faults in the formal consent criteria, which would have precluded the ICJ from exercising its jurisdiction in the affair, but these were set aside in the broader interests of justice.[193] Indeed, as noted elsewhere, such a broad construction of substance over form was highly controversial in this case, and was the subject of heated doctrinal debate. However, this merely serves to demonstrate that the World Court has, albeit very occasionally, been prepared to lay itself open to charges of judicial prevarication in order to give effect to equitable general principles in the interests of justice.

[190] H Delany, *Equity and the Law of Trusts in Ireland,* 3rd edn (Dublin, Thomson Roundhall, 2003) 34.

[191] *Brown County Bank v Freie Presse Printing Co* 174 Minn 143 (1928), 218 NW 557.

[192] Rossi (1993) (n 13) 173–74.

[193] *Case Concerning Military and Paramilitary Activities in and against Nicaragua (Nicaragua v United States)* (Judgment) [1984] ICJ Rep 14.

This aversion towards formalist interpretations and the idea that form may never be used as a shield for an illicit activity or purpose combine toward a more qualified interpretation of Article 2(4) of the UN Charter. The general prohibition upon the use of force may be perceived teleologically, much as the ICJ chose to view the formal consent criteria in the *Nicaragua* affair. Even the most superficial perusal of the UN Charter's general prohibition upon the use of force by States indicates that the purpose of this prohibition is to prevent the emergence of armed conflicts between States. Indeed, given the context of its drafting in the aftermath of the Second World War, this interest may be held to constitute the most fundamental single rationale for the Charter's coming into being. The purpose on the ban on the use of force is clearly a measure intended to limit armed conflicts and thus protect people. The purpose is not, however, to ensure an all-encompassing notion of State sovereignty that allows people to be tortured and murdered at the whim of a madman dictator. Such conduct – to the extent it was anticipated at all – is intended to give rise to action by the Security Council in its role as protector of international peace and security (the ambit of which may be determined by the Security Council itself). Evidently this situation is further complicated by the fact that many human rights norms only gained their normative 'teeth' subsequent to the Charter's adoption. If and when circumstances render it impossible for the Security Council to act to protect those suffering gross human rights abuses, the maxim *ex re sed non ex nomine* shall render it possible to look at the substance of the UN Charter – and indeed all international law, including human rights treaties and customary international law – rather than the Charter's form alone. Any such position which prioritises substance over form must take cognisance of the fact that the formal machinery of the UN Charter's general prohibition upon the use of force by States was created not to protect human rights abusers, but rather to prevent large-scale war and to preserve international peace and security. This is demonstrated by the non-absolute nature of the prohibition, whereby the Charter allows for two limited exceptions to the general prohibition, namely self-defence and enforcement action sanctioned by the Security Council, each of which is a reactive device, to be used as a response to serious incursions upon international peace and security. The substance of the Charter's prohibition, then, is the preservation of international peace and respect for the norms of international law. Hence, should a situation emerge whereby international peace and security are threatened by gross human rights abuses, the substance of the Charter may allow for humanitarian intervention.

It is perhaps worth noting here that the substance of the phrase 'international peace and security' itself has substantially changed since the Charter's inception. While Chesterman, amongst others, argued that refugee flows resulting from Pakistan's human rights abuses against the Bengali population destabilised the region, and partly acted as justification for India's subsequent intervention,[194] such refugee flows are hardly necessary for a threat to international peace and security to be established. Human rights abuses, when committed on a significant scale, have been enough to destabilise entire regions. When one considers events in the Balkans in the 1990s, for example, one is left with ample evidence of this trend. This is not to say, of course, that every instance of gross violations of human rights will trigger a right to humanitarian intervention. *Au contraire*, the point here is that the Charter's general prohibition upon the use of force may be viewed purposively rather than from a purely formalist perspective, and that such a purposive interpretation must take cognisance of the fact that gross human rights abuses may themselves contribute – to a greater or a lesser degree – to a threat to international peace and security, which is what the general prohibition upon the use of force purports to protect. In such situations, the *Nicaragua* formula of substance over form, combined with *ubi ius, ubi remedium*, may lend a certain amount of further legal impetus to legal arguments which would countenance humanitarian intervention.

vi. Principles in Practice – Drafting an Equitable Framework

Combining the weight of the principles discussed above, one is left with a distinctly more flexible picture of the Charter prohibition upon the use of force, and of international law in general. However, before tackling the effect of equitable principles upon the Charter regime on the use of force, it is perhaps useful to remind ourselves of the rules on treaty interpretation, noted in chapter two, concerning the interaction between general principles of law and international treaties. Article 31 of the Vienna Convention on the Law of Treaties represents a codification of the customary law position regarding the general rule of treaty interpretation.[195] Article 31(1) prescribes the 'basic rule', that a treaty is to be interpreted in good faith, with the ordinary meaning accorded to its terms in light of its object and purpose. Article 31(2) stipulates that due regard must be given to the treaty's context, while Article 31(3) places similar stipulations regarding subsequent agreements and subsequent practice. Article 31(4) prescribes that any special meaning must be taken into account; while Article 32 deals with supplementary means of interpretation. However, for the present purposes, the critical section of the VCLT is Article 31(3)(c), which prescribes that

[194] See repeated references to historical 'test cases for humanitarian intervention', including that of India/Pakistan in S Chesterman, *Just War or Just Peace? Humanitarian Intervention and International Law* (Oxford, Oxford University Press, 2001).

[195] M Villiger, *Commentary on the 1969 Vienna Convention on the Law of Treaties* (Leiden, Martinus Nijhoff, 2009) 415–41.

> [t]here shall be taken into account, together with the context: . . . (c) any relevant rules of international law applicable in the relations between the parties.

Villiger notes that such rules need have no particular relationship with the treaty in question other than assisting in the interpretation of its terms.[196] Although Article 31(3)(c) has long since been marginalised through infrequent explicit usage,[197] the ILC has noted that it remains an important component of the general rule and its importance should not be obscured through lack of overt references to it.[198] It is worth reiterating that Article 31 in its entirety is entitled the 'general rule of interpretation'. It is of course true that not all elements of Article 31 will be relevant in all cases. However, when they are, to whatever extent, they must be utilised. Article 31(2) and (3) are not merely discretionary appendages, but rather prescriptive and mandatory components of the general rule of treaty interpretation. Article 31(3) is unambiguous about this, stating 'There shall be taken into account' and leaving no room for judicial discretion in this regard. Earlier in this chapter, a series of examples were furnished in order to demonstrate the fact that extraneous norms, including customary international law and subsequent practice of the Security Council, have impacted upon the regime on the use of force as prescribed by the UN Charter, and must therefore be taken into account in any interpretation thereof. However, in interpreting the Charter, 'any relevant rules of international law' must be taken into account, per the VCLT. This necessarily includes general principles (as extraneous norms), insofar as they may potentially impact upon other rules of international law, including the Charter.

Hence, general principles of law – as relevant rules of international law – must be considered in the interpretation of international treaties, including the UN Charter. This was confirmed by the ICJ in the *Namibia* Advisory Opinion.[199] The question of how they may effect upon other more orthodox and less controversial interpretations of treaties is not entirely settled, though some observations in this regard have been made in this regard in chapter two. In short, logically, the further that general principles and other extraneous norms of international law push interpretation of international treaties away from an interpretation which accords with the 'basic rule' contained in Article 31(1), the more controversial such an interpretation becomes. This is due to the fact that such interpretations cleave significantly from a voluntarist conception of international law.

[196] ibid, 432.

[197] D French, 'Treaty Interpretation and the Incorporation of Extraneous Legal Rules' (2006) 55 *ICLQ* 281, 300.

[198] 'Report of the Group Established by the ILC on the Fragmentation of International Law', Report of the 56th Session (2004) A/59/10, 301.

[199] *Legal Consequences for States of the Continued Presence of South Africa in Namibia (South West Africa) notwithstanding Security Council Resolution 276 (1970)* (Advisory Opinion) [1971] ICJ Rep 16, 31.

Convened and precise terms in treaties being altered by occasionally unclear general principles would further seem to run contrary to the *lex specialis* principle. This also helps to explain why, with regards to equitable general principles, *infra legem* and occasionally *praeter legem* invocation are relatively uncontroversial, but *contra legem* usage may only be countenanced in truly exceptional circumstances.

As regards the shaping of an equitable framework for humanitarian intervention, several preliminary points must be noted. The first of these is that the third source of international law must certainly be factored into the equation when the topic of humanitarian intervention and the broader question of the use of force by States are raised, since, as demonstrated in the previous sections, this source of law may have significant relevance for interpreting, qualifying, and impacting upon the rules on the use of force by States. The second point is that, given the ample evidence provided by the case law of the World Court that this legal source may be both pertinent and potent in the solutions to a multiplicity of legal conundrums, it is somewhat surprising that the leading scholars on this subject have paid so little heed to general principles of law in framing the humanitarian intervention debate.

Thirdly, although not dealt with directly in this chapter, there is evidence, particularly that provided in the *Corfu Channel* case, that human rights or analogous humanitarian considerations may themselves form part of the general principles *corpus*. These 'elementary considerations of humanity', which the Court held were 'even more exacting in peace than in war',[200] would also seem to transcend the *ius ad bellum*/*ius in bello* divide, and are apparently not directly connected with either the wartime humanitarian law *corpus* or its peacetime human rights counterpart.[201] This would seem to add further weight to the notion that general principles may be equipped to traverse the traditional divide between the laws of war and the laws governing the use of force by States, adding weight to any notions of legal restrictions upon the conduct of States in undertaking humanitarian interventions. However, I am mindful of the *South West Africa* judgment – discussed in chapter four – which afforded a distinctly less central role to such principles, and it is for this reason that I have chosen not to employ such 'elementary considerations of humanity' directly in drafting a framework for equitable humanitarian intervention.[202]

[200] *Corfu Channel Case* (*United Kingdom v Albania*) (Merits) [1949] ICJ Rep 4, 22.

[201] As noted in ch 4, from what basis such elementary considerations are held to derive is unclear, but Rossi places them under the aegis of equitable principles in international law, while noting that the fact that the Court 'did not pause to spell out the legal basis of this obligation is unfortunate because such an explanation could have provided fertile ground for the further explanation of both the international minimum standards of protection for individuals under international law and the law of state responsibility'. Rossi (1993) (n 13) 180.

[202] See *South West Africa (Liberia and Ethiopia v South Africa)* [1966] ICJ Rep 34; see futher II. E in ch 4.

Another key point to note at this juncture is the fact that general principles, and more particularly equitable general principles such as those discussed in this chapter, while an inherent part of the international legal *corpus* itself, will only operate *infra legem* and *praeter legem* in normal circumstances. Usage *contra legem* – that is, against the letter of the (usually written) law – will only occur in exceptional circumstances. Again, we do not have a concrete test for when this may occur in international law due to the aforementioned lack of candour on the part of the World Court in its judgments which have dealt with general principles of law. However, what would seem clear is that it is possible for specific formal rules to be set aside if they clash with general principles where deep interests of justice are involved. This is demonstrated, inter alia, by the aforementioned *Nicaragua* jurisdiction decision, by Manley Hudson J's separate opinion in the *Meuse* case,[203] and by the *Chorzów Factory* case.[204] The lack of a precisely-defined threshold test for *contra legem* operability of general principles in international law does not entail that *contra legem* usage of such principles is impossible. On the contrary, it is an inherent characteristic of such principles that they may operate against the law as well as within it, albeit only in extremely exceptional circumstances, usually determined by the criterion of unconscionability. This is demonstrated by the experience of such principles within various national legal systems as well as the limited World Court case law that may guide us in this regard.

Since the test for *contra legem* applicability is cloudy at best, one must tread carefully when applying general principles against written rules. However, for the purposes of drafting a test for equitable humanitarian intervention, it would appear that it is perhaps not necessary after all to go as far as *contra legem* invocation of equitable principles in the strictest sense. Per Francioni, international law differs from national law, insofar as

> legal rules and principles are very general and with an ambit of appreciation that may be indeterminate and adaptable to different circumstances. This may permit [one] to present resort to equity as a set of considerations and criteria within the law or associated with the law, rather than outside or contrary to the law.[205]

Examining the United Nations Charter framework, it is clear that there is room for argument that the Charter does not prescribe a clear, codified, exhaustive list of situations where the general prohibition upon the use of force by States may be derogated from. There is no systematic link between Articles 2(4) and Article 42. Although Article 51 is linked to Article 42, the

[203] *Diversion of Water from the Meuse* PCIJ Rep Series A/B No 70, individual opinion of Manley Hudson J, 76–78.

[204] *Case Concerning the Factory at Chorzów* (Claim for Indemnity) (Jurisdiction) PCIJ Rep Series A No 9, 31.

[205] F Francioni, 'Equity in International Law' in R Wolfrum (ed), *The Max Planck Encyclopedia of Public International Law* (Oxford, Oxford University Press, 2008) para 14.

wording of these Articles does not go so far as to render these situations an exhaustive list of derogations to the general rule, which one might perhaps expect if the drafters had truly wished to devise a 'closing rule' with no scope for potential future developments. Further, the Charter itself, and particularly its Preamble, supports the possibility of a contrary conclusion. The Preamble prescribes that:

> WE THE PEOPLES OF THE UNITED NATIONS, DETERMINED . . .
>
> to reaffirm faith in fundamental human rights, in the dignity and worth of the human person, in the equal rights of men and women and of nations large and small, and
>
> to establish conditions under which justice and respect for the obligations arising from treaties and *other sources of international law* can be maintained . . .
>
> AND FOR THESE ENDS . . .
>
> to unite our strength to maintain international peace and security, and
>
> to ensure, by the acceptance of principles and the institution of methods, that armed force shall not be used, *save in the common interest* (emphasis added).[206]

The wording of the Preamble is perhaps revealing if one is to give credence to the position that Articles 42 and 51 may not constitute a definitive list of exceptions. The reference to 'other sources of international law' in the first paragraph reinforces the link between human rights (also mentioned), general principles of law as an extraneous source of international law, and the Charter itself. Further, the second paragraph prescribes that force shall not be used 'save in the common interest', which is clearly not identical to the combined effect of Articles 51 and 42. Article 51 in particular, concerns self-defence, which is necessarily suggestive of self-interest (though it may have some rule–utilitarian benefits). Further, if there was no clear wish to leave the door at least a fraction ajar for the development of further exceptions, then why not make a more concrete and systemic link between Articles 2(4), 42, 51 and the Preamble?

Of further note is the fact that Article 92 of the UN Charter itself recognises the ICJ Statute as an integral part of the Charter. This lends support to the fact that Article 38(1) of the ICJ Statute represents the definitive encapsulation of the sources of international law, certainly if not for all purposes, at least for those which concern interaction with the United Nations Charter. This being the case, Article 38(1) and its explicit reference to 'general principles of law recognised by civilised nations', the content of which has been examined in some depth in this volume, may, as an extraneous source of law per Article 31(3)(c) VCLT, act to inform an interpretation of the Charter that does not define Articles 42 and 51 as an exhaustive enumeration of permissible situations for the use of force by

[206] Charter of the United Nations 1945, 1 UNTS XVI.

States. In such a scenario, rather than derogating the Charter per se, the possibility of force 'in the common interest' through use of 'other sources of international law' to protect human rights could be held to be a legal interaction of the Charter, human rights norms and general principles of law. The fact that the Charter does not provide machinery on how such action should be undertaken constitutes, if anything, a lacuna. The shaping of a third exception to the prohibition upon the use of force in this manner also further supported by the principle that equity will look to the substance of a provision rather than its form. This would suggest that any model of equitable humanitarian intervention would be *praeter legem* rather than *contra legem*. This is supported to some degree by Francioni's contention that certain situations which appear to represent equity *contra legem* may in fact be *infra-* or *praeter legem* when seeming rule-breaking is supported by another rule of law, stating that a demarcation of equity *contra legem* from the use of equity within the law or as a gap-filler 'is extremely problematic, both conceptually and practically'.[207]

Infra legem and *praeter legem* applicability of general principles of law are less controversial and more widely accepted, though it is notable that the World Court has nonetheless been reticent about even these doctrines. Despite this limitation, however, the weight of the principles discussed in this chapter upon the UN Charter regime governing the use of force by States is significant. This is doubly so when they are considered together. The idea that States may be estopped from denying the fulfilment of promises which they have made (or are held to have assented to) to respect human rights may be combined with the principle that for every wrong there must be a remedy. Ergo, if States ignore the estoppel which has arisen, thereby acting *mala fides*, and if treaty law and customary international law fail to provide a remedy to the wrong which is being committed, and if the circumstances are sufficiently extreme and the conduct sufficiently unconscionable, then equitable general principles may intervene to craft an appropriate remedy. However, to be able to claim an estoppel against another State, any complainant State must itself be free of iniquity, have 'clean hands', and must undertake to conduct itself equitably if it is to participate in the administration of any remedy.[208]

Based upon the applicability of the principles discussed above, a model for humanitarian intervention that may be held to be legal by virtue of equity, or more properly, equitable general principles of international law,

[207] Francioni (2008) (n 205) paras 17–18. The author uses the example of sovereign immunity being used to defeat State jurisdiction, though it could perhaps be argued that this is merely a situation of a more specific rule derogating from the general one.

[208] Something similar has been suggested by Pattison, who argues that the question of 'who intervenes' is both morally and potentially legally relevant in determining the legitimacy and legality of any intervention. J Pattison, 'Humanitarian Intervention and International Law: the Moral Importance of an Intervener's Legal Status' (2007) 10 *Critical Review of International Society and Political Philosophy* 301.

and their interaction with the UN Charter regime on the use of force, emerges. It represents the culmination of a process of multi-source legal reasoning, employing general principles, and particularly those of an equitable nature, to temper the rigour of strict written rules when faced with a situation of a serious and extremely grave legal wrong existing but being without an adequate and effective remedy, a situation, which further, in this instance, amounts to a manifest injustice. Its tenets are as follows:

1) A series of gross and systematic human rights violations is committed;
2) By a State which has either signed human rights instruments or which has not consistently objected to the inclusion of human rights as part of customary international law.[209]
3) It must be determined beyond reasonable doubt that a peaceable means of putting an end to the violations will not be achievable in a sufficiently proximate time frame to prevent (further) gross human rights abuses from occurring or continuing.[210]
4) There must be no means of immediate ending these violations via the machinery of the UN Charter, that is the Security Council.
5) It must be reasonably determined that only armed military intervention will suffice as an immediate and effective means of ending the violations.
6) Intervention is only permitted where it may be an effective solution and is not undertaken in vain.

[209] In essence, this requirement is unnecessary. All States basically qualify under this criterion.

[210] It must be conceded that the formulation of this criterion is rather cumbersome and inelegant. In earlier drafts of this text, the concept of impossibility of putting a peaceful end to abuses had been used in its stead. However, the notion of 'impossibility' is very difficult indeed to prove or demonstrate to any satisfying degree. A possible alternative would be to say that 'all peaceable means of putting an immediate end to these violations must have been exhausted'. However, this is perhaps not suitable either. It would suggest that would-be intervening States must first exhaust all peaceable means of ending the violations which are occurring, even in situations where they are fully aware that such measures are highly unlikely to be heeded. For example, this entails that the would-be intervening States must make diplomatic entreaties towards the transgressor State, perhaps convene both the General Assembly and the Security Council in order to secure Resolutions, use sanctions regimes and trade embargoes, and any other measures which are commonly used to secure a non-violent end to gross human rights violations by a State against its own citizens in situations where there is no prospect of procuring Chapter VII action from the Security Council. After each of these measures, the would-be intervening State must presumably wait to see if the measure in question has had the desired effect of halting the gross human rights abuses that are continuing in the transgressor State. Such a formulation requires a temporal lapse greatly at odds with the urgency of real-life situations of humanitarian intervention. Of course the idea of determination beyond reasonable doubt is still far from an objective measurement, but it gives a steady, negatively-framed barometer as a threshold for intervention. If any State can advance convincing evidence that peaceable action will be successful in ending abuses, then intervention will not be permitted.

It is my contention that the evidence presented in this chapter suggests that if the six-fold test is satisfied, the equitable general principles of international law will allow a remedy – namely armed intervention – to be created to fill the lacuna in the legal framework *praeter legem*, and that this remedy may be invoked to supplement the strictures of the UN Charter regime. An estoppel may be held to arise from the conduct of the transgressor State in its acceptance of human rights obligations, with a change of position from other States, which acted in good faith based upon their perception that the transgressor State would stand by its obligations. The lack of a remedy through the United Nations machinery leads to the creation of a remedy *praeter legem* via the *ubi ius, ubi remedium* principle, its invocation being necessitated by the manifest injustice (gross human rights violations on a massive scale) that will result if no remedy is found. However, in accordance with this principle, armed intervention will only be permitted where peaceable means will not suffice and where such armed intervention is likely to be an effective remedy.

However, this is not the end of the story, since, as mentioned above, the strict separation between *ius ad bellum* and *ius in bello* would not seem to apply so rigidly to general principles of law. Hence, the legitimacy, legality and permissibility of any putative intervention are also predicated upon the conduct of the States which undertake it. Particular attention must be had to the clean hands doctrine, bona fides (and the doctrine of the abuse of rights) upon which the legal permission to intervene is necessarily predicated. More particularly:

1) No state which itself engages in gross and systematic human rights violations may intervene ('clean hands').
2) States must intervene with the principal purpose of ending such violations. Any right to intervene must not be used as a cloak for other ends, otherwise this will constitute *mala fides.*
3) States must act equitably in enforcing equity and must refrain from unnecessary loss of civilian life and unnecessary suffering in attempting to accomplish the operation, the purpose of which is to protect life and end suffering. To do otherwise will constitute an abuse of rights.

IV. CONCLUSION

The above represents equity's formula for humanitarian intervention. Its two-part nature sets it apart from that of most commentators, and makes it unique. In particular, its attention to the duties owed by the intervening power creates a series of safeguards against any abusive employment of the right to intervene. The utility of these safeguards must not be underestimated. If States wish to intervene, they must themselves boast a respectable human rights record, and must conduct the operation with the highest regard for the lives of those civilians whom they are supposed to be protecting.

The formulation which I have thus presented shares many common elements with the formulae advanced by various scholars discussed in the first chapter of this work, who have made use of the legal/legitimate dichotomy or who have attempted to mix law with ethics, politics or justice. In addition, the equitable formulation is mirrored in much of its import by the ICISS 'Responsibility to Protect' principles. However, the superiority of the equitable solution must immediately be obvious, insofar as it is rooted in the law, not merely in ethics, politics, or hazy philosophy. Here I am inclined to agree with Alf Ross' predilection for law rather than a broad conception of 'justice':

> To invoke justice is the same thing as banging on a table: an emotional expression which turns one's demand into an absolute postulate. That is no proper way to mutual understanding. It is impossible to have a rational conversation with a man who mobilises justice, because he says nothing that can be argued for or against. His words are persuasion, not argument.[211]

Nonetheless, there will doubtless be those who will seek to argue that the equitable model allows for the importation of moral reasoning, or even principles of natural law, into the legal framework on the use of force by States. Indeed, as mentioned in chapter two, Lauterpacht's conception of general principles of law included natural law in tandem with analogies from municipal legal systems.[212] However, responses to any charges that the equitable framework proposed above represents naturalist, rather than positivist, legal reasoning may be answered with two observations. The first brief point is that international law as a body of norms is not amoral in nature. The long-standing ban on the slave trade, the ever-increasing body of international human rights norms, international criminal law, international humanitarian law and the emerging *corpus* of international environmental law all represent normative categories closely linked to moral concerns. These categories demonstrate that international law does not exist in some sort of moral vacuum, and that it may be shaped, inter alia, by certain moral concerns when they are commonly held by States. However, long before most of these normative categories attained their contemporary importance, general principles of law such as good faith existed in order to regulate conduct and ensure ethical and moral dealing in contractual relations between individuals (and, in time, between States). It should therefore be acknowledged that while this work has sought to propose a legal, rather than a moral, framework for humanitarian inter-

[211] A Ross, *On Law and Justice* (Berkeley, University of California Press, 1959) 274.

[212] H Lauterpacht, *International Law and Human Rights* (London, Stevens and Sons, 1950) 115.

vention, that there are certain communalities between general principles and some tenets of moral and ethical theory, including natural law theory, as opined by Lauterpacht. This may go some way toward explaining why the test presented above bears similarities to those presented by some of the 'moralist' scholars criticised in the first chapter of this volume.[213]

The second point in riposte to those who would paint the test presented as an exercise in moral reasoning is (once again) to refer sceptics to the ICJ Statute, which, per Article 92 of the UN Charter, forms an integral part of the Charter text itself. While one may agree or disagree over the proximity of natural law to equity and general principles as described in this work, one must surely recognise that Article 38(1) of the ICJ Statute is generally recognised as the 'sources clause' for international law. International legal scholars rarely dispute this point.[214] The nature of general principles as a legal source is a matter for which I pursued an inductive analysis in order to better determine. While custom and treaty are, up to a point, sources of law an understanding of which may be agreed upon by international legal scholars, the same may not be said of 'general principles of law recognised by civilised nations'. It was therefore my goal to use the most representative and non-subjective barometer that I could find to delineate the content of this normative category. ICJ and PCIJ judgments provided the closest approximation to what I sought. As noted in chapter one Koskenniemi has outlined via an intricate and relatively cogent process, eight steps through which international lawyers are transformed into moralists by the logic of the argument for humanitarian intervention, passing from: (1) formal law *stricto sensu*, to (2) formal law *lato sensu*, to (3) instrumentalism (international law being an activity oriented toward a particular human purpose), to (4) utilitarianism, to (5) rights as trumps (per Dworkin), to (6) legislative discourse, to (7) law as procedure, and finally to (8) the turn to ethics, as Koskenniemi brands it. I find the logic of this model to be useful, and I believe that certain apologists for intervention *à la* Kosovo, such as Cassese and Nicholas Wheeler, have gone a long way down this eight-step road. I have roundly criticised them for doing so. However, at best (or, perhaps, better, at worst), the equitable model in this volume gets as far as point two. If I am guilty of using formal law *au sens large*, then I feel that this is justified, given that it is done with full and

[213] See Sections IV, V, VI, VII, IX, X, and XI in ch 1.

[214] See A D'Amato, *The Concept of Custom in International Law* (Ithaca, NY, Cornell University Press, 1971) 88; H Thirlway, *International Customary Law and its Codification* (Leiden, AW Sijthoff, 1972) 58; O Schachter, 'The Evolving International Law of Development' (1976) 15 *Columbia Journal of Transnational Law* 20; Cheng (1987) (n 4) 21–27; P Dallier and A Pellet, *Droit International Public*, 7eme (Paris, Librairie Générale de Droit et Jurisprudence, 2002) 114; P Kooijmans, *Internationaal publiekrecht in vogelvlucht*, 9th edn (Deventer, Kluwer, 2002); D Ruzié, *Droit international public*, 17eme (Paris, Dalloz, 2004) 15; M Karg, *IGH vs ISGH Die Beziehung zwischen zwei völkerrechtlichen Streitbeilegungsorganen* (Baden-Baden, Nomos, 2005); A Zimmermann (ed), *The Statute of the International Court of Justice: A Commentary* (Oxford, Oxford University Press, 2006); Raimondo (2008) (n 13) 20–21.

clear reference to the sources of law (Article 38(1) ICJ) and treaty interpretation (Article 31(3)(c) VCLT).

The fact that formal logic leads us to a similar finishing point, and to a similar 'test' to those of scholars like Cassese whom I so roundly criticised in chapter one is certainly interesting. Similar criteria would perhaps have emerged from an examination of the morally-inspired ideas of St Thomas Aquinas, the Spanish scholastics, or Grotius. However, while ultimately the criteria proposed for equitable humanitarian intervention in chapter five are doubtless similar to the tests proposed by Cassese and others, their distinctive quality is that they are based upon the law itself (even law *lato sensu*, if we must go this far), and not on political, ethical or moral philosophy.

The equitable model allows States the right to humanitarian intervention without straying outside international law and thereby destabilising international relations and the international legal order. In return for this right, however, they must present clean hands, and comport themselves equitably in the execution of the operation. A good many problems remain with the equitable formulation. While I feel I have demonstrated that there is good reason to follow the interpretation of equitable general principles that I have presented in this work, principles are by their nature less rigid than rules. Hence, other interpretations are certainly possible. While the equity model which I tentatively propose at the end of this chapter contains certain safeguards against abuse, these will be difficult to police. It would seem rather awkward to award a State a legal right to intervene in its neighbour's territory, only to retrospectively vitiate that right due to the State's conduct in executing said intervention, branding that State an aggressor – rather than a good Samaritan – in the process. States could even use such a code of conduct as justification for not intervening, for fear of being branded as international lawbreakers if they fail to maintain clean hands throughout the operation.

Such concerns, combined with the plethora of – admittedly mostly very patchy – literature on humanitarian intervention that has been penned in the last 13 years, means that States may be slow to adhere to the equitable model when considering humanitarian intervention. However, given that a firm and overbearing consensus in favour of any significant revision to the current regime on the use of force by States is – despite what Messrs Cassese et al would have the world believe – unlikely to emerge, equitable humanitarian intervention represents the sole legal avenue for military intervention to end gross human rights abuses. This is largely because it is predicated upon usage of the only source of international law that is not entirely voluntaristic in nature, requiring neither *usus* nor ratification to confirm its existence. Important to note is the fact that the nine conditions necessary to satisfy the test for legal equitable humanitarian intervention should be interpreted strictly. Six, seven, or even eight of the conditions together will not suffice to lend legality to any military operation. Rather, all nine must necessarily be satisfied. This is a restrictive measure for States, and will serve to limit the ambitions of those who would wish to cloak opportunistic military plundering in legal clothing. Again, this measure will reduce still further the range of States which might become proponents of such a doctrine, though it is germane to note that since this model is rooted in general principles rather than in customary international law, a lack of popular usage of the doctrine will not expunge it from the legal framework, where it will continue to exist until such a time as either the Charter regime or general principles of law are changed substantially. Since neither of these normative categories is likely to substantially change in the near future, we are left with the real possibility that, despite the likely reticence of States to be bound by the strictures of what is an extremely circumscribed third exception to the general prohibition on the use of force, it is by no means far-fetched to speculate that one day in the future a State or group thereof may consent to these constraints in order to avail of an opportunity to legally intervene to help those who cannot help themselves.

Until now, international law has seemed to be stuck between a rock and a hard place, as it were, when discussing humanitarian intervention. States and commentators were left with a stark choice. Cling to the machinery of the UN Charter, and one was labelled an apologist for *génocidaires*. Adopt a more 'adventurous' approach to justify humanitarian intervention, and one was accused of ignoring international law, thereby weakening global stability and peace. The lack of a third way, a third option, meant that one was open to condemnation in either case. Preserve international peace and the international legal system, or protect people against gross human rights abuses? The choice was necessary because international law did not seem to offer a means to do both. It is my contention that this choice is no longer necessary. The third source of international law offers a third perspective on the problem, crafting a third, albeit limited, exception to the general prohibition upon the use of force.

This is by no means the end of the story. Clearly, test cases will be necessary to see how equity's model works in practice. Certainly, no State has thus far purported to use anything similar in executing an intervention. However, perhaps it is not wildly optimistic to speculate that States may be tempted by the unearthing of a doctrine that would legally permit them to come to the rescue of those being murdered and tortured by tyrannical governments, even in the absence of Security Council authorisation. The previous position left any legal advisor wishing to frame even the most altruistically minded intervention carried out by his or her government without Security Council approbation in a difficult position. Resort to alternative languages – of ethics, political theory, necessity and philosophy – was the inevitable, and inenviable result, short of admitting illegality. The law was cast aside, and with it, one of the principal pillars of international order and stability.

The equitable framework presented in these pages offers another alternative. Through multi-source legal reasoning, those seeking to justify intervention to put a halt to gross and systematic human rights abuses may now ground their reasoning in the logic and the language of international law. Admittedly, problems remain with the framework presented. However, its tenets present those who wish to effectively prevent gross human rights abuses, while simultaneously upholding the stability and order offered by international law, with a means of accomplishing both in tandem. Such a solution may potentially prove attractive to States dissatisfied with failed initiatives like the R2P; States that wish to prevent slaughter without destabilising the international legal regime. If this is indeed the case, then equity and general principles could yet provide the basis for a fresh category of legal humanitarian intervention.

Conclusion

IN RECENT YEARS, discussions regarding the potential legality, legitimacy and consequences of unsanctioned humanitarian intervention have again come to the fore in international affairs. This trend has been fuelled by the crises in Libya and Syria in 2011 and 2012 respectively. While neither of these two recent events present a situation identical to Kosovo, or one that demonstrates the humanitarian intervention conundrum in such a stark light, it is nonetheless true that in both cases, world leaders, and particularly Western leaders, have come under intense pressure to react to the crises as they unfolded. It is also true that in both situations, certain Permanent Members of the UN Security Council seemed reticent to sanction armed intervention. In both cases, the civilian population was suffering due to abuses meted out by its own government. The moral outcry was clearly audible. Something, it seemed, needed to be done.

At the time of writing, the Syrian crisis is still unfolding, while the Libyan civil war, and the Western (Security Council-sanctioned) intervention remain fresh in the memory. The proverbial 'fog of war' has obscured some of the happenings in both contexts, and it may yet be some time before the details of what really transpired in either case become fully known. Despite this, both situations may serve as interesting case studies for models of humanitarian intervention, and for our present purposes, for the equitable framework presented in this volume. In these concluding pages, I shall make use of both scenarios in order to test the equitable framework in a scenario shaped by real-life circumstances – although in both cases, counterfactual elements will also be utilised.

I. LIBYA 2011

On 19 March 2011, a multi-State coalition began a military intervention in Libya to implement United Nations Security Council Resolution 1973, which was taken in response to events during the 2011 Libyan civil war.[1]

[1] UN Security Council SC/10200, 6498th Meeting (Night), 'Security Council Approves "No-Fly Zone" over Libya, Authorizing "All Necessary Measures" to Protect Civilians, by Vote of 10 in Favour with 5 Abstentions': www.un.org/News/Press/docs/2011/sc10200.doc.htm.

Military operations began with US and British forces firing over 110 Tomahawk cruise missiles, the French Air Force and British Royal Air Force undertaking sorties across Libya and a naval blockade by the Royal Navy. Since the beginning of the intervention, the initial coalition of Belgium, Canada, Denmark, France, Italy, Norway, Qatar, Spain, UK and US has expanded to 17 States, with newer States mostly enforcing the no-fly zone and naval blockade or providing military logistical assistance. The effort was initially largely led by France and the United Kingdom, with command shared with the United States.[2] NATO took control of the arms embargo on 23 March, named Operation Unified Protector. On 24 March, NATO agreed to take control of the no-fly zone, while command of targeting ground unit's remains with coalition forces. The handover occurred on 31 March 2011 at 0600 GMT.

The intervention itself was, like Kosovo before it, primarily conducted from the air. Initial operations were undertaken via warships and submarines firing Tomahawk missiles, and F-16 and other jets flying sorties and targeting Libyan military targets from high altitudes. In order to achieve better targeting and more effective engagement of Libyan ground units, British Prime Minister David Cameron confirmed, on 27 May 2011, the deployment of an unspecified number of Apache attack helicopters to aid the intervention. NATO command confirmed that French helicopters would also participate.[3] A limited amount of support in the form of military training and logistics has also been supplied to rebel forces in Libya fighting the Gaddafi Government.[4] Further, the European Union on 1 April approved a mission that would see troops from EU Member States deployed in Libya, under the title 'EUFOR Libya'. The proposed force would number less than 1,000, and be deployed solely to render humanitarian aid to civilians in the country.[5]

The legal authority upon which the military intervention in Libya was undertaken rested upon Security Council Resolution 1973. Resolution 1973 gives explicit permission for the maintenance of a no-fly zone over Libyan territory, as well as demanding the immediate establishment of a ceasefire and a complete end to violence and all attacks against, and abuses of, civilians. The resolution further authorises the use of 'all necessary measures' to protect civilians and civilian-populated areas, except for measures amounting to permanent occupation of the territory. It further strengthens the pre-existing arms embargo and particularly action against

[2] 'Libya: US, UK and France attack Gaddafi forces', BBC News Online, 20 March 2011, available at: www.bbc.co.uk/news/world-africa-12796972.

[3] 'May 27th updates', LibyaFeb17.com archive site, 27 May 2011, available at: archive.libyafeb17.com/2011/05/may-27th-updates/.

[4] 'Number Crunching: Hague to Send British Soldiers to Train Ragtag Rebel Army', *Private Eye*, London, no 1287, April/May 2011, 5.

[5] J Bajoria, 'Libya and the Responsibility to Protect', Council on Foreign Relations, 24 March 2011, available at: www.cfr.org/libya/libya-responsibility-protect/p24480.

mercenaries, by allowing for forcible inspections of ships and planes; imposes a ban on all Libyan-designated flights; imposes a freeze upon assets owned by the Libyan authorities, and reaffirms that such assets should be used for the benefit of the Libyan people; extends the travel ban and assets freeze of United Nations Security Council Resolution 1970 to a number of additional individuals and Libyan entities; and establishes a panel of experts to monitor and promote the implementation of sanctions.

Resolution 1973, undertaken under Chapter VII of the United Nations Charter, confers NATO and other intervening States with the necessary legal authority to intervene. The *'all necessary measures'* clause, contained in paragraph 4 of the resolution, gives unfettered discretion to intervening States in their choice of methods of intervention, provided that they are undertaken to protect civilians. Any military measures which go beyond the basic maintenance of the no-fly zone must be interpreted as being undertaken under the authority of this paragraph. This may well extend to the arming of rebel forces. Although the arms embargo imposed by paragraph 9 of Resolution 1970 would prevent arms being supplied to anyone in Libya, Resolution 1973 qualifies resolution 1970 with the wording 'all necessary measures . . . notwithstanding paragraph 9 of resolution 1970'. Hillary Clinton has argued that it would therefore be legal to arm rebel forces.[6] This was also the argument used by British Foreign Secretary William Hague.[7]

The legal basis for the Libyan intervention, then, is uncontroversial. However, what I wish to explore is a counterfactual hypothesis. Russia and China had reservations about the wording of Resolution 1973, particularly as regards the no-fly zone, including the practicalities of enforcing such a zone and concerns about the use of force when other means had not been exhausted.[8] However, noting the position of the Arab League and the 'special situation' in Libya, they therefore abstained rather than vetoing the Resolution.[9] However, what if, concerned by another NATO-led intervention in an area which had traditionally been outside the Western sphere of influence, and citing concerns about the use of force where there was no obvious threat to international peace and security (required for Chapter VII action), one or both of Russia and China had vetoed the draft Resolution, making it clear that they would not support military intervention against Libya in any circumstances? And what if, as

[6] L Trevelyan, 'Libya: Coalition divided on arming rebels, BBC News Online, 29 March 2011, available at: www.bbc.co.uk/news/world-africa-12900706.

[7] 'Number Crunching: Hague to Send British Soldiers to Train Ragtag Rebel Army', *Private Eye*, London, no 1287, April/May 2011, 5.

[8] 'UN Security Council adopts resolution on Libya', *RIA Novosti*, 18 March 2011, available at: en.rian.ru/world/20110318/163067336.html.

[9] S Dasgupta, 'China Opposed UN Resolution on Libya', *The Times of India*, New Dehli, 18 March 2011, available at: articles.timesofindia.indiatimes.com/2011-03-18/china/29144182_1_libya resolution countries.

in Kosovo 12 years previously, NATO had decided that humanitarianism and respect for human rights demanded action? The question arises as to whether the equitable framework might furnish permission for NATO action analogous to that which has in fact been undertaken in lieu of Security Council authorisation.

As noted in the previous chapter, the putative model for equitable humanitarian intervention proposes a two-part test for legality. The first part consists of six criteria which must be fulfilled before intervention will be permitted; the second of three conditions relating to the conduct of warfare and the actual operation of the intervention itself. The first part of the test runs thus:

1) A series of gross and systematic human rights violations is committed;
2) By a State which has either signed human rights instruments or which has not consistently objected to the inclusion of human rights as part of customary international law.
3) It must be determined beyond reasonable doubt that a peaceable means of putting an end to the violations at hand will not be achievable in a sufficiently proximate time frame to prevent (further) gross human rights abuses from occurring or continuing.
4) There must be no means of immediate ending these violations via the machinery of the UN Charter, that is the Security Council.
5) It must be reasonably determined that only armed military intervention will suffice as an immediate and effective means of ending the violations.
6) Intervention is only permitted where it may be an effective solution and is not undertaken in vain.

Sequentially relating the above criteria to the concrete situation in Libya, we can see that the first criterion would seem, prima facie, to be satisfied. Although information is occasionally contradictory from the various media sources, it would seem that the Gaddafi regime perpetrated severe human rights abuses against its own civilian population. This was the reason behind the 'all necessary measures' clause, which the UN Security Council saw fit to insert in Resolution 1973. Hence, in our counterfactual situation, we may suppose that the same level of abuses have taken place, and that therefore our first criterion is reached. The second, linked, criterion is, as noted in the previous chapter, close to superfluous, being inserted purely for the sake of clarity, since all States are bound by most of the international *corpus* dealing with gross human rights abuses in any case. Further for the present purposes, while the Libyan regime under Gaddafi has a poor human rights record,[10] Libya has

[10] In 2005, Freedom House rated political rights in Libya as 'seven' (one representing the most free and seven the least-free rating), civil liberties as 'seven' and gave it the freedom rating of 'Not Free'. Freedom House, *Freedom in the World 2006*, available at: www.freedomhouse.org/uploads/pdf/Charts2006.pdf.

nonetheless ratified the ICCPR, the ICESCR and the UN Convention Against Torture, has acceded to the Genocide Convention, and is party to a further host of international human rights instruments. In addition, Libya has not been a consistent objector to human rights norms in customary law and is further bound by the norms of *ius cogens*.

It would further seem that a peaceable means of ending the human rights violations was beyond the reach of the international community by this time. While, on 18 March, the Libyan Foreign Minister, Moussa Koussa, declared a ceasefire in accordance with Security Council Resolution 1973,[11] artillery shelling on the cities of Ajdabiya and Misrata continued, while tanks entered Benghazi the day after.[12] Hence, we may confidently conclude that this deception by the Libyan Government was indicative of their unwillingness to respond to peaceful entreaties on the part of the international community. In addition, the immediacy of the violence against civilians was such that to wait any longer and to continue to negotiate with slim hope of coercing Gaddafi's regime to cooperate could have led to further unfettered opportunities for violence by the Libyan Government against its own civilians.

So to the fourth criterion proposed, namely the impossibility of action through the machinery of the UN Charter. In our counterfactual example, Russia and China made it clear that the procurement of a Resolution to intervene militarily in Libya will be met with a veto from one or both of them for the reason that, in their opinion, there is no immediate threat to international peace and security. Hence, this criterion is also met. The equitable model of humanitarian intervention represents the only *legal* possibility for intervention.

The reasonable determination that only military intervention will suffice to put an end to the ensuing atrocities would also seem rather straightforward. The Gaddafi Government had repeatedly demonstrated that its word could not be trusted. Its human rights record was consistently abominable, and it has already been demonstrated that a peaceable means of ending the violence against civilians was impossible. Under such circumstances, the fulfilment of this criterion seems both logical and natural. So too the fact that intervention will only be permitted if it is an effective solution and not undertaken in vain. Destruction of Libya's military capacity would seem an ideal solution to ending the atrocities which were taking place, being perpetrated by and large by military and police forces.

[11] 'Libya: Foreign minister announces immediate ceasefire', BBC News Online, 18 March 2011, available at: www.bbc.co.uk/news/world-middle-east-12787056.

[12] T Amara and M Karouny, 'Gaddafi forces shell west Libya's Misrata, 25 dead', *Reuters*, Tunis, 18 March 2011, available at: uk.reuters.com/article/2011/03/18/us-libya-misrata-bombard-idUKTRE72H4L520110318; 'Libya: Gaddafi forces attacking rebel-held Benghazi', BBC News Online, 19 March 2011, available at: www.bbc.co.uk/news/world-africa-12793919

The six above criteria would thus seem to be fairly unequivocally satiated in the case of Libya. Even without a Security Council Resolution, NATO's intervention would thus seem legally permissible under the equitable model. However, this is not the end of the story. Unlike the UN Charter system, where the mandate accorded to interveners is generally separated from *ius in bello* issues, the equitable model, based upon equitable principles, is composed of two parts, the first relating to threshold criteria, the second to conditions concerning the conduct of warfare. These conditions are:

1) No state which itself engages in gross and systematic human rights violations may intervene ('clean hands').
2) States must intervene with the principal purpose of ending such violations and may not profit unduly as a result of doing so. Above all, any right to intervene must not be used as a cloak for other ends; otherwise this will constitute *mala fides*.
3) States must act equitably in enforcing equity and must refrain from unnecessary loss of civilian life and unnecessary suffering in attempting to accomplish the operation, the purpose of which is to protect life and end suffering.

As regards the conditions relating to the conduct of warfare, the question of the legality of our hypothetical Libyan intervention becomes somewhat more nuanced. While the majority of those States intervening would seem to have clean hands as far as gross human rights abuses are concerned, some questions may be asked regarding, for example, the practice of public stoning of women for adultery in Qatar and the treatment of terrorism suspects by the United States. As noted in chapter five, there is no easy answer to the question as to where to draw the line in terms of 'clean hands'. However, while states like the US and Qatar have committed serious human rights abuses and while such abuses should certainly not be taken lightly, they do not qualify as gross and systematic human rights abuses on a large scale, which must represent our threshold criterion in determining the cleanliness of the hands of any potential intervening State. Such a formulation does not entirely eschew questions of subjectivity, but it does add the requirement that a discernible systematic pattern must be identifiable, and that isolated incidents of human rights abuses by States may not be used as a pretext for abusive and disingenuous invocation of the equitable model, or, *a contrario*, the debarring of would-be interveners on the basis of isolated elements of their own human rights record. The hands of the intervening States' may not be glistening, but they are still sufficiently clean for the job at hand.

Regarding the purpose of the intervention, whether or not NATO and other States were genuinely intervening to rescue Libyan civilians remains a matter of some conjecture. It has been argued that European States, principally Italy, have a strong interest in gaining control of Libyan oil reserves. Additionally, the significant gold reserves of the Libyan Central Bank have been proposed as an alluring asset.[13] In addition, Gaddafi's history of sponsoring terrorist groups such as the IRA in Northern Ireland and Libyan involvement in the Lockerbie bombing have long made him a pariah for the West. Revenge and the wish to eliminate a troublesome leader may have led Western European and American leaders to use the crisis in Libya as an excuse for something they wished to accomplish in any case.[14] However, this is by no means clear. It is also perfectly possible that, as stated in the Security Council deliberations, the Libyan intervention genuinely was undertaken to save civilians. This case is supported by the fact that no attempts to militarily intervene were undertaken until the 2011 crisis came about. In addition, concerns that the West was attempting to 'murder' Gaddafi out of some sort of vengeful motive were unfounded. Gaddafi was the supreme military commander of the Libyan army, and is thus a legitimate military target under international humanitarian law. Hence, any attempts to remove him from the military equation are entirely legal, particularly if this leads to a speedier end to hostilities and abuses against civilians. In fact, one may state that due to the human rights record of his regime, missions to kill Gaddafi may well be amongst the most effective possible means to protect civilians.[15] This is a happy coincidence for the purpose of the equitable test. While, realistically, it is unlikely that the Libyan intervention was undertaken with the sole purpose of ending atrocities and rescuing civilians by all intervening parties, the equitable test does not require this. Rather it requires that the *principal* purpose is to save civilians, and while questions may be asked about the conduct of warfare by air to protect people being attacked by soldiers and tanks, there is nonetheless no compelling reason available which leads to the conclusion that protecting civilians (through the removal of Gaddafi, regime change or otherwise) was not the principal purpose of this mission.

The third and final condition relating to the conduct of warfare by intervening States stipulates that States must act equitably in enforcing equity and must refrain from unnecessary loss of civilian life and unnecessary suffering in attempting to accomplish the operation, the purpose of which is to protect life and end suffering. This is perhaps the most difficult condition, both to assess and to fulfil. What one may term as 'unnecessary loss of life' is notoriously difficult to quantify, even to military planners

[13] D Walker, 'Libya: the After Dinar Mint', *Ground Report*, 27 May 2011, available at: www.groundreport.com/Business/Libya-The-After-Dinar-Mint/2939257.

[14] P McKay, 'Gaddafi and the £1bn battle to save Dave's face', *Daily Mail*, London, 30 May 2011, available at: www.dailymail.co.uk/debate/article-1392253/Gaddafi-1bn-battle-save-Daves-face.html?ito=feeds-newsxml.

[15] P Preston, 'Remember Srebrenica? The west's intervention in Libya is a no-brainer', *The Guardian*, London, 29 May 2011, available at www.guardian.co.uk/commentisfree/2011/may/29/srebrenica-libya-intervention-no-brainer.

and experts in international humanitarian law. The ideas of mixed-use (civilian and military) targets and collateral damage divide opinion. However, what is clear from literature on international humanitarian law is that indiscriminate targeting is not permitted, and that States must take care to ensure that their targeting is as accurate as it can be. The lack of a media presence with access to all the available information in Libya has led to contradictory reports about the number of civilian and (allied) rebel-held targets hit by NATO missiles. Even in the weeks and months subsequent to the conclusion of hostilities, further clarity in this regard has not been forthcoming. However, the very fact that missiles have been launched from battleships and submarines off the coast and jets flying at high altitudes leads to serious concern about military targeting. Similar tactics in Serbia a decade earlier led to a series of civilian targets being hit, including a passenger train and the Chinese embassy. In addition, while France and the UK proffered limited helicopter support, the failure to deploy significant numbers of ground troops suggests that this alone may not be enough to protect civilians. It is clear that many of the intervening powers have sufficient military resources at their disposal to have deployed a significant number of ground troops into Libya, far beyond the meagre number of troops that were eventually sent to the country. Such a deployment would be more in keeping with the protection of civilians than unassisted bombing campaigns against villas and other mixed-use targets.[16]

On the face of it, then, it would seem that on this unique condition, the Libyan intervention falls foul of the equitable test. However, it may be necessary to take a somewhat broader view. When the choice is between doing something and doing nothing – that is, when bombing from 10,000m is all putative interveners are prepared to offer – is the equitable humanitarian intervention of such a nature that it would prefer to see Libyan civilians massacred rather than allow action which might potentially help them? The answer, of course, is no. The shadow of Mogadishu – where the loss of American military personnel during the Black Hawk Down operation evoked public outcry – coloured American tactics in Serbia and elsewhere.[17] Television images of American soldiers being dragged through the streets by Somalis were too graphic for the American public to endure. The Clinton Administration responded by altering its regional humanitarian efforts by scaling down United States involvement in Africa, and it became obvious to many Western democratic leaders that such images could cost them elections. The unpopularity of the Iraq war

[16] 'Libya crisis: UN leaves Tripoli amid mob attacks', BBC News Online, 2 May 2011, available at: www.bbc.co.uk/news/world-africa-13253896.

[17] R Thornton, *Asymmetric Warfare: Threat and Response in the Twenty-First Century* (Cambridge, Polity Press, 2007) 10.

has again highlighted such concerns.[18] The idea that State governments should intervene in situations where humanitarian concerns must represent the primary purpose of intervention, that they should not unduly profit from doing so, and that they should nonetheless agree to commit their soldiers' lives to a war from which they have little to gain may indeed be a bridge too far. In addition, in the Libyan context, it is necessary to take account of the de facto alliance that emerged between the anti-Gaddafi rebel forces (the Libyan National Liberation Army, which later became the National Transitional Council) and intervening forces. In some respects, the rebels' ground forces acted as the intervening powers' land army, offsetting the failure to deploy ground troops by NATO and others.

Equity, itself devised to deal with legal rigidity, should not itself impose legal strictures which would rob otherwise legal operations of their validity without due cause. As stated in chapters three and five, assessments under equity are generally made on a case-by-case basis. If indeed the political reality dictates that aerial intervention with no initial commitment of ground troops is all that NATO and its allies can muster, given that all the other criteria have been satisfied, a flexible interpretation of the final condition may be undertaken, if indeed it transpires to be the case that aerial bombing is effective in eliminating military targets and thereby protecting the civilian population. This was not the case in Kosovo. However, based on the best information available at present, the Libyan story would seem to be different, with military planners and governments learning from the past to make Libya a success story. If this is indeed the case, then the legality of our hypothetical Libyan intervention is assured under the equitable model.

Once again, it is worth highlighting the fact that our Libyan example is partly predicated upon the counterfactual circumstance of a Security Council Resolution being unprocurable. Nonetheless, the factual events surrounding the remainder of the Libyan crisis render it a useful test case for our purposes. In it, we see that the threshold criteria are all satisfied, and that all but one of the conduct conditions are also fulfilled, with the final condition somewhat uncertain, but ultimately also likely to be satisfied, since bombing (and coordination with rebel forces) indeed transpired to be an effective manner of ending gross human rights abuses and halting Gaddafi's campaign against his own civilians. In such circumstances, the equitable model would have conferred legality upon the operation in lieu of Security Council approbation.

Other counterfactual examples may be proffered in the Libyan context. It is possible for an intervention analogous to that described to fall foul of

[18] 'Iraq War as Unpopular as Vietnam: Experts', *Agence France Presse*, 23 March 2006, available at: www.commondreams.org/headlines06/0323 13.htm.

the equitable test for humanitarian intervention for a variety of reasons. Let us briefly imagine a couple of potential scenarios.

Suppose, for example, that immediately prior to the intervention described above, and with Western troops poised to embark, Colonel Gaddafi had offered to cease abuses against his own citizens and to allow United Nations inspectors to enter Libyan territory in order to supervise immediate reforms which would result in concrete human rights guarantees being afforded to Libyan citizens. A new UN-supervised Libyan human rights commission and court are established, with rights of individual petition, and free, State-funded legal counsel. Generous damages are offered to those who have suffered or who have lost family or property at the hands of the Libyan State. The gross human rights abuses have, it would seem, been remedied, and therefore, the equitable test is not satisfied, given that a peaceful means of putting an end to the violations has been found. In the meantime, however, Gaddafi's troops continue their war against the rebel forces, which, in conformity with the laws of war, in lieu of a proper uniform, have taken to displaying a distinctive sign – a white star – on their clothing and vehicles. Gaddafi's forces are scrupulous only to target those enemy units which carry the white star emblem, but are widely rumoured to be using excessive force and illegal means – shooting wounded enemies rather than taking them prisoner where possible, using 'dum-dum' guns and booby traps which maim and disfigure enemies, torturing interned prisoners in order to extract information and for punishment purposes, and failing to provide adequate medical facilities for internees, leading to death and disease in internment camps, where 500,000 detainees are held without Red Cross supervision, with another 80,000 having reportedly already died. There are also reports of rape of detainees by the Libyan forces, and that Libyan soldiers have taken to painting white stars on the shirts of any civilians which they kill, either by accident or otherwise. The few Western journalists who have ventured into the warzone have been attacked by military units painted with white stars, but rumours abound that these are actually Gaddafi's forces, chasing observers out so that they may have 'a free hand' in how they conduct the conflict. Reports of this conduct are not entirely uniform and are sometimes contradictory, but the United Nations inspectors which Gaddafi has allowed into Libya are unable to independently verify the extent of the violations of international humanitarian law and general human rights law which are taking place, and most NGOs have withdrawn their personnel after being attacked by unidentified militants. Gaddafi's total control of the machinery of State renders information-gathering still more difficult, but the rebels are struggling without any air or logistical support, and it appears that their forces are gradually being depleted. Trips to the warzone itself for inspectors, Gaddafi warns, could put their lives in danger.

Whether in such circumstances, a potential humanitarian intervention using the equitable criteria would be permissible is harder to say than our original example. Certainly, one could argue that the original human rights abuses have been dealt with and that Libya's civilian population is safe. However, the alleged excesses in the execution of military strategy could potentially constitute gross human rights violations if confirmed. The 'fog of war', the fact that information is not readily available in such circumstances, adds yet more to the difficulties in ascertaining exactly what may or may not permissible. And yet, such a circumstance is not entirely implausible. It is in such circumstances and with such fractured and incomplete information that military strategists, politicians and international legal advisors must contend on a regular basis. Decisions that are taken in such circumstances are hard to relate to abstract rules of international law, whether under the UN Charter system or via the framework of equity and general principles proposed here. A decision would need to be taken on the basis of the best possible information available at the time as to whether intervention would be warranted in the circumstances. If the decision to proceed with intervention were to be taken, intervening States would be obliged to demonstrate that their actions were undertaken in good faith in order to put an end to gross human rights abuses which they genuinely believed existed and that no peaceable means of stopping such abuses was available.

II. SYRIA 2012

On 15 March 2011, public demonstrations took place throughout Syria as part of the wider Arab Spring. In time, these demonstrations developed into a nationwide uprising. Protesters assembled throughout the country, demanding democratic reform, the end to nearly five decades of Ba'ath Party rule, and the resignation of President Bashar al-Assad. In the spring of 2011, the Syrian Government deployed the army to quell the revolts. Several cities were besieged, with troops reportedly instructed to fire on civilian protesters.[19] Civilians and army defectors began forming fighting units, and unified under the banner of the Free Syrian Army, began to engage in conflict with the Syrian Government police and army officials. However, the Assad regime styled this movement as 'terrorism', and undertook increasedly strident efforts to suppress and defeat it.[20] Since the opening of hostilities, tens of thousands have died, both combatants and civilians, though reliable figures are difficult to ascertain, particularly

[19] 'Defected Syria security agent speaks out', *Al Jazeera,* 8 June 2011, available at: www.aljazeera.com/news/middleeast/2011/06/201168175624573155.html.

[20] 'Opposition: 127 Dead As Syrian Forces Target Civilians', *The Denver Channel,* 7 April 2012, available at: www.thedenverchannel.com/news/30852733/detail.html

in view of the fact that the civilian/combatant distinction applicable in international humanitarian law is blurred by the informal nature of many members of the Free Syrian Army.

The crisis continued, and escalated into 2012, with tens of thousands of refugees fleeing Syria to neighbouring countries. UN Secretary-General Ban Ki-moon warned of the dire consequences of continuing violence, while his predecessor Kofi Annan – appointed by the UN and Arab League as an envoy to Syria – stated that 'there is an urgent need to stop the killing'.[21] International reaction to the situation was mixed. The Arab League suspended Syria's membership in response to the Government's actions against its own civilians, but sent an observer mission in December 2011 in order to foster a peaceable resolution to the crisis.[22] The League along with the United States, the European Union, and other countries have condemned the use of violence against the protesters. However, Russia and China have consistently blocked efforts to procure a UN Security Council Resolution condemning Mr Assad's actions,[23] and advised against sanctions, warning that any such actions could act as the first step on the road to armed intervention.[24] Efforts to procure further Security Council Resolutions in July 2012, either condemning the Syrian regime, or levelling sanctions upon the Assad regime, were also vetoed by the Russian and Chinese representatives, a situation the US representative described at 'highly regrettable'.[25]

As with Serbia 13 years before, Syria provides a real-world picture of the Security Council at an impasse over how to respond to a crisis involving multiple grave instances of human rights abuses by a State government against its own citizens. However, the circumstances of the Syrian crisis are somewhat more complicated. While the Syrian Government's human rights record has been condemned as abominable for many years,[26] and while conditions have certainly deteriorated since the beginning of the crisis, the International Committee of the Red Cross has classified the

[21] 'Syria crisis: Turkey refugee surge amid escalation fear', BBC News Online, 6 April 2012, available at: www.bbc.co.uk/news/world-middle-east-17635434.

[22] N MacFarquhar, 'Arab League Votes to Suspend Syria', *New York Times*, 12 November 2011.

[23] 'Syria's leadership making mistakes, says Russia', BBC News Online, 20 March 2012, available at: www.bbc.co.uk/news/world-middle-east-17450284.

[24] G Lopez, 'Russia and China: Sabotaging UN with Vetoes', CNN Online News, 8 February 2012, available at: edition.cnn.com/2012/02/08/opinion/lopez-russia-sanctions-cold-war/index.html.

[25] A Gabbatt, 'Syria: US condemns UN veto as "highly regrettable"', *The Guardian*, London, 19 July 2012, available at: www.guardian.co.uk/world/middle-east-live/2012/jul/19/syria-crisis-russia-china-veto-un-resolution-live-updates.

[26] Human Rights Watch, *World Report 2010: The Events of 2009* (New York, Seven Stories Press, 2010) 555; I Black, 'Syrian human rights record unchanged under Assad, report says', *The Guardian*, London, 16 July 2010.

current situation as a non-international armed conflict.[27] This entails the application of international humanitarian law rather than human rights law *simpliciter*, which derogates certain core norms of the peacetime human rights *corpus*. However, while the *ius in bello* framework does confer the right, inter alia, to kill human beings if they constitute legitimate military targets, by virtue of their involvement in the machinery of war (as well as, in limited circumstances, civilians not involved in the conflict, but who may constitute 'collateral damage'), the international humanitarian law system does not preclude the occurrence of gross and systematic human rights abuses. Indeed, it should be noted that many of the most serious instances of such abuses have occurred in periods of (international or non-international) armed conflict.[28]

Since it would seem exceedingly unlikely that Russian and China will acquiesce to a Security Council Resolution authorising recourse to armed force to deal with the Syrian crisis, we may ask whether the equitable framework proposed in this volume may be useful in conferring legality to a hypothetical non-sanctioned intervention. Again, we must return to the six threshold criteria. First, it is necessary to demonstrate that the Syrian Government has committed a series of gross and systematic human rights violations. Here, as is often the case in conflict zones, it is somewhat difficult to determine exactly what is occurring within Syria, especially since the situation is still in the process of evolution. If reports of widespread slaughter of civilians – and summary execution of soldiers who refuse to fire upon them[29] – are to be believed, then the threshold is surely met. Reports of widespread and systematic torture of prisoners add further weight to this conclusion.[30] The army has also been accused of using civilians as human shields.[31] However, as ever, the 'fog of war' means that the occurrence and extent of many such events are disputed and that reports from secondary sources are difficult to adequately verify. Nonetheless, it would seem clear that reputable international organs including the United Nations Human Rights Council have concluded that the situation on the ground amounts to a series of gross and systematic

[27] 'Syria in civil war, Red Cross says', BBC News Online, 15 July 2012, available at: www.bbc.co.uk/news/world-middle-east-18849362.

[28] One may cite, by way of brief examples, the National Socialist campaign against gypsies, Jews, homosexuals and other groups during the Second World War; the Bosnian Serb atrocities against ethnic Albanians at Srebrenica in 1995 during the Bosnian War; and the Rwandan Genocide during the 1994 Rwandan Civil War.

[29] 'Defected Syria security agent speaks out', *Al Jazeera*, 8 June 2011, available at: www.aljazeera.com/news/middleeast/2011/06/201168175624573155.html.

[30] E Peralta, 'Rights Group Says Syrian Security Forces Detained, Tortured Children', *National Public Radio*, 3 February 2012, available at: www.npr.org/blogs/thetwo-way/2012/02/03/146346490/rights-group-says-syrian-security-forces-detained-tortured children.

[31] 'Syria: Local Residents Used as Human Shields', *Huffington Post*, 26 March 2012, available at: www.huffingtonpost.com/human-rights-watch/syria-local-residents-usc_b_1380609.html.

human rights abuses, in certain cases rising to the status of international crimes.[32] Ergo, the first criterion of the equitable test is certainly met.

The second criterion is also relatively unproblematic. Syria is party to a myriad of human rights instruments, including the ICCPR, the ICESCR, the UN Convention on the Rights of the Child, and the UN Convention Against Torture. In addition, Syria has not been a persistent objector to human rights norms in customary law and is further bound by the norms of *ius cogens*.

The third criterion requires a determination beyond reasonable doubt that a peaceable means of putting an end to the violations at hand will not be achievable in a sufficiently proximate time frame to prevent (further) gross human rights abuses from continuing. This condition would also seem to be comparatively easily satisfied, despite the 'high bar' constituted by the burden of proof beyond reasonable doubt. Efforts have been made by the international community, and especially by the Arab League and the United Nations, to resolve the conflict in a peaceable manner, through intercession, negotiation, condemnation of atrocities, and the sending of special envoys to the region. However, despite the fact that Special Envoy Annan's peace plan – launched in February 2012 – provided for a ceasefire, while negotiations for it were being conducted, Syrian armed forces attacked a number of towns, summarily executing civilians while doing so.[33] Annan was later forced to admit that the ceasefire attempt had been a failure.[34] While the situation in Syria is clearly still evolving, the intransigence of the Assad regime, and the fact that China and Russia do not seem disposed to level even economic sanctions via the Security Council mean that there is little to suggest that a peaceable outcome to the conflict may emerge. While certain news agencies purport to present a situation whereby the rebels may eventually topple the Assad administration from within, such a scenario remains uncertain, and the subject of some conjecture.[35] In addition, it is unclear how long such a sit-

[32] UN Human Rights Council, 'Preliminary Report of the High Commissioner on the Situation of Human Rights in the Syrian Arab Republic' (14 June 2011) UN Doc A/HRC/17/CRP.1; UN Human Rights Council, 'Report of the Independent International Commission of Inquiry on the Syrian Arab Republic' (23 November 2011) UN Doc A/HRC/S-17/2/Add.1; UN Human Rights Council, 'Periodic Update of the Independent International Commission of Inquiry on the Syrian Arab Republic' (24 May 2012) available at: www.ohchr.org/Documents/HRBodies/HRCouncil/SpecialSession/CISyria/PeriodicUpdateCISyria.pdf.

[33] Amnesty International, 'Deadly Reprisals: Deliberate Killings and other Abuses by Syria's Armed Forces' (London, Amnesty International, 2012) available at: www.amnesty.org/en/library/asset/MDE24/041/2012/en/30416985-883b-4e67-b386-0df14a79f694/mde240412012en.pdf.

[34] 'Iran reaffirms full support for Annan's Syria peace plan', *Al Arabiya News*, 10 July 2012, english.alarabiya.net/articles/2012/07/10/225485.html.

[35] J Burch and S Al-Khalidi, 'Syria rebels emboldened after seizing border posts', *Chicago Tribune*, 23 July 2012, available at: www.chicagotribune.com/news/sns-rt-us-syria-crisis-border-postbre86m0jz-20120723,0,6885849.story.

uation may take to materialise, and how many gross human rights abuses might be meted out by the Assad regime in the interim. Taking the above into consideration, it would seem that a peaceable end to the conflict is beyond reach, and that the third criterion of the equitable framework is also satisfied.

The fourth criterion – whether there may be a means of immediately ending the violations through the machinery of the United Nations Charter – is closely linked. The Security Council is the competent organ in such instances, and it is abundantly clear that Russia and China are not of a mind to agree to any Resolution authorising the use of armed force by intervening States as a means of putting an end to the ongoing atrocities. Ergo, this condition is also fulfilled.

The fifth tenet in the six-part test demands a reasonable determination that only armed military intervention will suffice as an immediate and effective means of ending the violations. Again, it is necessary to take account of the current on-the-ground circumstances in making an informed assessment. The Assad regime has not responded to the condemnation of multiple States and groupings thereof regarding its conduct during this crisis. Further, it has breached the ceasefire agreed under the Annan plan, thereby vitiating the plan itself. All-out destruction of their enemies within the country – without adequate distinction between civilians and combatants – would seem to be the *modus operandi* of the Government forces. Peaceable attempts to intercede have failed, and the strength of the rebel forces is uncertain. China and Russia remain intransigent, ergo sanctions levied by the Security Council – or sanctioned intervention – are out of the question. It would appear, indeed, that unsanctioned intervention by forces of adequate strength and numbers may represent the only realistic way of putting a swift end to the ongoing atrocities.

The sixth and final criterion relates to the effectiveness of the intervention, demanding that prospective interventions must be undertaken in good faith as an effective solution to the ongoing abuses and may not be undertaken in vain. In the Syrian case, this would entail, a priori, intervention by a State or group of States with vastly superior military capabilities to those of the Syrian army, in order to put an end to the atrocities as swiftly as possible. Any such force would need to take account of the fact that Syria has threatened to use chemical weapons against any foreign invasion.[36] As a result, initial aerial bombardment might be most suitable, in order to nullify such capabilities. In theory, NATO would be an excellent candidate to lead such an intervention.

[36] 'Syrian regime makes chemical warfare threat', *The Guardian*, 23 July 2012, available at: www.guardian.co.uk/world/2012/jul/23/syria-chemical-warfare-threat-assad.

The Syrian case would, therefore, seem to meet all six of the threshold criteria for humanitarian intervention under the equitable framework. Even absent a Security Council Resolution, a potential intervention, provided that it would be effective and not in vain, would be permissible. However, as noted earlier, the equitable framework also requires three further conditions relating to the conduct of warfare by would-be interveners, namely the requirement of clean hands; the requirement that States intervene with the principal purpose of ending the gross human rights abuses; and that they refrain from unnecessary suffering in conducting the operation.

In the Syrian case, as with Libya before it, the most likely intervener is perhaps NATO. While no intervention has, as yet, been embarked upon, were one to occur, many would expect NATO to lead it. Again, as in the Libyan case, qualms may be voiced about the human rights record of some of NATO's key members, including the United States and Turkey. However, the transgressions of these States do not amount to human rights violations on a gross and systematic scale, and they are therefore not debarred from intervening under the equitable test.

The second conduct condition stipulates that States must intervene with the principal purpose of ending such violations and may not profit unduly as a result of doing so. Above all, any right to intervene must not be used as a cloak for other ends; otherwise this will constitute *mala fides*. In the Syrian context, this must entail that any potential intervention does not amount to a resource-grabbing operation, or an effort to oust Assad alone, without due attention to who replaces him and whether the human rights abuses have been stopped by doing so. It may, of course, be the case that the ousting of Assad will constitute the most effective means of putting an end to the abuses that are taking place. It would at least seem that his removal would constitute an indispensible condition of any meaningful reform vis-à-vis human rights in the country.

The final conduct criterion, prescribing that States must comport themselves in an equitable manner, abstaining from unnecessary loss of civilian life and unnecessary suffering in accomplishing the operation, calls both for overwhelming military strength and for careful military planning and targeting to be employed in the Syrian case. A sustained and forthright intervention by a powerful coalition like NATO would have the potential to strike a crushing blow upon the Syrian army, crippling their military capabilities and ensuring a swift conclusion to the conflict. However, this may not be done at the expense of the civilian population of Syria. In seeking to intervene and save lives, the intervening powers must not unnecessarily destroy the lives of Syrian civilians, either through killing them in the course of operations, or through engineering circumstances whereby they suffer unnecessarily. Caution must be exercised throughout.

III. TO BE OR NOT TO BE?

It must be admitted that our Libyan example is highly impressionistic, and that of Syria perhaps still more so. The reasons for this are connected with the unreliable and often contradictory information reporting which emanates from warzones. Being entirely sure of one's facts in such circumstances is by no means easy. And yet, for the equitable theory of humanitarian intervention to function, certain factual conditions need to be satisfied. However, this is by no means a new problem. Before the US-led coalition invaded Iraq in 2003, the United States delegation presented evidence garnered by its own intelligence services that the Hussein regime was developing so-called 'weapons of mass destruction'. This evidence failed to convince the doubters in the Security Council. The subsequent invasion found no evidence of such weapons. That the pre-eminent State intelligence agency could have erred in such circumstances indicates how difficult fact-finding regarding certain preconditions for conflict is. These difficulties are only exacerbated when the violence itself actually commences.[37] Equity's inherent flexibility may leave it better placed to allow some margin of appreciation for States that intervene, with good faith and a reasonable determination that the abuses are taking place, and that no peaceful means of ending them exists, all constituting key preconditions for the permissibility of intervention. This same flexibility may, of course, lay equitable principles open to a certain degree of abuse. However, that the framework presented here includes a code of conduct, both as a threshold requirement for would-be interveners, and as a prospective requirement in terms of comportment during the intervention itself, limits the potential for abuse of the doctrine significantly.

Theories of the legality and/or legitimacy of humanitarian intervention are increasingly common. Scholarship post-Kosovo witnessed a marked upsurge of interest in the area, with a proliferation of such literature. However, most justificatory theories either hinted at possible future law reform, or discarded the law in favour of morality, ethics and philosophy. The equitable model's greatest strength is that it points to a possible framework for humanitarian intervention that is deeply rooted in one of the principal sources of international law. Through it, States may intervene to stop gross human rights abuses when the UN Security Council is

[37] Of course, one must be conscious of the potential for subterfuge. That the US knew full well that Saddam Hussein was not developing weapons of mass destruction has been argued by many political commentators in the media, but even in such a scenario, the fact that governments are prepared to present fraudulent information to the UN Security Council in order to attempt to secure legal authority for a military invasion merely proves the point that fact-finding regarding legal preconditions for going to war is a process which is fraught with difficulties. If the US Government lies to its colleagues on the Security Council, then can any information reported by States be trusted?

unable to act, provided they behave in accordance with equity's guiding criteria.

While the Libyan intervention did not require the equitable theory to grant it legality in reality, and while NATO's Kosovo intervention is now long since past, no one can tell when a government will next turn its guns on its own civilians. The current Syrian crisis is ample evidence of this fact. The global interests of the Permanent Members of the Security Council are so widespread and varied that it will regularly be the case that one or more members may be diametrically opposed to intervention for a myriad of reasons. If such a case occurs, and if a State or coalition of States raises its banner and deploys troops for the humanitarian cause, perhaps rather than either condemn such action as illegal, or resort to morality and political theory – in lieu of legality – to justify it, the international community will look to equity, that is, to the law, for a solution. If States indeed decide to do so, they may well discover that what seems to be the right thing to do may well also be the legal thing.

Bibliography

BOOKS

Abiew, F, *The Evolution of the Doctrine and Practice of Humanitarian Intervention* (The Hague, London, Boston, Kluwer Law International, 1999).

Alston, P, and MacDonald, E, *Human Rights, Intervention and the Use of Force: The Collected Courses of the Academy of European Law* (Oxford, Oxford University Press, 2008).

Anzilotti, D, *Cours de Droit International* (Paris, Recueil Sirey, 1929) 117.

Aquinas, T, *Summa Theologiae – A Concise Translation* (Indiana USA, Christian Classics Press 1989 – Originally published in 1274).

Aristotle, *The Nicomachean Ethics*, Martin Ostwald Translation (Washington, The Library of Liberal Arts, 1962).

Ashburner, W, *Principles of Equity*, 2nd edn (London, Butterworths, 1933).

Austin, J, *The Province of Jurisprudence Determined* (1832).

Bell, J, Boyron, S and Whittaker, S, *Principles of French Law* (Oxford, Oxford University Press, 1998).

Bentham, J, *The Limits of Jurisprudence Defined* (New York, Columbia University Press, 1945).

Black, L, *Law Dictionary*, 3rd edn (St Paul, Minnesota, West, 1933).

Blackstone, W with St George Tucker, HG, *Blackstone's Commentaries: With Notes of Reference to the Constitution and Laws, of the Federal Government of the United States, and of the Commonwealth of Virginia: In Five*, 1996 reprint of 1765 edn (Philadelphia, Birch and Small).

Bloed, A and van Dijk, P (eds), *Forty Years of the International Court of Justice* (Utrecht, Europa-Instituut, 1988).

Bodde, D and Morris, C, *Law in Imperial China* (Cambridge, Harvard University Press, 1967).

Boehmer, G, *Grundlagen der bürgerlichen Rechtsordnung: Praxis der Richterlichen Rechtsschöpfung*, vol II (Tübingen, Archiv des öffentlichen Rechts, 1952).

Boisson de Chazournes, L and Gowlland-Debbas, V (eds), *L'Ordre Juridique International, Un Système en Quête d'Équité, Liber Amicorum Georges Abi-Saab* (den Haag, Martinus Nijhoff, 2001).

Bonichot, J-C, Cassia, P and Poujade, B, *Les Grands Arrêts du contentieux administratif* (Paris, Dalloz, 2006).

Bossuyt, M and Wouters, J, *Grondlijnen van internationaal recht* (Antwerpen, Intersentia, 2005).

Bricmont, O, *Impérialisme Humanitaire* (Brussels, Arden, 2005).

Brierly, JL, *The Law of Nations*, 6th edn (Oxford, Oxford University Press, 1963).

Brownlie, I, *International Law and the Use of Force by States* (Oxford, Oxford University Press, 1963).

——*The Rule of Law in International Affairs* (The Hague, Martinus Nijhoff Publishers, 1998).

Buchanan, A, *Justice, Legitimacy, and Self-Determination: Moral Foundations for International Law* (Oxford, Oxford University Press, 2004).

Buckland, WW and McNair, AD, *Roman Law and Canon Law: A Comparison in Outline*, 2nd edn, revised by FH Lawson (Cambridge, Cambridge University Press, 1965).

Bull, H, *The Anarchical Society – A Study of Order in World Politics* (New York, Columbia University Press, 2001).

——(ed), *Intervention in World Politics* (Oxford, Clarendon Press, 1984).

Burke, E, *Reflections on the Revolution in France and on the Proceedings in Certain Societies in London Relative to that Event* (London, J Dodsley of Pall-Mall, 1790).

Calvo, R, *L'equitá nel diritto privato. Individualitá, valori e regole nel prisma della contemporaneitá* (Milan, Giuffrè, 2010).

Cannizzaro, E and Palchetti, P (eds), *Customary International Law on the Use of Force: A Methodological Approach* (Leiden Koninklijke Brill, 2005).

Carr, EH, *The Twenty Years Crisis* 1919–39 (London, Macmillan, 1939).

Chapuis, R, *Droit du contentieux administratif* (Paris, Montchrestien, 2006).

Cheng, B, *General Principles of Law as Applied by International Courts and Tribunals* (Cambridge, Grotius Publications, 1987. Originally printed 1953).

Chesterman, S, *Just War or Just Peace? Humanitarian Intervention and International Law* (Oxford, Oxford University Press, 2001).

Chomsky, N, *The New Military Humanism: Lessons from Kosovo* (Monroe, ME, Common Courage Press, 1999).

Chü, T-T, *Law and Society in Traditional China* (den Haag, Mouton & Co, 1961).

Clark, GL, *Principles of Equity* (Mississippi, Columbia Press, 1919).

Cohn, EJ (ed), *Manual of German Law: General Introduction and Civil Law*, vol I (London, British Institute of International and Comparative Law and Oceana Publications, 1968).

Corten, O, *Le retour des guerres préventives* (Brussels, Labor, 2003).

Crawford, J, *The Creation of States in International Law*, 2nd edn (Oxford, Oxford University Press, 2006).

Dallier, P and Pellet, A, *Droit International Public*, 7eme (Paris, Librairie Générale de Droit et Jurisprudence, 2002).

D'Amato, A, *The Concept of Custom in International Law* (Ithaca, New York, Cornell University Press, 1971).

——*International Law: Process and Prospects* (New York, Transnational Publishers, 1987).

——*International Law Sources. Collected Papers*, vol III (Martinus Nijhoff, Leiden, 2004).

David, R and Brierley, JEC, *Major Legal Systems in the World Today, An Introduction to the Comparative Study of Law*, 2nd edn (London, Stevens and Sons, 1978).

de los Mozos, JL, *Metodología y ciencia en el Derecho Privado contemporáneo* (Madrid, Editorial de derecho privado, 1977).

Degan, VD, *L'équité et le droit international* (den Haag, Martinus Nijhoff, 1970).

Delany, H, *Equity and the Law of Trusts in Ireland*, 3rd edn (Dublin, Thomson Roundhall, 2003).

Deng, FM, et al, *Sovereignty as Responsibility: Conflict Management in Africa* (Washington, DC, Brookings Institution, 1996).

Der Derian, J, *Virtuous Wars, Mapping the Military-Industrial-Media-Entertainment Network* (Westview Press, 2001).

Donnelly, J, *Universal Human Rights in Theory and Practice,* 2nd edn (Ithaca, NY, Cornell University Press, 2003) 251.

Dworkin, R, *Taking Rights Seriously* (Cambridge, Harvard University Press, 1977).

Enneccerus, L and Lehmann, H, *Recht der Schuldverhältnisse,* 15th edn (Tübingen, Mohr, 1958).

——and Nipperdey, G, *Allgemeiner Teil des BGB,* vol I (Tübingen, Mohr, 1959).

Escott, PD, *After Secession: Jefferson Davis and the Failure of Confederate Nationalism* (Baton Rouge, Louisiana State University Press 1992).

Esser, J, *Schuldrecht: Allgemeiner Teil,* 4th edn, vol I (Karlsruhe, Müller, 1970).

Feenstra R and Zimmermann R (eds), *Das römisch-holländische Recht. Fortschritte des Zivilrechts im 17. und 18. Jahrhundert* (Berlin, Duncker and Humblot, 1992).

Fitzmaurice, M and Elias, O, *Contemporary Issues in the Law of Treaties* (Utrecht, Eleven International Publishing, 2005).

Franck, T, *Recourse to Force – State Actions Against Threats and Armed Attacks,* Hersch Lauterpacht Memorial Lectures (Cambridge, Cambridge University Press, 2002).

Freud, S, *The Interpretation of Dreams* (New York, Avon Press, 1980).

Fuller, L, *The Morality of Law,* Revised edn (Cambridge, Yale University Press, 1964).

Garcia Enterria, E, *Legislación delegada, potestad reglamentaria y control judicial* (Madrid, Tecnos, 1970).

Gény, F, *Método de interpretación y Fuentes en Derecho Privado Positivo* (Madrid, Hijos de Reus, 1902).

Grapin, P, *Valeur internationale des principes généraux du droit* (Paris, Ripert, 1934).

Harris, DJ, *Cases and Materials on International Law* (London, Thomson, Sweet & Maxwell, 2004).

Hart, HLA, *The Concept of Law* (London, Clarendon Law Series, 1961).

Hesselink, M, *The Harmonisation of European Contract Law* (London, Hart Publishing, 2006).

Higgins, R, *Problems and Process: International Law and How We Use It* (Oxford, Oxford University Press, 1994).

Holtman, RB, *The Napoleonic Revolution* (Baton Rouge, Louisiana State University Press, 1981).

Holzgrefe, JL and Keohane R (eds), *Humanitarian Intervention: Ethical, Legal and Political Dilemmas* (Cambridge, Cambridge University Press, 2003).

Hsia, TT, *Guide to Selected Legal Sources of Mainland China* (Washington DC, Library of Congress, 1967).

Hudson, MO, *The Permanent Court of International Justice 1920–42* (New York, Macmillan, 1943).

Janis, M and Noyes, J, *International Law: Cases and Commentary*, 3rd edn (St Paul, Minnesota, Thomson, 2006).

Jenks, CW, *The Prospects of International Adjudication* (London, Stevens and Sons, 1964).

Jones, H, *To the Webster-Ashburton Treaty: A Study in Anglo-American Relations, 1783–1843* (Chapel Hill, N Carolina, University of North Carolina Press, 1977).

Kant, I, *Zum ewigen Frieden. Ein philosophischer Entwurf* (Königsberg, erste Auflage, 1795).

Karg, M, *IGH vs ISGH. Die Beziehung zwischen zwei völkerrechtlichen Streitbeilegungsorganen* (Baden-Baden, Nomos, 2005).

Keane, R, *Equity and the Law of Trusts in the Republic of Ireland* (Dublin, Butterworths, 1988).

Kohn, L, *Die Verfassung des Irischen Freistaats* (Tübingen, Archiv des öffentlichen Rechts, 1928).

Kooijmans, P, *Internationaal publiekrecht in vogelvlucht,* 9th edn (Deventer, Kluwer, 2002).

Koskenniemi, M, *The Gentle Civilizer of Nations: The Rise and Fall of International Law 1870–1960,* Hersch Lauterpacht Memorial Lectures (Cambridge, Cambridge University Press, 2001).

Kouchner, B and Bettati, L, (eds) *Le Devoir d'Ingerence* (Paris, Denoël, 1987).

Kozma, J, Nowak, M and Scheinin, M, *A World Court of Human Rights – Consolidated Statute and Commentary* (Wien/ Graz, COST/European Science Foundation, 2010).

Krishnaswamy, S, *Democracy and Constitutionalism in India: A Study of the Basic Structure Doctrine* (Oxford, Oxford University Press, 2009).

Lauterpacht, H, *Private Law Sources and Analogies of International Law (With Special Reference to International Arbitration)* (London, Longman, Green & Co, 1927).

——*The Function of Law in the International Community* (London, Longman, Green & Co, 1933).

——*The Development of International Law by the Permanent Court of International Justice* (London, Longman, Green & Co, 1934).

——*International Law and Human Rights* (London, Longman, Green & Co, 1950).

Long, M, Weil, P, Braibant, G, Delvové, P, and Genevois, B, *Les Grands Arrêts de la jurisprudence administrative* (Paris, Dalloz, 2007).

Ludwig, E, *Bismarck. Ungekürzte Neuausgabe* (München, Herbig, 1975).

Mahoney, J, *The Challenge of Human Rights: Origin, Development and Significance* (Oxford, Blackwell Publishing Ltd, 2007).

Maine, H, *Ancient Law* (London, JM Dent & Sons, 1861).

Maitland, FW, *Equity – A Course of Lectures,* 2nd edn (Cambridge, Cambridge University Press, 1936).

Manaï, D, *Le juge entre la loi et l'équité : essai sur le pouvoir d'appréciation du juge en droit Suisse* (Lausanne, Payot, 1985).

Martin, J, *Hanbury and Martin: Modern Equity,* 16th edn (London, Sweet and Maxwell, 2001).

Meagher, RP, Gummow, WMC and Lehane, JRF, *Equity: Doctrines and Remedies,* 3rd edn (London, Butterworths, 1992).

Meron, T, *Human Rights and Humanitarian Norms as Customary Law* (Oxford, Clarendon Press, 1989).

Montesquieu, *Défense de l'esprit des loix* (Genève, Chez Barillot et Fils, 1748).

Morgenthau, H, *In Defence of National Interest: A Critical Examination of American Foreign Policy* (Washington DC, University Press of America, 1982).

Morris, C, *The New Turkey: The Quiet Revolution on the Edge of Europe* (London, Granta Books, 2005).

Murphy, S, *Humanitarian Intervention: The United Nations in an Evolving World Order* (Philadelphia, University of Pennsylvania Press, 1996).

Neff, S, *War and the Law of Nations* (Cambridge, Cambridge University Press, 2005).

Newman, RA, *Equity in the World's Legal Systems* (Brussels, Établissements Émile Bruylant, 1973).

Newton, I, *The Principia,* a new translation by IB Cohen and A Whitman (Berkeley, University of California Press, 1999).

Oleck, HL, *Creditor's Rights and Remedies* (Oxford, Oxford University Press, 1949).

Orakhelashvili, A, *Peremptory Norms in International Law* (Oxford, Oxford University Press, 2006).

Orwell, G, *Nineteen Eighty-Four* (London, Secker and Warburg, 1949).

Palmer, VV, *Mixed Jurisdictions Worldwide: The Third Legal Family* (Cambridge, Cambridge University Press, 2001).

PCIJ / Advisory Committee of Jurists (ACJ), *Procès-verbaux of the Proceedings of the Committee, 16 June–24 June* (den Haag, van Langhuysen Brothers, 1920).

Pekkanen, R, *Japan's Dual Civil Society: Members Without Advocates,* Contemporary Issues in Asia and Pacific (Standford, California, Stanford University Press, 2006).

Petman, J and Klabbers, J, *Nordic Cosmopolitanism: Essays in International Law for Martti Koskenniemi* (Leiden, Martinus Nijhoff, 2003).

Pieterse, JN (ed), *World Orders in the Making: Humanitarian Intervention and Beyond* (London, Macmillan,1998).

Pomeroy, J, *Equity Jurisprudence and Equitable Remedies,* 5th edn (London, General Books, 1941).

Puig Brutau, J, *La Jurisprudencia como fuente del derecho (Interpretación creadora y arbitrio judicial)* (Barcelona, Bosch, 1954).

Radbruch, G, *Rechtsphilosophie* (Stuttgart, Koehler, 1950).

Raimondo, FO, *General Principles of Law in the Decisions of International Criminal Courts and Tribunals* (Leiden, Martinus Nijhoff Publishers, 2008).

Rawls, J, *The Law of Peoples, with the Law of Public Reason Revisited* (Cambridge, ME, Harvard University Press, 1999).

Reinicke, D, *Rechtsfolgen formwidrig abgeschlossener Verträge* (Bad Homburg, Gehlen, 1969).

Richards, L, *Shays' Rebellion: The American Revolution's Final Battle* (Philadelphia, University of Pennsylvania Press, 2002).

Robb, C, *International Environmental Law Papers: Early Decisions,* vol I (Cambridge, Cambridge University Press, 1999).

Roosevelt, FD, *The Public Papers and Addresses of Franklin D. Roosevelt,* vol 4, 1940 volume (London, Macmillan, 1941).

Ross, A, *On Law and Justice* (Berkeley, University of California Press, 1959).

Rossi, C, *Equity and International Law: A Legal Realist Approach to International Decision Making* (Irvington, New York, Transnational Publishers Inc, 1993).

Rousseau, C, *Droit International Public* (Paris, Sirey, 1970).

Rubin, AP, *Ethics and Authority in International Law* (Cambridge, Cambridge University Press, 1997).

Rumpf, C, *Recht und Wirtschaft der Türkei* (Stuttgart, Local Global, 2007).

Ruzié, D, *Droit international public,* 17eme (Paris, Dalloz, 2004).

Sadat-Akhavi, SA, *Methods of Resolving Conflicts between Treaties* (Leiden, Martinus Nijhoff, 2003).

Salmond, J, *Jurisprudence, or, the Theory of the Law* (London, Stevens & Haynes, 1902).

Scerni, M, *I principi generali di diritto riconosciuti dalle nazioni civili nella giurisprudenza della Corte Permanente di Giustizia Internazionale* (Rome, Cedam, 1932).
Schachter, O, *International Law in Theory and Practice* (Leiden, Martinus Nijhoff, 1991).
Schmitt, C, *Der Nomos der Erde im Völkerrecht des Jus Publicum Europaeum* (Berlin, Duncker & Humblot, 1960).
——*Political Theology*, translated by G Schwab (Cambridge, MA, MIT Press, 1985).
——*Die wending zum diskriminierenden Kriegsbegriff* (Berlin, Duncker & Humblot, 1988).
——*Constitutional Theory* (London, Duke University Press, 2008).
Schulte, C, *Compliance with Decisions of the International Court of Justice* (New York, Oxford University Press, 2004)
Schwarzenberger, G, *A Manual of International Law*, vol 1, 4th edn (London, Stevens & Sons, 1960).
Selden, J, *The Table Talk of John Selden (with notes by David Irving)* (Edinburgh, Constable, 1854).
Séroussi, R, *Introduction au Droit Comparé*, 3rd edn (Paris, Dunod, 2008).
Shakespeare, W, *Hamlet* (London, Penguin, 2001).
Shirer, W, *The Rise and Fall of the Third Reich*, 1st Touchstone edn (London, Simon & Schuster, 1990).
Sieyès, EJ, *Political Writings* (Hackett Publishing, London, 2003).
Simpson, AWB, *Human Rights and the End of Empire: Britain and the Genesis of the European Convention* (Oxford, Oxford University Press, 2001).
Simpson, G, *Great Powers and Outlaw States: Unequal Sovereigns in the International Legal Order*, Cambridge Studies in International and Comparative Law (Cambridge, Cambridge University Press, 2004).
Spiermann, O, *International Legal Argument in the Permanent Court of International Justice, The Rise of the International Judiciary* (Cambridge Studies in International and Comparative Law, Cambridge, Cambridge University Press, 2005).
Stiegler, A, *Der kirchliche Rechtsbegriff, Elemente und Phasen seiner Erkenntnisgeschichte* (München, Schnell & Steiner, 1958).
Stone, J, *Non Liquet and the Function of Law in the International Community* (Oxford, Oxford University Press, 1960).
Stürchler, N, *The Threat of Force in International Law* (Cambridge, Cambridge University Press, 2007).
Tesón, F, *Humanitarian Intervention: An Inquiry into Peace, Law and Morality*, 2nd edn (New York, Transnational Publishers, 1997).
Thirlway, H, *International Customary Law and its Codification* (Leiden, AW Sijthoff, 1972).
Thomashausen, S, *Humanitarian Intervention in an Evolving World Order: The Cases of Iraq, Somalia, Kosovo and East Timor* (Pretoria, Africa Institute of South Africa, 2002).
Thompson, J, *Acceso a la justicia y equidad : estudio en siete países de América Latina* (San José, Costa Rica, Instituto Interamericano de Derechos Humanos, 2000).
Thornton, R, *Asymmetric Warfare: Threat and Response in the Twenty-First Century* (Cambridge, Polity Press, 2007).
van der Merwe, CG and du Plessis, JE, *Introduction to the Law of South Africa* (den Haag, Kluwer International, 2004).

Van Hove, A, *De legibus ecclesiasticis* (Mechelen, Belgium, Dessain, 1930).
Villiger, M, *Commentary on the 1969 Vienna Convention on the Law of Treaties* (Leiden, Martinus Nijhoff, 2009).
Vogel, FE, *Islamic Law and Legal System, Studies of Saudi Arabia* (Leiden, Brill, 2000).
von Glahn, G, *Law Among Nations: An Introduction to Public International Law,* 4th edn (New York, Macmillan, 1981).
von Savigny, FC, *Das Recht des Besitzes: Eine civilistische Abhandlung* (Giessen, Germnay, Heyer, 1803).
—— *Vom Beruf unserer Zeit für Gesetzgebung und Rechtswissenschaft* (Goldbach, Germany, Keip, 1814 reprinted 1997).
von Staudiger, J, *Kommentar zum Bürgerlichen Gesetzbuch, mit Einführungsgesetz und Nebengesetzen,* Zweite Auflage (Berlin, de Gruyter, 1954).
Walzer, M, *Just and Unjust Wars – A Moral Argument with Historical Illustrations* (New York, Basic Books, 1992).
Warendorf, H, Thomas, R and Curry-Summer, I, *The Civil Code of the Netherlands* (Leiden, Kluwer International, 2009).
Wellmer, A, *Revolution und Interpretation, Demokratie ohne Letztbegründung* (Assen, Van Garam, 1998).
Wheeler, N, *Saving Strangers: Humanitarian Intervention in International Society* (Oxford, Oxford University Press, 2000).
Wieacker, F, *Zur rechtstheoretischen Präzisierung des §242 BGB* (Tübingen, Archiv des öffentlichen Rechts, 1956).
Zimmermann, A (ed), *The Statute of the International Court of Justice: A Commentary* (Oxford, Oxford University press, 2006).
Zimmermann, R, *The Law of Obligations* (Cape Town, 1990).
—— and Visser DP (eds), *Southern Cross: Civil Law and Common Law in South Africa* (Oxford, Clarendon Press, 1996).
Zweigert, K and Kötz, H, *Einführung in die Rechtsvergleichung auf dem Gebiete des Privatrechts,* 3rd edn (Tübingen, Mohr, 1996).

ARTICLES

Abi-Saab, G, 'The Uses of Article 19' (1999) 10 *European Journal of International Law* 341.
Akehurst, M, 'Equity and the General Principles of Law' (1976) 25 *ICLQ* 801.
Albert, R, 'Nonconstitutional Amendments' (2009) 22 *Canadian Journal of Law and Jurisprudence* 5.
Ambos, K, 'Prosecuting Guantanamo in Europe: Can and Shall the Masterminds of the "Torture Memos" be held Criminally Responsible on the Basis of Universal Jurisdiction?' (2009) 42 *Case Western Reserve Journal of International Law* 405.
Aubert, W, 'Law as a Way of Resolving Conflicts: The Case of a Small Industrialised Society' in L Nader (ed), *Law in Culture and Society* (Chicago, Aldine, 1969) 282.
Bassiouni, MC, 'A Functional Approach to "General Principles of International Law"' (1990) 11 *Michigan Journal of International Law* 768.
—'International Crimes and Obligations Erga Omnes' (1996) 59 *Law and Contemporary Problems* 63.

Bellamy, AJ, 'Responsibility to Protect or Trojan Horse? The Crisis in Darfur and Humanitarian Intervention After Iraq' (2005) 19 *Ethics and International Affairs* 31.

——'Whither the Responsibility to Protect? Humanitarian Intervention and the 2005 World Summit' (2006) 20 *Ethics and International Affairs* 143.

Benjamin, BM, 'Unilateral Humanitarian Intervention: Legalising the Use of Force to Prevent Human Rights Atrocities' (1992) *Fordham International Law Journal* 120.

Berkowitz, D, Pistor, K and Richard, JF, 'The Transplant Effect' (2003) 51 *American Journal of Comparative Law* 163.

Berman, N, 'Intervention in a Divided World: Axes of Legitimacy' in P Alston and E MacDonald, *Human Rights, Intervention and the Use of Force: The Collected Courses of the Academy of European Law* (Oxford, Oxford University Press, 2008) 215.

Bettati, M, 'Du droit d'ingérence à la responsabilité de protéger' (2007) 20 *Outre-terre* 381.

Bhuta, N, 'Paved with Good Intentions – Humanitarian War, the New Interventionism and Legal Regulation of the Use of Force, Review Essay' (2001) 25 *Melbourne University Law Review* 843.

Bianchi, A, 'Human Rights and the Magic of Jus Cogens' (2008) 19 *European Journal of International Law* 504.

Bilder, RB, 'The Implications of Kosovo for International Human Rights Law' in P Alston and E MacDonald, *Human Rights, Intervention and the Use of Force: The Collected Courses of the Academy of European Law* (Oxford, Oxford University Press, 2008) 139.

Bouwman, N, 'A New Regime for the Meuse' (1996) 5 *Review of EC and International Environmental Law* 161.

Bowett, DW, 'Estoppel Before International Tribunals and its Relation to Acquiescence' (1957) 33 *British Yearbook of International Law* 176.

Brownlie, I, 'Thoughts on Kind-Hearted Gunmen' in R Lillich (ed), *Humanitarian Intervention and the United Nations* (Charlottesville, University of Virginia Press, 1973).

——'Humanitarian Intervention' in JN Moore (ed), *Law and Civil War in the Modern World* (Baltimore, John Hopkins University Press, 1974).

——'The United Nations Charter and the Use of Force, 1945–85' in A Cassese (ed), *The Current Legal Regulation of the Use of Force* (Dordrecht, Martinus Nijhoff Publishers, 1986).

——and Apperley, CJ, 'Kosovo Crisis Inquiry: Memorandum on the International Law Aspects' (2000) 49 *ICLQ* 878.

Bruha, T, 'Use of Force, Prohibition of' in R Wolfrum (ed), *United Nations: Law, Policies and Practice*, vol 2 (1995) 1387.

Brunner, CJH, 'Abuse of Rights in Dutch Law' (1976–77) 37 *Louisiana Law Review* 729.

Buchanan, A, 'Reforming the International Law of Humanitarian Intervention' in JL Holzgrefe and RO Keohane (eds), *Humanitarian Intervention: Ethical, Legal and Political Dilemmas* (Cambridge, Cambridge University Press, 2003) 131.

——'From Nuremburg to Kosovo: The Morality of Illegal International Legal Reform' (2001) 111 *Ethics* 673.

Buckland, WW, 'Praetor and Chancellor' (1939) 13 *Tulane Law Review* 163.

Byers, M and Chesterman, S, 'Changing the Rules about Rules? Unilateral Humanitarian Intervention and the Future of International Law' in JL Holzgrefe and RO Keohane (eds), *Humanitarian Intervention: Ethical, Legal and Political Dilemmas* (Cambridge, Cambridge University Press, 2003) 177.

Cameron, E, 'Constructive Trusts in South African Law: The Legacy Refused' (1999) *Edinburgh Law Review* 341.

Cassese, A, 'Ex iniuria ius oritur: Are We Moving towards International Legitimation of Forcible Humanitarian Countermeasures in the World Community?' (1999) *European Journal of International Law* 23.

——'A Follow-Up: Forcible Humanitarian Countermeasures and Opinio Necessitatis' (1999) *European Journal of International Law* 791.

Castberg, J, 'La méthodologie du droit international public' (1933) 43 *Recueil de La Haye* 313.

Cecioni, CG, 'La Traducibilità del linguaggio giuridico inglese' in G Cortese (ed), *Tradurre i linguaggi settoriali. Atti del seminario di Anglistica nell'ambito del progetto strategico CNR 'I problemi della traduzione nell'Italia dell'Europa': Università degli studi di Torino, Facoltà di Scienze Politiche, 27–28 maggio 1993* (Turin, Libreria Cortina, 1996) 155–73.

Chan, PCW, 'Acquiescence/Estoppel in International Boundaries: Temple of Preah Vihear Revisited' (2004) 3 *Chinese Journal of International Law* 421.

Charney, JI, 'Anticipatory Humanitarian Intervention in Kosovo' (1999) 93 *American Journal of International Law* 834.

Cheng, B, 'General Principles of Law as a Subject for International Codification' (1951) 4 *Current Legal Problems* 35.

——'United Nations Resolutions on Outer Space: "Instant" International Customary Law?' (1965) 5 *Indian Journal of International Law* 23.

——'Custom: The Future of General State Practice in a Divided World' in RStJ Macdonald and DM Johnston (eds), *The Structure and Process of International Law: Essays in Legal Philosophy Doctrine and Theory* (Dordrecht, Martinus Nijhoff, 1983) 513.

Chiba, M, 'Japan' in P-L Tan, *Asian Legal Systems* (London, Butterworths, 1997).

Choi, C, 'On the Reception of Western Law in Korea' (1981) 9 *Korean Journal of Comparative Law* 141.

Christenson, GA, 'The World Court and Jus Cogens' (1987) 81 *American Journal of International Law* 93.

Clarke, O, 'The State (Ryan) v Lennon: A Victory for Man Over God?' (2007) 15 *Irish Student Law Review* 136.

Corten, O, 'Breach and Evolution of Customary International Law on the Use of Force' in E Cannizzaro and P Palchetti (eds), *Customary International Law on the Use of Force: A Methodological Approach* (Leiden, Koninklijke Brill NV, 2005) 42.

——and Klein, P, 'L'autorisation de recourir à la force à des fins humanitaires: droit d'ingérence ou retour aux sources ?' (1993) 4 *European Journal of International Law* 506.

——'Vers une "Déterritorialisation " de l'Interdiction du Recours à la Force dans les Relations Internationales?' (2009) 5 *Annuário Brasileiro de Direito Internacional* 207.

Crook, JR, 'The International Court of Justice and Human Rights' (2003) 1 *Northwestern University Journal of International Human Rights* 2.

Crouzatier, J-M, 'Le Principe de la Responsabilité de Protéger: Avancée de la Solidarité Internationale ou Ultime Avatar de L'Impérialisme?' (2008) 2 *Revue Aspects* 13.

Cryer, R, 'One Appeal, Two Philosophies, Four Opinions and a Remittal: The Erdemovic Case at the ICTY Appeals Chamber' (1997) 2 *Journal of Armed Conflict* 193.

Danish Institute of Foreign Affairs, *Humanitarian Intervention: Legal and Political Aspects* (Copenhagen, Danish Institute of Foreign Affairs, 1999).

de Funiak, WQ, 'Equitable Protection of Personal or Individual Rights' (1947) 36 *Kentucky Law Journal* 7.

De Nicola, CP, 'Shield for the Knights of Humanity: The ICC Should Adopt a Humanitarian Necessity Defence to the Crime of Aggression' (2008–09) 30 *University of Pennsylvania Journal of International Law* 641.

Dekker, I and Werner, W, 'The Completeness of International Law and Hamlet's Dilemma (Non Liquet, The Nuclear Weapons Case and Legal Theory)' (1999) 68 *Nordic Journal of International Law* 225.

Deng, FM, 'Frontiers of Sovereignty' (1995) 8 *Leiden Journal of International Law* 249.

Deschenaux, H, 'Le traitement de l'equité en droit suisse' in M Bridel (ed), *Recueil de travaux suisses présentés au VIIIème Congrès international de droit comparé* (Basel, Helbing and Lichtenhahn, 1970) 29.

Du Bois, F, 'Introduction: History, System and Sources' in CG van der Merwe and JE du Plessis, *Introduction to the Law of South Africa* (The Hague, Kluwer, 2004) 40.

—— and Visser, DP, 'Der Einfluss des europäischen Rechts in Südafrika' (2001) *Jahrbuch für Europäische Geschichte* 47.

Eames, L, 'The Protection of Personal Rights in Equity Since 1946' (1952) 32 *Boston University Law Review* 419.

Eichensehr, KE, 'Defending Nationals Abroad: Assessing the Lawfulness of Forcible Hostage Rescues' (2008) 88 *Virginia Journal of International Law* 451.

Ellis, J, 'General Principles and Comparative Law' (2011) 22 *European Journal of International Law* 949.

Engisch, K, 'Der Rechtsfreie Raum' (1952) 108 *Zeitschrift für die Gesamte Staatwissenschaft* 385.

Faber, MJ, 'R2P, Humanitarian Intervention and Independence: The Proof of the Pudding is in the Eating' (2009) 1 *Amsterdam Law Forum* 4.

Falk, R, 'Humanitarian Intervention After Kosovo' in L Boisson de Chazournes and V Gowlland-Debbas (eds), *L'Ordre Juridique International, Un Système en Quête d'Équité, Liber Amicorum Georges Abi-Saab* (The Hague, Martinus Nijhoff, 2001) 177.

Farer, T, in S Murphy, *Humanitarian Intervention: The United Nations in an Evolving World Order* (Philadelphia, University of Pennsylvania Press, 1996) 70.

Fenstein, L and Slaughter, AM, 'A Duty to Prevent' (2004) 83 *Foreign Affairs* 136.

Flach, J, 'Le Code de Hammourabi et la constitution originaire de la propriété dans l'ancienne Chaldée' (1907) 5 *Revue historique* 272 (v 94, a 32, 1907, II).

Francioni, F, 'Of War, Humanity and Justice: International Law after Kosovo' in JA Frowein and R Wolfrum (eds), *Max Planck Yearbook of UN Law*, vol 4 (2000) 107.

——'Balancing the Prohibition of Force with the Need to Protect Human Rights: A Methodological Approach' in E Cannizzaro and P Palchetti (eds), *Customary International Law on the Use of Force: A Methodological Approach* (Leiden, Koninklijke Brill NV, 2005) 269.

——'Equity in International Law' in R Wolfrum (ed), *The Max Planck Encyclopedia of Public International Law* (Oxford, Oxford University Press, 2008).

Franck, T, 'Who killed Article 2(4)?' (1970) 64 *American Journal of International Law* 809.

——and Rodley, N, 'After Bangladesh: The Law of Humanitarian Intervention by Military Force' (1973) 67*American Journal of International Law* 290.

——and Sugrue, D, 'The International Role of Equity-as-Fairness' (1992–93) 81 *Georgetown Law Journal* 563.

French, D, 'Treaty Interpretation and the Incorporation of Extraneous Legal Rules' (2006) 55 *ICLQ* 281.

Frowein, JA, 'Ius Cogens' in R Wolfrum (ed), *The Max Planck Encyclopedia of Public International Law* (OUP, 2008) para 8.

——and Krisch, N, 'Chapter VII: Action with Respect to Threats to the Peace, Breaches of the Peace, and Acts of Aggression' in B Simma (ed), *The Charter of the United Nations: A Commentary*, 2nd edn (Oxford, Oxford University Press, 2002) 701–807.

Fukuyama, F, 'The End of History?' (1989) *National Interest* 3.

Fuller, L, 'The Case of the Speluncean Explorers' (1949) 42 *Harvard Law Review* 3.

Garcia Enterria, E, 'Reflexiones sobre la ley y los principios generales del derecho en el Derecho Administrativo' (1963) 40 *Revista de Administración Publica* 211.

Giliker, P, 'Barclay's Bank v O'Brien Revisited: What a Difference Five Years Can Make' (1999) 62 *MLR* 609.

Glenn, G and Redden, K, 'Equity – A Visit to the Founding Fathers' (1945) 31 *Virginia Law Review* 757.

Goodman, R, 'Humanitarian Intervention and Pretexts for War' (2006) 100 *American Journal of International Law* 107.

Graver, C, 'The Role of Equity in the Jurisprudence of the World Court' (1979) 37 *University of Toronto Faculty of Law Review* 101.

Green, J, 'Questioning the Peremptory Status of the Prohibition of the Use of Force' (2011) 32 *Michigan Journal of International Law* 215.

Green, LC, 'Drazen Erdemovic: The ICTY in Action' (1997) 10 *Leiden Journal of International Law* 363.

Greenwood, C, 'Humanitarian Intervention: The Case of Kosovo' (1999) 10 *Finnish Yearbook of International Law* 141.

Habermas, J, 'Bestiality and Humanity: A War on the Border between Legality and Morality' (1999) 6 *Constellations* 263.

Hafkin, G, 'The Russo-Georgian War of 2008: Developing the Law of Unauthorized Humanitarian Intervention after Kosovo' (2010) 28 *Boston University International Law Journal* 219.

Hannikainen, L, 'The World After 11 September 2001: Is the Prohibition on the Use of Force Disintegrating?' in J Petman and J Klabbers, *Nordic Cosmopolitanism: Essays in International Law for Martti Koskenniemi* (Leiden, Martinus Nijhoff, 2003) 445.

Hannum, H, 'The Status of the Universal Declaration of Human Rights in National and International Law' (1995) *Georgia Journal of International and Comparative Law* 287.
——'The UCHR in National and International Law' (1998) 3 *Health and Human Rights* 144.
Hartkamp, A, 'Judicial Discretion under the New Civil Code of the Netherlands' (2002) 40 *American Journal of Comparative Law* 551.
Heinze, EA, 'Humanitarian Intervention and the War in Iraq: Norms, Discourse and Practice (Spring 2006) *Parameters* 20.
Hendrickson, DC, 'In Defence of Realism: A Commentary on Just and Unjust Wars' (1997) 11 *Ethics and International Affairs* 46.
Henkin, L, 'NATO's Kosovo intervention: Kosovo and the Law of Humanitarian Intervention' (1999) 93 *American Journal of International Law* 826.
Hering, CJ, 'Die Billigkeit im kanonischen Recht' in E Wolff, *Deutsche Landesreferate zum III. Internationalen Kongreß für Rechtsvergleichung in London* (Berlin, de Gruyter, 1950).
Higgins, R, 'International Law and the Avoidance, Containment and Resolution of Disputes' (1991) 230 *Recueil des Cours de l'Académie de Droit International* 9.
——'Human Rights in the International Court of Justice' (2007) 20 *Leiden Journal of International Law* 745.
Hilpold, P, 'The Kosovo Case and International Law: Looking for Applicable Theories' (2009) 8 *Chinese Journal of International Law* 47.
Hogan, G, 'A Desert Island Case set in the Silver Sea: The State (Ryan) v Lennon (1934)' in E O'Dell (ed), *Leading Cases of the Twentieth Century* (Dublin, Roundhall Sweet & Maxwell, 2000) 81.
Holzgrefe JL, 'The Humanitarian Intervention Debate' in JL Holzgrefe and RO Keohane (eds), *Humanitarian Intervention: Ethical, Legal and Political Dilemmas* (Cambridge, Cambridge University Press, 2003) 18.
Hudson, MO, 'The Succession of the International Court of Justice to the Permanent Court of International Justice' (1957) 51 *American Journal of International Law* 569.
Hutt, M, 'Drafting the Nepal Constitution' (1990) 30 *Asian Survey* 1020.
Jalet, FT, 'The Quest for the General Principles of Law Recognized by Civilized Nations – A Study' (1962–63) 10 *University of California at Los Angeles Law Review* 1041.
Janis, MW, 'Equity and International Law: The Comment in the Tentative Draft' (1982) 57 *Tulane Law Review* 80.
Janssen, D, 'Humanitarian Intervention and the Prevention of Genocide' (2008) 10 *Journal of Genocide Research* 289.
Jennings, R, 'The Principles Governing Marine Boundaries' in K Hailbronner et al (eds), *Staat und Völkerrechtsordnung: Festschrift für Karl Doehring* (Berlin, Springer-Verlag, 1989) 397.
Kaeckenbeeck, G, 'Upper Silesia and the League of Nations' (1946) 243 *Annals of the American Academy of Political and Social Science* 129.
Kammerhofer, J, 'Gaps, the Nuclear Weapons Advisory Opinion and the Structure of International Legal Argument between Theory and Practice' (2009) 80 *British Yearbook of International Law* 337.
Kim, YS, 'The Responsibility to Protect, Humanitarian Intervention and North Korea' (2006) 5 *Journal of International Business and Law* 74.

Knopp, G, 'Schuldrecht (vol II)' in HAT Soergel, *Bürgerliches Gesetzbuch, ein Kommentar, (neu herausgeben von Wolfgang Siebert)*, Zehnte Auflage (Stuttgart, Kohlhammer, 1967) 193.

Koskenniemi, M, 'The Lady Doth Protest Too Much: Kosovo, and the Turn to Ethics in International Law' (2002) 65 *MLR* 159.

Kritsiotis, D, 'Reappraising Policy Objections to Humanitarian Intervntion' (1998) 19 *Michigan Journal of International Law* 1005.

Lauterpacht, E, 'Equity, Evasion, Equivocation and Evolution in International Law' (1977–78) *American Branch International Law Association Procedure and Commission Report* 34.

Lauterpacht, H, 'The Grotian Tradition in International Law' (1946) 23 *British Yearbook of Intlernationa Law* 48.

——'Some Observations on the Prohibition of "Non Liquet" and the Completeness of the Law' in *Symbolae Verzijl. Présentées au Prof JHW Verzijl à l'occasion de son LXX-ième anniversaire* (The Hague, Martinus Nijhoff, 1958) 204.

Le Pillouer, A, 'Pouvoir constituent originaire et pouvoir constituent derive: à propos de l'émergence d'une distinction conceptuelle' (2005–06) 25–26 *Revue d'histoire des facultés de droit et de la science juridique* 123.

Leclerc-Gagné, E and Byers, M, 'A Question of Intent: The Crime of Aggression and Unilateral Intervention' (2009) 41 *Case Western Reserve Journal of International Law* 379.

Lillich, R, 'The Growing Importance of Customary International Human Rights Law' (1995) 25 *Georgia Journal of International and Comparative Law* 1.

LJH, 'Clean Hands Doctrine' (1939) 18 *Texas Law Rev* 506.

Luban, D, 'The Romance of the Nation-State' (1980) 9 *Philosophy and Public Affairs* 395.

Lutz, DS, 'The Articles of Confederation' in SL Schechter, *Roots of the Republic: American Founding Documents Interpreted* (Oxford / Madison Wisconsin, Madison House, 1990) 227.

MacFarlane, SN, Thielking, CJ and Weiss, TG, 'The Responsibility to Protect: Is Anyone Interested in Humanitarian Intervention?' (2004) 25 *Third World Quarterly* 977.

MacGibbon, IC, 'The Scope of Acquiescence in International Law' (1954) 31 *British Yearbook of International Law* 181.

——'Estoppel in International Law' (1958) 7 *ICLQ* 468.

Makkonen, Y, 'Western Attitudes to International Equity' (1975) 42/43 *Annuaire de l'AAA* 86.

Massa, AS, 'Does Humanitarian Intervention Serve Human Rights? The Case of Kosovo' (2009) 1 *Amsterdam Law Forum* 50.

Maudsley, RH, 'Constructive Trusts' (1977) *Northern Ireland Law Quarterly* 123.

Mazzone, J, 'Unamendments' (2004–05) 90 *Iowa Law Review* 1747.

McCoy, A, 'Canonical Equity Versus the Proliferation of Dispensations and Privileges' (1966) *The Jurist* 95.

McDougal, M, Laswell, HD and Reisman, M, 'The World Constitutive Process of Authoritative Decision Making' in R Falk and C Black (eds), *The Future of the International Legal Order*, vol I (Princeton, NJ, Princeton University Press, 1969) 73.

McNair, A, 'The Legality of the Occupation of the Ruhr' (1924) 5 *British Yearbook of International Law* 17.

Meijer, G, 'The Influence of the Code Civil in the Netherlands' (2002) 14 *European Journal of Law and Economics* 228.

Mendelson, MH, 'The Formation of Customary International Law' (1998) 272 *Hague Academy Collected Courses* 155.

Meron, T, 'On a Hierarchy of International Human Rights' (1986) 80 *American Journal of International Law* 1.

Merz, H, 'Einleitung: Art 1-10 ZGB' in M Gmür, et al, *Berner Kommentar zum Schweizerischen Zivilgesetzbuch* (Berne, Stämpfli, 1962) 258–73.

Milanovic, M, 'The ICJ and Evolutionary Treaty Interpretation' *European Journal of International Law: Talk!* (14 July 2009).

Mill, JS, 'A Few Words on Non-Intervention' in Mill, JS, *Dissertations and Discussions,* vol III (Boston, Spencer, 1867) 171.

Millet, P, 'Equity – The Road Ahead' (1995) 9 *Trust Law International* 35.

Milo, JM, 'General Principles' in D Busch and HN Schnelhaas (eds), *The Principles of European Contract Law (Part III) and Dutch law,* vol II (den Haag, Kluwer, 2006) 77–91.

Mohamed, S, 'Restructuring the Debate on Unauthorised Humanitarian Intervention' (2010) 88 *North Carolina Law Review* 1275.

Mohr, T, 'British Involvement in the Creation of the Constitution of the Irish Free State' (2008) 30 *Dublin University Law Journal* 166.

Molier, G, 'Humanitarian Intervention and the Responsibility to Protect after 9/11' (2006) 53 *Netherlands International Law Review* 37.

Moreland, R, 'Injunctive Control of Family Relations' (1930) 18 *Kentucky Law Journal* 207.

Morelli, G, 'La théorie générale du procès international' (1937) 61 *Recueil de La Haye* 253.

Murphy, SD, 'Criminalizing Humanitarian Intervention' (2009) 41 *Case Western Reserve Journal of International Law* 341.

Nardin, T, 'Humanitarian Imperialism' (2005) 19 *Ethics and International Affairs* 21.

Newman, RA, 'The Place and Function of Pure Equity in the Structure of Law' (1965) 16 *Hastings Law Journal* 402.

——'The principle of equity as a source of World Law' (1966) 1 *Israel Law Review* 616.

——'The Hidden Equity' (1967) 19 *Hastings Law Journal* 48.

O'Connell, ME, 'Taking Opinio Juris Seriously, A Classical Approach to International Law on the Use of Force' in E Cannizzaro and P Palchetti (eds), *Customary International Law on the Use of Force: A Methodological Approach* (Leiden, Koninklijke Brill NV, 2005) 9–30.

Oleck, HL, 'Historical Nature of Equity Jurisprudence' (1951) 20 *Fordham Law Review* 27.

——'Maxims of Equity Reappraised' (1952) 63 *Rutgers Law Review* 520.

Opsahl, T, 'Struggling with Equity in the Modern World' (1975) 42/43 *Annuaire de l'Association des auditeurs et anciens auditeurs de l'Academie de droit international de la Haye* 72.

Orakhelashvili, A, 'Restrictive Interpretation of Human Rights Treaties in the Recent Jurisprudence of the European Court of Human Rights' (2003) 14 *European Journal of International Law* 537.

Özbudun, E, 'Judicial Review of Constitutional Amendments in Turkey' (2009) 15 *European Public Law* 533.

Parker, K and Neylon, LB, 'Jus Cogens: Compelling the Law of Human Rights' (1989) 12 *Hastings International and Comparative Law Review* 411.
Pattison, J, 'Humanitarian Intervention and International Law: The Moral Importance of an Intervener's Legal Status' (2007) 10 *Critical Review of International Social and Political Philosophy* 301.
Perreau, EH, 'Origine et développement de la théorie de l'abus du droit' (1913) *Revue générale du droit* 481.
Petman, J, 'The Problem of Evil and International Law' in J Petman and J Klabbers, *Nordic Cosmopolitanism: Essays in International Law for Martti Koskenniemi* (Leiden, Martinus Nijhoff, 2003) 111–40.
Petro, NN, 'Legal Case for Russian Intervention in Georgia' (2008) 32 *Fordham International Law Journal* 1524.
Phillimore, L, 'Scheme for the Permanent Court of International Justice' (1920) 6 *Grotius Transactions* 89.
Picone, P, 'La "Guerra del Kosovo" e il Diritto Internazionale Generale' (2000) 2 *Rivista di diritto internazionale* 309.
Pospishil, T, 'Equitable Estoppel' (1940) 19 *Nebraska Law Bulletin* 222.
Pound, R, 'Comparative Law and History as Bases for Chinese Law' (1948) 61 *Harvard Law Review* 749.
Prall, S, 'The Development of Equity in Tudor England' (1964) 8 *American Journal of Legal History* 9.
Prince, JD, 'Review: The Code of Hammurabi' (1904) 8 *American Journal of Theology* 601.
Quirico, O, 'A Formal Prescriptive Approach to General Principles of (International) Law' (2007) 19 *European University Institute Working Papers: Law*.
Radbruch, G, 'Die Erneuerung des Rechts' (1947) 2 *Die Wandlung* 8.
Ramsbotham, O, 'Humanitarian Intervention 1990–95: A Need to Reconceptualise?' (1997) 23 *Review of International Studies* 445.
Randelzhofer, A, 'Article 2(4)' in B Simma (ed), *The Charter of the United Nations: A Commentary*, 2nd edn (Oxford, Oxford University Press, 2002) 112.
Reisman, WM, 'Kosovo's Antimonies' (1999) 93 *American Journal of International Law* 860.
Ripert, 'Règles du droit civil applicables aux rapports internationaux' (1933) 44 *Recueil La Haye* 569.
Roberts, A, 'NATO's Humanitarian War over Kosovo' (1999) 41 *Survival* 110.
——'Traditional and Modern Approaches to Customary International Law: A Reconciliation' (2001) 95 *American Journal of International Law* 757.
——'Legality Verses Legitimacy: Can Uses of Force be Illegal but Justified?' in P Alston and E MacDonald (eds), *Human Rights, Intervention and the Use of Force: The Collected Courses of the Academy of European Law* (Oxford, Oxford University Press, 2008) 179–214.
Rodogno, D, 'Réflexions liminaires à propos des interventions humanitaires des Puissances européens au XIXème siècle' (2007) 131 *Relations internationales* 22.
Rosenne, S, 'The Perplexities of Modern International Law' (2001) 291 *Recueil des Cours de l'Academie de Droit International de la Haye* 63.
Rostow, N, 'The International Use of Force after the Cold War' (1991) 32 *Harvard Journal of International Law* 416.

——'International Law and the Use of Force: A Plea for Realism' (2009) 34 *Yale International Law Journal* 549.

Sacco, R, 'Codificare : Modo Superato di Legiferare?' (1983) 5 *Rivista di Diritto Civile* 117.

Sachs, A, 'Making Rights Work: The South African Experience' in P Smith (ed), *Making Rights Work* (Dartmouth, Ashgate, 1999) 1.

Samar, VJ, 'Can a Constitutional Amendment be Unconstitutional?' (2008) 33 *Oklahoma City University Law Review* 667.

Sands, P, 'Sustainable Development: Treaty, Custom, and the Cross-fertilization of International Law' in A Boyle and D Freestone (eds), *International Law and Sustainable Development – Past Achievements and Future Challenges* (Oxford, Oxford University Press, 1999) 49.

Schachter, O, 'The Evolving International Law of Development' (1976) 15 *Columbia Journal of Transnational Law* 20.

Scheffer, D, 'Toward a Modern Doctrine of Humanitarian Intervention' (1991–92) 23 *University of Toledo Law Review* 253.

Schlesinger, R, 'Research on the General Principles of Law Recognised by Civilised Nations' (1957) 51 *American Journal of International Law* 734.

Schmitt, MN, 'Military Necessity and Humanity in International Humanitarian Law: Preserving the Delicate Balance' (2010) 50 *Virginia Journal of International Law* 795.

Scholtz, W, 'The Changing Rules of Ius ad Bellum: Conflicts in Kosovo, Iraq and Afghanistan' (2004) 7 *Potchefstroomse Elektroniese Regsblad* 1.

Schwartz, BI, 'On Attitudes Toward Law in China' in JA Cohen, *The Criminal Process in the People's Republic of China 1949–63; An Introduction* (Cambridge, Mass, Harvard University Press, 1967).

Schwarzenberger, G, 'The Fundamental Principles of International Law' (1955) 87 *Recueil de la Haye* 303.

——'International Ius Cogens?' (1964–65) 43 *Texas Law Review* 455.

Scialosa, V, 'Del diritto positive e dell'equità' (1932) *Studi giuridici* 35.

Scobbie, IGM, 'The Theorist as Judge: Hersch Lauterpacht's Concept of the International Judicial Function' (1997) 2 *European Journal of International Law* 274.

Scott, C, 'Interpreting Intervention' (2001) *Annuaire Canadien de Droit International* 355.

Shue, H, 'The Shortcomings of the "New Humanitarianism"' in A Paolini, A Jarvis and C Reus-Smit (eds), *Between Sovereignty and Global Governance: The United Nations, the State and Civil Society* (London, Macmillan, 1998) 73.

Simma, B, 'NATO, the UN and the Use of Force: Legal Aspects' (1999) *European Journal of International Law* 1.

Skordas, A, 'Hegemonic Intervention as Legitimate Use of Force' (2007) 16 *Minnesota Law Journal* 407.

Slaughter, AM, 'An American Vision of International Law?' (2003) 97 *American Society of International Law Proceedings* 125.

Sohn, L, 'Sources of International Law III: The Status and Future of the Customary International Law of Human Rights' (1995) 25 *Georgia Journal of International and Comparative Law* 399.

Sorensen, M, 'Principes de droit international public, Cours Général' (1960) 101 *Recueil des Cours* 18.

Stanulova, M, 'Has Humanitarian Intervention Become an Exception to the Prohibition on the Use of Force in Article 2(4) of the UN Charter?' (2010) *Atlantic Community* 1.
Stone, J, 'Non Liquet and the International Judicial Function' in Ch Perelman (ed), *Le problème des lacunes en droit* (Bruylant, Brussels, 1968) 305.
Strupp, K, 'Le droit du juge international de statuer selon l'équité' (1930) 33 *Recueil La Haye* 357.
Sur, S, 'Quelle légalité pour le conflit armé en droit international ?' (2005) 24 *Cités* 103.
Tan, K-C, 'Enforcing Global Justice: The Problem of Intervention' in R Pierik and W Werner (eds), *Cosmopolitanism in Context: Perspectives from International Law and Political Theory* (Cambridge, Cambridge University Press, 2009).
Terreblanche, S, 'Privelegie teen selfinkriminasie: "n tyd om weer te dink"' (1994) 7 *South African Journal of International Justice* 177.
Tesón, F, 'The Liberal Case for Humanitarian Intervention' in JL Holzgrefe and RO Keohane (eds), *Humanitarian Intervention: Ethical, Legal and Political Dilemmas* (Cambridge, Cambridge University Press, 2003) 93–129.
——'Self-Defence in International Law and Rights of Persons' (2004) 18 *Ethics and International Affars* 87.
——'Ending Tyranny in Iraq' (2005) 19 *Ethics and International Affairs* 1.
——'Eight Principles of Humanitarian Intervention' (2006) 5 *Journal of Military Ethics* 93.
——'Kosovo: A Powerful Precedent for the Doctrine of Humanitarian Intervention' (2009) 1 *Amsterdam Law Forum* 42.
Thierry, H, 'Réflexions sur le 'Droit d'Ingérence Humanitaire' in L Boisson de Chazournes and V Gowlland-Debbas (eds), *L'Ordre Juridique International, Un Système en Quête d'Équité, Liber Amicorum Georges Abi-Saab* (den Haag, Martinus Nijhoff, 2001) 224.
Treves, T, 'Piracy, Law of the Sea, and the Use of Force: Developments off the Coast of Somalia' (2009) 20 *European Journal of International Law* 399.
Tsagourias, N, 'The Inevitable Independence of Kosovo' (2009) 1 *Amsterdam Law Forum* 39.
Verdross, A, 'Les principes généraux du droit dans la jurisprudence internationale' (1935) 52 *Recueil des Cours* 207.
——'Jus Dispositivum and Jus Cogens in International Law' (1966) 60 *American Journal of International Law* 55.
Verwey, W, 'Humanitarian Intervention in the 1990s and Beyond: An International Law Perspective' in JN Pieterse (ed), *World Orders in the Making: Humanitarian Intervention and Beyond* (London, Macmillan, 1998) 200.
Waldock, CHM, 'The Anglo-Norwegian Fisheries Case' (1951) 28 *British Yearbook of International Law* 114.
Walzer, M, 'The Moral Standing of States: A Resposnse to Four Critics' (1980) 9 *Philosophy and Public Affairs* 209.
——'The Argument about Humanitarian Intervention' (Winter 2002) *Dissent* 29.
Warner, D, 'Ethics, Law and Unethical Compassion in the Kosovo Intervention' in L Boisson de Chazournes and V Gowlland-Debbas (eds), *L'Ordre Juridique International, Un Système en Quête d'Equité, Liber Amicorum Georges Abi-Saab* (den Haag Martinus Nijhoff, 2001) 199–217.

Watson, JS, 'A Realistic Jurisprudence of International Law' (1980) *Yearbook of World Affairs* 265.

Weidenbaum, P, 'Necessity in International Law' (1938) 24 *Grotius Transactions* 105.

Weil, P, 'Le droit international en quête de son identité' (1992) 237 *Recueil des Cours de l'Academie de Droit International de la Haye* 147.

——'L'équité dans la jurisprudence de la Cour Internationale de Justice: Un mystère en voie de dissipation ?' in V Lowe and M Fitzmaurice (eds), *Fifty Years of the International Court of Justice* (Cambridge, Cambridge University Press, 1996) 121–44.

Weinrib, EJ, 'Legal Formalism, on the Immanent Reality of Law' in D Patterson (ed), *Philosophy of Law and Legal Theory: An Anthology* (Oxford, Blackwell Publishing, 2003) 325.

Weisburd, AM, 'Consistency, Universality, and the Customary Law of Interstate Force' in E Cannizzaro and P Palchetti (eds), *Customary International Law on the Use of Force: A Methodological Approach* (Leiden, Koninklijke Brill, 2005) 31–77.

Weiss, TG, 'The Sunset of Humanitarian Intervention? The Responsibility to Protect in a Unipolar Era' (2004) 35 *Security Dialogue* 135.

Werner, W, 'From Justus Hostis to Rogue State: The Concept of the Enemy in International Legal Thinking' (2004) 17 *International Review for the Semiotics of Law* 155.

White, M, 'Equity – A General Principle of Law Recognised by Civilised Nations?' (2003) 4 *Queensland Law Journal* 103.

Whitman, J, 'A Cautionary Note on Humanitarian Intervention' (1994) 34 *GeoJournal* 167.

Williams, G, 'The Defence of Necessity' (1953) 6 *Crim LR* 216.

Williams, P and Stewart, M, 'Humanitarian Intervention: The New Missing Link in the Fight to Prevent Crimes against Humanity and Genocide' (2008) 40 *Case Western Reserve Journal of International Law* 97.

Yiannopoulous, AN, 'Louisiana Civil Law: A Lost Cause?' (1980) 54 *Tulane Law Review* 830.

Zajadlo, J, 'Legality and Legitimization of Humanitarian Intervention: New Challenges in the Age of the War on Terrorism' (2005) 8 *American Behavioral Scientist* 653.

ADDITIONAL DOCUMENTS

British Foreign Office (Foreign Policy Document No 148) (1986) 57 *British Yearbook of International Law* 619.

Documents of the United Nations Conference on International Organisation, vol I: Closing Plenary Session, 26 June 1945, Doc 1209 P/16; 27 June 1945, San Francisco.

Declaration on Principles of International Law Concerning Friendly Relations and Co-operation (1970) General Assembly Resolution 3314 (XXIX).

ICISS, *Research, Bibliography, Background* (to the R2P Report) (2001).

ICISS, *The Responsibility to Protect* (Report) (2001).

Institut de Droit International, *L'autorisation du recours à la force par les Nations Unies, 10ème Commission, Session de Rhodes, 2011 Plenière* (9 septembre 2011).

Preliminary Report of the High Commissioner on the Situation of Human Rights in the Syrian Arab Republic, UN Human Rights Council (14 June 2011) UN Doc A/HRC/17/CRP 1.

Report of the Independent International Commission of Inquiry on the Syrian Arab Republic, UN Human Rights Council (23 November 2011) UN Doc A/HRC/S-17/2/Add 1.

Report of the Group Established by the ILC on the Fragmentation of International Law (Report of the 56th Session) (2004) A/59/10.

Report of the Informal Inter-Allied Committee on the Future of the Permanent Court of International Justice, 10 February 1944 (1944) Cmd 6531.

Report of the International Law Commission, 53rd Session, 23 April–1 June; 2 July–10 August 2001, at 283, UN Doc A/56/10, GAOR, 56th Session, Supp No 10 (2001).

Report on the Law of Treaties, UN Doc A/CN 4/63, 24 March (1953) 157.

United Nations: Survey of International Law in Relation to the Work of Codification of the International Law Commission (Memorandum submitted by the Secretary-General) (1949) UN Doc A/CN 4/1/Rev 1.

United States – Standards for Reformulated and Conventional Gasoline, Report of the WTO Appellate Body (AB-1996-1) (29 April 1996) (WT/DS2/AB/R).

World Summit Outcome 2005 A/60/L (15 September 2005).

Index